Essays on economic decisions under uncertainty

To Monique

'Without uncertainty,
love,
which always entails risks as well as the joy of discovery,
loses its sharp edge.'

Essays on economic decisions under uncertainty

JACQUES H. DRÈZE

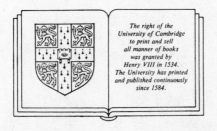

*The right of the
University of Cambridge
to print and sell
all manner of books
was granted by
Henry VIII in 1534.
The University has printed
and published continuously
since 1584.*

CAMBRIDGE UNIVERSITY PRESS

Cambridge
New York   Port Chester   Melbourne   Sydney

Published by the Press Syndicate of the University of Cambridge
The Pitt Building, Trumpington Street, Cambridge CB2 IRP
40 West 20th Street, New York, NY 10011, USA
10 Stamford Road, Oakleigh, Melbourne 3166, Australia

First published 1987
First paperback edition 1990

Printed in Great Britain at Woolnough Bookbinding,
Irthlingborough, Northamptonshire.

British Library cataloguing in publication data

Drèze, Jacques H.
Essays on economic decisions under uncertainty.
1. Economics – Decision making   2. Uncertainty
I. Title
330   HB199

Library of Congress cataloguing in publication data

Drèze, Jacques H.
Essays on economic decisions under uncertainty.

Includes bibliographies.
1. Decision-making – Addresses, essays, lectures.
2. Uncertainty – Addresses, essays, lectures.
3. Consumers' preferences – Addresses, essays, lectures.
I. Title.
HD30.23.D74 1986   338.5   85–19541

ISBN 0 521 26484 7 hard covers
ISBN 0 521 38697 7 paperback

TM

Contents

Acknowledgements

The author would like to thank the publishers of the following for their kind permission to reprint them in this book.

Axiomatic Theories of Choice, Cardinal Utility and Subjective Probability: A Review. In J.H. Drèze (ed.) (1974), *Allocation under Uncertainty: Equilibrium and Optimality*, pp. 3–23. London: Macmillan

Logical Foundations of Cardinal Utility and Subjective Probability. Translated from: Fondements logiques de la probabilité subjective et de l'utilité. In *La Décision*, Colloques Internationaux du CNRS (Paris), (1961), pp. 73–87

A Paradox in Information Theory. Translated from: Le paradoxe de l'information, *Economie Appliquée*, 13 (1960): 71–80

Inferring Risk Tolerance from Deductibles in Insurance Contracts, *The Geneva Papers on Risk and Insurance*, 20 (1981): 48–52

Market Allocation under Uncertainty, *European Economic Review*, 2 (1971) (2): 133–65

Demand Estimation, Risk Aversion and Sticky Prices, *Economies Letters*, 4 (1979) (1): 1–6

State-Dependent Utility, the Demand for Insurance and the Value of Safety. In M.W. Jones-Lee (ed.) (1982), *The Value of Life and Safety*, pp. 41–65. Amsterdam: North-Holland Publishing Company (with Pierre Dehez)

Consumption Decisions under Uncertainty, *Journal of Economic Theory*, 5 (1972) (3): 308–55 (with Franco Modigliani)

Earnings, Assets and Savings: A Model of Interdependent Choice. Translated from Section 6 of Epargne et consommation en avenir aléatoire, *Cahiers du Séminaire d'Econométrie*, 9 (1966): 7–33 (with Franco Modigliani) (*Partim*)

Demand Fluctuations, Capacity Utilisation and Prices, *Operations Research Verfahren*, 3 (1967): 119–41 (with Jean Jaskold Gabszewicz) (*Partim*)

Demand Fluctuations, Capacity Utilisation and Costs, *American Economic Review*, 66 (1976) (5): 731–42 (with Eytan Sheshinski)

On Industry Equilibrium under Uncertainty, *Journal of Economic Theory* 33 (1984) (1): 88–97 (with Eytan Sheshinski)

Investment under Private Ownership: Optimality, Equilibrium and Stability. In J.H. Drèze (ed.) (1974), *Allocation under Uncertainy: Equilibrium and Optimality*, pp. 129–66. London: Macmillan

Decision Criteria for Business Firms. In M. Hazewinkel and A.H.G. Rinnooy Kan (eds) (1982), *Current Developments in the Interface: Economics, Econometrics, Mathematics*, pp. 27–53. Dordrecht: D. Reidel Publishing Company

(Uncertainty and) the Firm in General Equilibrium Theory, Harry Johnson Lecture, Royal Economic Society, Association of University Teachers of Economics Meeting, Bath, 1984 *Economic Journal*, 95 (1985), Supplement: 1–20

Human Capital and Risk-Bearing, *The Geneva Papers on Risk and Insurance*, 12 (1979): 5–22

Some Theory of Labour Management and Participation, *Econometrica*, 44 (1976): 1125–39

Pricing, Spending and Gambling Rules for Non-Profit Organisations, In R.E. Grieson (ed.) (1976), *Public and Urban Economics*, pp. 58–89. Lexington, Mass: Lexington Books (with Maurice Marchand) (*Partim*)

Econometrics and Decision Theory, *Econometrica*, 40 (1972) (1): 1–17

Foreword

'Uncertainty is an intimate dimension of our daily lives. For some, it is the zest of life. Without uncertainty, the distinction between the present and the future is blurred; there are no surprises and no anticipations, hence no thrills; there is no scope for achievement, hence no rewards; and love, which always entails risks as well as the joy of discovery, loses its sharp edge. Yet, for others, uncertainty is the curse of life. It is so for those who feel threatened with loss of life or individual freedom, who have no assured shelter or subsistence, who lack job security and fear unemployment.

'Uncertainty is thus an intimate dimension of economics as well. Decisions of households, firms or policy makers seldom entail fully deterministic consequences; uncertainty is "generic". (Still, many titles in economics include the precision "under uncertainty", not even parenthetical; whereas it should be natural to include the warning "under certainty", when appropriate.)[1]

The present book collects twenty papers on economic decisions by households, firms or policy makers. (The title sacrifices to tradition by including the qualification 'under uncertainty', not even parenthetical. . . .) These papers were written over the past 25 years and span my professional career. Yet, there is a common thread running through most of them.

'Uncertainty has been introduced formally into the model of *Theory of Value* by recognising that the primitive data or *environment* – in particular resources, tastes and technology – are not known and given, but are part of the unfolding history of the world. As of any future date, the world is apt to find itself in any one of several alternative, mutually exclusive *states* – each

[1] Quoted from pp. 322–323 infra.

of which corresponds, among other things, to a history up to that date of resources, tastes and technology. Recognising that "the environment is state-dependent" draws a credible boundary between the exogenous sources of uncertainty and economic analysis; we should be grateful to Savage (1953, 1954) and Arrow (1953) in particular for introducing that approach, which is more satisfactory than earlier formulations in terms of probability distributions of economic variables (like prices or incomes).'[2]

The representation of uncertainty through a set of alternative, mutually exclusive *states of the environment* was an important break-through, which conveniently occurred during my graduate school days.[3] The common thread linking the essays in the present book is that the theory of individual decision, as developed for the 'states' model by Savage, 'provides a starting point for research on the economics of uncertainty that is both natural and satisfactory'.[4] In particular, it fits naturally into the general equilibrium model of allocation under uncertainty introduced by Arrow and developed by Debreu (1953, 1959).[5] That model, in turn, provides a suitably general framework within which the specific decisions of households, firms or policy makers can be studied and fitted together. In that way, general equilibrium theory takes life and acquires operational substance.

The broad organisation of the book flows directly from these remarks. Part I deals with the theory of individual decision, and Part II with market equilibrium. The following chapters deal successively with decisions of consumers (Part III) and producers (Part IV); then with their interaction through the stock market (Part V) and labour contracts (Part VI); and finally with public decisions (Part VII). The more specific Parts III to VII thus explore, in a number of directions, the operational characteristics of the unified general model of individual decision and market equilibrium.

Undoubtedly, the presence of a linking thread is more visible to the author than it will be to the readers of separate chapters. And the thread is sometimes broken, or lost in technical detours. Still, I invite my readers to look for the thread, to detect missing links, and hopefully to supply these through their own contributions.

To those readers who would like to follow the general substantive argument without paying attention to details or technical developments, I suggest a short route consisting of Chapter 1, Section 1 of Chapter 2, then Chapters 6, 16, 17 and 20 – possibly skipping Section 5 of Chapter 20, or adding Chapters 9 and 11 or 12.

[2] Quoted from pp. 323 infra.
[3] See the 'Historical Perspective' given on pp. 4–5 infra.
[4] Quoted from p. 19 infra. Chapter 1, written for the opening of the International Economic Association Conference held in 1971 in Bergen, elaborates on that remark. Dréze (1974) contains partial proceedings of that conference, and includes Chapter 14 of the present volume as well.
[5] Chapter 6, drafted during my visit to the University of Chicago in 1964, elaborates on that remark.

A few more specific guidelines may be helpful.

The general representation of uncertainty through states of the environment calls for modelling consumer tastes in terms of preferences over vectors of state-contingent consumption (including labour services). 'These preferences reflect simultaneously time preferences, probability beliefs, attitudes to risk and interactions between states and consumption.'[6] In the work of Arrow and Debreu, these preferences enter as a primitive concept, and obey standard assumptions (including continuity and convexity).[7] In the theory of individual decision presented by Savage, these preferences satisfy more specific axioms leading to a representation in terms of a probability measure over the states and a utility over the 'consequences' – where a consequence is 'anything that happens to the decision-maker'.[8] The axioms impose that consequences, hence utility, be independent of the state that obtains. Integrating the two frameworks requires an extension of the Savage model to allow for state-specific consequences and a state-dependent utility for consumption. That extension was the subject of my (unpublished) PhD Dissertation, presented in 1958 at Columbia University.

The extension also covers situations where the probabilities of the states are affected by unobserved strategies of the decision-maker – situations of 'moral hazard' in currently accepted terminology. Chapter 2, published here for the first time, presents a generalisation of the more limited results contained in my dissertation and in a summary presentation published in French in 1961 (translated here as Chapter 3). Chapter 2 is not easy to read in full (Sections 7 and 8 are quite technical); but the extensive introduction and final comments may help.[9]

The central result in Chapters 2 and 3 is a 'generalised moral expectation theorem': there exist a state-dependent utility function, and a closed convex set of probability measures over the states; decisions are ordered by their expected utility, evaluated at the element in the set of feasible probability measures for which expected utility is maximal. That is, maximisation of expected utility characterises the choices of strategies as well as the choices of state-distributions of consequences. The proof relies crucially on the assumption that the value of information is non-negative. The restrictive nature of that assumption, and its inapplicability to games of strategy (as opposed to games against nature with moral hazard), are illustrated in the anecdotal Chapter 4 – the translation of a paper published in French in 1960.

[6] Quoted from p. 324 infra.

[7] As for firms, they maximise the net value of production at prices for contingent deliveries. More realistic decision criteria for firms are introduced in Part V.

[8] Savage (1954), p. 13.

[9] The present version is the outcome of three complete drafts produced over the summers of 1983, 1984 and 1985 respectively. I mention this, not as an advocate of the labour theory of value, but to help my graduate students understand why I urge them to write their own dissertations in a form suitable for immediate publication ... in English!

Chapter 5 shows how a lower bound on relative risk aversion can be deduced from the relative size of deductibles in insurance policies. 'It seems to suggest an order of magnitude for the relative risk-aversion measure which is substantially higher than estimates based on portfolio composition.'[10]

The modelling of moral hazard and state-dependent preferences is essential for some applications, in particular to problems of life assurance and life protection. An early contribution to a debate over the value of saving a life published in French in 1962 and introducing what later became known as the 'willingness-to-pay' approach to the value of safety, was generalised twenty years later in Chapter 8, written in collaboration with Pierre Dehez.

The general equilibrium model with uncertainty about the states of the environment is reviewed in Chapter 6, for a pure exchange economy.

'A model where the environment is state-dependent is amenable to the same formal analysis as a model where the environment is given, if one is willing to assume the existence of a complete set of insurance markets, one for each physical commodity contingent on each state of the environment. In that case, business decisions reduce to arithmetic, because each production plan has a well-defined present value on the insurance markets. In particular, a firm contemplating a new investment could simultaneously protect itself against demand uncertainties by selling its output at each date on futures market, and against supply uncertainties by purchasing insurance against output deficiencies, whether they be due to machine breakdowns, low labour productivity or mismanagement.'[11]

The insurance markets referred to in that quotation are usually labelled 'markets for contingent claims', or more briefly 'contingent-markets'. Chapter 6 records that competitive prices for contingent claims to a numeraire commodity satisfy all the properties of a probability measure, including the definition of conditional probability. Yet, these prices should be interpreted as products of a probability by a relative marginal utility (p. 135).

Chapter 6 (Section 2.1) also substantiates the observation that risk aversion is the rule, in an economy where there exist opportunities for gambling at fair odds.

Chapter 7 points out that 'uncertainty about the price elasticity of demand has an effect comparable to a kink in the demand curve, for a risk-averse firm; the kink being located at the prevailing price and quantity'.[12] Hence the reference to sticky prices in the title of that chapter.

Turning to Part III, Chapters 9 and 10 (written with Franco Modigliani) deal with consumer decisions about occupational choice, savings and

[10]Quoted from p. 114 infra.
[11]Quoted from p. 323 infra.
[12]Quoted from p. 144 infra.

portfolio choices. An interesting purely ordinal condition under which these decisions can be taken sequentially (and thus become separable), when there exist markets for contingent claims, is given in Chapter 9. Chapter 10 investigates the relationship between portfolio choices and income uncertainty, in a mean-variance framework. These two chapters aim at specific results, and for that reason ignore the interaction between states and preferences. Some of the results could usefully be reconsidered in the broader framework of state-dependent preferences.[13]

Part IV contains three papers on industry equilibrium in a special uncertainty context where competitive investment can be efficient; namely a context where firms only decide whether or not to build specific plants, knowing the probability distribution of future spot prices. Although these papers are presented in terms of maximisation of expected profits, they can also be interpreted in terms of maximisation of present value at prices for contingent claims (see Section 4 of Chapter 12). Or they could be interpreted in terms of investment guided by the stock market, if each plant were incorporated separately and built provided its value on the stock market covers building costs; that is, provided its q à la Tobin (1980, Chapter IV) were not less than unity. A process where investment is guided by these criteria will converge to an efficient equilibrium of the industry, under correct expectations about future prices.

In parts II to IV, no explicit attention is given to the important issue of existence of markets for contingent claims. Either that issue is not directly relevant (as in Chapter 10), or it is assumed (as in Chapter 6) that a complete set of contingent market exists. The latter assumption 'is clearly an excessive idealisation. Existing insurance opportunities are limited by transaction costs, moral hazard, adverse selection and the like. (Note also that the set of potential buyers on a long-term futures market may include as yet unborn consumers....) Incomplete markets are the rule, and firms come to life as they face the non-insurable uncertainties of history in the making. At once, they become concerned with forecasting and risk taking, which involve more than arithmetic (fortunately, say the econometricians and decision theorists). But as firms come to life, they fit less easily into the envelope of general equilibrium theory: there is today no formal description of "live" firms which is both generally accepted and suitable for the purposes of general equilibrium theory'.[14]

Part V is devoted to the theory of the firm in a world of incomplete insurance markets. The three papers collected there, written over the period 1970–1984, use the same simple two-period model, introduced by Diamond (1967), of an economy with a single commodity and two periods – the present and the future. The true state of the environment is unknown in the

---

[13]The concept of risk aversion has been extended to state-dependent preferences by Karni (1985). Consumer decisions about savings and portfolio choices, under state-dependent preferences, are introduced and broadly characterised in Chapters 14 and 15.
[14]Quoted from pp. 323–324 infra.

present but will be known in the future. Firms are endowed with production sets linking present inputs to state-distributions of future outputs. In contrast to the special cases of 'multiplicative uncertainty' treated by Diamond or of mean-variance analysis treated in the Capital Asset Pricing Model, firms must choose among alternative state distributions of outputs (of profits). There are no markets for contingent claims, but there is a stock market where shares of stock are traded. Households choose savings levels and portfolios, so as to maximise the expected utility of their present consumption and of the state-distribution of future consumption permitted by their shares in the profits (outputs) of the firms.

That simple model of temporary equilibrium captures an essential feature of private ownership economies, where the firms gamble with the savings of consumers. 'Do the preferences of shareholders, and the prices of shares on the stock market, influence the choices of firms among alternative state distributions of profits?' 'The question arises because firms, unlike consumers, are not human beings whose preferences could be introduced as primitive data' (p. 326).

Chapter 14, written 15 years ago, introduces and investigates an equilibrium concept, called 'stockholders' equilibrium', where each firm adopts a production (investment) plan which is *Pareto-optimal from the viewpoint of its own shareholders, given their portfolios and the production plans of other firms*; and where consumers buy their preferred portfolios on a competitive stock exchange. That chapter brings out several important features of the model: the set of attainable allocations is not convex (due to the interaction between production decisions and portfolio choices), resulting in sub-optimality of the stockholders' equilibria; the production plans of firms have the formal attributes of public goods; under standard assumptions, stockholders' equilibria exist; a mixed tâtonnement/non-tâtonnement process whereby tentative revisions of the production plans of the firms alternate with meetings of the stock exchange is quasi-stable, and limit points are stockholders' equilibria.

Chapter 15 relates stockholders' equilibria to other approaches to the theory of the firm and portfolio choices. Chapter 16, which draws on the forthcoming manuscript of the 1983 Yrjö Jahnsson Lectures, takes a further step towards realism. It models firms as managed by boards of directors, the composition of which reflects the ownership of the stock, and the decisions of which are subject to approval by majority voting at shareholders' meetings. The boards of directors may also delegate some of their prerogatives to managing directors. In equilibrium, the production plan of the firm is not dominated by another plan apt to be chosen in accordance with these rules (given the portfolios of consumers and the production plans of other firms); and consumers buy optimal portfolios on a competitive stock exchange. Under a simple continuity assumption on the composition of the boards of directors, an equilibrium exists.

A further extension, sketched briefly in Chapter 16, brings in labour contracts. 'On several occasions, I have characterised firms as fulfilling three roles: they realise physical investments, that match consumer savings; they create jobs, which consumers fill; they produce commodities, which consumers buy.'[15] The first role has received extensive attention, in the theory of finance as well as in the theory of general equilibrium in stock-market economies. The second role is a central concern of the macro-economic theory of employment. At the microeconomic level, it has received attention more recently in the theory of 'implicit labour contracts', where risk-sharing between risk-averse workers and less risk-averse firms is analysed. It is surprising that the obvious connection between stock-market models (where the risk aversion of firms is determined) and labour contract models had not been investigated before.[16]

That topic is the main subject covered in my 1983 Jahnsson Lectures, on which Chapter 16 is based. Earlier thoughts on the same theme are presented in two survey lectures, namely the Second Annual Lecture of the Geneva Association (1979) reprinted as Chapter 17 and the Walras Lecture to the Third World Meeting of the Econometric Society (1975) reprinted as Chapter 18.

As noted by Meade (1972): 'While property owners can spread their risks by putting small bits of their property into a large number of concerns, a worker cannot put small bits of his effort into a large number of different jobs. This presumably is a main reason why we find risk-bearing capital hiring labour rather than risk-bearing labour hiring capital.' Chapters 17 and 18 explore that theme, first from the viewpoint of labour contracts in a capitalist economy, next from the viewpoint of a labour-managed firm resorting to equity financing. Linking these microeconomic attributes of risk-sharing between property owners and workers to macroeconomic wage policies, in a general equilibrium framework, stands high on my current research agenda.[17]

Parts V and VI thus relate the decision criteria of business firms to the preferences of consumers, through the stock market and labour contracts. Part VII, entitled 'Public Decisions', starts with a chapter devoted to decision criteria for non-profit organisations (NPOs). These have no shareholders and no market value. On what basis do they evaluate risks, in the absence of contingent markets? Chapter 19 derives the risk aversion of an NPO as a sum of two terms, namely the elasticity of the 'willingness-to-

---

[15]Quoted from p. 337 infra. Part V uses a single-commodity model, which does not bring out the interactions between producer decisions and consumer preferences over commodities. That interaction is the subject of a forthcoming paper with John Geanakopoulos and Michael Magill, which substantiates my early intuition that price rigidities may serve a useful risk-sharing function, in the absence of contingent markets. That intuition provided the initial motivation for my work on equilibrium with price rigidities and quantity constraints – Drèze (1975).

[16]See p. 335 for a deep sociological explanation of that puzzle.

[17]See e.g. Drèze (1986).

pay' of beneficiaries for the NPO's services, and the output elasticity of the marginal cost of these services. That chapter is thus complementary to Part V. But the approach in Chapter 19 is less general, as it does not allow for state-dependent preferences. There is scope for further work in this neglected area.

Finally, Chapter 20 reproduces my Presidential Address to the Econometric Society in 1970, entitled 'Econometrics and Decision Theory'. The theme of that address was that 'we should now regard as a realistic challenge the formal analysis of decision problems in economics, resting on a specification of ends and means firmly rooted in economic theory, incorporating a probabilistic treatment of econometric information, and making use of the possibilities offered by mathematical programming techniques to compute optimal policies'.[18] A central part of the address dealt with advances in Bayesian econometrics paving the way to an operational realisation of the second goal.[19]

The integration of economic models and Bayesian inference is already stressed in Chapter 1 (written in the same year). The circle is thus closed, even if statistical inference is otherwise ignored throughout the book.[20]

In the concluding section of Chapter 20, I wrote fifteen years ago: 'We are still a long way from operational routines for a formal analysis of economic decision problems under uncertainty, but the goal is in sight, and the task is challenging. The challenges come on several fronts: normative economics, statistical methods of econometrics, and mathematical programming. I have no doubt that these challenges will be answered; this is just a matter of time. When problems of practical relevance and scientific importance are clearly defined, they attract talent. The problems of decision-making under uncertainty have all these attributes.'[21] The integration of economic theory, econometrics and mathematical programming is the platform of the Center for Operations Research and Econometrics (CORE), which has over the past twenty years provided an exceptional environment for my professional activity. Several aspects of the program outlined in Chapter 20 have been pursued there. In March, 1986, I attended a seminar by my colleague Yves Smeers on the development of gasfields in the North Sea and the design of contracts between Norway and other European countries for gas deliveries. His model involves estimates of demand functions, computation of equilibrium prices and the use of sequential stochastic programming techniques to compute optimal policies. That model could replace advantageously the agricultural policy illustration used in Chapter 20.[22] We are

---

[18] Quoted from p. 402.
[19] See Drèze and Richard (1983) for a progress report on that topic.
[20] I had initially hoped to include in Part VII an essay on the risk aversion of governments and the treatment of estimation uncertainties in public decisions – but time constraints did not permit me to do so.
[21] Quoted from p. 417 infra.
[22] See Boucher et al. (1985, 1986) for non-technical expositions of the model and of simulation results.

still a long way from routine applications of formal decision theory – but the example just mentioned shows that it can be done. It remains a matter of time...

The decision to publish this book was made several years ago, after I had read (with great interest) the survey paper by Hirshleifer and Riley (1979) on 'The Analytics of Uncertainty and Information'. I felt at the time that the main focus of research was shifting from the problems of exogenous or 'technological' uncertainty considered in this book, towards the more sophisticated problems of acquisition and dissemination of information. To a large extent, that has indeed happened. But there remain a number of important issues worthy of further research in the more limited framework considered here. The theory of the firm in an environment of uncertainty and incomplete markets remains a central issue; in particular, the integration in a canonical model of the interactions of the firm with its shareholders, its employees and its customers remains incomplete. And the macroeconomic implications of theories of risk-sharing remain to be spelled out. I am thus inclined today to regard some of the essays in this book as dealing with issues which are still in the foreground of the research scene.

In thanking all those who have contributed directly or indirectly to the research effort presented in this book, I wish first of all to express my immense gratitude to my teacher and thesis supervisor William Vickrey.[23] My professional orientation was much influenced by the congenial welcome and intellectual stimulation received from the graduate students and the Faculty at Columbia University, in particular from Abram Bergson, Albert Gailord Hart, George Stigler and William Vickrey.

As a novice struggling with unwieldy research problems, I had the good fortune of a close association with Franco Modigliani. Through joint work with him, I learned the tricks of the trade, and became contaminated with his obsession for linking theory to real issues. More importantly, there resulted a lifetime friendship, which I treasure.

At a later stage, I have received much inspiration, and derived great pleasure, from my contacts with graduate students at Université Catholique de Louvain – some of whom became lasting associates. Many of them are mentioned in the acknowledgements of specific chapters. I beg my co-authors Pierre Dehez, Jean Jaskold Gabszewicz and Maurice Marchand to accept, on behalf of all of them, my deep gratitude for their friendship and for the privilege of sharing their intellectual adventures.

I had not met Eytan Sheshinski until we discovered that we had independently developed the contents of Chapter 12. He handled that situation graciously. There resulted a more valuable discovery, namely that

---

[23]Vickrey's encouragement was instrumental towards the preparation of Chapter 2. Chapter 19 was written for a volume in his honour. Chapter 20 is dedicated to him, and it was a special pleasure to deliver that address in his presence.

a true friendship can develop among adult colleagues. It has a special flavour.

All but three of the essays in this book were written at the Center for Operations Research and Econometrics. I have already stated that CORE had provided an exceptional environment for my professional activity. It has also been a delightful environment. I am grateful to the members, visitors, research associates and administrative assistants of CORE for the continuing demonstration that work can be fun. And I am grateful to Université Catholique de Louvain, the Ford Foundation and the Belgian agencies Services de Programmation de la Politique Scientifique, Fonds National de la Recherche Scientifique and Fonds de la Recherche Fondamentale Collective for their support of CORE in general and of my own research in particular.

All but two of the essays in this book were initially typed and processed by Ginette Vincent, who has painstakingly kept a measure of order in my professional activities over the past 22 years. Her competence and dedication have repeatedly shifted the frontier of what was possible. Witness this book, which she prepared, proofread and indexed. Beyond my deep gratitude for the friendly and always reliable assistance, I am glad that she shares my conviction that one can do serious work without taking oneself seriously ...

As I take a last look at the galleys of this book, I am reminded of all the efforts aimed at mastering problems lying beyond my understanding and my technical competence – efforts that often cut into evenings, week ends and holidays. To my wife and our five sons, I wish to express my regrets for the demands thus placed on their patience, and my gratitude for their understanding. They have been a source of motivation and guidance about academic standards and economic priorities.

Walcheren, April 1986.

References

Arrow, K.J. (1953). 'Le rôle des valeurs boursières pour la répartition la meilleure des risques'. In *Econométrie*, pp. 41–7. Paris CNRS. Translated (1964) as 'The Role of Securities in the Optimal Allocation of Risk-Bearing'. *Review of Economic Studies*, 31: 91–6.

Boucher, J., P.M. Herzet and Y. Smeers (1985). 'Security of Gas Supply: How Much is it worth?' Mimeo. CORE, Louvain-la-Neuve.

Boucher, J., T. Hefting, P. Pinson and Y. Smeers (1986). 'Economic Analysis of Natural Gas Contracts'. Mimeo, CORE, Louvain-la-Neuve.

Debreu, G. (1953). 'Une économie de l'incertain' [mimeographed]. Paris EDF.

Debreu, G. (1959), *Theory of Value*. New York: Wiley.

Diamond, P.A. (1967). 'The Role of a Stock Market in a General Equilibrium Model with Technological Uncertainty'. *American Economic Review*, 57: 759–76.

Drèze, J.H. (1974) (ed.) *Allocation under Uncertainty: Equilibrium and Optimality*. Proceedings of an International Economic Association Conference. London: Macmillan.

Drèze, J.H. (1975). 'Existence of an Exchange Equilibrium under Price Rigidities'. *International Economic Review*, 16, (2): 301–20.

Drèze, J.H. (1986). 'Work-Sharing: Why? How? How Not...'. CEPS Paper n° 27. Bruxelles.

Drèze, J.H. and J.-F. Richard (1983). 'Bayesian Analysis of Simultaneous Equations Models'. In Z. Griliches and M. Intriligator (eds.), *Handbook of Econometrics*, Chap. 9, pp. 517–598.

Hirshleifer, J. and J.G. Riley (1979). 'The Analytics of Uncertainty and Information: An Expository Survey', *Journal of Economic Literature*, 17: 1375–421.

Karni, E. (1985). *Decision-Making under Uncertainty: The Case of State-Dependent Preferences*. Boston: Harvard University Press.

Meade, J. (1972). 'The Theory of Labour-Managed Firms and of Profit Sharing'. *Economic Journal*, **82**: 402–28.

Savage, L.J. (1953). 'Une axiomatisation du comportement raisonable face à l'incertitude'. In *Econométrie*, pp. 29–34. Paris: CNRS.

Savage, L.J. (1954). *The Foundations of Statistics*. New York: Wiley.

Tobin, J. (1980). *Asset Accumulation and Economic Activity*. Oxford: Blackwell.

I Decision-making under uncertainty: general theory

1 Axiomatic theories of choice, cardinal utility and subjective probability: a review*

Most of the papers collected in this volume rely, explicitly or implicitly, upon (i) a formal description of uncertainty situations in terms of the concepts of events, acts and consequences; and (ii) an axiomatic theory of individual choices, which justifies the representation of preferences among acts by their expected utility.

The purpose of this introductory essay is to review these concepts and axioms against the background of their economic applications.[1] The essay is not a systematic exposition of the theory (results will be stated without proofs); neither is it a survey of contributions to the theory (only a few key references will be used). Rather, it is a *review* of the main properties of the concepts and of the axiomatic theory, with a discussion of their usefulness and limitations in economic applications.[2]

Section 1 provides an element of historical perspective. Section 2 reviews the concepts of events, acts and consequences. Section 3 reviews the axioms of a normative theory of individual choice under uncertainty and their main implication (the moral expectation theorem). Section 4 reviews some objections that have been raised against the normative appeal of the

*Opening lecture for the Workshop in Economic Theory organised by the International Economic Association in Bergen in 1971.

[1] I am grateful to Louis-André Gérard Varet, Louis Gevers, Roger Guesnerie, Agnar Sandmo and Dieter Sondermann for their comments on a first draft of this paper.
[2] Participants in the conference had been urged to become acquainted before hand with the theory of individual choice under uncertainty, as exposed for instance by Savage (1954) or Arrow (1970) and with the model of allocation of resources under uncertainty introduced by Arrow (1953) and Debreu (1959).

3

axioms. Section 5 is devoted to a general discussion of the usefulness and limitations of the theory. Section 6 relates the concepts of the general theory to those underlying economic applications presented elsewhere in this volume.

1 Historical perspective

On 13 May 1952, the participants in a symposium on 'Foundations and Applications of the Theory of Risk-Bearing' (CNRS, 1953) held in Paris heard successively Savage (1953) present 'An Axiomatisation of Reasonable Behavior in the Face of Uncertainty' and Arrow (1964) analyse 'The Role of Securities in the Optimal Allocation of Risk-Bearing'. These two papers have influenced deeply the development of the theory of resource allocation under uncertainty. In order to appreciate the significance of these two papers, one must look back at the state of the theory of risk-bearing prior to the 1952 symposium in Paris.

Those who have the privilege of youth and who received their training in this field after these two papers were published,[3] can still get a picture of the previous state of affairs from the survey paper published by Arrow (1951b). Actually, that paper presents, in an orderly manner, a spectrum of approaches and results that could, at that time, be grasped only by those who had fully mastered a highly diversified literature.

Arrow (1951b) surveys the status of theories 'explaining how individuals choose among alternate courses of actions when the consequences of their actions are incompletely known to them' (p. 1). It is noteworthy that he proceeds from the following premise (p. 9): 'It is understood that in economic situations the consequences about which uncertainty exists are commodity bundles or money payments over future dates.' His survey deals successively with two topics: the description of uncertain consequences, and the ordering of courses of actions (whose uncertain consequences have been described in some way).

With reference to the *description of the consequences* resulting from a given course of action, the major distinction is between 'those [descriptions] which use exclusively the language of probability distributions and those which call for some other principle, either to replace or to supplement' (Arrow, 1951b, p. 8). The first category is further subdivided according to the chosen interpretation of probability (see Savage, 1954, p. 3 for a concise description of alternative approaches). The second category reflects the views of scholars of no lesser standing than the economists Keynes, Knight and Shackle, the statisticians Neyman, Pearson and Wald.

[3]The proceedings of the Conference appeared (in French) in November 1953; Savage's contribution was fully developed in his book, *The Foundations of Statistics* (Savage, 1954); Arrow's paper did not become available in English until 1963, but the material in his paper is covered and extended by Debreu (1959) in the *Theory of Value* (ch. 7).

With reference to the *ordering of courses of action*, sharper issues arise when the problem has been recognised as that of ordering probability distributions of consequences. In the 1930s and early 1940s, economists like Hicks (1931), Marschak (1938) and Tintner (1941) were debating whether the ordering of such distributions could be based on their means and standard deviations alone (as given by Hicks (1931)), or on these two and other parameters as well (as given by Marschak (1938)), or should more generally be represented by a 'risk preference functional' (as given by Tintner (1941)).

An axiomatic approach to the ordering of probability distributions, recognising explicitly the 'mutually exclusive' nature of alternative consequences, had been introduced by Ramsey (1931). This approach was revived in successively clearer and simpler terms by von Neumann and Morgenstern (1947) and Marschak (1950), gaining increasing recognition for the existence of a utility function which permits the representation of an ordering among probability distributions of consequences by the mathematical expectation of the utility of these consequences.

Still, by 1951, this approach was far from being generally accepted (see, for instance, the various papers by Allais (CNRS, 1953, and elsewhere)); and its applicability was limited to those situations where the probability distribution of consequences was somehow given. The main suggestions contained in Arrow's survey, in so far as other situations are concerned, came from the minimax school of Wald (1971) (extended to 'minimax regret' by Savage (1951)) and from the specific theory of Shackle (1952). The shortcomings of these approaches are exposed by Arrow.[4]

The defects of this state of affairs were numerous. The lack of agreement among specialists was rather confusing for the beginning student. There was no general conceptual framework, within which one could identify the difficulties specific to certain classes of problems, and assess the significance of specific results.

The most useful theoretical contribution seemed to be that of von Neumann and Morgenstern – yet it was still surrounded by rather obscure discussions. Its applicability seemed restricted to situations where probabilities reflecting the beliefs of the decision-maker could be objectively defined; its relation to the neo-classical theories of consumer choice and of the firm had not been spelled out; and its exposition in terms of 'consequences' identified with wealth was a continuous source of misunderstandings.[5] The need for a more general theory was thus acute.

---

[4] Arrow's survey devotes a few pages to the work of de Finetti, Ramsey, Rubin and Chernoff on axiomatic theories of '*a priori* probabilities'. However, little emphasis is placed on these developments, the significance of which was by no means evident at that time.
[5] This is perhaps best evidenced by the famous article of Friedman and Savage (1948), where a single function is assumed to describe satisfactorily the utility of wealth to both a consumer and his heirs; and by the attention paid to the reinterpretation by Markowitz (1952) of the Friedman–Savage analysis.

2 The conceptual framework

It is by now standard practice to describe a problem of individual decision under uncertainty (or a 'game against nature') in terms of a matrix where:

(i)   the rows correspond to alternative, mutually exclusive courses of action open to the decision-maker;

(ii)   the columns correspond to alternative, mutually exclusive courses of future events;

(iii)   the entries of the matrix correspond to the consequences for the decision-maker resulting from a given course of action under a specific course of events.

Such a description aims at starting from primitive concepts, endowed with an operational meaning in terms of observable phenomena. Thus, the uncertainty is traced back to its source (the future course of events), instead of being described in derived terms – a probability distribution, for instance. And the consequences need not be commodity bundles or money payments; their description may encompass any relevant consideration – from which, possibly, a consumption vector or budget constraint may eventually result.

The trilogy of rows, columns and entries of the matrix, corresponding to 'what the decision-maker does, what nature does, what happens to the decision-maker' admits of a natural abstract representation in terms of two sets. Denoting a course of action by a, a course of future events by s, one then considers the set A of elements $a, a', \ldots$ and the set S of elements $s, s', \ldots$;[6] every entry of the matrix may then be denoted by an ordered pair (a, s). This formal structure is fully adequate as a starting point of the theory. In the same way as 'the currently prevalent axiomatic treatment of probability as a branch of measure theory seems designed to keep the technical development of the theory from being bogged down in the difficulties of the 'foundations' (Arrow, 1951b, p. 406) so the exclusive reliance upon the sets A, S and their Cartesian product $A \times S$ makes it possible to develop the theory of choice under uncertainty without facing explicitly any difficulties of interpretation.

Expositors of the theory discuss concisely the interpretation of the basic concepts. Thus, Savage (1954, p. 9) proposes 'the following nomenclature... as brief, suggestive, and in reasonable harmony with the usages of statistics and ordinary discourse:

> the *world*: the object about which the person is concerned;
> a *state* (of the world): a description of the world, leaving no relevant aspect undescribed;
> the *true* state (of the world): the state that does in fact obtain, i.e. the true description of the world.'

---

[6] The words 'course of action', 'action' and 'act' are here treated as synonyms; the same remark applies to 'course of future events', 'state of the world' and 'state'.

He then completes his set of definitions as follows:

> an *event*: a set of states;
> a *consequence*: anything that may happen to the person;
> an *act*: a function attaching a consequence to each state of the world.[7]

The primitive concepts are thus states and consequences. The formal theory is based upon a set of states S, a set of events (to be denoted $E, E', \ldots$) given by the σ-algebra of S, a set of consequences C and a set of acts given by the mappings of S into C. To consider every such mapping as an act means, of course, to consider hypothetical acts, which do not correspond to courses of action effectively open to the decision-maker.[8]

Some of these hypothetical acts (e.g. constant acts) are needed in the construction of the theory.

The cardinality of the sets S and C has important technical implications. S must be at least denumerably infinite. On the other hand, the theory is easier to develop for acts with only a finite number of distinct consequences.

Before turning to the axioms, three properties of the concepts of events, acts and consequences should be stressed. These properties define the class of decision situations which the theory aims at encompassing; the reasonableness of the axioms should be appraised with reference to those situations only.

2.1 About events

Events must be defined with *interpersonal objectivity* and their occurrence must lie *beyond the control of the decision-maker*. These two aspects are covered by the interpretation of events as circumstances upon which bets can be placed, since the very idea of a bet[9] presupposes that (i) it can be ascertained with interpersonal objectivity who has won the bet, and (ii) neither party to the bet can unilaterally enforce his winning.

The relevance of these remarks for economic applications is the following: (i) uncertainty of the decision-maker about his own tastes at a future date cannot be described through distinct events corresponding to distinct preference structures, since this would violate the condition of

---

[7]This definition is motivated as follows: 'If two different acts had the same consequences in every state of the world, there would from the present point of view be no point in considering them two different acts at all. An act may therefore be identified with its possible consequences' (Savage, 1954, p. 14).

[8]For instance, many consumers could buy a lottery ticket giving them a very small chance of winning a million dollars, but very few have access to a course of action giving them the certainty of winning that amount.

[9]As distinct from a 'challenge'.

interpersonal objectivity;[10] (ii) 'moral hazards', that is uncertainties that lie (at least in part) under the control of the decision-maker, cannot be described through events either.[11]

2.2 About consequences

'In the description of a consequence is included all that the agent values' (Arrow, 1970, p. 45); accordingly, commodity bundles will generally prove inadequate to define consequences. To quote Savage:

> Before going on a picnic with friends, a person decides to buy a bathing suit or a tennis racket.... The possession of the tennis racket and the possession of the bathing suit are to be regarded as acts, not consequences.... The consequences relevant to the decision are such as these: a refreshing swim with friends, sitting on a shadeless beach twiddling a brand new tennis racket while one's friends swim, etc.... (Savage, 1954, p. 25).

Even in those cases where commodity bundles prove adequate to define consequences, a careful definition of commodities may be required. Thus, a person buying 6 eggs, some of which may conceivably be bad, is in fact buying x good eggs and $6-x$ bad eggs, where x is an *unknown* integer, $0 \leqslant x \leqslant 6$. This purchase may be described by a point in the two-dimensional space of 'good' and 'bad' eggs, the location of the point being a function of the state of the world (x).[12]

2.3 About constant acts

The assumption that every consequence can be attained in any state (which implies the existence of constant acts) precludes the explicit consideration of events that are of significant value to the decision-maker; thus, a person's death is clearly a circumstance on which bets can be placed (e.g. through a life-insurance contract), but it is also a 'vital' element in the description of consequences. In defining constant acts, a consequence like 'being alive, poor and healthy' should be attainable in the event that the decision-maker dies – which stretches the imagination of mere mortals a bit too far, in my

[10]With reference to the economics of insurance, a contract specifying that 'I shall receive a certain capital if I develop a taste for Bourbon whisky' would be viewed by the company as equivalent to a sure promise of that capital, since the event mentioned in the contract is not amenable to their verification.

[11]With reference to the economics of insurance again, 'moral hazards' (e.g. arson) occur when the person's actions (as opposed to his tastes) escape verification.

[12]Whereas '6 good eggs' is arithmetically equal to two times '3 good eggs', the same property of addition does not hold for '6 eggs, some of which are good', unless specific assumptions about the determinants of the quality of the eggs are added.

opinion. It thus seems best to exclude such circumstances from explicit consideration.[13]

These properties being understood, it should be clear that the basic concepts offer a medium for the description of problems of decision under uncertainty, which is far more general and flexible than previously available alternatives. To some extent, the gain in clarity and generality is comparable to that achieved by relying upon the formal concept of probability space as the starting point of probability theory. The general conceptual framework can always be particularised to handle specific problems – but the nature of the particular assumptions is then easily assessed.

3 Axioms of a normative theory

Consistency of preferences is traditionally identified with the existence of a simple ordering among the objects of choice; that is, of preferences which are complete and transitive. The preference relation itself is a primitive concept.

To assume that a preference relation is a simple ordering is to assume that the decision-maker behaves neither like Buridan's ass, who died of starvation half-way between a bale of hay and a pail of water, because he could not decide which, his hunger or his thirst, he should satisfy first; nor like Grimm's Hans in Glück, who received a precious gift, then made a series of exchanges, each of which looked favourable to him, and eventually reverted to his initial position.

In the theory of choice under uncertainty reviewed here, the assumption that there exists a simple ordering is successively applied to

(i)   acts;
(ii)   acts, conditionally on events;
(iii)   consequences;
(iv)   events.

Using the symbol $\gtrsim$ to mean 'preferred or indifferent', the first assumption reads:
    For all a, a', $a'' \in A$:

(i)   either $a \gtrsim a'$ or $a' \gtrsim a$;
(ii) $a \gtrsim a'$ and $a' \gtrsim a'' \Rightarrow a \gtrsim a''$.

Some definitions are needed to state the other three assumptions. It will be said that 'a' is not preferred to a, given E (or conditionally on E)' if and only if $b \gtrsim b'$ whenever:

$$\left. \begin{array}{l} c(a,s) = c(b,s) \\ c(a',s) = c(b',s) \end{array} \right\} \forall s \in E; \quad c(b,s) = c(b',s) \forall s \in \tilde{E}.[14]$$

---

[13]See, however, note 22.
[14]$\tilde{E}$ denotes the complement of E (in S).

To assume that conditional preference, given an arbitrary event E, is well defined (is a simple ordering) is to say that the consequences $c(b,s) = c(b',s), s \in \tilde{E}$, are irrelevant to the choice between b and b': if two acts have identical consequences under a certain event ($\tilde{E}$), then the choice between them should proceed as if that event did not exist as a possibility; that is, the choice should not depend in any way upon the nature of these identical consequences. The justification for this assumption (sometimes called 'Sure Thing Principle', as given by Savage (1954), and sometimes called 'Strong Independence Axiom', as given by Marschak (1950)) is that an event E and its complement $\tilde{E}$ are mutually exclusive, so that the attractiveness of the consequences associated with E should be assessed independently of those consequences associated with $\tilde{E}$. The logic of this reasoning seems compelling, even though the implications of the assumption are very strong, as one may realise with the help of an example introduced in the next section.

With conditional preferences well defined, one may define the 'nullity' (subjective impossibility) of an event E either by the condition '$a \gtrsim a'$ given E for all $a, a' \in A$' or by the condition '$a \gtrsim a'$ given $\tilde{E}$ if and only if $a \gtrsim a'$'. A preference relation among consequences is then easily defined as follows: $\bar{c} \gtrsim \bar{c}'$ if and only if $a \gtrsim a'$ given E whenever $c(a,s) = \bar{c}, c(a',s) = \bar{c}'$ for all $s \in E$, E being non-null (but otherwise arbitrary). To assume that this relation is well defined (is a simple ordering) is to assume that consequences are so defined that preferences among them are never modified by knowledge of the event that obtains.

Finally, if $\bar{c}$ and $\bar{c}'$ are two consequences such that $\bar{c} \gtrsim \bar{c}'$, the event E is said to be 'revealed at least as likely' as the event E' if and only if

$a \gtrsim a'$ whenever:
$c(a,s) = \bar{c}, s \in E; \quad c(a,s) = \bar{c}', s \in \tilde{E};$
$c(a',s) = \bar{c}, s \in E'; \quad c(a',s) = \bar{c}', s \in \tilde{E}'.$

This definition states that if a person prefers to stake a prize on E rather than on E', then we may infer that the person regards the occurrence of E as more likely than the occurrence of E'. To assume that this relation is well defined (is a simple ordering among events) is to assume that which one of two events a person prefers to stake a prize on, does not depend upon the nature of the prize.[15] Within the conceptual framework of the theory, it seems hard to object to this assumption, even though the implications of the assumption are very strong, as one may realise with the help of an example introduced in the next section.

The four assumptions just reviewed may be summarised by saying that a consistent decision-maker is assumed always to be able to compare (transitively) the attractiveness of acts, of hypothetical acts and of

---

[15]Remember that a 'prize' is a consequence, and consequences are defined so comprehensively that preferences among them are never modified by knowledge of the event that obtains.

consequences as well as the likelihood of events. These requirements are minimal, in the sense that no consistency of behaviour may be expected if any one of them is violated; but they are very strong, in the sense that all kinds of comparisons are assumed possible, many of which may be quite remote from the range of experience of the decision-maker. This is also the reason why the axioms have more normative appeal than descriptive realism; few people would insist on maintaining, consciously, choices that violate them, but their spontaneous behaviour may frequently fail to display such rigorous consistency.

In order to avoid the trivial case of generalised indifference, it is further assumed that one does not have $c \gtrsim c'$ for all c, c'.

In the theory of consumer choice under certainty, one typically starts with an assumption of simple ordering among commodity bundles.[16] Specific theorems in economics rely upon assumptions about preferences that have no counterpart in the general theory reviewed here; such is the case for the assumptions of desirability and convexity frequently made about preferences among vectors in Euclidian space. There is, however, another assumption which plays an important role in many economic models, and which has a counterpart in the theory of decision under uncertainty; namely, the assumption of continuity. The intuitive concept of continuity of preference is that consequences which are 'close' to each other in some real (physical) sense must also be 'close' to each other in terms of preferences: $c \not\lesssim \bar{c}$ implies $c' \not\lesssim \bar{c}$ for all c' sufficiently close to c (in terms of Euclidian distance).

Continuity of preferences is necessary (and almost sufficient) for the representation of preferences by a continuous real-valued function.

Continuity is frequently described as a 'technical' assumption, to distinguish its nature from the 'logical' assumption of consistency (identified with the existence of a simple ordering). A certain structure must be placed on the objects of choice in order for the technical assumption of continuity to be meaningful. In general, no particular structure applies to the sets A, C or S. But a rich structure can be created by assuming that non-null events can be partitioned at will into other non-null events (for instance, by means of such random mechanisms as dice or coins). This possibility is introduced by means of the assumption of *atomlessness* (if E is non-null, E contains E' less likely than E and non-null). Sequences of non-null events, each of which is contained in, and is less likely than, the preceding one (i.e. monotonic decreasing sequences) are then used to introduce a *continuity* assumption which has the desired implications for representation of preferences by real-valued functions.[17] Atomlessness and continuity are 'technical' assumptions, that bear upon the structure of

---

[16] Some results of economic interest do not require the assumption of complete preferences (see e.g., Schmeidler (1969)).

[17] For precise statements of these assumptions, see Arrow (1970), pp. 48 and 77.

events as well as upon preferences; and in so far as they bear upon preferences, they reflect 'convenience' rather than logical necessity. Thus, Arrow (1970) refers to a simple ordering among objects of choice as being 'the hallmark of rationality' (p. 47), and to the axiom of continuity as being 'the harmless simplification almost inevitable in the formalisation of any real-life problem' (p. 48).

From the assumptions reviewed so far, one deduces the celebrated 'moral expectation theorem' for acts with finitely many distinct consequences,[18] namely:

- there exists a (countably-additive) probability measure P,
- there exists a real-valued function of consequences U, defined up to a linear transformation,

such that

if $c(a, s) = c_i$ for all $s \in E_i$, $c(a', s) = c'_i$ for all $s \in E'_i$,

$a \lesssim a'$ if and only if $\sum_i P(E_i)U(c_i) \leqslant \sum_i P(E'_i)U(c'_i)$.

The theorem states that the orderings of consequences and events are representable, respectively, by a cardinal utility function and by a probability measure, in such a way that the ordering among acts is representable by the expected utility. In particular, the ordering among acts can be constructed by first constructing independently P and U, and then computing expected utilities.[19]

By way of concluding this section, I will illustrate by a simple example how the utility of *information about events* can be inferred from the expected utility of acts. Consider the events E and E', with $P(E) = \frac{1}{2}$, $P(E') = \frac{1}{4}$, $P(E \cap E') = \frac{1}{8}$. Let the act a have two possible consequences c and c', with

$$U(c) = 1, U(c') = -1$$

and

$$c(a, s) = c \text{ for all } s \in E \cap \tilde{E}' \text{ and for all } s \in \tilde{E} \cap E'$$

$$c(a, s) = c' \text{ otherwise.}$$

Clearly, the expected utility of a is zero, with conditional expectations of $\frac{1}{2}$ given E and $-\frac{1}{2}$ given $\tilde{E}$. Let, finally, the act a' be such that $c(a', s) = c$ for all s such that $c(a, s) = c'$, $c(a', s) = c'$ for all s such that $c(a, s) = c$. Again, the expected utility of a' is equal to 0, with conditional expectations of $-\frac{1}{2}$ given E and $\frac{1}{2}$ given $\tilde{E}$.

If the decision-maker is offered the choice between a and a', he will be indifferent between these two acts, and his expected utility will be equal to 0.

---

[18] An additional assumption of 'dominance', namely: '$a \lesssim c(a', s)$ given E for every $s \in E$ implies $a \lesssim a'$ given E', is required to extend the theorem to acts with infinitely many distinct consequences.

[19] An example of these constructions, which may serve as a useful revision of the theory, is given by Pratt et al. (1964).

Should he know whether E is true or not, he could choose a if E is true, a' if E is not true, with an expected utility of $\frac{1}{2}$ in either case. Hence, information about E would have a utility value of $\frac{1}{2}$.

4 Objections to the normative appeal of the axioms

Although objections to the descriptive realism of the theory have been numerous, objections to its normative appeal have been addressed almost exclusively to the assumption regarding conditional preference. The objections have been sustained by examples of simple choice situations, where violations of the axioms of conditional preference are frequently observed among rankings of acts elicited through casual or systematic questionnaires. Two clever examples, due respectively to Maurice Allais and Daniel Ellsberg, will be reproduced here.

The example of Allais consists of four acts, the consequences of which depend upon the drawing of a ball from an urn containing 100 numbered balls. The consequences consist of prizes, expressed say in thousands of dollars, and described in Table 1.1.

Many people report the ranking $a \not\precsim a' \not\precsim b' \not\precsim b$: the certainty of 50 thousand dollars is preferred to a lottery offering 89 chances in a hundred of 50 thousand and 10 chances in a hundred of 250 thousand; but a lottery offering 10 chances in a hundred of 250 thousands is preferred to a lottery offering 11 chances in a hundred of 50. On the other hand, the axiom of conditional preference requires: $a \not\precsim a'$ if and only if $b \not\precsim b'$, since the identical consequences associated, by either a and a' or b and b', with the event '11–99' should not affect the rankings within these two pairs of acts.

The example of Ellsberg consists of four acts, the consequences of which depend upon the drawing of a ball from an urn containing 90 coloured balls. It is specified that 30 balls are red, the other 60 being either black or white; the number of black (white) balls is *not* specified. Accordingly only the events 'red' and 'black or white' have objectively defined numerical probabilities. The acts are described in Table 1.2.

Many people report the ranking $b' \not\precsim b \not\precsim a \not\precsim a'$, which violates the axiom of conditional preference. Reportedly, a is better than a' because a entails an 'objective' probability of $\frac{1}{3}$ of winning the prize, whereas no 'objective'

Table 1.1 *Number on ball drawn at random*

Acts	0	1–10	11–99
a	50	50	50
a'	0	250	50
b	50	50	0
b'	0	250	0

Table 1.2 *Colour of ball drawn at random*

Acts	Red	Black	White
a	50	0	0
a'	0	50	0
b	50	0	50
b'	0	50	50

probability of gain is offered by a'. A similar argument applies to $b' \lessgtr b$.

These two examples rely upon an illusory complementarity operating across mutually exclusive events. In the example of Allais, the consequence associated with the event '11–99' looks 'complementary' to the other consequences in the case of act a, but not in the case of act b. The illusory nature of this 'complementarity' is perhaps best evidenced by the fact that a person insisting on the preferences '$a \lessgtr a', a' \lessgtr a$ given 0–11' would prefer a to an act a^0 whereby the person would first be informed whether the event '11–99' obtains; if it obtains, the person receives 50; otherwise, the person may choose between a and a' (and would choose a'). The ranking would then be $a^0 \lessgtr a \lessgtr a'$ – but a^0 (with the assumed strategy) is *identical* to a'!

In the example of Ellsberg, the event 'white' looks complementary to the event 'black' in the case of act b', but not in the case of act a'. To bring out the illusory nature of that complementarity, it is helpful to consider also an act a^0 promising 50 if the ball is *white*, zero otherwise. One then typically finds that persons preferring a to a' are indifferent between a' and a^0. It may then be remarked that 50–50 chance of either a' or a^0 entails an objective probability of $\frac{1}{3}$ of winning the prize, *irrespective* of the number of black (white) balls, and should be indifferent to a; thus (in an obvious notation): $a \lessgtr a' \sim a^0 \sim (a', a^0; \frac{1}{2}, \frac{1}{2}) \sim a$, which brings out the contradiction quite explicitly.

In both examples, the root of the difficulty is that a decision-maker must decide upon his preferences between a and a' conditionally on a certain event (0–11 in Table 1.1, red or black in Table 1.2); once that ranking is ascertained, consistent choices follow. The temptation to avoid facing squarely the issue of conditional preference is cleverly exploited in constructing the examples. I feel strongly that they belong to the family of 'optical illusions', their main purpose being to remind us of the strength of the assumptions of consistency and of the usefulness of decomposing logically complex choice situations into their elementary components.

Finally, I would like to mention another example, which was constructed during the Bergen Conference. Four acts are involved, with consequences depending upon the toss of a coin. Some consequences are monetary prizes ($\lessgtr 0$), others are tickets for a concert (the person is assumed to be fond of classical music, and equally eager to attend either one of two concerts

Table 1.3 *Outcome of coin toss*

Acts	Heads	Tails
a	$1,000	hear Beethoven's Ninth Symphony (concert A)
a'	$1,000	hear Mozart's Requiem (concert B)
b	$ –1,000	Concert A
b'	$ –1,000	Concert B

planned for the same evening). Several participants at the conference mentioned the ranking $a' \lesssim a \lesssim b \lesssim b'$ (Table 1.3).

One may try to reconcile this understandable ranking with the axiom of conditional preference by claiming that 'concert A' or 'concert B' are not consequences, whereas 'attending concert · in an elated mood', and 'attending concert · in a depressed mood' are consequences. This reinterpretation raises, however, a subtle issue of dependence of the consequences upon the *acts*. Alternatively (or consequently?) one may recognise this type of situation as a limitation to the realm of applicability of the theory – a limitation, however, that may be regarded as innocuous from the viewpoint of economics.

5 Merits and limitations of the theory

In this section, I will propose an evaluation of the merits and limitations of the theory under review from the successive viewpoints of its relevance, usefulness, generality and integration with other theories. In each case, merits and limitations will be mentioned successively, in that order. I will then conclude with an overall evaluation.

5.1 Relevance

5.1.1 The theory has strong normative appeal. The normative appeal of a theory may be measured by the acceptability of its premises and the strength of the conclusions derived from them. As indicated in section 4, I personally regard the axioms of the theory under review as perfectly acceptable. It seems generally agreed that the moral expectation theorem is a strong conclusion based upon these premises. Yet, my interest in the theory derives, in large part, from a slightly different consideration.

Scientists should not attempt, in a professional capacity, to prescribe values or norms of behaviour; but they should explain how, and under what conditions, scientific methods can be brought to bear upon realistic problems. If we accept the view that the values and judgements of a person are eminently relevant to his own decisions, then it seems clear that a consistent assessment of these values and judgements is a necessary condition for scientific reasoning to be brought to bear on his decision problems; and the theory under review has the great merit of telling us that the condition is also sufficient.

To be more specific: whether a person wants to accept a bet involving one chance in eleven of losing 50 thousand dollars, and ten chances in eleven of winning 200 thousand dollars, seems to be for that person to decide; but if a scientist is to use that person's choice in this simple situation to prescribe solutions in more complex situations, then it is a minimal requirement that the choice be unambiguous; (unstable or) intransitive preferences do no meet that minimal requirement; consequently, persons with (unstable or) intransitive preferences not only risk having unfair bets placed against them, they also deprive themselves of the potential assistance of scientists in solving decision problems.

In other words, a person who does not accept the axioms of simple ordering for conditional acts, consequences and events, should not expect any assistance from scientific methods in handling decision problems.

5.1.2 The theory has doubtful descriptive realism. Three remarks will be made in this respect:

(i)   casual empiricism suggests that spontaneous behaviour of reasonable persons may fail to satisfy the axioms of the theory;

(ii)   the formalisation of even the simplest decision problems proves amazingly intricate, and this casts doubts upon the possibility of using the theory as a model within which future choices could be predicted on the basis of past observations;

(iii)   it may still be true (but remains to be demonstrated?) that economic theories based upon the behavioural assumption of expected utility maximisation will have implications that are borne out by empirical tests, and have predictive power.

5.2 Usefulness

5.2.1 The theory is of substantial theoretical usefulness. A normative theory of decision can be helpful in two ways:

(i)   in resolving logical difficulties connected with the statement of problems and criteria for solving them;

(ii)   in bringing powerful scientific methods to bear upon the solution of decision problems.

On both counts, the theory under review is extremely helpful.

(i)   The description of decision problems in terms of acts, events and consequences, is 'far more general and flexible than previously available alternatives' (*supra*, p. 9). The maximisation of expected utility is a generally applicable decision criterion, which resolves logical difficulties previously regarded as serious.

(ii)   The theory brings the powerful mathematical theory of probability to bear upon decision problems. Since a decision-maker's judgements about the likelihood of events are summarised in a probability measure, the rules of conditional probability and Bayes' theorem can be used to incorporate new information.[20]

5.2.2 The theory is of limited practical usefulness. The practical usefulness of the theory is subject to limitations stemming from three problems, which the theory, as such, leaves entirely open, namely:

(i)   the calibration of probabilities;
(ii)   the calibration of utilities;
(iii) the discovery of an optimal act from a given set.

Experiments dealing with individual ability to make realistic probability assessments point strongly towards systematic biases (Raiffa, 1969). This is not surprising, since hardly anybody has ever been trained in assessing probabilities; and it is by no means clear how such training could be effective. As for individual ability to calibrate utilities, very little is known on that score.

The third problem is the subject-matter of optimisation theory, operations research and statistical decision theory. The class of decision problems under uncertainty which can be handled formally is still very limited, and problems of sequential decision raise very serious difficulties.[21]

5.3 Generality

5.3.1 The theory has almost complete formal and logical generality. The formal generality of the theory derives from its ability to encompass situations that were previously distinguished as calling for distinct formalisms – for instance, situations of 'risk' where the relative frequencies in repeated observations invited the formalism of probability, as opposed to situations of 'uncertainty' where the absence of such observations precluded the use of that formalism.

The logical generality of the theory derives from its main conclusion, which justifies the use of expected utility as a single decision criterion. This result provides a single answer to a variety of questions with which economists and statisticians were concerned, and to which they were tempted to offer distinct answers (ranging from 'risk preference functional' to minimax solutions).

Although this view is not generally accepted, I personally understand the expected utility criterion to be applicable to (non-cooperative) games of

---

[20]Arrow (1970, p. 46) remarks: 'The influence of experience on beliefs is of the utmost importance for a rational theory of behaviour under uncertainty, and failure to account for it must be taken as a strong objection to theories such as Shackle's (1952)'.
[21]On this topic, see the last section of Drèze (1972).

strategy as well. If the pure strategies of the opponent(s) are treated as events and if the pay-off of the game is understood to be expressed in utility terms, then one may regard the specific object of the theory of games as being the assessment of the probabilities of events, the ultimate decision criterion being the maximisation of expected utility (under due recognition for the influence of strategy choices on the probabilities of the events).

5.3.2 The applicability of the theory is limited by its conceptual structure. It was emphasised in section 2 that events and consequences had to be defined in such a way that:

(i)   every consequence can be attained in any state;
(ii)   the occurrence of any event can be verified with interpersonal objectivity and lies beyond the control of the decision-maker.

As was noted there, these conditions preclude explicit consideration of events which are themselves of value to the decision-maker (e.g. his own death), or which have a dimension of 'moral hazard'. This is a serious limitation for economic applications.[22]

5.4 Integration with other theories

5.4.1 Economics, statistics and decision theory. A major merit of the theory under review lies in the provision of an integrated framework within which the disciplines of economics, statistics and decision theory can be developed jointly. Uncertainty in economics can best be described through events and consequences. Utility analysis is only natural for economists. The existence of a probability measure on events provides the bridge with statistical theory, whereby empirical information can be used to revise previous judgements. A systematic development of statistical procedures, designed to facilitate such revisions, is currently under way, and goes under the name of 'Bayesian statistics'.[23]

5.4.2 Individual versus group decisions. The theory under review is presented with reference to a single decision-maker. Yet it must be recognised that many, if not most, decision problems of interest to social scientists call for group decisions. In economics, the abstract 'consumer' is typically a family, and most families consist of more than a single person; the abstract 'producer' is typically a firm, grouping many individuals; and

[22] I have shown elsewhere (Drèze, 1961) that such situations could be encompassed in a generalised theory, at the cost of considerable formal complexity, and within the limitations of a serious identification problem.

[23] An additional axiom is required to validate these procedures, namely an axiom which states that the probability of any event E, *after* making an observation x, is equal to the prior probability of E conditionally on x (that is the probability of E given x *before* making the observation).

problems of 'social choice' arise specifically from the presence of several decision-makers, with distinct values and judgements, and typically with conflicting interests. Savage (1954, p. 154) also advances the view that '... *statistics proper* can perhaps be defined as the art of dealing with vagueness and *with interpersonal difference* in decision situation'. One is thus naturally led to wonder about the integration of the theory with other work dealing explicitly with group decisions.

The most important theorem on group decisions in economics is Arrow's impossibility theorem (Arrow, 1951a), which has drawn attention to the difficulties inherent in group decisions based on ordinal preferences (rankings) of the members. Cardinal preferences (a utility function defined up to a linear transformation) open a natural avenue to overcome these difficulties. When there is unanimous agreement about the probabilities, reasonable axioms proposed by Harsanyi (1955) lead to a group utility function, which is a weighted average of individual utility functions. In the absence of agreement about the probabilities, a group probability measure may be defined as a weighted average of the individual measures, but Madansky (1964) has shown that the weights must be revised in the light of new information. And Zeckhauser has proved another important impossibility theorem: there does not exist, in general, a group utility function which aggregates individual utilities, and a group probability measure which aggregates individual probability measures, in such a way that admissible group decisions maximise the expectation of the group utility (in terms of the group probabilities). Further results on this problem have been established by Wilson (1968).[24]

5.5 Overall evaluation

If one refers to the earlier situation, as outlined in section 1, the merits of the theory under review are substantial, and generally outweigh its limitations. In my opinion, the theory provides a starting point for research on the economics of uncertainty that is both natural and satisfactory. Specific applications may call for further specifications or for specific extensions; and one should remain conscious of the doubtful descriptive realism of the theory. But that being understood, it seems fruitful to investigate economic models relying, explicitly or implicitly, upon the axioms or conclusions of the theory.

[24]When the group decisions concern the production and allocation of commodities, Pareto-optimal decisions can be sustained by a price system for contingent claims to commodities (see Guesnerie and de Montbrial (1974). These prices admit of an expected utility interpretation: under appropriate normalisation, undiscounted prices for a numeraire commodity have all the properties of a probability measure on the events; prices for other commodities, expressed in terms of the numeraire conditionally on any given event, measure the utility of these commodities (see Guesnerie and de Montbrial (1974) and Drèze (1971)). In this sense, efficient group decisions sustained by a price system admit of an expected utility interpretation.

6 Link with economic applications

Several writers (Guesnerie and de Montbrial, 1974; Guesnerie and Jaffray, 1974; Gevers, 1974; Drèze, 1974) proceed from a description of uncertainty in terms of events and states of the world. In these models, decisions about production and allocation of commodities are evaluated from the viewpoint of consumer preferences. Given a list of commodities and a list of possible states, a consumption plan for a consumer is a vector specifying his consumption of every commodity in every state. Such a consumption plan corresponds to an act in the terminology used here. Thus, acts are functions from the state of the world to the commodity space. Does it follow that points in the commodity space define consequences? It was noted on p. 8 above that 'commodity bundles will generally prove inadequate to define consequences'. This is also the reason why it is *not* assumed in these papers that preferences among consumption vectors are independent of the state that obtains. It is thus natural to think about consequences as being elements of the Cartesian product of the state space and the commodity space.[25]

These papers rely upon the assumption of a simple ordering among acts. Typically, assumptions of continuity and convexity are made about this ordering. As was explained in section 3, continuity of preferences among acts with values in a Euclidian space is a rather different assumption from the monotone continuity axiom of the theory of subjective probability, and convexity assumptions have no place in the general theory.

Under continuity, the simple ordering of acts is representable by a continuous real-valued function, defined up to a *monotonic* transformation. Values of that function correspond to expected utilities of the acts in the general theory. Under the assumption of conditional preference, the simple ordering of acts with finitely many consequences is representable by an *additive* function, that is by a sum, over the states, of continuous real-valued functions of the consumption in those states. (Of course, the additive property is not preserved by non-linear transformations.) Each such function then corresponds to the product of the probability of the state by the utility of the consequences attained in that state. The assumption of conditional preference, which is equally justified in these models as in the general theory, is not introduced explicitly so long as it is not required to establish general results.

A discussion of the convexity assumption, and of its relation to risk aversion when points in the commodity space define consequences, is given by Arrow (1964, section 4).

Delbaen's work on stochastic preferences (Delbaen, 1974) deserves a

---

[25]That is also the approach followed by Drèze (1961).

special mention. At first sight, it might appear that stochastic preferences among the objects of choice are the very negation of consistent preferences, i.e. of a simple ordering of the objects of choice. Earlier work on this subject (by Georgescu-Roegen (1958) or Luce (1959) for instance) seemed to proceed in that spirit. But the same remark does not apply to the approach introduced by Hildenbrand (1971) and followed by Delbaen. Indeed, the work of these authors seems better described in terms of consequences belonging to the Cartesian product of a state-space and a commodity-space – a formal structure already discussed above. The new element seems to be that the relevant state-space is specific to each consumer, so that states are implicitly defined by uncertainty about consumer tastes. Given the state, commodity vectors are ordered consistently.

References

Arrow, K.J. (1951a). *Social Choice and Individual Values*. New York: Wiley
—(1951b). Alternative Approaches to the Theory of Choice in Risk-Taking Situations. *Econometrica*, 19: 404–37
—(1953). Le rôle des valeurs boursières pour la répartition la meilleure des risques. In *Econométrie*, pp. 41–7. Paris: CNRS. Translated (1964) as The Role of Securities in the Optimal Allocation of Risk-Bearing. *Review of Economic Studies*, 31: 91–6
—(1970). Exposition of the Theory of Choice under Uncertainty. In K.J. Arrow (ed.), *Essays in the Theory of Risk-Bearing*, pp. 44–89. Amsterdam: North-Holland
CNRS (1953). *Econométrie*, Colloque International XL. Paris: CNRS
Debreu, G. (1959). *Theory of Value*. New York: Wiley
Delbaen, F. (1974). Stochastic Preferences and General Equilibrium Theory. In J.H. Drèze (ed.), *Allocation under Uncertainty: Equilibrium and Optimality*, Ch. 7. London: Macmillan
Drèze, J.H. (1961). Les fondements logiques de la probabilité subjective et de l'utilité. In *La Décision*, pp. 73–87. Paris: CNRS (Translated as Chapt. 3 infra.)
—(1971). Market Allocation under Uncertainty. *European Economic Review*, 2: 133–65 (Chapter 6 infra.)
—(1972). Econometrics and Decision Theory. *Econometrica*, 40: 1–17 (Ch. 20 infra.)
—(1974). Investment under Private Ownership: Optimality, Equilibrium and stability. In J.H. Drèze (ed.), *Allocation under Uncertainty: Equilibrium and Optimality*, Ch. 9. London: Macmillan (Chapter 14 infra.)
Friedman, M. and L.J. Savage (1948). The Utility Analysis of Choices Involving Risk. *Journal of Political Economy*, 56: 279–304
Georgescu-Roegen, N. (1958). Threshold in Choice and the Theory of Demand. *Econometrica*, 26: 157–68
Gevers, L. (1974). Competitive Equilibrium of the Stock Exchange and Pareto Efficiency. In J.H. Drèze (ed.), *Allocation under Uncertainty: Equilibrium and Optimality*, Ch. 10. London: Macmillan
Guesnerie, R. and T. de Montbrial (1974). Allocation under Uncertainty: A Survey.

In J.H. Drèze (ed.), *Allocation under Uncertainty: Equilibrium and Optimality*, Ch. 4. London: Macmillan

Guesnerie, R. and J.Y. Jaffray (1974). Optimality of Equilibrium of Plans, Prices and Price Expectations. In J.H. Drèze (ed.), *Allocation under Uncertainty: Equilibrium and optimality*, Ch. 5. London: Macmillan

Harsanyi, J. (1955). Cardinal Welfare, Individualistic Ethics and Interpersonal Comparisons of Utility. *Journal of Political Economy*, 63: 309–21

Hicks, J.R. (1931). The Theory of Uncertainty and Profit. *Economica*, 11: 170–89

Hildenbrand, W. (1971). Random Preferences and Equilibrium Analysis. *Journal of Economic Theory*, 3: 414–29

Luce, R.D. (1959). *Individual Choice Behavior*. New York: Wiley

Madansky, A. (1964). Externally Bayesian Groups, Memorandum RM-4141-PR, The Rand Corporation

Markowitz, M. (1952). The Utility of Wealth. *Journal of Political Economy*, 60: 151–8

Marschak, J. (1938). Money and the Theory of Assets. *Econometrica*, 6: 311–25

—(1950). Rational Behaviour, Uncertain Prospects, and Measurable Utility. *Econometrica*, 18: 111–41

Neumann, J. von and O. Morgenstern (1947). *Theory of Games and Economic Behavior*. Princeton: Princeton University Press

Pratt, J., H. Raiffa and R. Schlaifer (1964). The Foundations of Decision under Uncertainty: An Elementary Exposition. *Journal of the American Statistical Association*, 59: 353–75

Raiffa, H. (1969). Assessment of Probabilities [mimeographed]

Ramsey, F.P. (1931). Truth and Probability. In *The Foundations of Mathematics and Other Logical Essays*, pp. 156–98. London: Routledge and Kegan Paul

Savage, L.J. (1951). The Theory of Statistical Decision. *Journal of the American Statistical Association*, 46: 55–67

—(1953). Une axiomatisation du comportement raisonnable face à l'incertitude. In *Econométrie*, Colloque International XL. Paris: CNRS

—(1954). *The Foundations of Statistics*. New York: Wiley

Schmeidler, D. (1969). Competitive Equilibria in Markets with a Continuum of Traders and Incomplete Preferences. *Econometrica*, 37: 578–85

Shackle, G.L.S. (1952). *Expectation in Economics*. Cambridge University Press

Tintner, G. (1941). The Theory of Choice under Subjective Risk and Uncertainty. *Econometrica*, 9: 298–304

Wald, A. (1950). *Statistical Decision Functions*. New York: Wiley (2nd edn, Bronx, NY: Chelsea Publ. Co., 1971)

Wilson, R. (1968). On the Theory of Syndicates. *Econometrica*, 36: 119–32

2 Decision theory with moral hazard and state-dependent preferences*

1 Introduction

1.1 Scope and example

In the theory of *utility*, as presented in modern terms by von Neumann and Morgenstern (1947) and their followers, one starts from a set of prizes, say the finite set B with elements $b_q, q = 1, \ldots, t$. One then defines probability mixtures of prizes, by means of numerical probability vectors β on B, and observes the preferences of a decision-maker among such probability mixtures. When these preferences satisfy three simple axioms (complete order, independence and continuity – see Section 3 below), there exists a real-valued function u on B, called utility, such that preferences among probability mixtures of prizes are isomorphic with expected utilities. That is, the mixture β is preferred to the mixture β' if and only if

$$\sum_q \beta(b_q)u(b_q) > \sum_q \beta'(b_q)u(b_q). \tag{1.1}$$

In the theory of *games against nature*, as presented in modern terms by Savage (1954) and his followers, one starts from a set of alternative, mutually exclusive states of the world, say the finite[1] set S with elements

*I have benefited greatly from discussions with Robert Aumann, Claude d'Aspremont, Yossi Greenberg, Heraklis Polemarchakis and Shmuel Zamir, as well as from comments on a previous draft by George Dionne and Ngo van Long. My deepest gratitude goes to William Vickrey, who supervised my Ph.D. Dissertation on which this chapter is based and who repeatedly encouraged me to bring out this material in print.
[1]A finite set is considered here for ease of exposition at a non-technical level. The formal development of the theory requires reliance on arbitrarily fine partitions of S, or else (as in Section 4) on probability mixtures of acts.

$s^1, \ldots, s^n$. Using, as before, a set B of prizes ('consequences'), acts $f, f', \ldots$, are defined as mappings of S into B – that is, as state distributions of prizes (instead of the probability distributions of prizes considered in utility theory). One then observes the preferences of a decision-maker among acts. When these preferences satisfy certain axioms (about which more below), there exists a utility u on B and a (subjective) probability p on S, such that preferences among acts are isomorphic with (subjectively) expected utilities. Denote by $b(f, s^m)$ the prize associated with state s^m by act f; then act f is preferred to act f' if and only if

$$\sum_m p^m u(b(f, s^m)) > \sum_m p^m u(b(f', s^m)). \tag{1.2}$$

Thus, the theory of Savage *extends* that of von Neumann and Morgenstern to events for which no agreed numerical probabilities exist. It also *validates* the von Neumann–Morgenstern theory, by showing that numerical probabilities emerge naturally in a consistent approach to decisions under uncertainty.

This last observation also suggests how the theories of utility and of subjective probability can be developed 'sequentially'. In a first step, one uses a single pair of prizes (say, $b_1 =$ status quo and $b_2 =$ status quo plus \$100) to define acts by staking either prize on the outcomes of *random devices* (roulette wheels, cards, dice, coins, ...). Imposing the Savage axioms on the choices among such acts yields numerical probabilities for the random outcomes.[2]

In a second step, *these probabilities* are used to form probability mixtures of prizes (from the whole set B), and to develop the theory of utility. The third step then leads to subjective probabilities. Starting from numerical probabilities for random outcomes, this is a small additional step. For each state s^m, it suffices to find a random outcome (with known probability) such that the decision-maker would *indifferently* stake a prize on s^m or on that outcome. That simple procedure is well defined, provided the indifference relation in question is invariant to the prize used in eliciting it. That is, 'on which of two events the person will choose to stake a given prize does not depend on the prize itself' (Savage, 1954, p. 31).

Intuitively, there are two aspects to this last requirement. First, the subjective probability of an event should be fixed, independently of the prize (or penalty) staked on the event; (otherwise, one faces a situation of 'moral hazard'). Second, the utility of a prize should be fixed, independently of the event that obtains; (otherwise, one faces a situation of 'state-dependent preferences'). When the theory is developed sequentially, as suggested in the previous paragraph, each of these two aspects is covered by

[2]Authors following a 'sequential' approach typically omit this first step altogether, and treat the numerical probabilities for random outcomes as a given primitive; for an exception, see Drèze (1961. Section 14).

a simple, plausible axiom; the elegant 'Definition of Subjective Probability' by Anscombe and Aumann (1963), restated in Section 4, brings this out.[3]

A simple example illustrates the two requirements, and the corresponding postulates. A bowman is about to participate in an Olympic archery contest, where his chances of winning are quite good. Two events are considered: 'winning' or 'losing'. Let it be observed that the bowman would indifferently stake a $100 prize on 'winning', on 'losing' or on observing 'head' in a coin toss. Does it follow that he would also be indifferent between staking a $100 000 prize on 'winning', on 'losing' or on 'head'? Not necessarily.

First, a $100 000 prize staked on 'losing' *might* induce the bowman to aim amiss and lose the contest for sure; if this prospect appeals to him more than staking the prize on 'head' or on 'winning', a situation of moral hazard arises.

The postulate ruling out moral hazard goes as follows. Let the bowman be told that he will be offered a $100 000 prize, but *a coin toss will decide whether the prize is staked on* 'winning' *or on* 'losing'. Does it matter to him that the coin be tossed after, or before, the contest?[4] If the bowman *insists* on having the coin tossed *before* the contest, it may be surmised that he wants the information to aim accordingly; moral hazard prevails, and his (subjective) probability of winning will depend upon which way the prize goes. A simple postulate, ruling out moral hazard, is called by Anscombe and Aumann 'Reversal of Order'. It requires that when a random device is to decide which of two acts obtains, the device may *indifferently* be activated before or after observing the true state.[5]

Second, winning the contest may change the bowman's life altogether – say, from being a happy college instructor to becoming famous and a wealthy executive in a sport goods company. This *might* change his attitude towards wealth fundamentally – say, from being highly risk averse to becoming nearly risk neutral; if he then prefers to stake the $100 000 prize on 'winning' than on either 'losing' or 'head', a situation of 'state-dependent preferences' arises.

The postulate ruling out state-dependent preferences is well known. It calls for eliciting preferences over prizes (or probability mixtures of prizes) *conditionally* on alternative states, and imposing that these conditional

[3]The extension of the theory of games against nature, successively to situations of moral hazard (Section 6) and to situations of state-dependent preferences (Section 8), calls for relaxing each axiom in turn. ·
[4]The significance of postponing the activation of a random device is clearly brought out in the following more realistic example, suggested to me by J. Greenberg. When income tax returns are checked on a sample basis, the sample is drawn *after* the returns come in; and yet it would be more efficient to notify the taxpayers beforehand: those to be checked would document their returns carefully, speeding up verification; while others could save themselves the trouble of detailed justification....
[5]As in note 25 below, this postulate implies the 'Sure Thing Principle' advocated by Savage (1954, Section 2.7).

preferences be invariant with respect to the states. Thus, the bowman could be told the $100 prize will be replaced by a 50–50 chance of either $20 or $200. If he finds this alternative prize just as attractive as $100 when staked on 'winning', then (says the postulate) he should also find it equally attractive when staked on 'losing' or on 'head'.

Two further points should be noted about this example. First, whether the bowman aims carefully, or aims amiss, is not observable – an essential aspect of 'moral hazard'. Second, whether and how the event 'winning' will affect the bowman's preferences over prizes cannot be ascertained a priori, but should be inferred from his choices among acts – an essential aspect of 'state-dependent preferences'.

The purpose of this chapter is to present, in simple terms, the extensions of the theory of games against nature to situations of moral hazard and state-dependent preferences, initially developed by Drèze (1958, 1961).

The nature of these two extensions, and their status in the literature, is quite different.

1.2 Moral hazard

The words 'moral hazard' are used here to denote a variety of situations where the decision-maker chooses simultaneously an act, as defined above, and a 'strategy' susceptible of influencing the course of events. These situations include 'games of strength and skill', in the terminology of von Neumann and Morgenstern (1947). The term 'moral hazard' comes from the literature on insurance, where it is recognised that 'the insurance policy might itself change incentives and therefore the probabilities upon which the insurance company has relied. Thus, a fire insurance policy for more than the value of the premises might be an inducement to arson or at least to carelessness' (Arrow, 1965, p. 142).

I am not aware of any attempt by others at developing an axiomatic approach to decision theory with moral hazard.[6] But there exists a fair amount of applied work on that subject.[7] That work proceeds from models where the decision-maker has access to a given set of strategies, say Σ with elements $\sigma, \sigma', \ldots$. With each strategy σ in Σ is associated a probability measure p_σ on S.[8] It is then *assumed* that the decision-maker chooses, for each act, the strategy which maximises expected utility. Preferences among acts are then isomorphic with expected utilities *under the maximising strategies*. That is, act f is preferred to act f' if and only if[9]

$$\text{Max}_{\sigma \in \Sigma} \sum_m p_\sigma^m u(b(f, s^m)) > \text{Max}_{\sigma' \in \Sigma} \sum_m p_{\sigma'}^m u(b(f', s^m)). \tag{1.3}$$

---

[6]In private conversations, I have heard expressions of scepticism about the very idea of eliciting personal probabilities for events lying, partly or entirely, under the control of the decision-maker.

[7]See, for example, Dionne (1982) and the references given there.

[8]As σ ranges over Σ, a set P of probability measures on S is generated.

[9]In (1.3), the maximisation could equivalently be stated in terms of $p \in P$, $p' \in P$.

Inequality (1.3) embodies an extension of the principle of expected utility maximisation from the realm of games against nature (choice of an act) to the realm of moral hazard (simultaneous choice of an act and a strategy).

The same extension underlies much of the theory of *games of strategy*, where players are continually assumed to maximise expected utility, both with respect to choices of strategies (due account being taken of the interactions among players) and with respect to choices of games or payoffs.[10]

It is somewhat surprising that the rule (1.3) is invariably used *without specific justification*, as if it were implicitly covered by the axioms of consistent behaviour in games against nature. Clearly, if such were the case, then it would be worthwhile to bring out the logical connection explicitly; and if it is not the case, then it is worthwhile to exhibit a set of behavioural axioms from which the rule follows.

Drèze (1958, 1961) makes allowance for moral hazard by relaxing the 'Reversal of Order' assumption into the following weaker requirement:[11] when a random device is to decide which of two acts obtains, the decision-maker *never prefers* (strictly) that the device be activated *after* observing the true state *instead of beforehand*. Thus, when told that a coin toss will decide whether a $100 000 prize is to be staked on 'winning' or on 'losing', the bowman in my example should not *insist* on having the coin tossed *after* the contest.[12] As shown in Section 6, this (in conjunction with the postulates of utility theory and of state-independent preferences) validates the rule (1.3): there exists a (closed convex) set of probability measures P on S, and a utility u on B, such that act f is preferred to act f' if and only if

$$\underset{p \in P}{\text{Max}} \sum_m p^m u(b(f, s^m)) > \underset{p' \in P}{\text{Max}} \sum_m p'^m u(b(f', s^m)). \tag{1.4}$$

That result (stated formally and proved as theorem 6.1 below) provides the missing axiomatic foundations for the applied work on moral hazard. It is gratifying that no new assumptions are needed. The main implications of the result for analysis of strategy choices and for elicitation of subjective probabilities are given in Sections 6.3, 6.4 and 7.

Some implications of the result for the theory of games of strategy (where a strict preference for postponing information about choices is sometimes reasonable) are outlined in Section 9.4.

Furthermore, the result has useful implications for my second topic, i.e. state-dependent preferences.

1.3 State-dependent preferences

The extension of decision theory to situations of state-dependent preferences raises an altogether different problem, which has been recognised

---

[10]See, for example, Luce and Raiffa (1958, Ch. 3).
[11]See assumption 5.1, labelled 'Value of Information', and the comments in Section 9.3.
[12]This is not an altogether vacuous requirement; see the discussion in Section 9.3.

(but not solved) in the literature on games against nature.[13] Situations where preferences over such prizes as money amounts or commodity bundles vary with the state that obtains are frequent. The most obvious example is life insurance, which is motivated (in spite of the unfair odds of most contracts) by the consideration that 'wealth in case of death' is not the same thing as 'wealth in case of life'. In the terminology of Savage (1954, pp. 13, 25), these define different 'consequences', which are, however, *specific to certain events*. It is therefore impossible to associate a *given* consequence (like death cum \$10 000) with *every* state.[14] But it remains possible to associate *prizes* (like \$10 000) with every state, and to accept that preferences over prizes are state-dependent. (This amounts to redefining consequences as pairs, consisting of a prize and a state.) One must then omit the requirement that conditional preferences over prizes be state invariant, while retaining the requirement that they be well defined.

As suggested in my bowman example, one can elicit *conditional preferences over prizes* (or probability mixtures of prizes) under every state. If these preferences satisfy the axioms of von Neumann and Morgenstern, they are representable *under each state* by a utility function on B, specific to that state – say, $u^m(b)$ for state s^m. *Each of these conditional utilities is defined up to a positive linear transformation*. There remains the problem of relating the scales and origins of the n state-specific (conditional) utilities. In the context of games against nature, that problem remains unsolved, and insolvable.[15]

Thus, introducing state-specific utilities in expression (1.2), one may rewrite the inequality as:

$$\sum_m p^m[u^m(b(f,s^m)) - u^m(b(f',s^m))] > 0, \tag{1.5}$$

where $u^m(b)$ has received an arbitrary scale normalisation.

Rescaling each function u^m by a specific constant $1/c^m > 0$, and adjusting simultaneously each probability p^m by a factor $c^m/\sum_l p^l c^l$, we can verify:

$$\sum_m \frac{p^m c^m}{\sum_l p^l c^l}\left[\frac{1}{c^m}u^m(b(f,s^m)) - \frac{1}{c^m}u^m(b(f',s^m))\right]$$

$$:= \sum_m \hat{p}^m[\hat{u}^m(b(f,s^m)) - \hat{u}^m(b(f',s^m))] > 0. \tag{1.6}$$

In (1.6), $\hat{u}^m(b) := (1/c^m)(u^m(b))$ is a utility for prizes conditionally on s^m if and only if $u^m(b)$ is such a utility; $\hat{p}^m := p^m c^m/\sum_l p^l c^l$ is a probability measure ($m = 1,\ldots,n$) on S if and only if p^m is such a probability; and preferences among acts are isomorphic with (1.6) if and only if they are isomorphic with

---

[13]See Section 9.1 for references.
[14]This point is discussed further in Section 9.1.
[15]See Section 9.1 for particulars.

(1.5). But p and $\hat{p}$ are *different probability measures*. In short, (subjective) *probabilities and the scales of conditional utilities are not separately identified on the basis of observed preferences among acts.*

It is shown in Section 8, following Drèze (1958, 1961), how that identification problem receives a solution (at least a partial solution) in the broader context of games with moral hazard. Returning to my example, suppose that when a coin toss must decide whether a $100 000 prize is to be staked on 'winning' (act 1) or on 'losing' (act 2), the bowman *insists* on having the coin tossed *before* the contest. Suppose furthermore that an act 3, staking a $50 000 prize on 'losing', has the following property: if a coin toss must decide whether act 1 or act 3 holds, the bowman is *indifferent* between having the coin tossed *before or after* the contest; and the same indifference prevails if a coin toss must decide whether act 2 or act 3 holds. We could then draw the following inferences:

(i)   a $100 000 'prize' for losing induces the bowman to aim amiss;
(ii)   a $50 000 'prize' for losing leaves him *indifferent* between aiming amiss (losing the contest and collecting the prize), or aiming carefully (with some chance of winning, some chance of losing and collecting the prize);
(iii)   therefore, the bowman is indifferent, in the behavioural sense, between 'losing cum $50 000' and 'winning cum $0' – a conclusion which *relates the levels of the two conditional utilities.* Using another similarly revealed indifference relation – say, between 'losing cum $60 000' and 'winning cum $15 000' – would relate unambiguously the *scales* of the two conditional utilities.

The reason why this approach works should be intuitively clear. Under moral hazard, a decision-maker chooses states (through his strategies) as well as prizes. His observed preferences among acts (with accompanying strategies) reveal implicit preferences among 'prize and state' pairs.[16] If strategies were directly observable, implementation of the approach would be straightforward. With unobserved strategies, implementation requires a detour: that two acts call for distinct strategies, is inferred from the positive value of early information as to which act prevails; in this way, strategy choices become indirectly observable.

Thus, 'moral hazard' introduces a complication into the Savage model; but that complication is easily handled formally (by a natural relaxation of the 'Reversal of Order' assumption); and that complication, in addition to being of independent interest, resolves the identification problem associated with state-dependent preferences.[17]

It is thus natural to treat both extensions in a single paper, even though

---

[16]The approach only works to the extent that every state is, to some extent, 'chosen'. In general, that is not the case and the identification problem receives a partial solution only; see theorem 8.2 and the ensuing comments.

[17]A small price must be paid, however: the elicitation of conditional preferences requires additional precautions under moral hazard; indeed, a given state may be regarded as impossible under *some but not all* strategies. That technicality is treated in Section 8.2.

they are of a different nature. The treatment of moral hazard extends the *logic* of utility maximisation to strategy choices. The treatment of state-dependent preferences extends the *elicitation* of probabilities and utilities to a state-dependent utility – in situations where the logic of choice remains the same.

1.4 Organisation and concepts

The contents of this chapter are organised as follows:

Section 2: The model and notation
Section 3: The von Neumann–Morgenstern theorem
Section 4: The Anscombe–Aumann theorem
Section 5: The value of information and equipotence
Section 6: Decision theory with state-independent preferences and moral hazard
Section 7: Properties of the set of attainable probabilities
Section 8: Decision theory with state-dependent preferences and moral hazard
Section 9: Comments

Assumptions and definitions are listed with page references in Appendix D, p. 88.

This organisation follows a gradual sequence, from utility theory (Section 3) to games against nature (Section 4) to moral hazard (Section 6) to state-dependent preferences (Section 8). Specific results of relevance to both Section 6 and Section 8 are isolated in the separate Sections 5 and 7.

The presentation in Sections 2–8 is mostly technical, with additional comments collected in the final section. Technical demands are not heavy, but the reasoning must handle carefully one aspect typically absent from axiomatic theories of decision: whether a random device is activated before or after observing the true state makes a crucial difference.

The sequential presentation here is at variance with my earlier work (Drèze, 1958, 1961) where the general model of decisions with state-dependent preferences and moral hazard was tackled at once (and without reliance on previously elicited numerical probabilities for random outcomes). That earlier approach had the (youthful?) drawback of introducing too many complications at once, thereby obscuring the specific nature of individual difficulties and the specific role of individual assumptions. Hopefully, the presentation here will prove easier to follow. It has, of course, benefited substantially from intervening contributions, in particular the closely related contribution by Anscombe and Aumann (1963). The preliminary step of eliciting formally the numerical probabilities for outcomes of random devices is omitted altogether – on grounds summarised in Section 9.2.

Although the presentation is sequential, the basic model and notation are the same throughout. Assumptions specific to individual sections (namely, 4 and 6) restrict the applicability to certain classes of situations. The basic concepts are geared to the more general case ('with state-dependent preferences and moral hazard'). The added generality, also reflected in the terminology, carries an advantage: the concepts are more clear-cut and operational.

My basic concepts are states and events; prizes (or probability mixtures of prizes); and games (or probability mixtures of games called 'lotteries'). I conclude this introduction with some comments on these concepts and their interpretation.

An event is any circumstance on which a wager can be placed. Thus, an event must be so defined that its occurrence can be verified with interpersonal objectivity. But the description of an event may include activities of the decision-maker himself (like his running a mile in 7 minutes, his presence at a certain time and place,...), or circumstances influenced by the decision-maker's unobserved behaviour (like his winning an archery contest, his survival over a given period,...). The objective verification makes the concept operational.

An event which is not the union of other events is a state. In other words, there exists a finest partition of the set of events, and elements of that partition ('elementary events') are called states. Although that concept is at best an idealisation, states play an important role in some parts of the theory below. Some comments on this limitation are offered in Section 9.7.

There is a set of prizes, each of which can be associated with any state (in defining wagers). It is natural to think about prizes as consisting of commodity bundles, sums of money, and the like. Because preferences over prizes will be allowed to become state-dependent, there is no need to aim at a 'comprehensive' concept, like the 'consequences' of Savage (1954, p. 13: 'A consequence is anything that may happen to the person'). Any given set of prizes will do, and the concept is perfectly operational. (Pairs consisting of a state and a prize will eventually play the role of 'consequences'.)

For convenience, I use a finite set of prizes, and introduce continuity by forming *probability mixtures of prizes, or prize mixtures.*

A game is a function associating a prize mixture with every state. The term 'game' is substituted for 'act' to remind us that the decision-maker is also choosing an (unobserved) 'strategy', in situations involving 'moral hazard'. The term 'game' is thus a short cut for 'game against nature with moral hazard'. Strategies themselves are not introduced as a formal concept; the term is used only in heuristic, intuitive interpretations.

Under the definition of a game, the random device selecting a specific prize, from the prize mixture associated with a given state, is to be activated *after the true state is observed.* In contrast, when a *probability mixture of games* is considered, it is understood that the random device selecting a specific game from the mixture is to be activated *at once*. Probability mixtures of games are called *lotteries*. The importance of the distinction between immediate and postponed information about random choices was illustrated in Sections 1.1–1.2. It is reflected in the notation introduced in Section 2.

The theory of utility is introduced in Section 3 for probability mixtures of games (lotteries). The three simple axioms of the theory are then definitely convincing. The von Neumann–Morgenstern theorem asserts the existence of *a function on games*, here called 'value', such that preferences among lotteries are isomorphic with their expected 'values'. That result is used as a stepping stone in the sequential development of the theory, successively for 'games against nature' (Section 4), 'games with moral hazard' (Section 6) and 'games with moral hazard and state-dependent preferences' (Section 8).

Precisely what class of situations is encompassed by a theory must ultimately be decided by assessing the reasonableness of the assumptions in a given context. The present theory does not apply to general game situations (games of strategy) because the assumption that information has non-negative value is not reasonable in that context – a point illustrated and discussed in Section 9.4. Two other kinds of situations sometimes referred to under the heading of moral hazard do not fit into my model: situations where 'strategies' are an object of preference *by themselves,* and not only through their influence on prizes and states;[18] and situations where the set of available 'strategies' depends upon the prizes.[19] Sections 9.3 and 9.5 take up the possibility of extending the model to these cases.

2 The model and notation

The set S of *states* comprises finitely many elements $s^1,\ldots,s^m,\ldots,s^n$, with subsets (*events*) denoted $S^A, S^B,\ldots$. The complement of S^A in S is denoted $S^{\sim A}$; the complement of s^m is denoted $S^{\sim m}$.

There is a given finite[20] set B of *prizes* $b_0, b_1,\ldots, b_q,\ldots, b_t$. The set B contains at least two distinct elements – say, b_0 and b_1.

A probability mixture of prizes, or more concisely a *prize mixture,* is defined by a probability measure β on B. The set of all such probability measures is denoted $\mathbb{B}$. Specific elements of $\mathbb{B}$ will be identified below by appropriate indices.

The set $\mathbb{B}$ is closed under (finite) compounding of probabilities. For β and β' in $\mathbb{B}$ and α in $[0, 1]$, $\alpha\beta + (1 - \alpha)\beta'$ in $\mathbb{B}$. Following Luce and Raiffa (1958) and Fishburn (1982), I also write $\beta\alpha\beta'$ for $\alpha\beta + (1 - \alpha)\beta'$, and note that $\mathbb{B}$ is a 'mixture set'.[21]

---

[18]Unobserved effort, in principal-agent problems, offers an example.
[19]Think about a 'nervous bowman' whose shooting accuracy is reduced when the stakes are high.
[20]It would make no difference whatever to use an infinite set of prizes, while restricting attention to simple probability measures on that set. I have a partiality for finite sets.
[21]Thus, for λ in $[0, 1]$, $(\beta\alpha\beta')\lambda\beta' \equiv \beta(\alpha\lambda)\beta'$.

A *game* is a mapping of S into $\mathbb{B}$. That is, a game assigns a prize mixture to each state in S. The set of games is denoted G, with elements $g_0, g_1, \ldots, g_h, g_i, \ldots$. I shall denote by β_h^m the prize mixture associated with state s^m by the game g_h, $m = 1, \ldots, n$. Thus, $g_h := (\beta_h^1, \ldots, \beta_h^n)$ and $G := \mathbb{B}^n$.

This definition should be understood as follows: *after the true state is observed, a random device will be activated, to determine a prize from B* – according to the probabilities β_h^m, if the game was g_h and the state is s^m.

It is sometimes convenient to describe a game succinctly by $g_h := (\beta_h^m, \beta_h^{-m})$, where β_h^{-m} is a concise notation for the $(n-1)$-tuple of prize mixtures $(\beta_h^1, \ldots, \beta_h^{m-1}, \beta_h^{m+1}, \ldots, \beta_h^n)$. A natural extension of this notation consists in writing (β, β_h^{-m}) for a game associating the prize mixture β with state s^m and the same prize mixtures as g_h with all other states.

A *constant game* is a game assigning the same prize mixture to every state. Thus, g_h is constant when $\beta_h^l = \beta_h^m$ for all $l, m = 1, \ldots, n$.

A probability mixture of games is defined by a simple probability measure γ on G; that is, by a probability measure γ on G such that $\gamma(g_h) \neq 0$ for finitely many elements g_h of G only. Such a probability mixture of games is here called a *lottery*, and the word lottery is used exclusively with this specific technical meaning.[22] The set of lotteries is denoted by Γ, with elements $\gamma, \gamma', \gamma'', \ldots$.

The set Γ is closed under (finite) compounding of probabilities, and is again a 'mixture set'.

The definition of a lottery should be understood as follows: under lottery γ, *a random device will be activated at once, to determine a game from G,* according to the probabilities γ; afterwards, when the true state is observed, a random device will in turn determine a prize from B, according to the probabilities β_h^m if the game is g_h and the state s^m.

The foregoing definitions have specific and important implications for the *timing of information*. To every lottery γ, there corresponds *numerically* a uniquely defined game, obtained by *postponing the draw of lottery γ* until after the true state is observed. That game is denoted g_γ and called 'the game *corresponding* to lottery γ'. It is defined as follows (using a summation sign to denote an integral with respect to the *simple measure* γ, over the set G with generic element g_h):

Definition 2.1: The game g_γ corresponding to lottery γ is defined by

$$g_\gamma := (\beta_\gamma^1, \ldots, \beta_\gamma^n), \quad \text{where } \beta_\gamma^m = \sum_h \gamma(g_h)\beta_h^m, m = 1, \ldots, n. \text{[23]} \tag{2.1}$$

The lottery under which the games g_h and g_i receive probabilities α and

---

[22]This is in contrast to the terminology of Anscombe and Aumann (1963), who refer to my prize mixtures as 'roulette lotteries', to my games as 'compound horse lotteries' and to my lotteries as 'roulette lotteries whose prizes are such horse lotteries' (pp. 200–1).

[23]Thus, β_γ^m is the marginal distribution on $\mathbb{B}$ implied by γ if s^m obtains. Drèze (1958, 1961) called γ an 'immediate lottery' and g_γ 'the corresponding delayed lottery'. The terminology adopted here is simpler: all lotteries are drawn immediately, all games entail delayed draws.

$1 - \alpha$ respectively is denoted $g_h \alpha g_i$. The *corresponding game* is accordingly denoted $g_{g_h \alpha g_i}$. When state s^m is of particular interest, I use the notation $g_h := (\beta_h^m, \bar{\beta}_h^{-m})$, $g_i := (\beta_i^m, \bar{\beta}_i^{-m})$. Then $g_h \alpha g_i := (\beta_h^m, \bar{\beta}_h^{-m}) \alpha (\beta_i^m, \bar{\beta}_i^{-m})$ and, by (2.1),

$$g_{g_h \alpha g_i} := g_{(\beta_h^m, \bar{\beta}_h^{-m}) \alpha (\beta_i^m, \bar{\beta}_i^{-m})} \equiv (\beta_h^m \alpha \beta_i^m, \bar{\beta}_h^{-m} \alpha \bar{\beta}_i^{-m}). \tag{2.2}$$

It must be stressed emphatically that

$$(\beta_h^m, \bar{\beta}_h^{-m}) \alpha (\beta_i^m, \bar{\beta}_i^{-m}) \not\equiv (\beta_h^m \alpha \beta_i^m, \bar{\beta}_h^{-m} \alpha \bar{\beta}_i^{-m}). \tag{2.3}$$

Indeed, the *lottery* on the left entails *immediate* drawing of either g_h (with probability α) or g_i; whereas the *game* on the right entails the single compound drawing, *after observing the true state*, of a prize from B – according to the probabilities $\beta_h^l \alpha \beta_i^l = \alpha \beta_h^l + (1 - \alpha) \beta_i^l$ if the true state is s^l.

In the theory presented here, lotteries are the only object of choice. It will be assumed that the decision-maker has observable preferences among lotteries. The theory rests on these, and *only on these*, preferences.

When γ is not preferred to γ', I write $\gamma \precsim \gamma'$. In case of indifference (both $\gamma \precsim \gamma'$ and $\gamma' \precsim \gamma$), I write $\gamma \sim \gamma'$. In case of strict preference, I write $\gamma \prec \gamma'$.

In the notation, greek letters are reserved for probabilities, with the exception of ι (iota) which denotes a vector $(1, \ldots, 1)$ with all elements equal to unity; and δ^m, which denotes the Kronecker unit vector $(0, \ldots, 1, \ldots, 0)$, with element m equal to unity. Closed and open intervals are denoted by $[,]$ and $(,)$ respectively. Scalar products are identified by a dot as in $p \cdot c = \sum_l p^l c^l$.

3 The von Neuman–Morgenstern theorem

Throughout this chapter, it is assumed, *without reminder*, that preferences *over lotteries* satisfy the postulates of von Neumann and Morgenstern (1947), stated here as follows:[24]

PO (Weak Order)

(i)   For all γ, γ' in Γ, either $\gamma \precsim \gamma'$ or $\gamma' \precsim \gamma$;

(ii)   For all $\gamma, \gamma', \gamma''$ in Γ, if $\gamma \precsim \gamma'$ and $\gamma' \precsim \gamma''$, then $\gamma \precsim \gamma''$.

PI (Independence)

For all $\gamma, \gamma', \gamma''$ in Γ, for all α in $(0, 1]$, $\gamma \alpha \gamma'' \precsim \gamma' \alpha \gamma''$ if and only if $\gamma \precsim \gamma'$.

PC (Continuity)

For all $\gamma, \gamma', \gamma''$ in Γ, if $\gamma \prec (\succ) \gamma'$, then there exists α in $[0, 1)$ such that $\gamma \alpha \gamma'' \prec (\succ) \gamma'$.

The well-known 'expected utility' theorem of von Neumann and Morgenstern (1947) follows from these postulates. Because I want to reserve the term 'utility' for a function defined on the set B of prizes, I shall retain the

[24]See also Fishburn (1982, Section 2.2).

terminology of Drèze (1961) and call *value* a function on *games*, whose expectation represents preferences among lotteries.

Theorem 3.1: Under **PO, PI, PC**, there exists a real-valued function V, defined on G up to a positive linear transformation, such that $\gamma \precsim \gamma'$ if and only if $\sum_h \gamma(g_h)V(g_h) \leqslant \sum_h \gamma'(g_h)V(g_h)$.

Because games are special (degenerate) lotteries, preferences over lotteries imply preferences over games. Also, preferences over constant games may be interpreted as a kind of preferences over prize mixtures; namely preferences over these prize mixtures *when promised with certainty*, no matter what state obtains. Again, prizes are special (degenerate) prize mixtures. Hence, preferences over prize mixtures imply preferences (of the same kind) over prizes. All these preferences are weak orders, in view of **PO**. They will be denoted by the same symbols $\precsim, \prec, \sim$. Thus, $g_h \precsim g_i, \beta \precsim \beta'$ or $b_q \precsim b_r$ are successive specialisations of the basic preference relation $\gamma \precsim \gamma'$. And these specialisations can be combined in statements like $g_h \precsim \gamma, \beta \precsim \gamma$, a.s.o. Similarly, the values of constant games may be interpreted as values of the corresponding prize mixtures (or prizes), when promised no matter what state obtains. These values are accordingly denoted $V(\beta)$, or $V(b_q)$.

4 The Anscombe–Aumann theorem

Relying upon probability mixtures and the von Neumann–Morgenstern theorem, Anscombe and Aumann (1963) derive the Savage theorem from two additional assumptions, which they call 'Monotonicity' and 'Reversal of Order' respectively. In the notation adopted here, these two assumptions read as follows:

Assumption 4.1 (Monotonicity): Let the games g_h and g_i be such that $\beta_h^{\sim m} = \beta_i^{\sim m}$; then $\beta_h^m \precsim \beta_i^m$ implies $g_h \precsim g_i$.

Assumption 4.2 or **RO** (Reversal of Order): Every lottery is indifferent to the corresponding game; that is, for all γ in Γ, $\gamma \sim g_\gamma$.

Assumption 4.2 (RO) formalises the idea that postponing the draw of a lottery is a matter of indifference, in the absence of moral hazard.

In order to facilitate comparisons with Sections 6 and 8, I shall substitute for assumption 4.1 an alternative formulation which, although definitely weaker, is *equivalent under* **RO**. The alternative assumption rests on two definitions, which are again formulated in terms tailored to later needs.

Definition 4.1 (Conditional Preferences): For all s^m in S, for all β, β' in $\mathbb{B}$:

(i) $\beta \prec \beta'$ *given* s^m if and only if there exists a $(g_h$ in G with) $\beta_h^{\sim m}$ such that $(\beta, \beta_h^{\sim m}) \prec (\beta', \beta_h^{\sim m})$;

(ii) $\beta \sim \beta'$ *given* s^m if and only if neither $\beta \prec \beta'$ *given* s^m nor $\beta' \prec \beta$ *given* s^m.

Definition 4.2 (Null States): State s^m in S is null, if and only if $\beta \sim \beta'$ given s^m for all β, β' in $\mathbb{B}$.

Assumption 4.3 or SIP (State-Independent Preferences): For all s^l, s^m in S, for all β, β' in $\mathbb{B}$, if $\beta \prec \beta'$ given s^m, then it is not true that $\beta' \prec \beta$ given s^l.

Assumption 4.3 (SIP) states that conditional preferences are *not reversed* when the same prize mixtures are associated with alternative states. But strict preference conditionally on some states does not rule out indifference conditionally on other states (for instance, on null states). By itself, assumption SIP entails a weak form of monotonicity.[25]

Lemma 4.1: Under assumption SIP, for all g_h, g_i in G, if $\beta_h^m \precsim \beta_i^m$ given s^m for all s^m in S, then $g_h \precsim g_i$.

Proof: Let g_h and g_i be given. For each $m = 1, \ldots, n$, define a game $\tilde{g}_m$ by:

$$\tilde{\beta}_m^l = \begin{cases} \beta_h^l, & l = 1, \ldots, m \\ \beta_i^l, & l = m+1, \ldots, n. \end{cases}$$

Because $\beta_h^m \precsim \beta_i^m$ given s^m for all s^m in S, it follows from definition 4.1 and assumption SIP that $\tilde{g}_1 \precsim g_i$ and, for all $m = 2, \ldots, n$,

$$\tilde{g}_m = (\beta_h^1, \ldots, \beta_h^{m-1}, \beta_h^m, \beta_i^{m+1}, \ldots, \beta_i^n)$$
$$\precsim (\beta_h^1, \ldots, \beta_h^{m-1}, \beta_i^m, \beta_i^{m+1}, \ldots, \beta_i^n) = \tilde{g}_{m-1};$$

indeed, if $\beta_h^m \sim \beta_i^m$ given s^m, then definition 4.1 (ii) implies $\tilde{g}_m \sim \tilde{g}_{m-1}$ (or $\tilde{g}_1 \sim g_i$ if $m = 1$); if $\beta_h^m \prec \beta_i^m$ given s^m, then assumption SIP implies $\tilde{g}_m \precsim \tilde{g}_{m-1}$ (or $\tilde{g}_1 \precsim g_i$ if $m = 1$). Consequently $g_h = \tilde{g}_n \precsim \tilde{g}_{n-1} \cdots \precsim \tilde{g}_1 \precsim g_i$. $\square$

The monotonicity property of lemma 4.1 falls short of the monotonicity assumption 4.1 because the lemma does not relate conditional preferences given a state s^m to unconditional preferences. The next lemma provides the missing link.

Lemma 4.2: Under assumptions RO and SIP, for all β and β' in $\mathbb{B}$, $\beta \precsim \beta'$ implies $\beta \precsim \beta'$ given s^m for all s^m in S.

Proof: (i) Let $\beta \prec \beta'$. If there exists s^m in S with $\beta \succ \beta'$ given s^m, then $\beta \succsim \beta'$ given s^l for all s^l in S by assumption SIP, so that $\beta \succsim \beta'$ by lemma 4.1, a contradiction.

(ii) Let then $\beta \sim \beta'$. If there exists s^m in S with $\beta \succ \beta'$ given s^m, then there

[25]This is theorem 2 in Savage (1954, p. 24), obtained there as an implication of the 'Sure Thing Principle'. By a reasoning similar to that used in step (ii) of the proof of lemma 4.2, one easily verifies that RO *by itself* entails that conditional preferences given s^m define a weak order on $\mathbb{B}$.

exists (a game g_h in G with) $\beta_h^{\sim m}$ such that $(\beta, \beta_h^{\sim m}) \succ (\beta', \beta_h^{\sim m})$. It then follows from PI that $(\beta, \beta_h^{\sim m})\frac{1}{2} \beta' \succ (\beta', \beta_h^{\sim m})\frac{1}{2} \beta' \sim (\beta', \beta_h^{\sim m})\frac{1}{2} \beta$, and from RO that

$$(\beta\tfrac{1}{2}\beta', \beta_h^{\sim m}\tfrac{1}{2}\beta') \succ (\beta'\tfrac{1}{2}\beta, \beta_h^{\sim m}\tfrac{1}{2}\beta) \tag{4.1}$$

where $\beta_h^{\sim m}\frac{1}{2}\beta$ denotes the $(m-1)$-tuple of prize mixtures $\beta_h^l\frac{1}{2}\beta$, $l = 1, \ldots, n$, $l \neq m$.

If it were the case that $(\beta_h^l\frac{1}{2}\beta') \precsim (\beta_h^l\frac{1}{2}\beta)$ given s^l for all s^l in S, $l \neq m$, then lemma 4.1 would imply

$$(\beta\tfrac{1}{2}\beta', \beta_h^{\sim m}\tfrac{1}{2}\beta') \precsim (\beta'\tfrac{1}{2}\beta, \beta_h^{\sim m}\tfrac{1}{2}\beta),$$

contradicting (4.1). Therefore

$$\exists s^l \text{ in } S, (\beta_h^l\tfrac{1}{2}\beta') \succ (\beta_h^l\tfrac{1}{2}\beta) \text{ given } s^l. \tag{4.2}$$

Consider the constant game β_h^l. It follows again from PI that $(\beta, \beta_h^{\sim m})\frac{1}{2}\beta_h^l \succ (\beta', \beta_h^{\sim m})\frac{1}{2}\beta_h^l$, and from RO that

$$(\beta\tfrac{1}{2}\beta_h^l, \beta_h^{\sim m}\tfrac{1}{2}\beta_h^l) \succ (\beta'\tfrac{1}{2}\beta_h^l, \beta_h^{\sim m}\tfrac{1}{2}\beta_h^l). \tag{4.3}$$

It then follows from definition 4.1 (i) that

$$(\beta\tfrac{1}{2}\beta_h^l) \succ (\beta'\tfrac{1}{2}\beta_h^l) \quad \text{given } s^m. \tag{4.4}$$

Assumption SIP rules out the simultaneous occurrence of (4.2) and (4.4), and the proof is complete. □

Remark 4.1: In the proof of lemma 4.2, assumption RO is used only in (4.1) and (4.3) to the effect that a lottery between an arbitrary game and a *constant* game $(\beta', \beta$ or $\beta_h^l)$ is indifferent to the corresponding game. This remark is used in Section 6.

In order to elicit subjective probabilities, one must still exclude the trivial case where all lotteries (hence all games and all prizes) are indifferent.

Assumption 4.4 or ND (Non-Degeneracy): It is not true that $g_h \precsim g_i$ for all g_h, g_i in G.

Because the set B is finite, it contains a most preferred prize – say b_1 – and a least preferred prize – say b_0. By assumption PI, for all β in $\mathbb{B}$, $b_0 \precsim \beta \precsim b_1$. By assumption SIP and lemma 4.1, for all g_h in G, $b_0 \precsim g_h \precsim b_1$. Therefore, $b_0 \prec b_1$. The prizes b_0 and b_1 provide a convenient normalisation for the value V of theorem 3.1. They will be identified with games labelled g_0 and g_1 respectively.

Normalisation N.4: $V(g_0) = V(b_0) = 0$, $V(g_1) = V(b_1) = 1$.

Theorem 4.1 (Moral Expectation): Under assumptions ND, RO and SIP, there exists a probability measure p on S and a real-valued function u on B, called state-independent utility, such that, for all g_h in G,

$$V(g_h) = \sum_m p^m \sum_q \beta_h^m(b_q) u(b_q);$$

p is unique and u is unique up to the same positive linear transformation as V.

Proof: Define the utility u on B by $u(b_q) = V(b_q)$ for all b_q, where $V(b_q)$ is the value of the constant game promising b_q with certainty. Under the normalisation N.4, the range of u is contained in $[0, 1]$.

It follows from theorem 3.1 and assumption RO that, for all β in $\mathbb{B}$,

$$V(\beta) = \sum_q \beta(b_q) u(b_q).^{26}$$

The range of V is $[0, 1]$.

For every game g_h and every state s^m, define

$$v_h^m := \sum_q \beta_h^m(b_q) u(b_q) = V(\beta_h^m),$$

the expected utility of the prize mixture associated with s^m by g_h. For all g_h and s^m, v_h^m belongs to $[0, 1]$. By lemma 4.2, $v_h^m \leqslant v_i^m$ implies $\beta_h^m \precsim \beta_i^m$ given s^m. By lemma 4.1, $v_h = v_i$ implies $g_h \sim g_i$, so that the value of any game g_h is uniquely determined by the n-vector of expected utilities $v_h := (v_h^1, \ldots, v_h^n)$.

Thus, there exists a function f, $[0, 1]^n \to R$, such that, for all g_h in G, $V(g_h) = f(v_h^1, \ldots, v_h^n) = f(v_h)$. By assumption RO, the function f is linear. (Indeed RO states precisely that, for all α in $[0, 1]$, for all g_h and g_i in G, $\alpha f(v_h) + (1 - \alpha) f(v_i) = f(\alpha v_h + (1 - \alpha) v_i)$; and $f(0, \ldots, 0) = 0$, under N.4.) Thus, there exists a vector p in R^n such that, for all g_h in G,

$$V(g_h) = \sum_m p^m v_h^m.$$

Under the normalisation N.4, $f(1, \ldots, 1) = 1$, so that $\sum_m p^m = 1$. Also, $f(1, 0, \ldots, 0) \geqslant 0$, so that $p^1 \geqslant 0$, and similarly for p^m, $m = 2, \ldots, n$. Thus p is a probability measure on S, and, for all g_h in G,

$$V(g_h) = \sum_m p^m v_h^m = \sum_m p^m \sum_q \beta_h^m(b_q) u(b_q).$$

Applying this formula to constant games and invoking theorem 3.1

---

[26]Assumption RO states that the *game* assigning β to each state, with value $V(\beta)$, is indifferent to the *lottery* assigning a probability $\beta(b_q)$ to the game promising b_q with certainty; the value of that lottery is

$$\sum_q \beta(b_q) V(b_q),$$

according to theorem 3.1.

establishes the uniqueness of u, up to the same positive linear transformation as V. Generalising the definition of v_h^m to

$$v_h^m := \sum_q \beta_h^m(b_q) \cdot \frac{u(b_q) - u(b_0)}{u(b_1) - u(b_0)}, \quad v_h^m \text{ in } [0,1]$$

the function f, $[0,1]^n \to R$, is unique, with

$$f(v_h) = \frac{V(g_h) - V(g_0)}{V(g_1) - V(g_0)}.$$

The uniqueness of p^1 then follows from $f(1,0,\ldots,0) = p^1$, and similarly for $p^2, \ldots, p^n$.[27]   □

The elicitation of p is very simple. Formally (to facilitate comparisons later), for each s^m in S, $p^m = V((\beta_1^m, \beta_0^{\sim m}))$; that is, p^m is the value (as per theorem 3.1) of a game $(\beta_1^m, \beta_0^{\sim m})$ promising a prize of utility 1 if s^m obtains, of utility 0 if s^m does not obtain.[28] The value of such a game is also equal to the probability α_m, for which $(\beta_1^m, \beta_0^{\sim m}) \sim g_1 \alpha_m g_0$. Indeed, by theorem 3.1, $(\beta_1^m, \beta_0^{\sim m}) \sim g_1 \alpha_m g_0$ if and only if

$$V((\beta_1^m, \beta_0^{\sim m})) = \alpha_m V(g_1) + (1 - \alpha_m) V(g_0) = \alpha_m.$$

Thus, p^m is equal to the probability α_m such that the decision-maker would indifferently stake a prize (of utility 1) on s^m, or on a random outcome of probability α_m. This is the elicitation scheme announced in the introduction. And theorem 4.1 guarantees that α_m (hence p^m) will not be affected, if any other 'prize' is substituted for β_1^m.

Remark 4.2: Theorem 4.1 asserts the uniqueness of the *state-independent utility* u on B (up to normalisation) and of the associated probability p on S. If one allowed representation of preferences by a *state-dependent utility* on $B \times S$, and a probability on S, then uniqueness would be lost. Indeed, as noted in Section 1.3,[29] defining $\hat{u}(b_q, s^m) = (1/c^m)$ $[u(b_q) + d^m]$ and $\hat{p}^m = p^m c^m$ (with $c^m > 0$ for all m and $\sum_m p^m c^m = 1$, $\sum_m p^m d^m = 0$) would entail, for all g_h in G:

$$\sum_m \hat{p}^m \sum_q \beta_h^m(b_q) \hat{u}(b_q, s^m) = \sum_m p^m \sum_q \beta_h^m(b_q) u(b_q) = V(g_h).$$

5 Value of information and equipotence

The example in the introduction indicates unambiguously that assumption RO must be relaxed if the theory is to encompass situations of moral

[27]Thus, $p^m = 0$ if and only if s^m is null.
[28]Reminder: $\beta_1^m(b_1) = 1$, $\beta_0^m(b_0) = 1$, $m = 1, \ldots, n$.
[29]See also Fishburn (1982, p. 110), Rubin (1983) and Section 8.2.

hazard. A natural relaxation, repeatedly used by decision theorists,[30] asserts that information about the outcome of a lottery has non-negative value. Thus, when a lottery is compared to the *corresponding game* (which entails the same marginal prize mixtures, in all states, but less early information), the game is never preferred to the lottery.

Assumption 5.1 or VI (Value of Information): Every lottery is *preferred or indifferent* to the corresponding game; that is, for all γ in Γ, $\gamma \gtrsim g_\gamma$.

The dichotomy 'strict preference–indifference' defines a *relation among games*, called *equipotence* by Drèze (1958, 1961).[31]

Two games are equipotent, if and only if information about the outcome of a lottery among them has zero value.

Definition 5.1 (Equipotence): The games g_h and g_i are equipotent, written $g_h E g_i$, if and only if, for all α in $[0, 1]$, the lottery $g_h \alpha g_i$ is *indifferent* to the corresponding game.

Equipotence is clearly a reflexive and symmetric relation. There is no reason to expect that it be a transitive relation, and we shall see below (lemma 6.2) that transitivity of the equipotence relation is instructive. Because equipotence is not in general transitive, *simultaneous equipotence* must be defined, for (finite) sets of games.

Definition 5.2 (Simultaneous Equipotence and Equipotent Sets): The elements of a finite set of games G' in G are simultaneously equipotent if and only if every lottery among elements of G' is indifferent to the corresponding game; in which case, G' is called an 'equipotent set'.

In other words, *an equipotent set is a set of games for which assumption RO is satisfied*. It is useful to note at once that (simultaneous) equipotence is well defined, and can be verified empirically from a minimal number of observations: if *some* lottery assigning positive probabilities to a set of games is indifferent to the corresponding game, then the same property holds for *all* lotteries among these games.

Lemma 5.1: Under assumption VI, if γ is any lottery such that $\gamma \sim g_\gamma$, then the set of games g_h with $\gamma(g_h) > 0$ is an equipotent set.

Proof: We must show that $\gamma \sim g_\gamma$ implies $\gamma' \sim g_{\gamma'}$ for all γ' in Γ such that $\gamma'(g_h) = 0$ for all g_h in G with $\gamma(g_h) = 0$.

[30]See, for example, Marschak (1954), also quoted in Section 9.3.

[31]The term 'equipotence' was suggested to me by L.J. Savage. Although equipotence is related to 'strategic equivalence' (see von Neumann and Morgenstern (1947, p. 245)), the two notions are distinct. As noted below, equipotence is *not* an equivalence relation.

1. Assume first that $\gamma'(g_h) > 0$ for all g_h in G with $\gamma(g_h) > 0$; denoting by G' the set of games for which $\gamma'(g_h) > 0$, γ and γ' are probabilities on G'. Define

$$\lambda = \underset{g_h \in G'}{\text{Min}} \frac{\gamma(g_h)}{\gamma'(g_h)}.$$

By construction, $\lambda > 0$; also, $\lambda \leqslant 1$, because $\gamma \cdot \iota = \gamma' \cdot \iota = 1$. If $\lambda = 1$, then $\gamma' = \gamma$ and the conclusion follows trivially. Otherwise, there exists γ'' in Γ such that $\gamma = \gamma'\lambda\gamma''$; that is,

$$\gamma'' = \frac{1}{1-\lambda}(\gamma - \lambda\gamma').$$

Indeed, for all g_h in G',

$$\gamma''(g_h) = \frac{\gamma'(g_h)}{1-\lambda}\left(\frac{\gamma(g_h)}{\gamma'(g_h)} - \lambda\right) \geqslant 0;$$

and

$$\gamma'' \cdot \iota = \frac{1}{1-\lambda}(\gamma \cdot \iota - \lambda\gamma' \cdot \iota) = 1.$$

Now assumption VI implies $\gamma' \succsim g_{\gamma'}$, $\gamma'' \succsim g_{\gamma''}$ and $g_{\gamma'}\lambda g_{\gamma''} \succsim g_{g_{\gamma'}\lambda g_{\gamma''}}$. Assumption PI therefore implies $\gamma'\lambda\gamma'' \succsim g_{\gamma'}\lambda\gamma'' \succsim g_{\gamma'}\lambda g_{\gamma''}$. Together, VI and PI imply:

$$\gamma = \gamma'\lambda\gamma'' \succsim g_{\gamma'}\lambda\gamma'' \succsim g_{\gamma'}\lambda g_{\gamma''} \succsim g_{g_{\gamma'}\lambda g_{\gamma''}} = g_\gamma \sim \gamma.$$

Hence, $\gamma' \sim g_{\gamma'}$, as was to be shown.

2. If there exists g_h with $\gamma(g_h) > 0$ but $\gamma'(g_h) = 0$, partition the vector γ into $(\gamma_\mathrm{I}, \gamma_\mathrm{II})$ so that $\gamma'(g_h) > 0$ for all g_h in G with $\gamma_\mathrm{I}(g_h) > 0$, $\gamma'(g_h) = 0$ otherwise.

For $\mu = \gamma_\mathrm{I} \cdot \iota > 0$, define the lotteries $\tilde{\gamma}_\mathrm{I} = (1/\mu)\gamma_\mathrm{I}$ and $\tilde{\gamma}_\mathrm{II} = (1/1-\mu)\gamma_\mathrm{II}$. Then, $\gamma = \tilde{\gamma}_\mathrm{I}\mu\tilde{\gamma}_\mathrm{II}$ and, using again VI and PI in the same way as under step 1,

$$\gamma \sim \tilde{\gamma}_\mathrm{I}\mu\tilde{\gamma}_\mathrm{II} \succsim g_{\tilde{\gamma}_\mathrm{I}}\mu\tilde{\gamma}_\mathrm{II} \succsim g_{\tilde{\gamma}_\mathrm{I}}\mu g_{\tilde{\gamma}_\mathrm{II}} \succsim g_{g_{\tilde{\gamma}_\mathrm{I}}\mu g_{\tilde{\gamma}_\mathrm{II}}} = g_\gamma \sim \gamma.$$

Hence, $\tilde{\gamma}_\mathrm{I} \sim g_{\tilde{\gamma}_\mathrm{I}}$.

Repeating step 1 with $\tilde{\gamma}_\mathrm{I}$ substituted everywhere for γ completes the proof. $\square$

Actually, a slightly stronger property holds, that will prove useful below. If a set of games are simultaneously equipotent, then not only are *all* the lotteries among them indifferent to the corresponding games (lemma 5.1); in addition, these 'corresponding games' can be added to the original set, and simultaneous equipotence is preserved. In other words, if G' is an equipotent set, so is the union of G' with all the games whose n-tuple of prize mixtures is a convex combination of the n-tuples of prize mixtures of the elements of G'. Formally:

Lemma 5.2: If G' is an equipotent set and γ satisfies

$$\sum_{g_h \in G'} \gamma(g_h) = 1, \text{ then } G' \cup \{g_\gamma\} \text{ is an equipotent set.}$$

Proof: Let γ' be any lottery such that $\gamma'(g_h) > 0$ for *all* g_h in G' and

$$\sum_{g_h \in G'} \gamma'(g_h) = 1.$$

We need only show that $g_\gamma \alpha \gamma' \sim g_{g_\gamma \alpha g_\gamma}$ for some α in $(0, 1)$.

Define $\gamma'' = \gamma \alpha \gamma'$, a lottery on G'. Because G' is an equipotent set, $\gamma'' \sim g_{\gamma''}$. Using again VI and PI as in the proof of lemma 5.1:

$$\gamma'' = \gamma \alpha \gamma' \gtrsim g_\gamma \alpha \gamma' \gtrsim g_\gamma \alpha g_{\gamma'} \gtrsim g_{g_\gamma \alpha g_{\gamma'}} = g_{\gamma''} \sim \gamma'',$$

so that $g_\gamma \alpha \gamma' \sim g_{g_\gamma \alpha g_{\gamma'}}$.   □

Games which are *equipotent with every other game* will play a special role in the sequel. Following Drèze (1961), I shall call such games 'omnipotent'.

Definition 5.3 (Omnipotence): The game g_h is omnipotent if and only if $g_h E g_i$ for all g_i in G.

Existence of omnipotent games is asserted by assumptions CGO in Section 6 and NDO in Section 8. It follows from lemma 5.1 that games corresponding to lotteries over omnipotent games are themselves omnipotent.

6 Decision theory with state-independent preferences and moral hazard

6.1 Constant games are omnipotent

The motivation for replacing assumption RO by the weaker assumption VI is to allow for the possibility that early information about the outcome of a lottery is 'valuable', because it gives access to a more flexible course of action ('strategy'). Still, there are cases where the added flexibility is worthless, because the same course of action would be taken, irrespective of the outcome of the lottery. *In general*, nothing can be said *a priori* about the occurrence of such cases: they are *revealed* by the indifference of the decision-maker between a lottery and the corresponding game. There is one exception, however, which can be used to advantage under state-independent preferences; it involves *constant games*. If the decision-maker is concerned about prizes only (i.e. does not care which state obtains, so long as he ends up with the same prize), and if a game assigns the same prize mixture to every state, then no motivation exists for influencing the course of events. This has an important implication. Let g_c be a constant game, g_h be an arbitrary game, and $\gamma = g_c \alpha g_h$ be a lottery among them. Early information about the outcome of that lottery should be immaterial.

Indeed, under the corresponding game g_y, the decision-maker, though not knowing whether g_c or g_h will determine the prize mixture, could always *act as if g_h were the relevant game*. Should g_h come out, the chosen course of action was optimal; should g_c come out, the same conclusion holds, since all courses of action are equally good for g_c. This line of reasoning, akin in spirit to that underlying the Sure Thing Principle, suggests that *a constant game should be equipotent with every other game*, i.e. should be omnipotent (in terms of definitions 5.1 and 5.3). This very reasonable requirement will be introduced as assumption 6.1.

Assumption 6.1 or CGO (Constant Games are Omnipotent): Every constant game is omnipotent.

Assumption CGO could be viewed as a mild strengthening of assumption VI in the 'direction' of RO; I think that it is better understood as complementary to assumption SIP in vindicating a state-independent utility. I may 'prefer' to see event S^A occur, rather than event S^B, even though my preferences over prizes (commodity bundles a.s.o.) will remain the same in both cases. (The operational meaning of 'prefer' is that I will try to make S^A more likely, and S^B less likely, if that is within my reach – and if I am not otherwise motivated by prizes staked on these events.[32]) In such cases, assumption CGO is apt to be violated, and the more general analysis of Section 7 (leading to a state-dependent utility) is called for.

6.2 Generalised moral expectation theorem

Theorem 6.1 (Generalised Moral Expectation): Under assumptions ND, VI, SIP and CGO, there exist a closed convex set P of probability measures on S, and a state-independent utility u on B, such that, for all g_h in G,

$$V(g_h) = \underset{p \text{ in } P}{\text{Max}} \sum_m p^m \sum_q \beta_h^m(b_q)u(b_q);$$

P is unique and u is unique up to the same positive linear transformation as V.

Proof: 1. Proceeding as in the proof of theorem 4.1, define the utility u uniquely (under normalisation N.4) by $u(b_q) = V(b_q)$. Because all constant games are omnipotent, it still follows from theorem 3.1 that, for all β in $\mathbb{B}$,

$$V(\beta) = \sum_q \beta(b_q)u(b_q).$$

Define the expected utility of the prize mixture associated with state s^m by

[32]Example: I would 'prefer' to see A rather than B become a Nobel laureate in economics....

game g_h as

$$v_h^m := \sum_q \beta_h^m(b_q)u(b_q).$$

In view of remark 4.1, assumption CGO may be substituted for assumption RO in the statement of lemma 4.2. Thus, $v_h^m \leqslant v_i^m$ still implies $\beta_h^m \precsim \beta_i^m$ given s^m. Using lemma 4.1, there exists again a unique function f, $[0,1]^n \to R$, such that, for all g_h in G, $V(g_h) = f(v_h^1,\ldots,v_h^n) = f(v_h)$.

2. By assumption VI, the function f is convex. Indeed, VI states precisely that, for all α in $[0,1]$, for all g_h and g_i in G,

$$\alpha f(v_h) + (1-\alpha)f(v_i) \geqslant f(\alpha v_h + (1-\alpha)v_i).$$

The function f is 1-homogeneous. Indeed, the constant game g_0 with $v_0 = (0,\ldots,0)$ is omnipotent, so that for all g_h in G, for all α in $[0,1]$,

$$\alpha f(v_h) + (1-\alpha)f(v_0) = \alpha f(v_h) = f(\alpha v_h + (1-\alpha)v_0) = f(\alpha v_h).$$

And if $k > 1$ is such that $kv_h \leqslant \iota$,

$$\frac{1}{k}f(kv_h) = f(v_h).^{33}$$

The function f is continuous.[34] Thus, f is a finite, closed, positively homogeneous convex function. By corollary 13.2.1 in Rockafellar (1970, p. 114), f is the support function of a uniquely defined closed convex set P^*, namely:

$$P^* = \{p \in R^n | \forall v \in [0,1]^n : p \cdot v \leqslant f(v)\}.$$

Thus

$$f(v) = \operatorname*{Sup}_{p \in P^*} p \cdot v.$$

3. Define P uniquely as $P = P^* \cap \Delta^n$, where Δ^n is the unit simplex of R_+^n. P is a closed convex set of probability measures. I will show, in three easy steps, that for all g_h in G, there exists a p in P such that $f(v_h) = p \cdot v_h$.

(i) For the game g_1, with $v_1 = \iota$,

$$f(v_1) = \operatorname*{Sup}_{p \in P^*} p \cdot \iota = 1,$$

so that $p \cdot \iota \leqslant 1$ for all p in P^*.
For the game $(\beta_1^m, \beta_0^{\tilde{m}})$, with $v(\beta_1, \beta_0^{\tilde{m}}) = \delta^m$,

$$f(\delta^m) = \operatorname*{Sup}_{p \in P^*} p^m \leqslant 1,$$

so that $p^m \leqslant 1$ for all $m = 1,\ldots,n$, for all p in P^*.
Because P^* is closed, and f is continuous, either

---

[33]This is the lemma given by Anscombe and Aumann (1963, p. 202).
[34]At the risk of being pedantic: for arbitrary v_h, if $|v_i^m - v_h^m| \leqslant \varepsilon$ for all $m = 1,\ldots,n$, then $|f(v_i) - f(v_h)| \leqslant \varepsilon$. Indeed, Min $[(1+\varepsilon)v_h^m, 1] \geqslant v_i^m \geqslant (1-\varepsilon)v_h^m$ for all m implies $(1+\varepsilon)f(v_h) \geqslant f(v_i) \geqslant (1-\varepsilon)f(v_h)$.

$$\operatorname*{Sup}_{p \in P^*} p \cdot v$$

is attained as

$$\operatorname*{Max}_{p \in P^*} p \cdot v$$

at some finite p in P^*, or else the supremum corresponds to $v^m = 0$, $p^m = -\infty$ for some state(s) s^m.

(ii) For an arbitrary game g_h, form the lotteries $g_h \alpha g_1$, $\alpha \in (0, 1)$, and consider the corresponding games $g_{g_h \alpha g_1}$. Because $\alpha v_h + (1 - \alpha)\iota$ is a strictly positive vector,

$$V(g_{g_h \alpha g_1}) = f(\alpha v_h + (1 - \alpha)\iota) = \operatorname*{Max}_{p \in P^*} p \cdot (\alpha v_h + (1 - \alpha)\iota).$$

Denote by P_α an element of P^* where the maximum is attained. Because g_1 is omnipotent (constant), $g_{g_h \alpha g_1} \sim g_h \alpha g_1$. Thus,

$$V(g_{g_h \alpha g_1}) = \alpha p_\alpha \cdot v_h + (1 - \alpha)p_\alpha \cdot \iota = \alpha V(g_h) + (1 - \alpha)V(g_1) = \alpha \operatorname*{Sup}_{p \in P^*} p \cdot v_h + 1 - \alpha.$$

Because

$$\operatorname*{Sup}_{p \in P^*} p \cdot v_h \geqslant p_\alpha \cdot v_h$$

and $1 \geqslant p_\alpha \cdot \iota$, it must be the case

$$p_\alpha \cdot v_h = \operatorname*{Sup}_{p \in P^*} p \cdot v_h$$

and $p_\alpha \cdot \iota = 1$. Thus, there exists p_α in P^* with $p_\alpha \cdot \iota = 1$ such that $V(g_h) = f(v_h) = p_\alpha \cdot v_h$.

(iii) For the game $(\beta_0^m, \beta_1^{-m})$, with $v((\beta_0^m, \beta_1^{-m})) = \iota - \delta^m$,

$$f(\iota - \delta^m) = \operatorname*{Sup}_{p \in P^*} p \cdot (\iota - \delta^m) = 1 - \operatorname*{Inf}_{p \in P^*} p^m \leqslant 1,$$

so that $p^m \geqslant 0$ for all $m = 1, \ldots, n$, for all p in P^*.

In particular, $p_\alpha \geqslant 0$ in step (ii) so that, for all g_h in G, there exists $p \in P$ with $p \cdot v_h = f(v_h) = V(g_h)$.

4. Because constant games are omnipotent, so that RO applies to lotteries among them, it still follows from theorem 3.1 that u is unique, up to the same positive linear transformation as V. Generalising again the definition of v_h^m to

$$v_h^m := \sum_q \beta_h^m(b_q) \frac{u(b_q) - u(b_0)}{u(b_1) - u(b_0)}, \quad v_h^m \text{ in } [0, 1],$$

the function f is unique and therefore so is P^*. $\qquad\square$

Remark 6.1: $p^m = 0$ for *all* p in P if and only if state s^m is null.

Proof: Repeating the argument in step 3 (iii) of the proof of theorem 6.1,

$$f(v_1^m, \tilde{v}_0^m) = f(\delta^m) = \operatorname*{Max}_{p \in P^*} p^m = 0 \quad \text{if } s^m \text{ is null.}$$

If $p^m = 0$ for all p in P, then $V(g_h)$ is unaffected by v_h^m and $\beta \sim \beta'$ given s^m for all β, β' in $\mathbb{B}$. □

Theorem 6.1 accomplishes the first goal stated in the introduction (Section 1.2), namely to extend the principle of moral expectation (subjectively expected utility) from games against nature to games with moral hazard. As announced there, a natural relaxation of the Reversal of Order assumption (into VI and CGO) has proved adequate for this extension.

The theorem establishes the existence of a unique compact convex set of probability measures (P), intuitively related to a set of unobservable strategies. Preferences over games are consistent with a representation in terms of expected utilities, where the expected utility of a game is computed with the element(s) of P for which it is maximal ('generalised' moral expectation).

The convexity of P may be viewed as reflecting the availability of mixed strategies. If the decision-maker has access (through suitable strategies) to the probability vectors p and p' in P, then randomisation gives access to all convex combinations of p and p'. Two other properties of the set P are of interest, both in themselves and for the purpose of elicitation (of P itself in this section, of a state-dependent utility in Section 8). A first property is *dimensionality*, i.e. the maximal member of linearly independent elements of P. A second property is the *cardinality of the set of extreme points*, which is finite if and only if P is a polyhedron (generated by a finite set of vectors, corresponding to 'pure strategies'). When P is a polyhedron, some convenient implications follow. These two properties are discussed in Section 7.

I now recall some basic properties of the maximisation of a linear function over a compact convex set, and relate them to equipotence (Section 6.3). Then I exhibit formulae for eliciting probability vectors in P and computing the conditional value of a game given any probability vector in P (Section 6.4).

Throughout Sections 6.3, 6.4 and 7, assumptions ND, VI and the existence conclusion for P in theorem 6.1 are assumed without explicit reminder. Assumptions SIP and CGO are not used explicitly, but only implicitly through the existence of P; accordingly the results established here will remain applicable in conjunction with theorem 8.1 in Section 8 (where assumptions SIP and CGO are relaxed).

6.3 Equipotence and probabilities

A basic property used repeatedly in what follows is the numerical verification of the intuitive idea that two games are equipotent (it is unnecessary to know beforehand which of the two prevails), if and only if there exists a probability measure in P (a 'strategy') which is simultaneously optimal for both; that is, if and only if the two games admit a 'common optimal strategy'. More generally:

Lemma 6.1: The subset G' of G is an equipotent set, if and only if there exists a probability measure p' in P such that $V(g_h) = p' \cdot v_h$ for all g_h in G'.

Proof: Let γ be such that

$$\sum_{g_h \in G'} \gamma(g_h) = 1,$$

with $\gamma(g_h) > 0$ for all g_h in G'.

Sufficiency: If, for all g_h in G', $V(g_h) = p' \cdot v_h$ for some p' in P, then:

$$\sum_h \gamma(g_h) V(g_h) = \sum_h \gamma(g_h) p' \cdot v_h = \underset{p \in P}{\text{Max}} \sum_m p^m \sum_h \gamma(g_h) v_h^m = V(g_\gamma).$$

Thus, $\gamma \sim g_\gamma$ and the elements of G' are simultaneously equipotent, according to lemma 5.1.

Necessity: If the elements of G' are simultaneously equipotent, then:

$$V(g_\gamma) = \underset{p \in P}{\text{Max}} \sum_m p^m \sum_h \gamma(g_h) v_h^m = \sum_h \gamma(g_h) V(g_h) = \sum_h \gamma(g_h) \underset{p \in P}{\text{Max}} \, p \cdot v_h$$

and there exists an element of P, say p', such that

$$\underset{p \in P}{\text{Max}} \, p \cdot v_h = p' \cdot v_h$$

for all g_h in G'. $\qquad \square$

A linear function $(p \cdot v_h)$ attains its maximum on a compact convex set (P) at an *extreme point*.[35] If the set is strictly convex, then the maximum is attained at a single extreme point, or else the function is constant over the whole set (as is the case for $p \cdot v_h$ if and only if g_h is omnipotent). If the set is convex but not strictly convex, then it contains (one or more) *exposed faces*; if the function attains its maximum at some point belonging to the relative interior of an exposed face, then the function is constant over that whole face.

Definition 6.1: $P^*(g_h)$ is the set of probability vectors for which

$$p \cdot v_h := \sum_m p^m \sum_q \beta_h^m(b_q) u(b_q)$$

---

[35]See Rockafellar (1970) for details regarding this and the next paragraph.

attains its maximum $V(g_h)$ on P; that is,

$$P^*(g_h) := \{p \in P \mid V(g_h) = p \cdot v_h\}$$
$$= \{p \in P \mid p \cdot v_h \geqslant p' \cdot v_h \quad \text{for all} \quad p' \text{ in } P\}. \tag{6.1}$$

Games g such that $P^*(g)$ is a singleton play an important role in eliciting subjective probabilities (Section 6.4). The next two lemmas establish that such games exist, and are characterised by a qualitative, directly observable property.

Lemma 6.2: If p is an extreme point of the set P, there exists a game g in G such that $P^*(g) = \{p\}$.

Proof: Let p be an extreme point of the compact convex set P. The 'cone of normals to P at p',[36] i.e. $N_P(p) := \{x \in R^n \mid p \cdot x \geqslant p' \cdot x \forall p' \in P\}$, contains $\bar{x}$ such that $p \cdot \bar{x} > p' \cdot \bar{x}$ for all p' in P, $p' \neq p$. The same property holds for $\lambda \bar{x}, \lambda > 0$. Because $P \subset \Delta^n, p \cdot \iota = p' \cdot \iota$ for all p' in P. Accordingly, for any $\mu \in R$, $p \cdot (\lambda \bar{x} + \mu \iota) > p' \cdot (\lambda \bar{x} + \mu \iota)$ for all p' in P, $p' \neq p$; and there exist λ, μ such that $\lambda \bar{x} + \mu \iota \in [0, 1]^n$. To $v = \lambda \bar{x} + \mu \iota$ corresponds a game g in G with $P^*(g) = \{p\}$. □

Lemma 6.3: $P^*(g_h)$ *is a singleton if and only if equipotence with* g_h *is transitive (if and only if* $g_h \text{E} g_i$ *and* $g_h \text{E} g_j$ *imply* $g_i \text{E} g_j$).

Proof: Necessity: Let $P^*(g_h) = \{p_h\}$. By lemma 6.1, $g_h \text{E} g_i$ if and only if $p_h \in P^*(g_i)$; and $p_h \in P^*(g_i) \cap P^*(g_j)$ implies $g_i \text{E} g_j$.
Sufficiency: If $P^*(g_h)$ is not a singleton, then $P^*(g_h)$ contains at least two distinct extreme points of P, say p_i and p_j. To p_i there corresponds a v_i in $[0, 1]^n$ such that $p_i \cdot v_i > p \cdot v_i$ for all p in P, $p \neq p_i$, and v_i corresponds to a game g_i with $P^*(g_i) = \{p_i\}$. Similarly, to p_j there corresponds a game g_j with $P^*(g_j) = \{p_j\}$. By lemma 6.1, it is not true that $g_i \text{E} g_j$, since $P^*(g_i) \cap P^*(g_j) = \phi$. □

6.4 Conditional values and subjective probabilities

When P is a set, and not a singleton, the elicitation of subjective probabilities is thereby complicated. In the first place, the elicitation is of necessity game-specific: subjective probabilities vary from game to game, in function of their state-vectors of expected utilities. To avoid ambiguities, the elicitation should be based on games g_h implying a unique probability vector, i.e. games g_h for which $P^*(g_h)$ is a singleton.

Furthermore, the n specific games used to elicit subjective probabilities in Section 4, namely the games $(\beta_1^m, \beta_0^{-m})$ staking a prize of utility 1 on s^m alone $(m = 1, \ldots, n)$, will not suffice to elicit a *set* of probabilities. Indeed,

$$V((\beta_1^m, \beta_0^{-m})) = p_h^m \quad \text{if and only if} \quad p_h \in P^*((\beta_1^m, \beta_0^{-m}));$$

[36] Cf. Rockafellar (1970, p. 15).

otherwise

$$V((\beta_1^m, \beta_0^{\tilde{m}})) = \text{Max}_{p \in P} p^m > p_h^m.$$

In order to generate the required information, one must rely on the concept of *conditional value*, introduced by Drèze (1961, definition 2.8). For an arbitrary game g_i in G and probability $\bar{p}$ in P, one defines

$$V(g_i|\bar{p}) := \bar{p} \cdot v_i. \tag{6.2}$$

Theorem 6.1 asserts that conditional values are uniquely defined (up to the same linear transformation as V). Although formula (6.2) involves the numerical probability $\bar{p}$, it is possible to evaluate conditional values without prior elicitation of probabilities, as the next lemma shows. The evaluation is obtained in the same way as a directional derivative.

Lemma 6.4: Let g_h be such that $P^*(g_h) = \{p_h\}$. Then for all g_i in G,

$$V(g_i|p_h) = \lim_{\alpha \to 1} \frac{1}{1-\alpha} [V(g_{g_h \alpha g_i}) - V(g_{g_h \alpha g_0})]. \tag{6.3}$$

Proof: By theorem 6.1, for each α in $[0,1]$, there is a p_α in P (not necessarily unique) such that

$$V(g_{g_h \alpha g_i}) = p_\alpha \cdot (\alpha v_h + (1-\alpha)v_i) \geq p_h \cdot (\alpha v_h + (1-\alpha)v_i)$$
$$= \alpha V(g_h) + (1-\alpha)V(g_i|p_h). \tag{6.4}$$

By the theorem of the maximum (Debreu, 1957, p. 19), the correspondence defining p_α is upper semi-continuous in α. Because $P^*(g_h) = \{p_h\}$,

$$\lim_{\alpha \to 1} p_\alpha = p_h.$$

Also, (6.4) implies

$$(1-\alpha)V(g_i|p_h) \leq V(g_{g_h \alpha g_i}) - \alpha V(g_h) = V(g_{g_h \alpha g_i}) - V(g_{g_h \alpha g_0}),$$
$$(1-\alpha)p_\alpha \cdot v_i = V(g_{g_h \alpha g_i}) - \alpha p_\alpha \cdot v_h \geq V(g_{g_h \alpha g_i}) - \alpha V(g_h)$$
$$= V(g_{g_h \alpha g_i}) - V(g_{g_h \alpha g_0}).$$

Dividing by $1 - \alpha$ and letting α tend to 1, we have

$$\lim_{\alpha \to 1} \frac{V(g_{g_h \alpha g_i}) - V(g_{g_h \alpha g_0})}{1-\alpha} \geq V(g_i|p_h) = \lim_{\alpha \to 1} p_\alpha \cdot v_i$$
$$\geq \lim_{\alpha \to 1} \frac{V(g_{g_h \alpha g_i}) - V(g_{g_h \alpha g_0})}{1-\alpha},$$

so that the limit exists and satisfies (6.3). $\qquad \square$

Combining formulae (6.2) and (6.3), applied to the game $(\beta_1^m, \beta_0^{-m})$ staking a prize of utility 1 on s^m alone, we obtain the following:

Elicitation formula

$$V((\beta_1^m, \beta_0^{-m})|p_h) = p_h \cdot \delta^m = p_h^m$$

$$= \lim_{\alpha \to 1} \frac{1}{1-\alpha} [V(g_{g_h\alpha(\beta_1^m, \beta_0^{-m})}) - V(g_{g_h\alpha g_0})]. \qquad (6.5)$$

The added complication introduced by moral hazard, as regards elicitation of subjective probabilities, is thus twofold: (i) the elicitation must be repeated for each extreme point of P; (ii) the elicitation calls for computing conditional values, and not only values, of specific games (staking a prize of utility 1 on s^m alone).

One can also interpret, or elicit, p_h^m directly as the partial derivative of the value $V(g_h)$ of a game g_h with $P^*(g_h) = \{p_h\}$ with respect to the expected utility v_h^m of the prize mixture staked by that game on s^m. To see this, consider the convex 1-homogeneous function $f(v)$ introduced in the proof of theorem 6.1; and take without loss of generality a game g_h such that $v_h^m < 1$.[37] Then, (6.5) is equivalent to[38]

$$p_h^m = \lim_{\alpha \to 1} \frac{f(\alpha v_h + (1-\alpha)\delta^m) - f(\alpha v_h)}{1-\alpha}$$

$$= \lim_{\alpha \to 1} \left(\left[\alpha f\left(v_h + \frac{1-\alpha}{\alpha}\delta^m\right) - \alpha f(v_h) \right] \Big/ (1-\alpha) \right)$$

$$= \lim_{\varepsilon \to 0} \frac{f(v_h + \varepsilon\delta^m) - f(v^h)}{\varepsilon}$$

$$= \frac{\partial f(v_h)}{\partial v_h^m} = \frac{\partial V(g_h)}{\partial v_h^m}. \qquad (6.6)$$

It is shown in Section 7.2 that a simpler formula is obtained when P is a polyhedron.

7 Properties of the set of attainable probabilities

7.1 Dimensionality of P

I turn now to a brief discussion of the dimensionality of P. The next two lemmas, which play an important role in Section 8.3, bring out the significance of that dimensionality.

[37]There is no loss of generality, because $P^*(g_h) = \{p_h\}$ implies $P^*(g_{h\lambda g_0}) = \{p_h\}$ for all λ in $(0, 1]$ and $\lambda v_h^m + (1 - \lambda)v_0^m = \lambda v_h^m < 1, m = 1, \ldots, n$.
[38]Although one-sided directional derivatives of convex functions exist universally, the equality of the left and right derivatives is not universal; it is here a consequence of the fact that $P^*(g_h)$ is a singleton.

Lemma 7.1: If P contains n linearly independent elements, then a game g_h is omnipotent *if and only if* it assigns to all states prize mixtures with equal expected utilities; that is, if and only if it is a 'constant expected utility game', with $v_h = V(g_h)\iota$.

Proof: Let there exist n linearly independent vectors $p_1, \ldots, p_n$ in P, and let g_h be a game with the property $V(g_h) = p_j \cdot v_h$, $j = 1, \ldots, n$. Defining w_h in R^n by $w_h^m = v_h^m - V(g_h)$, $m = 1, \ldots, n$, we have $p_j \cdot w_h = 0$ for each $j = 1, \ldots, n$. Because the n vectors p_j are linearly independent, $w_h = 0$ and $v_h^m = V(g_h)$ for all $m = 1, \ldots, n$. □

The constant games of assumption CGO form a subset of the constant expected utility games.

Lemma 7.2: If P contains l, and at most $l < n$, linearly independent elements, then the expected utility vectors associated with omnipotent games form an $(n - l + 1)$-dimensional subset of $[0, 1]^n$.

Proof: Proceeding as in the proof of lemma 7.1, the set of vectors w_h associated with omnipotent games g_h belongs to the null space of the l linearly independent vectors $p_1, \ldots, p_l$ in R^n; that null space is $(n - l)$-dimensional. The values $V(g_h)$ of these games vary from 0 to 1, which adds one dimension. □

Corollary 7.1: If P contains $l \leqslant n$ linearly independent elements, then there exists a set of $n - l$ states defining an event S^A such that, if two games g_h and g_i are both omnipotent with $g_h \sim g_i$ and $\beta_h^m \sim \beta_i^m$ given s^m for all s^m in S^A, then $\beta_h^l \sim \beta_i^l$ given s^l for all s^l in $S^{\sim A}$.

In other words, for all g_h omnipotent, v_h is uniquely determined by $V(g_h)$ and $n - l$ elements of the vector v_h; the remaining l elements of v_h being single-valued functions of these $n - l + 1$ numbers. For $l = 1$, P is a singleton (no moral hazard), every game is omnipotent and one element of v_h can always be deduced from the remaining $n - 1$ elements and $V(g_h) = p \cdot v_h$. For $l = n$, g_h is omnipotent only if g_h is constant, so that $v_h = V(g_h)\iota$ is uniquely determined by $V(g_h)$ alone.

Proof of corollary 7.1: Let $\bar{p}_1, \ldots, \bar{p}_l$ be linearly independent elements of P, and denote by $\bar{P}$ the $l \times n$ matrix with row i equal to $\bar{p}_i$, $i = 1, \ldots, l$. Denote by $\bar{P}^{\sim A}$ an $l \times l$ submatrix from $\bar{P}$ with rank l, by $\bar{P}^A$ the remaining $n - l$ columns of $\bar{P}$, and re-index columns (states) so that $\bar{P} = [\bar{P}^{\sim A}, \bar{P}^A]$.

Let g_h be omnipotent. Then, $V(g_h) = \bar{p}_i \cdot v_h$, $i = 1, \ldots, l$, or $V(g_h)\iota = \bar{P} \cdot v_h$. Partitioning v_h into $v_h^{\sim A}$ and v_h^A, we may solve explicitly for $v_h^{\sim A} = [\bar{P}^{\sim A}]^{-1}[V(g_h)\iota - \bar{P}^A v_h^A]$. Thus, if g_i is another omnipotent game, with $V(g_i) = V(g_h)$ and $v_i^A = v_h^A$, then solving for $v_i^{\sim A}$ yields $v_i^{\sim A} = v_h^{\sim A}$. □

Using lemma 7.2 and corollary 7.1, one can test for the dimensionality of P by attempting to construct omnipotent games $g_h, g_i, \ldots$ with linearly independent expected utility vectors $v_h, v_i, \ldots$. If one can construct $n - l$ such vectors, then P contains at most $l + 1$ linearly independent elements.

An alternative test, based on conditional values, may prove more operational, because it does not involve omnipotent games. (It is easy to verify that a game is *not* omnipotent, but the converse is less easy; see also the comments in Section 8.3.)

Lemma 7.3: The set of probability vectors P contains l linearly independent elements, say $\bar{p}_1, \ldots, \bar{p}_l$, if and only if there exist l games, say $\bar{g}_1, \ldots, \bar{g}_l$, such that the $l \times l$ matrix of conditional values $[V(\bar{g}_j | \bar{p}_i)]$, $i, j = 1, \ldots, l$, has full rank.

Proof: The matrix $[V(\bar{g}_j | \bar{p}_i)] = [\bar{p}_i \cdot \bar{v}_j]$ is the product of two matrices, say the $l \times n$ matrix $\bar{P}$ and the $n \times l$ matrix $\bar{V}$, where the l rows of $\bar{P}$ are the vectors $\bar{p}_1, \ldots, \bar{p}_l$ and the l columns of $\bar{V}$ are the vectors $\bar{v}_1, \ldots, \bar{v}_l$. Sufficiency follows from the observation that the rank of $\bar{P}$ is at least equal to the rank of the product $\bar{P} \cdot \bar{V}$. Necessity follows from the observation that, for every $\bar{P}$ in $(\Delta^n)^l$, there exists a $\bar{V}$ in $([0, 1]^n)^l$ such that rank $(\bar{P} \cdot \bar{V}) = $ rank $(\bar{P})$. (For instance, let $\bar{V}$ consist of a set of Kronecker delta vectors corresponding to linearly independent columns of $\bar{P}$.) $\qquad \square$

The last sentence in the proof of lemma 7.3 reveals that evaluating a matrix of conditional values, or evaluating a matrix of probabilities, amounts basically to the same thing. Still if there existed for each $j = 1, \ldots, l$ a game $\bar{g}_j$ such that $V(\bar{g}_j | \bar{p}_j) \neq V(\bar{g}_j | \bar{p}_i) = V(\bar{g}_j | \bar{p}_k)$, all i and k different from j, then the matrix of conditional values would have full rank – a property ascertained in that case from preference comparisons, without recourse to numerical evaluations.

It seems appropriate to conclude that qualitative indicators of the dimensionality of P exist *in principle*.

For the purposes of Section 8, I introduce a definition:

Definition 7.1 (Linearly Independent Games): If the l probability vectors $\bar{p}_1, \ldots, \bar{p}_l$ in P are linearly independent, and the games $\bar{g}_1, \ldots, \bar{g}_l$ in G are such that $P^*(\bar{g}_j) = \{\bar{p}_j\}$, $j = 1, \ldots, l$, then $\bar{g}_1, \ldots, \bar{g}_l$ are called 'linearly independent games'.

The *existence* of l linearly independent games may be inferred by application of corollary 7.1, or of lemma 7.3 (or again of lemma 7.6 below).

7.2 Finitely many pure strategies

When P is a polyhedron, corresponding to the availability of finitely many pure strategies, all the results in Sections 6.4 and 7.1 can be sharpened.

Lemma 6.2 permits a direct, qualitative verification of the fact that P is a polyhedron.

Lemma 7.4: If there exists a *finite* subset G' of G such that:

(i)   for every g_h in G', $P^*(g_h)$ is a singleton;

(ii)   for every g_i in G, there exists a g_h in G' with $g_i E g_h$;

then P contains finitely many extreme points (at most as many as the number of elements of G').

Proof: For each g_h in G', $P^*(g_h)$ is an extreme point of P. If there existed an extreme point p_k not contained in

$$\bigcup_{g_h \in G'} P^*(g_h),$$

then there would exist a game g_k such that

$$P^*(g_k) = \{p_k\}, P^*(g_k) \cap \left(\bigcup_{g_h \in G'} P^*(g_h) \right) = \varnothing, \text{ contradicting (ii).} \quad \square$$

When P is a polyhedron, and the game g_h is such that $P^*(g_h)$ is a singleton (an extreme point of P), then small perturbations of g_h (of v_h) do not affect the choice of an optimal probability vector in P. This useful property is established in the next lemma.[39]

Lemma 7.5: Let P contain finitely many extreme points. If $P^*(g_h)$ is a singleton, then there exists $\bar{\alpha}$ in $[0, 1)$ such that, for all g_i in G and all $\alpha \geq \bar{\alpha}$, $P^*(g_{h \alpha g_i})$ contains p_h and $g_{h \alpha g_i} E g_h$.

Proof: See Appendix B.

Using lemma 7.5, one can restate formula (6.3) in exact, discrete form. When $p_h \in P^*(g_h) \cap P^*(g_{h \alpha g_i})$, then

$$V(g_{h \alpha g_i}) = \alpha V(g_h) + (1 - \alpha) V(g_i | p_h)$$
$$= V(g_{h \alpha g_0}) + (1 - \alpha) V(g_i | p_h),$$
$$V(g_i | p_h) = \frac{1}{1 - \alpha} [V(g_{h \alpha g_i}) - V(g_{h \alpha g_0})]. \tag{7.1}$$

Taking $g_i = (\beta_1^m, \beta_0^{-m})$ in (7.1), we obtain a discrete counterpart of (6.5), namely,

$$p_h^m = \frac{1}{1 - \alpha} [V(g_{h \alpha(\beta_1^m, \beta_0^{-m})}) - V(g_{h \alpha g_0})]. \tag{7.2}$$

---

[39] Lemma 7.5 corresponds to *assumption* P. 2.3 in Drèze (1961). Note that the lemma also holds at an extreme point of a strictly convex set, if that point is a 'corner'. More specifically, let p_h be an extreme point of P; if there exists a convex polyhedron $\bar{P} \subset \Delta^n$ such that $P \subset \bar{P}$ and p_h is an extreme point of $\bar{P}$, then lemma 7.5 holds for all g_h such that $P^*(g_h) = \{p_h\}$.

Formula (7.2) admits of a suggestive interpretation. When it is not true that $(\beta_1^m, \beta_0^{-m})Eg_h$, so that $V((\beta_1^m, \beta_0^{-m})) > p_h^m$, then one can still *embed* $(\beta_1^m, \beta_0^{-m})$ in a broader game, $g_{g_h\alpha(\beta_1^m, \beta_0^{-m})}$, for which p_h is an optimal probability. In formula (7.2), the term in square brackets measures the incremental value of staking a prize of utility 1 on s^m alone, with probability $1 - \alpha$, within a game for which p_h is the only optimal probability. Dividing by $1 - \alpha$ yields p_h^m.

Finally, I state two lemmas which provide a relatively straightforward qualitative test of the dimensionality of P. Lemma 7.6 gives a sufficient condition for P to contain l linearly independent elements. The condition is sufficient, whether P be a polyhedron or not. But the condition is not operational (is never satisfied) when P is a strictly convex set. Lemma 7.7 states that the condition is *always* operational when P is a polyhedron.[40,41]

Lemma 7.6: If there exists an ordered sequence of l non-empty equipotent sets $G^1, \ldots, G^l$ such that, for each $k = 2, \ldots, l$,

$$\bigcap_{j=1,\ldots,k-1} G^j \neq \bigcap_{j=1,\ldots,k} G^j, \tag{7.3}$$

then P contains l linearly independent elements.

Proof: See Appendix B.

Lemma 7.7: If P is a polyhedron containing l linearly independent elements, then there exist l non-empty equipotent sets $G^1, \ldots, G^l$ such that, for $k = 2, \ldots, l$, (7.3) holds.

Proof: See Appendix B.

8 Decision theory with state-dependent preferences and moral hazard

8.1 Conditional preferences and conditional utilities

Examples of state-dependent preferences proposed in the literature include situations where some states specify that 'you' are alive and others that 'you' are dead; or situations where 'you' plan a winter vacation at a ski resort and some states specify 'snow' while others specify 'no snow', as in Fishburn (1982, p. 111) a.s.o.

---

[40]The geometrical intuition behind the condition (as revealed by the proof of lemma 7.7) is the following: when P is a polyhedron, there exist nested sequences of faces of successively higher dimensionality, starting with an extreme point (zero dimensional face) and ending with the relative interior of P (face of highest dimensionality); the cones of normals to P at a sequence of points belonging to the relative interiors of these faces are also nested, and define the sequence of equipotent sets $G^1, \ldots, G^l$ in the statement of the lemma.

[41]A related condition, appearing as theorem 3.2 in Drèze (1961), is not reproduced here, because it is not always operational, even when P is a polyhedron.

In the framework adopted here, a situation of state-dependent preferences may be diagnosed from *either or both* of the following symptoms: (i) conditional preferences over prize mixtures differ across states – in violation of assumption SIP; (ii) some constant games are not omnipotent – in violation of assumption CGO.

We must accordingly replace SIP and CGO by suitably weakened assumptions. In so far as assumption SIP is concerned, the task is easy; I shall simply assume that conditional preferences *given any state* are free of inconsistencies – though being allowed to vary from state to state.

Assumption 8.1 or CP (Conditional Preferences): For all s^m in S, for all β, β' in $\mathbb{B}$, if $\beta \prec \beta'$ given s^m, then it is not true that $\beta' \prec \beta$ given s^m.

Remember from definition 4.1 that $\beta \prec \beta'$ given s^m if there exists $\beta_h^{\tilde{m}}$ such that $(\beta, \beta_h^{\tilde{m}}) \prec (\beta', \beta_h^{\tilde{m}})$. Thus, assumption 8.1 states that there do *not* exist $\beta_h^{\tilde{m}}$ and $\beta_i^{\tilde{m}}$ with $(\beta, \beta_h^{\tilde{m}}) \prec (\beta', \beta_h^{\tilde{m}})$ and $(\beta', \beta_i^{\tilde{m}}) \prec (\beta, \beta_i^{\tilde{m}})$.

This is certainly a minimal and reasonable requirement. In particular, it does *not* rule out the existence of $\beta_h^{\tilde{m}}$ and $\beta_i^{\tilde{m}}$ such that $(\beta, \beta_h^{\tilde{m}}) \prec (\beta', \beta_h^{\tilde{m}})$ and $(\beta, \beta_i^{\tilde{m}}) \sim (\beta', \beta_i^{\tilde{m}})$.[42] Such preferences could arise if state s^m, though not null, is regarded impossible *in the particular comparison* $(\beta, \beta_i^{\tilde{m}}) \sim (\beta', \beta_i^{\tilde{m}})$.[43]

The proposed weakening of assumption CGO is somewhat less intuitive. It embodies a first requirement which one would prefer to dispense with (namely, the existence of at least two omnipotent games), as well as some more technical requirements (weak form of the independence and continuity assumptions) which I regard as perfectly reasonable when the former holds.

As announced in the introduction (Section 1.3), the two omnipotent games will be used to relate the scales of conditional utilities, elicited separately for each state thanks to assumption CP. The assumption that there exist omnipotent games is definitely stronger under state-dependent preferences than under state-independent preferences, where constant games could be assumed omnipotent. That point is taken up in Section 9.6 where the definite possibility of replacing assumption 8.2 by a more innocuous alternative is outlined.

Assumption 8.2 or NDO (Existence of Omnipotent Games): There exist two omnipotent games, say g_0 and g_1, with $g_0 \prec g_1$.

(The labelling NDO reflects the assumption that the non-degeneracy condition ND is fulfilled by omnipotent games.)

---

[42]The precise wording of definition 4.1 was chosen so that SIP still allowed for this possibility.
[43]Thus, if $\beta_i^{\tilde{m}}$ says that our bowman receives \$100 000 in case he misses, he may well be indifferent between receiving \$10 (β) or \$100 (β') in case he wins; whereas if $\beta_h^{\tilde{m}}$ says that he receives \$0 in case he misses, he will prefer receiving \$100 rather than \$10 in case he wins.

The two omnipotent games singled out by assumption NDO will be used for normalisation purposes, thereby replacing b_0 and b_1. (Under state-dependent preferences, constant games need not be omnipotent.)

Normalisation N.4′: $V(g_0) = 0$, $V(g_1) = 1$ for g_0, g_1 as in assumption NDO.

The rationale for the next and last assumption may now be presented. Readers uninterested in technicalities or desirous to acquire first a general understanding of the contents of this chapter may wish to proceed directly to Section 8.2.

Reasoning heuristically, if the game g_0 is omnipotent, all 'strategies' are optimal for that game. These may include some strategies under which s^m is null, as well as other strategies under which s^m is not null. Let now g_0 be modified on s^m *alone*, with a *more attractive* prize mixture substituted for β_0^m. For that modified game, it becomes desirable to choose a strategy whereby the probability of s^m is *maximised*; if s^m is not null, such a strategy entails a positive probability for s^m, and the modified game is *strictly preferred* to g_0. Also, *all* games of the form $(\beta, \beta_0^{\sim m})$ strictly preferred to g_0 should be simultaneously equipotent, since a strategy maximising the probability of s^m is optimal for any of them.

Do there exist games of the form $(\beta, \beta_0^{\sim m})$ strictly preferred to g_0? I shall assume that, for all s^m not null, $(\beta_1^m, \beta_0^{\sim m}) \succ g_0$, where β_1^m is the prize mixture associated with s^m by the omnipotent game g_1 preferred to g_0.[44]

In addition, I shall assume that, for all β in $\mathbb{B}$, there exists α in $[0, 1)$ such that $(\beta_1^m \alpha \beta, \beta_0^{\sim m}) \succ g_0$. This is an extension of continuity assumption PC from preferences over lotteries to *conditional* preferences over prize mixtures given a state. That extension could be introduced as a general principle (If $\beta \prec \beta'$ given s^m, then for all β'' in $\mathbb{B}$ there exists α in $[0, 1)$ such that $\beta \alpha \beta'' \prec \beta'$ given s^m and $\beta \prec \beta' \alpha \beta''$ given s^m) justified on the same grounds as PC. But it is sufficient to state the assumption for β_1^m and β_0^m only.

Assumption 8.3 or ICC (Independence and Continuity of Conditional Preferences): For all s^m not null:

(i)   the set $G_0^m := \{g_h \in G \mid g_h := (\beta_h^m, \beta_0^{\sim m}), g_h \succ g_0\}$ is an equipotent set;
(ii)   for each β in $\mathbb{B}$, there exists α in $[0, 1)$ such that $(\beta_1^m \alpha \beta, \beta_0^{\sim m}) \succ g_0$.

The labelling 'ICC' is motivated by the fact that (ii) is an assumption of continuity for conditional preference, as explained in the previous paragraph; and (i) is equivalent to an assumption of independence for conditional preference, as shown in lemma 8.1 (which is otherwise a digression).

---

[44] This places on g_1 and g_0 a further requirement, consistent with our hope that g_1 and g_0 may have the 'constant expected utility property'.

Taken *together*, assumptions NDO, PC and ICC are a *weakening* of assumptions CGO and SIP, which imply the independence and continuity properties for conditional preferences (see lemma 4.2 and remark 4.1).

    Lemma 8.1: Under assumptions NDO and VI, the following two statements are mutually equivalent:

(a)   for all g_h, g_i in G_0^m, $g_h E g_i$ (i.e. G_0^m is an equipotent set);

(b)   for all g_h, g_i, g_j in G_0^m, for all α in $(0, 1]$, $g_{g_h \alpha g_j} \precsim g_{g_i \alpha g_j}$ if and only if $g_h \precsim g_i$.

    Proof: Let g_h, g_i and g_j belong to G_0^m.

(a) *implies* (b): under (a), for all α in $[0, 1]$, $g_{g_h \alpha g_j} \sim g_h \alpha g_j$ and $g_{g_i \alpha g_j} \sim g_i \alpha g_j$; in view of PO, then PI: $g_{g_h \alpha g_j} \precsim g_{g_i \alpha g_j}$ if and only if $g_h \alpha g_j \precsim g_i \alpha g_j$ if and only if $g_h \precsim g_i$.

(b) *implies* (a): assume w.l.o.g. that $g_h \precsim g_i$; in view of theorem 3.1, there exists λ in $(0, 1]$ such that $g_i \lambda g_0 \sim g_h \succ g_0$; because g_0 is omnipotent (NDO), $g_{g_i \lambda g_0} \sim g_i \lambda g_0$; by construction, $g_{g_i \lambda g_0} \in G_0^m$; by (b), for all α in $(0, 1]$, $g_{g_h \alpha (g_i \lambda g_0)} \sim g_{g_h \alpha g_h} = g_h$ because $g_h \sim g_i \lambda g_0$; accordingly, $g_{g_h \alpha (g_i \lambda g_0)} \sim g_h \sim g_h \alpha (g_i \lambda g_0)$, so that g_h, g_i and g_0 are simultaneously equipotent. $\square$

An important lemma establishes the existence of 'conditional utilities'. The statement and the proof of the lemma are a bit awkward, due to the recurrent complication arising when a state, though not null, is regarded as impossible in specific comparisons.

    Lemma 8.2: Under assumptions NDO, VI, CP and ICC, there exists for each s^m in S a real-valued function u^m, defined on B up to a positive linear transformation and called conditional utility, such that, for all β and β' in $\mathbb{B}$,

$$\sum_q \beta(b_q) u^m(b_q) > (\text{resp.} =) \sum_q \beta'(b_q) u^m(b_q)$$

if and only if

$$\beta_1^m \alpha \beta \succ (\text{resp.} \sim) \ \beta_1^m \alpha \beta' \text{ given } s^m \text{ for some (resp. all) } \alpha \text{ in } [0, 1),$$

only if

$$\beta \succsim (\text{resp.} \sim) \beta' \text{ given } s^m.$$

    Proof: 1. For all s^m in S, for all b_q in B, define:

$$u^m(b_q) = 0 \quad \text{if } s^m \text{ is null;} \tag{8.1}$$

$$u^m(b_q) = \left[\frac{V((\beta_1^m \alpha b_q, \beta_0^{\tilde{m}}))}{V((\beta_1^m, \beta_0^{\tilde{m}}))} - \alpha \right] \frac{1}{1 - \alpha} \quad \text{for } \alpha \text{ such that} \tag{8.2}$$

$(\beta_1^m \alpha b_q, \beta_0^{\tilde{m}}) \succ g_0$, if s^m is not null.

The function $u^m(b_q)$ is thereby uniquely defined, under normalisation N.4'. When s^m is not null, this is verified as follows:

1. *First*, $V((\beta_1^m, \beta_0^{\sim m})) > 0$, by theorem 3.1, since $(\beta_1^m, \beta_0^{\sim m}) \succ g_0$ by assumption 8.3(ii) and $V(g_0) = 0$. *Second*, the value of $u^m(b_q)$ in (8.2) is independent of α, so long as $(\beta_1^m \alpha b_q, \beta_0^{\sim m}) \in G_0^m$. Indeed, let $(\beta_1^m \alpha' b_q, \beta_0^{\sim m}) \succ g_0$ as well. Assuming w.l.o.g. that $\alpha' > \alpha$, there exists λ in $(0, 1)$ such that $\alpha' = \alpha\lambda + 1 - \lambda$. By assumption 8.3(i) $V((\beta_1^m \alpha' b_q, \beta_0^{\sim m})) = \lambda V((\beta_1^m \alpha b_q, \beta_0^{\sim m})) + (1 - \lambda)V((\beta_1^m, \beta_0^{\sim m}))$,

$$\left[\frac{V((\beta_1^m \alpha' b_q, \beta_0^{\sim m}))}{V((\beta_1^m, \beta_0^{\sim m}))} - \alpha' \right] \frac{1}{1 - \alpha'} = \left[\lambda \frac{V((\beta_1^m \alpha b_q, \beta_0^{\sim m}))}{V((\beta_1^m, \beta_0^{\sim m}))} + 1 - \lambda - \alpha' \right] \frac{1}{\lambda(1 - \alpha)}$$

which is the same as $u^m(b_q)$ in (8.2), since $1 - \lambda - \alpha' = - \lambda\alpha$.

2. If s^m is null, then for all β, β' in $\mathbb{B}$, for all α in $[0, 1]$, $\beta_1^m \alpha\beta \sim \beta_1^m \alpha\beta'$ given s^m, by definition 4.2; and

$$\sum_q \beta(b_q)u^m(b_q) = \sum_q \beta'(b_q)u^m(b_q) = 0$$

by (8.1). The lemma is thus proved for all s^m null.

3. If s^m is not null, then for all β, β' in $\mathbb{B}$,

$$\sum_q \beta(b_q)u^m(b_q) \geq \sum_q \beta'(b_q)u^m(b_q) \tag{8.3}$$

if and only if, for some α in $[0, 1)$

$$(\beta_1^m \alpha\beta, \beta_0^{\sim m}) \succsim (\beta_1^m \alpha\beta', \beta_0^{\sim m}) \succ g_0.$$

Because B is finite, there exists, by assumption 8.3(ii), some $\dot{\alpha}$ in $[0, 1)$ such that $(\beta_1^m \dot{\alpha} b_q, \beta_0^{\sim m}) \succ g_0$ for *all* b_q. It then follows from assumption 8.3(i) that

$$V((\beta_1^m \dot{\alpha}\beta, \beta_0^{\sim m})) = \sum_q \beta(b_q)V((\beta_1^m \dot{\alpha} b_q, \beta_0^{\sim m}))$$

and

$$V((\beta_1^m \dot{\alpha}\beta', \beta_0^{\sim m})) = \sum_q \beta'(b_q)V((\beta_1^m \dot{\alpha} b_q, \beta_0^{\sim m})).$$

Using (8.2), we find that $V((\beta_1^m \dot{\alpha}\beta, \beta_0^{\sim m})) - V((\beta_1^m \dot{\alpha}\beta', \beta_0^{\sim m})) \geq 0$ if and only if

$$\sum_q \beta(b_q)u^m(b_q) - \sum_q \beta'(b_q)u^m(b_q) \geq 0,$$

as required by (8.3).

4. I use (8.3) to show next that $\beta_1^m \tilde{\alpha}\beta \succ \beta_1^m \tilde{\alpha}\beta'$ given s^m for some $\tilde{\alpha}$ in $[0, 1)$, implies that there exists α in $[0, 1)$ such that $(\beta_1^m \alpha\beta, \beta_0^{\sim m}) \succ (\beta_1^m \alpha\beta', \beta_0^{\sim m})$. (The converse implication, with $\tilde{\alpha} = \alpha$, is definition 4.1.)

Suppose on the contrary that $(\beta_1^m \alpha\beta, \beta_0^{\sim m}) \precsim (\beta_1^m \alpha\beta', \beta_0^{\sim m})$ for *all* α in $[0, 1)$; and let w.l.o.g. $\tilde{\alpha}$ be such that $(\beta_1^m \tilde{\alpha}\beta', \beta_0^{\sim m}) \succ g_0.$[45]

---

[45]Because g_1 is omnipotent, $(\beta_1^m \tilde{\alpha}\beta, \beta_0^{\sim m}) \succ (\beta_1^m \tilde{\alpha}\beta', \beta_h^{\sim m})$ implies, for all λ in $[0, 1)$. $((\beta_1^m \tilde{\alpha}\beta)\lambda\beta_1^m, \beta_h^{\sim m}\lambda\beta_1^{\sim m}) \succ ((\beta_1^m \tilde{\alpha}\beta')\lambda\beta_1^m, \beta_h^{\sim m}\lambda\beta_1^{\sim m})$ so that $\beta_1^m(\tilde{\alpha}\lambda + 1 - \lambda)\beta \succ \beta_1^m(\tilde{\alpha}\lambda + 1 - \lambda)\beta'$ given s^m for all λ in $[0, 1)$.

Consider first the case where $(\beta_1^m, \beta_0^{-m}) \succ (\beta_1^m \tilde{\alpha} \beta, \beta_0^{-m})$. Then, by PI, for all λ in $[0,1)$, $(\beta_1^m \tilde{\alpha} \beta', \beta_0^{-m}) \lambda (\beta_1^m, \beta_0^{-m}) \succ (\beta_1^m \tilde{\alpha} \beta, \beta_0^{-m})$. By assumption 8.3(i), $(\beta_1^m \tilde{\alpha} \beta', \beta_0^{-m}) \lambda (\beta_1^m, \beta_0^{-m}) \sim ((\beta_1^m \tilde{\alpha} \beta') \lambda \beta_1^m, \beta_0^{-m})$, so that (definition 4.1)

$$(\beta_1^m \tilde{\alpha} \beta') \lambda \beta_1^m \succ \beta_1^m \tilde{\alpha} \beta \quad \text{given } s^m, \text{ for all } \lambda \text{ in } [0,1). \tag{8.4}$$

On the other hand, $\beta_1^m \tilde{\alpha} \beta \succ \beta_1^m \tilde{\alpha} \beta'$ given s^m means that there exists β_h^{-m} such that $(\beta_1^m \tilde{\alpha} \beta, \beta_h^{-m}) \succ (\beta_1^m \tilde{\alpha} \beta', \beta_h^{-m})$. By assumption PC, there exists λ in $[0,1)$ such that $(\beta_1^m \tilde{\alpha} \beta, \beta_h^{-m}) \succ (\beta_1^m \tilde{\alpha} \beta', \beta_h^{-m}) \lambda (\beta_1^m, \beta_h^{-m})$; hence, by assumption VI, $(\beta_1^m \tilde{\alpha} \beta, \beta_h^{-m}) \succ ((\beta_1^m \tilde{\alpha} \beta') \lambda \beta_1^m, \beta_h^{-m})$, contradicting (8.4).

Consider now the case where $(\beta_1^m \tilde{\alpha} \beta, \beta_0^{-m}) \succsim (\beta_1^m, \beta_0^{-m}) \succ g_0$. Then, by PI, for all λ in $[0,1)$, $(\beta_1^m \tilde{\alpha} \beta', \beta_0^{-m}) \succsim (\beta_1^m \tilde{\alpha} \beta, \beta_0^{-m}) \succ (\beta_1^m \tilde{\alpha} \beta, \beta_0^{-m}) \lambda g_0$. Because g_0 is omnipotent, $(\beta_1^m \tilde{\alpha} \beta, \beta_0^{-m}) \lambda g_0 \sim ((\beta_1^m \tilde{\alpha} \beta) \lambda \beta_0^m, \beta_0^{-m})$, so that

$$\beta_1^m \tilde{\alpha} \beta' \succ (\beta_1^m \tilde{\alpha} \beta) \lambda \beta_0^m \quad \text{given } s^m, \text{ for all } \lambda \text{ in } [0,1). \tag{8.5}$$

On the other hand, there exists β_h^{-m} such that $(\beta_1^m \tilde{\alpha} \beta, \beta_h^{-m}) \succ (\beta_1^m \tilde{\alpha} \beta', \beta_h^{-m})$. By assumption PC, there exists λ in $[0,1)$ such that $(\beta_1^m \tilde{\alpha} \beta, \beta_h^{-m}) \lambda g_0 \succ (\beta_1^m \tilde{\alpha} \beta', \beta_h^{-m})$, and λ' in $[0,1)$ such that $(\beta_1^m \tilde{\alpha} \beta, \beta_h^{-m}) \lambda g_0 \succ (\beta_1^m \tilde{\alpha} \beta', \beta_h^{-m}) \lambda' (\beta_1^m \tilde{\alpha} \beta', \beta_0^{-m})$. For $\bar{\lambda} = \text{Max } (\lambda, \lambda')$, by PI,[46] $(\beta_1^m \tilde{\alpha} \beta, \beta_h^{-m}) \bar{\lambda} g_0 \succ (\beta_1^m \tilde{\alpha} \beta', \beta_h^{-m}) \bar{\lambda} (\beta_1^m \tilde{\alpha} \beta', \beta_0^{-m})$. Using the omnipotence of g_0 in the left-hand side of this relation and assumption VI in the right-hand side, $((\beta_1^m \tilde{\alpha} \beta) \bar{\lambda} \beta_0^m, \beta_h^{-m} \bar{\lambda} \beta_0^{-m}) \succ (\beta_1^m \tilde{\alpha} \beta', \beta_h^{-m} \bar{\lambda} \beta_0^{-m})$, contradicting (8.5).

We may thus conclude that $\beta_1^m \tilde{\alpha} \beta \succ \beta_1^m \tilde{\alpha} \beta'$ given s^m for some $\tilde{\alpha}$ in $[0,1)$ if and only if $(\beta_1^m \alpha \beta, \beta_0^{-m}) \succ (\beta_1^m \alpha \beta', \beta_0^{-m})$ for some α in $[0,1)$.

5. The proof is now almost complete. First,

$$\sum_q \beta(b_q) u^m(b_q) > \sum_q \beta'(b_q) u^m(b_q)$$

if and only if (step 3) $(\beta_1^m \alpha \beta, \beta_0^{-m}) \succ (\beta_1^m \alpha \beta', \beta_0^{-m})$ for some α in $[0,1)$, if and only if (step 4) $\beta_1^m \tilde{\alpha} \beta \succ \beta_1^m \tilde{\alpha} \beta'$ given s^m for some $\tilde{\alpha}$ in $[0,1)$. Next,

$$\sum_q \beta(b_q) u^m(b_q) = \sum_q \beta'(b_q) u^m(b_q)$$

consequently rules out '$\beta_1^m \tilde{\alpha} \beta \succ (\prec) \beta_1^m \tilde{\alpha} \beta'$ given s^m for some $\tilde{\alpha}$ in $[0,1)$', implying $\beta_1^m \alpha \beta \sim \beta_1^m \alpha \beta'$ given s^m for all α in $[0,1)$.

Finally, $\beta \succ \beta'$ given s^m implies $(\beta, \beta_h^{-m}) \succ (\beta', \beta_h^{-m})$ for some β_h^{-m}. By PI, for all α $[0,1)$, $g_1 \alpha(\beta, \beta_h^{-m}) \succ g_1 \alpha(\beta', \beta_h^{-m})$. By omnipotence of g_1, $(\beta_1^m \alpha \beta, \beta_1^{-m} \alpha \beta_h^{-m}) \succ (\beta_1^m \alpha \beta', \beta_1^{-m} \alpha \beta_h^{-m})$, so that $\beta_1^m \alpha \beta \succ \beta_1^m \alpha \beta'$ given s^m for all α in $[0,1)$. It follows that $\beta_1^m \alpha \beta \succ \beta_1^m \alpha \beta'$ given s^m for some α in $[0,1)$ rules out $\beta' \succ \beta$ given s^m and implies $\beta \succsim \beta'$ given s^m; whereas $\beta_1^m \alpha \beta \sim \beta_1^m \alpha \beta'$ for all α in $[0,1)$ rules out both $\beta \succ \beta'$ given s^m and $\beta' \succ \beta$ given s^m, implying $\beta \sim \beta'$ given s^m. All the implications in the lemma are thus proved.

6. It is clear from the statement of the lemma that its conclusion is not altered if a positive linear transformation is applied to u^m. Non-linear transformations are ruled out by the requirement that, for *all* β and β' in $\mathbb{B}$,

$$\sum_q \beta(b_q) u^m(b_q) \geqslant \sum_q \beta'(b_q) u^m(b_q)$$

[46]When $g_h \succ g_i$ and $g_h \lambda g_j \succ g_i$, then $g_h \mu g_j \succ g_i$ for all μ in $[\lambda, 1]$; similarly, when $g_h \succ g_i$ and $g_h \succ g_i \lambda' g_k$, then $g_h \succ g_i \mu' g_k$ for all μ' in $[\lambda', 1]$.

if and only if, for some α in $[0,1)$, $\beta_1^m \alpha \beta \gtrsim \beta_1^m \alpha \beta'$ given s^m if and only if $(\beta_1^m \alpha \beta, \beta_0^{\sim m}) \gtrsim (\beta_1^m \alpha \beta', \beta_0^{\sim m})$. □

Remark 8.1: Under normalisation N.4′, the convex hull of the range of the function $u^m(b_q)$ defined by (8.1)–(8.2), say I^m, *includes* $[0,1]$, and that function satisfies:

Normalisation N.8: For each s^m not null,

$$v_0^m = \sum_q \beta_0^m(b_q) u^m(b_q) = 0,$$

$$v_1^m = \sum_q \beta_1^m(b_q) u^m(b_q) = 1.$$

Proof of remark 8.1: By the reasoning in step 3 in the proof of lemma 8.2,

$$V((\beta_1^m \hat{\alpha} \beta_0^m, \beta_0^{\sim m})) = \sum_q \beta_0^m(b_q) V((\beta_1^m \hat{\alpha} b_q, \beta_0^{\sim m}))$$

so that, by (8.2),

$$\sum_q \beta_0^m(b_q) u^m(b_q) = \sum_q \beta_0^m(b_q) \left[\frac{V((\beta_1^m \hat{\alpha} b_q, \beta_0^{\sim m}))}{V((\beta_1^m, \beta_0^{\sim m}))} - \hat{\alpha} \right] \frac{1}{1 - \hat{\alpha}}$$

$$= \left[\frac{V((\beta_1^m \hat{\alpha} \beta_0^m, \beta_0^{\sim m}))}{V((\beta_1^m, \beta_0^{\sim m}))} - \hat{\alpha} \right] \frac{1}{1 - \hat{\alpha}}$$

$$= \left[\frac{\hat{\alpha} V((\beta_1^m, \beta_0^{\sim m})) + (1 - \hat{\alpha}) V(g_0)}{V((\beta_1^m, \beta_0^{\sim m}))} - \hat{\alpha} \right] \frac{1}{1 - \hat{\alpha}} = 0,$$

where use has been made of the fact that g_0 is omnipotent, with $V(g_0) = 0$.
By the same reasoning,

$$\sum_q \beta_1^m(b_q) u^m(b_q) = \sum_q \beta_1^m(b_q) \left[\frac{V((\beta_1^m \hat{\alpha} b_q, \beta_0^{\sim m}))}{V((\beta_1^m, \beta_0^{\sim m}))} - \hat{\alpha} \right] \frac{1}{1 - \hat{\alpha}}$$

$$= \left[\frac{V((\beta_1^m \hat{\alpha} \beta_1^m, \beta_0^{\sim m}))}{V((\beta_1^m, \beta_0^{\sim m}))} - \hat{\alpha} \right] \frac{1}{1 - \hat{\alpha}}$$

$$= \left[\frac{V((\beta_1^m, \beta_0^{\sim m}))}{V((\beta_1^m, \beta_0^{\sim m}))} - \hat{\alpha} \right] \frac{1}{1 - \hat{\alpha}} = 1. \qquad □$$

The remark also shows that normalisations N.4′ and N.8 are mutually consistent. Whereas normalisation N.4′ is perfectly innocuous, normalisation N.8 is not, as will be explained in Section 8.3.

I now introduce a counterpart of lemma 4.1 stated in terms of conditional expected utilities.

Corollary 8.1: Under the terms of lemma 8.2, for all g_h, g_i in G, if

$$\sum_q \beta_h^m(b_q) u^m(b_q) \leqslant \sum_q \beta_i^m(b_q) u^m(b_q)$$

for each $m = 1, \ldots, n$, then $g_h \precsim g_i$.

Proof: For each $m = 1, \ldots, n$, define a game g_{hm} by

$$\beta_{hm}^l = \begin{cases} \beta_h^l, & l = 1, \ldots, m \\ \beta_i^l, & l = m+1, \ldots, n. \end{cases}$$

Thus, $g_{h^1} = (\beta_h^1, \beta_i^2, \ldots, \beta_i^n)$ and $g_{h^n} = g_h$.

For each $m = 1, \ldots, n$, $g_{hm} \precsim g_{h^{m-1}}$. Indeed, $\beta_{hm}^l = \beta_{h^{m-1}}^l$ for all $l \neq m$, $l = 1, \ldots, n$, so that $g_{hm} := (\beta_h^m, \beta_{h^{m-1}}^{-m})$. Because

$$\sum_q \beta_h^m(b_q) u^m(b_q) \leqslant \sum_q \beta_i^m(b_q) u^m(b_q),$$

it follows from lemma 8.2 that $\beta_h^m \precsim \beta_i^m$ given s^m, so that (assumption 8.1) $g_{hm} = (\beta_h^m, \beta_{h^{m-1}}^{-m}) \precsim (\beta_i^m, \beta_{h^{m-1}}^{-m}) = g_{h^{m-1}}$.

Thus,

$$g_h = g_{h^n} \precsim g_{h^{n-1}}, \ldots, \precsim g_{h^1} \precsim g_i. \qquad \square$$

8.2 Main results

After this lengthy preparation, it is relatively easy to extend the results of Section 6 for the case of state-dependent preferences. The existence result (theorem 8.1) is quite straightforward. The uniqueness, or 'identification' result, is less straightforward and therefore presented separately, in two propositions (theorem 8.2).

I wish to remind the reader that assumptions NDO and VI together are a weakening of assumptions ND and RO, whereas assumptions NDO, CP and ICC together are a weakening of assumptions SIP and CGO.

Theorem 8.1: Under assumptions NDO, VI, CP and ICC there exist a closed convex set P of probability measures on S, and a real-valued function U on $S \times B$, called state-dependent utility, such that, for all g_h in G,

$$V(g_h) = \underset{p \in P}{\text{Max}} \sum_m p^m \sum_q \beta_h^m(b_q) U(s^m, b_q), \quad \text{with } p^m = 0 \text{ whenever } s^m \text{ is}$$
null.

Proof: The proof follows closely that of theorem 6.1. For each s^m in S, let $u^m(b_q)$ be as defined in (8.1)–(8.2), and let, for each g_h in G,

$$v_h^m := \sum_q \beta_h^m(b_q) u^m(b_q).$$

Then $v_h^m \in I^m$, the range of u^m. In view of corollary 8.1, there exists a function $f, \times_m I^m \to R$, such that, for all g_h in G, $V(g_h) = f(v_h^1, \ldots, v_h^n) = f(v_h)$. By the reasoning in step 2 of the proof of theorem 6.1, the function f is finite, closed, convex and positively homogeneous. (To establish homogeneity, note first that g_0 is omnipotent by NDO, with $v_0 = (0, \ldots, 0)$ by N.8; hence, for all α in $[0, 1]$, $\alpha f(v_h) = f(\alpha v_h)$ and $\alpha v_h \in \times_m I^m$; if $k > 1$ is such that $k v_h \in \times_m I^m$, then $(1/k) f(k v_h) = f(v_h)$.)

Thus, there exists a closed convex set $P^* \subset R^n$ such that, for all g_h in G,

$$v(g_h) = \operatorname*{Sup}_{p \in P^*} p \cdot v_h.$$

Let again $P := P^* \cap \Delta^n$. To retrace steps 3(i)–3(iii) in the proof of theorem 6.1, renumber the states so that $s^1, \ldots, s^k$ are not null, $s^{k+1}, \ldots, s^n$ are null ($k \leqslant n$). Then $v_1 = (\iota, 0)$, $\iota \in R^k$, and the reasoning in steps 3(i)–3(iii) shows successively that: for all $p \in P^*$, $p \cdot v_1 \leqslant 1$; for all g_h in G, there exists p_α in P^*, with $p_\alpha \cdot v_1 = 1$ and $p_\alpha \cdot v_h = f(v_h)$; and for all p in P^*, $p^m \geqslant 0$, $m = 1, \ldots, k$. Setting $p_\alpha^m = 0$ for all $m = k+1, \ldots, n$, there exists for each g_h in G a p in P such that $V(g_h) = p \cdot v_h \geqslant p' \cdot v_h$ for all p' in P, with $p^m = 0$ whenever s^m is null.

Defining $U(s^m, b_q) := u^m(b_q)$, $m = 1, \ldots, n$, completes the proof. $\square$

The existence results in theorems 6.1 and 8.1 are analogous, and carry the logical implication that 'strategies' are chosen so as to maximise (subjectively) expected utility. The uniqueness result of theorem 6.1 is analogous to that in part (i) of theorem 8.2, where a new condition (based on definition 7.1) appears. When that condition is not satisfied, the separate identification of probabilities and scales of conditional utilities is incomplete, as indicated in part (ii) of the theorem.

Theorem 8.2: Under the terms of theorem 8.1, let there be $k \leqslant n$ states which are not null, with union $S^K \subset S$;

(i)   if there exist k linearly independent games, then P is unique, and v is unique on $S^K \times B$ up to the same positive linear transformation as V;

(ii)   if there exist l, and at most $l < k$, linearly independent games, then P and U are defined on S^K and $S^K \times B$ respectively, up to a set of joint transformations which, for all p in P, s^m in S^K and b_q in B, take p^m and $U(s^m, b_q)$ into $p^m c^m$ and $(1/c^m)[U(s^m, b_q) + d^m]$ respectively, $c^m > 0$; the set of admissible vectors c (resp. d) satisfies, for all p in P, $\sum_K p^m c^m = 1$ (resp. $\sum_K p^m d^m = 0$) and lies in a $(k - l)$-dimensional subspace of R^k; besides, U remains subject to the same positive linear transformation as V.

Proof: The statement of theorem 8.2 recognises explicitly that U remains subject to the same positive linear transformation as V. Accordingly, we may proceed under normalisation N.4′.

Let the states be numbered so that $s^1, \ldots, s^k$ are not null, $s^{k+1}, \ldots, s^n$ are null. Suppose that there exist an alternative set of probability measures R on S^K and an alternative state-dependent utility W on $S^K \times B$ such that, for all g_h in G,

$$V(g_h) = \operatorname*{Max}_{r \in R} \sum_{m=1}^{k} r^m \sum_q \beta_h^m(b_q) W(s^m, b_q).$$

(Inside this proof, R does not denote Euclidian 1-space, but rather a subset of Δ^k, the unit simplex of Euclidian k-space.)

As noted in the proof of lemma 8.2 (step 6), on $s^m \times B$, W must be a positive linear transformation of $U = u^m$, say $W(s^m, b_q) = (1/c^m)[U(s^m, b_q) + d^m]$, $c^m > 0$. Thus,

$$\sum_q \beta_h^m(b_q) W(s^m, b_q) = \frac{1}{c^m} \sum_q \beta_h^m(b_q)[U(s^m, b_q) + d^m]$$

$$= \frac{1}{c^m}(v_h^m + d^m) =: w_h^m.$$

For each g_h in G,

$$V(g_h) = \underset{r \in R}{\text{Max}} \sum_{m=1}^{k} r^m w_h^m.$$

Using NDO, VI and theorem 8.1, all the results derived in Section 6.3 apply. In particular, if equipotence with the game g_h is transitive, so that $R^*(g_h)$ is a singleton, $R^*(g_h) = \{r_h\}$, then by (6.6) or its discrete counterpart (7.2),

$$r_h^m = \frac{\partial V(g_h)}{\partial w_h^m} = c^m \frac{\partial V(g_h)}{\partial v_h^m} = c^m p_h^m.$$

It follows that R and W are related to P and U of theorem 8.1 by a pair of k-dimensional vectors, $c \gg 0$ and d, with $W(s^m, b_q) = (1/c^m)[U(s^m, b_q) + d^m]$ on $S^K \times B$ and with $R = \{r \in \Delta^k | \exists p \in P : \forall m = 1, \dots, k, r^m = p^m c^m\}$.

The requirement that $R \subset \Delta^k$ places restrictions on c: for all p in P,

$$\sum_{m=1}^{k} p^m c^m = 1.$$

Writing p^K for $(p^1, \dots, p^k)$, and noting that $p^K \iota = 1$, we may write this requirement as

$$p^K(c - \iota) = 0 \quad \text{for all } p \text{ in } P. \tag{8.6}$$

If P contains k linearly independent elements, (8.6) implies $c - \iota = 0$, or $c^m = 1$ for all $m = 1, \dots, k$, so that P is unique. If P owns l, and at most $l < k$, linearly independent elements $p_1, \dots, p_l$, (8.6) implies that $c - \iota$ lies in the null space of the l vectors $p_1^K, \dots, p_l^K$, which is $(k - l)$-dimensional; so that c itself lies in a $(k - l)$-dimensional subspace of Euclidian k-space.

Turning to admissible vectors d, the omnipotent game g_0, with $v_0 = (0, \dots, 0)$ and $V(g_0) = 0$, imposes that

$$\sum_{m=1}^{k} r^m \frac{d^m}{c^m} = 0$$

for all r in R, or equivalently

$$\sum_{m=1}^{k} p^m d^m = 0$$

for all p in P. By the reasoning in the previous paragraph, $d = 0$ when P owns k linearly independent elements, and d lies in a $(k - l)$-dimensional subspace of Euclidean k-space when P owns l linearly independent elements.

By definition 6.1, if there exist $l(\leqslant k)$ linearly independent games, P contains l linearly independent elements. $\square$

8.3 Elicitation and identification of subjective probabilities

Part (i) of theorem 8.2 substantiates the claim in the introduction (Section 1.3) that 'moral hazard... resolves the identification problem associated with state-dependent preferences'. The resolution is complete (P is unique, and U is unique on non-null states up to monotone linear transformations) when *all* states are subject to the decision-maker's influence – a remote possibility. Otherwise, the identification is only partial, as explained in part (ii) of the theorem.

In order to interpret these results, it is helpful to consider first how subjective probabilities are elicited, in this case. The guiding principle is the same as in Sections 4 and 6.4 and calls for looking at the value of the game $(\beta_1^m, \beta_0^{\sim m})$ staking a 'prize of utility one' on s^m alone. Under state-independent preferences, one could stake the *same* prize b_1 on any state s^m (with the less preferred prize b_0 accruing otherwise). In other words, a single normalisation (N.4) could define a 'prize of utility one' *simultaneously for all states*.

Under state-dependent preferences, it is no longer appropriate to assume that a given physical prize entails the same utility (or utility increment relative to a fixed reference prize) conditionally on every state. Instead, a 'prize of utility one' must be defined *separately for each state*. In other words, conditional utilities given alternative states are subject to *independent normalisations*.

The procedure followed here consists in using a pair of omnipotent games to normalise all the conditional utilities. The rationale for the procedure is intuitively clear. Ignore provisionally null states. If a game assigns to all states prize mixtures entailing identical utility levels, that game must be omnipotent (all 'strategies' are equally good for that game). Hence, the set of omnipotent games *includes all* the games with the 'constant expected utility' property; the latter are also the only games suitable for normalising the levels, then the scales of conditional utilities.

The open question is the complementary one: does the set of omnipotent games contain *additional* elements, *not* endowed with the 'constant expected utility' property? The answer depends upon the extent of moral hazard. Under 'general moral hazard', when every state is subject to the decision-maker's influence, then P contains as many linearly independent elements as there are states; and we know from lemma 7.1 (which holds under the terms of theorem 8.1) that a game is omnipotent *only if* it has the 'constant expected utility' property. In that favourable case, our procedure is validated: we have adopted the *only* normalisation of conditional utilities consistent with the a priori requirement that constant expected utility games should be omnipotent.[47] Hence the claim in theorem 8.2(i) that P is unique, and U is unique up to the same positive linear transformation as V.[48]

To complete the analysis of that favourable case, it suffices to note that *subjective probabilities are elicited exactly as in* Section 6.4 – with $(\beta_1^m, \beta_0^{-m})$ given by the two omnipotent games g_1 and g_0 of assumption NDO. The only added difficulty comes from the fact that *omnipotent games must be identified on the basis of observed equipotence relations, instead of being constructed trivially as constant games*. That added difficulty is discussed further in Section 8.4 below.

Turning to the less favourable case of 'limited moral hazard', let there exist fewer linearly independent games than states. Then, we know from lemma 7.2 that the expected utility vectors associated with omnipotent games span an $(n-l+1)$-dimensional subset of R^n. Accordingly, *it is not true that all omnipotent games are constant expected utility games*. Our normalisation procedure for conditional utilities is accordingly fraught with arbitrariness: there remain $n-l$ 'degrees of freedom' in setting the levels and scales of these utilities, without violating the a priori requirement that constant expected utility games should be omnipotent. In other words, there remain $n-l$ degrees of freedom in defining 'prizes of utility one' for the different states. Since the subjective probabilities of the states s^m are obtained from the values of games 'staking a prize of utility one on s^m alone', there are $n-l$ degrees of freedom in eliciting subjective probabilities. These 'degrees of freedom', or degrees of arbitrariness, are brought out in theorem 8.2(ii). In the limiting case of *no* moral hazard (all games are simultaneously equipotent, and RO is satisfied), there are $n-1$ degrees of freedom, and subjective probabilities are completely arbitrary (are not identified).[49] Otherwise, the extent to which probabilities are identified is reflected in the statement of theorem 8.2(ii). *The elicitation still proceeds exactly as in* Section 6.4, but the interpretation of the results is different – due to the explicitly recognised degrees of arbitrariness.

A simple example may be in order. Let there be three states, but only two linearly independent equipotent sets. If omnipotent games are characterised by the property[50] 'g_h is omnipotent if and only if $v_h^1 = v_h^2$',

---

[47] Specifically: any other normalisation of conditional utilities would have the undesirable consequences that omnipotent games do not have the constant expected utility property, whereas constant expected utility games are not omnipotent!

[48] Thus, origins and scales of the conditional utilities are uniquely related to each other, but remain subject to a single common positive transformation.

[49] That is also the situation considered and the conclusion reached, by Fishburn (1982, p. 110), Rubin (1983) or remark 4.2.

[50] Reminder:

$$v_h^1 = \sum_q \beta_h^1(b_q) u^1(b_q) = \sum_q \beta_h^1(b_q) U(s^1, b_q),$$

where $u^1(b_q) = U(s^1, b_q)$ is normalised by N.8.

irrespective of v_h^3, then it may be inferred that p_3 is fixed; the elicitation will identify uniquely $p_1/(p_1 + p_2)$ and $p_2/(p_1 + p_2)$ (separately for each equipotent set); but $p_1 + p_2 = 1 - p_3$ is arbitrary.

If omnipotent games are characterised instead by the property that 'g_h is omnipotent if and only if $\frac{1}{2}v_h^1 + \frac{1}{2}v_h^2 = v_h^3$', then it may be inferred that p^1/p^2 is fixed, and equal to 1; but $p_3 = 1 - 2p_2$ is variable, with arbitrary limits.[51]

8.4 Identification of omnipotent games

The next question concerns the identification of omnipotent games. As remarked above, under state-dependent preferences, one cannot expect constant games to be omnipotent; instead, one must *construct* games that are equipotent with any other game. There are two aspects to this question: first, given two games which are not equipotent, how does one construct a third game which is equipotent with both; second, when does one accept that a game is omnipotent?

The first aspect is a practical one, for which my advice boils down to 'trial and error'. Thus, in Section 1.3, I entertained the possibility that a \$100 000 prize staked on 'losing' induced my hypothetical bowman to aim deliberately amiss; whereas a \$50 000 prize staked on 'losing' left him *indifferent* between aiming amiss and aiming carefully (omnipotence). In practice, the prize (here \$50 000) such that indifference obtains can only be elicited by trial and error.[52] With many states and complex 'strategies' the elicitation may not be easy; but the outcome of the elicitation procedure (a game equipotent with two other games, which are not equipotent with each other) is conceptually well defined.

The second aspect is logically more subtle. If a set of *linearly independent games* has been identified (again by 'trial and error'), one knows that a game must be equipotent with *every* member of that set in order to be omnipotent. If furthermore the cardinality of the set is equal to the number of (non-null) states, then one may safely conclude that a game g_0 which is equipotent with every member of the set is definitely omnipotent. The reason is again that g_0 must have the 'constant expected utility' property, as shown in lemma 7.1.

On the other hand, if only $l < k$ linearly independent games have been identified, there remains the *possibility* that some 'strategies' have been overlooked, i.e. that there exist $l + 1$, or more, linearly independent games. (In other words, the dimensionality of the set P has been underestimated.) In that case, further investigation might reveal that a game, equipotent with the initial set of l linearly independent games, is *not* equipotent with the 'l + first'. The only way to guard against this possibility is to adopt a

---

[51] The limits could still be identified if they were equal to 0 or 1 – but only then.
[52] The same problem arises in standard utility theory: the exact sure amount which I regard equivalent to a 50–50 chance of 0 or \$100 000 can only be elicited by trial and error.

systematic search procedure for linearly independent games. The results of Section 7 (in particular corollary 7.1, lemma 7.3 and lemma 7.6) indicate how such games can be *recognised* operationally. The construction of a search procedure lies beyond the scope of the present paper. I will simply note here that the consequences of misjudging the dimensionality of the set P are not severe. In view of theorem 8.2(ii), one would recognise $k - l$ degrees of arbitrariness in eliciting subjective probabilities. This is also the extent of arbitrariness present in the elicitation as carried out. The fact that only $k - l - 1$, or fewer, degrees of arbitrariness might result from additional observations, does not invalidate the conclusions already reached. These conclusions are not 'wrong' – they are simply less 'sharp' than would be the case under a more extensive search.

8.5 Null states

It remains to comment upon 'null states'. Here again, state-dependent preferences create an identification problem. A state s^m is null (definitions 4.1–4.2) if the prizes staked on that state never affect preferences among games; in which case $p^m \equiv 0$ under theorem 8.1. Let an heirless bachelor express indifference between the games $(\beta, \beta_h^{\sim m})$ and $(\beta', \beta_h^{\sim m})$, identically in β, β' and $\beta_h^{\sim m}$, whenever s^m stipulates that he is dead; is the bachelor immortal, or selfish? The model studied here provides no answer[53] and common sense must take over. In *interpreting* the results, one should treat the probabilities of null states as arbitrary and entertain the alternative possibility of generalised indifference over prizes, given such states.

9 Comments

9.1 State-dependent and conditional preferences

The point that probabilities cannot be separated from utilities, when 'consequences' must be described with reference to the state that obtains, is stressed emphatically by Drèze (1961). It has also been recognised by various authors, including Luce and Krantz (1971, p. 263), Fishburn (1973, p. 2), Arrow (1974, p. 61), Karni *et al.* (1983, p. 1022) and Rubin (1983); see also the letter from Aumann to Savage, dated 8 January 1971, reproduced in Appendix A (with Aumann's permission).

In *The Foundations of Statistics* (Savage, 1954), this difficulty is circumvented by assuming that consequences like (s^m, b_q) can be associated

---

[53]In the example, one would hope to find an answer in the fact that a person's death is subject to moral hazard; if p^m varies with strategies, then $p^m \equiv 0$ is ruled out, and $U(s^m, b_q) \equiv 0$ (all b_q in B) must be the answer. That avenue is barred by assumptions NDO *and* ICC, which rule out $U(s^m, b_q) \equiv 0$ when s^m is not null. The extension outlined in Section 9.6 might get round that difficulty.

with *any state*, and not only with state s^m. Savage's justification for making the assumption is stated unambiguously in the following quotation from the letter in Appendix A:[54] 'To some it will seem grotesque if I say that I should not mind being hung so long as it be done without damage to my health or reputation, but I think it desirable to adopt such language so that the danger of being hung can be contemplated in the framework of *The Foundations of Statistics*'.

If there are two states, s^m implying death and s^l implying survival, the consequence (s^m, b_q) *associated with the state* s^l amounts precisely to 'being hung without damage to health or reputation'. Such consequences do not seem to appear in realistic decision problems – but they must be entertained, if one assumes the existence of acts which associate the same 'consequence' with every state, and if one relies on such acts to identify subjective probabilities uniquely.

Authors who find that assumption unacceptable sought escape in various directions. Some, like Arrow (1974), are careful to restrict application of the theory to situations where either the Savage assumptions are realistic, or probabilities are objectively defined.

Others like Luce and Krantz (1971) or Fishburn (1973), assume that such consequence as (s^l, b_q) and (s^m, b_r) are *directly comparable*; preferences among such consequences ('conditional acts') are introduced as a *primitive concept*, and define *a complete ordering*. Thus, these authors assume that a decision-maker can meaningfully answer questions like: Would you rather see (s^l, b_q) happen, or (s^m, b_r)? This is a well-defined question, but a verbal answer to that question does not lend itself to verification through material behaviour – *unless you could somehow choose between these alternatives*, for instance by committing suicide (an instance of 'moral hazard').

In a recent paper, Karni *et al.* (1983) assume that a person is able and willing to express preferences among acts, *conditionally on some exogenously given probability measure* p' on the set of states. Write $\succsim'$ for this conditional preference relation, to distinguish it from the actual (unconditional) preference relation $\succsim$. Then, choices under $\succsim'$ can be analysed in the light of known p', thereby defining *utility* up to monotone linear transformations. The theorem by Karni *et al.* is that, given $\succsim$, $\succsim'$ and p', a unique p can be associated with $\succsim$ (under suitable consistency assumptions). This useful result is perhaps not surprising, if one realises from the above discussion that one is in fact allowing the experimenter to ask questions of the following kind: 'You are indifferent between signing, or not, a given 12 months' life insurance contract; would you remain indifferent, if you *knew* that death within 12 months has probability 0.067?' Although

---

[54]In 1957, I had the privilege of extended conversations with Professor Savage on this subject. The contents of his letter to Aumann agree perfectly with my recollection of these conversations. Reproducing the letter seemed preferable to quoting the conversations from memory after 25 years. I am grateful to Robert Aumann for sharing this viewpoint and making the private correspondence available.

the questions considered by Karni *et al.* seem more natural (to me at least) than the questions entertained in defining conditional References, they share the defect that verbal answers to these questions do not lend themselves to verification through material behaviour – *unless*, again, *the decision-maker could somehow choose between alternative probability measures*, as in the 'moral hazard' case.

The approach followed by Drèze (1961) and here, in contrast to the alternative approaches of *The Foundations of Statistics*, of the 'Conditional Preferences' theory and of Karni *et al.*, proceeds exclusively from observed preferences among acts (games). This is usually construed as a distinct advantage. For instance, in *The Foundations of Statistics*, Savage writes (p. 17): '...I think it of great importance that preference, and indifference,... be determined at least in principle by decisions between acts and not by response to introspective questions'. He expands on this theme in his introduction to the chapter on 'Personal Probability' (pp. 27–28). There he contrasts the 'direct' and the 'behavioral' approaches toward eliciting personal probabilities. He writes: 'Attempts to define the relative probability of a pair of events in terms of the answers people give to direct interrogation has justifiably met with antipathy from most statistical theorists... If the state of mind in question is not capable of manifesting itself in some sort of extraverbal behavior, it is extraneous to our main interest. If, on the other hand, it manifests itself through more material behavior, that should, at least in principle, imply the possibility of testing whether a person holds one event to be more probable than another, by some behavior expressing, and giving meaning to, his judgement.'[55]

In 1961, I was much impressed with the strength of that argument. Having witnessed the limited scope and success of attempts at empirical validation of the theory,[56] and having lived with the issue for another 20 years, I now hold less sanguine views. Instead of defending the approach followed here as the only true behavioural model of state-dependent preferences, I would present it as a *systematic exploration of the exact limitations of a fully behavioural theory of decision under moral hazard and state-dependent preferences.*

9.2 *Random devices*

Random devices have played a crucial role in several steps of my argument. Most prominent perhaps is the role of random devices in withholding

[55]The concluding paragraph on that subject (Savage, 1954, p. 28) is also instructive. 'There is a mode of interrogation intermediate between what I have called the behavioral and the direct. One can, namely, ask the person, not how he feels, but what he would do in such and such a situation. Insofar as the theory of decision under development is regarded as an empirical one, the intermediate mode is a compromise between economy and rigour. But in the theory's more important normative interpretation as a set of criteria of consistency for us to apply to our own decisions, the intermediate mode seems to me to be just the right one.'

[56]See Schoemaker (1982).

information from the decision-maker as to which one of two or more reward structures will be effective. More broadly, random devices are used to generate events about which information is easily controlled, which are independent of real events, whose occurrence does not affect preferences, and whose probabilities cannot be manipulated. These requirements are akin to those underlying the use of random devices in game theory, for the purpose of defining mixed strategies.

In *The Foundations of Statistics*, Savage took the view that assumptions about the existence of random devices would be *ad hoc*, and found it more convincing to state all his postulates in terms of arbitrary events. This is also the basic approach followed by Drèze (1961), except that purely random events are identified as such, and used to construct lotteries. Stronger postulates apply to preferences conditional on random events than to preferences conditional on arbitrary events, reflecting the fact that random events should not affect preferences, should not convey information about 'real' events and should not be manipulable. (That is, random events are not conducive to state-dependent preferences or to moral hazard.)

Other authors have accepted numerical probabilities for outcomes of random devices as a primitive concept in developing theories of personal probabilities for more interesting contingencies; see in particular Anscombe and Aumann (1963), Fishburn (1973) or Karni *et al.* (1983). The same approach was followed here, to simplify exposition.

As intimated in the introduction, I would now regard the two presentations as equivalent. It is only natural to rely systematically on random devices in developing a theory of consistent behaviour under uncertainty. Indeed, purely random events are often helpful to clarify one's own ideas and I would find it foolhardy to attempt to elucidate the subtle concepts of consistent choice under uncertainty with someone who did not apply probability theory to the analysis of random events in the same way as I would.[57] Accordingly, I am quite satisfied to use numerical probabilities for random events as a primitive concept.

9.3 Value of information

In the theory presented here, it is assumed, following Drèze (1961), that *the value of information about a lottery draw is never negative.*

This postulate reflects the standard inequality

$$E_x \underset{d \in D}{\text{Max}} f(x, d) \geqslant \underset{d \in D}{\text{Max}} E_x f(x, d);$$

see, for example, Marschak (1954). That inequality is predicated upon the

[57]See the comments on this point by Anscombe and Aumann (1963, p. 204). Reference could also be made to the fundamental work of Ramsey (1931) and de Finetti (1937), for illustration of the constructive uses to which random devices can be put in developing theories of personal probability.

specification that neither the feasible set D, nor the probability distribution of the random variable x, is modified, when the maximisation and expectation operators are interchanged. Counterexamples to this specification are easy to find in daily life or game theoretic models. Here are three simple illustrations.

(i)   I know an 'anxious bowman' who feels that his accuracy is adversely affected by the size of prizes staked on his shots. Let Δv measure the incremental (expected) utility of such prizes, $1 \geqslant \Delta v \geqslant 0$. For a specific target, he assesses his probability of success as

$$\tfrac{7}{10} - \tfrac{2}{10}\Delta v.$$

A coin toss is to decide whether $\Delta v = 0$ or $\Delta v = 1$. If the coin is tossed before he shoots, his expected utility is

$$\tfrac{1}{2}(\tfrac{7}{10})0 + \tfrac{1}{2}(\tfrac{7}{10} - \tfrac{2}{10})1 = 0.25;$$

if the coin is tossed after he shoots, corresponding to $\Delta v = \tfrac{1}{2}$, his expected utility is

$$(\tfrac{7}{10} - \tfrac{2}{10}\tfrac{1}{2})\tfrac{1}{2} = 0.3 > 0.25,$$

violating VI.

(ii)   A risk-averse person being offered the choice between a ticket for this week's sweepstake and a ticket for next week's sweepstake, may well strictly prefer the latter, in apparent conflict with assumption VI. This is because the risk-averse person will try to resell the ticket, and will have less difficulty in doing so with an extra week's notice.[58]

(iii)   A famous two-person non-cooperative game, the 'battle of the sexes' (see Luce and Raiffa, 1957, p. 90), is defined by payoff matrix A below.

	L	R		L	R		L	R
T	(2, 1)	(−1, −1)		(2, 5)	(−1, −1)		(2, 3)	(−1, −1)
B	(−1, −1)	(1, 2)		(−1, −1)	(1, 2)		(−1, −1)	(1, 2)
	Matrix A			Matrix B			Matrix C	

Consider the alternative matrix B. A coin toss is to decide whether the payoff is defined by matrix A or by matrix B. If the coin is tossed *after* both players select their moves, the relevant payoff matrix is C. Both players may well prefer selecting their move before the coin is tossed–in violation of VI.

These three simple illustrations are logically distinct, and call for distinct extensions of the theory presented here. Reasoning heuristically, the first illustration corresponds to general situations where the set P of attainable probabilities on S varies with the game g_h – say with the associated vector of expected utilities v_h. One would then like to show that, *for each g_h in*

---

[58]This example is taken from Drèze (1960); for examples borrowed from market exchange and production situations, see Hirshleifer (1971) and Arrow (1978).

G, there exists a closed convex set of probability measures $P(v_h)$ such that

$$V(g_h) = \underset{p \in P(v_h)}{\text{Max}} \; p \cdot v_h.$$

Clearly, this is not a very exciting result. It simply states that $V(g_h)$ belongs to the convex hull of $(v_h^1, \ldots, v_h^n)$. In order to say more, one should place some structure on the mapping $P(v_h)$. While recognising (as a tennis fan) that situations of this kind are fairly common in 'games of strength and skill', I have no specific suggestion to offer about extending the analysis.

The second and third illustrations describe situations of interaction between a decision-maker and third parties, where earlier information accruing to the former simultaneously accrues to the latter. In the second illustration, that information restricts opportunities for mutually advantageous trading; in the third illustration, it replaces harmonious expectations (matrix C) by conditional conflict (matrix A).

9.4 Implications for game theory

The third illustration of Section 9.3 substantiates the statement, at the end of Section 1.4, that 'the present theory does not apply to general game situations (games of strategy) because the assumption that information has non-negative value is not reasonable in that context'. Yet as remarked in Section 1.2, the theory of games of strategy typically proceeds on the *assumption* that players maximise expected utility, both with respect to choices of strategies and with respect to choices of games or payoffs. That is, the theory typically assumes the 'generalised moral expectation' property, instead of deriving it from primitive axioms, as is done here (theorems 6.1 and 8.1).

Even though the present theory is not directly applicable to general game situations, it has a number of potential implications that deserve further investigation.

Let the decision-maker be engaged in some 'real game', described in extensive form (see, for example, Luce and Raiffa (1958, Ch. 3, especially p. 54)). Each end point of the game tree corresponds to a state in the terminology used here. A payoff function for the decision-maker, assigning a prize mixture to each end point, corresponds to a game in the terminology used here. Variations to that payoff function – keeping the outcomes to all other players unchanged – define alternative games, over which 'lotteries' can be defined. Preferences over such lotteries (and over the 'corresponding games') could meaningfully be elicited. The framework of 'moral hazard and state-dependent preferences' seems appropriate to analyse these preferences. (In particular, which end point will obtain typically depends, at least in part, upon the strategy choices of the decision-maker.)

If it were a property of the 'real game' that (in the terminology used here) *lotteries* over variations to the decision-maker's payoff function are always preferred or indifferent to the *corresponding games* (VI), then the present theory would be applicable to that particular 'real game', and its associated variations; and theorem 8.1 would validate the 'generalised moral expectations' property for that real game. One could conclude that a player in the 'real game' (the decision-maker) associates with each of his own strategies a probability measure over the end points of the game tree, and chooses that strategy for which the expected utility of the outcome is highest. Such a conclusion would be independent of any 'solution concept' for the 'real game'. Rather, the spirit of that conclusion would be that substantive results of game theory (like for instance the minimax theorem) consist precisely in *guiding the formation of reasonable probabilistic beliefs* (of reasonable subjective probabilities) over the end points of the game tree under each strategy. This role is analogous to that of physics, meteorology, a.s.o., in guiding the formation of reasonable probabilities about physical events.

The heuristic discussion in the preceding paragraph suggests that it would be of interest to characterise the set of 'real games' endowed with the property that the 'value of information' assumption is reasonable. Alternatively, one might investigate the possibility of building that property into the construction of particular sets of games, or again of redefining 'states' in such a way that the property becomes reasonable (for instance, by including the 'types' of the other players in the definition of the states). These proposed investigations, which go beyond the scope of the present paper, would aim at validating 'generalised moral expectation' as the basic behavioural foundation of game theory, antecedent to but compatible with the complementary analysis of solutions concepts.

9.5 Strategies

As explained in Section 9.3, my assumptions (in particular VI) do not allow the *set* of feasible strategies to vary with the state-distribution of prizes (or prize mixtures). There remains to stress another limitation: my assumptions (in particular assumption 8.1 or CP) do not allow strategies to affect preferences. This rules out from the domain of applications of the theory certain situations where unobservable strategies affect utility by themselves, and not only through their influence on states and prizes. This limitation was already mentioned at the end of Section 1; an obvious example is unobserved effort, in principal–agent problems.

To the best of my present understanding, the theory of decision with moral hazard and *state-independent preferences* in Section 6 could be extended to accommodate *strategy-dependent preferences*, at least in the case where there exist finitely many pure strategies. On the other hand, under *state-and-strategy dependent preferences*, the identification problem preventing separate elicitation of probabilities and utility scales would remain unsolved. I must confine myself here to list these conjectures as subjects of further investigation.

9.6 Constant utility games

It was noted in Section 8 that assumption NDO, to the effect that there exist constant utility games, is quite strong. In the standard example where s^m entails immediate death and s^l survival, the assumption asserts the existence of prizes b_q, b_r such that $u(s^m, b_q) = u(s^l, b_r)$; that is, of a reward b_q in case of death, and a penalty b_r in case of life, such that life or death becomes immaterial. That assumption is admittedly not realistic. Thus, Karni *et al.* (1983, p. 1023) write: 'This is irreconcilable with some applications (e.g. life insurance problems) that motivated our research.'

There may exist events which carry so much 'utility' of their own that a decision-maker will always restrict himself to strategies which maximise (or minimise) the probability of such an event. If that is the case, the event in question is not *effectively* subject to moral hazard – even if it could be *in principle*. (Although I do not contemplate suicide, I still recognise that logical possibility.) And if that is the case, there will not exist as many linearly independent *effective* strategies as there are states (the probability of some event is kept fixed), so that some personal probabilities are not identified, in the present model.

More frequently, however, suitable rewards and penalties will be effective in inducing a decision-maker to seek or accept a *small change* in the probability of events that carry substantial 'utility' of their own. Although I could not be compensated outright for the loss of my life, or my wife's life, still I shun certain expenses which would unquestionably increase *somewhat* my, or her, probability of survival. Thus, we could replace the family car by a safer, more expensive model; we could carry additional expensive safety equipment when we go sailing; and so on.

In such cases, alternative strategies are chosen in response to alternative prize structures, and the theory developed in this paper is relevant. Although the extreme assumption 8.2 (NDO) is violated, the logic of the theory remains valid. It should be a straightforward, though possibly tedious, technical task to extend the model, in the spirit of the examples just given. That possibility is confirmed by the illustrative calculations in Appendix C, for the special case of only two states.

9.7 Small worlds

An obvious limitation of the theory presented in this paper is that it takes the concept of 'state' much too seriously. Even in the weak form implied by assumption CP, conditional preferences given a state must be well defined; which means that states could not be subdivided more finely into 'substates', the conditional probabilities of which (given the state) might be influenced by the decision-maker. In *The Foundations of Statistics*, Savage devotes a section (5.5, 'Small Worlds') to the same problem and concludes (p. 90): '...the difficulty I find in defining an operationally applicable criterion is, to say the least, ground for caution'. I cannot do any better here. And the more ambitious framework, where moral hazard and state-dependent preferences are attacked formally, aggravates the difficulty.

A more satisfactory approach of the whole problem of decisions under uncertainty would recognise explicitly the *sequential* nature of such decisions, instead of collapsing the dynamics into the elementary dichotomy 'at once' – 'after observing the true state'. Any realistic treatment of sequential decision-making under uncertainty would seem to call for an appropriate concept of *bounded rationality*, outside of the rare situations where decision horizons can be defined endogenously. In spite of an earlier expression of optimism,[59] I would not regard that program today as readily accessible.

In the present state of our knowledge, applications of decision theory require a skillful combination of formal analysis and judgement. I have tried to push the formal analysis ahead, in the twin directions of moral hazard and state-dependent preferences. But judgement remains essential to formulate isolated decision situations, in terms of a short list of well-chosen states, so that the formal theory could be implemented. And judgement is indispensable when observed preferences do not permit a full identification of probabilities and utilities, whereas stronger conclusions are sought.

[59]Cf. Drèze (1972).

Appendix A

Letter from Robert Aumann to Leonard Savage,
8 January 1971

There is a conceptual question regarding subjective probabilities that has been puzzling me, about which I would like to consult you.

Consider the following two acts:

Act A: You get an umbrella if it rains, nothing if it does not rain.
Act B: You get an umbrella in either case.

Suppose your utility for an umbrella is 1, and for no umbrella is 0; suppose further that your subjective probability for rain is 1/2. Then acts A and B have utilities 1/2 and 1 respectively. On the other hand, I don't think it would be unreasonable for you to be indifferent between the two acts, since an umbrella is useless in fine weather.

Obviously, the answer is that your utility for umbrellas depends on the weather, i.e. on the state of the world. But that leads rather quickly to the conclusion that your postulate P3 is unreasonable; for example, all in all, I prefer an umbrella to a nickel, but if it does not rain, I prefer the nickel.

The only conclusion seems to be that it is improper to call an umbrella a 'consequence'. An umbrella is really an act; the consequence is getting wet or not. But that does not quite get us out of trouble. Most people prefer to get wet in fine weather; the fact is, most swimming pools are poorly attended when it rains. So even the utility of getting wet is state-dependent. The appropriate answer then seems to be: 'Getting wet is also an act; the consequence is getting wet in the rain or getting wet in the sunshine.' But you will agree that that isn't very satisfactory; we have now made the *description* of the consequence state-dependent. By the same token, sunshine and rain themselves could be called 'consequences', and then one could construct nonsensical acts such as 'You get sunshine if it rains, and rain otherwise.'

It seems that the notions of 'state', 'act', and 'consequence' have rather fuzzy interpretations; in particular, it is not always easy conceptually to distinguish between them. But to make sense of the axioms, it is essential to have a fairly sharp idea of what these notions mean.

The main question that is puzzling me is more basic, though; it does not concern your derivation of the subjective probability notion, but the very possibility of defining this notion – in any way – via preferences. Suppose Mr X loves his wife very much, he feels that if he should lose her, life would be somehow less interesting, less attractive – less 'worth living.' His wife falls ill, and it is decided that if she is to survive, she must undergo an operation. This operation is well-known in medicine, one might even say routine; but it is very dangerous. In fact, 1/2 of the patients die on the operating table, whereas the remaining 1/2 survive the operation and then are entirely cured. (Of course the whole scenario is oversimplified, but I think it captures the essentials of some very important real-life situations.) Now the man is asked whether he would rather bet $100 on his wife's survival, or on heads in a coin-toss. I think he would not be unreasonable strongly to prefer the bet on his wife's survival. If she should not survive, the $100 is somehow worthless; and if he bets on the coin toss, he might get the $100 in a situation in which he would not be able to enjoy it. Nevertheless, Mr X might well agree with the medical information with which he is supplied, and estimate his 'personal probability' for her survival – whatever that may mean – at 1/2. The point of the example, of course, is that in this situation there is *nothing* that one could truly call a 'consequence' in the sense in which I think you meant it, i.e. something whose 'value' is state-independent.

Let's change the scene. Professor Y is a fifty-year-old nineteenth-century physicist, whose life-work is strongly based on the notion of 'ether' (again the scenario is oversimplified). He hears of the Michelson–Morley experiment, is very upset, and decides to repeat it. Now what about his a priori? I think it's fair to say that Y's feelings toward the ether are at least qualitatively comparable to X's feelings towards his wife. Can we at all *define* the a priori?

Lester Dubins was here for a few days, and we discussed this matter. He said he had heard this question before, and that you probably had an appropriate answer.

Finally, I'd like to mention that there is no particular difficulty in extending utility theory to this kind of situation. For each state, one can define the conditional utility of a consequence (or an act) *given the state*, and one can also define numbers that behave mathematically like subjective probabilities of the states. The trouble is that utilities that are conditional on disjoint states can be normalized independently, as long as one adjusts appropriately the so-called 'subjective probabilities'. Thus mathematically, the subjective probabilities and the utilities get all mixed up, and cannot be separated from each other. Conceptually, of course, that is exactly what happens also.

Since Frank Anscombe and I once did some joint work on subjective probabilities, I am taking the liberty of sending him a copy of this letter. I hope very much that you will be able to clear me up on this.

Letter from Leonard Savage to Robert Aumann, 27 January 1971

Thank you for your letter of 8 January. It is the sort of letter that one is tempted to postpone answering until there is time to reflect and prepare a thorough answer. For me, this temptation often results in letters altogether unanswered, so let me say something promptly and perhaps return to the theme later, especially if you raise new questions.

The difficulties that you mention are all there; I have known about them in a confused way for a long time; I believe they are serious but am prepared to live with them until something better comes along. The theory of personal probability and utility is, as I see it, a sort of framework into which I hope to fit a large class of decision problems. In this process, a certain amount of pushing, pulling, and departure from common sense may be acceptable and even advisable. There are minds that think it absurd to accept zero as a number and the null set as a set; it seems idle to say that these minds are objectively wrong, but you and I prefer the other way and have come to think it natural. To some – perhaps to you – it will seem grotesque if I say that I should not mind being hung so long as it be done without damage to my health or reputation, but I think it desirable to adopt such language so that the danger of being hung can be contemplated in the framework of F. of S. An extremely able discussion of such pushing and pulling is Quine's famous essay, 'Two Dogmas of Empiricism', *Philosophical Review*, vol. 60, pp. 20–43 (reprinted in *From a Logical Point of View*, Harvard University Press, Cambridge, 1953).

Let me point out some passages in F. of S. that speak a little to the problems raised in your letter, though of course they cannot really put the problems to rest. Perhaps the first complete paragraph on page 15 is relevant. On page 14, the sentence, 'Consequences might appropriately be called states of the person, as opposed to states of the world', seems suggestive. The lower half of page 25 describes an example much like some of yours. Finally, Section 5.5 of F. of S., 'Small Worlds', is about philosophical problems that seem to be close to, or at any rate entangled with, yours.

Now let us see what specific comments the examples in your letter may suggest. On the first page, you take an example, at first it is carelessly described, and subjected to increasingly more careful descriptions, much as

I would do myself. The very last line of the page is telling. I would regard it as fanciful but not as nonsense to say, 'You experience sunshine if it rains, and rain otherwise'. In this, I have changed your 'get' into 'experience' to emphasize my notion that a consequence is in the last analysis an experience. The insistence that consequences are experiences or sensations does not of course sweep all problems away. These terms may be suggestive, but they might defy definition. Also, the appreciation of uncertainty is itself an important aspect of sensation, and that seems to contradict the notion of a sure consequence.

This returns to what was hinted at early in this letter. I believe, and examples have confirmed, that decision situations can be usefully structured in terms of consequences, states, and acts in such a way that the postulates of F. of S. are satisfied. Just how to do that seems to be an art for which I can give no prescription and for which it is perhaps unreasonable to expect one – as we know from other postulate systems for application. Thus to paraphrase the middle of your first page, I would be glad to pay a nickel to rent an umbrella for a fall football match but given that it will not rain, I would prefer the nickel. I analyze this in terms of several consequences: the status quo, being miserably drenched, and being undrenched but out a nickel. These 'consequences' seem to enable me to describe the situation in terms of, and consistent with, the postulates in F. of S. Of course, they are not ultimate. A nickel is itself a lottery ticket, and one objection to getting miserably drenched is that it seems conducive to illness. If the problem were concerned with illness or the possibility of accidentally buying poisoned food, then of course the notion of consequence would have to be further analyzed. An ultimate analysis might seem desirable, but probably it does not exist and certainly threatens to be cumbersome.

The first paragraph on the second page of your letter seems excellent to me. The terms are indeed 'fuzzy' and it is indeed 'essential to have a fairly sharp idea of what these notions mean'. My own notion seems to be fairly sharp in that I seem to be able to couch decision problems in terms of them, and while these formulations involve various choices, tempting choices do not seem to lead to different practical conclusions. It seems something like the following familiar phenomenon. We usually couch probability problems in terms of the Kolmogorov theory and in particular in terms of atomic, or unsubdividable, events; these are the points of the probability space. But in practice, any event can be further subdivided by flipping still another coin. Yet we feel, and find, that there is no harm in this ambiguity. I do not mean to insist that the ambiguities of 'state', 'act', and 'consequence' are that innocuous but only to remind you of a certain kind of floating flexibility that we expect in the formulation of applied problems.

Let us try to reflect on the medical example in the middle of your page 2. It is quite usual in this theory to contemplate acts that are not actually available. These serve something like construction lines in geometry. A typical decision theoretic argument runs, 'If B were available, I would clearly prefer A to B and B to C, therefore, my momentary impression that C is more attractive than A will not bear inspection'.

In particular, I can contemplate the possibility that the lady dies medically and yet is restored in good health to her husband. Put a little differently, I can ask Mr. Smith how he would bet on the operation if the continuance of his family life were not dependent on its outcome. Make believe is certainly involved, and indeed it is extremely difficult to make believe to the required extent. Yet, it does seem to be a helpful goal. Incidentally, it would not be nonsensical, though unmannerly, for the experimenter to guarantee to execute Mrs. Smith if she recovers from the operation. And I see no real objection to Mr. Smith imagining this cruel situation if it helps him appraise his own probabilities.

Another line of thought to which it might be well to return more thoroughly is this. By betting both on and off the recovery, Mr. Smith's hedging could be detected and perhaps measured and corrected for. It would be good to know how much can and cannot be done thus in principle.

Yes, a bet on the survival of one's favorite theory does seem somewhat like a bet on the survival of one's wife. If Professor Y wants to know his own personal probability for the event he has a very severe problem in detaching himself. Whether it is in principle different from any other such introspection such as telling himself the price at which he would sell his car is hard for me to decide. Any statement of the form, 'I would do this if that.' is somewhat mysterious philosophically; are the ones you emphasize so much worse than the others? When you underline the word 'define' I understand that you want to try to be operational in eliciting this chap's probability that his favorite theory is true and you find it difficult to imagine any bet on the issue that would not encourage hedging. I can imagine some procedures that have the defect of being extremely expensive and possibly extremely cruel but that might yet have the merit of showing certain things to be possible in principle, as in disposing of Mrs. Smith. We might be able to find some way to so blacken Mr. Y's reputation, painting him as a plagiarist and a fool, that he no longer cares whether his favorite theory is true or not and can bet on it dispassionately.

One of the problems raised about a Professor Y is that of his optimism or pessimism and what it actually means for him to combat those tendencies in himself. I have some tendency to confuse that with your riddle which is really a different one, namely that of insulating Mr. Y from consequences normally associated with the events about which we want his opinion.

I suppose that the mixing up of things that you mention on page 3 is the same as, or closely related to, a mixing up of things mentioned in my section on small worlds but have not checked closely.

As promised this reply is prompt. I am sorry that it is not more satisfactory. There is certainly much in what you say. What is not clear to me is what, if anything, had best be done about it. A person who has published much in the spirit of your example is Jacques Drèze. One reference of his of which I have record is: 'Fondements logiques de la probabilité subjective et de l'utilité', pp. 73–87 in *La Décision*, 1961, Paris, Centre National de la Recherche Scientifique.

I shall give Frank a copy of this letter and shall be as interested as you to hear his reactions to these matters.

Under separate cover are a few reprints and preprints of possible interest including a little reading note about the Michelson–Morley experiment. Michelson himself, incidentally, fully believed in the ether–drift effect even after his most refined and successful experiment.

Appendix B

This appendix contains the proofs of lemmas 7.5–7.7.

Lemma 7.5: Let P contain finitely many extreme points; if $P^*(g_h)$ is a singleton, then there exists $\bar{\alpha}$ in $[0, 1)$ such that $g_{g_h\alpha g_i} E g_h$ for all g_i in G and all $\alpha \geqslant \bar{\alpha}$.

Proof: Let $P^*(g_h) = \{p_h\}$, and let g_i be an arbitrary element of G. For each α in $[0, 1)$, let $p_\alpha \in P^*(g_{g_h\alpha g_i})$ be an extreme point of P. Then:

$$V(g_{g_h\alpha g_i}) = p_\alpha \cdot (\alpha v_h + (1 - \alpha)v_i) \geqslant p_h \cdot (\alpha v_h + (1 - \alpha)v_i). \tag{B.1}$$

If $\{\alpha_v\}_{v = 1, 2, \ldots}$ is an increasing sequence converging to 1, the corresponding sequence $\{p_{\alpha_v}\}_{v = 1, 2 \ldots}$ contains converging subsequences (P is compact) and (B.1) implies

$$\lim_{\alpha_v \to 1} p_{\alpha_v} \cdot v_h \geqslant p_h \cdot v_h.$$

Because $P^*(g_h)$ is a singleton,

$$\lim_{\alpha_v \to 1} p_{\alpha_v} = p_h.$$

Because p_h is one of the finitely many extreme points of P and p_{α_v} is an extreme point of P for each v, there exists $\bar{v}$ such that $p_{\alpha_v} = p_h$ for all $v \geqslant \bar{v}$, and $\alpha_{\bar{v}} \in [0, 1)$. Thus, for all p' in P,

$$p_h \cdot (\alpha v_h + (1 - \alpha)v_i) \geqslant p' \cdot (\alpha v_h + (1 - \alpha)v_i) \tag{B.2}$$

both when $\alpha = \alpha_{\bar{v}}$ and when $\alpha = 1$. By convexity, (B.2) also holds for any $\hat{\alpha} \in [\alpha_{\bar{v}}, 1]$, implying $g_{g_h\hat{\alpha}g_i} E g_h$.

82

For each subset S^A of S, define a game $g_A := (\beta_1^A, \beta_0^{\sim A})$ by $\beta_A^m = \beta_1^m$ if $s^m \in S^A$, $\beta_A^m = \beta_0^m$ if $s^m \in S^{\sim A}$. There are finitely many (2^n) distinct subsets of S. hence finitely many games g_A so defined. Denote by G' that finite set. For each game g_A in G', there exists $\bar{\alpha}_A$ such that $g_{g_h \alpha g_A} E g_h$ for all $\alpha \geqslant \bar{\alpha}_A$. Let

$$\bar{\alpha} := \underset{g_A \in G'}{\text{Max}}\ \bar{\alpha}_A.$$

Then, for *all* g_A in G', $g_{g_h \alpha g_A} E g_h$ whenever $\alpha \geqslant \bar{\alpha}$.

For each game g_A in G', v_A is a vector with all entries equal to either 1 (if that coordinate corresponds to $s^m \in S^A$) or 0 (otherwise). Thus v_A is an extreme point of the cube $[0,1]^n$ and $\{v_A | g_A \in G'\} = V'$ is the set of these extreme points. For every game g_i in G, v_i belongs to $[0,1]^n$, so that v_i is a convex combination of the vectors v_A in V'. It then follows from lemma 5.2 that $g_{g_h \alpha g_i} E g_h$ whenever $\alpha \geqslant \bar{\alpha}$. $\square$

Lemma 7.6: If there exists an ordered sequence of l non-empty equipotent sets $G^1, \ldots, G^l$ such that, for each $k = 2, \ldots, l$,

$$\bigcap_{j=1,\ldots,k-1} G^j \neq \bigcap_{j=1,\ldots,k} G^j, \tag{7.3}$$

then P contains at least l linearly independent elements.

Proof: For each $G^j, j = 1, \ldots, l$, there exists by lemma 6.1 an element p_j of P such that, for all g_h in G^j, $V(g_h) = p_j \cdot v_h$. These l vectors are linearly independent, as can be verified recursively. Thus, $G^1 \neq G^1 \cap G^2$ implies that there exists a $g_h \in G^1, g_h \notin G^2$, so that $p_2 \neq p_1$. Hence, p_1 and p_2 in Δ^n are linearly independent. Next, let $p_1, \ldots, p_{k-1}$ be linearly independent. From condition (7.3), there exists a

$$g_h \in \bigcap_{j=1,\ldots,k-1} G^j, \quad g_h \notin G^k.$$

If there existed a vector d' in $R^k \backslash \{0\}$ such that

$$\sum_{j=1}^k d'_j p_j = 0,$$

then $d'_k \neq 0$, since $p_1, \ldots, p_{k-1}$ are linearly independent. Defining $d_j = -(d'_j/d'_k), j = 1, \ldots, k-1$, we could write

$$p_k = \sum_{j=1}^{k-1} d_j p_j,$$

with

$$1 = p_k \cdot \iota = \sum_{j=1}^{k-1} d_j p_j \cdot \iota = \sum_{j=1}^{k-1} d_j.$$

But

$$V(g_h) = p_1 \cdot v_h = \cdots = p_{k-1} \cdot v_h > p_k \cdot v_h$$

$$= \sum_{j=1}^{k-1} d_j p_j \cdot v_h$$

$$= \sum_{j=1}^{k-1} d_j V(g_h)$$

$$= V(g_h),$$

a contradiction. Therefore, $p_1, \ldots, p_k$ are linearly independent, $k = 2, \ldots, l$.
□

Lemma 7.7: If P is a polyhedron containing l linearly independent elements, then there exist l non-empty equipotent sets $G^1, \ldots, G^l$ such that, for all $k = 2, \ldots, l$, (7.3) holds.

Proof: The compact convex polyhedron $P \subset R^n$ is the set of solutions to some finite set of inequalities of the form $p \cdot a_k \leqslant b_k, k = 1, \ldots, N$. To each *face* of P (see Rockafellar (1970, p. 162) for a definition), there corresponds a maximal subset of inequalities, with linearly independent vectors $\{a_k\}$, which are satisfied as equalities. Thus, at each extreme point (zero-dimensional face) of P, n such inequalities are satisfied as equalities. On the relative interior of one-dimensional faces, $n-1$ such inequalities are satisfied as equalities; and so on. On the relative interior of P itself (face of maximal dimension), r such inequalities are satisfied exactly. When P contains l linearly independent elements, then the relative interior of P has dimension $l-1$ (at least) and r is equal to $n-l+1$ (at most).

Starting from some extreme point p_0 of P and from the corresponding set of (linearly independent) equalities, one can relax successively at least $l-1$ of these equalities into inequalities. In the process, one defines an ordered sequence of l faces of P with respective dimensions $0, 1, \ldots, l-1$. Each face is strictly contained in the next one, but is disjoint from the relative interior of that next face.[60]

Let $p_0, p_1, \ldots, p_{l-1}$ be an ordered set of elements of P, with p_j contained in the relative interior of the face of dimension j just defined, $j = 0, 1, \ldots, l-1$. Let $N_P(p_j)$ denote the (convex) cone of normals to P at $p_j, N_P(p_j) := \{x \in R^n | p_j \cdot x \geqslant p \cdot x \forall p \in P\}$. If the j-dimensional face is defined by the $n-j$

---

[60]The existence of a nested sequence *without gaps* requires proof. I have not been able to find that particular result in standard reference works. But it appears in Pulleyblank (1973, p. 2.17), and I also have a self-contained proof. (I am grateful to my colleague Laurence Wolsey for advice on this point.) That each face of a polyhedron is disjoint from the relative interior of other faces is theorem 18.2 in Rockafellar (1970, p. 164).

equalities (suitably reindexed) $p \cdot a_i = b_i$, $i = j + 1, j + 2, \ldots, n$, then

$$N_P(p_j) = \left\{ x \in R^n \mid \exists \lambda \in R_+^{n-j}, x = \sum_{i=j+1}^{n} \lambda_i a_i \right\}^{61}$$

It follows that $N_P(p_j) \subset N_P(p_{j-1})$, and $N_P(p_j) \neq N_P(p_{j-1})$ since the n vectors $a_1, \ldots, a_n$ are linearly independent. Because $P \subset \Delta^n$, $p \cdot \iota = 1$ for all $p \in P$ and $\iota \in N_P(p_j)$ for all $j = 0, 1, \ldots, l - 1$. Consequently $[N_P(p_{j-1}) \backslash N_P(p_j)] \cap [0, 1]^n \neq \emptyset$.[62]

Then let $G^j := \{ g_h \in G \mid v_h \in N_P(p_j) \} \neq \emptyset$, $j = 0, 1, \ldots, l - 1$. We have just shown that, for all $j = 1, \ldots, l - 1$, $G^j \subset G^{j-1}$ with $G_j \neq G^{j-1}$; hence, for each $k = 1, \ldots, l - 1$,

$$\bigcap_{j=0,1,\ldots,k-1} G^j = G^{k-1} \neq G^k = \bigcap_{j=0,1,\ldots,k} G^j,$$

as was to be proved. □

[61] Indeed, the definition implies

$$p_j \cdot x = \sum_i \lambda_i b_i.$$

Since every p in P satisfies $p \cdot a_i \leqslant b_i$, $i = j + 1, \ldots, n$, it follows that

$$p \cdot x \leqslant \sum_i \lambda_i b_i = p_j \cdot x.$$

And $p \cdot x$ must be constant over the whole j-dimensional face.

[62] Indeed, with $a_j \in N_P(p_{j-1}) \backslash N_P(p_j)$ and $\iota \in N_P(p_{j-1})$, there exists $\lambda > 0$ such that $\iota + \lambda a_j \in [N_P(p_{j-1}) \backslash N_P(p_j)] \cap R_+^n$ (remember that a_j is linearly independent of the elements of $N_P(p_j)$); hence there exists $\mu > 0$ such that $\mu(\iota + \lambda a_j) \in [N_P(p_{j-1}) \backslash N_P(p_j)] \cap [0, 1]^n$.

Appendix C

This appendix illustrates the possibility of dispensing with assumption 8.2 (NDO), while still achieving unique identification of probabilities and state-dependent utilities. The illustration is presented for two states only. Start from two conditional utilities, u^1 and u^2, defined on B as per lemma 8.2. Both u^1 and u^2 are defined up to a positive linear transformation. The simultaneous normalisation N.8 is not available because there do not exist omnipotent games. A single normalisation may still be chosen freely; so, normalise u^1. To recognise that the level and scale of u^2 still need to be somehow related to those of u^1, write $au^2 + c$, with a and c undetermined. Write p and $1 - p$ for p^1 and p^2 respectively; and p', $1 - p'$ for alternative probabilities.[63] We thus have four unknowns to determine, a, c, p and p'. To that end, we can use four relations of indifference among games, namely one involving p, one involving p', and two involving both p and p'. For instance,

$$pu^1(b_1) + (1 - p)[au^2(b_2) + c] = pu^1(b_3) + (1 - p)[au^2(b_4) + c]^{64}$$

(C.1)

$$p'u^1(b_5) + (1 - p')[au^2(b_6) + c]$$
$$= p'u^1(b_7) + (1 - p')[au^2(b_8) + c]^{65}$$

(C.2)

---

[63] For instance: s^1 = drowning, s^2 = safe crossing; p = probability (s^1|acquisition of expensive safety equipment), p' = probability (s^1|no acquisition of said equipment).
[64,65] If we do (resp. do not) acquire the safety equipment (presumably, at a price $b_1 - b_5 = b_2 - b_6$), we would be indifferent between buying or not buying an insurance policy, paying a net indemnity of $b_3 - b_1$ (resp. $b_7 - b_5$) in case of drowning, against a premium of $b_2 - b_4$ (resp. $b_6 - b_8$).

$$pu^1(b_1) + (1-p)[au^2(b_2) + c]$$
$$= p'u^1(b_9) + (1-p')[au^2(b_{10}) + c]^{66} \qquad (C.3)$$

$$pu^1(b_{11}) + (1-p)[au^2(b_{12}) + c]$$
$$= p'u^1(b_{13}) + (1-p')[au^2(b_{14}) + c].^{67} \qquad (C.4)$$

We can solve (C.1) and (C.2) for

$$(1-p)a = p\frac{u^1(b_1) - u^1(b_3)}{u^2(b_4) - u^2(b_2)} := pk \qquad (C.5)$$

$$(1-p')a = p'\frac{u^1(b_5) - u^1(b_7)}{u^2(b_8) - u^2(b_6)} := p'k', \qquad (C.6)$$

where $k' \neq k$, since $p' \neq p$.
We can also deduce from (C.5) and (C.6):

$$p' = \frac{pk}{pk + (1-p)k'}. \qquad (C.7)$$

Subtracting (C.4) from (C.3) yields:

$$p[u^1(b_1) - u^1(b_{11})] + (1-p)a[u^2(b^2) - u^2(b_{12})]$$
$$= p\{u^1(b_1) - u^1(b_{11}) + k[u^2(b_2) - u^2(b_{12})]\}$$
$$:= pK$$
$$= p'[u^1(b_9) - u^1(b_{13})] + (1-p')a[u^2(b_{10}) - u^2(b_{14})]$$
$$= p'\{u^1(b_9) - u^1(b_{13}) + k'[u^2(b_{10}) - u^2(b_{14})]\}$$
$$:= p'K'. \qquad (C.8)$$

Combining (C.7) and (C.8) leads to the unique solution

$$p = \frac{kK' - k'K}{K(k - k')}. \qquad (C.9)$$

Thus, p is identified uniquely, and we can then solve for p' in (C.7), for a in (C.5) and for c in (C.3) or (C.4).

[66]We are indifferent between buying and not buying the safety equipment at a price $b_1 - b_9 = b_2 - b_{10}$.
[67]If we did receive an unexpected tax refund in the amount $b_{11} - b_1 = b_{12} - b_2$, we would then become indifferent between buying and not buying the safety equipment at a price of $b_{11} - b_{13} = b_{12} - b_{14}$.

Appendix D: Assumptions and definitions

List of assumptions

PO (Weak Order), PI (Independence) and PC (Continuity): p. 34
4.2 or RO (Reversal of Order): p. 35
4.3 or SIP (State-Independent Preferences): p. 36
4.4 or ND (Non-Degeneracy): p. 37
5.1 or VI (Value of Information): p. 40
6.1 or CGO (Constant Games are Omnipotent): p. 43
8.1 or CP (Conditional Preferences): p. 55
8.2 or NDO (Existence of Omnipotent Games): p. 55
8.3 or ICC (Independence and Continuity of Conditional Preferences):
p. 56

List of definitions

D2.1 (The game g_γ corresponding to lottery γ): p. 33
D4.1 (Conditional Preferences) and D4.2 (Null States): pp. 35–6
D5.1 (Equipotence) and D5.2 (Equipotent Sets): p. 40
D5.3 (Omnipotence): p. 42
D6.1 (The Set of Probability Vectors for which the Value of a Game is Attained): p. 47
D7.1 (Linearly Independent Games): p. 52

References

Anscombe, F.J. and R.J. Aumann (1963). A Definition of Subjective Probability, *Annals of Mathematical Statistics*, 43: 199–205

Arrow, K.J. (1965). *Aspects of the Theory of Risk-Bearing*, Helsinki: Yrjö Jahnssonin Säätiö

—(1974). Optimal Insurance and Generalized Deductibles, *Scandinavian Actuarial Journal*, 1: 1–42

—(1978). Risk Allocation and Information: Some Recent Theoretical Developments, *The Geneva Papers on Risk and Insurance*, 8: 5–19

Debreu, G. (1957). *Theory of Value*, New York: Wiley

Dionne, G. (1982). Moral Hazard and State-Dependent Utility Function, *Journal of Risk and Insurance*, pp. 405–22

Drèze, J.H. (1958). *Individual Decision Making Under Partially Controllable Uncertainty*, unpublished Ph.D. thesis, Columbia University

(1960). Le paradoxe de l'information, *Economie Appliquée* (Paris), 13: 71–80. (Translated as Chapter 4 infra.)

—(1961). Les fondements logiques de l'utilité cardinale et de la probabilité subjective. In *La Décision*, Colloques Internationaux du CNRS (Paris), pp. 73–87. (Translated as Chapter 3 infra.)

—(1972). Econometrics and Decision Theory, *Econometrica*, 40(1): 1–17. (Chapter 20 infra.)

Finetti, B.de (1937). La prévision: ses lois logiques, ses sources subjectives, *Annales de l'Institut Poincaré*, 7: 1–68

Fishburn, P.C. (1970). *Utility Theory for Decision Making*, New York: Wiley

—(1973). A Mixture-Set Axiomatization of Conditional Subjective Expected Utility, *Econometrica*, 41: 1–25

—(1982). *The Foundations of Expected Utility*, Dordrecht: Reidel

Hirshleifer, J. (1971). The Private and Social Value of Information and the Reward to Inventive Activity, *American Economic Review*, 61: 561–74

Karni, E., D. Schmeidler and K. Vind (1983). On State-Dependent Preferences and Subjective Probabilities, *Econometrica*, 51: 1021–32

Luce, D.C. and D.H. Krantz (1971). Conditional Expected Utility, *Econometrica*, 39(2): 253–71

Luce, D.C. and H. Raiffa (1957). *Games and Decisions*, New York: Wiley

Marschak, J. (1954). Towards an Economic Theory of Organization and Information. In R.M. Thrall, C.H. Coombs and R.L. Davis (eds.), *Decision Processes*, New York: Wiley

Neumann, J. von and O. Morgenstern (1947). *Theory of Games and Economic Behavior*, 2nd edn Princeton, N.J.: Princeton University Press

Pulleyblank, W.R. (1973). *Faces of Matching Polyhedra*, unpublished Ph.D. thesis, University of Waterloo

Ramsey, F.P. (1931). Truth and Probability. In *The Foundations of Mathematics and Other Logical Essays*, London: Kegan Paul, Trench, Trubner and Co.

Rockafellar, R.T. (1970). *Convex Analysis*, Princeton, N.J.: Princeton University Press

Rubin, H. (1983). A Weak System of Axioms for 'Rational' Behavior and the Non-Separability of Utility from Prior, Technical Report 83–27, Purdue University

Savage, L.J. (1954). *The Foundations of Statistics*, New York: Wiley

Schoemaker, P.J.H. (1982). The Expected Utility Model: Its Variants, Purposes, Evidence and Limitations, *Journal of Economic Literature*, 20: 529–63

3 Logical foundations of cardinal utility and subjective probability*

1 A formal model

Consider a set S of possible states $s^1, s^2, \ldots$, with subsets $S^A, S^B, \ldots$ called events; and a finite set B of commodity prizes $b_1, b_2, \ldots, b_r$ (each b_i is a vector, the elements of which can be positive, negative or zero). G will denote the set of mappings from S to B, i.e. the set of functions $g_1, g_2, \ldots$, hereafter called games, which associate an element of B with every element of S.

The prize associated by g_i with s^j will be denoted a_i^j; if g_i associates the same prize with every $s^j \in S^J$, that prize will be denoted a_i^J. When a person 'reveals' that (s)he does not prefer g_i to g_j, or that s(he) is indifferent between g_i and g_j, I shall write $g_i \leqslant g_j$, or $g_i \doteq g_j$.

2 Definition of utility and probability

In the theory of subjective probability developed by Ramsey (1931), de Finetti (1937) and more recently Savage (1953), two events S^A and S^B are defined equally probable if and only if $g_i \doteq g_k$ whenever $a_i^A = a_k^B$, $a_i^{\tilde{A}} = a_k^{\tilde{B}}$.

In the theory of utility developed by Ramsey (1931), von Neumann and Morgenstern (1947), then various authors including Savage (1953), the difference between the utility of the prize b_i and that of the prize b_j is defined as equal to the difference between the utility of b_j and that of b_k if and only if $g_l \doteq g_m$ whenever, for S^A and $\sim S^A$ equally probable, $a_l^A = b_i$, $a_l^{\tilde{A}} = b_k$ and $a_m^A = a_m^{\tilde{A}} = b_j$.

3 Interpretation of the basic concepts

These definitions, and more basically the consistency postulates which

*Translated from a paper published in French in 1961.

accompany them, are acceptable only in so far as the preferences between prizes are independent of the event which obtains; that is, in so far as there is no interaction (preference complementarity) between the events and the prizes associated with them. Accordingly, Savage emphasises that prizes should, in his model, be so defined as to exclude any interaction with the events. This viewpoint is built into a postulate, on which Savage has commented thus (1953, p. 32): 'I wish it understood that, on no account, should preferences among (prizes)[1] be modified by the discovery of which event obtains. The usefulness of an umbrella at a certain time and place depends, to be sure, upon the contingency of rain at that time and place. To my mind, this does not contradict the principle stated above; rather, it reminds us that having an umbrella when it rains, or when the sun shines, defines a (prize) in this example, whereas simply having an umbrella does not.'

This perfectly sensible warning raises, unfortunately, a difficult logical problem. Indeed, from the very definition of subjective probability, to every pair of events there must exist a pair of (commodity) prizes defined independently of these events – otherwise statements like $a_i^A = a_k^B$ become meaningless.

One is thus led to wonder whether such commodity prizes generally exist, and whether their existence can be verified objectively. The answer to these questions depends upon the interpretation given to the primitive concepts (prizes and events), an interpretation that depends in turn upon the formal structure of the model.

4 Savage's interpretation and a difficulty

Savage assumes that every prize can be freely associated with each of the possible states. Indeed, preference among prizes, a key element in the definition of subjective probability, is defined as follows: $b_i \leqslant b_j$ if and only if $g_i \leqslant g_j$ whenever $a_i^k = b_i, a_j^k = b_j$ for all $s^k \in S$. Now the prize 'having an umbrella in Paris on July 14 in the rain' would not be logically associated with the event 'it will not rain in Paris on July 14'; so that the following condition is needed to maintain the logical consistency of the model: 'Any circumstance (e.g. it will rain in Paris on July 14) may appear either in the definition of prizes, or in the definition of events, but never simultaneously in the definition of prizes and events'.

Given this condition, is one free to decide whether a given circumstance will appear in the definition of prizes, or else in the definition of events? Certainly not. In the quotation above, Savage actually suggests that a circumstance such as 'it will rain in Paris on July 14' definitely belongs with the description of prizes – otherwise preferences among prizes would depend upon the events. This interpretation, however, raises another difficulty. Let the description of b_i state that it will rain in Paris on July 14; to

[1]Savage uses the term 'consequence', which I reserve for another use – see Section 5.

consider a game g_i such that $a_i^k = b_i$ for all $s^k \in S$ amounts to asserting that it will definitely rain in Paris on July 14. On the one hand, such games are needed to define preferences among prizes; on the other hand, asserting that it will definitely rain in Paris on July 14 also presents logical difficulties. By similar reasoning, we could be led to assert, for instance, that a person is immortal, or that cancer is always curable, which is grotesque.

5 State-dependent consequences and preferences

In order to escape this dilemma, we must revise both the interpretation of the primitive concepts and the formal structure of the model. A more general formulation consists in defining objectively prizes as well as events, then letting preferences among prizes depend upon the event which obtains. Thus, we may describe prizes minutely, and accept calling 'event' any circumstance on which a wager could be placed. Under this approach, it becomes legitimate to describe 'events' in terms of circumstances controlled by the decision-maker, or by any other person, whenever these circumstances can be defined objectively. The only additional restriction concerns the nature of 'prizes', which must be defined independently of the events, so they can be associated with every possible event – granted that preferences among prizes could be modified by the discovery of which event obtains. I shall accordingly call 'consequence' a pair (b^i, s^j), i.e. an element of the Cartesian product of B and S; and I shall attempt to define a preference relation among consequences, rather than among prizes.

For two consequences such as (b_i, s^j) and (b_k, s^j), the preference relation is easily defined. Let g_i and g_k be such that $a_i^j = b_i$, $a_k^j = b_k$, $a_i^l = a_k^l$ for all $s^l \neq s^k$; one then defines $(b_i, s^j) \leqslant (b_k, s^j)$ if and only if $g_i \leqslant g_k$. This definition, however, is not applicable for two consequences like $(b_i, \ s^j)$ and (b_k, s^l) – and preference between such consequences is at the root of subjective probability.

6 Identification of utility and probability

At this stage, our inability to identify in a unique way subjective probabilities and utilities can be set out as follows. Consider an event S^A and two games, g_i and g_k, such that: (i) $a_i^A = a_k^{\sim A} = b_l$, $a_i^{\sim A} = a_k^A = b_m$; (ii) $(b_l, S^A) < (b_m, S^A)$, $(b_l, \sim S^A) < (b_m, \sim S^A)$; (iii) $g_i \doteq g_k$. As previously mentioned, these relations are usually interpreted as implying that S^A and $\sim S^A$ are equally probable, or again that the subjective probability of S^A, say p^A, is equal to 0.5. Such is indeed the only solution of the equation linking the expected utilities:

$$p^A u(b_l) + (1 - p^A)u(b_m) = p^A u(b_m) + (1 - p^A)u(b_l).$$

However, when utility is defined on the set of consequences $B \times S$, rather than on the set of prizes B, that equation becomes:

$$p^A u(b_l, S^A) + (1 - p^A)u(b_m, \sim S^A)$$
$$= p^A u(b_m, S^A) + (1 - p^A)u(b_l, \sim S^A)$$

with solution

$$p^A = \frac{u(b_l, \sim S^A) - u(b_m, \sim S^A)}{[u(b_l, S^A) - u(b_m, S^A)] + [u(b_l, \sim S^A) - u(b_m, \sim S^A)]}.$$

Let $u(b_l, \sim S^A) - u(b_m, \sim S^A) = \beta[u(b_l, S^A) - u(b_m, S^A)]$. Then: $p^A = \beta/(1 + \beta)$. To conclude that $p^A = 0.5$, one should know that $\beta = 1$; more generally, to conclude that p^A has a specific numerical value, one should assign to β a specific numerical value – and relations like $(b_l, S^A) < (b_m, S^A)$ and $(b_l, \sim S^A) < (b_m, \sim S^A)$ place no restrictions on the value of β beyond the sign condition $\beta > 0$. There is an infinity of possible values for β, and a corresponding infinity of possible values for p^A; in the terminology of Wald (1950), p^A is not identifiable. This feature is mentioned, albeit vaguely, in the section of Savage's book entitled 'Small Worlds' (1954, pp. 89–90).

7 The ordering of consequences

In order to assign a precise numerical value to β, it is absolutely necessary to rely on relations like $(b_i, S^A) \doteq (b_j, \sim S^A)$. Savage has proposed that these relations be obtained by defining prizes in such a way that (b_i, S^A) and $(b_j, \sim S^A)$ be identical consequences, hence indifferent, which automatically entails $\beta = 1$. Chipman (1957) has proposed to set $\beta = 1$ by definition whenever: $(b_l, S^A) \leqslant (b_m, S^A)$ if and only if $(b_l, \sim S^A) \leqslant (b_m, \sim S^A)$ identically in $b_l, b_m \in B$. Although this definition conforms to the 'Principle of Insufficient Differentiation' put forward by Harsanyi (1955), it remains entirely arbitrary, since even in this case every positive value for β is equally consistent with observed preferences. Davidson and Suppes (1957) are aware of the difficulty, but simply evade it by suggesting that two consequences like (b_i, S^A) and $(b_j, \sim S^A)$ which are not directly comparable may nevertheless 'in many cases' become indirectly comparable via other consequences, like (b_k, S^A) and $(b_k, \sim S^A)$ which could be treated as identical. Whether or not these are identical is again a matter of subjective opinion, and is not amenable to empirical testing.

8 Moral hazard and the ordering of consequences

The difficulty which we face in trying to define operationally a preference relation between the consequences (b_i, s^j) and (b_k, s^l) comes from the fact, already mentioned above, that states are not chosen by a person, in the way that prizes are. That states become themselves objects of choice would be enough for consequences to be chosen as well; one could then postulate that preferences among games induce a complete ordering on the set of consequences, instead of a partial ordering only.

In the traditional model, that approach is blocked, because states and events are so defined as not to be influenced by the decision-maker. That interpretation is chosen to guarantee that the (subjective) probability of an event be independent of the consequences which it entails – a property which would not be generally true if the decision-maker could influence the likelihood of events, since his influence would be exerted in a direction geared to the respective utilities of the consequences associated with the events.

This point calls for two remarks. First, the traditional interpretation is not the only one, and it is possible to develop a theory from alternative premises. Second, and more fundamentally, the definition of events in the traditional model raises serious problems of interpretation, which I will emphasise by means of an example.

9 Moral hazard and the definition of events

Suppose that I wish to evaluate the subjective probability attached by Mr X to the contingency that his car be stolen within a year. What would happen if I were to offer Mr X a prize of, say, one million francs, leaving it up to him to choose whether the prize be staked on the theft of his car within a year, or on the opposite contingency? Clearly, the alternative chosen by Mr X will exert a definite influence on the caution with which he uses his car, and it will be very difficult for me to draw from this experiment any conclusion whatever regarding the probability which Mr X did attach to the possible theft of his car before he accepted the wager. The situation brought about by my offer would anyhow be most ambiguous. For instance, is Mr X entitled to choose the second alternative, and then to sell his car at once, thereby ruling out the possibility that it be stolen from him? Is he entitled to lock up his car in a well-protected garage, and to depend on taxicabs for the next twelve months? These 'strategies' can of course be stipulated away under the terms of the wager, but how far would this take us? We could, in principle at least, stipulate that 'you will not tamper with the devices protecting your car or your garage against thieves', or that 'you will drive as many miles this year as last year'; but it is difficult to enforce the only adequate stipulation, namely: 'You will use your car exactly as you would have done in the absence of a wager.' Indeed, such a stipulation has no operational meaning; the range of behaviour open to a car owner contains many subtle variations, which are not adequately represented by a finite list of objective stipulations. (This is also the reason why von Neumann and Morgenstern refer to 'games of strength and skill' in situations where a player's personal behaviour is decisive, and is not adequately represented by a set of 'anonymous' strategies carried out by an agent or umpire.)

10 Moral hazard and identification

What meaning could then be given to 'the' subjective probability that Mr X's car be stolen within a year? For many authors, that notion is not well defined, or not even susceptible of being well defined. Indeed by the definition of Ramsey, de Finetti and Savage, that probability could only be defined objectively if it were possible, when placing wagers, to stipulate objective terms preventing Mr X from departing in any way from his usual behaviour – an impossible task, as we have just seen.

If the restrictions imposed on the behaviour of the decision-maker are of necessity incomplete, then it must be recognised that the subjective probability of a given event is not unique; there exist several probabilities, each of which corresponds to some game or set of games. We must accordingly try to evaluate each of these probabilities separately.

The preceding remarks bring out the relevance of that project. For suppose that we could specify under what conditions Mr X will try to have his car stolen, or will on the contrary try to prevent the theft from taking place; then we could also, in principle at least, specify under what conditions he will be indifferent between having his car stolen or retaining it; in such a case, we could conclude that the consequences associated with the theft of the car, and with the absence of theft, are indifferent; and this would define a relation $(b_i, S^A) \doteq (b_j, \sim S^A)$, which is precisely the type of relation required to identify subjective probabilities!

11 Equipotence

Can we define operationally (and without reference to numerical probabilities) the conditions under which Mr X will be indifferent between having his car stolen or retaining it? I believe we can, and I wish to propose a definition which, though not necessarily unique, appears adequate to me. That definition is based on the work of various authors, including Marschak (1954), on the theory of information. For the purpose of this definition, I will call 'strategy' an exhaustive plan, prescribing all the decisions which the decision-maker might take, and the manner in which these decisions will be carried out. This concept of a strategy – which extends the concept used by von Neumann and Morgenstern – is of course not operational, but this does not matter for my purposes, because strategies will never appear explicitly in the formal theory.

Let us suppose that the decision-maker is offered choices, not only among games, but also among lotteries over games; where lotteries are defined in the usual way, namely as staking certain prizes – games in our case – on the outcomes of some random device. Two kinds of lotteries will be considered: lotteries with immediate draw, under which the outcome is disclosed to the decision-maker straight away; and lotteries with postponed draw, under which the outcome is disclosed to the decision-maker only after it is known which state obtains. If two lotteries are identical, except for the timing of their draw, I shall postulate that the lottery with postponed draw is never preferred to the lottery with immediate draw. Finally, if the decision-maker reveals his indifference between two such lotteries, I shall conclude that there exists at least one strategy which is simultaneously optimal for all the games appearing as prizes in the two lotteries.

The rationale for this conclusion is straightforward. If these lotteries were to include two games for which there is no common optimal strategy, the decision-maker would benefit from adapting his behaviour to the game which accrues to him as a prize; now this is not possible in the case of a postponed draw, but only in the case of an immediate draw; hence the two lotteries could not be indifferent.

Note that existence of a common optimal strategy for two games is a broader concept than 'strategic equivalence' as defined by von Neumann and Morgenstern (1947, p. 245). To avoid confusion between the two concepts, I shall call the former 'equipotence', a term suggested to me by Savage. When a game is equipotent with every other game, I shall call it 'omnipotent' – and I shall rely on omnipotent games to draw inferences about the preference relation between consequences like (b_i, s^j) and (b_k, s^l). The precise meaning of that preference relation can only be spelled out after developing a formal theory of decision based on the concepts which have just been presented.

12 Towards a more general theory

That development is of necessity long and tedious; the definitions, axioms and main theorems only are listed below, without comments. The aim of the present paper was to discuss the basic concepts of the theory, and not the deductive properties which are, as Samuelson (1953) aptly noted, the less important part. The analysis proceeds in three steps. The first step is an axiomatic theory of choices among lotteries with immediate draw, the lotteries being defined over games; this step is an exact replication of Savage's model, *mutatis mutandis* (where his states become random choices, his consequences become games and his acts become lotteries with immediate draw). The second step is an axiomatic theory of equipotence and choices among lotteries with postponed draw. Special precautions must be taken there. First, as shown by Drèze (1960), the dominance of lotteries with immediate draw over lotteries with postponed draw is not as clear-cut as one might think offhand, and must be imposed axiomatically. Next conditional preference (the Sure-thing Principle) is well defined only in the case of equipotent lotteries, and some (weak) conditions must be imposed on the 'richness' of equipotence classes if conditional preferences are to be used at all. Finally, the fact that equipotence classes are incomplete sets complicates the proofs of some theorems (proofs are omitted here). The third step comprises only two axioms, one of them about conditional preferences among games and the other one about preferences among consequences; these preferences define partial orderings, the former because it is defined only for equipotent games and the latter because it is defined only for consequences involving the same state. Yet, these two axioms are sufficient, in combination with earlier results, to prove an important theorem, about which some comments are proffered.

For convenience, the theory is stated here for finite sets of states and prizes – hence of games – as well as of implicit optimal strategies (equipotence classes). This restriction is avoided only for the set of random choices. The extension to infinite, or countable, sets is of little practical interest, but raises technical difficulties which do not belong in this presentation.

The reader who is familiar with the works of Savage will realise that my set of axioms P1.1–P3.2 is a weakening of his axioms. The differences lie with Savage's axioms 2, 3 and 4, the scope of which is restricted in my model. The relationship of the axioms given by Savage[2] to mine is as follows:

> Axiom 1 in Savage: axiom P1.1 below
> Axiom 2 in Savage: axioms P1.2, P2.5 and P3.1 below
> Axiom 3 in Savage: axioms P1.2, P2.6 and P3.2 below
> Axiom 4 in Savage: axioms P1.4 and P2.7 below
> Axiom 5 in Savage: axioms P1.5 and P2.4 below
> Axiom 6 in Savage: axiom P1.6 below.

On the other hand, my axioms P2.1–P2.3 about equipotence have no counterpart in Savage – although in the second part of his book, and especially in Chapter 6, P2.1 and P2.2 are implicitly assumed. Finally, P2.3 formalises the hypothesis that the set of optimal strategies is finite and introduces a topological hypothesis about the contents of equipotence classes.[3]

13 Notation and definitions

The set of states S contains a finite number n of elements $s^1, s^2, \ldots, s^n$, with subsets denoted $S^A, S^B, \ldots$ An event is any occurrence on which a bet can be

---

[2]See the end-papers of Savage (1954). Morlat (1961) gives the following concise but vivid description of the axioms:

1. There is a complete ordering on the set of (games).
2. It induces a complete conditional ordering.
3. It induces a complete ordering on the set of consequences.
4. It induces a complete ordering on the set of events.
5. There is no universal indifference.
6. Preferences have a continuity property, with respect to partitions of the events. Formally, these axioms are identical with P1.1–P1.6 below, under the *'mutatis mutandis'* proviso in the text.

[3]Readers who are not interested in the formal structure of the model may turn directly to the theorems of Section 16.

placed. In addition, there exists a random device, whose choices are not included in the description of the states. When the random device is used at once, R denotes the set of random choices, with subsets $r^1, r^2, \ldots, r^k, \ldots$. When the random device is used after observing which state obtains, $\mathscr{R}$ denotes the set of random choices, and ρ^1, ρ^2, $\rho^k, \ldots$ the subsets of $\mathscr{R}$ corresponding to $r^1, r^2, \ldots, r^k, \ldots$ respectively.

G denotes the finite set of games $g_1, g_2, \ldots, g_q$, that is the set of mappings from S to B, where B is the finite set of (commodity) prizes. A mapping from $R \times \mathscr{R}$ to G is called a lottery, and Γ denotes the set of lotteries $G_A, G_B, \ldots$ Thus, $G \subset \Gamma$. A lottery is called *immediate* ('with immediate draw') when it associates the same game with (r^k, ρ^i) and (r^k, ρ^j) for all ρ^i, $\rho^j \subset \mathscr{R}$; otherwise, it is called *delayed* (with delayed draw).

$G_{ij}(r^k)$ denotes the immediate lottery which associates g_i with r^k and g_j with $\sim r^k$. $G_{IJ}(r^k)$ denotes the lottery whose games are defined by G_I when r^k obtains and by G_J when $\sim r^k$ obtains. In case of a delayed draw, the corresponding lotteries are $G_{ij}(\rho^k)$ and $G_{IJ}(\rho^k)$. Finally, r_I^j or ρ_I^j denotes the random event with which the game g_j is associated by the lottery G_I.[4] The letter P is used for postulates, the letter D for definitions.

14 Theory of choices among immediate lotteries

P1.1   (i) For all G_I, $G_J \in \Gamma$, either $G_I \leqslant G_J$, or $G_J \leqslant G_I$.
         (ii) If $G_I \leqslant G_J, G_J \leqslant G_K$, then $G_I \leqslant G_K$.

D1.1 $G_I \leqslant G_J$ given r^k, if and only if $G_{IK}(r^k) \leqslant G_{JK}(r^k)$ for all $G_K \in \Gamma$.

P1.2   For all $G_I, G_J \in \Gamma$ and $r^k \subset R$, either $G_I \leqslant G_J$ given r^k, or $G_J \leqslant G_I$ given r^k.

D1.2 r^k is null, if and only if $G_I \leqslant G_J$ given r^k for all $G_I, G_J \in \Gamma$.

P1.3   If r^k is not null, then $G_{ik}(r^k) \leqslant G_{jk}(r^k)$ if and only if $g_i \leqslant g_j$.

D1.3 $r^l \leqslant r^m$ if and only if $G_{ij}(r^l) \leqslant G_{ij}(r^m)$ or $g_i \leqslant g_j$, for all $g_i, g_j \in G$.

P1.4   For all $r^l, r^m \subset R$, either $r^l \leqslant r^m$ or $r^m \leqslant r^l$.

P1.5   It is not true that $g_i \leqslant g_j$ for all $g_i, g_j \in G$.

P1.6   If $G_I < G_J$, there exists a finite partition of R into $r^{p_1}, \ldots, r^{p_m}$ such that $G_{kI}(r^{p_i}) < G_J$ and $G_I < G_{kJ}(r^{p_i})$ for all g_k and r^{p_i}.

D1.4   A probability measure on a set R is a function $P(r^k)$ attaching to each $r^k \subset R$ a real number such that:
         (i) $P(r^k) \geqslant 0$ for all r^k;
         (ii) If $r^l \cap r^m = \varnothing$, $P(r^l \cup r^m) = P(r^l) + P(r^m)$;
         (iii) $P(R) = 1$.

Theorem 14.1: There exists a probability measure on R.

D1.5   A 'value' is a real-valued function V defined on G such that, if G_I and G_J are immediate lotteries, then $G_I \leqslant G_J$ if and only if

$$\sum_{i=1}^{q} P(r_I^i) V(g_i) \leqslant \sum_{i=1}^{q} P(r_J^i) V(g_i).$$

*This notation is used only in definitions D1.5 and D2.8.

Theorem 14.2: There exists a value.

Note that the probability measure and the value are not separately identified, as was shown in Section 6. This element of arbitrariness is unimportant for later developments, and has no material implications – especially if one is not directly interested in the subjective probabilities of random events.

15 Equipotence classes and theory of choices among delayed lotteries

Notice: Henceforth, no random event is null.

P2.1   A delayed lottery is never preferred to the corresponding immediate lottery.

D2.1   When a delayed lottery is indifferent to the corresponding immediate lottery, these lotteries are called 'informationally neutral', or in short 'neutral'.

P2.2   If a lottery is neutral, every other lottery among the same games, or a subset thereof, is also neutral.

D2.2   The games in any given subset of G are simultaneously equipotent if and only if all the lotteries among these games are neutral.

D2.3   A set G' of simultaneously equipotent games is maximal if there exists no distinct set G'' of simultaneously equipotent games such that $G' \subset G''$.

D2.4   An equipotence class is a subset of Γ comprising:
   (i)   A maximal set of simultaneously equipotent games;
   (ii) All the lotteries, immediate or delayed, which are simultaneously equipotent with all the games in that maximal set.[5]
   Equipotence classes are henceforth denoted $\Gamma_A, \Gamma_B, \ldots, \Gamma_I, \Gamma_J, \ldots$

P2.3   If $g_j \in \Gamma_J$, $g_j \notin \Gamma_I$, for all $I \neq J$, there exists ρ^k such that $G_{ij}(\rho^k) \in \Gamma_J$ for all $g_i \in G$.[6]

P2.4   The intersection of all the equipotence classes contains at least two games which are not indifferent.

D2.5   For $G_I, G_J \in \Gamma_J$, $G_I \leqslant G_J$ given ρ^k if and only if $G_{IK}(\rho^k) \leqslant G_{JK}(\rho^k)$ for all $G_K \in \Gamma_J$.[7]

P2.5   For all $G_I, G_J \in \Gamma_J$, for all Γ_J and ρ^k, either $G_I \leqslant G_J$ given ρ^k, or $G_J \leqslant G_I$ given ρ^k.

---

[5] So far, equipotence between a game and a delayed lottery has not been defined formally. The concept is intuitively transparent, if one considers 'superlotteries', with either games or delayed lotteries as prizes, and neutrality of these 'superlotteries'. A formal definition requires more care, and in particular rests on random choices which are independent in probability. It is not presented here so as to avoid introducing still more notation.

[6] This amounts, in fact, to postulating that available strategies define a convex polyhedron in state space, not an arbitrary convex set.

[7] It can be seen readily that definition D2.5 could not be extended to games which are not equipotent. If $g_i \doteq g_j$, the definition should entail $g_i \doteq g_j$ given ρ^k, hence $G_{ik}(\rho^k) \doteq G_{jk}(\rho^k)$, for all ρ^k; however, for g_k equipotent with g_i but not with g_j, $G_{ik}(\rho^k) > G_{jk}(\rho^k)$ for all ρ^k; whereas, g_k equipotent with g_j but not with g_i would entail $G_{ik}(\rho^k) < G_{jk}(\rho^k)$.

D2.6 $g_i \leqslant g_j$ given Γ_J, if and only if $G_{iK}(\rho^k) \leqslant G_{jK}(\rho^k)$ for all $G_{iK}(\rho^k)$, $G_{jK}(\rho^k) \in \Gamma_J$.

P2.6   For all g_i, g_j and Γ_J, either $g_i \leqslant g_j$ given Γ_J, or $g_j \leqslant g_i$ given Γ_J.

D2.7 $\rho^l \leqslant \rho^m$ if and only if $G_{ij}(\rho^l) \leqslant G_{ij}(\rho^m)$ or $g_i \leqslant g_j$ given Γ_J, for all $G_{ij}(\rho^l)$, $G_{ij}(\rho^m) \in \Gamma_J$ and for all Γ_J.

P2.7 $\rho^l \leqslant \rho^m$ if and only if $r^l \leqslant r^m$.

D2.8   A conditional value for an equipotence class Γ_J is a real-valued function V_J defined on G such that, if G_I and G_J are delayed lotteries belonging to Γ_J, then $G_I \leqslant G_J$ if and only if

$$\sum_{i=1}^{q} P(\rho_I^i) V_J(g_i) \leqslant \sum_{i=1}^{q} P(\rho_J^i) V_J(g_i).$$

Theorem 15.1: There exists a conditional value for each equipotence class.

Corollaries:

(a)   For $g_i \in \Gamma_J \cap \Gamma_K$, $V_J(g_i) = V_K(g_i)$.

(b)   For $g_j \in \Gamma_J$, $V_J(g_j) \geqslant V_I(g_j)$ for all I.

Remark: These results imply, in particular:

(i)   That strategies for delayed lotteries are chosen according to a kind of 'moral expectation' principle.

(ii)   That postponing the draw of a lottery may restrict, but not extend, the range of feasible strategies.

16 Theory of subjective probability and utility

D3.1   If $G_I, G_K \in \Gamma_J, G_I \leqslant G_K$ given Γ_J and S^A if and only if $G_{LJ}(\rho^k) \leqslant G_{MJ}(\rho^k)$ for all $G_{LJ}(\rho^k)$, $G_{MJ}(\rho^k) \in \Gamma_J$ such that $a_L^A = a_I^A$, $a_M^A = a_K^A, a_L^{\tilde{A}} = a_M^{\tilde{A}}$.

P3.1   For all $G_I, G_K \in \Gamma_J$ and for all Γ_J and S^A, either $G_I \leqslant G_K$ given Γ_J and S^A, or $G_K \leqslant G_I$ given Γ_J and S^A.

D3.2 s^m is null given Γ_J if and only if $G_I \leqslant G_K$ given Γ_J and s^m for all $G_I, G_K \in \Gamma_J$.

P3.2   For all $G_I, G_K \in \Gamma_J$, and $G_K, G_L \in \Gamma_K$ such that $a_I^m = a_K^m$ and $a_J^m = a_L^m$, for all s^m not null given Γ_J and given Γ_K, and for all $\Gamma_J, \Gamma_K, G_I \leqslant G_J$ given Γ_J and s^m if and only if $G_K \leqslant G_L$ given Γ_K and s^m.

Theorem 16.1: For every equipotence class Γ_J, there exists a non-negative vector $(\alpha_J^1, \ldots, \alpha_J^n)$; and for every state s^k there exists a real-valued function E^k defined on B, such that for all g_i and Γ_J,

$$V_J(g_i) = \sum_{k=1}^{n} \alpha_J^k E^k(a_i^k).$$

D3.3   The N equipotence classes $\Gamma_A, \ldots, \Gamma_N$ are linearly independent, if and only if the vectors $\alpha_A, \ldots, \alpha_N$ are linearly independent.

Theorem 16.2: The N equipotence classes $\Gamma_A, \ldots, \Gamma_N (N \leqslant n)$ are linearly independent if

$$\bigcap_{\substack{I = A, \ldots, N}} \Gamma_I \neq \bigcap_{\substack{I = A, \ldots, N \\ I \neq J}} \Gamma_I \quad \text{for all } J = A, \ldots, N.$$

Fundamental theorem

For every Γ_J, there exists a probability measure on S. That measure is unique if and only if there exist n linearly independent equipotence classes (more generally: That measure is subject to as many linear restrictions as there are linearly independent equipotence classes).

D3.4   Let $P_J = (P_J^1, \ldots, P_J^n)$ and $P_K = (P_K^1, \ldots, P_K^n)$ be probability measures on S, associated with Γ_J and Γ_K respectively. A utility is a real-valued function U defined on $B \times S$ such that, if $g_j \in \Gamma_J$ and $g_k \in \Gamma_K$,
(i) $g_j \leqslant g_k$ if and only if

$$\sum_{l=1}^{n} P_J^l U(a_j^l, s^l) \leqslant \sum_{l=1}^{n} P_K^l U(a_k^l, s^l);$$

(ii) $\sum_{l=1}^{n} (p_J^l - P_K^l) U(a_j^l, s^l) \geqslant 0 \quad \text{and} \quad \sum_{l=1}^{n} (P_J^l - P_K^l) U(a_k^l, s^l) \leqslant 0.$

Theorem 16.3: There exists a utility. The utility is defined up to a linear transformation if and only if there exist n linearly independent equipotence classes.

Corollary: For every game g_i belonging to the intersection of all equipotence classes, $U(a_i^k, s^k) \equiv U(a_i^l, s^l)$, $k, l = 1, \ldots, n$, if and only if there exist n linearly independent equipotence classes.

17 Summary and conclusions

The theorems in the previous section do not require extensive comments, for they fit naturally in the general theory of identification in econometrics. As could be expected, these theorems tell us that the subjective probability of an event can only be defined precisely when that probability is chosen by the decision-maker. My analysis thus leads to a less powerful decision theory, since the subjective probabilities of many events must remain arbitrary; but it does, in my opinion, validate that theory in a deeper sense. For I have established the logical possibility of defining objectively the subjective probabilities of events influenced by human behaviour; of course, I have done so at the cost of non-trivial technical complications, and under specific assumptions, regarding in particular the richness of 'equipotence classes'. It seems clear that the concept of subjective probability is much more valuable to analyse situations involving personal strategies than to analyse games against nature. Moreover, those regretting the pruning of the traditional theory may perhaps find comfort in noting that whenever the subjective probabilities are not identified, the products of subjective probabilities and utilities are identified, and that is enough to guide decisions. In all cases, one can identify the parameters entering a decision rule, neither more nor less – this makes sense, and no more is needed.

Undoubtedly, it is still helpful to analyse many decisions in terms of utilities and probabilities, even when these concepts cannot be identified separately. Probability theory is a powerful tool, and we have known for a long time that it could be applied fruitfully, even though the idea of probability remained vague. In many applications, it is only natural to adopt non-operational procedures in specifying the numerical values of unidentifiable probabilities and utilities. Provided one remembers what these measures mean, there is no objection to using them.

A positive by-product of the theory outlined in this paper is the formulation of necessary and sufficient conditions under which cardinal utility can be evaluated not only for commodity prizes but also for events; this development opens new possibilities towards formal analysis of those situations – like life insurance – where utility depends more critically on the events themselves than on the commodity prizes normally associated with them.

Some may wonder whether it is meaningful to develop formally a model so complex that any practical application seems out of the question. Things are not quite that bad. But even if they were, I would not mind too much. Decision theory is much more valuable, in our current state of knowledge, to guide our thinking about foundations and our selection of decision criteria than to produce specific choices or forecasts. I thus found it important to try and clarify at least my own understanding of the concepts of subjective probability and utility.

In the process, a model has emerged, which may have some general validity. Until recently, I used to distinguish three types of situation: games against nature, games of strategy, games of strength and skill. I realise today that the basic postulates defining consistent behaviour can be formulated in a unified framework – up to extensions specific to each area, like the principle of cogent reason and laws of large numbers, for games against nature, or the minimax theory for games of strategy. If the unified theory withstands detailed criticism, its complexity may be justified by its comprehensiveness.

Postscript

The proofs of the theorems and corollaries were not included in the 1961 publication. The original proofs, which are sometimes cumbersome and unnecessarily involved, are of no particular interest. They are superseded by the more general treatment in Chapter 2 of this book.

The relation between the approach in Chapter 2 and the original approach of 1961 is basically as follows. Section 14 of the present chapter derives the existence of numerical probabilities *for random outcomes*, and the von Neumann–Morgenstern theorem *for games*, from a set of axioms corresponding exactly to those of Savage. Theorems 14.1 and 14.2 are immediate corollaries of the Savage theorem. Section 14 of the present chapter is thus replaced by Section 2 of Chapter 2, which proceeds directly from accepted numerical probabilities for random outcomes (see also Section 9.2 of Chapter 2).

Section 15 of the present chapter starts (P2.1) with assumption VI (non-negative value of information) of Chapter 2. It then introduces as an assumption (P2.2) a property which is established as lemma 5.1 in Chapter 2; the assumption is thus redundant. Next, Section 15 introduces an assumption (P2.3) which corresponds to lemma 7.5 in Chapter 2. That lemma spells out a property which holds when the set P of subjective probabilities on the states contains finitely many extreme points – a property described heuristically as 'finitely many pure strategies'. In Chapter 2, lemma 7.5 is used to obtain simpler formulae for 'conditional values' (7.1) and subjective probabilities (7.2). In the present chapter the result in lemma 7.5 is postulated (the general case of a continuum of pure strategies is not treated), and used to establish directly the existence of conditional values (theorem 15.1). The line of reasoning is different from that of Chapter 2, where existence of conditional values is obtained as a corollary of the generalised moral expectation theorem, instead of being an intermediate step towards that theorem. The approach of Chapter 2 is needed to treat the general case (infinitely many pure strategies). Theorem 15.1 here is again an immediate corollary of the Savage theorem, under assumptions (P2.5, P2.6 and P2.7) which are largely redundant. As for P2.4, it is the counterpart of NDO in Chapter 2.

Section 16 of the present chapter starts with two assumptions on conditional preferences (P3.1 and P3.2). Assumption P3.2 corresponds to CP in Chapter 2. As for assumption P3.1, which corresponds to the Sure Thing Principle restricted to equipotent sets, it turns out to be redundant. (In the terms of Chapter 2: over an equipotent set, the 'Reversal of Order' assumption holds; as noted in footnote 25 of Chapter 2, this in itself implies the 'Sure Thing Principle'.)

The fundamental theorem and theorem 16.3 correspond to theorems 8.1 and 8.2 of Chapter 2. (Theorem 16.1 is an intermediate step, which comes very close to the final results. Theorem 16.2 and the corollary correspond to material treated at greater length in Section 7.1 of Chapter 2.) As explained in the introduction to Chapter 2, the presentation in Chapter 3 deals at once with state-dependent preferences *and* moral hazard, instead of treating these two extensions of standard decision theory sequentially one at a time.

Thanks to the organisation of Chapter 2, the specific role of each assumption will hopefully become more transparent. Yet, the sequence of the present chapter, going from 'values' to 'conditional values' to 'generalised moral expectation', is also instructive.

References

Chipman, J. (1957). Stochastic Choice and Subjective Probability, Econometric Society Meeting, Philadelphia, December 30, 1957

Davidson, D. and P. Suppes (1957). *Decision Making, an Experimental Approach*, Palo Alto: Stanford University Press

Drèze, J.H. (1960). Le paradoxe de l'information, *Economie Appliquée*, 13, 55–70 (Translated as Chapter 4 infra).

Finetti, B. de (1937). *La prévision, ses lois logiques, ses sources subjectives*, Annales de l'Institut Henri Poincaré, VII, Paris

Harsanyi, J. (1955). Cardinal Welfare, Individualistic Ethics and Interpersonal Comparisons of Utility, *Journal of Political Economy*, 63: 309–321

Marschak, J. (1954). Towards an Economic Theory of Organisation and Information. In R.M. Thrall, C.H. Coombs and R.L. Davis (eds.), *Decision Processes*, New York: Wiley

Morlat, G. (1959). L'incertitude et les probabilités, unpublished

Neumann, J. von and O. Morgenstern (1947). *Theory of Games and Economic Behavior*, Princeton, N.J: Princeton University Press

Ramsey, F.-P. (1931). Truth and Probability. In *The Foundations of Mathematics and Other Logical Essays*, London: Routledge and Kegan

Samuelson, P.A. (1953). Utilité, préference et probabilité. In *Econométrie*, Rapport du Colloque International du CNRS, Paris, May 12–17, 1952, pp. 141–50

Savage, L.J. (1953). Une axiomatisation de comportement raisonnable face à l'incertitude. In *Econométrie*, Rapport du Colloque International du CNRS, Paris, May 12–17, 1952, pp. 29–34

—(1954). *The Foundations of Statistics*, New York: Wiley

Wald, A. (1950). Note on the Identification of Economic Relations. In T. Koopmans (ed.), *Statistical Inference in Dynamic Economic Models*, New York: Wiley, pp. 238–44

4 A paradox in information theory*

In order to evaluate aptly the significance of uncertainty about the outcome of a decision, it is often helpful to ask oneself how different the situation would be if the uncertainty disappeared, totally or partly; i.e. if additional information accrued to the decision-maker. A familiar method of analysis consists in imputing a 'value' to such additional information;[1] the imputation rule is clearly explained in the following quotation from Marschak: (1954, pp. 200–1):

> A person's profit (utility) is $u(a, x)$ where a is his action and x is the state of environment (an element of the set X). The person knows the distribution $F(x)$. Assuming that he tries to maximize expected profit, how much should he be willing to pay for exact information on x?
>
> Compare the maximum expected profit U under two alternatives: when the person has not inquired, and when he has inquired about the actual value of x. If he has not inquired, he will choose an action which is independent of x and which will maximize the expectation of the profit. This expectation will therefore be
>
> $$U = U_0 = \max_a \mathrm{E}u(a, x).$$
>
> If, on the other hand, the person has inquired about the actual value of x he will be able to choose an action that will

---

*Translated from a paper published in French in 1960.

[1] This 'value' should not be mistaken for the 'quantity of information' (entropy) defined in communication theory, see, e.g. Shannon and Weaver (1949).

maximize the actual profit. The action chosen will depend on x. The actual profit will be $\max_a u(a, x)$. The expectation of profit will be

$$U = U_1 = E \max_a u(a, x).$$

The difference $U_1 - U_0$ can be called w, the value of inquiry:

$$(3.1.1) \quad w = E \max_a u(a, x) - \max_a E u(a, x) \geqslant 0,$$

for U_1 can never be smaller than U_0.

The result that the value of information cannot be negative follows, according to Marschak, from the following reasoning. The action which is chosen after observing the true value of x is a function of x – say $\alpha(x)$. To choose a decision rule is to choose a function $\alpha(x)$ from the set of admissible functions. On the other hand, the action which is chosen without information does not depend upon x; it may be viewed as a constant function of x. To choose a decision rule boils down in this case to choosing a function $\alpha(x)$ from the set of admissible functions restricted to constant functions only. So Marschak concludes (p. 202): 'It is clear that if one is restricted in the choice of the rule of action one can never obtain a better result than if one is not so restricted.'

An even more intuitive argument is presented by Savage (1954, p. 107). After all, says Savage, the action which is chosen without information remains feasible after inquiry; therefore, the expected gain from a given action, chosen before the inquiry, can always be reaped by choosing uniformly the same action after the inquiry, no matter what information is received. 'In short, the person is free to ignore the observation. That obvious fact is the theory's expression of the commonplace that knowledge is not disadvantageous.'

The property that the value of information cannot be negative leads directly to the maxim: 'Never make today a decision which could wait until tomorrow'[2] – a maxim which qualifies aptly the common saying that a task which could be carried out today should never be postponed until tomorrow! This property of the value of information provides also a natural explanation of some market phenomena. When comparing uncertain prospects, one should indeed consider not only their respective payoff structures, but also their 'information structures' – i.e. the set of dates at which new information reduces, and finally eliminates, the uncertainty about the payoff. Thus, if two lotteries offer identical payoff structures, but differ in that the first is to be drawn a year hence whereas the second is to be drawn tomorrow (still with the payoff accruing a year hence), tickets for the first lottery will command today a lower price than tickets for

---

[2] 'Tomorrow' stands for any future date at which more information will be available.

the second lottery; the difference in price represents the value of additional information accruing tomorrow under the second lottery.[3]

Noting that lottery tickets are usually offered for sale shortly before the draw, whereas the uncertainty surrounding portfolio investments extends over a more distant future, one finds in the 'value of information' a partial explanation of the fact that lottery tickets typically sell for more than their actuarial values, which is less true for shares of stock. Again, the 'value of information' provides a rationale for some forms of arbitration between long-term and short-term risks; an example of such arbitration would be the simultaneous purchase of an insurance policy and a lottery ticket.[4]

There are many other areas where the value of information plays an important role – like the theory of teams and organisations, successfully investigated by Marschak, Radner, Beckmann and others. My purpose here is not to review these applications, but rather to draw attention to paradoxical situations where the 'value of information' turns out to be negative. Although the existence of such situations has already been noted in the literature, I feel that one of the main reasons giving rise to these paradoxical situations has received insufficient attention, and I would like to illustrate it with a few examples. Prior to that, however, I will recall through quotations the more familiar reservations.

The first of these is psychological in nature, and related to the observation that the reading of a detective story should not start with the last pages! Here are some relevant comments by Savage (1954, p. 107):

> It sometimes happens that a real person avoids finding
> something out or that his friends feel duty bound to keep
> something from him, saying that what he doesn't know can't
> hurt him; the jealous spouse and the hypochondriac are familiar
> tragic examples. Such apparent exceptions to the principle that
> forewarned is forearmed call for analysis. At first sight, one
> might be inclined to say that the person who refuses freely
> proffered information is behaving irrationally and in violation
> of the postulates. But perhaps it is better to admit that
> information that *seems* free may prove expensive by doing
> psychological harm to its recipient. Consider, for example, a
> sick person who is certain that he has the best of medical care
> and is in a position to find out whether his sickness is mortal.
> He may decide that his own personality is such that, though he
> can continue with some cheer to live in the fear that he may

---

[3]In Chapter 9, co-authored with Franco Modigliani, the value of this information is connected to a consumer's preferences, in particular to the interest elasticity of his savings.

[4]An altogether different rationale of such phenomena is offered in the classical paper by Friedman and Savage (1948). Although the ingeniosity of these authors is praiseworthy, I am afraid that their conclusions are biased because they neglect time – hence information – and take a narrow view of utility (defined on monetary gains only, instead of being state-dependent).

possibly die soon, what is left of his life would be agony, if he knew that death were imminent. Under such circumstances, far from calling him irrational, we might extol the person's rationality, if he abstained from the information. On the other hand, such an interpretation may seem forced.

Whether the interpretation runs in terms of 'value' or of 'cost', the psychological contents of a piece of information can undoubtedly prove so harmful as to offset the advantages of flexibility in choosing a course of action. This should not surprise us. Let us now look at another type of situation, coming from the field of game theory. Two players must each choose between two alternatives (say, player 1 must choose between α_1 and α_2; player 2 between β_1 and β_2). These choices jointly determine outcomes of concern to both. It would seem to follow from the principle 'information cannot have negative value' that preplay communication should be advantageous, or at least not harmful, to both of them. Yet, it is easy to construct examples where this conclusion is invalid. The following example is due to Luce and Raiffa (1957, p. 111).

Let the outcomes of the decisions of the two players yield the utility levels[5] given in Table 4.1 (in each cell, the first number is a utility level for player 1, the second number is a utility level for player 2):

Table 4.1

		Choice of player 2	
		β_1	β_2
choice of player 1	α_1	1, 2	3, 1
	α_2	0, − 200	2, − 300

Luce and Raiffa analyse this game as follows: 'If there is no preplay communication, the analysis of the game is simple because α_1 strictly dominates α_2 and β_1 strictly dominates β_2. Furthermore, the pair (α_1, β_1) is the unique equilibrium point which is jointly admissible, so it is the solution (in any sense) of this non-cooperative game. Now suppose the players were forced into preplay communication. Player 1 can demand that they enter into a binding agreement to choose (α_1, β_2) by the threat to choose α_2 if 2 does not agree. To be sure, 1 does not want to take α_2, which would give him only 0, but if he does 2 is faced with a loss of 200 (which cannot be said to give 1 any satisfaction beyond 0 since we are already dealing with utilities). It is reasonable to suppose 2 will succumb to the "threat" if the same numbers for players 1 and 2 somehow denote changes of comparable

[5]Reliance upon cardinal utilities – a subject treated more fully by Luce and Raiffa (1957, Ch. 2) – is of course not essential for my purpose here.

importance. Regardless of some of the potential pitfalls of the above analysis, it is to 2's advantage to refuse to come to a conference table, for to confer would only allow 1 to browbeat him into an agreement.'

Here again, it could be argued that seemingly costless information is actually costly – because the associated negotiation enlarges the set of strategies available to the opponent. More generally, it is known that a player may find it advantageous to forego some information, because acquiring the information would entail a risk that the opponent benefits from it as well. Such is, after all, the main argument offered by von Neumann and Morgenstern (1947, p. 146) in defence of mixed strategies.

Beyond these familiar situations, where the superiority of ignorance rests on psychological or strategic motivations, there exist other situations where these motivations are not present, as some examples will show. In one way or another, these situations involve the fact that availability of information precludes concluding certain transactions. Were these transactions to a person's advantage, then that person will gain from foregoing the information.

Here is a limiting case. A man and wife hear on the radio some preliminary forecasts, on the eve of a presidential election. Partial results keep coming in, and they listen attentively. After a while, the husband says: 'I bet that the republican candidate wins'. His wife expresses willingness to take up the bet. So they turn off the radio by common consent to discuss stakes before new information settles the issue definitely.

The lesson of this example is simple: it is hardly possible to arrange a bet on some event, when either or both players already know whether the event has occurred! And this remark applies equally to those eager to bet and to those eager to avoid betting. If presented with a lottery ticket as a gift, I would hope that the draw be delayed enough, so as to allow my reselling the ticket! Similarly, if important political changes, of unknown direction, are taking place in a distant country where I hold mining interests, I may hope that no further information arises before I have a chance to sell my shares on the stock exchange – a hope that some prospective buyers might entertain as well! In the same vein, when President Eisenhower attended a NATO Conference two months after the successful launching of the first Russian artificial satellite, he could conceivably have preferred that the first US attempt at a similar launching be postponed until after the conference. Indeed, he could have endeavoured to elicit support from his allies on the basis of a prospective launching, to be attempted soon with high probability of success; the additional strengthening of his political position in case of successful launching might not compensate adequately for the risk of desertion in case of failure.[6]

---

[6]Admittedly, a secret attempt would seem optimal; but concealing failure would be dishonest, would be risky should the information leak, would undermine the President's persuasiveness, a.s.o.

To sum up, it is often advisable to 'trade' risks, letting a third party, a market or even an opponent evaluate them, rather than bearing the risks on one's own; this sometimes requires foregoing (costless) information. A final example, less direct but not less convincing, may help drive the point home.[7]

A millionaire has two charming twin daughters, Ann and Barbara. You are in love with Ann, and intend proposing to her; but she is afraid that your primary interest might lie with her father's money. If she refuses, you intend covering up your chagrin by marrying Barbara, who is more than willing, and for whom you have no aversion (period). The millionaire does not wish to split his fortune, so he plans bequeathing it all to one daughter, who will then pay a modest alimony to her less favoured sister. In order to guard himself from prejudice, he will choose the lucky beneficiary at random, by tossing a coin. Being aware of your inclinations, he summons you to the office of his solicitor, informs you of his plan, and extracts from his waistcoat a golden sovereign which he is about to toss.

A rapid assessment of the situation brings you to the following conclusions:

(1)   Assume that Ann becomes the heir, if you then propose to her, she will be convinced that your interest is mercenary and she will refuse you; you will end up marrying poor Barbara.

(2)   Assume that Barbara becomes the heir; you will propose to Ann who, being penniless, will realise that your motivations are non-pecuniary and will marry you.

That is, you are assured of marrying the unwealthy daughter, who may be either Ann or Barbara with even chance.

If you could convince the millionaire to postpone his toss by a couple of days, the situation would be entirely different. You could explain to Ann her father's plan, and your request for a delay enabling you to propose under ignorance of the wealth. Had you been chasing her dowry, you would have acted quite differently! This reasoning seems compelling enough to dispel Ann's suspicions, and you are confident that she will react positively. Whereafter, chance will decide about her wealth. In short, you are assured of marrying Ann, who may be either rich or poor with even chance.

Look at the two situations (immediate toss or delayed toss). If Ann is poor, you marry her in both cases; if she is rich, you marry her in the second case but not in the first. It is thus to your advantage to forego momentarily information about her wealth, i.e. to act (propose) before becoming informed.

A similar, though less colourful, situation would be experienced by a small firm facing a big firm as opponent in a court trial about ownership of a revolutionary patent. The trial has been conducted, and the verdict of the

[7]The example was inspired by a situation described in the paper by Strotz (1958).

court is pending, with both parties feeling that their chances of winning are equal. The small firm might seek to negotiate a merger with its opponent prior to hearing the verdict – i.e. prior to acquiring a piece of information apt to influence the terms of the merger – if it felt that:

(a)   in case of defeat, it is doomed;
(b)   in case of victory, it should anyhow seek through a merger the capital needed to exploit the patent.[8]

These sundry examples reveal that the 'value of information' should be handled with care, and need not be non-negative unless one resorts to strained interpretations of doubtful validity or usefulness.

To sum up, the significance of additional information in a decision context is generally twofold. First, information adds flexibility to the course of action, since the decision may vary with the message received. The benefit arising from this flexibility is usually called 'value of information'. Second, information may modify the set of feasible courses of action; in particular, information that an event is true precludes betting on that event; more generally, it precludes 'trading' (or negotiating) under ignorance about that event. This modification of the set of feasible courses of actions can be advantageous or disadvantageous, depending upon circumstances. It entails a sort of 'opportunity cost', which is logically distinct from the value of information.

In practice, the distinction between the opportunity cost and the value of a piece of information may be hard to draw. The usual comparison mentioned in the opening paragraph of this note does not bring out the distinction explicitly, and measures only the algebraic sum of the two factors. The sign of the sum can well be negative, when the restriction of the set of feasible courses of action dominates the gain in flexibility. In general, separation of the two factors requires an exact delimitation of the set of feasible courses of action before and after receiving the information. This is sometimes possible on logical grounds, but may also require probability assessments. Information theory is then closely linked to the theory of subjective probabilities.

References

Friedman, M. and L.J. Savage (1948). The Utility Analysis of Choices Involving Risk, *The Journal of Political Economy*, 56: 279–304
Luce, D.C. and H. Raiffa (1957). *Games and Decisions*, New York: Wiley
Marschak, J. (1954). Towards an Economic Theory of Organization and Information. In R.M. Thrall, C.H. Coombs and R.L. Davis (eds), *Decision Processes*, New York: Wiley

[8]Without invoking the *deus ex machina* of the trial, one could seek in attitudes towards future uncertainties an explanation of the puzzling fact that mergers typically occur in 'waves', appearing simultaneously for no obvious reason in different industries.

Neumann, J. von and O. Morgenstern (1947). *Theory of Games and Economic Behaviour*, 2nd edn, Princeton: Princeton University Press
Savage, L.J. (1954). *The Foundations of Statistics*, New York: Wiley
Shannon, C.E. and W. Weaver (1949). *The Mathematical Theory of Communication*, Urbana: University of Illinois Press
Strotz, R. (1958). How Income Ought to be Distributed: A Paradox in Distributive Ethics, *Journal of Political Economy*, 66

5   Inferring risk tolerance from deductibles in insurance contracts*

Of the numerous results provided over the past 30 years by the theory of decision under uncertainty, none has proved more helpful to me in solving practical problems than the following elegant proposition due to Arrow: '*Proposition*: If an insurance company is willing to offer any insurance policy against loss desired by the buyer at a premium which depends only on the policy's actuarial value, then the policy chosen by a risk-averting buyer will take the form of 100 percent coverage above a deductible minimum.

Note: The premium will, in general, exceed the actuarial value; it is only required that two policies with the same actuarial value will be offered by the company for the same premium.'[1]

The purpose of this note is to show that Arrow's proposition is helpful to economists not only in solving daily life problems[2] but also in drawing inferences about the degree of risk aversion of insurance purchasers. This

* *The Geneva Papers on Risk and Insurance*, 20 (July 1981): 48–52. The result presented in this note was obtained during the IMSSS workshop at Stanford University under support from NSF grant SOC 75-31820-A01. Helpful comments from Louis Phlips are gratefully acknowledged.
[1] Arrow (1971, p. 212). For a more recent contribution to the same topic and additional references, see Raviv (1979).
[2] Arrow's proposition came to my attention at a very opportune time, when I had just become a house owner and was trying to use the results of Mossin (1968) to decide on a value assessment for which to insure the house against fire. The insurance contract made no provision for a deductible. After reading Arrow's paper, I insured the house for its replacement cost, and took a deductible indirectly by assessing the furniture below replacement cost. After writing the present note, I did revise downward the insurance coverage on the furniture, thereby increasing the implied deductible.

new approach is applicable to a broader class of consumers than the prevailing alternative based upon asset portfolio composition.[3] Also, it seems to suggest an order of magnitude for the relative risk-aversion measure which is substantially higher than estimates based on portfolio composition.

Let $W =$ initial wealth of the individual

$\quad\quad X \quad$ his loss, a random variable with distribution $\Phi(X)$

$\quad\ I(X) \quad$ amount of insurance paid if loss X occurs

$\quad\quad P \quad$ insurance premium

$\quad\ Y(X) \quad$ wealth of the individual after paying the premium, incurring the loss, and receiving the insurance benefit

$\ u[Y(X)] \quad$ cardinal utility function for terminal wealth, assumed twice differentiable concave

and let E   denote the expected value operator.

Arrow's result states that if $P = P[EI(X)]$, then any optimal policy must stipulate

$$I(X) = \text{Max}\,(X - D, 0) \tag{1}$$

where D is a constant – the 'deductible'.
Under (1),

$$EI(X) = E(X - D \,|\, X \geqslant D) = \int_{X \geqslant D} (X - D)\mathrm{d}\Phi(X), \tag{2}$$

so that $EI(X)$ is a function of D – say $\bar{I}(D)$. Accordingly, $P = P(D)$ and

$$Y(X) = W - P(D) - \text{Min}\,(X, D), \tag{3}$$

$$Eu[Y(X)] = \int_{X \leqslant D} u[W - P(D) - X]\mathrm{d}\Phi(X)$$
$$+ \int_{X \geqslant D} u[W - P(D) - D]\mathrm{d}\Phi(X) =_{\text{def}} \bar{u}(D). \tag{4}$$

The optimal insurance contract (deductible) is obtained by maximising (4) with respect to D. For ease of notation, define

$$u[W - P(D) - X] = u_X, \quad u[W - P(D) - D] = u_D. \tag{5}$$

The first-order condition for an interior maximum is[4]

$$0 = \frac{\mathrm{d}\bar{u}(D)}{\mathrm{d}D} = \int_{X \leqslant D} u'_X \left(-\frac{\mathrm{d}P}{\mathrm{d}D} \right) \mathrm{d}\Phi(X)$$
$$+ \int_{X \geqslant D} u'_D \left(-\frac{\mathrm{d}P}{\mathrm{d}D} - 1 \right) \mathrm{d}\Phi(X). \tag{6}$$

---

[3]See, for example, Blume and Friend (1975).
[4]The second-order condition is satisfied; it follows from risk aversion and $P[EI(X)] > EI(X)$ that $W \geqslant D \geqslant 0$ at the optimum.

For $X \leqslant D$, I will use the approximation

$$u'_X \approx u'_D - (X - D)u''_D, \tag{7}$$

and rewrite (6) as

$$0 = -\frac{dP}{dD}\left[u'_D \int_{X \leqslant D} d\Phi(X) - u''_D \int_{X \leqslant D} (X - D)d\Phi(X) \right]$$

$$-\left(\frac{dP}{dD} + 1 \right)u'_D \int_{X \geqslant D} d\Phi(X)$$

$$0 = -\left(\frac{dP}{dD} + \int_{X \geqslant D} d\Phi(X) \right)u'_D + \frac{dP}{dD}u''_D \int_{X \leqslant D} (X - D)d\Phi(X), \tag{8}$$

$$-\frac{u''_D}{u'_D} = -\frac{\dfrac{dP}{dD} + \displaystyle\int_{X \geqslant D} d\Phi(X)}{\dfrac{dP}{dD} \displaystyle\int_{X \leqslant D} (X - D)d\Phi(X)}. \tag{9}$$

It follows from (2) that

$$\frac{dP}{dD} = -\frac{dP}{d\bar{I}} \int_{X \geqslant D} d\Phi(X) =_{\text{def}} -k \int_{X \geqslant D} d\Phi(X), \tag{10}$$

thereby defining k as one plus the (marginal) loading factor. Substituting into (9), we obtain

$$-\frac{u''_D}{u'_D} = \frac{1 - k}{k \displaystyle\int_{X \leqslant D} (X - D)d\Phi(X)}$$

$$= \frac{k - 1}{kD + k\left[\displaystyle\int_{X \leqslant D} (D - X)d\Phi(X) - D \right]} > \frac{k - 1}{kD} \tag{11}$$

$$R_D =_{\text{def}} -\frac{Y(D)u''_D}{u'_D} > \frac{k - 1}{k}\frac{Y(D)}{D}. \tag{12}$$

Formula (12) places a lower bound on the relative risk-aversion measure, R, evaluated at the minimal wealth level $Y(D) = W - P(D) - D$. To aid intuition, let $k = 2$, a reasonable figure for many contracts of insurance against loss. Then a lower bound for R is given by half the ratio of $Y(D)$ to D, i.e. by the reciprocal of twice the uninsured fraction of wealth. The figure $R = 2$, sometimes found in the literature, would imply deductibles as high as one-fourth of the consumer's wealth $Y(D)$, or equivalently one-fifth of the consumer's initial wealth W (if $P(D)$ is small in relation to W).

Table 5.1 gives the lower bounds for R corresponding to alternative

Table 5.1 *Lower bounds for R as a function of k and D/Y(D)*

k	\multicolumn{6}{c}{$D/Y(D)$}
	1/3	1/4	1/5	1/10	1/15	1/20
2	1.5	2	2.5	5	7.5	10
5/3	1.2	1.6	2	4	6	8
3/2	1	1.3	1.7	3.3	5	6.7
5/4	.6	.8	1	2	3	4

assumptions about the values of k and $D/Y(D)$. The striking feature of this table is that reasonable assumptions suggest rather large values of R.

In order to explain the cumbersome term

$$k\left[\int_{X \leqslant D} (D - X)\mathrm{d}\Phi(X) - D\right]$$

in (11) and to gain insight in the degree of tightness of the lower bound, assume that the loading factor is constant so that

$$P(D) = kEI(X) = k\int_{X \geqslant D} (X - D)\mathrm{d}\Phi(X). \tag{13}$$

Under that assumption,

$$k\int_{X \leqslant D} (X - D)\mathrm{d}\Phi(X) = k\left[\int_{X \geqslant 0} X\,\mathrm{d}\Phi(X) - D\right] - P(D)$$

$$= P(0) - kD - P(D) \tag{14}$$

$$-\frac{Y(D)u''_D}{u'_D} = \frac{(k-1)Y(D)}{kD - [P(0) - P(D)]}. \tag{15}$$

When the savings on the insurance premium due to the deductible, $P(0) - P(D)$, is small in relation to the deductible itself, then the lower bound in formula (12) will be close to the more exact formula (15).

References

Arrow, K.J. (1971). *Essays in the Theory of Risk-Bearing*, Amsterdam: North-Holland

Blume, M.E. and I. Friend (1975). The asset structure of individual portfolios and some implications for utility functions, *Journal of Finance*, 30 (May): 585–603

Mossin, J. (1968). Aspects of rational insurance purchasing, *Journal of Political Economy*, 76 (July–August): 553–68

Raviv, A. (1979). The design of an optimal insurance policy, *American Economic Review*, 69 (March): 84–96

II Markets and prices

6   Market allocation under uncertainty*

This paper discusses the interpretation and implications of the analysis of efficient resource allocation under uncertainty initiated by Arrow (1953) in 'The Role of Securities in the Optimal Allocation of Risk-Bearing'. Arrow's model and results are reviewed. It is shown that prices for contingent claims to a numeraire commodity have all the formal properties of a probability measure on the states, but still reflect the relative scarcities under alternative states as well as the probabilities of these states. Some implications of the analysis for asset prices, portfolio selection, and investment criteria are mentioned.

1 Arrow's model

1.1 Opportunity sets

Arrow (1953) considers an economy consisting of I individuals whose endowments (points in C-dimensional commodity space) will depend upon which one of S mutually exclusive states of the world obtains.[1] Let x^i_{sc} denote the quantity of commodity c accruing to individual i if state s

*European Economic Review, 2 (1971): 133–65. This is a slightly revised version of the paper presented at the First World Congress of the Econometric Society, Rome, September 1965. The research underlying this paper was started at the University of Chicago, where Merton H. Miller provided much stimulation and constructive advice; the paper was completed in Louvain, where Paul Van Moeseke provided helpful suggestions and criticisms.
[1] Production was fitted into Arrow's model of a pure exchange economy by Debreu (1953, 1959). The implications of the model for investment decisions are discussed by Hirshleifer (1964, 1965). Lesourne (1964) has attempted to use the model for cost-benefit analysis.

obtains. Then the total amount of commodity c available for consumption by all individuals if state s obtains is:

$$x_{sc} = \sum_i x_{sc}^i \quad s = 1, \ldots, S, \quad c = 1, \ldots, C. \tag{1.1}$$

It is *not* assumed that $x_{sc} = x_{tc}$. Let q_{sc}^i denote the quantity of commodity c consumed by individual i if state s obtains. In the absence of exchange, $q_{sc}^i = x_{sc}^i$ for all $i, s,$ and c. If exchange is possible, consumptions may differ from endowments, but must satisfy the conservation equations,

$$x_{sc} = \sum_i q_{sc}^i \quad s = 1, \ldots, S, \quad c = 1, \ldots, C, \tag{1.2}$$

as well as some budget constraints for the individuals. The nature of the budget constraints depends upon the organisation of exchange.

Suppose, first of all, that no exchange is to take place until it is known what state s obtains. Let p_{sc}^0 denote the market price that would, under these circumstances, prevail for commodity c if state s obtains – using, for example, the first commodity as a numeraire, so that $p_{s1}^0 = 1$. Then budget constraints are of the form:

$$\sum_c p_{sc}^0(q_{sc}^i - x_{sc}^i) = 0, \quad i = 1, \ldots, I. \tag{1.3}$$

In this case, exchange takes place in a world of certainty, and each individual himself bears the uncertainty arising from the dependence of his endowment upon the state of the world.

Arrow introduces instead competitive markets for 'contingent claims' to commodities; SC such markets are supposed to exist, with prices $\bar{p}_{sc}$, $s = 1, \ldots, S, c = 1, \ldots, C$. $\bar{p}_{sc}$ is the price, to be paid irrevocably before it is known what state of the world obtains, for a claim to one unit of commodity c, to be delivered *if and only if* state s obtains.[2] With such markets for 'contingent claims', exchange takes place immediately, and deliveries take place after it is known what state obtains. Since the states form a partition, an unconditional claim to one unit of commodity c is equivalent to S contingent claims, one for each state of the world, and its price is equal to $\sum_s \bar{p}_{sc}$. Using again the first commodity as a numeraire, one may normalise prices by setting:

$$\sum_s \bar{p}_{s1} = 1. \tag{1.4}$$

Each individual i now trades on the SC markets for contingent claims, under the single budget constraint:

$$\sum_{s,c} \bar{p}_{sc}(q_{sc}^i - x_{sc}^i) = 0, \quad i = 1, \ldots, I. \tag{1.5}$$

---

[2] Since all deliveries are postponed, 'payment' takes the form of exchanging 'claims'. Arrow actually introduces 'money' in his construction, but that is not essential.

This constraint is less strict than (1.3) in that transfers of individual endowments across states are now permitted. The individual who would be relatively well endowed if state s obtains, but relatively poorly endowed if state t obtains, may sell claims to commodities contingent on s and buy claims to commodities contingent on t (thus, for him, $\sum_c \bar{p}_{sc} q_{sc}^i < \sum_c \bar{p}_{sc} x_{sc}^i$, $\sum_c \bar{p}_{tc} q_{tc}^i > \sum_c \bar{p}_{tc} x_{tc}^i$).

1.2 Expected utility

Let $V^i(q_{11}^i, \ldots, q_{1C}^i, q_{21}^i, \ldots, q_{SC}^i)$ be a utility function representing the preference-preordering of individual i on the SC-dimensional space of contingent consumption claims. The assumption that V^i is *quasi-concave* is equivalent to the assumption that all indifference surfaces are convex toward the origin in that space.

Similarly, let $U_s^i(q_{s1}^i, \ldots, q_{sC}^i)$ be a utility function representing the conditional preference-preordering of individual i, *given state s*, on the C-dimensional space of consumption vectors. If preferences among consumption vectors vary with the state that obtains, then: $U_s^i(\bar{q}_{s1}^i, \ldots, \bar{q}_{sC}^i) > U_s^i(\hat{q}_{s1}^i, \ldots, \hat{q}_{sC}^i)$, and $U_t^i(\bar{q}_{t1}^i, \ldots, \bar{q}_{tC}^i) < U_t^i(\hat{q}_{t1}^i, \ldots, \hat{q}_{tC}^i)$ may well hold simultaneously, when $\bar{q}_{sc}^i = \bar{q}_{tc}^i$, $\hat{q}_{sc}^i = \hat{q}_{tc}^i$.[3]

If the preference-preordering of individual i on the space of contingent consumption claims satisfies certain postulates of consistent choice under uncertainty, then there exist utility functions V^i, U_s^i, and subjective probabilities π_s^i, such that:

$$V^i(q_{11}^i, \ldots, q_{SC}^i) = \sum_s \pi_s^i U_s^i(q_{s1}^i, \ldots, q_{sC}^i), \qquad (1.6)$$

where V^i is defined up to a linear transformation[4] and all conditional utility functions U_s^i are defined up to an arbitrary origin and a *common* scale factor.[5] V^i thus admits of an expected utility interpretation.

Arrow (1953, theorem 3) has shown that when U_s^i and U_t^i are identical functions for all s and t, they must also be *concave* in order for V^i to be quasi-concave. Concavity of U_s^i is then equivalent to *risk aversion*. In the general case, where U_s^i and U_t^i are allowed to differ, quasi-concavity of V^i has weaker

---

[3]Thus, let state s involve rainfall; state t, sunshine; if the consumption vector $\bar{q}$ differs from the vector $\hat{q}$ by the substitution of an umbrella for a straw hat, then the inequalities in the text would only be natural. Notice that a consumption vector is not a 'consequence' as defined in the theory of decision under uncertainty – see, for example, Savage (1954, pp. 13, 25).

[4]This is a well-known result for the case where U_s^i and U_t^i are identical (preferences are independent of the state of the world). See, for example, Savage (1954). When U_s^i and U_t^i are allowed to differ, the analysis is more complicated and a difficult identification problem arises. See Drèze (1961). Yet the logic of choice remains the same and the expected utility theorem is still valid. The identification problem need not concern us here, since no attempt at being operational is made.

[5]If $V^i = \sum_s \pi_s^i U_s^i$ is a utility, then $\alpha + \beta V^i$, $\beta > 0$, is also utility, with $\alpha + \beta V^i = \sum_s \pi_s^i (\alpha_s + \beta U_s^i)$, $\sum_s \pi_s^i \alpha_s = \alpha$. If the states were so defined that π_s^i may vary, then $\alpha_s \equiv \alpha$; see Drèze (1961).

implications. U_s^i need not be concave for all s, if lack of concavity for some states is properly offset by concavity for others, so that V^i remains quasi-concave.[6]

1.3 Expected utility maximisation: the problem

If no exchange were possible until it is known what state s obtains, one assumes that each individual i would *then* trade as if he were maximising his *conditional* utility U_s^i subject to the budget constraint (1.3), i.e. as if he were solving the problem:

$$\underset{q_{s1}^i,\ldots,q_{sC}^i}{\text{Max}}\ U_s^i(q_{s1}^i,\ldots,q_{sC}^i)\quad\text{subject to}\quad\sum_c p_{sc}^0(q_{sc}^i - x_{sc}^i) = 0, \qquad (1.7)$$

or

$$\underset{q_{s1}^i,\ldots,q_{sC}^i}{\text{Max}}\ U_s^i(q_{s1}^i,\ldots,q_{sC}^i) - \lambda_s^{0i}\left(\sum_c p_{sc}^0 q_{sc}^i - y_s^{0i}\right) \qquad (1.7')$$

where λ_s^{0i} is a Lagrange multiplier, and where y_s^{0i}, the conditional market value of the individual's endowment, is defined by:

$$y_s^{0i} = \sum_c p_{sc}^0 x_{sc}^i. \qquad (1.8)$$

His expected utility would then be:

$$\sum_s \pi_s^i \underset{q_{s1}^i,\ldots,q_{sC}^i}{\text{Max}}\left\{ U_s^i(q_s^i,\ldots,q_{sC}^i) - \lambda_s^{0i}\left(\sum_c p_{sc}^0 q_{sc}^i - y_s^{0i}\right)\right\}. \qquad (1.9)$$

With markets for contingent claims to commodities, each individual i is supposed to behave as if he were maximising his *expected utility* V^i, subject to the budget constraint (1.5), i.e. as if he were solving the problem

$$\underset{q_{11}^i,\ldots,q_{SC}^i}{\text{Max}}\ V^i(q_{11}^i,\ldots,q_{SC}^i)\quad\text{subject to}\quad\sum_{s,c} \bar{p}_{sc}(q_{sc}^i - x_{sc}^i) = 0, \qquad (1.10)$$

[6] Let $g(x) = g(x_1,\ldots,x_s,\ldots,x_S) = \sum_s \pi_s f_s(x_s)$. g is quasi-concave if $g(\bar{x}) \geqslant g(\hat{x})$ implies $g[\alpha\bar{x} + (1-\alpha)\hat{x}] \geqslant g(\hat{x})$ for all $0 \leqslant \alpha \leqslant 1$. $f_s(x_s)$ is concave if $f_s[\alpha\bar{x}_s + (1-\alpha)\hat{x}_s] \geqslant \alpha f_s(\bar{x}_s) + (1-\alpha)f_s(\hat{x}_s)$ for all $\bar{x}_s, \hat{x}_s$, and $0 \leqslant \alpha \leqslant 1$. Suppose that $f_s(x_s)$ is not concave and let $\bar{x}, \hat{x}$ be such that $g(\bar{x}) = g(\hat{x})$, with $f_s(\bar{x}_s) \neq f_s(\hat{x}_s)$. Then $g[\alpha\bar{x} + (1-\alpha)\hat{x}] \geqslant \alpha g(\bar{x}) + (1-\alpha)g(\hat{x})$, since g is quasi-concave; but $f_s[\alpha\bar{x}_s + (1-\alpha)\hat{x}_s] < \alpha f_s(\bar{x}_s) + (1-\alpha)f_s(\hat{x}_s)$ since f_s is not concave. No contradiction arises so long as:

$$\sum_{t \neq s} \{\pi_t f_t[\alpha\bar{x}_t + (1-\alpha)\hat{x}_t] - \alpha f_t(\bar{x}_t) - (1-\alpha)f_t(\hat{x}_t)\}$$
$$\leqslant \pi_s\{\alpha f_s(\bar{x}_s) + (1-\alpha)f_s(\hat{x}_s) - f_s[\alpha\bar{x}_s + (1-\alpha)\hat{x}_s]\} > 0.$$

The analogy in terms of the theory of consumer choice under certainty is the following: a diminishing marginal rate of substitution does not require diminishing marginal utility for each commodity, as long as increasing marginal utility for one commodity is properly offset by diminishing marginal utility for the other. See also Hirshleifer (1965, p. 20) for a related but distinct remark.

or

$$\underset{q^i_{11},\dots,q^i_{SC}}{\text{Max}} \sum_s \pi^i_s U^i_s(q^i_{s1},\dots,q^i_{SC}) - \lambda^i\left(\sum_{s,c} \bar{p}_{sc}q^i_{sc} - \bar{y}^i\right) \qquad (1.10')$$

where λ^i is a Lagrange multiplier and where $\bar{y}^i$, the present (non-stochastic) market value of the individual's (stochastic) endowment, is defined by

$$\bar{y}^i = \sum_{s,c} \bar{p}_{sc}x^i_{sc}. \qquad (1.11)$$

1.4 Expected utility maximisation: the conditions

Let us introduce the new symbol p_{sc}, defined by:

$$p_{sc} = \frac{\bar{p}_{sc}}{\bar{p}_{s1}}, \quad s = 1,\dots,S, \; c = 1,\dots,C. \qquad (1.12)$$

Thus, p_{sc} is the ratio of the prices for claims to one unit of commodities c and 1, respectively, both contingent on state s. It is the rate of exchange between commodities c and 1, contingent on state s. This may also be interpreted as the price, prevailing *before* it is known what state s obtains, for exchange between commodities c and 1, when the exchange is *conditional* upon state s (see Section 3.1 below).[7]

Similarly, let the new variable y^i_s be defined by:

$$y^i_s = \sum_c p_{sc}q^i_{sc} \quad \text{or} \quad \bar{p}_{s1}y^i_s = \sum_c \bar{p}_{sc}q^i_{sc}. \qquad (1.13)$$

That is, $\bar{p}_{s1}y^i_s$ is the total present value of individual i's claims to *consumption* contingent on state s;[8] and y^i_s is the same total expressed in units of claims to the numeraire commodity 1 contingent on state s. Thus, y^i_s is equal to the number of units of numeraire against which individual i's total consumption could be exchanged conditionally on state s.

We may now restate problem (1.10') in the equivalent form:

$$\underset{y^i_1,\dots,y^i_S}{\text{Max}} \sum_s \pi^i_s \left\{ \underset{q^i_{s1},\dots,q^i_{sC}}{\text{Max}} \left[U^i_s(q^i_{s1},\dots,q^i_{sC}) \right. \right.$$
$$\left. \left. - \lambda^i_s\left(\sum_c p_{sc}q^i_{sc} - y^i_s\right) \right] \right\} - \lambda^i\left(\sum_s \bar{p}_{s1}y^i_s - \bar{y}^i\right). \qquad (1.14)$$

---

[7] Thus, p_{sc} differs from p^0_{sc} in that p_{sc} refers to a conditional contract, agreed upon *before* it is known what state obtains whereas p^0_{sc} refers to an unconditional contract, agreed upon *after* it is known that state s obtains; the objects of the contracts are the same (exchange of commodity c for commodity 1), but one contract takes place immediately and is conditional, whereas the other will eventually take place later on and be unconditional. p_{sc} and p^0_{sc} need not be numerically equal, for a reason given below.

[8] This may differ from the market value of individual i's endowment under state s, $\sum_c \bar{p}_{sc}x^i_{sc}$.

The equivalence between the two problems follows immediately from the identity of the first-order conditions for a maximum, which define the solution together with (1.5). The variables y_s^i play a dummy role in (1.14).

Indeed, let us call F^i the function to be maximised in (1.14). The first-order conditions for a maximum are:

$$\frac{\partial F^i}{\partial y_s^i} = \pi_s^i \lambda_s^i - \bar{p}_{s1} \lambda^i = 0, [9] \tag{1.15}$$

$$\frac{\partial F^i}{\partial q_{sc}^i} = \pi_s^i \frac{\partial U_s^i}{\partial q_{sc}^i} - \pi_s^i \lambda_s^i p_{sc} = 0. \tag{1.16}$$

Consequently, in equilibrium:

$$\pi_s^i \frac{\partial U_s^i}{\partial q_{sc}^i} = \bar{p}_{s1} \lambda^i p_{sc} = \bar{p}_{sc} \lambda^i, \tag{1.17}$$

so that

$$\frac{\pi_s^i}{\bar{p}_{sc}} \frac{\partial U_s^i}{\partial q_{sc}^i} = \frac{\pi_t^i}{\bar{p}_{td}} \frac{\partial U_t^i}{\partial q_{td}^i}, \quad s, t = 1, \ldots, S; c, d = 1, \ldots, C. \tag{1.18}$$

Conditions (1.18) are also the first-order conditions for a maximum in (1.10′).

The formulation (1.14) is useful in two respects. First, it brings out two interdependent aspects of the allocation process: allocation of total resources among states, on the one hand (y_s^i), and allocation of total consumption for each state among commodities on the other hand (q_{sc}^i).[10]

When no exchange takes place before it is known what state obtains, the first aspect disappears; a comparison of (1.9) with (1.14) is illustrative in this respect.

Second, (1.14) reminds us that, should state s obtain and individual endowments be given by y_s^i, all markets would then be cleared by the price vector $(p_{s1}, \ldots, p_{sC})$, just as they would be by the vector $(p_{s1}^0, \ldots, p_{sC}^0)$ if individual endowments were given by y_s^{0i}. The difference between these two price vectors is thus seen to result from differences in the distribution of endowments among individuals.

1.5 Two theorems on optimum allocation

What is meant by an optimum allocation of resources under uncertainty? Arrow (1953) defines an allocation as optimum if no other allocation exists, under which *expected utility* is higher for at least one individual without being lower for any individual. This leads to:

---

[9]The implications of these conditions are further discussed in Section 4.
[10]This budgeting procedure has been discussed by Strotz (1957, 1959) and Gorman (1959) in connection with 'utility-trees', of which expected utility is a special case.

Theorem 1.1 (Arrow, 1953): If V^i is quasi-concave for all i, every optimum allocation of resources under uncertainty can be obtained by a system of competitive markets for contingent claims to commodities.

The same allocation would have resulted, in the absence of markets for contingent claims, if the market value, at prices $(p_{s1}, \ldots, p_{sC})$, of individual i's endowment – given state s – had been y_s^i, $i = 1, \ldots, I$, $s = 1, \ldots, S$. In general, however:

$$\sum_c p_{sc} x_{sc}^i \neq y_s^i. \tag{1.19}$$

The equality could be restored in (1.19) if it were only possible to exchange contingent claims to the numeraire commodity 1. Arrow's statement of this proposition reads:[11]

Theorem 1.2 (Arrow, 1953): If V^i is quasi-concave for all i, every optimum allocation of resources under uncertainty can be obtained by perfect competition on the markets for contingent claims to a single (numeraire) commodity.

Arrow comments upon this result as follows (Arrow, 1953, p. 45): 'Socially, the significance of theorem 2 is that it permits economizing on the number of markets. An optimum allocation can be obtained through $S + C$ markets only instead of SC in theorem 1.'

2 Some salient features of the model

2.1 Quasi-concavity of utility functions

I will not attempt to discuss systematically all the features that distinguish Arrow's model from other formalisations of the allocation process under uncertainty. My comments will be limited to the theorems themselves.

Both theorems rest upon a definition of optimum allocations and a hypothesis about the individual preference-preorderings. The hypothesis that V^i is quasi-concave for all i strikes me as perfectly innocuous, if one is willing: (a) to assume the possibility for each individual to gamble at odds that he regards as fair; (b) to leave the analysis of such gambling behaviour out of the picture, when dealing with resource allocation under uncertainty – at least in a first approach; and (c) to assume that V^i is bounded from above.

Indeed, Arrow (1953, theorem 3, see also note 6 above) has shown that concavity of U_s^i for all s was sufficient to guarantee quasi-concavity of V^i. Using the indirect utility function[12]

$$\psi_s^i(1, p_{s2}, \ldots, p_{sC}, y_s^i) =$$

$$\underset{q_{s1}^i, \ldots, q_{sC}^i}{\text{Max}} \; U_s^i(q_{s1}^i, \ldots, q_{sC}^i) - \lambda_s^i\left(\sum_c p_{sc} q_{sc}^i - y_s^i\right) \tag{2.1}$$

[11] I have slightly altered the original wording of the theorem.
[12] See Houthakker, (1961, pp. 716–17).

and holding the prices constant, the crucial hypothesis is one of concavity of ψ_s^i with respect to y_s^i, i.e. of non-increasing marginal utility of income (endowment), given state s.[13] If individual i knows, when reallocating his endowment among states, that he will have the possibility of gambling at fair odds with that endowment, no matter what state obtains, then he should substitute for $\psi_s^i(y_s^i | p_{s2}, \ldots, p_{sC})$ the expected utility of the most attractive bet that y_s^i can buy. Let ψ_s^{*i} be the function obtained upon that substitution. The availability of fair gambles and the boundedness of V^i (hence, of ψ_s^i if S is finite) guarantee the existence of a *concave* ψ_s^{*i}.

This point is illustrated graphically in Figure 6.1, where the value of an individual's endowment is measured horizontally and utility is measured vertically. The function $\psi_s^i(y_s^i | p_{s2}, \ldots, p_{sC})$ is not concave over the range $A \leqslant y_s^i \leqslant B$. Let the individual's endowment under state s be equal to C, which is halfway between A and B; the individual would gladly exchange C for even chances of A *and* B, a prospect with expected utility $1/2\,\overline{AG} + 1/2\,\overline{BF} = \overline{CE} > \overline{CD}$. If he takes such possibilities into account, the individual will trade in claims to the numeraire commodity contingent on state s as if his utility function for y_s^i were ψ_s^{*i} (the curve $OGEF$ in Figure 6.1), which is concave by *construction*, and not ψ_s^i (the curve $OGDF$ in Figure 6.1) which is not concave everywhere.[14]

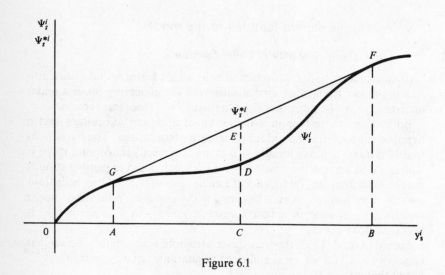

Figure 6.1

[13]Indeed if ψ_s^i is concave with respect to y_s^i, then the usual assumption that ordinal preferences among consumption vectors $(q_{si}^i, \ldots, q_{sc}^i)$ are convex is sufficient to guarantee that V^i is quasi-concave.

[14]ψ_s^{*i} is the 'concavification' of ψ_s^i, that is: ψ_s^{*i} is a concave function of y_s^i, $\psi_s^{*i} \geqslant \psi_s^i$ for all y_s^i, and there exists no concave function $\Phi_s^i(y_s^i)$ such that $\Phi_s^i \geqslant \psi_s^i$ for all y_s^i but $\Phi_s^i < \psi_s^{*i}$ for some y_s^i.

The assumption that gambling opportunities at fair odds exist seems rather innocuous.[15] Excluding redistributive gambling with random devices from the scope of the analysis is a minor limitation, which has proved helpful in related contexts as well.[16] *I will accordingly assume throughout what follows that V^i is quasi-concave for all i.*

2.2 Pareto-optimality and Arrow-optimality

Pareto-optimality is achieved whenever it is impossible to make some individual better off without making any other individual worse off. The limitations of that concept in an economy of certainty are well known. In particular, an appropriate redistribution policy is required to link Pareto-optimality with the maximisation of a social welfare function.

Arrow applies the concept of Pareto-optimality to the expected utilities of the individuals, and derives the important result (theorem 1.1) that perfect competition on the SC markets for contingent claims to commodities is sufficient to achieve Pareto-optimality in that sense. Actually, he shows something more: not only will the allocation be Pareto-optimal *ex ante*, in terms of the expected utilities V^i with prices $(\bar{p}_{11},\ldots,\bar{p}_{SC})$ and market values of endowment $(\bar{y}^1,\ldots,\bar{y}^I)$; it will also be Pareto-optimal (in the usual sense) *ex post*, given that state s has obtained, in terms of utilities U^i_s, with prices $(p_{s1},\ldots,p_{sC})$ and market values of endowments $(y^1_s,\ldots,y^I_s)$. Indeed it was noticed in the closing paragraph of 1.4 above that all markets would be cleared and all consumers would be in equilibrium, given state s, with those prices and endowment values; sufficient conditions for an equilibrium relative to a price system to be a Pareto-optimum are well known (see, e.g. Debreu (1959)).

It must be noticed, however, that if no exchange takes place before it is known what state obtains, the resulting allocation would also be Pareto-optimal *ex post*, given that state s has obtained, in terms of utilities U^i_s, with prices $(p^0_{s1},\ldots,p^0_{sC})$ and market values of endowments $(y^{01}_s,\ldots,y^{0I}_s)$. Thus, *ex post*, what distinguishes Arrow's allocation from the allocation brought about by deferred trading is not existence versus absence of Pareto-optimality, but simply the distribution of a given social endowment $(x_{s1},\ldots,x_{sC})$ among individuals – with the usual price implications of these distributive differences.

Someone who is interested in maximising a specific social welfare function, and who can enforce the implied redistribution policy,[17] might argue that Pareto-optimality in terms of expected utilities – say Arrow-optimality for brevity – is irrelevant, for he will in any event redistribute

[15]The implications for income distribution of this hypothesis, both without and with transaction costs, are dealt with by Friedman (1953).

[16]See Pratt *et al.* (1964) or Drèze (1961).

[17]'Le Petit père du peuple', as Lesourne (1964) puts its.

endowments *ex post*, after state s has obtained, so as to achieve his preferred allocation. A social optimum could thus be obtained by *ex post* trading and redistribution alone.

Could it be that a distribution of endowments that is regarded as optimal *ex ante*, given the existence of competitive markets for contingent claims to commodities, would automatically remain optimal *ex post*? This possibility is very remote, as the following argument shows. Under the proposed allocation system, $\partial V^i/\partial \bar{y}^i$, the 'marginal expected utility' of endowment – or wealth – to individual i is equal to λ^i; similarly, $\partial U^i_s/\partial y^i_s$, the marginal utility of wealth to individual i if state s obtains, is equal to λ^i_s. By (1.15), we must have in equilibrium:

$$\lambda^i_s = \frac{\bar{p}_{s1}}{\pi^i_s} \lambda^i. \tag{2.2}$$

Consequently,

$$\frac{\lambda^i_s}{\lambda^j_s} = \frac{\pi^j_s}{\pi^i_s} \frac{\lambda^i}{\lambda^j} = \frac{\pi^i_t \lambda^i_t}{\pi^j_t \lambda^j_t} \frac{\pi^j_s}{\pi^i_s}. \tag{2.3}$$

Thus, *the ratios of marginal utilities for two individuals are not independent of the state that obtains, unless the subjective probabilities of every state are the same for both individuals.*

No matter what significance one attaches to Arrow-optimality in a model of pure exchange, the concept becomes essential in a model of production. In the model of pure exchange, social endowments $(x_{s1},\ldots,x_{sC})$, $s = 1,\ldots,S$, are *given* quantities of consumption goods. In the model of production, one starts instead with a vector of total resources and a total production set in SC-dimensional commodity space. The quantities of all commodities available for consumption depend upon the *choice* of a point in the production set. Of two such points, one may involve more total consumption of some commodities, given state s, but less total consumption of some commodities, given state t. For the choice among such points, an *ex ante* concept of optimality is needed: redistribution for a given state is constrained by the social endowment available, an endowment that reflects prior choices of economic agents as well as nature's choice. Arrow-optimality seems to provide a natural extension of Pareto-optimality in such situations, while leaving open the problem of redistribution – whether *ex ante* or *ex post*.

2.3 Price information and optimum allocation

If we assume that V^i is quasi-concave for all i, and if we attach significance to Arrow-optimality, theorem 1.1 is a very important result. It is not a surprising result, for the shortcomings of alternative systems of resource allocation under uncertainty are well known. Thus, futures markets are helpful to dispose of uncertainty about prices, but not about yields; insurance companies have discovered the usefulness of exchanging contingent claims instead of sharing policies globally.[18]

The forbidding aspect of theorem 1.1 lies in the number of markets required to achieve Arrow-optimality. Theorem 1.2 addresses itself to that question, in suggesting that only $S + C$ markets would be sufficient: S markets for claims to the numeraire commodity contingent upon the alternative states of the world, and C markets for the exchange of commodities after it is known what state obtains.

One should, however, be careful in understanding precisely the significance of theorem 1.2. It is indeed true that, *if all individuals knew the prices that would prevail given any state s,* they could reallocate their endowments among states by trading in contingent claims to the numeraire alone. But how could they know these prices if no exchange of commodities is to take place until it is known what state of the world obtains? Detailed knowledge of these prices ceases to be necessary for Arrow-optimality only if either one of the following two conditions is satisfied: (a) the price system is independent of the state of the world; (b) the demand functions for contingent claims to the numeraire are independent of the price structures for commodities. Aside from these two limiting cases, allocation of resources under uncertainty cannot be optimal in an *exact* sense without simultaneous clearing of all markets for contingent claims to commodities (or a substitute for these, to be introduced in the next section). This is not to deny that *nearly* optimal allocations could be achieved with substantially less than SC markets. Price uncertainty may be of secondary importance as compared with uncertainty about endowments. Again, some *sets of states* may be identified for which the price system would be nearly constant, or some commodities may be identified, whose prices permit the construction of an index that could efficiently guide the reallocation of endowments.[19] In the general case, however, the significance of theorem 1.2 has to be sought in a different direction.

3 Markets and prices

3.1 Conditional markets for commodities

So far, only two kinds of markets have been considered: markets for contingent claims, where delivery of a commodity if a certain state obtains is promised in exchange for immediate payment; and spot markets where unconditional exchanges take place.

I will now introduce a third type of markets, to be called 'conditional markets' – namely, markets for exchanges that are conditional upon a

---

[18]On this point, see Borch (1962).
[19]See note 10 for references to work on that problem.

certain state. These markets correspond to the notion of 'conditional contracts': if a certain state obtains, the traders are committed to carry out a certain exchange. This differs from markets for contingent claims in that no payment will take place unless a given state obtains. It differs from spot markets in that exchange is neither immediate nor postponed until it is known what state obtains, but agreed upon immediately for realisation conditional upon a certain state. Let us call the prices prevailing on such markets 'conditional prices'.

Suppose that there exist SC markets for contingent claims to commodities with prices $(\bar{p}_{11}, \ldots, \bar{p}_{SC})$ normalised by (1.4) and $S(C-1)$ conditional markets, where commodities $2, \ldots, C$ are exchanged against the numeraire commodity 1 conditionally upon state $s, s = 1, \ldots, S$. Thus, conditional prices are normalised by using the same numeraire, no matter what state s obtains. It is readily verified that, under those circumstances, the conditional prices are given by (1.12), that is, $p_{sc} = \bar{p}_{sc}/\bar{p}_{s1}$ is the conditional price of commodity c, given state s.

Indeed, a claim to one unit of commodity c contingent upon state s may now be acquired in two ways: either by purchasing it outright for a price $\bar{p}_{sc}$; or by purchasing it conditionally, thus promising to pay p_{sc} units of numeraire against delivery of one unit of c should s obtain, while purchasing simultaneously a claim to p_{sc} units of numeraire contingent on state s for a price $p_{sc}\bar{p}_{s1}$. If $\bar{p}_{sc} \neq p_{sc}\bar{p}_{s1}$, arbitrage between contingent claims and conditional contracts will take place until equality is restored; such arbitrage would be perfectly riskless, the 'real' position of the trader being identical in both cases.

The implication of this observation is clearly that conditional markets and markets for contingent claims serve the same function, provided S markets for contingent claims to some numeraire commodity exist, one for each state of the world. One may thus substitute up to $S(C-1)$ conditional markets for the corresponding markets for contingent claims, while still providing individuals with full information about the price structure that would prevail if state s obtains; but no further substitution is possible: at least as many markets for contingent claims as there are states of the world must exist for Arrow-optimality to be achieved in a competitive market economy.

I understand this proposition to convey correctly the significance of Arrow's theorem 1.2, which may be restated as follows:

Theorem 1.2': If V^i is quasi-concave for all i, every optimum allocation of resources under uncertainty can be obtained by perfect competition on the markets for contingent claims to commodities *or* on the markets for contingent claims to a single (numeraire) commodity and on the conditional markets for all other commodities.[20]

[20]Of course, a different choice of numeraire could be made for each state: that would only result in unnecessary complication; 'money' is specifically referred to in Section 5.

3.2 A digression: uncertainty about tastes

An understanding of the equivalence, from the viewpoint of allocation, of conditional markets and markets for contingent claims to commodities other than the numeraire may help to explain why so few such markets exist in reality. Aside from the formidable accounting problem, reference should be made to the uncertainty of individuals about their own future tastes. To say that individual preference-preorderings may vary with the state that obtains is *not* to say that preference-preorderings for a given state are known with certainty, or, equivalently, that the preferences of an individual may enter into the definition of states. The latter must be defined with enough objectivity for contingent and conditional contracts to be possible among different individuals. For individual i to expect delivery of some commodity if his tastes call for it is equivalent to expecting delivery if he should so desire, and one may hardly conceive of such conditions being entered in a contract!

If, in the absence of conditional markets, an individual feels more uncertain about his own tastes, given state s,[21] than about the price structure, given state s, he has no incentive to organise such conditional markets and will be satisfied to reallocate his endowment among states without precommitting his consumption under state s. Under such circumstances, one should not expect conditional markets, or markets for contingent claims to commodities other than the numeraire, to be organised.

Uncertainty about tastes for a given state (as distinct from dependence of tastes upon the states) is not ruled out by the assumptions of the model, but it is ignored, which may well be a reasonable simplification in the present state of the arts.

3.3 Conditional markets for contingent claims

The extent to which conditional markets may replace markets for contingent claims may be specified further if we consider the possibility of sequential information in terms of an 'event tree' (Debreu, 1959, pp. 98–9). It will simplify exposition if we restrict attention to a two-stage information structure. Consider a partition of the set of states into subsets $A, B, \ldots$, called 'events', and suppose that it will be known what event obtains before it is known what state obtains. Figure 6.2 depicts the information structure – or event tree – for a hypothetical case with six states and three events.

A set of prices for claims to the numeraire commodity contingent on the states is a six-dimensional vector $(\bar{p}_{11}, \ldots, \bar{p}_{61})$. A claim to one unit of that commodity contingent on either state 1 or state 2 must then command a

---

[21] Who knows well his own preferences for new commodities or for existing commodities in situations hitherto unexperienced?

States   1   2   3   4   5   6

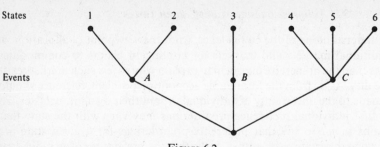

Events

Figure 6.2

price equal to $\bar{p}_{11} + \bar{p}_{21}$, for otherwise perfectly riskless arbitrages would be possible.[22] This joint claim may be called 'a claim contingent on event A', and its price denoted by $\bar{p}_{A1}$. Thus $\bar{p}_{A1} = \bar{p}_{11} + \bar{p}_{12}$; $\bar{p}_{B1} = \bar{p}_{31}$; $\bar{p}_{C1} = p_{41} + \bar{p}_{51} + \bar{p}_{61}$.

At the risk of stretching the reader's imagination beyond reason, let us now consider *conditional markets for contingent claims*. For example, consider a contract in terms of which, if *event A* obtains, a claim to one unit of numeraire *contingent on state 1* will be purchased. The price specified in that contract – say ϕ – is a number of units of numeraire, to be paid if event A obtains. That price ϕ can only be equal to $\bar{p}_{11}/\bar{p}_{A1}$, for otherwise arbitrage would again be possible. Indeed, a claim contingent on state 1 must command the same price, whether it be acquired outright, for a price $\bar{p}_{11}$, or indirectly: by purchasing it conditionally on event A at a price ϕ and purchasing at the same time a claim to ϕ units of numeraire contingent on A. Unless $\bar{p}_{11} = \phi\bar{p}_{A1}$, arbitrage between contingent claims and conditional contracts for claims will take place until ϕ is brought into equality with $\bar{p}_{11}/\bar{p}_{A1}$.

Conditional markets for contingent claims thus provide the same price information and the same allocation opportunities as spot markets for these claims, as long as spot markets exist for claims contingent on events that: (i) form a partition and (ii) will prove true or false before it is known what state obtains. This proposition, which is apt to play an important role in further developments of the theory, may be restated as follows: if V^i is quasi-concave for all i, and if events $A, B, \ldots, E$ form a partition, every optimum allocation of resources under uncertainty can be obtained by perfect competition on the markets for claims to a numeraire commodity contingent on *events*, on the conditional markets for contingent claims to that numeraire (conditional on events, contingent on states), and on the conditional markets for all other commodities (conditional on states).

---

[22]This is *not* to say that in the absence of *separate* markets for claims, contingent on states 1 and 2, the price of a claim contingent on event A would still be $\bar{p}_{11} + \bar{p}_{21}$.

3.4 Prices for contingent claims and probability

It is now easy to verify that *the vector* $(\bar{p}_{11}, \ldots, \bar{p}_{S1})$ *is a probability measure on the set of states.* Indeed:

$$1 \geqslant \bar{p}_{s1} \geqslant 0, \quad s = 1, \ldots, S. \tag{3.1}$$

$$\sum_s \bar{p}_{s1} = 1. \tag{3.2) or (1.4}$$

$$\bar{p}_{A1} = \sum_{s \in A} \bar{p}_{s1}. \tag{3.3}$$

Furthermore, the conditional price of a claim contingent on state s given event $A, s \in A$, is equal to $\bar{p}_{s1}/\bar{p}_{A1}$.

Does this mean that the price $\bar{p}_{s1}$ may be interpreted as the 'market evaluation' of the probability of state s? Such an interpretation would be ill-founded, for *our probability measure will not, in general, be independent of the choice of the numeraire.* To see this, consider the contingent prices $(\bar{p}_{11}, \ldots, \bar{p}_{S1})$ and the conditional prices $(p_{1c}, \ldots, p_{Sc})$, and suppose that commodity c were to replace commodity 1 as numeraire. The prices for contingent claims to commodity c (the new numeraire) will be:

$$\bar{p}_{sc} = \bar{p}_{s1} p_{sc}. \tag{3.4}$$

For renormalisation, each $\bar{p}_{sc}$ may be divided by $\sum_s \bar{p}_{sc} = \sum_s \bar{p}_{s1} p_{sc}$. In order for the new probability measure to coincide with $(\bar{p}_{11}, \ldots, \bar{p}_{S1})$, it is necessary and sufficient that p_{sc} be a constant independent of s, for otherwise $(\bar{p}_{11}, \ldots, \bar{p}_{S1})$ and $(\bar{p}_{1c}, \ldots, \bar{p}_{Sc})$ could not be proportional.

Thus, unless the conditional prices of all commodities are independent of the state that obtains, equivalently, unless the S prices for contingent claims to any commodity are strictly proportional to the S prices for contingent claims to any other commodity, there will exist several different probability measures defined on the set of states by the prices for contingent claims. The choice of a numeraire commodity being arbitrary, its contingent prices cannot be said to provide *the* 'market evaluations' of the probabilities of the states.

4 Probability and utility

4.1 The equilibrium conditions revisited

In an economy where there exist competitive markets for claims to a numeraire commodity contingent on every state of the world, and where the price p_{sc} of every commodity c in terms of the numeraire is known for every state s, the first-order conditions for an optimal allocation of individual i's endowment among states are:

$$\pi_s^i \lambda_s^i - \bar{p}_{s1} \lambda^i = 0, \quad s = 1, \ldots, S, \tag{4.1) or (1.15}$$

where λ_s^i is the marginal utility of the numeraire commodity, given state s, and λ^i is the marginal expected utility of wealth, for individual i. Furthermore, in view of (1.4):

$$\sum_s \pi_s^i \lambda_s^i = \lambda^i \sum_s \bar{p}_{s1} = \lambda^i. \tag{4.2}$$

As one might have guessed: in equilibrium, the *marginal expected utility of wealth is equal to the expected marginal utility of the numeraire*.

Notice that $\lambda_s^i = \lambda^i$ if and only if $\pi_s^i = \bar{p}_{s1}$: the marginal utility of the numeraire, given state s, will be equal to the marginal expected utility of wealth if and only if the subjective probability of state s for individual i is equal to the price of a claim to the numeraire contingent on state s. We may look at this relationship in another way, by rewriting (4.1) as follows, using (4.2) and (1.4):

$$\bar{p}_{s1} = \frac{\lambda_s^i}{\lambda^i} \pi_s^i = \frac{\lambda_s^i}{\sum_t \pi_t^i \lambda_t^i} \pi_s^i = \frac{\bar{p}_{s1}}{\sum_t \bar{p}_{t1}}. \tag{4.3}$$

Thus, in order for individual i to be in equilibrium, he must so allocate his wealth among states that the price of a claim to the numeraire contingent on state s is equal to the product of two terms: (a) his subjective probability for state s, or the probability for him that his claim will be delivered; (b) his marginal utility for the numeraire, given state s, or the increment of utility that delivery would bring about if it occurs. The denominators come in for normalisation and to ensure commensurability.[23]

4.2 An interpretation of prices for contingent claims

If all individuals agreed on the probability of state s, so that $\pi_s^i = \pi_s^j, i, j = 1, \ldots, I$, then (4.3) would imply that the ratio λ_s^i / λ^i be the same for all individuals; the indices i might then be dropped and (4.3) rewritten as:

$$\bar{p}_{s1} = \frac{\lambda_s}{\lambda} \pi_s. \tag{4.4}$$

In this case the probability of state s is unambiguously defined by unanimous agreement, and the interpretation of $\bar{p}_{s1}$ becomes straightforward: it is equal to the probability of s times the relative marginal utility of the numeraire, given s.

This is a natural extension of the usual interpretation of price ratios as marginal rates of substitution. Probability comes in because we deal with the price of a contingent claim. The fact that V^i is defined up to a linear transformation enables us to refer to ratios of marginal utilities, or 'relative marginal utilities', instead of marginal rates of substitution.

[23]Indeed, λ_s^i / λ^i is a pure number; if V^i were normalised by setting $\lambda^i = 1$ (arbitrary choice of scale), then (4.3) would reduce to $\bar{p}_{s1} = \lambda_s^i \pi_s^i$.

It may come as a surprise to the reader that, *while the prices for contingent claims to the numeraire* $(\bar{p}_{11}, \ldots, \bar{p}_{S1})$ *have all the properties of a probability measure, they are to be interpreted as the products of a probability by a relative marginal utility*. There is, however, nothing paradoxical about such a situation. In the more familiar context of expected utility analysis for the individual, if we normalise V^i by setting $\lambda^i = 1$, then the marginal expected utilities of contingent claims to the numeraire $\pi_s^i \lambda_s^i$ also behave like probabilities; still, they are not to be confused with the subjective probabilities π_s^i.[24]

In the light of this observation, it is easy to understand why the C probability measures defined by the price vectors for contingent claims to commodities $(\bar{p}_{1c}, \ldots, p_{Sc})$, $c = 1, \ldots, C$, are not identical: each one of them is the product of the same probabilities π_s by different relative marginal utilities, namely, the relative marginal utilities of different commodities. *If a commodity existed, the marginal utility of which is independent of the state of the world, then the prices of contingent claims to that commodity would be equal to the probabilities of the states*, in our special case of unanimous agreement about these probabilities. Such a commodity would provide a very useful numeraire, for the prices of contingent claims to commodities, $\bar{p}_{sc} = p_{sc}\bar{p}_{s1}$, would then be equal to the product of the probabilities of the states by the conditional prices of the commodities. Conversely, under unanimous agreement about the probabilities, a numeraire with constant marginal utility would be identified by the condition that prices to its contingent claims be equal to the probabilities of the states.

4.3 An illustration

If there exist competitive markets for contingent claims to a numeraire commodity, and if all individuals agree about the probability of s, why would $\lambda_s^i/\lambda^i = \lambda_s/\lambda$ differ from unity? The answer lies naturally in relative scarcities. Let there be only two states, s and t, so that $\lambda^i = \pi_s \lambda_s^i + (1 - \pi_s)\lambda_t^i$, and let s be a state of abundance (prosperity?) and t be a state of poverty (depression?), for society as a whole. Then one would expect to find $\lambda_s^i < \lambda^i < \lambda_t^i$ for all i, and accordingly, $\lambda_s/\lambda < \lambda_t/\lambda$.

The interested reader may find it helpful to work out the following simple illustration. Let there be a single commodity (whose subscript will be dropped) and two individuals, i and j, with identical utility functions:

$$V^i = \pi_s \log q_s^i + (1 - \pi_s) \log q_t^i. \tag{4.5}$$

Let η_s denote the quantity $q_s^i - x_s^i$, i.e. the number of claims to the single commodity contingent on s bought by i; automatically, $q_s^j = x_s^j - \eta_s$.

---

[24]This is the reason why the identification of subjective probabilities is so difficult, when preference-preorderings are not independent of the state that obtains; see Drèze (1961).

Similarly, $\eta_t = q_t^i - x_t^i$. From the budget balancing condition:

$$\bar{p}_s \eta_s + \bar{p}_t \eta_t = 0, \tag{4.6}$$

it follows that

$$\eta_t = \eta_s \frac{\bar{p}_s}{\bar{p}_s - 1}.$$

Solving this model for η_s and $\bar{p}_s$, we get:

$$\bar{p}_s = \pi_s \frac{x_t}{\pi_s x_t + (1 - \pi_s) x_s}, \quad 1 - \bar{p}_s = (1 - \pi_s) \frac{x_s}{\pi_s x_t + (1 - \pi_s) x_s}, \tag{4.7}$$

$$\eta_s = (1 - \pi_s) \left(\frac{x_s}{x_t} x_t^i - x_s^i \right) = (1 - \pi_s) \left(x_s^j - \frac{x_s}{x_t} x_t^j \right). \tag{4.8}$$

Furthermore,

$$\lambda_s^i = \frac{1}{q_s^i} = \left[\pi_s x_s^i + (1 - \pi_s) \frac{x_s}{x_t} x_t^i \right]^{-1}, \quad \frac{\lambda_s^i}{\lambda^i} = \frac{x_t}{\pi_s x_t + (1 - \pi_s) x_s}. \tag{4.9}$$

If $x_s > \pi_s x_t + (1 - \pi_s) x_s > x_t$, we have indeed $\bar{p}_s < \pi_s$, $\lambda_s/\lambda < 1$ and $1 - \bar{p}_s > 1 - \pi_s$, $\lambda_t/\lambda > 1$. Thus, a claim to one unit of the commodity contingent on abundance sells for less than its actuarial value π_s, whereas a claim to one unit of the commodity contingent on poverty sells for more than its actuarial value. To repeat, *prices for contingent claims reflect relative scarcities as well as probabilities.*

In this example, if $x_s = x_t$, then $\bar{p}_s = \pi_s$, no matter what the distribution of endowments among the individuals may be; both contingent claims sell for their actuarial value, π_s or $1 - \pi_s$ as the case may be, and $\lambda_s/\lambda = \lambda_t/\lambda = 1$. In terms of a distinction used by Allais (1953), when $x_s \neq x_t$ society's endowment is uncertain (*risques globalement inéliminables*); whereas, when $x_s = x_t$, only individual endowments are uncertain (*risques globalement inexistants*). It is not surprising that, in our simple context, contingent claims would sell for their actuarial value in the latter case but not in the former (cf. Allais (1953, p. 13)).

Notice further that, if $x_s = x_t$ but $U_s^i \neq U_t^i$, then $p_s \neq \pi_s$. To verify this, suppose that:

$$V^i = \pi_s \log (q_s^i)^{a_s} + (1 - \pi_s) \log (q_t^i)^{a_t}, \quad a_s \neq a_t, \tag{4.10}$$

$$\pi_s a_s + (1 - \pi_s) a_t = 1, \tag{4.11}$$

where (4.11) is simply a choice of unit of scale for V^i. Then $\bar{p}_s = \pi_s a_s$, no matter what the distribution of endowments among individuals may be: the solution will be the same in this case as in a hypothetical case where the subjective probabilities would be $\pi_s a_s$ and $(1 - \pi_s)a_t$, respectively. This shows that constancy of society's endowments, in terms of physical quantities, does not eliminate social risks unless tastes are constant as well.[25]

4.4 Significance of the interpretation

One must be careful not to attach to the preceding remarks more significance than they deserve. To say that, in equilibrium, prices for contingent claims are equal to the product of a probability and a relative marginal utility is an *interpretation* of the equilibrium, not a theorem about *price formation*. In particular, it is not claimed that, had the probabilities been different, then the prices for contingent claims would have stood in the same ratios to these hypothetical probabilities as they stand to the actual probabilities. Indeed, different probabilities mean a different distribution of expected endowments among individuals; hence a distortion of the price structure, reflecting distributional effects as well as probability effects.[26]

Furthermore, should the probabilities change *because it is known that a certain event A obtains*, then both the prices for contingent claims and the probabilities of states would change *in a predictable way*, albeit *not proportionally*. Indeed, let $\bar{p}_{s1}|_A$ denote the price for a claim contingent on state s that would prevail if it were known that A obtains.[27] Since prices for contingent claims behave like a probability measure (see Section 3.4 above), we know that

$$\bar{p}_{s1}|_A = \frac{\bar{p}_{s1}}{\bar{p}_{A1}} = \frac{\bar{p}_{s1}}{\sum_{s \in A} \bar{p}_{s1}} = \frac{\dfrac{\lambda_s}{\lambda}\pi_s}{\sum_{s \in A} \dfrac{\lambda_s}{\lambda}\pi_s} = \frac{\lambda_s \pi_s}{\sum_{s \in A} \lambda_s \pi_s}. \tag{4.12}$$

---

[25]A society confronted with two states – say, rain or sunshine – may have the same endowment under both states; still, there is uncertainty about the scarcity of such commodities as straw hats or umbrellas; that is enough to generate prices for contingent claims to the numeraire that differ from the probabilities of the states.

[26]Indeed, suppose again that there are only two states, with probabilities π_s and $1 - \pi_s$, and that prices are $\bar{p}_{s1}$ and $1 - \bar{p}_{s1}$. Had the probabilities been $\pi_s \mu_s$ and $1 - \pi_s \mu_s$, we cannot assert that the prices would have been $\bar{p}_{s1}\mu_s$ and $1 - \bar{p}_{s1}\mu_s$, unless $\lambda_s/\lambda = \lambda_t/\lambda$; indeed for individual i,

$$\bar{p}_{s1} = \frac{\lambda_s^i}{\pi_s \lambda_s^i + (1 - \pi_s)\lambda_t^i}\pi_s,$$

so that:

$$\bar{p}_{s1}\mu_s = \frac{\lambda_s^i}{\pi_s \lambda_s^i + (1 - \pi_s)\lambda_t^i}\pi_s\mu_s \neq \frac{\lambda_s^i}{\pi_s\mu_s \lambda_s^i + (1 - \pi_s\mu_s)\lambda_t^i}\pi_s\mu_s;$$

but $\lambda_s^i = \lambda_t^i$ implies $\pi_s \lambda_s^i + (1 - \pi_s)\lambda_t^i = \pi_s\mu_s \lambda_s^i + (1 - \pi_s\mu_s)\lambda_t^i$.

[27]This is also the conditional price for a contingent claim referred to in Section 3.3.

Similarly, let $\pi_s|_A$ denote the conditional probability of s given A,

$$\pi_s|_A = \frac{\pi_s}{\pi_A} = \frac{\pi_s}{\sum\limits_{s \in A} \pi_s}, \tag{4.13}$$

and define:

$$\lambda_A = \sum_{s \in A} \lambda_s \pi_s|_A = \sum_{s \in A} \lambda_s \frac{\pi_s}{\pi_A} = \frac{\sum\limits_{s \in A} \lambda_s \pi_s}{\sum\limits_{s \in A} \pi_s}. \tag{4.14}$$

We then have:

$$\frac{\bar{p}_{s1}|_A}{\pi_s|_A} = \frac{\lambda_s \pi_s}{\sum\limits_{s \in A} \lambda_s \pi_s} \frac{\sum\limits_{s \in A} \pi_s}{\pi_s} = \frac{\lambda_s \sum\limits_{s \in A} \pi_s}{\sum\limits_{s \in A} \lambda_s \pi_s} = \frac{\lambda_s}{\lambda_A}, \tag{4.15}$$

$$\bar{p}_{s1}|_A = \frac{\lambda_s}{\lambda_A} \pi_s|_A. \tag{4.16}$$

λ_s/λ_A measures the relative marginal utility of the numeraire given A. Thus, as information about events accrues, the interpretation of prices remains valid; but prices stay in the same ratios to probabilities if and only if the relative marginal utility of the numeraire remains unaffected.

4.5 Aggregation of subjective probabilities

When the subjective probabilities of the various individuals trading in contingent claims are not identical, then the relative marginal utilities λ_s^i/λ^i differ from unity, not only because of relative scarcities but also because of individual differences of opinion – since $\lambda_s^i/\lambda^i \neq \lambda_s^j/\lambda^j$ whenever $\pi_s^i \neq \pi_s^j$. The *interpretation* of prices for contingent claims as products of probabilities and relative marginal utilities is still valid for the individual, but it is no longer straightforward from the standpoint of society – since these two components vary from individual to individual. It is still doubtless true that prices for contingent claims must still *reflect in some way* both the probabilities of the states and the relative marginal utilities of the numeraire commodity, *as seen by the various individuals*. But in order to carry out the interpretation of these prices as products of *a* probability measure and *a* measure of relative marginal utility, some meaning should first be attached either to a 'social' or 'market' probability measure *or* to a 'social' measure of relative marginal utility.[28]

---

[28]The present analysis does not throw any new light on the difficult problems encountered in attempting to define meaningfully either of these concepts. An earlier version of this paper includes a demonstration of the following proposition (which bears some relation to the work of Madansky (1964) on the aggregation of subjective probabilities): if there exist markets for contingent claims to a numeraire commodity, and if some aggregate probability measure is to be defined as a linear combination of individual probability measures, then as information about events accrues, the revisions of the weights assigned to the individuals in that aggregate will be inversely proportional to the revisions of the marginal utilities of wealth to the individuals.

5 Some implications of the model

5.1 Conclusion

By way of conclusion, attention will be drawn to a few implications of the notion that competitive prices for contingent claims to a numeraire commodity would reflect both the probabilities of the states and the relative marginal utilities of that commodity. It will be left for the reader to decide whether he wants to think about the implications as holding only in cases of unanimous agreement on the probabilities, or whether he finds the notion equally suggestive (even if not operational) in a more general context as well.

5.2 Money

Money as a numeraire has the property that its scarcity is not determined by physical circumstances of the kind that would naturally enter into the definition of states of the world (such as the yield of a crop, the results of mine prospecting, the impact of technological progress, etc.). Instead, the quantity of money is determined by the choices of economic agents – private and public – within the framework of monetary institutions.

As indicated above, if the marginal utility of the numeraire were independent of the state that obtains, then prices for contingent claims to the numeraire would measure the probabilities of states; prices for contingent claims to commodities other than the numeraire would be equal to the prices of these commodities given a state times the probability of that state; etc. There would undoubtedly be some virtue to such a state of affairs: the absence of uncertainty about the utility value of the numeraire might well facilitate many a decision.

Money could in principle come closer to meeting that requirement than any commodity, the scarcity of which is state-dependent (like wheat, oil or electricity). On the other hand, the choices of economic agents are in a sense less predictable than the choices of nature, so that another element of uncertainty must be reckoned with in forecasting the relative scarcity of money.

5.3 Assets

In terms of our model, assets (e.g. inventories or shares of stock) are *collections of contingent claims*. The price or market value of an asset should thus be equal to the sum of the prices of these contingent claims, if the markets for assets are competitive.[29] Consider then an asset, like a bond or a share of stock, which is a collection of claims to money. If the relative marginal utility of money were independent of the state of the world, so that prices for contingent claims to money were equal to the probabilities of the

[29]See also Hirshleifer (1965, Section VI).

states, then the market value of an asset at time t would also be the (discounted) expectation of its market value at time $t + \Theta$. When the relative marginal utility of money is not independent of the state that obtains, such a conclusion is no longer valid: an asset that corresponds mostly to claims contingent on states where the relative marginal utility of money is low will sell for *less* than its (discounted) expected future market value, and vice versa. To be more specific, at the risk of oversimplification, an asset that promises to pay back a lot in case of prosperity, where the relative marginal utility of money may be regarded as low, but that would become worthless in case of depression, where the relative marginal utility of money may be regarded as high, should sell today for less than the expectation of its future market value; indeed, it should sell today for the weighted expectation of its future market value, the weights being the relative marginal utilities of money given the states. Thus, if a share of stock possesses roughly the characteristics of the hypothetical asset just mentioned, whereas a bond pays back the same amount no matter what state obtains, then their present market values should imply a higher *expected* rate of return for the stock than for the bond – but equal *weighted* expectations. *Ex post*, one should then also find that the rates of return on stocks exceed the rates of return on bonds, after a suitable averaging over the shares of various companies and over time.[30] Loosely speaking, market rationality and arbitrages should not result in equating the prices of assets having the same expected money value, but only of assets having the same expected utility value; the two expectations coincide only when the relative marginal utility of a dollar is independent of the state that obtains.

5.4 Portfolio selection

If there existed markets for contingent claims as well as markets for assets, then individuals could indifferently hold their wealth in the form of contingent claims or in the form of assets, so long as their total wealth were optimally allocated among states. If the price of an asset were equal to the sum of the prices for the collection of contingent claims which it represents, and if an unbalanced allocation of wealth among states could always be corrected by trading in contingent claims, then the composition of his portfolio should be a matter of indifference to the individual – aside from transaction costs. It is the very absence of markets for contingent claims that raises the problem of portfolio selection, by forcing individuals to use assets as a means of reallocating their endowments among states. It is perhaps doubtful that assets provide enough flexibility for an efficient allocation of resources under uncertainty to be achieved in this way.

Under existing arrangements, an efficient portfolio for the individual

---

[30]This seems to conform with the findings of Lorie and Fisher (1964) whose interpretation of the phenomenon is, however, quite different.

cannot be selected in terms of some general representation of his attitude toward risk: the dependence of his endowment upon states must also be taken into account. Thus, an individual whose earning capacity would be severely reduced by a state of depression should hold his tangible wealth in another way than an individual whose earning capacity would remain unchanged there, even if the tastes and subjective probabilities of both individuals are identical.[31] In particular, shares of stock are apt to be an advantageous investment for the second individual even if he is conservative, but not for the former even if he is less conservative!

5.5 Firms

If the equity of a firm represents a collection of contingent claims, then maximising the market value of the firm is equivalent to maximising the present value, on the markets for contingent claims, of the firm's future profits.[32] If the prices for contingent claims to the numeraire were equal to the probabilities of the states, that present value would also be the firm's (discounted) expected profit, and firms should maximise expected profit *without regard for risk*. When prices for contingent claims reflect relative scarcities as well as probabilities, maximising the firm's present value is equivalent to maximising a weighted (and discounted) expectation of profit, where *the weights vary with the states but not with the size of profits given the states*. This remark may help dispel existing confusion about the notion of a firm's utility function:[33] an optimal allocation of resources under uncertainty – properly sustained by competitive markets for contingent claims to the numeraire – would require that all firms act as if they were maximising the expectation of the *same* expected utility function, namely a function in terms of which *utility is linear in profit for any given state, but with a different proportionality constant for each state*.[34] Thus, the tastes of the owners of the firm are irrelevant, under competitive markets for assets and optimal allocation of endowments among states by individuals. This remark applies, of course, to all firms regarded as owners of production sets, to independent practitioners as well as to joint stock companies. The failure of existing arrangements to dissociate effectively the tastes of owners or

[31]This proposition casts some doubt on the realism of the proposition, due to Tobin (1958), Markowitz (1959), and Brownlee and Scott (1963), that various individuals with different but quadratic utility functions should hold stocks in fixed proportions, with only the proportion of the portfolio invested in stocks being specific to the individuals; the proposition does not even hold for two individuals with identical utility functions, once the dependence of endowments upon states is recognised.

[32]That Arrow's model leads to an immediate proof of the theorem of Modigliani and Miller (1958) on the cost of capital has been shown by Hirshleifer (1965).

[33]See, for example, Lesourne (1964, p. 226).

[34]This proposition remains valid only so long as competition prevails on all markets – for commodities and assets as well as contingent claims.

managers from the attitude of firms toward risks is undoubtedly a source of misallocation that seems to be serious enough to motivate further research, empirical as well as theoretical.

5.6 Two open questions

This list of illustrations could be extended in several directions – such as futures prices, public investment, the term-structure of interest rates, and so on. The pragmatic value of such an exercise remains limited by two major considerations that also define priorities for further research: (i) markets for contingent claims are conspicuously non-existent for many states; the analysis should thus be extended to second-best models, recognising these limitations on exchange opportunities; (ii) many economic decisions should be regarded as *choices about events* rather than as means of reallocating resources among events; thus, whether or not a particular research effort undertaken in connection with air pollution will prove successful is a choice of nature – but the decision to undertake the effort is a choice of man; what matters to that decision is not the relative *marginal* utility of a dollar, given success or failure, but the *total* utility of success or failure; when a decision influences the subjective probabilities of the states, the expected utilities of all individuals are affected, and external effects are much more decisive than market effects.[35] The limitations of classical welfare theory and the need for advances on the front of social choice analysis are particularly evident in the economics of uncertainty; in both respects, the present paper raises more questions than it answers.

References

Allais, M. (1953). Généralisation des théories de l'équilibre économique général et du rendement social au cas du risque. In *Econométrie*, pp. 81–110. Paris: CNRS

Arrow, K.J. (1953). Le rôle des valeurs boursières pour la répartition la meilleure des risques. In *Econométrie*, pp. 41–7. Paris: CNRS. Translated (1964) as The Role of Securities in the Optimal Allocation of Risk-Bearing. *Review of Economic Studies*, 31: 91–6

Borch, K. (1962). Equilibrium in a Reinsurance Market. *Econometrica*, 30(3): 424–44

Brownlee, O. and I.O. Scott (1963). Utility, Liquidity, and Debt-Management. *Econometrica*, 31(3): 349–62

Debreu, G. (1953). Une economie de l'incertain [mimeographed]. Paris: EDF (1959). *Theory of Value*. New York: Wiley

Drèze, J. (1961). Les fondements logiques de la probabilité subjective et de l'utilité. In *La Décision*, pp. 73–87. Paris: CNRS (Translated as Chapter 4 supra.)

—(1964). Some Postwar Contributions of French Economists to Theory and Public Policy. *American Economic Review*, 54(4), Pt 2: 1–64

[35]For a specific example, see the problem of choosing a probability of shortage in electricity supply; Drèze (1964, pp. 18ff.).

Friedman, M. (1953). La théorie de l'incertitude et la distribution des revenus selon leur grandeur. In *Econométrie*, pp. 65–79. Paris: CNRS

Gorman, W.M. (1959). Separable Utility and Aggregation. *Econometrica*, 27(3): 469–81, 489

Hirshleifer, J. (1964). Efficient Allocation of Capital in an Uncertain World. *American Economic Review*, 54(3): 77–85

—(1965). Investment Decision under Uncertainty: Choice-Theoretic Approaches. *The Quarterly Journal of Economics*, 79: 509–36

Houthakker, H. (1961). The Present State of Consumption Theory. *Econometrica*, 29(4): 704–40

Lesourne, J. (1964). *Le calcul économique.* Paris: Dunod

Lorie, J. and L. Fisher (1964). Rates of Return on Investments in Common Stock. *Journal of Business*, 37: 1–21

Madansky, A. (1964). Externally Bayesian Groups. Memorandum RM–4141–PR, The Rand Corporation

Markowitz, H. (1959). *Portfolio Selection.* New York: Wiley

Modigliani, F. and M. Miller (1958). The Cost of Capital, Corporation Finance and the Theory of Investment. *American Economic Review*, 48(3): 261–97

Pratt, J.H., H. Raiffa and R. Schlaifer (1964). The Foundations of Decision under Uncertainty: An Elementary Exposition. *Journal of the American Statistical Association*, 59(7): 353–75

Savage, L.J. (1954). *The Foundations of Statistics.* New York: Wiley

Strotz, R.H. (1957). The Empirical Implication of a Utility Tree. *Econometrica*, 25(2): 269–80

—(1959). The Utility Tree – A Correction and Further Appraisal. *Econometrica*, 27(3): 482–8

Tobin, J. (1958). Liquidity Preference as Behavior Towards Risk. *Review of Economic Studies*, 25: 65–86

7 Demand estimation, risk aversion and sticky prices*

1 Introduction and summary

The purpose of this chapter is to point out that uncertainty about the price elasticity of demand has an effect comparable to that of a kink in the demand curve, for a risk-averse firm; the kink being located at the prevailing price and quantity. The reason for this effect, namely estimation uncertainty, is entirely distinct from the standard reason invoked in the literature on kinky demand curves, since Sweezy (1939), namely asymmetrical reactions of competitors. Thus symmetrical, but imperfectly known, reactions would produce asymmetrical effects. And asymmetrical, but imperfectly known, reactions would produce doubly asymmetrical effects – the asymmetry generated by uncertainty being compounded with that generated by the reactions themselves.

The effect of uncertainty in the context considered here is analogous to the effect of uncertainty about rates of return on savings decisions by consumers. Variance of rates of return affects these decisions in the same way as *adverse* changes in expected returns – see Drèze and Modigliani (1972) or Sandmo (1974). Thus, uncertainty about rates of return has an effect comparable to that of a kink in the budget line constraining present and future consumption; the kink being located at the endowment point. (The reason for that kink is again distinct from the standard reason, namely a difference between lending and borrowing rates; both asymmetries must again be compounded.)

We first illustrate our point for the special case of a linear demand curve, a linear cost curve, and a 'truncated minimax' decision criterion – see Van Moeseke (1965) for a discussion of that criterion, which calls for maximising

*Economics Letters, 4 (1979): 1–6; © North-Holland Publishing Co.

expected value minus a multiple of standard deviation. In that special case, the effect of uncertainty about the price elasticities of demand is precisely equivalent to that of a kink in the demand curve. We then extend our argument to local analysis of a general situation.

Whether firms are risk-averse or not is a sometimes debated issue, which is not taken up here. The author's current views on that issue are summarised by Drèze (1979).

A number of possible extensions (uncertainty about the level of demand at the prevailing price, uncertainty about costs, price decisions aimed at gathering information about the demand elasticity, costs associated with price changes, multiperiod problems,...) seem to raise unrewarding analytical difficulties and are therefore left as exercises for the readers!

2 A special case

We consider first the linear demand and cost functions

$$q = a - bp, \tag{2.1}$$

$$C(q) = cq + d, \tag{2.2}$$

where q denotes quantity, p denotes price, and (a, b, c, d) are positive scalars. Starting from a point (q_0, p_0) on the demand function, we may express profits Π as a function of price,

$$\Pi(p) = pq - C(q) = (p - c)[q_0 + b(p_0 - p)] - [C(q_0) - cq_0]$$
$$= \Pi(p_0) + (p - p_0)[q_0 - b(p - c)]. \tag{2.3}$$

If b is unknown, but estimated by means of a probability density, then $\Pi(p)$ is a random variable with moments

$$E[\Pi(p)] = (p - c)[q_0 + E(b)(p_0 - p)] - [C(q_0) - cq_0], \tag{2.4}$$
$$V[\Pi(p)] = V(b)(p - c)^2(p_0 - p)^2, \tag{2.5}$$

and standard deviation

$$\sigma[\Pi(p)] = \sigma(b)(p - c)|p_0 - p|, \tag{2.6}$$

over the relevant range where $p > c$.

The 'truncated minimax' criterion calls for maximising the linear homogeneous function of Π,

$$E[\Pi(p)] - \alpha\sigma[\Pi(p)]$$
$$= (p - c)[q_0 + E(b)(p_0 - p) - \alpha\sigma(b)|p_0 - p|] - [C(q_0) - cq_0]$$
$$= (p - c)\left[q_0 + \left\{E(b) + \alpha\sigma(b)\frac{|p_0 - p|}{p - p_0}\right\}(p_0 - p)\right]$$
$$\quad - [C(q_0) - cq_0]$$
$$= (p - c)[q_0 + \beta(p)\cdot(p_0 - p)] - [C(q_0) - cq_0]$$
$$= \Pi(p_0) + (p - p_0)[q_0 - \beta(p)\cdot(p - c)], \tag{2.7}$$

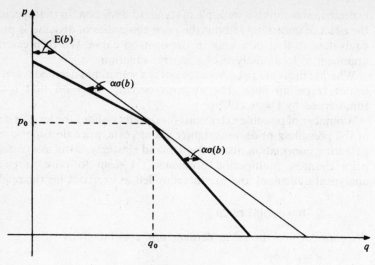

Figure 7.1

where

$$\beta(p) = E(b) + \alpha\sigma(b) \cdot s(p - p_0),$$

$$s(x) = \text{sign of } x = 1 \qquad \text{if } x > 0$$
$$= -1 \quad \text{if } x < 0$$
$$= 0 \qquad \text{if } x = 0.$$

We thus verify that, in this special case, uncertainty about b is equivalent to an *adverse* change in $E(b)$; indeed, the term in $\sigma(b)$ works like an increase in the response of demand to price increases, and a decrease in the response of demand to price decreases, i.e. it is equivalent to a kink in the demand function at (q_0, p_0), see Figure 7.1.

3 The general case (local analysis)

For a local analysis of the general case, we write

$$\Pi(p) = p \cdot q(p) - C(q), \tag{3.1}$$

with

$$q(p_0) = q_0, \quad \left.\frac{dq}{dp}\right|_{p_0} = -b, \quad \left.\frac{dC}{dq}\right|_{q_0} = c,$$

and expand the utility function of the firm, $u[\Pi(p)]$, in a Taylor-series around $u[\Pi(p_0)]$,

$$u[\Pi(p)] \simeq u[\Pi(p_0)] + (p - p_0)\frac{du}{d\Pi}\frac{d\Pi}{dp}\bigg|_{p_0}$$

$$+\frac{(p-p_0)^2}{2}\left[\frac{d^2u}{d\Pi^2}\left(\frac{d\Pi}{dp}\right)^2\bigg|_{p_0}+\frac{du}{d\Pi}\frac{d^2\Pi}{dp^2}\bigg|_{p_0}\right]$$

$$\simeq u[\Pi(p_0)]+\frac{du}{d\Pi}\bigg|_{p_0}\{(p-p_0)[q_0-b(p_0-c)]$$

$$-(p-p_0)^2b\}$$

$$+\frac{d^2u}{d\Pi^2}\bigg|_{p_0}\frac{(p-p_0)^2}{2}[q_0-b(p_0-c)]^2. \tag{3.2}$$

Expression (3.2) is meant to hold for p close to p_0. Accordingly, the fourth-order terms $(p-p_0)^2(d^2q/dp^2)$ and $(p-p_0)^2(d^2c/dq^2)$ have been dropped.

Uncertainty about the demand elasticity means uncertainty about b in (3.2). The expected utility associated with a given p is then

$$Eu[\Pi(p)]\simeq u[\Pi(p_0)]+\frac{du}{d\Pi}\bigg|_{p_0}(p-p_0)[q_0-E(b)(p-c)]$$

$$+\frac{d^2u}{d\Pi^2}\bigg|_{p_0}\frac{(p-p_0)^2}{2}E[q_0-b(p_0-c)]^2. \tag{3.3}$$

Let $\phi[\Pi(p_0)]=\phi_0$ denote the absolute risk-aversion function of the firm evaluated at $\Pi(p_0)$, i.e.

$$\phi_0=-\frac{d^2u}{d\Pi^2}\bigg|_{\Pi(p_0)}\bigg/\frac{du}{d\Pi}\bigg|_{\Pi(p_0)}\geq 0. \tag{3.4}$$

Under risk aversion, $\phi_0>0$, under risk neutrality, $\phi_0=0$, see Pratt (1964) or Arrow (1965). We may then rewrite (3.3) as

$$\frac{Eu[\Pi(p)]-u[\Pi(p_0)]}{du/d\Pi|_{\Pi(p_0)}}\simeq(p-p_0)[q_0-E(b)(p-c)]$$

$$-\frac{\phi_0}{2}(p-p_0)^2E[q_0-b(p_0-c)]^2, \tag{3.5}$$

or equivalently as

$$\frac{Eu[\Pi(p)]-u[\Pi(p_0)]}{du/d\Pi|_{\Pi(p_0)}}\simeq(p-p_0)\bigg\{q_0-(p-c)\bigg[E(b)$$

$$+\frac{\phi_0}{2}\frac{p-p_0}{p-c}\{(p_0-c)^2V(b)$$

$$+[q_0-E(b)(p_0-c)]^2\}\bigg]\bigg\}$$

$$=(p-p_0)\{q_0-(p-c)\beta(p)\}, \tag{3.6}$$

where $\beta(p)\lessgtr E(b)$ as $p\lessgtr p_0$, when $\phi_0>0$.

The expression for $\beta(p)$ plays the same role in (3.6) as in (2.7). In both

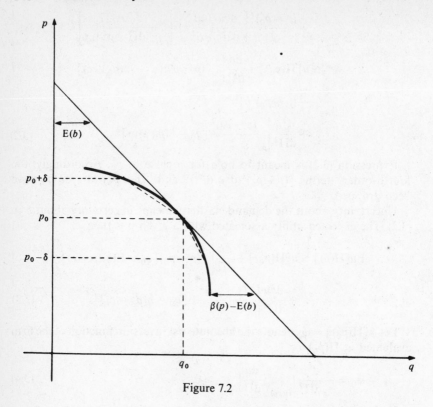

Figure 7.2

cases, the sign of $\beta(p) - E(b)$ is the sign of $(p - p_0)$. Unfortunately, the expression for $\beta(p)$ is much more complicated in (3.6) than in (2.7). (This is of course the reason for considering the special case first.) In (2.7), the difference $\beta(p) - E(b)$ is equal to a constant times the sign of the difference $p - p_0$; in (3.6), the difference $\beta(p) - E(b)$ is a non-linear function of $(p - p_0)$. In other words, the 'certainty equivalent' demand derivative $\beta(p)$ is not constant over half lines but moves away from $E(b)$ in a non-linear way as p moves away from p_0, see Figure 7.2.[1]

If changes in p (away from p_0) must take place in multiples of a certain 'unit' δ, this non-linearity implies that $\beta(p_0 + \delta) - \beta(p_0) \neq \beta(p_0) - \beta(p_0 - \delta)$; finite differences will be evaluated as if the 'certainty equivalent' demand function had a kink at (p_0, q_0).

Maximisation of the left-hand side of (3.5) or (3.6) with respect to p is equivalent to maximisation of expected utility. A risk-neutral firm would simply maximise the first term on the right-hand side. This would also

---

[1]It is readily verified that $\beta(p)$ is a concave function of $p - p_0$. A few printing errors have been corrected in this section.

maximise $(p - p_0)[q_0 - E(b)(p - c)] - (\phi_0/2)(p - p_0)^2[q_0 - E(b)(p - c)]^2$, over the range where the quadratic approximation is valid. The remaining term, $-(\phi_0/2)(p - p_0)^2(p - c)^2 V(b)$, is maximal at $p = p_0$ and therefore pulls the optimal p towards p_0 in the case of a risk-averse firm. (This justifies the reference to sticky prices in the title of this note.)

References

Arrow, K.J. (1965). *Aspects of the theory of risk bearing*, Helsinki: Yrjö Jahnsson Foundation

Drèze, J.H. and F. Modigliani (1972). Consumption decisions under uncertainty, *Journal of Economic Theory*, 5: 308–35 (Chapter 9 infra.)

Drèze, J.H. (1979). Human capital and risk-bearing, *Second annual lecture of the Geneva Association*, The Geneva Papers on Risk and Insurance, 12 (Chapter 17 infra.)

Moeseke, P. van (1965). Stochastic linear programming: A study in resource allocation under risk, *Yale Economic Essays*, 5: 196–254

Pratt, J. (1964). Risk aversion in the small and in the large, *Econometrica*, 32: 127–36

Sandmo, A. (1974). Two-period models of consumption decisions under uncertainty. In J.H. Drèze (ed.), *Allocation under uncertainty: Equilibrium and optimality*, London: Macmillan

Sweezy, P. (1939). Demand under conditions of oligopoly, *Journal of Political Economy*, 47: 568–73

III Consumer decisions

8   State-dependent utility, the demand for insurance and the value of safety[*]

Public projects increasing safety, or entailing risks of human deaths, have inescapably raised the question: 'How much should a society spend for the safety of its members?'; alternatively stated: 'What is the social value of a human life?' Answers provided by economists, public administrators and other scientists[1] have come to be classified under two headings: The 'human capital' approach and the 'willingness-to-pay' approach.[2] Broadly speaking, the first approach seeks an objective measure of the value of a person's life in his or her earning ability, whereas the second approach takes as its starting point the person's subjective tastes. Some of the literature is directed towards relating the two approaches and in particular towards formulating assumptions under which a person's human capital provides a lower bound to the value placed by that person on his/her life.

It seems to be now generally recognised that 'willingness-to-pay' is the logical approach to assessing the benefits of public safety. The approach becomes operational when coupled with the modern theory of public expenditure, initiated by Samuelson (1954). Yet, the methodological foundations of the subjective approach – state-dependent preferences – do not seem to be universally understood, leaving room for occasional doubt or error. This chapter starts (Section 1) with a review of these foundations, which involve preferences revealed through gambling, insurance and life

*Paper prepared with Pierre Dehez for the Geneva Conference on *The Value of Life and Safety*, Geneva, March–April 1981. The authors are grateful to Paul Champsaur and Denis Moffet for interesting discussions and helpful suggestions.
[1]The contributors known to us include medical doctors, actuaries, sociologists, civil engineers, statisticians, economists,....
[2]See Jones-Lee (1976) and Linnerooth (1979) for a survey of the literature.

protection. The economics of individual demand for insurance and safety are the subjects of Sections 2 and 3 respectively. The 'public goods' aspect is taken up briefly in Section 4.[3]

Decisions affecting survival probabilities should preferably be analysed in an intertemporal framework. But such an analysis is at once quite complicated, and methodological issues are more conveniently discussed in the simpler static framework used here.

1 Revealed preferences and expected utility

1.1 State-dependent utility

Economic choices affecting survival probabilities are of necessity choices with uncertain consequences; they must accordingly be studied within the framework of a theory of decision-making under uncertainty. The behavioural theory of 'expected utility' (or 'moral expectation'), in the modern treatment due to von Neumann and Morgenstern (1947) and Savage (1954), provides the starting point for developing such a framework.

In its simplest form, it concerns an individual choosing among bets $b, b', \ldots$, involving sums of money $w_i, w'_i, \ldots$, staked on events i generated by random devices with objectively known probabilities p_i. The other circumstances affecting the person (health and wealth, the prices at which money buys commodities, family status and so on) are taken as given and unaffected by the bets. The theory defines axiomatically 'consistent behaviour': Choices among arbitrary bets should be well defined and transitive; if two bets stake identical prizes on some events, the choice among these bets is unaffected by identical modifications of the common prizes ('strong independence' axiom or 'sure-thing principle'). Under a technical continuity assumption, these axioms lead to the 'moral expectation theorem':

(i)   There exists a real-valued function of money wealth, $u(w)$, called utility, such that a bet b entailing a higher level of expected utility is always preferred to a bet b' entailing a lower level of expected utility; that is

$$\sum_i p_i u(w_i) > \sum_i p_i u(w'_i) \quad \text{if and only if } b \text{ is preferred to } b'.$$

(ii)   The function u is defined up to positive linear transformations; that is $v(w) = \alpha + \beta u(w), \beta > 0$, is also a utility.

---

[3]We draw freely on the contents of an earlier paper by one of us (Drèze, 1962). That paper, published in the *Revue Française de Recherche Opérationnelle*, apparently contains the first exposition of the 'willingness-to-pay' approach. It did influence the work of Michael Jones-Lee (1976), but seems to have otherwise escaped attention, so that some repetition may be in order.

It should be emphasised that no other interpretation is proposed for *u* besides the fact that it represents correctly the choices among bets, made by a particular person under given circumstances.

The extension to choices involving consequences more diversified than payments of money, staked on events more substantive than the outcomes of random devices, requires some care. Suppose, for example, that a person setting out for a day of sailing is offered two 'bets', of which the first promises a pint of beer if the day is warm and a bowl of soup if the day is cold; whereas the second promises a pint of beer if the day is cold and a bowl of soup if the day is warm. No valid analysis of this situation could ignore the obvious point that 'beer on a hot day' and 'beer on a chilly day' are two different 'consequences'. Similarly, in the analysis of life insurance, one cannot ignore the obvious point that 'an indemnity in case of death' is not the same consequence as 'an indemnity in case of life'.

We shall not treat here the case where the definition of consequences includes references to events with unknown, subjective probabilities.[4] Assuming that probabilities are objectively known entails a drastic simplification (at a logical, not only technical level), and enables us to concentrate attention on the utility aspects, which are our primary concern.

Consider the simple case of two events, the event of life indexed $i = 1$, and the event of death, indexed $i = 0$. (These two events could be associated with the outcome of the sailing trip mentioned above...) Recognising that payments of money in case of life, and payments of money in case of death, are different 'consequences', we begin with the definition of two utility functions for money wealth, $u_1(w_1)$ for the case of life and $u_0(w_0)$ for the case of death. Each of these reflects (is constructed from) *conditional bets* involving sums of money staked on occurrences generated by a random device. Thus, $u_1(w_1)$ is constructed from bets conditioned on the event of life: if and only if you ('the person') return safely from the sailing trip, a roulette wheel is to be spun, and according to the outcome you receive prizes w_{1i} with probabilities p_i. It is assumed that 'you' make consistent choices among such bets, i.e. (conditional) choices that can be represented by a (conditional) function $u_1(w_1)$, *defined up to a positive linear transformation*.

Similarly, $u_0(w_0)$ is constructed from bets conditioned on the event of death: if and only if you die at sea, a roulette wheel is to be spun, and your heirs receive prizes w_{0i} with probabilities p_i. Again, $u_0(w_0)$ is thereby defined *up to a positive linear transformation*.

So far, we have simply applied the expected utility theory of von Neumann and Morgenstern to conditional bets. We have constructed two utility functions, say $\alpha_1 + \beta_1 u_1(w_1)$ and $\alpha_0 + \beta_0 u_0(w_0)$, with $\alpha_1, \beta_1, \alpha_0$ and β_0 still undefined ($\beta_1 > 0, \beta_0 > 0$). And we are assuming that the two events (life and death) have known probabilities p_1, p_0, with $p_1 + p_0 = 1$.

As a next step, we can introduce choices among money payments staked

---

[4]See Drèze (1961), Karni *et al.* (1983) and the references cited there.

upon the events 'life' and 'death'. A simple example is the straight life insurance contract whereby 'you' pay (now) a premium y to receive an indemnity 1 (at the end of the day) in case of death.[5] Suppose that, for $y = \bar{y}$, you are *indifferent* between signing and not signing such a contract. We will then *define* your 'utility gain' in case of death, $\alpha_0 + \beta_0 u_0(w_0 + 1 - \bar{y}) - \alpha_0 - \beta_0 u_0(w_0) = \beta_0[u_0(w_0 + 1 - \bar{y}) - u_0(w_0)]$, weighted by its probability p_0, as equal to your 'utility loss' in case of life, $\beta_1[u_1(w_1) - u_1(w_1 - \bar{y})]$, weighted by its probability $p_1 = 1 - p_0$:

$$p_0\beta_0[u_0(w_0 + 1 - \bar{y}) - u_0(w_0)]$$
$$+ (1 - p_0)\beta_1[u_1(w_1 - \bar{y}) - u_1(w_1)] = 0 \tag{1.1}$$

$$\frac{\beta_0}{\beta_1} = \frac{1 - p_0}{p_0} \frac{u_1(w_1) - u_1(w_1 - \bar{y})}{u_0(w_0 + 1 - \bar{y}) - u_0(w_0)}. \tag{1.2}$$

Consistency requires that the ratio β_0/β_1 be independent of the particular insurance contract used to define it, so long as indifference prevails. Denoting the right-hand side of (1.2) by r_β, we have that $\beta_0 = r_\beta\beta_1$, so that the utility in case of death is $\alpha_0 + r_\beta\beta_1 u_0(w_0)$.[6]

It should be emphasised that no other interpretation is proposed for r_β besides the fact that it represents correctly the choices made among insurance contracts.

The final step consists in offering the person (you) an opportunity to reduce the probability of death, say from p_0 to $p_0 - \delta$, by acquiring a special safety equipment at a cost x. Suppose that, for $x = \bar{x}$, you are indifferent between acquiring and not acquiring the equipment. We will then *define* your expected utility gain, through higher safety, $\delta[\alpha_1 + \beta_1 u_1(w_1 - \bar{x}) - \alpha_0 - r_\beta\beta_1 u_0(w_0 - \bar{x})]$, as equal to your expected utility loss due to the cost $\bar{x}$,[7]

$$p_0 r_\beta\beta_1[u_0(w_0) - u_0(w_0 - \bar{x})] + (1 - p_0)\beta_1[u_1(w_1) - u_1(w_1 - \bar{x})];$$

thus

$$p_0[\alpha_0 + r_\beta\beta_1 u_0(w_0)] + (1 - p_0)[\alpha_1 + \beta_1 u_1(w_1)]$$
$$= (p_0 - \delta)[\alpha_0 + r_\beta\beta_1 u_0(w_0 - \bar{x})]$$
$$+ (1 - p_0 + \delta)[\alpha_1 + \beta_1 u_1(w_1 - \bar{x})], \tag{1.3}$$

$$\alpha_0 - \alpha_1 = \beta_1 u_1(w_1 - \bar{x}) - r_\beta\beta_1 u_0(w_0 - \bar{x})$$
$$+ \frac{1}{\delta}[p_0 r_\beta\beta_1\{u_0(w_0 - \bar{x}) - u_0(w_0)\}$$
$$+ (1 - p_0)\beta_1\{u_1(w_1 - \bar{x}) - u_1(w_1)\}]. \tag{1.4}$$

[5] Your wealth is thus reduced from w_1 to $w_1 - y$ in case of life, but increased from w_0 to $w_0 + 1 - y$ in case of death.

[6] It should be clear from equation (1.2) that an unknown p_0 raises a logical difficulty; indeed (1.2) is then a relation between the products $p_0\beta_0$ and $p_1\beta_1$, and provides no information on the ratio β_0/β_1 as distinct from the ratio p_0/p_1.

[7] This is an expectation, because it takes on different values under life and death respectively.

Consistency requires that the difference $\alpha_0 - \alpha_1$ be independent of the particular safety gain used to define it, so long as indifference prevails. Denoting the right-hand side of (1.4) by $d_\alpha \beta_1$, we have that $\alpha_0 = \alpha_1 + d_\alpha \beta_1$, so that the utility in case of death is $\alpha_1 + \beta_1 [d_\alpha + r_\beta u_0(w_0)]$.

It should be emphasised that no other interpretation is proposed for d_α besides the fact that it represents correctly the choices made among safety levels. We return to this important point below.

Putting pieces together, and using again the moral expectation theorem, we have a representation of choices in terms of an expected utility which is state-dependent and defined up to a *single* positive linear transformation, namely:

$$
\begin{aligned}
Eu(w_0, w_1; p_0, \alpha_1, \beta_1) \\
= p_0[\alpha_1 + \beta_1\{d_\alpha + r_\beta u_0(w_0)\}] + (1 - p_0)[\alpha_1 + \beta_1 u_1(w_1)] \\
= \alpha_1 + \beta_1[p_0\{d_\alpha + r_\beta u_0(w_0)\} + (1 - p_0)u_1(w_1)].
\end{aligned} \tag{1.5}
$$

The choices of origin and unit of scale for u_0 and u_1 have been arbitrary throughout – for instance, $u_0(0) = u_1(0) = 0$; $u_0(1) = u_1(1) = 1$. The choice of α_1 and β_1 is still open, and there is no loss of generality in setting $\alpha_1 = 0$, $\beta_1 = 1$, so that

$$
Eu(w_0, w_1; p_0) = p_0[d_\alpha + r_\beta u_0(w_0)] + (1 - p_0)u_1(w_1). \tag{1.6}
$$

The important point is that d_α and r_β are *uniquely* defined (given our conventions) by (1.2) and (1.4), and relate unambiguously the origins and units of scale of u_0 and u_1. *No additional degree of freedom is left to rescale or relocate either u_0 or u_1 separately.* We emphasise this feature because it is overlooked in a number of otherwise valuable contributions to the literature.[8]

1.2 Willingness-to-pay for safety

Formula (1.6) is the more general formulation of the expected utility approach to the valuation of survival probabilities, as introduced by Drèze (1962) and given by Bergström (1978), Cook and Graham (1977) and Jones-Lee (1974, 1976). It is usually presented in the form

$$
Eu(w_0, w_1; p_0) = p_0 u_0(w_0) + (1 - p_0)u_1(w_1) \tag{1.7}
$$

without explicit reference to d_α and r_β. It must then be understood that the respective scalings of u_0 and u_1 satisfy (1.2) and (1.4). That is, if $u_1(0) = 0$, $u_1(1) = 1$, then $u_0(0) = d_\alpha$, $u_0(1) = d_\alpha + r_\beta$ as defined there. The only other

---

[8]See, for instance, Linnerooth (1979): 'The utility of the state of death can be arbitrarily set at zero...' (p. 60); 'Without any loss in generality the level of consumption at which a person can no longer survive can be set at zero...' (p. 61); 'Again without any loss in generality the utility of this point can be arbitrarily set at zero' (p. 64).

standard restriction placed on u_0 and u_1 is concavity – i.e. risk aversion.[9]

This formulation is consistent with the propositions that a reduction of p_0 by δ increases expected utility by $\delta[u_1(w_1) - u_0(w_0)]$, if w_0 and w_1 are taken as given; and that such a reduction, accompanied with a reduction of both w_0 and w_1 by $\bar{x}$, leaves expected utility unchanged. But these propositions are tautological, to the extent that they merely retrieve a step in the construction of (1.7).

In other words, the magnitude of $\bar{x}$ is *in no way* restricted by the abstract formulation (1.7): *A person's willingness-to-pay for increased safety is a matter for that person to decide*; the consistency axioms underlying (1.7) have no implications whatever for that decision. *This is precisely as it should be*, considering the variety of motives which may influence the decision. Thus, a rich bachelor without heirs may still be unwilling to buy additional safety at any positive price, thereby suggesting that he goes through life without enjoying it at all and would just as well face death as a reduction in his lavish (but unrewarding) consumption standard. At the same time, a poor widow working overtime to keep her children at subsistence might decline a well-paid but riskier job, thereby suggesting that she does not want to take chances with her children becoming orphans.

Yet, additional assumptions about either behaviour, or market opportunities, or both enable the theorist to draw some implications from the abstract formulation (1.7). Such assumptions, and their implications, are considered in Sections 2 and 3.

2 The demand for insurance

2.1 Model and assumptions

State-dependent utility functions provide the proper tool to study the demand for insurance, when the indemnities are staked on events which are relevant for the definition of final consequences (events which affect preferences). Life insurance is an obvious example – see Drèze (1962). Insurance of irreplaceable commodities, like heirlooms, is another example – see Cook and Graham (1977).

To study the demand for insurance – which has some implications for the demand for safety – we retain and simplify the notation of Section 1, in particular of (1.7):

$$Eu(w_0, w_1; p) = pu_0(w_0) + (1 - p)u_1(w_1), \qquad (2.1)$$

where w_0 is 'wealth in case of death', w_1 is 'wealth in case of life' and $p(= p_0,$ subscript omitted) is the probability of death. Denoting non-human wealth

---

[9]For a justification of the concavity assumption based on the existence of opportunities for gambling at nearly fair odds, see Drèze (1971, Section 2.1) and Raiffa (1968, Section 4.13).

by w, we write $w_0 = w + a_0$ and $w_1 = w + a_1$. About u_0 and u_1, we make the following assumption:

Assumption 2.1: u_0 and u_1 are twice differentiable non-decreasing concave functions; u_1 is strictly increasing.

Differentiability is assumed for convenience, so that we can use derivatives instead of the heavier formalism of subgradients. Concavity is justified by the existence of opportunities to gamble at (nearly) fair odds; see the references in footnote 9. We assume that more wealth is strictly preferred to less wealth in case of life, whereas more wealth is preferred or indifferent to less wealth in case of death. Our comments will be geared to the more typical situation where u_0 is strictly increasing.

Both u_0 and u_1 depend upon other variables which are kept constant, and ignored, in our static analysis. In particular, they depend upon future contingencies; the conditional probabilities of which (given the states of death 0 or life 1) are assumed constant. Thus, u_0 and u_1 may be viewed as well-defined conditional expected utilities (where the expectation is taken over the future contingencies).

We wish to study insurance contracts, involving the definite payment of an initial premium y, giving right to a gross indemnity $k(y; p)$ in case of death. For the holder of such a contract, expected utility is given by

$$Eu(y) = pu_0(w_0 + k(y; p) - y) + (1 - p)u_1(w_1 - y). \tag{2.2}$$

An optimal policy corresponds to the value of y for which (2.2) is maximal. Properties of optimal policies stand out more clearly under the following assumptions, motivated by convenience:

Assumption 2.2

$$\lim_{w \to 0} u'_1(w) = \infty.$$

Assumption 2.3

$$k(y; p) = \frac{\alpha}{p} y.$$

Assumption 2.2 guarantees that y maximising (2.2) is strictly less than w_1, thereby dispensing with the need to introduce a liquidity constraint explicitly. Assumption 2.3 introduces the standard stipulation that price is independent of quantity. The parameter α is an index of *fairness*. When $\alpha = 1$, insurance is fair in the sense that $pk(y; p) = y$. The premium is equal to the actuarial value of the policy. For $\alpha > 1$ (resp. < 1), the insurance is more than fair (resp. less than fair). Although the loading factor typically results in less than fair insurance, still tax provisions may restore fairness – see Jones-Lee (1976). Some implications of fairness are exhibited below.

2.2 General theory

Necessary and sufficient conditions for an optimal insurance contract, i.e. for a maximum of (2.2), are:

$$(\alpha - p)u_0'\left(w_0 + \frac{\alpha}{p}y - y\right) - (1 - p)u_1'(w_1 - y) = 0; \tag{2.3}$$

$$D =_{\text{def}} (\alpha - p)^2 u_0''\left(w_0 + \frac{\alpha}{p}y - y\right) + p(1 - p)u_1''(w_1 - y) \leqslant 0. \tag{2.4}$$

Under Assumption 2.1, the second-order condition is automatically satisfied. If it were stipulated that y must be non-negative, condition (2.3) should be replaced by

$$y[(\alpha - p)u_0' - (1 - p)u_1'] = 0, \quad (\alpha - p)u_0' - (1 - p)u_1' \leqslant 0. \tag{2.5}$$

The first-order condition implies

Proposition 2.1

(i)   Under (2.3), $u_1' - u_0' \gtrless 0$ according as $\alpha \gtrless 1$.
(ii)   Under (2.5), $\alpha \geqslant 1$ implies $u_0' \leqslant u_1'$.
(iii)   When $\alpha \leqslant 1$ (resp. $\alpha = 1$), then $y > 0$ only if (resp. if and only if) $u_1'(w_1) < u_0'(w_0)$.

Implicit differentiation of (2.3) leads to the following formulae ($D \neq 0$):

$$\frac{\partial y}{\partial w_0} = \frac{-p(\alpha - p)u_0''}{D}, \quad \frac{\partial y}{\partial w_1} = \frac{p(1 - p)u_1''}{D}; \tag{2.6}$$

$$\frac{\partial y}{\partial w} = \frac{\partial y}{\partial w_0} + \frac{\partial y}{\partial w_1} = p(1 - p)u_1'\left(\frac{u_1''}{u_1'} - \frac{u_0''}{u_0'}\right)\bigg/ D; \tag{2.7}$$

$$\frac{\partial y}{\partial p} = \left[p(u_0' - u_1') + (\alpha - p)\frac{\alpha}{p}yu_0''\right]\bigg/ D$$

$$= \left[p\frac{1 - \alpha}{1 - p}u_0' + (\alpha - p)\frac{\alpha}{p}yu_0''\right]\bigg/ D; \tag{2.8}$$

$$\frac{\partial\left(\frac{\alpha}{p}y - y\right)}{\partial p} = \left[\frac{\alpha - p}{1 - p}(1 - \alpha)u_0' - \frac{\alpha}{p}y(1 - p)u_1''\right]\bigg/ D$$

$$= \left[1 - \alpha + \frac{\alpha}{p}y(1 - p)\left(-\frac{u_1''}{u_1'}\right)\right]u_1'\bigg/ D; \tag{2.9}$$

$$\frac{\partial y}{\partial \alpha} = \frac{-[pu_0' + (\alpha - p)yu_0'']}{D}; \tag{2.10}$$

$$\frac{\partial\left(\dfrac{\alpha}{p}y - y\right)}{\partial\alpha} = \frac{[(1-p)yu_1'' - (\alpha - p)u_0']}{D};$$

(2.11)

$$\left.\frac{\partial y}{\partial p}\right|_{\alpha/p = \text{constant}} = -\frac{u_1'}{D}.$$

(2.12)

The main implications of these formulae are:

Proposition 2.2: Under (2.3) and strict risk aversion ($D < 0$):

(i) $\dfrac{\partial y}{\partial w_0} \leqslant 0, \ 0 \leqslant \dfrac{\partial y}{\partial w_1} \leqslant 1, \ \dfrac{\partial y}{\partial w} \leqslant 1, \ \dfrac{\partial y}{\partial w} \gtrless 0$ according as $-\dfrac{u_1''}{u_1'} \gtrless -\dfrac{u_0''}{u_1'}$;

(ii) $-1 \leqslant \dfrac{\partial\left(\dfrac{\alpha}{p}y - y\right)}{\partial w_0} \leqslant 0; \ \alpha \geqslant 2p$ implies $\dfrac{\partial y}{\partial w_0} \geqslant -1$;

(iii) $\dfrac{\partial y}{\partial p} > 0$ if and only if $-\left(w_0 + \dfrac{\alpha}{p}y - y\right)\dfrac{u_0''}{u_0'} > (1-\alpha)\dfrac{p}{1-p}\dfrac{w_0 + \dfrac{\alpha}{p}y - y}{\dfrac{\alpha}{p}y - y}$;

$\alpha \geqslant 1$ implies $\dfrac{\partial y}{\partial p} \geqslant 0; \ \left.\dfrac{\partial y}{\partial p}\right|_{\alpha/p = \text{constant}} > 0$;

(iv) $\dfrac{\partial\left(\dfrac{\alpha}{p}y - y\right)}{\partial p} \leqslant 0$ if $\alpha \leqslant 1$;

(v) $\dfrac{\partial y}{\partial\alpha} < 0$ if and only if $-\left(w_0 + \dfrac{\alpha}{p}y - y\right)\dfrac{u_0''}{u_0'} > \dfrac{w_0 + \dfrac{\alpha}{p}y - y}{\dfrac{\alpha}{p}y - y} \geqslant 1$;

$\dfrac{\partial y}{\partial\alpha} < 0$ implies $\dfrac{\partial y}{\partial p} > 0$;

(vi) $\dfrac{\partial\left(\dfrac{\alpha}{p}y - y\right)}{\partial\alpha} > 0; \ \left(-\dfrac{u_0''}{u_0'}\right) \leqslant \left(-\dfrac{u_1''}{u_1'}\right)$ implies $\dfrac{\partial\left(\dfrac{\alpha}{p}y\right)}{\partial\alpha} > 0.$

The first of these propositions is straightforward. The demand for insurance increases with wealth in case of life (say labour income), and decreases with wealth in case of death (say survivors' annuity); an increase in non-human wealth w is never spent entirely on insurance; because such an increase raises w_0, it may even lead to less insurance if (but only if) death strengthens risk aversion.

Two measures of risk aversion, introduced by Arrow (1971) and Pratt (1964), are commonly used. Absolute risk aversion is measured by $R^A = -u''/u'$ ('twice the risk premium per unit of variance, for infinitesimal risks'). Relative risk aversion is measured by $R^R = -w(u''(w)/u'(w))$, a quantity that has the advantage of being dimensionless.[10] Clearly, both measures may differ when evaluated from u_0 or u_1 respectively.

[10]Reasonable values of R^R suggested in the literature range from 1 (characterising logarithmic

When $R_0^A > R_1^A$, an increase in non-human wealth w reduces the purchase of insurance because, then, the marginal utility of w decreases faster in case of death than in case of life.

Somewhat surprising is the fact that an increase in w_0 could possibly lead to a *larger* reduction of the amount y spent on insurance ($\partial y/\partial w_0 < -1$). However, the second proposition indicates that the reduction in *net insurance benefits* never exceeds the reduction in w_0, and this is the more relevant comparison. When $p > \alpha/2$, ($p > \frac{1}{2}$ in case of fair insurance), then the premium exceeds the net benefit ($y > (\alpha/p)y - y$). An increase in w_0 matched by an equivalent reduction in net benefits (leaving final wealth in case of death unchanged) would be accompanied by a larger reduction in y.

The effect on y of an increase in the probability of death p is unambiguously positive if one assumes that the terms of the insurance contract (α/p) remain unchanged. (An optimally insured person taking up a new risky activity covered under the terms of his policy should increase the amount of converage.) However, when the terms of the policy are adjusted to the increase in p

$$\left(\frac{d(\alpha/p)}{dp} = \frac{-\alpha}{p^2} \right)$$

then the sign of $\partial y/\partial p$ remains unambiguously non-negative in case of fair insurance, but depends upon the degree of risk aversion when insurance is less than fair.

Proposition 2.2 (iii) states that an increase in death probability, fully reflected in the terms of the insurance contract, leads to an increase in the amount spent on insurance if and only if R_0^R, the relative risk-aversion measure in case of death, exceeds a certain quantity. For α not too far from unity and p not too far from zero, this quantity is apt to be small, suggesting again an increase in y when p increases. The role of R_0^R is understandable, considering that wealth in case of death,

$$w_0 + \frac{\alpha}{p}y - y,$$

would decrease by an amount $(\alpha/p^2)ydp$ if p increased without y being adjusted; how markedly this decrease affects u_0' (u_1' unchanged) matters, and is measured by R_0^A or R_0^R.

Using formula (2.9), proposition 2.2(iv) states that the net insurance benefit $(\alpha/p)y - y$ is a decreasing function of p whenever insurance is less than fair. In case of fair or more than fair insurance, the effect depends upon R_1^A or R_1^R. This is again understandable since unchanged benefits would require a higher y, hence a lower $w_1 - y$, affecting u_1' (u_0' unchanged) to an extent measured by R_1^A or R_1^R.

---

utility functions – see Arrow (1971)) to 2 (rationalising some observed portfolio choices – see Blume and Friend (1975)) or more (if one wishes to rationalise low deductibles in property or liability insurance – see Drèze (1981)).

Propositions 2.2(v) and 2.2(vi) consider the effect of the 'degree of fairness' α on the premium y and the net benefits $(\alpha/p)y - y$. It is seen that a reduction of the loading factor always leads to more net coverage. The effect on the premium paid may go in either direction, because the savings due to increased fairness may offset the costs of increased coverage. The premium will invariably be reduced when

$$R_0^R \geqslant \frac{w_0 + \dfrac{\alpha}{p}y - y}{\dfrac{\alpha}{p}y - y},$$

an inequality that may be expected to hold when the net benefits $(\alpha/p)y - y$ are a major component of wealth in case of death.

2.3 A special case

For the sake of completeness, we shall make reference to special circumstances where the premium takes the form of a deduction from w_1 *leaving w_0 unchanged*, i.e. a deduction from a_1. This is the case, in particular, for flight insurance bought at an airport with currency. If the plane crashes, it could well happen that whatever cash a passenger was carrying is also lost. In that case, the cost of insurance is zero in case of death. The optimal insurance corresponds to

$$\underset{y}{\text{Max}} \left[pu_0 \left(w_0 + \frac{\alpha}{p}y \right) + (1 - p)u_1(w_1 - y) \right] \tag{2.13}$$

with the first-order condition

$$y[\alpha u_0' - (1 - p)u_1'] = 0, \quad \alpha u_0' - (1 - p)u_1' \leqslant 0. \tag{2.14}$$

By implicit differentiation of this condition when $y > 0$, $D < 0$, we find

$$\frac{\partial y}{\partial p} = -\frac{u_1' + \dfrac{\alpha^2 y}{p^2}(-u_0'')}{\dfrac{\alpha^2}{p}u_0'' + (1 - p)u_1''} > 0. \tag{2.15}$$

Thus, in this case, the sign of $\partial y/\partial p$ is unambiguously positive. Further calculations reveal however that the sign of

$$\frac{\partial \dfrac{\alpha}{p}y}{\partial p}$$

is now ambiguous for all α and depends upon R_1^R.

As a side comment on this situation, it may be remarked that a passenger for whom $u_0'(w_0) = u_1'(w_1)$ would definitely buy flight insurance at a fair price, or at a less than fair price such that $\alpha > 1 - p$. Indeed, for such a passenger, (2.14) is violated at $y = 0$.[11]

3 The demand for safety

3.1 Willingness-to-pay

3.1.1: We now turn to the implications of consistent behaviour for an individual's demand for safety. This issue can be approached in two ways. First, one could assume that the probability of death p is a function of the expenses x incurred to 'buy safety': $p = p(x)$, $p' < 0$. Interest then centres on a characterisation of optimal expenditures on safety and of the impact on these expenditures of marginal changes in w_0, w_1 and p. Alternatively, one could define an individual's marginal willingness-to-pay for safety as the amount of wealth, here denoted ϕ, which would exactly compensate the individual for an infinitesimal increase in death probability, at a constant level of expected utility. Interest then centres on evaluation of the marginal willingness-to-pay for safety, and of the impact on this quantity of marginal changes in w_0, w_1 and p.

We begin with the characterisation of optimal expenditures, and the evaluation of the marginal willingness-to-pay, for safety. We consider first an individual who either carries no life insurance or carries a policy the terms of which (y and $(\alpha/p)y$) are kept constant in the face of a change in the safety level p; we turn next to an individual who carries an optimal life insurance policy, satisfying (2.3), the terms of which (y and $(\alpha/p)y$) are adjusted to a change in p. The 'comparative statics' analysis of changes in w_0, w_1 and p are treated in the (increasingly technical) Sections 3.2, 3.3 and 3.4.

Throughout, we shall use the following general expression for expected utility:

$$\mathrm{E}u(x, y) = p(x)u_0\left(w_0 + \frac{\alpha}{p}y - y - x\right) + [1 - p(x)]u_1(w_1 - y - x),$$

$$(3.1)$$

where the expenditures on safety, x, are deducted from both w_1 and w_0. Special cases are conveniently obtained by keeping y, $(\alpha/p)y$ and/or x fixed.

3.1.2: To begin with the simpler problem, assume that y and $(\alpha/p)y$ are given. Then optimal expenditures on safety are characterised by the first and second-order conditions for a maximum of (3.1) with respect to x, namely[12]

---

[11]The fact that the cash used to pay the premium would have been lost in case of a plane crash explains why our results are at variance with those obtained by Eisner and Strotz (1961).

[12]If it were stipulated that x must be non-negative as well as the arguments of u_0 and u_1, then equation (3.2) should be generalised, in the same manner that (2.3) was.

$$p'(u_0 - u_1) - pu_0' - (1 - p)u_1' = 0; \tag{3.2}$$

$$\Delta = 2p'(u_1' - u_0') + pu_0'' + (1 - p)u_1'' + p''(u_0 - u_1) \leqslant 0. \tag{3.3}$$

We return below to the second-order condition. As for (3.2), it is helpful to rewrite it as[13]

$$\frac{-1}{p'} = \frac{u_1 - u_0}{Eu'} \tag{3.4}$$

where $Eu' = pu_0' + (1 - p)u_1'$. The right-hand side of (3.4) is also the general expression for marginal willingness-to-pay for safety:

$$\phi = \frac{dw}{dp}\bigg|_{\overline{Eu}} = -\frac{\partial Eu}{\partial p}\bigg/\frac{\partial Eu}{\partial w} = \frac{u_1 - u_0}{Eu'}. \tag{3.5}$$

Hence, at the optimal level of expenditures on safety, the marginal willingness-to-pay is equal to the marginal cost of safety, i.e. to the reciprocal of the marginal product $(-p')$ of expenses on safety.

When (3.4) holds, ϕ is positive $(p' < 0)$. In general, ϕ is positive whenever suicide is undesirable $(u_1 > u_0)$. A sharper conclusion is reached under the minimal assumption that suicide is never desirable when the pecuniary consequences of death are not favourable:

Assumption 3.1

$$u_1(w_1) > u_0(w_0) \quad \text{whenever } w_0 \leqslant w_1.$$

The conclusion is stated in proposition 3.1 below.

When (3.2) is satisfied, $u_1 > u_0$. Therefore, assuming non-increasing returns to safety expenditures $(p'' \geqslant 0)$, a sufficient condition for the second order condition to hold is $u_1' \geqslant u_0'$ (at the optimal level of expenditures), a condition satisfied when fair or more than fair insurance is available. As is shown in Appendix A.1, Eu is quasi-concave in w and p if

$$2(u_1 - u_0)(u_0' - u_1')Eu' + (u_1 - u_0)^2 Eu'' \leqslant 0 \tag{3.6}$$

where $Eu'' = pu_0'' + (1 - p)u_1''$. Quasi-concavity is therefore satisfied whenever $(u_1' - u_0')(u_1 - u_0) \geqslant 0$ everywhere.

3.1.3: When the individual carries a life insurance contract, the terms of which are adjusted to a change in p, then

$$\frac{\partial Eu}{\partial x} = p'(u_0 - u_1) - pu_0'\left(1 + \frac{\alpha}{p^2}yp'\right) - (1 - p)u_1'. \tag{3.7}$$

---

[13]Equation (3.4) is a differential equivalent of (1.4), which could have been written as

$$\frac{1}{\delta} = \frac{-1}{dp} = \frac{u_1 - u_0}{dEu}.$$

The first-order condition for an optimal insurance coverage is still

$$(\alpha - p)u'_0 - (1 - p)u'_1 = 0,$$

implying $Eu' = \alpha u'_0$. Using this condition, and setting $\partial Eu/\partial x = 0$, we obtain:

$$\frac{-1}{p'} = \frac{u_1 - u_0}{Eu'} + \frac{y}{p} \tag{3.8}$$

the right-hand side being equal to ϕ, the marginal willingness-to-pay for safety. It now includes an additional term, reflecting the lower cost of insurance under reduced risks. In Appendix A.2, it is shown that the second-order conditions are satisfied when $\alpha = 1$. In Appendix A.3, it is shown that when $\alpha = 1$, Eu is quasi-concave in w and p.

Proposition 3.1: Under assumption 3.1, (3.8) implies

$$\phi \geq \frac{\alpha - p}{\alpha(1 - p)}(w_1 - w_0) + \frac{1 - \alpha}{1 - p}\frac{y}{p} = \frac{u'_1}{Eu'}\left(w_1 - w_0 - \frac{\alpha y}{p}\right) + \frac{y}{p} \tag{3.9}$$

whereas (3.5) implies

$$\phi \geq \frac{u'_1}{Eu'}\left(w_1 - w_0 - \frac{\alpha y}{p}\right). \tag{3.10}$$

Proof: By concavity of u_1 (assumption 2.1):

$$u_1(w_1 - y - x) \geq u_1\left(w_0 + \frac{\alpha y}{p} - y - x\right) + \left(w_1 - w_0 - \frac{\alpha y}{p}\right)$$
$$\times u'_1(w_1 - y - x),$$

$$\frac{u_1 - u_0}{Eu'} \geq \frac{u_1\left(w_0 + \dfrac{\alpha y}{p} - y - x\right) - u_0\left(w_0 + \dfrac{\alpha y}{p} - y - x\right)}{Eu'}$$
$$+ \left(w_1 - w_0 - \frac{\alpha y}{p}\right)\frac{u'_1}{Eu'};$$

using assumption 3.1,

$$\frac{u_1 - u_0}{Eu'} \geq \left(w_1 - w_0 - \frac{\alpha y}{p}\right)\frac{u'_1}{Eu'}.$$

This establishes (3.10). When (2.3) holds,

$$\frac{u'_1}{Eu'} = \frac{\alpha - p}{\alpha(1 - p)},$$

and (3.8) implies

$$\phi = \frac{u_1 - u_0}{Eu'} + \frac{y}{p} \geqslant \frac{\alpha - p}{\alpha(1-p)}\left(w_1 - w_0 - \frac{\alpha y}{p}\right) + \frac{y}{p}$$

$$= \frac{\alpha - p}{\alpha(1-p)}(w_1 - w_0) + \frac{1-\alpha}{1-p}\frac{y}{p}. \qquad \square$$

This proposition entails *sufficient conditions under which 'a person's life is worth more than her human capital'.*[14]

It seems indeed natural to regard $w_1 - w_0$ as a measure of 'human capital'. *If insurance is available at fair odds*, then proposition 3.1 implies $\phi \geqslant w_1 - w_0$ – either through (3.9) with $y > 0$ and $\alpha = 1$, or through (3.10) with $y = 0$ and $u_1' \geqslant Eu'$ (see proposition 2.1).

It may seem surprising that assumption 3.1 is not in itself sufficient to establish that a person's life is worth more than his/her human capital. There are two reasons for this. First, one must reckon with insurance benefits. Of course, one could *define* 'human capital' *net of insurance benefits*, i.e.

$$w_1 - \left(w_0 + \frac{\alpha}{p}y\right).$$

Proposition 3.1 implies that

$$\phi \geqslant w_1 - w_0 - \frac{\alpha}{p}y$$

whenever $u_1' \geqslant Eu'$, i.e. whenever $u_1' \geqslant u_0'$. This brings up the second point. Safety is bought by reducing w_0 as well as w_1. When $u_0' > u_1'$, the 'opportunity cost' of safety bought from non-human wealth exceeds the opportunity cost in terms of human wealth – explaining why ϕ may fall short of human wealth.

Indeed, assume that safety could be bought from human wealth alone.[15] Then, under a fixed insurance contract, we have:

$$\left.\frac{dw_1}{dp}\right|_{Eu} = -\frac{\partial Eu}{\partial p}\Big/\frac{\partial Eu}{\partial w_1} = \frac{u_1 - u_0}{(1-p)u_1'} \geqslant \frac{w_1 - w_0 - \dfrac{\alpha y}{p}}{1-p}, \qquad (3.11)$$

implying

$$(1-p)\frac{dw_1}{dp} \geqslant w_1 - w_0 - \frac{\alpha y}{p}. \qquad (3.12)$$

---

[14] See Bergström (1978).
[15] As when a person boarding a plane rents a parachute against cash....

When the terms of the insurance contract are adjusted to changes in risk, (3.12) becomes

$$(1-p)\frac{dw_1}{dp} \geqslant w_1 - w_0 - \frac{\alpha-1}{\alpha-p}\frac{\alpha y}{p} \geqslant w_1 - w_0 - \frac{\alpha y}{p}. \qquad (3.13)$$

The expected value of the amount which an individual is willing to pay in case of life to reduce the probability of death is at least equal to human capital net of insurance benefits, under assumption 3.1.[16]

3.2 Comparative statics: optimal expenses

Turning to 'comparative statics', we consider first the effect of marginal changes in w_0, w_1 and p on optimal safety expenditures x, for a person who either carries no life insurance or carries a policy the terms of which (y and $(\alpha/p)y$) are kept constant. (The more general case of simultaneous adjustments in x and y is more complicated, and no definite conclusions emerge.) By a change in p, we mean an exogenous change in death probability which does not affect p'.

Implicit differentiation of (3.2) leads to the following formulae ($\Delta \neq 0$):

$$\frac{\partial x}{\partial w_0} = \frac{-p'u_0' + pu_0''}{\Delta}, \quad \frac{\partial x}{\partial w_1} = \frac{p'u_1' + (1-p)u_1''}{\Delta}; \qquad (3.14)$$

$$\frac{\partial x}{\partial w} = \frac{p'(u_1' - u_0') + pu_0'' + (1-p)u_1''}{\Delta}; \qquad (3.15)$$

$$\frac{\partial x}{\partial p} = \frac{-(u_1' - u_0')}{\Delta}. \qquad (3.16)$$

The main implications of these formulae are:

Proposition 3.2: Under (3.2) and (3.3) with $\Delta < 0$:

(i) $\dfrac{\partial x}{\partial w_0} \gtreqless 0$ according as $\dfrac{-u_0''}{u_0'} \gtreqless \dfrac{-p'}{p}$;

(ii) $\dfrac{\partial x}{\partial w_1} > 0$;

(iii) $u_1' - u_0' \geqslant 0$ implies $\dfrac{\partial x}{\partial w} > 0$;

(iv) $u_1' - u_0' \geqslant 0$ and $p'' \geqslant 0$ imply $\dfrac{\partial x}{\partial w} \leqslant 1$;

(v) $\dfrac{\partial x}{\partial p} \gtreqless 0$ according as $u_1' - u_0' \gtreqless 0$.

---

[16]This is precisely the proposition found in Bergström (1978), who uses assumption 3.1 in the guise of a 'thought experiment' involving a rentier cousin.

The sign of $\partial x/\partial w_0$ is ambiguous, because an increase in w_0 has two conflicting effects on the marginal rate of substitution in (3.5). It reduces the *numerator* by a quantity $- u'_0 dw_0$, thereby reducing the demand for safety (the pecuniary consequences of death are less deterring). But it also reduces the *denominator* by a quantity $pu''_0 dw_0$ (the expected marginal utility of wealth, which defines the opportunity cost of buying safety, decreases with w_0).

The sign of $\partial x/\partial w_1$ is positive, conforming to intuition; An increase in w_1 increases the numerator *and* reduces the denominator of the right-hand side in (3.5). When fair insurance is available, so that $u'_1 - u'_0$ is non-negative, an increase in non-human wealth induces additional spending on safety (iii). When safety is acquired at non-decreasing marginal cost ($p'' \geqslant 0$), the marginal propensity to spend on safety is less than one. Note also that $p'' = 0$ would imply

$$\frac{\partial x}{\partial w} = \frac{p'(u'_1 - u'_0) + \mathrm{E}u''}{2p'(u'_1 - u'_0) + \mathrm{E}u''} = \frac{1}{2} + \frac{1}{2}\frac{\mathrm{E}u''}{\Delta} \geqslant \frac{1}{2}, \tag{3.17}$$

i.e. a marginal propensity to spend on safety of at least one half. Notice that, for an individual carrying an optimal *fair* insurance policy ($u'_0 = u'_1$), the terms of which are not adjusted, $p'' = 0$ would even imply $\partial x/\partial w = 1$: An increment in non-human wealth would be spent entirely on safety! (This is because insurance is bought at constant marginal cost whereas safety is bought at increasing marginal cost, and consumption is subject to diminishing marginal utility.) Casual empiricism thus suggests strongly that if (3.2) holds, $p'' > 0$ and $p''(u_0 - u_1)$ is a non-negligible component of Δ.

When $\partial x/\partial p > 0$, the expenses incurred to buy additional safety would be reduced if the individual experienced an exogenous decrease in death probability and conversely. This plausible reaction is entirely due to the change in the expected marginal utility of wealth (the opportunity cost of buying safety), the sign of which is given by the sign of $u'_1 - u'_0$.

3.3 Comparative statics: fixed insurance contracts

We turn next to the effect of marginal changes in w_0, w_1 and p on the marginal willingness to pay for safety ϕ. We begin with the case of a person who either carries no life insurance or carries a policy the terms of which are kept constant. And we assume that expenditures on safety x are also kept constant.

Differentiating the right-hand side of (3.5), we find:

$$\frac{\partial \phi}{\partial w_0} = -\frac{u'_0 + \phi pu''_0}{\mathrm{E}u'}; \tag{3.18}$$

$$\frac{\partial \phi}{\partial w_1} = \frac{u'_1 - \phi(1 - p)u''_1}{\mathrm{E}u'}; \tag{3.19}$$

$$\frac{\partial \phi}{\partial w} = \frac{u'_1 - u'_0 - \phi[pu''_0 + (1-p)u''_1]}{Eu'};$$ (3.20)

$$\frac{\partial \phi}{\partial p} = \phi \frac{u'_1 - u'_0}{Eu'}.$$ (3.21)

These formulae enable us to state the counterpart of proposition 3.2:

Proposition 3.3: Under (3.5):

(i) $\dfrac{\partial \phi}{\partial w_0} \gtrless 0$ according as $\dfrac{-u''_0}{u'_0} \gtrless \dfrac{1}{p\phi}$;

(ii) $\dfrac{\partial \phi}{\partial w_1} > 0$;

(iii) $u'_1 - u'_0 \geqslant 0$ implies $\dfrac{\partial \phi}{\partial w} \geqslant 0$;

(iv) $u'_1 - u'_0 \geqslant 0$ implies $\dfrac{\partial \phi}{\partial w_1} \geqslant 1$;

(v) $\dfrac{\partial \phi}{\partial p} \gtrless 0$ according as $u'_1 - u'_0 \gtrless 0$.

These propositions follow from (3.18)–(3.21), upon remembering that $u'_1 \geqslant u'_0$ also implies $u'_1 \geqslant Eu'$. These inequalities always hold when insurance is available on fair (or more than fair) terms.

The sign of $\partial \phi / \partial w_0$ is ambiguous, for the same reasons which explained why the sign of $\partial x / \partial w_0$ is ambiguous. For the sake of completeness, we note that the marginal rate of substitution between w_1 and p, namely

$$\phi_1 =_{\text{def}} \frac{dw_1}{dp}\bigg|_{Eu} = -\frac{\partial Eu}{\partial p} \bigg/ \frac{\partial Eu}{\partial w_1} = \frac{u_1 - u_0}{(1-p)u'_1},$$ (3.22)

unambiguously decreases with w_0. Indeed, from (3.22),

$$\frac{\partial \phi_1}{\partial w_0} = \frac{-u'_0}{(1-p)u'_1} < 0.$$ (3.23)

Proposition 3.3(iv) may seem startling: When human wealth increases, willingness-to-pay for safety increases *even more*. However, this does not imply a marginal propensity to spend on safety of one or more. Indeed, the marginal propensity is defined by $\partial x / \partial w_1$, with the properties listed in proposition 3.2.

Proposition 3.3(v) states that marginal willingness-to-pay for safety decreases with safety, when fair insurance is available.

3.4 Comparative statics: adjusted insurance contracts

For a person who carries an optimal life-insurance policy, satisfying (2.3), the results of Section 3.3 need to be extended. The starting point is the definition of ϕ in (3.8), instead of (3.5). More importantly, differentiation of the right-hand side of (3.8) requires allowance for the adjustments in the insurance premium y, and the indemnity $(\alpha/p)y$, associated with changes in w_0, w_1 or p. The relevant expressions were given in formulae (2.6)–(2.8) above. Thus, (3.18) now takes the form

$$\frac{\partial \phi}{\partial w_0} = -\frac{u_0' + (\phi p - y)u_0''}{Eu'} + \frac{\partial \phi}{\partial y}\frac{\partial y}{\partial w_0}, \tag{3.24}$$

and similarly for (3.19)–(3.21). (Indeed, $\partial Eu/\partial y = 0$ does *not* imply $\partial \phi/\partial y = 0$.) Details of the calculations are given in Appendix A.4, where use is made of the first-order condition (2.3). The resulting formulae are ($D \neq 0$):

$$\frac{\partial \phi}{\partial w_0} = \frac{-1}{\alpha} + \frac{1-\alpha}{\alpha(1-p)}\frac{\partial y}{\partial w_0} - \alpha p(1-p)\frac{u_1 - u_0}{(Eu')^2}\frac{u_0''u_1''}{D}; \tag{3.25}$$

$$\frac{\partial \phi}{\partial w_1} = \frac{1}{\alpha} + \frac{\alpha-1}{\alpha(1-p)}\left(1 - \frac{\partial y}{\partial w_1}\right) - \alpha(\alpha-p)(1-p)\frac{u_1 - u_0}{(Eu')^2}\frac{u_0''u_1''}{D}; \tag{3.26}$$

$$\frac{\partial \phi}{\partial w} = \frac{\alpha-1}{\alpha(1-p)}\left(1 - \frac{\partial y}{\partial w}\right) - \alpha^2(1-p)\frac{u_1 - u_0}{(Eu')^2}\frac{u_0''u_1''}{D}; \tag{3.27}$$

$$\frac{\partial \phi}{\partial p} = \frac{\alpha-1}{\alpha(1-p)}\left[\frac{u_1 - u_0}{Eu'}\alpha(\alpha-p)\frac{u_0''}{D} - \frac{\partial y}{\partial p}\right]$$
$$+ \alpha^2(1-p)\frac{y}{p}\frac{u_1 - u_0}{(Eu')^2}\frac{u_0''u_1''}{D}. \tag{3.28}$$

These formulae enable us to state a partial counterpart to proposition 3.3. With optimal life insurance, the sign of $u_1' - u_0'$ is also the sign of $(\alpha - 1)$, since (2.3) implies

$$u_1' = \frac{\alpha - p}{1 - p}u_0'.$$

A positive sign thus corresponds to more than fair terms.

The absence of moral hazard requires that

$$u_1(w_1 - x - y) > u_0\left(w_0 + \frac{\alpha}{p}y - x - y\right). \tag{3.29}$$

This does not necessarily follow from assumption 3.1, when

$$w_0 + \frac{\alpha}{p}y > w_1.$$

Proposition 3.4: Under (3.8) and (3.29), with strict risk aversion $(D < 0)$:

(i) $\alpha \geqslant 1$ implies $\dfrac{\partial \phi}{\partial w_1} \geqslant \dfrac{1}{\alpha}$;

(ii) $\alpha \geqslant 1$ implies $\dfrac{\partial \phi}{\partial w} \geqslant 0$;

(iii) $\alpha = 1$ implies $\dfrac{\partial \phi}{\partial p} \leqslant 0$.

Propositions 3.3(i) and 3.3(ii) have no meaningful counterparts here. Propositions 3.3(iii) and 3.3(iv) are closely matched by propositions 3.4(i) and 3.4(ii). But 3.3(v) is much sharper than 3.4(iii). Also, 3.4(iii) is somewhat counter-intuitive. Combining 3.3(v) and 3.4(iii), we remark: For a person who is optimally insured on fair terms, or a person who is not insured due to unfair terms, marginal willingness-to-pay for safety *increases* with safety. Thus, assertions regarding the sign of $\partial \phi / \partial p$ must be carefully justified in terms of underlying assumptions.

4 The provision of public safety

4.1 General theory

Public projects increasing safety, or entailing risks of human deaths, affect simultaneously the survival probabilities of many individuals. In such contexts, public safety has all the properties of a pure public good.[17] An efficient provision of public safety is thus governed by the same principles as an efficient production of public goods. This viewpoint, implicitly adopted by Jones-Lee (1974, 1976) and Mishan (1971) in the guise of cost-benefit analysis, is developed formally by Bergström (1978).

Restating their analysis in the notation of the present paper, let N denote a set of individuals indexed by $i = 1, \ldots, n$, whose death probabilities p^i depend upon the level z of expenditures on public safety; and let t^i be the tax levied on individual i to finance these expenditures,

$$\sum_i t^i = z.$$

Then, omitting the explicit reference to x^i and y^i, we may rewrite (3.1) as

$$\mathrm{E}u^i = p^i(z)u_0^i(w_0^i - t^i) + [1 - p^i(z)]u_1^i(w_1^i - t^i). \tag{4.1}$$

A Pareto-efficient program of public expenditures z and taxes t^i, $i = 1, \ldots, n$, solves

$$\operatorname*{Max}_{z, \{t^i\}} \sum_i \lambda^i \{ p^i(z)u_0^i(w_0^i - t^i) + [1 - p^i(z)]u_1^i(w_1^i - t^i) \} - \lambda \left(\sum_i t^i - z \right), \tag{4.2}$$

---

[17]See Samuelson (1954) for the original presentation, and Milleron (1972) for an excellent survey of the relevant theory.

where λ is a Lagrange multiplier and where the non-negative multipliers $\{\lambda^i\}$ characterise a particular Pareto-optimum.[18] The first order conditions for a solution of (4.2) are

$$\sum_i \lambda^i \left[\frac{\partial p^i}{\partial z}(u_0^i - u_1^i) \right] + \lambda = 0; \tag{4.3}$$

$$- \lambda^i [p^i u_0^{i\prime} + (1 - p^i)u_1^{i\prime}] - \lambda = 0, \quad i = 1, \ldots, n. \tag{4.4}$$

Eliminating the multipliers between (4.3) and (4.4), we obtain

$$\sum_i \frac{\partial p^i}{\partial z} \frac{u_1^i - u_0^i}{\mathrm{E}u^{i\prime}} = -1. \tag{4.5}$$

Using the definition of ϕ^i in (3.5), thus taking the terms of all insurance contracts as given, we may also write (4.5) as

$$\sum_i \frac{\partial p^i}{\partial z} \phi^i = -1. \tag{4.6}$$

Let then

$$\sum_i \frac{\partial p^i}{\partial z} = \frac{\partial \sum_i p^i}{\partial z} =_{\mathrm{def}} \frac{-1}{c}, \tag{4.7}$$

so that

$$c = - \frac{\mathrm{d}z}{\mathrm{d}\sum_i p^i}$$

is the marginal cost of saving one life through public expenditures. Then,

$$c = \sum_i \frac{\partial p^i}{\partial z} \phi^i \Big/ \sum_i \frac{\partial p^i}{\partial z}$$

$$= \frac{1}{n} \sum_i \phi^i + \sum_i \phi^i \left(\frac{\frac{\partial p^i}{\partial z}}{\sum_i \frac{\partial p^i}{\partial z}} - \frac{1}{n} \right)$$

$$= \frac{1}{n} \sum_i \phi^i - c \, \mathrm{Cov}\left(\phi^i, \frac{\partial p^i}{\partial z} \right). \tag{4.8}$$

If the reductions in death probabilities $\partial p^i / \partial z$ are uncorrelated, across individuals, with the measures of willingness-to-pay ϕ^i, then (4.8) reduces to

[18]That is, the set of Pareto-optima is generated by letting the relative weights

$$\lambda^i / \sum_j \lambda^j$$

range over the unit simplex in R^n.

$$c = \frac{1}{n} \sum_i \phi^i =_{\text{def}} \bar{\phi}. \tag{4.9}$$

An efficient provision of public safety is obtained when the marginal cost of saving a life is equal to the average willingness-to-pay for safety of the population members. This proposition seems now well understood. Note, however, the role of the lump-sum tax levies in (4.4).

4.2 Influence of wealth

Two implications of this analysis seem worth mentioning, in relation to Sections 2 and 3. First, public safety is typically in the nature of a *local* public good.[19] Traffic lights, sidewalks, highway lights or coatings provide obvious examples. The condition (4.9) must then be applied to a local population N, which will be different in each case. It follows that society's marginal expenditure to save a life (society's valuation of life) will also be different in each case. In particular, assume that individual preferences (u_0^i, u_1^i) are identically distributed over individuals in two distinct populations N and N'; the distribution of ϕ^i, $i \in N$, will still differ from the distribution of ϕ^i, $i \in N'$, if the distributions of wealth (w_0^i, w_1^i) or the risk levels p^i differ between the two populations. More specifically, we have seen in propositions 3.3 and 3.4 that $\partial \phi^i / \partial w_1^i$ is positive, and greater than or equal to one if life insurance is available on fair terms. *We may then expect $\bar{\phi}$ to increase with the average value of human wealth in the relevant population.*

It is not surprising that society should be prepared to spend more in order to save a 'statistical life' when more 'human capital' is at stake.

Propositions 3.3 and 3.4 also tell us that $\partial \phi^i / \partial w^i$ is non-negative, when fair insurance is available. *We may then expect $\bar{\phi}$ to increase with the average level of non-human wealth in the relevant population.* This conclusion is less appealing on ethical grounds, since the non-human wealth is not itself in jeopardy. The conclusion follows from the greater willingness of wealthier individuals to 'buy safety'. This greater willingness would also normally be reflected in higher taxes t^i levied to finance the public expenditures at stake.

As for differences in risk levels, we have seen in Section 3 that the sign of $\partial \phi^i / \partial p^i$ is in general ambiguous, so that no definite conclusions emerge on that score.

4.3 Participation of insurance companies

Formula (4.9) is based on the assumption that the terms of all insurance contracts $(y^i, (\alpha/p^i)y^i)$ are given, and unaffected by public safety. And the formula was obtained without taking explicitly into account private expenditures on safety x^i.

[19]On this notion, see, for example, Greenberg (1977), Stiglitz (1977) and Tiebout (1956).

If we start from the more general formulation

$$\mathrm{E}u^i = p^i(z, x^i)u_0^i\left(w_0^i + \frac{\alpha}{p^i}y^i - y^i - x^i - t^i\right)$$
$$+ [1 - p^i(z, x^i)]u_1^i(w_1^i - y^i - x^i - t^i), \tag{4.10}$$

extend (4.2) accordingly and use the first-order conditions (2.3) and (3.8), then (4.5) becomes

$$\sum_i \frac{\partial p^i}{\partial z}\left[\frac{u_1^i - u_0^i}{\mathrm{E}u^{i\prime}} + \frac{y^i}{p^i}\right] = -1. \tag{4.11}$$

This still leads to (4.6)–(4.9), but with ϕ^i now given by (3.8) instead of (3.5). The implications for individual expenditures on insurance and safety follow from (2.8) and (3.16).

In the light of formula (4.11), it is natural to raise the following issue. If the terms of individual insurance contracts are *not* adjusted to improvements in public safety, then individuals will reveal a willingness-to-pay for safety ϕ^i equal to $(u_1^i - u_0^i)/\mathrm{E}u^{i\prime}$, whereas the true benefit to society includes an additional term y^i/p^i, reflecting the savings accruing to life insurance companies. Under fair insurance ($\alpha = 1$), the expected savings of the life insurance companies is precisely equal to

$$\sum_i \frac{\partial p^i}{\partial z}\frac{y^i}{p^i}.$$

Given that life-insurance contracts are typically based on mortality tables which are up-dated at irregular intervals, our analysis provides a justification for the participation of insurance companies in the financing of public expenditures on safety.

Appendix

A.1

Let us consider the following expected utility function

$$Eu = pu_0(w + a_0) + (1 - p)u_1(w + a_1). \tag{A.1}$$

We have

$$\frac{\partial Eu}{\partial p} = u_0 - u_1; \tag{A.2}$$

$$\frac{\partial Eu}{\partial w} = pu_0' + (1 - p)u_1' = Eu'; \tag{A.3}$$

$$\frac{\partial^2 Eu}{\partial p^2} = 0, \quad \frac{\partial^2 Eu}{\partial p \partial w} = u_0' - u_1', \quad \frac{\partial^2 Eu}{\partial w^2} = pu_0'' + (1 - p)u_1'' = Eu''. \tag{A.4}$$

The condition for quasi-concavity of Eu, namely $d^2 Eu|_{Eu} \leqslant 0$ takes the form:

$$\frac{\partial^2 Eu}{\partial p^2}\left(\frac{\partial Eu}{\partial w}\right)^2 - 2\frac{\partial^2 Eu}{\partial p \partial w}\frac{\partial Eu}{\partial p}\frac{\partial Eu}{\partial w} + \frac{\partial^2 Eu}{\partial w^2}\left(\frac{\partial Eu}{\partial p}\right)^2 \leqslant 0, \tag{A.5}$$

or

$$2(u_0' - u_1')(u_1 - u_0)Eu' + (u_1 - u_0)^2 Eu'' \leqslant 0. \tag{A.6}$$

A.2

The first partial derivatives of the expected utility function (3.1) are given by:

$$\frac{\partial Eu}{\partial x} = p'(u_0 - u_1) - Eu' - \frac{\alpha y}{p}u_0'p'; \tag{A.7}$$

176

$$\frac{\partial Eu}{\partial y} = (\alpha - p)u'_0 - (1-p)u'_1. \tag{A.8}$$

Let (x^*, y^*) denote a point where these derivatives are simultaneously equal to zero. At such a point, the second partial derivatives are given by:

$$\frac{\partial^2 Eu}{\partial x^2} = \alpha u'_0 \frac{p''}{p'} + (1-p)u''_1 + p\left(1 + \frac{\alpha y}{p^2}p'\right)^2 u''_0 + 2\frac{\alpha-1}{1-p}u'_0 p' \tag{A.9}$$

$$\frac{\partial^2 Eu}{\partial y^2} = \frac{(\alpha-p)^2}{p}u''_0 + (1-p)u''_1 \tag{A.10}$$

$$\frac{\partial^2 Eu}{\partial x \partial y} = \frac{\alpha-1}{1-p}u'_0 p' + (1-p)u''_1 - (\alpha-p)\left(1 + \frac{\alpha y}{p^2}p'\right)u''_0. \tag{A.11}$$

When $\alpha = 1$, the determinant of the Hessian matrix at (x^*, y^*) is

$$\frac{\partial^2 Eu}{\partial x^2}\frac{\partial^2 Eu}{\partial y^2} - \left(\frac{\partial^2 Eu}{\partial x \partial y}\right)^2 = \alpha\frac{p''}{p'}u'_0\frac{\partial^2 Eu}{\partial y^2}$$

$$+ \alpha^2 \frac{1-p}{p}\left(1 + y\frac{p'}{p}\right)^2 u''_0 u''_1. \tag{A.12}$$

Assuming that $p'' \geqslant 0$ and $\alpha = 1$, we have

$$\frac{\partial^2 Eu}{\partial x^2} \leqslant 0; \quad \frac{\partial^2 Eu}{\partial y^2} \leqslant 0; \quad \frac{\partial^2 Eu}{\partial x^2}\frac{\partial^2 Eu}{\partial y^2} - \left(\frac{\partial^2 Eu}{\partial x \partial y}\right)^2 \geqslant 0 \tag{A.13}$$

i.e. the second-order conditions are verified at (x^*, y^*).

A.3

Let us fix $\alpha = 1$ and consider the following expected utility function

$$Eu = pu_0\left(w + a_0 + \frac{1-p}{p}y(p,w)\right) + (1-p)u_1(w + a_1 - y(p,w)) \tag{A.14}$$

where $y = y(p, w)$ satisfies the optimality condition (2.3), i.e. $u'_0 = u'_1$. Following (2.7) and (2.8), we have

$$\frac{\partial y}{\partial p} = \frac{(1-p)yu''_0}{pD} \tag{A.15}$$

$$\frac{\partial y}{\partial w} = \frac{p(1-p)(u''_1 - u''_0)}{D} \tag{A.16}$$

with $D = (1-p)(pu''_1 + (1-p)u''_0)$, $D \neq 0$. The first and second partial derivatives of Eu are given by

$$\frac{\partial Eu}{\partial p} = (u_0 - u_1) - \frac{yu'_1}{p} \tag{A.17}$$

$$\frac{\partial \mathrm{E}u}{\partial w} = \mathrm{E}u' = u'_1 \tag{A.18}$$

$$\frac{\partial \mathrm{E}u^2}{\partial p^2} = \frac{y}{p} u''_1 \frac{\partial y}{\partial p} = \frac{(1-p)y^2 u''_0 u''_1}{p^2 D} \tag{A.19}$$

$$\frac{\partial^2 \mathrm{E}u}{\partial w^2} = u''_1 \left(1 - \frac{\partial y}{\partial w}\right) = \frac{(1-p)u''_0 u''_1}{D} \tag{A.20}$$

$$\frac{\partial^2 \mathrm{E}u}{\partial p \partial w} = -u''_1 \frac{\partial y}{\partial p} = -\frac{(1-p)y u''_0 u''_1}{pD}. \tag{A.21}$$

The condition for quasi-concavity of $\mathrm{E}u$ is given by (A.5). Here, it takes the form

$$(1-p)u''_0 u''_1 \left(\frac{\partial \mathrm{E}u}{\partial p} + \frac{y}{p}\frac{\partial \mathrm{E}u}{\partial w}\right)^2 \bigg/ D \leqslant 0 \tag{A.22}$$

a condition which is verified under the assumption 2.1.

A.4

For a person carrying an optimal amount of insurance, we know that

$$(\alpha - p)u'_0 - (1-p)u'_1 = 0; \tag{2.3}$$

$$\phi = \frac{y}{p} + \frac{u_1 - u_0}{\mathrm{E}u'}. \tag{3.12}$$

The derivatives of ϕ are evaluated as follows:

$$\frac{\partial \phi}{\partial w_0} = \frac{-u'_0 \mathrm{E}u' - (u_1 - u_0)pu''_0}{(\mathrm{E}u')^2} + \frac{\partial \phi}{\partial y}\frac{\partial y}{\partial w_0}, \tag{A.23}$$

where $\partial y/\partial w_0$ is given by (2.6) and

$$\frac{\partial \phi}{\partial y} = \frac{1}{p}$$
$$+ \frac{\left[-u'_1 - u'_0\left(\frac{\alpha}{p} - 1\right)\right]\mathrm{E}u' - (u_1 - u_0)[(\alpha - p)u''_0 - (1-p)u''_1]}{(\mathrm{E}u')^2}. \tag{A.24}$$

It follows from (2.3) that

$$\mathrm{E}u' = \alpha u'_0 = \frac{\alpha(1-p)}{\alpha - p}u'_1,$$

so that

$$\frac{\partial \phi}{\partial y} = \frac{1}{p} - \frac{\alpha - p}{\alpha(1-p)} - \frac{\alpha - p}{\alpha p} - \frac{u_1 - u_0}{(\mathrm{E}u')^2}[(\alpha - p)u''_0 - (1-p)u''_1]$$

$$= \frac{1-\alpha}{\alpha(1-p)} - \frac{u_1 - u_0}{(Eu')^2}[(\alpha - p)u_0'' - (1-p)u_1''].\qquad(A.25)$$

Using (2.6) and (A.25) we obtain

$$\frac{\partial \phi}{\partial w_0} = \frac{-1}{\alpha} + \frac{1-\alpha}{\alpha(1-p)}\frac{\partial y}{\partial w_0} - \frac{u_1 - u_0}{(Eu')^2}$$

$$\times \left[pu_0'' + \frac{\partial y}{\partial w_0}\{(\alpha - p)u_0'' - (1-p)u_1''\} \right]$$

$$= \frac{-1}{\alpha} + \frac{1-\alpha}{\alpha(1-p)}\frac{\partial y}{\partial w_0} - \frac{u_1 - u_0}{(Eu')^2}\frac{pu_0''}{D}$$

$$\times [(\alpha - p)^2 u_0'' + p(1-p)u_1'' - (\alpha - p)^2 u_0'' + (\alpha - p)(1-p)u_1'']$$

$$= \frac{-1}{\alpha} + \frac{1-\alpha}{\alpha(1-p)}\frac{\partial y}{\partial w_0} - \frac{u_1 - u_0}{(Eu')^2}\frac{u_0'' u_1''}{D}p\alpha(1-p).\qquad(A.26)$$

By the same reasoning, using (2.6),

$$\frac{\partial \phi}{\partial w_1} = \frac{u_1' Eu' - (u_1 - u_0)(1-p)u_1''}{(Eu')^2}$$

$$+ \frac{\partial y}{\partial w_1}\left[\frac{1-\alpha}{\alpha(1-p)} - \frac{u_1 - u_0}{(Eu')^2}\{(\alpha - p)u_0'' - (1-p)u_1''\} \right]$$

$$= \frac{\alpha - p}{\alpha(1-p)} + \frac{1-\alpha}{\alpha(1-p)}\frac{\partial y}{\partial w_1} - \frac{u_1 - u_0}{(Eu')^2}\frac{(1-p)u_1''}{D}$$

$$\times [(\alpha - p)^2 u_0'' + p(1-p)u_1'' + p(\alpha - p)u_0'' - p(1-p)u_1'']$$

$$= \frac{1}{\alpha} + \frac{\alpha - 1}{\alpha(1-p)}\left(1 - \frac{\partial y}{\partial w_1}\right) - \frac{u_1 - u_0}{(Eu')^2}\frac{u_1'' u_0''}{D}\alpha(\alpha - p)(1-p).$$

$$(A.27)$$

Combining (A.26) and (A.27):

$$\frac{\partial \phi}{\partial w_0} + \frac{\partial \phi}{\partial w_1}$$

$$= \frac{\alpha - 1}{\alpha(1-p)}\left(1 - \frac{\partial y}{\partial w_0} - \frac{\partial y}{\partial w_1}\right) - \frac{u_1 - u_0}{(Eu')^2}\frac{u_0'' u_1''}{D}\alpha^2(1-p).\qquad(A.28)$$

Still by the same reasoning, using (2.8),

$$\frac{\partial \phi}{\partial p} = \frac{-y}{p^2} + \frac{\frac{\alpha y}{p^2}u_0' Eu' - (u_1 - u_0)\left(u_0' - u_1' - \frac{\alpha y}{p}u_0''\right)}{(Eu')^2}$$

$$+ \frac{\partial y}{\partial p} \left[\frac{1 - \alpha}{\alpha(1 - p)} - \frac{u_1 - u_0}{(Eu')^2} \{(\alpha - p)u_0'' - (1 - p)u_1''\} \right]$$

$$= \frac{1 - \alpha}{\alpha(1 - p)} \left[-\frac{u_1 - u_0}{Eu'} + \frac{\partial y}{\partial p} \right] + \frac{u_1 - u_0}{(Eu')^2}$$

$$\times \left[\frac{\alpha y}{p} u_0'' - \frac{\partial y}{\partial p} \{(\alpha - p)u_0'' - (1 - p)u_1''\} \right]$$

$$= \frac{1 - \alpha}{\alpha(1 - p)} \left[\frac{\partial y}{\partial p} - \frac{u_1 - u_0}{Eu'} \left\{ 1 + \frac{p}{D}((\alpha - p)u_0'' - (1 - p)u_1'') \right\} \right]$$

$$+ \frac{u_1 - u_0}{(Eu')^2} \frac{\alpha y}{p} u_0'' \left[1 - \frac{\alpha - p}{D} \{(\alpha - p)u_0'' - (1 - p)u_1''\} \right]$$

$$= \frac{1 - \alpha}{\alpha(1 - p)} \left[\frac{\partial y}{\partial p} - \frac{u_1 - u_0}{Eu'} \frac{u_0''}{D} \alpha(\alpha - p) \right]$$

$$+ \frac{u_1 - u_0}{(Eu')^2} \frac{\alpha^2 y}{p} (1 - p) \frac{u_0'' u_1''}{D}. \tag{A.29}$$

References

Arrow, K.J. (1971). *Essays in the Theory of Risk-Bearing*, Amsterdam: North-Holland

Bergström, Th.C. (1978). When is a Man's Life Worth More than his Human Capital? In M. Jones-Lee (ed.) *The value of Life and Safety*, pp. 3–26. Amsterdam: North-Holland

Blume, M.E. and I. Friend (1975). The Asset Structure of Individual Portfolios and Some Implications for Utility Functions, *Journal of Finance*, 30: 585–603

Cook, P.J. and D.A. Graham (1977). The Demand for Insurance and Protection: The Case of the Irreplaceable Commodity, *Quarterly Journal of Economics*, 9: 143–156

Drèze, J.H. (1961). Les fondements logiques de l'utilité cardinale et de la probabilité subjective. In *La Décision*, Paris: Colloques Internationaux du CNRS, 73–87 (Translated as Chapter 3 supra.)

—(1962). L'utilité sociale d'une vie humanine, *Revue Française de Recherche Opérationnelle*, 22: 139–55

—(1971). Market Allocation under Uncertainty, *European Economic Review*, 2: 133–65 (Chapter 6 supra.)

—(1981). Inferring Risk Tolerance from Deductibles in Insurance Contracts, *The Geneva Papers on Risk and Insurance*, 20: 48–52 (Chapter 5 supra.)

Eisner, R. and R.H. Strotz (1961). Flight Insurance and the Theory of Choice, *The Journal of Political Economy*, 69: 355–68

Greenberg, J. (1977). Pure and Local Public Goods: A Game Theoretic Approach. In A. Sandmo (ed.), *Public Finance*, Lexington, MA: Heath and Co.

Jones-Lee, M. (1974). The Value of Changes in the Probability of Death or Injury, *Journal of Political Economy*, 99: 835–49

Jones-Lee, M. (1976). *The Value of Life: An Economic Analysis*, London: Martin Robertson

Karni, E., D. Schmeidler and K. Vind (1983). On State-Dependent Preferences and Subjective Probabilities, *Econometrica*, 51: 1021–32

Linnerooth, J. (1979). The Value of Human Life: A Review of the Models, *Economic Inquiry*, 17: 52–74

Milleron, C. (1972). Theory of Value with Public Goods: A Survey Article, *Journal of Economic Theory*, 5: 419–77

Mishan, E.J. (1971). Evaluation of Life and Limb: A Theoretical Approach, *Journal of Political Economy*, 79: 685–705

Neumann, J. von and O. Morgenstern (1947). *Theory of Games and Economic Behavior*, Princeton: Princeton University Press

Pratt, J. (1964). Risk-Aversion in the Small and in the Large, *Econometrica*, 32: 122–36

Raiffa, H. (1968). *Decision Analysis; Introductory Lectures on Choices under Uncertainty*, Reading, MA: Addison-Wesley

Samuelson, P.A. (1954). The Pure Theory of Public Expenditures, *Review of Economics and Statistics*, 36: 387–89

Savage, L.J. (1954). *The Foundations of Statistics*, New York: Wiley

Stiglitz, J.E. (1977). The Theory of Local Public Goods. In M. Feldstein and R. Inman (eds), *The Economics of Public Services*, London: Macmillan

Tiebout, C.M. (1956). A Pure Theory of Local Expenditures, *Journal of Political Economy*, 64: 416–24

9   Consumption decisions under uncertainty*

This chapter deals with three issues related to consumption decisions under uncertainty, namely, (i) the determinants of risk aversion for future consumption; (ii) the impact of uncertainty about future resources on current consumption and (iii) the separability of consumption decisions and portfolio choices. These issues are discussed in the context of a simple model introduced, together with our assumptions, in Section 1. The first issue is motivated and treated in Section 2, the conclusions of which are summarised in proposition 2.5. The other two issues are treated in Section 3 under the assumption that there exist perfect markets for risks, and in Section 4 under the converse assumption.

Some technical results needed in the text are collected in Appendices A, B and C; a simple graphical illustration of our major result, theorem 3.3, is given in Appendix D.[1]

*Reprinted from *Journal of Economic Theory.* 5(1972)(3): 308–55, with Franco Modigliani. The research underlying this paper was initiated while the authors were both affiliated with the Graduate School of Industrial Administration, Carnegie-Mellon University; the support of, that institution, and at a later stage of the Sloan School of Management, Massachussets Institute of Technology, is gratefully acknowledged. The authors also wish to thank Albert Ando and Ralph Beals for their helpful assistance at an early stage of this work, as well as Louis Gevers, Agnar Sandmo and Joseph Stiglitz for their critical reading of the final manuscript.

[1]An earlier summary version of this paper, written in French, has appeared in the *Cahiers du Séminaire d'Econométrie* (Drèze and Modigliani, 1966).

1 The model and the assumptions

1.1 Model

Following Fisher (1930), we study the problem faced by a consumer who must allocate his total wealth y between a flow of current (or 'initial') consumption c_1 and a residual stock $(y - c_1)$ out of which future consumption c_2 (including bequests) will be financed. We restrict our attention to the aggregate values of present and future consumption, or equivalently to a single-commodity, two-period world.

We conceive of the consumer's wealth y as being the sum of two terms:

1. The (net) market value of his assets, plus his labour income during the initial period, to be denoted altogether by y_1.
2. The present value of his future labour income, plus additional receipts from sources other than his current assets.

Denote by y_2 the value of the second term, discounted back to the *end* of the initial period; and by r the real rate of interest prevailing over that initial period;[2] y and c_2 are then defined by

$$y = y_1 + y_2(1 + r)^{-1}; \quad c_2 = (y - c_1)(1 + r)$$
$$= (y_1 - c_1)(1 + r) + y_2. \tag{1.1}$$

Usually, when a decision about current consumption is made, y_1 may be taken as known with certainty, but y_2 and r may not: future labour income and real rates of return on assets are, in most cases, imperfectly known *ex ante*. In our simple two-period model, we conceive of the uncertainty about y_2 and r as being removed only at the end of the initial period – hence, *after* c_1 has been chosen. Accordingly, we refer to uncertain prospects for y_2 and/or r as *temporal uncertain prospects* (time will elapse before the uncertainty is removed), and we refer to this type of uncertainty as being 'temporal' or 'delayed'. By contrast, if the uncertainty is to be entirely removed before the choice of c_1, we speak of *timeless uncertain prospects*.

1.2 Assumptions

Relying upon the theory of decision under uncertainty, as developed by von Neumann and Morgenstern (1944), Savage (1954), etc., we start from assumptions about probability and utility, instead of the more natural axioms about choice.

For analytical convenience, their results are strengthened into:

Assumption 1.1: Every uncertain prospect is described by a (subjective) mass or density function $\phi(y_2, r)$ with finite moments of at least first

[2]In a single-commodity world, real rates are well defined; a multiplicity of assets, with different rates of return, is introduced in Section 3.

and second order. The distribution function corresponding to $\phi(y_2, r)$ will be denoted by $\Phi(y_2, r)$.[3]

Assumption 1.2: There exists a cardinal utility function $U(c_1, c_2)$, real valued, continuous and continuously differentiable at least three times.[4]

In addition, we introduce two assumptions that go beyond consistency requirements but reflect behaviour patterns that we regard as generally encountered in reality.

In the first place, we assume that neither present nor future consumption is an inferior commodity, so that both c_1 and c_2 increase when y (or y_1 with y_2 and r constant) increases. An alternative statement is that the 'marginal propensity to consume', as defined in appendix formula (A.4), is everywhere positive but less than one, that is:

Assumption 1.3: $1 > dc_1/dy_1 > 0$.

In the second place, we assume that the consumer's preferences among consumption vectors are convex, and that his choices among uncertain prospects reflect risk aversion, or possibly risk neutrality; that is,[5]

Assumption 1.4: U is concave.

Various properties of U, derived from assumptions 1.2, 1.3 and quasi-concavity of U, are collected in Appendix A.

1.3 Cardinal utility: wealth versus consumption

The (cardinal) indirect utility function corresponding to $U(c_1, c_2)$ may be written $V(y, r)$, where

$$V(y, r) = _{\text{def}} \underset{c_1}{\text{Max}}\, U(c_1, (y - c_1)(1 + r)).$$

Let $r = r^0$ be the sure and only rate of interest at which a consumer may lend and borrow; then $V(y, r^0)$, a function of y alone, is the *cardinal utility function for wealth* relevant to the analysis of choices among *timeless*

---

[3]For notational convenience, we use the integral symbol without introducing parallel statements in the notation of discrete random variables; the standard symbol E is used for the expectation operator when there is no ambiguity about the underlying mass or density function.

[4]Thus, U is defined up to a linear increasing transformation; if the consumer were to choose between the certainty of consuming (c_1, c_2) and the prospect of consuming either (c_1', c_2') or (c_1'', c_2'') with respective probabilities π and $1 - \pi$, he would never prefer the former alternative if $U(c_1, c_2) \leqslant \pi U(c_1', c_2') + (1 - \pi)U(c_1'', c_2'')$.

[5]As argued elsewhere by one of us (Drèze, 1971), risk preference may be excluded without loss of generality, if one assumes the availability on the market of fair gambling opportunities.

uncertain prospects. In other words, if a cardinal utility function for wealth were derived from observations about choices between *timeless* uncertain prospects, when the market rate of interest for safe loans is r^0 and y_2 is known, then such a function would coincide with $V(y, r^0)$ up to an increasing linear transformation.

In the language of demand theory, $V(y, r^0)$ measures utility cardinally for movements along the Engel curve corresponding to r^0, by assigning utility levels to the successive indifference curves crossed by that Engel curve. Provided dc_1/dy is continuous (as implied by assumption 1.2) and satisfies assumption 1.3, the Engel curve will have a point in common with every indifference curve and the assignment of utility levels to these curves will be exhaustive. One may then *construct* the cardinal utility function $U(c_1, c_2)$ by relying simultaneously on two independent and familiar tools, namely,

1. Indifference curves, as revealed by choices among sure vectors of present and future consumption.
2. A cardinal utility function for wealth, as revealed by choices among timeless uncertain prospects.

2 Temporal prospects, the values of information and risk preference

2.1 Temporal versus timeless uncertain prospects

If a consumer owns a temporal uncertain prospect $\phi(y_2, r)$ that he cannot or does not wish to exchange for some other prospect, his expected utility is given by

$$\underset{c_1}{\text{Max}} \int U\{c_1, (y_1 - c_1)(1 + r) + y_2\} d\Phi(y_2, r). \qquad (2.1)$$

The solution to this maximisation problem determines the optimal current consumption $\hat{c}_1$. Future consumption is a random variable defined by (1.1), with $c_1 = \hat{c}_1$. We shall assume that c_2 so defined is non-negative, identically in y_2 and r, so that the density of c_2 is defined by

$$\psi(c_2) = \int \phi\{c_2 - (y_1 - \hat{c}_1)(1 + r), r\} dr \qquad (2.2)$$

with first and second moments

$$\bar{c}_2 = (y_1 - \hat{c}_1)(1 + \bar{r}) + \bar{y}_2,$$
$$\sigma_{c_2}^2 = (y_1 - \hat{c}_1)^2 \sigma_r^2 + \sigma_{y_2}^2 + 2(y_1 - \hat{c}_1)\sigma_{ry_2}. \qquad (2.3)$$

Had the *same* uncertain prospect been timeless, so that the value of y_2 and r were known to our consumer before his choice of c_1, then his expected utility would have been

$$\int_{c_1} \text{Max}\, U\{c_1, (y_1 - c_1)(1 + r) + y_2\}\mathrm{d}\Phi(y_2, r)$$

$$= \int V\{y_1 + y_2(1 + r)^{-1}, r\}\mathrm{d}\Phi(y_2, r). \tag{2.4}$$

It is immediately verified, by application of a well-known theorem,[6] that

$$\text{Max}_{c_1} \int U\{c_1, (y_1 - c_1)(1 + r) + y_2\}\mathrm{d}\Phi(y_2, r)$$

$$\leqslant \int \text{Max}_{c_1} U\{c_1, (y_1 - c_1)(1 + r) + y_2\}\mathrm{d}\Phi(y_2, r). \tag{2.5}$$

The difference between the right- and left-hand sides of (2.5) is 'the expected value of perfect information' (EVPI), well known to the statisticians.[7]

The meaning of (2.5) may be conveyed somewhat informally, as follows:

Proposition 2.1: A temporal uncertain prospect is never preferred to the timeless uncertain prospect described by the same mass or density function, no matter what the consumer's utility function may be.[8]

2.2 A risk-aversion function for delayed risks

The general inferiority of temporal over timeless uncertain prospects has implications for the willingness to bear risk in a temporal context. One convenient way of capturing these implications rests upon the 'risk-aversion function' introduced by Pratt (1964) for timeless uncertainty about total resources (wealth).

Let $r = r^0$ be given; Pratt's (absolute) risk-aversion function is then given by $(-V_{yy}/V_y)_{r^0}$. This quantity, which is equal to 'twice the risk premium per

[6]See for example, Marschak (1954, p. 201). The theorem may be stated as follows: 'Let g be a function of the decision variable d and of the random variable x with density $f(x)$; then:

$$\int_\infty \text{Max}_d g(d, x)f(x)\mathrm{d}x \geqslant \text{Max}_d \int_\infty g(d, x)f(x)\mathrm{d}x.'$$

[7]In order to get a measure that does not depend upon the choice of units for the utility function, one should divide both sides of equation (2.5) by some appropriate index of marginal utility – like $U_1 = V_y$, or U_2 – so as to measure the EVPI in the same units as consumption, either current or future.

[8]The mass or density functions must, of course, be kept identical, not only 'theoretically' but also 'practically', if spurious contradictions are to be avoided; thus, a consumer with strong risk aversion may prefer a temporal prospect that is marketable to a similar timeless one that is not; the appropriate density for the temporal prospect is then given by the certainty of its market value and our proposition is not applicable.

unit of variance for infinitesimal risks' when the consumer's wealth is y and $r = r^0$, is a local measure of risk preference. It is, however, related to risk aversion in the large: if one consumer has a greater local risk aversion than another at all wealth levels y, then (and only then) he has greater risk aversion in the large – in the sense that he would exchange *any* timeless uncertain prospect $\chi(y)$ against the certainty of an amount which would be unacceptable to the other consumer.[9]

We shall now derive a (local) measure of risk aversion for *delayed* risks which, like the Pratt measure in the timeless context, represents 'twice the risk premium per unit of variance for infinitesimal risks'.

We begin with a given r (say $r \equiv r^0$) and income prospects $\phi(y_2)$. If such prospects are *timeless*, the random outcome will be known at time 1 but *paid* at time 2: the choice of c_1 still occurs under certainty. It is readily verified that the risk-aversion function relevant for such prospects is

$$\frac{-1}{1+r^0}\left(\frac{V_{yy}}{V_y}\right)_{r^0} = \left(\frac{-V_{y_2 y_2}}{V_{y_2}}\right)_{r^0}.$$

When such prospects become temporal, on the other hand, the appropriate risk-aversion function is $(-U_{22}/U_2)_{\hat{c}_1}$. This can be verified as follows. Let $\hat{c}_1$ be the first period consumption that is optimal for a given temporal uncertain prospect $\phi(y_2, r)$ and let $\psi(c_2)$ be defined as in (2.2). The expected utility of the prospect is then $\int U(\hat{c}_1, c_2)\mathrm{d}\Psi(c_2)$.

Clearly, if U_{22} does not change sign over the range of $\psi(c_2)$, then

$$\int U(\hat{c}_1, c_2)\mathrm{d}\Psi(c_2) \gtreqless U(\hat{c}_1, \bar{c}_2) \quad \text{according as } U_{22} \gtreqless 0. \tag{2.6}$$

Confining attention to infinitesimal risks, we have

$$\int U(\hat{c}_1, c_2)\mathrm{d}\Psi(c_2) \simeq U(\hat{c}_1, \bar{c}_2) + (\sigma_{c_2}^2/2)U_{22}(\hat{c}_1, \bar{c}_2) =_{\text{def}} U(\hat{c}_1, c_2'),$$

$$\tag{2.7}$$

thereby defining c_2' implicitly.

Furthermore, $U(\hat{c}_1, c_2') \simeq U(\hat{c}_1, \bar{c}_2) + (c_2' - \bar{c}_2)U_2(\hat{c}_1, \bar{c}_2)$, so that

$$c_2' \simeq \bar{c}_2 + \frac{\sigma_{c_2}^2}{2}\frac{U_{22}(\hat{c}_1, \bar{c}_2)}{U_2(\hat{c}_1, \bar{c}_2)}, \quad \text{implying} \quad \left(-\frac{U_{22}}{U_2}\right)_{\hat{c}_1, \bar{c}_2} \simeq \frac{2(\bar{c}_2 - c_2')}{\sigma_{c_2}^2}. \tag{2.8}$$

Thus $(-U_{22}/U_2)_{\hat{c}_1, \bar{c}_2}$ is equal to 'twice the risk premium per unit of variance y_2 for infinitesimal *delayed* risks'. For given $\hat{c}_1$, the function $(-U_{22}/U_2)_{\hat{c}_1}$ is a local measure of risk aversion at all levels of c_2 in the same

---

[9] See Pratt (1964, p. 122) and Sections 3–5; Arrow (1965) has independently introduced the same concept.

sense as $-V_{y_2y_2}/V_{y_2}$ provides such a measure at all levels of y_2 for timeless uncertain prospects. One must, however, be careful to realise that the value of $(-U_{22}/U_2)_{\hat{c}_1}$ is in general not independent of $\hat{c}_1$.[10] It measures risk aversion along a particular cut of the utility function orthogonal to the c_1 axis, but the measure may not be the same, at a given level of c_2, for different choices of c_1 (different cuts of the utility function by parallel planes).

2.3 Ordinal determinants of the aversion for delayed risks

It follows from appendix formula (A.15) that, *at any point in* (c_1, c_2) *space*,

$$\frac{-U_{22}}{U_2} = \frac{-V_{y_2y_2}}{V_{y_2}} + \left(\frac{dc_1}{dy_2}\right)^2 \left(\frac{d^2c_2}{dc_1^2}\bigg|_U\right) \geqslant -\frac{V_{y_2y_2}}{V_{y_2}}, \tag{2.9}$$

where $V_{y_2y_2}/V_{y_2}$ and dc_1/dy_2 are computed along the Engel curve going through *that point*, and where the inequality follows from assumptions 1.3 and 1.4.

The risk premium for a delayed risk must be equal to the sum of (i) the expected value of perfect information, and (ii) the risk premium for the same risk when timeless.[11] Thus the second term on the right-hand side of (2.9) measures 'twice the expected value of perfect information per unit of variance y_2 for infinitesimal risks'. That second term is invariant under monotonic transformations of the utility function;[12] it is the product of two factors, of which the second one is most easily interpreted. $d^2c_2/dc_1^2|_U$ is a (local) measure of curvature of the indifference loci. As shown in the appendix formulas (A.5), (A.6), it also measures the reciprocal of the substitution effect on c_1, of a rise in r.[13] That curvature of the indifference loci should be relevant to assess the superiority of timeless over temporal uncertain prospects is readily seen if one contrasts extreme situations. At one extreme, suppose that the indifference curves are nearly linear in the vicinity of the equilibrium point: the consumer is almost indifferent about the allocation of this total resources between c_1 and c_2, which are almost perfect substitutes, the curvature is close to nil, and the response of c_1 to a compensated change in the rate of interest would be very large. Obviously,

---

[10]A necessary and sufficient condition for $-U_{22}/U_2$ to be everywhere independent of c_1 is that $U = f(c_1) + g(c_1)h(c_2)$.

[11]Indeed, the total premium paid to dispose of a given delayed risk should be the same, whether the uncertain prospect be exchanged outright for a sure amount, or whether it be exchanged first (at some premium) for an identical but timeless prospect, to be converted next into a sure amount.

[12]It is thus observed that, for *infinitesimal* risks, the expected value of perfect information depends only upon ordinal properties of U; of course, this strong and somewhat surprising result does not hold more generally.

[13]This effect is usually referred to as the 'substitution term of the Slutsky equation'; it measures the response of c_1 to a *compensated* change in the rate of interest; the Slutsky equation, however, is typically expressed in terms of the 'price' $(1+r)^{-1}$ rather than in terms of the interest rate r.

for such a consumer, delayed uncertainty is not appreciably different from timeless uncertainty, since the opportunity to gear c_1 exactly to total resources matters little to him. At the other extreme, suppose that the indifference curves are very close to right angles in the vicinity of the equilibrium point: the consumer has very exacting preferences for the allocation of his total resources between c_1 and c_2, which are strongly complementary, the curvature is very pronounced, and the response of c_1 to a compensated change in the rate of interest would be negligible. For such a consumer, delayed uncertainty is very costly, due to the imperfect allocation which it entails: the utility of a consumption plan with given present value $c_1 + c_2(1 + r)^{-1}$ decreases rapidly when the allocation departs from the preferred proportions. Thus, as formula (2.9) shows, *the aversion for delayed risks grows as curvature of the indifference loci increases*, or, to use more operational terms, consumers who would respond strongly to a (compensated) change in the rate of interest are *relatively* better suited to carry delayed risks.

The role of the other factor, the marginal propensity to consume, is again most easily understood by looking at limiting situations. If $dc_1/dy = 0$, then the optimum c_1 can be chosen without exact knowledge of total resources, so that perfect information is worthless. At the other extreme, a person who wants to consume all his resources now because he derives no satisfaction from later consumption is ill-suited to bear delayed risks: since he can only afford to consume now the resources he is sure to own, the uncertain prospect carries no more utility for him than the certainty of its worst outcome. In general, *the inferiority of temporal over timeless uncertain prospects will be the more severe, the larger the marginal propensity to consume* (*other things being equal*).

2.4 Uncertainty about rates of return versus uncertainty about future income

We now turn briefly to the case where y_2 is given (say $y_2 = \bar{y}_2$) and r is a random variable with density $\phi(r)$. Our problem is to compare timeless with temporal uncertain prospects about r. One can readily verify that the Pratt 'risk-aversion function' for timeless gambles about r is $-(y_1 - c_1)$ $(V_{rr}/V_r)_{\bar{y}}$.[14] Similarly, when $\sigma_{c_2}^2 = (y_1 - \hat{c}_1)^2\sigma_r^2$, we see from (2.7) that $-(y_1 - \hat{c}_1)^2(U_{22}/U_2)_{\hat{c}_1}$ is the appropriate corresponding measure for temporal gambles. Furthermore, it follows from formula (A.15) that, *at any point in* (c_1, c_2) *space*,

$$
\begin{aligned}
-(y_1 - c_1)^2(U_{22}/U_2) &= -(y_1 - c_1)(V_{rr}/V_r) \\
&\quad + (dc_1/dr)^2(d^2c_2/dc_1^2|_U) \\
&\geqslant -(y_1 - c_1)(V_{rr}/V_r),
\end{aligned} \tag{2.10}
$$

---

[14] Note, from equation (A.11), that $V_r = V_{y_2}(y_1 - c_1)$ has the same sign as $(y_1 - c_1)$: an increase in r affects utility positively for a lender, negatively for a borrower.

where V_{rr}/V_r and dc_1/dr are computed along the offer-curve going through that point. Formula (2.10) admits of the same interpretation as (2.9), so that the second term on the right-hand side measures 'twice the expected value of perfect information per unit variance r for infinitesimal risks' – a non-negative quantity that is again invariant under *monotonic* transformations of the utility function. We notice that this quantity vanishes when $dc_1/dr = 0$: if current consumption is insensitive to r, it is also insensitive to σ_r^2 (at least locally), and uncertainty about r is of no concern in choosing c_1. For people with positive asset holdings $(y_1 - c_1 > 0)$, dc_1/dr is unrestricted as to sign on a priori grounds; the absence of empirical evidence pointing strongly to either a positive or a negative sign is perhaps an indication that dc_1/dr, whatever its sign, may not be appreciably different from zero, thus pointing towards a small value for the expected value of perfect information about r, and *a less pronounced inferiority of temporal over timeless uncertainty in the case of rates of return than in the case of income*.[15]

2.5 Summary

Summarising our discussion of (2.9)–(2.10), we have:

Proposition 2.2: A consumer's willingness to bear delayed risks, as measured by his risk-aversion function for temporal prospects $(-U_{22}/U_2)_{\hat{c}_1}$, will be the lower:

(i)   the lower his willingness to bear immediate risks, as measured by his risk-aversion function for timeless prospects $(-V_{yy}/V_y)_r$;

(ii)   the larger his marginal propensity to consume dc_1/dy, and/or the responsiveness of his current consumption to the rate of interest $|dc_1/dr|$;

(iii)   the lower, in absolute value, the substitution effect of a change in the rate of interest on his current consumption $|S|$.

---

[15]The general case of joint uncertainty about y_2 and r is a straightforward extension of the foregoing analysis; equations (2.9) and (2.10) combine to

$$\left(\frac{-U_{22}}{U_2}\right)\sigma_{c_2}^2 = \left(\frac{-U_{22}}{U_2}\right)(\sigma_{y_2}^2 + (y_1 - c_1)^2\sigma_r^2 + 2(y_1 - c_1)\sigma_{ry_2})$$

$$= -\left(\frac{V_{y_2y_2}}{V_{y_2}}\sigma_{y_2}^2 + \frac{V_{rr}}{V_r}(y_1 - c_1)\sigma_r^2 + 2\frac{V_{ry_2}}{V_r}(y_1 - c_1)\sigma_{ry_2}\right)$$

$$+ \left(\left(\frac{dc_1}{dy_2}\right)^2\sigma_{y_2}^2 + \left(\frac{dc_1}{dr}\right)^2\sigma_r^2 + 2\frac{dc_1}{dr}\frac{dc_1}{dy_2}\sigma_{ry_2}\right)\left(\frac{d^2c_2}{dc_1^2}\bigg|_U\right).$$

3 Consumption and portfolio decisions with perfect markets

3.1 Statement of the problem

We now turn to the following questions: (i) How does uncertainty about future resources affect current consumption? (ii) What is the relationship between consumption decisions and portfolio choices? The first question may be raised irrespective of the nature and source of uncertainty, but cannot be answered until some reference criterion is chosen; the second question is appropriate only when savings may be invested in a variety of assets, and the consumer is free to *choose* his portfolio mix.

The portfolio problem traditionally considered in the literature involves a perfectly safe asset, yielding a rate of return r_0, and n risky assets yielding uncertain rates of return. The consumer is free to allocate his savings (wealth) among these $n + 1$ assets. If there is no uncertainty about future income, then any uncertainty affecting future resources is 'chosen' or 'endogenous', since it results entirely from portfolio choices (all the savings could have been invested in the safe asset). And a natural reference criterion, in assessing the impact of uncertainty on current consumption, is the value of c_1 that would be optimal if indeed all the savings were yielding the *sure* rate r_0. This is a more natural reference than the (more traditional) optimal c_1, given the *expected* rate of return on the chosen portfolio. Indeed, under assumption 1.4, a consumer would not choose a risky portfolio unless its expected return were higher than r_0; but no portfolio yielding the certainty of that expected return is available on the market; and knowing how $\hat{c}_1$ stands relative to the expected value criterion would not tell us how endogenous uncertainty actually affects c_1.

This argument can be extended to income uncertainty if one assumes the existence of insurance markets where an uncertain future income with density $\phi(y_2)$ can be exchanged against the certainty of some sure income y_2^0. In the presence of perfect markets for both income and assets, all uncertainty is 'chosen' or 'endogenous' and it is natural to compare $\hat{c}_1$ with the consumption that would be optimal if c_2 were equal to $y_2^0 + (y_1 - c_1)$ $(1 + r_0)$ with certainty.

Such is the case treated in this section. It turns out that with perfect markets, a particular *ordinal* property of the utility function determines unambiguously how uncertainty affects consumption, *and* whether consumption and portfolio decisions are separable.

First-order conditions for optimal decisions are given in Section 3.2. We then prove a certainty equivalence theorem in 3.3 and interpret it in 3.4. The property of the utility function mentioned above is discussed in 3.5. In Section 4, we then turn to the case where the uncertain prospect faced by a consumer is not chosen, but given 'exogenously' (at least on the income side). And we conclude that section with some remarks on the response of current consumption to availability of market opportunities for sharing risks.

3.2 First-order conditions and their interpretation

We now introduce a general model designed to analyse simultaneous decisions about $\phi(y_2, r)$ and $\hat{c}_1$ under perfect insurance and asset markets.[16] These decisions are assumed to maximise expected utility over the class of all prospects, the market value of which does not exceed that of $\phi(y_2, r)$.

Let there be one perfectly safe asset, yielding a rate of return r_0, and n risky assets yielding the uncertain rates of return $r_j, j = 1, \ldots, n$. The amounts invested in these $n + 1$ assets will be denoted by $(x_0, x_1, \ldots, x_n)$. Let furthermore future earnings y_2 be the sum of m components $y_{i2}, i = 1, \ldots, m$; and let z_{i1} be the *present* value of y_{i2} on the insurance market.[17] Denote by $(1 - \alpha_i), i = 1, \ldots, n$, the fraction of y_{i2} that a consumer chooses to *sell* on the insurance market; his current wealth and future (net) earnings then become

$$y_1 + \sum_{i=1}^{m} (1 - \alpha_i) z_{i1} \quad \text{and} \quad \sum_{i=1}^{m} \alpha_i y_{i2},$$

respectively. Given a current consumption c_1, his portfolio of assets must satisfy the constraint

$$y_1 + \sum_{i=1}^{m} (1 - \alpha_i) z_{i1} - c_1 = x_0 + \sum_{j=1}^{n} x_j,$$

or   (3.1)

$$x_0 = y_1 - c_1 + \sum_{i=1}^{m} (1 - \alpha_i) z_{i1} - \sum_{j=1}^{n} x_j,$$

[16]Drèze and Modigliani (1966, Section 6) have used a slightly different formulation, based upon the notion that labour income (current and future) results from activities among which the consumer divides his *time*, of which a fixed quantity is available; it was also assumed that earnings from a given activity were proportional to the amount of time devoted to it, and that one of the activities entailed a perfectly safe income; the activities themselves did not appear as arguments of the utility function. Under that formulation, earnings per unit of time from the safe activity provide an implicit 'insurance value' for the earnings per unit of time from any of the risky activities.

[17]This 'insurance value' may be defined in a number of ways: one of them is straightforward insurance of professional income (including unemployment and medical insurance); another is suggested in note 16; another still is provided by the purchase (or short sale) of a portfolio of assets perfectly negatively (or positively) correlated with y_{i2}. One might also consider a 'states of the world' model (Arrow, 1953; Debreu, 1959; Hirshleifer, 1965) with m states and define:

$$y_{i2} = \begin{cases} \text{future earnings, if state } i \text{ obtains,} \\ 0, \text{ otherwise;} \end{cases}$$

$z_{i1} = y_{i2}$ times the current price of a unit claim contingent on state i.

Our formal analysis is consistent with any of these interpretations, or combinations thereof, so long as z_{i1} is well defined, independently of the amount of 'coverage' that our consumer buys on y_{i2}.

and his future consumption is defined by

$$c_2 = \sum_{i=1}^{m} \alpha_i y_{i2} + x_0(1 + r_0) + \sum_{j=1}^{n} x_j(1 + r_j)$$

$$= \sum_{i=1}^{m} \alpha_i y_{i2} + \left(y_1 - c_1 + \sum_{i=1}^{m} (1 - \alpha_i) z_{i1} \right)(1 + r_0) + \sum_{j=1}^{n} x_j(r_j - r_0)$$

$$= z_2 + (y_1 - c_1)(1 + r_0) + \sum_{i=1}^{m} \alpha_i(y_{i2} - z_{i2}) + \sum_{j=1}^{n} x_j(r_j - r_0),$$

$$(3.2)$$

where

$$z_{i2} =_{\text{def}} z_{i1}(1 + r_0) \quad \text{and} \quad z_2 =_{\text{def}} \sum_{i=1}^{m} z_{i2}.$$

Given the joint density $\phi(y_{12}, \ldots, y_{m2}, r_1, \ldots, r_n)$, the simultaneous choice of an asset portfolio $(x_1, \ldots, x_n)$, an insurance portfolio $(1 - \alpha_1, \ldots, 1 - \alpha_m)$ and a consumption level c_1, is then arrived at by solving the following problem:

$$\max_{c_1, \alpha_1, \ldots, \alpha_m, x_1, \ldots, x_n} \int U \left\{ c_1, z_2 + (y_1 - c_1)(1 + r_0) + \sum_{i=1}^{m} \alpha_i(y_{i2} - z_{i2}) \right.$$

$$\left. + \sum_{j=1}^{n} x_j(r_j - r_0) \right\} d\Phi(y_{12}, \ldots, y_{m2}, r_1, \ldots, r_n), \qquad (3.3)$$

subject to whatever constraints prevail on the maximising variables. We shall assume that such constraints, if any, are never binding, and that the solutions to (3.3) are given by the first order conditions (3.4)–(3.6)[18]

$$\partial EU/\partial c_1 = E(U_1 - U_2(1 + r_0)) = 0, \quad \text{or} \quad EU_1/EU_2 = 1 + r_0;$$

$$(3.4)$$

$$\partial EU/\partial x_j = E(U_2(r_j - r_0)) = 0 \quad \text{or} \quad EU_2 r_j/EU_2 = r_0; \qquad (3.5)$$

$$\partial EU/\partial \alpha_i = E(U_2(y_{i2} - z_{i2})) = 0, \quad \text{or} \quad EU_2 y_{i2}/EU_2 = z_{i2}. \qquad (3.6)$$

These results admit of the following economic interpretation:

Proposition 3.1: Under perfect insurance and asset markets, any solution to problem (3.3) has the following properties:

---

[18]Thus, we assume that all solutions to equations (3.4)–(3.6) satisfy $c_1 \geq 0$ and $c_2 \geq 0$ identically in $(y_{12}, \ldots, y_{m2}, r_1, \ldots, r_n)$, plus whatever conditions might be imposed on the α_i's and x_j's; clearly, the model lends itself to a more courageous formulation with inequality constraints. The second-order conditions follow naturally from assumption 1.4.

(3.4) The ratio of the expected marginal utilities of present and future consumption is equal to one plus the rate of return on the safe asset;

(3.5) The expected marginal utility of a unit investment in every asset is the same; the expected value of the rate of return on every asset, *weighted by the marginal utility of future consumption*, is equal to the rate of return on the safe asset;

(3.6) The expected marginal utility of a unit worth of insurance on every source of earnings is the same; the expected value of the earnings from any source, *weighted by the marginal utility of future consumption*, is equal to the insurance value of these earnings.

Clearly, if there exist perfect asset markets, but no insurance markets, the solution to (3.3) with all the α_i equated to one is still given by (3.4)–(3.5), and if there exist neither asset nor insurance markets, the solution is given by (3.4).

Furthermore, if the rate of return on the entire portfolio, namely

$$r_0 + \left(\sum_{j=1}^{n} (r_j - r_0)x_j \bigg/ \left(x_0 + \sum_{j=1}^{n} x_j \right) \right),$$

is still denoted by r, and since

$$y_2 =_{\text{def}} \sum_{i=1}^{m} y_{i2},$$

(3.5)–(3.6) imply

$$EU_2 r / EU_2 = r_0, \quad EU_2 y_2 / EU_2 = z_2$$

$$= EU_2 \sum_{i=1}^{m} (\alpha_i y_{i2} + (1 - \alpha_i)z_{i2}) / EU_2. \tag{3.7}$$

3.3 A theorem about the impact of uncertainty on consumption

We now state and prove a theorem that has an immediate bearing on consumption and portfolio decisions with perfect markets. It does, however, admit of a somewhat broader interpretation, which justifies the notation 'y_2^*, r^*, c_1^*' introduced in the statement of the theorem.

Theorem 3.1: Let $y_2^* =_{\text{def}} Ey_2 U_2(\hat{c}_1, c_2)/EU_2(\hat{c}_1, c_2)$, $r^* =_{\text{def}} ErU_2(\hat{c}_1, c_2)/EU_2(\hat{c}_1, c_2)$ and define $c_1^* = c_1^*(r^*, y_2^*)$ by

$$U_1(c_1^*, (y_1 - c_1^*)(1 + r^*) + y_2^*)$$

$$- (1 + r^*)U_2(c_1^*, (y_1 - c_1^*)(1 + r^*) + y_2^*) = 0.\text{[19]}$$

Then

$$\partial^2 \frac{U_1}{U_2} \bigg/ \partial c_2^2 \gtreqqless 0 \,(\text{identically in } c_2, \text{ given } \hat{c}_1) \text{ implies } \hat{c}_1 \gtreqqless c_1^*.$$

[19] That is, c_1^* is the level of current consumption that would be optimal given $y_2 \equiv y_2^*, r \equiv r^*$; $\hat{c}_1$ is still the optimal level given $\phi(y_2, r)$.

Proof: The proof is based upon lemma C.2 in Appendix C. Let $U_1(\hat{c}_1, c_2)/U_2(\hat{c}_1, c_2) - (1 + r^*) =_{\text{def}} f(c_2)$; we may rewrite (3.4) as

$$0 = \int U_2 f(c_2) \, d\Psi(c_2) =_{\text{def}} \int h(c_2) \, d\Psi(c_2), \tag{3.8}$$

where $U_2 = U_2(\hat{c}_1, c_2)$ is a function of c_2. Let then

$$c_2^* =_{\text{def}} \frac{Ec_2 U_2}{EU_2} = \frac{E((y_1 - \hat{c}_1)(1 + r) + y_2)U_2}{EU_2}$$

$$= (y_1 - \hat{c}_1)(1 + r^*) + y_2^* \text{ by } (3.7).$$

Lemma C.2 then implies

$$f(c_2) \begin{matrix} \text{concave} \\ \text{linear} \\ \text{convex} \end{matrix} \Rightarrow \int h(c_2) \, d\Psi(c_2) \lesseqgtr f(c_2^*) \int U_2 \, d\Psi(c_2). \tag{3.9}$$

Now, $\int U_2 \, d\Psi(c_2) > 0$, and $f(c_2)$ is a linear function of U_1/U_2, whose concavity properties (in c_2) are determined by the sign (assumed constant) of $\partial^2 (U_1/U_2)/\partial c_2^2$; consequently, (3.8) and (3.9) together imply

$$\frac{\partial^2 (U_1/U_2)}{\partial c_2^2} \lesseqgtr 0 \Rightarrow \frac{U_1(\hat{c}_1, c_2^*)}{U_2(\hat{c}_1, c_2^*)} - (1 + r^*) \gtreqless 0$$

$$\Rightarrow U_1(\hat{c}_1, c_2^*) - (1 + r^*)U_2(\hat{c}_1, c_2^*) \gtreqless 0. \tag{3.10}$$

Assumption 1.3 and the definition of c^* imply that

$$U_{11}(c_1^*, c_2^*) - (1 + r^*)U_{21}(c_1^*, c_2^*) < 0,$$

so that

$$U_1(\hat{c}_1, c_2^*) - (1 + r^*)U_2(\hat{c}_1, c_2^*) \gtreqless 0 \Leftrightarrow \hat{c}_1 \lesseqgtr c_1^*.$$

The theorem then follows from (3.10). □

3.4 A sufficient condition for separation of the consumption and portfolio decisions

When there exist perfect markets for income insurance and for assets, then (3.4)–(3.7) imply that y_2^* is equal to the insurance value of future income (z_2) and r^* is equal to the market sure rate of return (r_0).[20] Suppose that $\partial^2 (U_1/U_2)/\partial c_2^2 = 0$; theorem 3.1 then implies that current consumption $\hat{c}_1$ is equal to the level (c_1^*) that would be optimal if all income were insured ($y_2 \equiv y_2^*$) and all savings were held in the safe asset ($r \equiv r^*$). *This result holds independently of the actual insurance policy and asset portfolio chosen by the consumer.* Hence endogenous uncertainty has no impact on consumption. Furthermore, $y_2^*(= z_2)$ and $r^*(= r_0)$ being directly observable market

---

[20]Some readers may find it more convenient to transpose this interpretation to the situation where there is no uncertainty about future income, so that $y_2 \equiv y_2^*$.

values, $\hat{c}_1(=c_1^*)$ may be chosen first (as a function of z_2 and r_0), the optimal insurance policy and asset portfolio being determined thereafter (jointly, for this given $\hat{c}_1$). Consumption and portfolio decisions may be taken sequentially and are 'separable', in that sense.[21]

When $\partial^2(U_1/U_2)/\partial c_2^2 \neq 0$, then the sign of that quantity is also the sign of the impact of endogenous uncertainty on current consumption. It is noteworthy that U_1/U_2, hence its second derivative, is invariant under monotonic transformations of the utility function, and thus independent of risk aversion. There thus exist ordinal preferences, consistent with our assumptions, such that endogenous uncertainty results in increased consumption, and alternative preferences such that the opposite result holds. In the latter case, the consumer chooses an uncertain prospect which yields a higher expected utility than the sure prospect of identical market value, but he simultaneously chooses to consume less in the first period – postponing the (uncertain) benefit to the second period. Such behaviour is consistent with risk aversion, in spite of the saying that 'a bird in hand is worth two in the bush'.

3.5 *Interpretation of the condition*

It is appropriate at this point to inquire about the meaning of the rather unfamiliar quantity $\partial^2(U_1/U_2)/\partial c_2^2$ which controls the response of consumption to endogenous risk, and to inquire whether there is ground for supposing that some sign is more plausible than another.

First we recall that U_1/U_2 is a familiar quantity, the slope of the indifference curve; hence $\partial(U_1/U_2)/\partial c_2$ is the rate of change of the slope of the indifference curves as we increase c_2 for fixed c_1. That derivative must have a positive sign by assumption 1.3 (c_1 is not an inferior good). The function $(\partial^2(U_1/U_2)/\partial c_2^2)_{\hat{c}_1}$ measures the curvature of U_1/U_2 as a function of c_2.

An intuitive explanation of the relevance of $\partial^2(U_1/U_2)/\partial c_2^2$ for consumption decisions under uncertainty is provided in Appendix D, by means of a simple graphical illustration.

More generally, the following can be said:

(i) $\partial^2(U_1/U_2)/\partial c_2^2 = 0$ identically in c_1 and c_2 if and only if $U(c_1, c_2) = F(g(c_1) + h(c_1) \cdot c_2)$, $F' > 0$, $h > 0$ (see Appendix B). That is, $\partial^2(U_1/U_2)/\partial c_2^2 \equiv 0$ is the *ordinal* property of $U(c_1, c_2)$ that is *necessary* for risk neutrality in terms of c_2, and sufficient for such neutrality to obtain under a monotonic transformation of U.

(ii)   Given any $r > -1$, $y > 0$ and U, there exist y_1 and $y_2 = (y - y_1)(1 + r)$ such that $dc_1/dr = 0$; when $dc_1/dr = 0$, then d^2c_1/dr^2 has the sign of $\partial^2(U_1/U_2)/\partial c_2^2$ (see formulas A.7–A.8). That is, $\partial^2(U_1/U_2)/\partial c_2^2 = 0$ is the

---

[21] An extension of these propositions to an n-period model, $n > 2$, has been provided by Pestieau (1969), under the additional assumption of homothetic indifference surfaces.

ordinal property of $U(c_1, c_2)$ that is *necessary* for a zero interest-elasticity of consumption at all r and *sufficient* for this situation to obtain under an appropriate time-distribution of income.

Concluding heuristically about the case of perfect insurance and asset markets, we would like to suggest as *a rough first approximation* that uncertainty has little impact on current consumption, and that consumption decisions are for practical purposes separable from portfolio decisions. The lack of empirical evidence pointing towards a substantial interest-elasticity of consumption and the intuitive appeal of the separability proposition lend support to this conclusion.

4 Consumption and portfolio decisions without perfect markets

4.1 Implications of the previous section

When there do not exist perfect markets, with prices at which an arbitrary uncertain prospect can be evaluated and exchanged, then uncertainty is no longer endogenous, and a new reference criterion must be introduced to replace market value. Expected value then seems to be a natural criterion; it calls for comparing $\hat{c}_1$, that maximises EU given $\phi(y_2, r)$, with $\bar{c}_1$ that would maximise U given $y_2 \equiv \bar{y}_2$ and $r \equiv \bar{r}$.

Theorem 3.1 has some implications for the relation of $\hat{c}_1$ to $\bar{c}_1$, but these implications are limited in scope. Specifically, it follows from the definition in theorem 3.1 that

$$y_2^* = EU_2 y_2/EU_2 = \bar{y}_2 + [\text{cov}(U_2, y_2)/EU_2]. \tag{4.1}$$

When r is non-stochastic ($r \equiv r^*$), then it follows from $U_{22} < 0$ and $c_2 = y_2 + (y_1 - \hat{c}_1)(1 + r)$ that $\text{cov}(U_2, y_2) < 0$ and $y_2^* < \bar{y}_2$. In view of assumption 1.3, this entails $c_1^* < \bar{c}_1$. Consequently, $\partial^2(U_1/U_2)/\partial c_2^2 \leqslant 0$ implies $\hat{c}_1 \leqslant c_1^* < \bar{c}_1$; the relationship of $\hat{c}_1$ to $\bar{c}_1$ is indeterminate only when $\partial^2(U_1/U_2)/\partial c_2^2 > 0$.

Unfortunately, when r is stochastic, this line of reasoning is no longer valid. Indeed, $\text{cov}(U_2, y_2) = \text{cov}(U_2, c_2) - (y_1 - \hat{c}_1)\text{cov}(U_2, r)$. Whereas $\text{cov}(U_2, c_2) < 0$ still follows from $U_{22} < 0$, the sign of the second term is indeterminate: both $y_1 - \hat{c}_1$ and $\text{cov}(U_2, r)$ are arbitrary as to sign (r could be negatively correlated with c_2, if the returns on the *chosen* portfolio were negatively correlated with labour income).

4.2 Results by other authors

A different line of analysis has been pursued, still for the case where r is non-stochastic, by Leland (1968) and Sandmo (1970). Broadly speaking, their results point to diminishing absolute risk aversion as a sufficient condition for $\hat{c}_1 < \bar{c}_1$, where r is non-stochastic. Remember that $- U_{22}(c_2, \hat{c}_1)/U_2(c_2, \hat{c}_1)$ has been defined in Section 2 as the 'absolute risk-aversion' function relevant for temporal risks. Starting from any point in (c_1, c_2)-space, one may wonder whether $-(U_{22}/U_2)$ increases, decreases or remains constant when the starting point is displaced in some particular direction. Leland (1968) considers a move along the (tangent to the) indifference curve through (c_1, c_2): c_2 increases and c_1 is simultaneously decreased to keep utility constant. Leland assumes that such a move *decreases* absolute risk aversion, and derives as an implication that current consumption diminishes if the variance of y_2 increases, the expectation of y_2 being kept constant. In other words, such an 'increase in risk' reduces current consumption.

Sandmo (1970) assumes that $- U_{22}/U_2$ decreases with c_2 and increases with c_1; then defines an 'increase in risk' as a multiplicative shift in the distribution of y_2 combined with an additive shift that keeps the mean constant. His assumptions imply that such an increase in risk reduces current consumption.[22]

We will now state and prove (Section 4.3) a theorem and a corollary that generalise the analysis of Leland and Sandmo. An interpretation of our results is given in 4.4, where it is also explained how theorem 4.1 generalises these related results. Finally, we come back in Section 4.5 to the relevance of market opportunities for consumption decisions under uncertainty.

4.3 A second theorem about the impact of uncertainty on consumption

The condition appearing in theorem 4.1 refers to the behaviour of the absolute risk-aversion function along budget lines with slope $dc_2/dc_1 = -(1 + r^*)$. Define indeed

$$R(c_1, c_2, r^*) = \frac{\partial - (U_{22}/U_2)}{\partial c_1} - (1 + r^*)\frac{\partial - (U_{22}/U_2)}{\partial c_2}.$$

The sign of R determines whether absolute risk aversion increases (> 0), decreases (< 0) or remains constant ($= 0$) when c_1 increases and c_2 decreases along the budget line $c_2 = (y_1 - c_1)(1 + r^*) + y_2$. In this definition r^* is still given by (3.7) and satisfies $EU_1/EU_2 = 1 + r^*$.

Theorem 4.1: Let $y_2^\dagger$ be such that

$$\underset{c_1}{\text{Max}}\, U(c_1, (y_1 - c_1)(1 + r^*) + y_2^\dagger) = EU(\hat{c}_1, (y_1 - \hat{c}_1)(1 + r) + y_2)$$

$$(4.2)$$

---

[22]Related results have been established under the additional assumption of additive (cardinal) utility, for example by Mirman (1971) or by Rothschild and Stiglitz (1970). The latter paper clarifies in a basic way the concept of 'increase in risk'.

and let $c_1^\dagger$ be the value of c_1 maximising the left-hand side of (4.2). Then $R \gtreqless 0$ (identically in c_2 given $\hat{c}_1$) implies $\hat{c}_1 \lesseqgtr c_1^\dagger$.

Proof: The proof is based upon lemma C.1 in Appendix C. For convenience, it is broken into three easy steps.

(i)   We first notice that

$$U_1(\hat{c}_1, c_2) - (1 + r^*)U_2(\hat{c}_1, c_2) =_{\text{def}} h(c_2) = f(U(\hat{c}_1, c_2)), \tag{4.3}$$

with

$$f'(U) = \frac{U_{12} - (1 + r^*)U_{22}}{U_2}. \tag{4.4}$$

Indeed, differentiating both sides of (4.3) with respect to c_2, we verify: $dh/dc_2 = U_{12} - (1 + r^*)U_{22} = f'(U) \cdot U_2$, which satisfies (4.4);

$$d^2h/dc_2^2 = U_{122} - (1 + r^*)U_{222} = f''(U) \cdot U_2^2 + f'(U) \cdot U_{22}$$
$$= df'(U)/dc_2 \cdot (dc_2/dU) \cdot U_2^2 + f'(U) \cdot U_{22}$$
$$= \frac{(U_{122} - (1 + r^*)U_{222})U_2 - U_{22}(U_{12} - (1 + r^*)U_{22})}{U_2^2}$$
$$\times \frac{U_2^2}{U_2} + U_{22} \cdot \frac{U_{12} - (1 + r^*)U_{22}}{U_2},$$

and so on for higher derivatives. We notice in the process that

$$U_2 f''(U) = \frac{(U_{122} - (1 + r^*)U_{222})U_2 - U_{22}(U_{12} - (1 + r^*)U_{22})}{U_2^2}$$

$$= \frac{\partial(U_{22}/U_2)}{\partial c_1} - (1 + r^*)\frac{\partial(U_{22}/U_2)}{\partial c_2} = -R. \tag{4.5}$$

(ii)   In view of (4.5) and $U_2 > 0$, $R \gtreqless 0$ implies that

            concave

f is a linear function of U.

            convex

Let c_2' be such that $U(\hat{c}_1, c_2') = \int U(\hat{c}_1, c_2) \, d\Psi(c_2)$; Lemma C.1 then implies

$$R \gtreqless 0 \Rightarrow \int h(c_2) \, d\Psi(c_2) \lesseqgtr h(c_2'). \tag{4.6}$$

By (3.4) and the definition of h, $\int h(c_2) \, d\Psi(c_2) = 0$; therefore,

$$R \gtreqless 0 \Rightarrow h(c_2') = U_1(\hat{c}_1, c_2') - (1 + r^*)U_2(\hat{c}_1, c_2') \gtreqless 0. \tag{4.7}$$

(iii)   By definition,

$$U(\hat{c}_1, c_2') = U(c_1^\dagger, (y_1 - c_1^\dagger)(1 + r^*) + y_2^\dagger)$$

$$= \underset{c_1}{\text{Max}}\, U(c_1, (y_1 - c_1)(1 + r^*) + y_2^\dagger).$$

Since $d^2U/dc_1^2 < 0$, this implies

$$U_1(\hat{c}_1, c_2') - (1 + r^*)U_2(\hat{c}_1, c_2') \gtreqqless 0 \Leftrightarrow \hat{c}_1 \lesseqqgtr c_1^\dagger.$$

Combining this with (4.7), we conclude

$$R \gtreqqless 0 \Rightarrow \hat{c}_1 \lesseqqgtr c_1^\dagger. \qquad\qquad\qquad\qquad\qquad \square$$

Corollary: $r \equiv r^*$ implies $c_1^\dagger \leqslant \bar{c}_1$.

Proof: $U_{22} \leqslant 0$ implies

$$\begin{aligned}
U(c_1^\dagger, (y_1 - c_1^\dagger)(1 + r^*) + y_2^\dagger) &= EU(\hat{c}_1, (y_1 - \hat{c}_1)(1 + r) + y_2) \\
&\leqslant U(\hat{c}_1, (y_1 - \hat{c}_1)(1 + \bar{r}) + \bar{y}_2) \\
&\leqslant U(\bar{c}_1, (y_1 - \bar{c}_1)(1 + r^*) + \bar{y}_2).
\end{aligned}$$

It then follows from assumption 1.3 that $c_1^\dagger \leqslant \bar{c}_1$. $\qquad\qquad \square$

4.4 Endogenously diminishing absolute risk aversion

When $r \equiv r^*$, $R > 0$ means that absolute risk aversion $(-U_{22}/U_2)_{\hat{c}_1}$ diminishes when c_2 increases *thanks to* the additional savings implied in a decrease of c_1. We shall refer to this situation as 'endogenously diminishing absolute risk aversion'. Combining theorem 4.1 and its corollary, we have the result that $R \geqslant 0$ implies $\hat{c}_1 \leqslant \bar{c}_1$.

This conclusion is consistent with those reached by Leland and Sandmo. In the case of infinitesimal risks, the three conclusions are identical, although the assumptions are not quite identical – indicating that the assumptions used are sufficient, but not necessary, for the conclusion. Theorem 4.1 clarifies that issue, by showing that $R \geqslant 0$ is *necessary and sufficient for* $\hat{c}_1 \leqslant c_1^\dagger$; when $U_{22} < 0$ and $\sigma_{y_2}^2 > 0$, then $c_1^\dagger < \bar{c}_1$. Thus, $R > 0$ is not necessary for $\hat{c}_1 < \bar{c}_1$, but it is necessary for $\hat{c}_1 < c_1^\dagger$. The three-way implication in theorem 4.1 is thus a generalisation of the other results.

Our sharper result may be interpreted as follows. The impact of the uncertainty about future income on current consumption may be decomposed into an income effect and a substitution effect. The income effect corresponds to the fact that the expected utility of $\phi(y_2)$ is less than the utility of $\bar{y}_2$ – it is only equal to the utility of $y_2^\dagger \leqslant \bar{y}_2$. This income effect alone would call for setting $\hat{c}_1 = c_1^\dagger < \bar{c}_1$: the income effect is always negative under risk aversion. But in addition there is room for a substitution effect: keeping expected utility constant, uncertainty about y_2 may still affect current consumption. Theorem 4.1 states that the sign of the substitution effect is the sign of $-R$: risk aversion alone does not imply that the substitution effect is negative, but endogenously diminishing absolute risk aversion does. The implications of risk aversion are thus unambiguously defined.

A strong case may be made for regarding endogenous risk aversion as a meaningful, operational concept. Arrow (1965) argues as follows that absolute risk aversion for total wealth may reasonably be expected to decrease with wealth: 'If absolute risk aversion increased with wealth, it would follow that as an individual became wealthier, he would actually decrease the amount of risky assets held' (p. 35). In that argument, wealth is used as a primitive concept, and the increase in wealth is treated as exogenous. The argument may, however, be reformulated for the case where assets are acquired with savings and used to finance future consumption. One would then say: 'If absolute risk aversion for c_2 increased with c_2 along a budget line, it would follow that as an individual accumulated more wealth, he would actually decrease the amount of risky assets held.' One may thus consider that standard arguments invoked to discuss increasing versus decreasing absolute risk aversion for 'wealth' apply almost verbatim to 'risk aversion for c_2 along a budget line', that is, to endogenous risk aversion.

The arguments for decreasing absolute risk aversion are perhaps not compelling (the argument quoted above lacks generality when there are more than two assets), but it is a general conclusion that $\hat{c}_1$ is less than, equal to or greater than its 'expected utility' certainty equivalent according to whether absolute risk aversion for c_2 decreases, remains constant or increases with c_2 along budget lines defined by r^* – with some plausibility arguments in favour of the 'decreasing' case.

4.5 Consumption decisions with and without perfect markets

There remains now to relate the results of Sections 3 and 4. This will be done in three steps.

(i)   *When there exist perfect insurance and asset markets*, then y_2^* (as defined in theorem 3.1) $\leqslant y_2^\dagger$ (as defined in theorem 4.1). Indeed, define y_2^{00} by

$$\operatorname*{Max}_{c_1 \quad r} EU(c_1,(y_1 - c_1)(1 + r) + y_2^{00}) = U(c_1^\dagger,(y_1 - c_1^\dagger)(1 + r^*) + y_2^\dagger)$$

$$= \operatorname*{E}_{r,y_2} U(\hat{c}_1,(y_1 - \hat{c}_1)(1 + r) + y_2).$$

Because r is the rate of return on the *chosen* portfolio, whereas the sure rate r^* was available, we must have $y_2^\dagger \geqslant y_2^{00}$. Similarly, because the chosen future income could have been exchanged against the certainty of $y_2^*, y_2^{00} \geqslant y_2^*$. It follows that $c_1^* \leqslant c_1^\dagger$. Furthermore, if $\hat{c}_1 \leqslant c_1^*$, then $\hat{c}_1 \leqslant c_1^\dagger$, revealing that $\partial^2(U_1/U_2)/\partial c_2^2 \leqslant 0$ implies $R \geqslant 0$. This may be verified through formula (A.16) which may be rewritten as

$$\frac{\partial^2(U_1/U_2)}{\partial c_2^2} = -R - \frac{U_{22}\partial(U_1/U_2)}{\partial c_2} + \left(\frac{U_1}{U_2} - (1+r^*)\right)\frac{\partial - (U_{22}/U_2)}{\partial c_2}. \tag{4.8}$$

On the right-hand side of (4.8), the second term is positive, and the third vanishes when $U_1/U_2 = 1 + r^*$. Hence, at the value of c_2 for which $U_1/U_2 = 1 + r^*$, $\partial^2(U_1/U_2)/\partial c_2^2 \leqslant 0$ implies $R > 0$; if R does not change sign over the range of $\psi(c_2)$ that sign must be positive. We may then conclude that $\partial^2(U_1/U_2)/\partial c_2^2 \leqslant 0$ is consistent with endogenously diminishing absolute risk aversion.

(ii)   *When perfect insurance markets do not exist*, then: if $\hat{c}_1 = c_1^\dagger$, the availability of insurance would definitely increase $\hat{c}_1$; if $\hat{c}_1 = c_1^*$, the availability of insurance would increase (decrease) $\hat{c}_1$, if the insurance prices were such that the consumer would buy (sell) some insurance on his whole future income.

The first proposition is immediate: New insurance opportunities could only raise expected utility, irrespective of the insurance prices; this would also raise $y_2^\dagger$, hence $c_1^\dagger$, hence $\hat{c}_1 = c_1^\dagger$. The second proposition can be verified as follows: To say that insurance becomes available at a price such that the consumer would buy some on his whole future income means that $EU_2(y_2 - z_2) < 0$, or $EU_2 y_2/EU_2 < z_2$ (where z_2 is still the insurance value of future income). Hence, y_2^* would increase from its present level to the level z_2, through insurance purchase, and $\hat{c}_1 = c_1^*$ would similarly rise. A similar reasoning applies to the selling case.[23]

(iii) In the absence of perfect markets for assets *and* insurance, separability of consumption and portfolio decision is rather implausible; actually, we do not know of any reasonable conditions under which that situation obtains.

---

[23]The existence of markets with prices at which the consumer would *sell* insurance might seem remote, under generalised risk aversion. This remark is well taken when the risks of different consumers or groups of consumers are sufficiently independent, or even negatively correlated, so that insurance can reduce everybody's risks simultaneously. On the other hand, when the risks of most consumers are strongly positively correlated, equality of supply and demand in the insurance markets calls for prices at which there will be sellers as well as buyers; the less risk-averse consumers will then be sellers: they will find it profitable to accept a greater variability of c_2 but will offset partly this added variability by reducing c_1 (for reasons indicated in Appendix D). In such cases, the organisation of the insurance market need not stimulate total consumption.

Appendix A

Under certainty, the maximum of $U(c_1, c_2)$ under the budget constraint

$$c_2 = (y_1 - c_1)(1 + r) + y_2 \tag{A.1}$$

is defined by the first- and second-order conditions

$$U_1 - U_2(1 + r) = 0, \quad U_{11} - 2U_{12}(1 + r) + U_{22}(1 + r)^2 < 0. \tag{A.2}$$

Let

$$S =_{\text{def}} U_2(U_{11} - 2U_{12}(1 + r) + U_{22}(1 + r)^2)^{-1} < 0. \tag{A.3}$$

Through total differentiation of the first-order condition in (A.2), we find

$$\frac{dc_1}{dy} = \frac{dc_1}{dy_1} = -S(1 + r)\frac{\partial(U_1/U_2)}{\partial c_2},$$

$$\frac{dc_1}{dy_2} = -S\frac{\partial(U_1/U_2)}{\partial c_2}, \quad \text{where}$$

$$\frac{\partial(U_1/U_2)}{\partial c_2} = \frac{U_{12} - (U_1/U_2)U_{22}}{U_2}; \tag{A.4}$$

$$dc_1/dr = ((y_1 - c_1)/(1 + r))(dc_1/dy_1) + S$$

$$= -S\left((y_1 - c_1)\frac{\partial(U_1/U_2)}{\partial c_2} - 1\right). \tag{A.5}$$

In (A.5), $((y_1 - c_1)/(1 + r))(dc_1/dy_1)$ measures the income effect, and $S(<0)$ the substitution effect, of a change in r on c_1. The absolute value of S is also a measure of curvature of the indifference surfaces:

$$\frac{-1}{S} = \left(\frac{d^2 c_2}{dc_1^2}\right)_U = \left(\frac{-1}{U_2}\right)\left(\frac{d^2 U}{dc_1^2}\right)_{U_1 = U_2(1+r)}. \tag{A.6}$$

For any given values of r and $y = y_1 + y_2(1 + r)^{-1}$, dc_1/dr is equal to 0 provided $y_1 = \hat{y}_1$ and $y_2 = (y - \hat{y}_1)(1 + r)$, where

$$\hat{y}_1 = c_1 + \left(\frac{\partial(U_1/U_2)}{\partial c_2}\right)^{-1} > c_1. \tag{A.7}$$

One then finds that $(dc_2/dr)_{y_1 = \hat{y}_1} = \hat{y}_1 - c_1 = (\partial(U_1/U_2)/\partial c_2)^{-1}$ and

$$\frac{d^2 c_1}{dr^2}\bigg|_{y_1 = \hat{y}_1} = \frac{\partial(dc_1/dr)}{\partial c_2}\frac{dc_2}{dr} = -S(\hat{y}_1 - c_1)\frac{\partial^2(U_1/U_2)}{\partial c_2^2}$$

$$= -S\left(\frac{\partial(U_1/U_2)}{\partial c_2}\right)^{-1}\frac{\partial^2(U_1/U_2)}{\partial c_2^2}. \tag{A.8}$$

This expression has the sign of $\partial^2(U_1/U_2)/\partial c_2^2$, where

$$\frac{\partial^2(U_1/U_2)}{\partial c_2^2} = \frac{U_{122} - (U_1/U_2)U_{222}}{U_2} - 2\frac{U_{22}}{U_2}\frac{\partial(U_1/U_2)}{\partial c_2}. \tag{A.9}$$

The indirect utility function $V(y, r)$ is defined by

$$V(y, r) = U(c_1(y, r), c_2(y, r)| U_1 = U_2(1 + r)), \tag{A.10}$$

and its partial derivatives are evaluated by

$$\begin{aligned}
V_y &= U_1(dc_1/dy) + U_2(dc_2/dy) \\
&= U_1(dc_1/dy) + U_2(1 + r)(1 - (dc_1/dy)) \\
&= U_2(1 + r) = U_1, \\
V_r &= U_1(dc_1/dr) + U_2(dc_2/dr) \\
&= U_1(dc_1/dr) + U_2(y_1 - c_1 - (1 + r)(dc_1/dr)) \\
&= U_2(y_1 - c_1).
\end{aligned} \tag{A.11}$$

Proceeding further in this manner, one finds:

$$V_{yy} = U_{22}(1 + r)^2 - \frac{U_2}{S}\left(\frac{dc_1}{dy}\right)^2 \geq U_{22}(1 + r)^2; \tag{A.12}$$

$$V_{rr} = U_{22}(y_1 - c_1)^2 - \frac{U_2}{S}\left(\frac{dc_1}{dr}\right)^2 \geq U_{22}(y_1 - c_1)^2; \tag{A.13}$$

$$V_{ry} = U_{22}(1 + r)(y_1 - c_1) - \frac{U_2}{S}\frac{dc_1}{dy}\frac{dc_1}{dr}. \tag{A.14}$$

Since $dy/dy_2 = (1 + r)^{-1}$, one may define $V_{y_2} = (1 + r)^{-1}V_y = U_2$, $V_{y_2 y_2} = (1 + r)^{-2}V_{yy}$, and write in view of (A.12)–(A.14):

$$\begin{aligned}
-\frac{U_{22}}{U_2} &= -\frac{V_{y_2 y_2}}{V_{y_2}} + \left(\frac{dc_1}{dy_2}\right)^2\left(\frac{-1}{S}\right) \\
&= -\frac{V_{y_2 y_2}}{V_{y_2}} + \left(\frac{dc_1}{dy_2}\right)^2\left(\frac{d^2 c_2}{dc_1^2}\bigg|_U\right) \geq -\frac{V_{y_2 y_2}}{V_{y_2}},
\end{aligned}$$

$$-\frac{U_{22}}{U_2} = -\frac{V_{rr}}{V_r(y_1 - c_1)} + \frac{1}{(y_1 - c_1)^2}\left(\frac{dc_1}{dr}\right)^2\left(\frac{-1}{S}\right)$$

$$= -\frac{V_{ry_2}}{V_r} + \frac{1}{y_1 - c_1}\frac{dc_1}{dy_2}\frac{dc_1}{dr}\left(\frac{-1}{S}\right). \tag{A.15}$$

$-(U_{22}/U_2)$ is defined in the text as the absolute risk-aversion function for future consumption. Its partial derivatives satisfy:

$$\frac{\partial -(U_{22}/U_2)}{\partial c_1} - (1 + r)\frac{\partial -(U_{22}/U_2)}{\partial c_2}$$

$$= -\frac{U_{122} - (1 + r)U_{222}}{U_2} + \frac{U_{22}}{U_2}\frac{U_{12} - (1 + r)U_{22}}{U_2}$$

$$= -\frac{\partial^2(U_1/U_2)}{\partial c_2^2} - \frac{U_{22}}{U_2}\frac{\partial(U_1/U_2)}{\partial c_2}$$

$$+ \left(\frac{U_1}{U_2} - (1 + r)\right)\frac{\partial -(U_{22}/U_2)}{\partial c_2}, \tag{A.16}$$

$$\frac{\partial -(U_{22}/U_2)}{\partial c_1} - \frac{U_1}{U_2}\frac{\partial -(U_{22}/U_2)}{\partial c_2}$$

$$= -\frac{U_{122} - (U_1/U_2)U_{222}}{U_2} + \frac{U_{22}}{U_2}\frac{U_{12} - (U_1/U_2)U_{22}}{U_2}$$

$$= -\frac{\partial^2(U_1/U_2)}{\partial c_2^2} - \frac{U_{22}}{U_2}\frac{\partial(U_1/U_2)}{\partial c_2} \geqslant -\frac{\partial^2(U_1/U_2)}{\partial c_2^2}, \tag{A.17}$$

as can be readily verified, starting from (A.9).

Appendix B

Let $f(x, y)$ have the property that $f_x/f_y = a(x) + b(x)y$, $f_y \neq 0$. We wish to show that $f(x, y) = F(g(x) + h(x) \cdot y)$.

For $f(x, y) = \text{constant}$, we have $f_x + f_y y' = 0$, with $y' = dy/dx|_{f \text{ constant}}$, or $y' = -(f_x/f_y)$, so that:

$$y' = -a(x) - b(x)y. \tag{B.1}$$

The solution of this ordinary differential equation is readily verified to be

$$y = e^{-B(x)}(-\int a(x)e^{B(x)}dx + C), \tag{B.2}$$

where $B(x) = \int b(x)\,dx$; we may write (B.2) as

$$g(x) + h(x) \cdot y = c, \tag{B.3}$$

with $h(x) = e^{B(x)}$, $g(x) = \int a(x)e^{B(x)}dx$; since (B.3) is equivalent to '$f(x, y) = \text{constant}$', our hypothesis is verified.[24]

[24]We are grateful to Wlodzimierc Szwarc for this result.

Appendix C

Lemma C.1: Let $h(x) = f\{g(x)\}$ where f is differentiable in g and g is continuous in x; let furthermore $\phi(x)$ be any density such that $\int h(x)\,d\Phi(x)$ and $\int g(x)\,d\Phi(x)$ exist and are finite. Define x^0 (not necessarily unique) implicitly by $\int g(x)\,d\Phi(x) = g(x^0)$. Then

$$f\{g(x)\}\begin{matrix}\text{concave}\\\text{linear}\\\text{convex}\end{matrix}\ \text{in } g \text{ over the range of } \phi \text{ implies } \int h(x)\,d\Phi(x) \gtreqqless h(x^0).$$

Proof:

$$f\{g(x)\}\begin{matrix}\text{concave}\\\text{linear}\\\text{convex}\end{matrix}\ \text{in } g \Rightarrow h(x) = f\{g(x)\}$$

$$\gtreqqless f\{g(x^0)\} + \{g(x) - g(x^0)\}\cdot f'(g)|_{g(x^0)}.$$

This in turn implies

$$\int h(x)\,d\Phi(x) \gtreqqless f\{g(x^0)\} + f'(g)|_{g(x^0)}\int\{g(x) - g(x^0)\}\,d\Phi(x)$$

$$= f\{g(x^0)\} = h(x^0),$$

since $\int\{g(x) - g(x^0)\}\,d\Phi(x)$ vanishes by definition of x^0. $\qquad\square$

Lemma C.2: Let $h(x) = g(x)f(x)$, where f is differentiable and g is continuous in x; let furthermore $\phi(x)$ be any density such that $\int h(x)\,d\Phi(x)$,

$\int g(x)\,d\Phi(x)$ and $\int xg(x)\,d\Phi(x)$ exist and are finite. Define

$$x^0 = \int xg(x)\,d\Phi(x)\bigg/\int g(x)\,d\Phi(x).$$

Then $f(x)\begin{smallmatrix}\text{concave}\\\text{linear}\\\text{convex}\end{smallmatrix}$ in x over the range of ϕ implies

$$\int h(x)\,d\Phi(x)\gtreqqless f(x^0)\int g(x)\,d\Phi(x).$$

Proof: $f(x)\begin{smallmatrix}\text{concave}\\\text{linear}\\\text{convex}\end{smallmatrix}$ in $x\Rightarrow f(x)\lesseqqgtr f(x^0)+(x-x^0)f'(x)|_{x^0}.$

This in turn implies:

$$\int h(x)\,d\Phi(x)\gtreqqless f(x^0)\int g(x)\,d\Phi(x)+f'(x)|_{x^0}$$

$$\cdot\int (x-x^0)g(x)\,d\Phi(x)$$

$$= f(x^0)\int g(x)\,d\Phi(x)$$

since $\int(x-x^0)g(x)\,d\Phi(x)$ vanishes by definition of x^0. $\square$

Appendix D

Figure 9.1 may be helpful to illustrate the role of $\partial^2(U_1/U_2)/\partial c_2^2$ in our problem, as well as the way in which a reduction of c_1 is equivalent to a reduction in the risk about c_2.

In the figure, line I is the sure budget equation $c_2 = (y_1 - c_1)(1 + \bar{r}) + \bar{y}_2$ with slope $- (1 + \bar{r})$. The point $\bar{c}$ with coordinates $(\bar{c}_1, \bar{c}_2)$ represents the chosen point on this budget equation, and the rising line EE depicts the Engel curve through $\bar{c}$, drawn linear for graphical convenience. Now suppose $\bar{y}_2$ is replaced by a very simple uncertain prospect $\phi(y_2)$ in terms of which y_2 will assume the value $(\bar{y}_2 + \delta)$ or the value $(\bar{y}_2 - \delta)$ with equal probability. In the figure the lines labelled IIA and IIB represent the (mutually exclusive) budget equations corresponding to each of these alternatives. Suppose further that, when confronted with $\phi(y_2)$, the consumer wonders whether he should consume $\bar{c}_1$ or alternatively reduce his first period consumption from $\bar{c}_1$ to $c'_1 = \bar{c}_1 - \varepsilon$.

If the consumer stays at $\bar{c}_1$, we see from the figure that he will end up at the consumption points $\bar{a}$ or $\bar{b}$, with equal probability. Letting $\bar{a}$ and $\bar{b}$ denote also the c_2 coordinate of the corresponding points in the figure, the mutually exclusive and equally likely outcomes can be described by the two consumption vectors $(\bar{c}_1, \bar{a})$, $(\bar{c}_1, \bar{b})$ having expected utility: $\bar{U} = (1/2)(U(\bar{c}_1, \bar{a}) + U(\bar{c}_1, \bar{b}))$. Similarly, if he moves to c'_1, we see that his expected utility can be expressed as $U' = \frac{1}{2}(U(c'_1, a') + U(c'_1, b'))$. To compare the two consumption decisions, first draw the indifference curve through $\bar{a}$ and let it intersect the line $c_1 = c'_1$ at the point α. Hence by construction, $U(\bar{c}, \bar{a}) = U(c'_1, \alpha)$. By drawing similarly the indifference curve through $\bar{b}$, we locate the point β such that $U(\bar{c}_1, \bar{b}) = U(c'_1, \beta)$. Hence $\bar{U} = \frac{1}{2}(U(c'_1, \alpha) + U(c'_1, \beta))$. In other words, moving back from c'_1 to $\bar{c}_1$ is

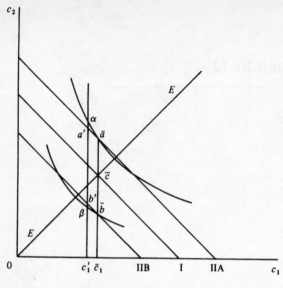

Figure 9.1

entirely equivalent, in terms of $E(U)$, to remaining at c'_1 but exchanging the random variable c'_2 taking the values a' and b' with equal probability against a new random variable, call it γ_2, which takes the values α and β with equal probability. Thus our problem can be reduced to the question: Given c'_1, is the prospect $\{c'_2\}$ better or worse than the prospect $\{\gamma_2\}$? One point is immediately apparent from Figure 9.1: since $\beta < b' < a' < \alpha$, it follows that $\text{var}(\gamma_2) > \text{var}(c'_2)$. In other words *increasing consumption* from c'_1 to $\bar{c}_1$ has the effect of *increasing the variance* of the outcome. The reason is not far to seek. Increasing c_1 is equivalent to gearing current consumption more nearly to the higher income; this will produce an improvement *if* the larger y_2 obtains, but a deterioration if the smaller y_2 obtains. It will thus make things even brighter when they would be bright anyway and even more dismal if the worse turns out, hence it increases the variance of the outcome.[25] On this account then, if there is risk aversion, c'_2 will be preferred to γ_2, and hence c'_1 will be preferred to $\bar{c}_1$. Or, to put it differently, uncertainty tends to increase savings because the increase in savings has the effect of trimming the uncertainty of the outcome.

But this 'variance effect' is not the end of the story: In choosing between the uncertain prospects $\{c'_2\}$ and $\{\gamma_2\}$, one must also compare their mean

[25]It can be verified from the figure that, for ε sufficiently small, the above conclusion must necessarily hold as long as the indifference curves are convex and the Engel curve has a finite positive slope. For an extension to more complicated densities, see Drèze and Modigliani (1966), theorem 5.1.

values.[26] If $\bar{\gamma}_2 = \frac{1}{2}(\alpha + \beta) < c'_2 = \frac{1}{2}(a' + b')$, then c'_2 dominates γ_2 in both respects and hence c'_1 will be unequivocally preferred to $\bar{c}_1$ (even under risk indifference). But if the above inequality is reversed, then no definite conclusion can be reached. We will now show that the relation between $\bar{\gamma}_2$ and $\bar{c}_2$ is precisely controlled by the sign of $\partial^2(U_1/U_2)/\partial c_2^2$.

To this end we first observe from Figure 9.1 that the two mutually exclusive values of c'_2, namely a' and b', can be expressed as follows:

$$a' = \bar{a} + \varepsilon(1 + \bar{r}), \quad b' = \bar{b} + \varepsilon(1 + \bar{r}). \tag{D.1}$$

We further note that, for ε small, the slope of the chord joining the points $\bar{a}$ and α in the figure can be approximated by that of the indifference curve through $\bar{a}$, namely, $U_1(\bar{c}_1, \bar{a})/U_2(\bar{c}_1, \bar{a}) =_{\text{def}} (U_1/U_2)_{\bar{a}}$. Similarly, the slope of the chord joining $\bar{b}$ and β can be approximated by the slope of the indifference curve through $\bar{b}$, $(U_1/U_2)_{\bar{b}}$. We therefore have

$$\alpha \simeq \bar{a} + \varepsilon(U_1/U_2)_{\bar{a}}, \quad \beta \simeq \bar{b} + \varepsilon(U_1/U_2)_{\bar{b}}. \tag{D.2}$$

Hence

$$\bar{c}_2 - \bar{\gamma}_2 \simeq \varepsilon\left((1 + \bar{r}) - \frac{1}{2}\left(\left.\frac{U_1}{U_2}\right|_{\bar{a}} + \left.\frac{U_1}{U_2}\right|_{\bar{b}} \right) \right)$$

$$= \varepsilon\left(\left.\frac{U_1}{U_2}\right|_{\bar{c}} - \frac{1}{2}\left(\left.\frac{U_1}{U_2}\right|_{\bar{a}} + \left.\frac{U_1}{U_2}\right|_{\bar{b}} \right) \right).^{27} \tag{D.3}$$

Since $\bar{a}$ and $\bar{b}$ are symmetrically located about $\bar{c}$, in the neighbourhood of that point, it follows that

$$\left.\frac{\partial^2(U_1/U_2)}{\partial c_2^2}\right|_{\bar{c}} \gtreqless 0 \Leftrightarrow \left\{ \frac{1}{2}\left(\left.\frac{U_1}{U_2}\right|_{\bar{a}} + \left.\frac{U_1}{U_2}\right|_{\bar{b}} \right) \right.$$

$$\left. \gtreqless \left.\frac{U_1}{U_2}\right|_{\bar{c}=(\bar{a}+\bar{b})/2} \right\} \Leftrightarrow \bar{c}'_2 - \bar{\gamma}_2 \lesseqgtr 0. \tag{D.4}$$

Accordingly, this 'mean effect' will reinforce the 'variance effect' whenever $\partial^2(U_1/U_2)/\partial c_2^2 \leqslant 0$, establishing unequivocally the superiority of c'_1 over $\bar{c}_1$; but it will work in the opposite direction when $\partial^2(U_1/U_2)/\partial c_2^2 > 0$. Theorem 3.1 may be interpreted as showing that the 'variance effect' vanishes at c_1^*, through optimal choice of the prospect ϕ; the sign of $\hat{c}_1 - c_1^*$ is then determined by the 'mean effect', i.e. by the sign of $\partial^2(U_1/U_2)/\partial c_2^2$.

---

[26]With infinitesimal risks, higher moments need not be considered.
[27]The last step follows from the fact that the point $\bar{c} = (c_1, c_2)$ is the point of tangency of the budget equation I in Figure 9.1 with an indifference curve; hence at $\bar{c}$, the slope of the indifference curve $(U_1/U_2)_{\bar{c}}$ is precisely $(1 + \bar{r})$.

References

Arrow, K.J. (1953). Le rôle des valeurs boursières pour la réparition la meilleure des risques. *Econométrie*, pp. 41–8. Paris: CNRS. Translated (1964) as The Role of Securities in the Optimal Allocation of Risk-Bearing. *Review of Economic Studies*, 31: 91–6

—(1965). *Aspects of the Theory of Risk-Bearing*. Helsinki: Yrjö Jahnsson Foundation

Debreu, G. (1959). *Theory of Value*. New York: Wiley

Drèze, J. (1971). Market Allocation under Uncertainty *European Economic Review* 2: 133–65 (Chapter 6 supra.)

Drèze, J. and F. Modigliani (1966). Epargne et consommation en avenir aléatoire. *Cahiers du Séminaire d'Econométrie*, 9: 7–33 (Partim: Chapter 10 infra.)

Fisher, I. (1930). *Theory of Interest*. New York: Macmillan

Hirshleifer, J. (1965). Investment Decisions Under Uncertainty: Choice-Theoretic Approaches. *The Quarterly Journal of Economics*, 79: 509–36

Leland, H.E. (1968). Saving and Uncertainty: The Precautionary Demand for Savings. *The Quarterly Journal of Economics*, 82: 463–73

Marschak, J. (1954). Towards an Economic Theory of Organization and Information. In *Decision Process*, R.M. Thrall, C.H. Coombs and R.L. Davis (eds.), pp. 187–220, New York: Wiley

Mirman, L.J. (1971). Uncertainty and Optimal Consumption Decisions. *Econometrica*, 39: 179–85

Neumann, J. von and O. Morgenstern (1944). *Theory of Games and Economic Behavior*. Princeton: Princeton University Press

Pestieau, P. (1969). Epargne et consommation dans l'incertitude: un modèle à trois périodes. *Recherches Economiques de Louvain*, 2: 63–88

Pratt, J.W. (1964). Risk Aversion in the Small and in the Large. *Econometrica*, 32: 122–36

Rothschild, M. and J.E. Stiglitz (1970). Increasing Risk, I and II. *Journal of Economic Theory*, 2: 225–43; *ibid.*, 3: 66–84

Sandmo, A. (1970). The Effect of Uncertainty on Saving Decisions. *Review of Economic Studies*, 37: 353–60

Savage, L.J. (1954). *The Foundations of Statistics*. New York: Wiley

10 Earnings, assets and savings: a model of interdependent choice*

1 Portfolio selection and occupational choice

After discussing the determinants of current consumption when $\phi(y_2, r)$ is given, we study here the behaviour of a consumer who chooses simultaneously an uncertain prospect ϕ and a level of initial consumption c_1. One aspect of this problem is well known, namely the 'portfolio selection problem' – see, for example, Markowitz (1959).

In that problem, one studies the allocation by a consumer of a given wealth level x among $m + 1$ assets with rates of return r_j, given the known rate of return r_{m+1} of a safe asset and the joint density $\phi(r_1, \ldots, r_m)$ of the remaining rates of return. If a fraction β_j of the wealth x is allocated to asset j, then

$$\beta_{m+1} = 1 - \sum_{j=1}^{m} \beta_j,$$

and the *overall* rate of return is equal to

$$r_{m+1} + \sum_{j=1}^{m} \beta_j(r_j - r_{m+1}).$$

The portfolio selection problem is stated as follows in our notation:

$$\begin{aligned}
\max_{\beta_1, \ldots, \beta_m} \int_{r_1}, \ldots, \int_{r_m} U\bigg[c_1, x\Big\{ 1 + r_{m+1} \\
+ \sum_{j=1}^{m} \beta_j(r_j - r_{m+1}) \Big\} + y_2 \bigg] d\Phi(r_1, \ldots, r_m).
\end{aligned} \tag{1.1}$$

*This chapter is a verbatim translation of Section 6 in 'Epargne et consommation en avenir aléatoire', J.H. Drèze and F. Modigliani, *Cahiers du Séminaire d'Econométrie*, 9 (1966): 7–33. It complements Section 3 of Chapter 9; see in particular note 16 there. The assumptions and definitions of Chapter 9 are retained here.

Writing $x = y_1 - c_1$ and maximising with respect to c_1 as well as $\beta_1, \ldots, \beta_m$, one would solve simultaneously the savings problem and the portfolio selection problem, when future income is known. In order to allow for uncertainty of future income, one should replace $\phi(r_1, \ldots, r_m)$ by $\psi(y_2, r_1, \ldots, r_m)$ and integrate in (1.1) with respect to $m + 1$ variables rather than m.

A further generalisation, introduced here, consists in treating the density of future income as chosen by the consumer on a par with the density of the *overall* rate of return on assets. To that end, we shall assume that the consumer has access to $n + 1$ professional activities with respective incomes $\{y_1(i), y_2(i)\}, i = 1, \ldots, n + 1$; and that he knows the first period incomes $y_1(i)$ for all activities as well as the second period income $y_2(n + 1) = y_2$ of a safe occupation. Defining n random variables

$$\tau_i = \frac{y_2(i)}{y_2(n+1)} - 1, \quad \text{so that } y_2(i) = (1 + \tau_i)y_2,$$

we shall assume that the joint density $\phi(\tau_1, \ldots, \tau_n, r_1, \ldots, r_m)$ is known.

To facilitate comparisons, we treat the two problems symmetrically, namely occupational choice and portfolio choice, by assuming that the consumer allocates to activity i a fraction α_i of his time,

$$\sum_{i=1}^{n+1} \alpha_i = 1.$$

An actual occupation is thus defined as a linear combination of $n + 1$ underlying activities. The same flexibility exists for occupational choices and for portfolio choices. As we shall verify, this amounts to considering an infinity of actual occupations, with a linear relationship between the expectations and standard deviations of the incomes associated with alternative occupations.

2 First-order conditions

It is convenient to use the following notation:

$$y_1(n + 1) = by_2; \quad y_1(i) = y_1(n + 1) + \eta_i y_2;$$

$A = $ net market value of the consumer's initial assets;

$$a = \frac{A}{y_2} + b, \quad \alpha = (\alpha_1, \ldots, \alpha_n)', \quad \eta = (\eta_1, \ldots, \eta_n)'.$$

Accordingly, the wealth of the consumer, inclusive of current savings, is given by

$$x = y_2\left(a + \sum_{i=1}^{n} \alpha_i \eta_i\right) - c_1 = y_2(a + \alpha'\eta) - c_1. \tag{2.1}$$

Furthermore let

$$r = 1 + r_{m+1}, \quad \rho_j = r_j - r_{m+1}, \quad \rho = (\rho_1, \ldots, \rho_m)',$$
$$\beta = (\beta_1, \ldots, \beta_m)', \quad \tau = (\tau_1, \ldots, \tau_n)';$$

then

$$c_2 = x\left(r + \sum_{j=1}^{m} \beta_j \rho_j\right) + y_2\left(1 + \sum_{i=1}^{n} \alpha_i \tau_i\right)$$

$$= x(r + \beta'\rho) + y_2(1 + \alpha'\tau). \tag{2.2}$$

The consumer's problem becomes:

$$\underset{c_1, \alpha, \beta}{\text{Max}} \int U[c_1, \{y_2(a + \alpha'\eta) - c_1\}(r + \beta'\rho) + y_2(1 + \alpha'\tau)] \, d\Phi(\tau, \rho). \tag{2.3}$$

First-order conditions for a maximum are:

$$\frac{\partial E(U)}{\partial c_1} = \int [U_1 - U_2(r + \beta'\rho)] \, d\Phi(\tau, \rho) = 0; \tag{2.4}$$

$$\frac{\partial E(U)}{\partial \alpha_i} = \int U_2[y_2 \eta_i(r + \beta'\rho) + y_2 \tau_i] \, d\Phi(\tau, \rho) = 0, \quad i = 1, \ldots, n; \tag{2.5}$$

$$\frac{\partial E(U)}{\partial \beta_j} = \int U_2[y_2(a + \alpha'\eta) - c_1] \rho_j \, d\Phi(\tau, \rho) = 0, \quad j = 1, \ldots, m. \tag{2.6}$$

Finally let $\pi = \tau + \eta r$ and denote by $\omega(\pi, \rho)$ the joint density of π and ρ obtained from $\phi(\tau, \rho)$ by shifting the origin. Conditions (2.4)–(2.6) simplify to:

$$\int (U_1 - rU_2) \, d\Omega(\pi, \rho) = 0; \tag{2.7}$$

$$\int U_2 \pi_i \, d\Omega(\pi, \rho) = 0, \quad i = 1, \ldots, n; \tag{2.8}$$

$$\int U_2 \rho_j \, d\Omega(\pi, \rho) = 0, \quad j = 1, \ldots, m. \tag{2.9}$$

Assume that second-order conditions are satisfied, and that there exists a solution $\hat{c}_1 > 0$, $\hat{\alpha} > 0$, $\hat{\beta} > 0$ with

$$\sum_{i=1}^{n} \hat{\alpha}_i < 1, \quad \sum_{i=1}^{m} \hat{\beta}_i < 1.$$

Our results admit of the following interpretation:

Proposition 2.1: The ratio of expected marginal utilities for c_1 and c_2 is equal to the exchange rate defined by the *safe* asset $m + 1$ (2.7).

Proposition 2.2: The expected marginal utility (in terms of c_2) of a unit of labour time is the same for each of the $n + 1$ activities (2.8).

Proposition 2.3: The expected marginal utility (in terms of c_2) of a unit worth of investment is the same for each of the $n + 1$ assets (2.9).

3 Separation of consumption decisions from portfolio and occupational choices

Let c_1^* be the optimal initial consumption when $\alpha = 0$, $\beta = 0$, i.e. when the consumer has only access to the safe occupation and the safe asset. The following theorem (which is proved in Chapter 9) holds for every consumer and every density ω.

Theorem 3.1:

$$\left. \partial^2 \frac{\dfrac{U_1}{U_2}}{\partial c_2^2} \right|_{\hat{c}_1} \equiv 0 \quad \text{implies} \quad \hat{c}_1 = c_1^*.$$

This theorem is our main result. It has the following meaning: Under a purely ordinal condition – namely that the slope of the indifference curves be a linear function of c_2 for fixed c_1 – the initial *consumption* of a consumer, allocating freely his time among alternative activities and his wealth among alternative assets, does not depend upon his degree of risk aversion nor upon his actual choices of occupations (hence of income) and of portfolio (hence of rate of return). The ordinal condition is equivalent to the absence of the 'mean effect' (mentioned in Appendix D to Chapter 9); the theorem reveals that the 'variance effect' vanishes under optimal occupational and portfolio choices on competitive markets. Of course, when $\hat{c}_1 = c_1^*$, initial savings $y_2(a + \alpha'\eta) - \hat{c}_1$ rise with initial income $y_2(a + \alpha'\eta)$, so that initial *savings* depend upon risk preferences and occupational choices.

Using formula (A.8) of Chapter 9, we can prove:

Theorem 3.2: If there exists an allocation of income between the initial period and the future such that $dc_1/dr = 0$ identically in r, then

$$\partial^2 \frac{\dfrac{U_1}{U_2}}{\partial c_2^2} = 0$$

identically in c_2.

Combining the two theorems yields:

Proposition 3.1: If there exists an intertemporal allocation of income for which $dc_1/dr \equiv 0$, then $c_1 = c_1^*$ identically in $\hat{\alpha}, \hat{\beta}$.

4 Mean-variance analysis

When $U_{222} \equiv 0$, or $U_{2222} \equiv 0$ and all third-order moments (around the mean) of (π, ρ) vanish, then (2.8) and (2.9) can be solved explicitly for α and β.

Let $\bar{\pi}, \bar{\rho}$ denote the expected values, Σ the covariance matrix, of π, ρ. Furthermore let

$$z = \frac{-1}{U_{22}} \left(U_2 + U_{222} \frac{\sigma_{c_2}^2}{2} \right). \tag{3.1}$$

It is then readily verified that (2.8)–(2.9) are solved by:

$$\begin{pmatrix} y_2 \hat{\alpha} \\ x \hat{\beta} \end{pmatrix} = z \Sigma^{-1} \begin{pmatrix} \bar{\pi} \\ \bar{\rho} \end{pmatrix}. \tag{3.2}$$

This vector equality generalises the well-known results obtained under similar assumptions for the portfolio problem. To see this, partition Σ as:

$$\Sigma = \begin{bmatrix} \Sigma_{\pi\pi} & \Sigma_{\pi\rho} \\ \Sigma_{\rho\pi} & \Sigma_{\rho\rho} \end{bmatrix}, \quad \Sigma^{-1} = \begin{bmatrix} \Sigma^{\pi\pi} & \Sigma^{\pi\rho} \\ \Sigma^{\rho\pi} & \Sigma^{\rho\rho} \end{bmatrix}. \tag{3.3}$$

Equation (3.2) can then be written in partitioned form as:

$$\hat{\alpha} = \frac{z}{y_2} (\Sigma^{\pi\pi} \bar{\pi} + \Sigma^{\pi\rho} \bar{\rho}), \tag{3.4}$$

$$\hat{\beta} = \frac{z}{x} (\Sigma^{\rho\pi} \bar{\pi} + \Sigma^{\rho\rho} \bar{\rho}). \tag{3.5}$$

Accordingly:

Proposition 4.1: If U is quadratic in c_2, or if U is cubic in c_2 and ω symmetrical, then the ratios

$$\frac{\hat{\alpha}_i}{\hat{\alpha}_k}, \quad i, k = 1, \ldots, n, \quad \text{and} \quad \frac{\hat{\beta}_j}{\hat{\beta}_l}, \quad j, l = 1, \ldots, m,$$

are independent of the consumer's tastes and wealth (both human and non-human wealth); they are identical for all consumers having access to the same occupational choices and asset markets.

The same property holds for the ratios

$$\frac{y_2 \hat{\alpha}_i}{x \hat{\beta}_j}, \quad i = 1, \ldots, n, j = 1, \ldots, m.$$

On the other hand, the ratios

$$\frac{\hat{\alpha}_i}{\hat{\beta}_j} \quad \text{and} \quad \frac{\sum\limits_{i=1}^{n} \hat{\alpha}_i}{\sum\limits_{j=1}^{m} \hat{\beta}_j}$$

are proportional to the ratio x/y_2 of non-human wealth to human wealth.[1]

Proposition 4.2: When $\Sigma_{\pi\rho} = 0$, i.e. when future earnings are uncorrelated with asset returns, then (3.4)–(3.5) simplify to

$$\hat{\alpha} = \frac{z}{y_2}\Sigma^{\pi\pi}\bar{\pi}, \tag{4.1}$$

$$\hat{\beta} = \frac{z}{x}\Sigma^{\rho\rho}\bar{\rho}. \tag{4.2}$$

Proposition 4.2 (4.2) is due to Tobin (1958). In general, portfolio choices are influenced by uncertainties surrounding labour income – a conclusion which is both logical and supported by experience. Since the ratios $\hat{\alpha}_i/\hat{\alpha}_k$ and $\hat{\beta}_j/\hat{\beta}_l$ are independent of tastes, we must look at the totals

$$\sum_{i=1}^{n}\hat{\alpha}_i \quad \text{and} \quad \sum_{j=1}^{m}\hat{\beta}_j$$

to conclude whether or not a given consumer has chosen a risky occupation or a risky portfolio. For given x and y_2, the ratio of these two totals does not depend upon tastes, so that a consumer choosing a riskier occupation will also hold a riskier portfolio (invest a smaller fraction of his wealth in the safe asset). Contrary to the intuition of some, this behaviour is consistent with diversification. A consumer holding a very risky occupation but a conservative portfolio should – if possible – shift to a less risky occupation and a less conservative portfolio, in order to diversify more effectively his overall risk. This is the meaning of proposition 4.1. In equilibrium, the fraction of labour time devoted to risky activities must stand to the fraction of wealth held in risky assets in the same ratio as non-human wealth stands to human wealth; thus, the asset portfolio will be the more risky, the smaller is the share of that portfolio in aggregate wealth.

5 Measuring risk aversion

Let $c_2^0 = (y_2 a - c_1)r + y_2$ denote the non-stochastic part of future consumption; substituting from (3.2) into (2.2), we get:

$$c_2 = c_2^0 + z(\bar{\pi}' \ \bar{\rho}')\Sigma^{-1}\begin{pmatrix}\pi\\\rho\end{pmatrix}, \tag{5.1}$$

$$\bar{c}_2 = c_2^0 + z(\bar{\pi}' \ \bar{\rho}')\Sigma^{-1}\begin{pmatrix}\bar{\pi}\\\bar{\rho}\end{pmatrix}, \tag{5.2}$$

[1]Note that this last ratio does not affect c_1, in the framework of theorem 3.1, in contrast to the views expressed by Friedman (1957).

$$\sigma_{c_2}^2 = z^2 (\bar{\pi}' \ \bar{\rho}') \Sigma^{-1} \left(\frac{\bar{\pi}}{\bar{\rho}} \right) = z(\bar{c}_2 - c_2^0), \tag{5.3}$$

$$\bar{c}_2 = c_2^0 + \sigma_{c_2} \left[(\bar{\pi}' \ \bar{\rho}') \Sigma^{-1} \left(\frac{\bar{\pi}}{\bar{\rho}} \right) \right]^{1/2}. \tag{5.4}$$

We thus exhibit the linear relationship between $\bar{c}_2$ and σ_{c_2} familiar in the portfolio literature and mentioned at the end of Section 1 for earnings. Finally, with $1/z$ being a measure of risk aversion, the quantity $\bar{c}_2 - c_2^0$ is inversely proportional to risk aversion. This suggests a way of inferring risk aversion from market data and using the measurement in other areas of economic theory like income distribution.

References

Friedman, M. (1957). *A Theory of the Consumption Function*, Princeton: Princeton University Press

Markowitz, H. (1959). *Portfolio Selection*, New York: Wiley

Tobin, J. (1958). Liquidity Preference as Behavior Towards Risk, *Review of Economic Studies*, 25: 65–86

IV Producer decisions

11 Demand fluctuations, capacity utilisation and prices*

1 Introduction

In this paper, we consider an industry supplying a single commodity, the demand for which is uncertain or shifting in time. We show that several standard propositions in the static theory of the firm no longer apply in that context. Consequently, a widely accepted inference about the nature of competition in such an industry becomes unwarranted under our more realistic assumptions.

Section 2 restates the propositions that are challenged later on. A simplified model is introduced in Section 3. Section 4 is devoted to counterparts, for that model, of the propositions listed in Section 2. Four methodological conclusions are presented in Section 6. The appendix collects some properties of the cost function used in the simplified model.

2 Some propositions from the static theory

Let us consider an industry operating under the following assumptions:

a. it produces a single commodity;
b. all firms are identical;
c. cost for each firm is a function of quantity alone; the total and variable average cost curves of those firms are U-shaped, continuously differentiable, and independent of the number of firms in the industry;
d. there is no restriction to entry, and the number of firms is not required to be an integer;
e. the quantity demanded at each price is fixed for the industry, independently of the number of firms; the demand function is continuous.

*Operations Research Verfahren, 3 (1967): 119–41, with Jean Jaskold Gabszewicz. The proofs of the propositions, and a section discussing generalisations, are omitted because they are covered by Chapter 12.

Let us furthermore adopt the following notation:

> p: price of the commodity;
> $Q = Q(p)$: demand function for the industry;
> n: number of firms;
> q: output of an individual firm;
> $F(q)$: total cost for a firm;
> $f(q)$: average cost for a firm;
> $\Phi(q)$: marginal cost for a firm;
> q^*: output for which average cost is minimum: $f(q^*) = \Phi(q^*)$;
> $C = C(Q, n) = nF(Q/n)$: total cost for the industry.[1]

The following propositions are then easily derived:[2]

Proposition 2.1: For every Q, $C(Q, n)$ is minimum for n such that

$$f\left(\frac{Q}{n}\right) = \Phi\left(\frac{Q}{n}\right),$$

or $q = q^*$; i.e. total cost for the industry is minimised when each firm is producing that output for which average cost is equal to marginal cost (so that average cost is minimum).

Proposition 2.2: If q is such that $\Phi(q) = p$, and if n increases (decreases) whenever $F(q) < (>)q\Phi(q)$, then in equilibrium

$$f\left(\frac{Q}{n}\right) = \Phi\left(\frac{Q}{n}\right) = p$$

and $F(q) = pq$; i.e. competition and free entry lead to a price equal to minimum average cost and to an optimal number of firms, each of which is breaking even.

These propositions apply to both the short run and the long run. If the long-run average cost curve is defined as the envelope of the short-run average cost curves, as plant sizes and designs are varied, then the output which minimises long-run average cost also minimises short-run average cost, for the right size and design of plant.

Furthermore, since equality of short- and long-run average costs implies equality of short- and long-run marginal costs, it follows that the relationship of average to marginal cost is the same for the short-run as for the long-run concepts, when plants are of the right size and design.

---

[1] In what follows, it is systematically assumed that the output produced by each firm is larger than the output for which marginal cost is minimum, so that $d\phi(q)/dq > 0$ – for otherwise $q = Q/n$ would not be an efficient allocation of output among firms.

[2] See, for example, Krelle (1961, Ch. 9).

These propositions are at the root of the inferences according to which:

$f(q) = \Phi(q)$ is an indication of perfect competition and free entry;
$f(q) > \Phi(q)$ is an indication of imperfect or monopolistic competition and free entry;
$f(q) < \Phi(q)$ is an indication of limitations to entry (restrictive practices, scarce inputs,...).

3 A simple model with uncertain demand

Propositions 2.1 and 2.2 describe a situation where the design of plants, and their number, are perfectly adjusted to the demand conditions. Such a situation may prevail in the long run if the demand function is stable – or conceivably if it is shifting over time in a regular and predictable way. In the latter case, a distinction must be drawn between increases and decreases in the rate of demand. Increases can be met by additional investment, if only they become known soon enough for the required building time to be available; otherwise they must be met (temporarily at least) by overloading the existing equipment. Decreases can be accompanied by natural depreciation without replacement – provided only the rate of decrease does not exceed the rate of depreciation; otherwise, they must be met by operating the existing equipment below capacity. Furthermore, decreases that are forseen may operate as a check on investment or replacement: a temporary overloading of the equipment is then preferred to the creation of a capacity that could be fully utilised today but would become excessive tomorrow. In such cases, propositions 2.1 and 2.2 fail to be continuously verified and the concept of optimal capacity must be redefined.

Similar difficulties arise when a decision to build a plant must be reached under imperfect knowledge about the demand – or equivalently the price – that will prevail when the plant will be in operation: it is impossible to adjust the design and number of plants optimally to a quantity that is as yet unknown! A conservative investment behaviour reduces the risk of creating excess capacity but increases the risk of under-capacity, and conversely.

Demand uncertainty may take two forms. First, one may be uncertain about the general level of demand over the lifetime of a plant. This is typical of situations where plants are short-lived. An almost perfect example is given by the provision of facilities (e.g. restaurants) for visitors at a fair, exhibition or similar event: facilities must be built under imperfect information about the number of visitors to be served – and no further capacity adjustment is possible once that number is known. Second, one may have reasonably accurate forecasts about the average level of demand over rather long periods, but at the same time be faced with substantial random fluctuations in the short run. By analogy with the previous example, we might refer to permanent facilities for serving tourists at a resort, when the daily number of customers responds sharply to weather conditions. Industries that are sensitive to cyclical fluctuations provide countless additional examples.

In all these situations, perfect adjustment of design and number of plants to quantity demanded or to market price is impossible, and rates of capacity utilisation are uncertain or variable in time. One may then investigate whether propositions 2.1 and 2.2 remain fulfilled *on the average* – either in terms of expectations or in terms of averages over time. In order to show that such is not the case, and to exhibit the systematic biases that result from uncertainty or fluctuations, we discuss a simple model where: (i) total cost for the firm is a cubic function of output; and (ii) demand for the industry is a random variable, with known symmetric density and zero price elasticity. More precisely, we replace assumptions c and e by:

c′: total cost for each firm is given by the expression:

$$F(q) = \gamma + q - \frac{\alpha}{2}q^2 + \frac{\beta}{3}q^3, \quad \alpha, \beta > 0, \gamma \geqslant 0^3; \tag{3.1}$$

e′: demand (and thus output) for the industry is a random variable Q, with finite expectation $E(Q) = \bar{Q}$, finite variance $E\{(Q - \bar{Q})^2\} = \sigma_Q^2 > 0$ and zero third moment $E\{(Q - \bar{Q})^3\} = 0$.

These assumptions enable us to derive exact results from Taylor-series expansions carried to three terms only. Demand is assumed perfectly inelastic so as to give a precise meaning to minimisation of expected total cost for the industry. Generalisations are discussed below.

One may think about Q as the total quantity that will be demanded from the industry during the lifetime of n plants to be built now – before Q is known; after Q is observed,[4] each plant will produce Q/n at a cost $F(Q/n)$. Again, one may think about Q as measuring demand during a particular time interval. Our analysis would then rest on the assumption that the density of demand is identical for all time intervals, independently of past realisations.[5]

With c′, we are assuming that all firms have identical cost functions. The existence of a cost function is predicated upon a priori choice of plant size and design. What determines that choice in our model? This problem has retained the attention of Hart (1951), who argues that uncertainty about

---

[3]γ is of course fixed costs; α and β must be strictly positive for average cost to be U-shaped, with $\alpha^2 < 4\beta$ for positive marginal cost.

[4]We retain the assumption that $Q/n > \alpha/2\beta$ – see note 1 above. For a model with output decisions under uncertainty, see Tisdell (1963).

[5]It is helpful, in this case, to think about γ as measuring the rental value, per time interval, of a plant. If the demand density and operating costs are constant over time, so will be γ. If the number of plants in existence at a given time reflects, in some sense, an optimum or an equilibrium, then the same property will be verified at other times, and the number of plants will remain constant over time, in spite of the random fluctuations of demand. This constancy is not due to the impossibility of setting up new plants, but to the stationarity of the demand density.

output puts a premium on plant flexibility (as reflected in a flat-bottomed average cost curve).[6] We comment further on the problem of plant design below. Suffice it to say at this stage that our results in the next section hold for *any* cubic cost function (3.1) – in particular, for the cost function of the optimal plant, so long as it is cubic. What use is made of optimally designed plants can be discussed independently of the problems to be faced in choosing the best size and design – a difficult problem under uncertainty.

Given these assumptions, we will discuss the conditions under which total expected cost for the industry is minimised, state their implications for expected output and expected price, and compare this situation with competitive equilibrium under free entry and maximisation of expected profit by the firms.[7]

4 Some properties of expectations in the simple model

Consider the problem:

$$\operatorname*{Min}_{n} \operatorname*{E}_{Q} \{C(Q, n)\} = \operatorname*{Min}_{n} \operatorname*{E}_{Q} \left\{ nF\left(\frac{Q}{n}\right) \right\} \quad \text{given } c', e'; \qquad (4.1)$$

i.e. find the number of identical firms, with cost functions given by (3.1), for which the *expected total cost* of producing a random output Q (with zero third moment) is minimum.

Denote by n^* the solution to problem (4.1), i.e. the optimal number of firms in the industry, if minimisation of *expected* total cost is chosen as a criterion. Then, each firm will produce a (random) output Q/n^*, with expectations $\bar{q} = \bar{Q}/n^*$ and variance $\sigma_q^2 = \sigma_Q^2/n^{*2}$.

The counterpart to proposition 2.1 is:

---

[6]There is thus no indication whatever that the plants under consideration here are the same as those that would be chosen if Q were no longer uncertain – a point that we owe to our colleague P. Rousseaux.

[7]Our analysis thus extends previous contributions by Oi (1961), Tisdell (1963) and Zucker (1965) by paying explicit attention to the entry phenomenon. Oi shows that, for a firm with increasing marginal cost producing an output that equates marginal cost to price, expected profit increases with the variance of price – a proposition that is referred to below; he does not, however, draw the implications of this proposition for entry under competition. Tisdell shows that Oi's result fails to hold if the firm must decide upon its output level before knowing the market price, instead of equating marginal cost to market price once the latter is observed; again, Tisdell does not address himself to the problem of entry; we start from Oi's rather than Tisdell's assumption but our analysis could easily be replicated for Tisdell's case. Zucker concentrates on variability of gross revenue; he points out that, under constant elasticity of supply (i.e. an exponential marginal cost function), expected profit is proportional to expected gross revenue, irrespective of the variability of gross revenue; he does not, however, discuss the influence of demand variability on entry – hence on expected price – in an industry with fixed costs. One should also mention an interesting paper by Nelson (1961) on forecasting and the cost of uncertainty; Nelson also assumes that total cost is a cubic function of output; he derives a short-run counterpart of our proposition 2.2″(i).

Proposition 2.1': n^* solving problem (4.1) is such that $\Phi(\bar{q}) < f(\bar{q})$, or $\bar{q} < q^*$, i.e. with the optimal number of firms, expected output for each firm is less than the output for which average cost is minimum, so that marginal cost is less than average cost at expected output.

In setting up problem (4.1), we have implicitly assumed that investment in our hypothetical industry was controlled by some central authority aiming at minimisation of expected cost. We will now assume that investment decisions are in the hands of private entrepreneurs, who are guided by a criterion of *profit expectation*.

If we assume that market price will definitely be such as to equate demand and supply, and that each firm will produce that quantity for which marginal cost is equal to price, then price may be expressed as a function of Q and n, namely the marginal cost of Q/n:

$$p = \Phi\left(\frac{Q}{n}\right). \tag{4.2}$$

Expected profit for a firm is then equal to

$$\mathop{E}_{Q}\left\{\frac{Q}{n}\Phi\left(\frac{Q}{n}\right) - F\left(\frac{Q}{n}\right)\right\} = \frac{1}{n}\mathop{E}_{Q}\left[Q\left\{\Phi\left(\frac{Q}{n}\right) - f\left(\frac{Q}{n}\right)\right\}\right]. \tag{4.3}$$

It is easily verified that:

$$\frac{1}{n}\mathop{E}_{Q}\left[Q\left\{\Phi\left(\frac{Q}{n}\right) - f\left(\frac{Q}{n}\right)\right\}\right]$$

is a monotonic decreasing function of n; i.e. expected profit for each firm decreases as the number of firms in the industry increases. Indeed,

$$\frac{d}{dn}\left[\frac{1}{n}\mathop{E}_{Q}\left\{Q\left\{\Phi\left(\frac{Q}{n}\right) - f\left(\frac{Q}{n}\right)\right\}\right\}\right]$$

$$= -\frac{1}{n}\mathop{E}_{q}[q\{\Phi(q) - f(q) + q\Phi'(q) - qf'(q)\}]$$

$$= -\frac{1}{n}\mathop{E}_{q}[\{q^2(2\beta q - \alpha)\}] < 0 \quad \text{for } q > \frac{\alpha}{2\beta}. \tag{4.4}$$

Consequently, the number of firms – say n^0 – for which expected profit is equal to zero is a stable equilibrium under free entry and competition: for $n < n^0$, expected profit is positive, and new firms will enter; for $n > n^0$, expected profit is negative, and firms will leave the industry until equilibrium is restored.

We may now state the counterpart of proposition 2.2 for quantities, namely:

Proposition 2.2′: If n increases (decreases) whenever

$$\mathop{E}_{q}\{F(q)\} < (>)\mathop{E}_{q}\{q\Phi(q)\},$$

then in equilibrium $n^0 = n^*$, so that

$$\Phi\left(\frac{Q}{n^0}\right) < f\left(\frac{Q}{n^0}\right) \quad \text{and} \quad \frac{Q}{n^0} = \bar{q} < q^*;$$

i.e. competition and free entry with maximisation of expected profit lead to an optimal number of firms in the sense of minimum expected total cost for the industry, but expected output for each firm is less than the output for which average cost is minimum.

Propositions 2.1′ and 2.2′ have two important implications. In the first place, competition and free entry guided by expected profit maximisation lead to the number of firms for which expected total cost of meeting demand is minimum. In other words, decentralised decisions are socially efficient. This result is due to the absence of external effects and to the linearity of the expectation operator. If firms were to adopt a different decision criterion (for instance, maximise the expectation of the logarithm of profit), this result would generally not obtain – a point to which we return below.

Second, the optimal number of firms is such that each firm expects to operate below capacity ($\bar{q} < q^*$). This result is due to the convexity of marginal cost, which puts a penalty on variability of output rates. Since the variance of a firm's output, σ_q^2, is inversely proportional to n^2, that penalty is reduced by increasing n (and thus reducing σ_q^2); of course, the increase in n leads to additional fixed costs, and to output rates that are no longer centred on q^*; this is another kind of penalty, which puts a limit to the process of increasing n for the sake of reducing σ_q^2: in equilibrium the two kinds of penalty offset each other at the margin. From the standpoint of the individual firm, if $\bar{q}$ were equal to q^*, expected profit would be positive because the large profit margins at high rates of output would overcompensate the losses at small rates of output, as noted by Oi (1961). Consequently, entry would not stop when $\bar{q} = q^*$.

Turning to *prices* and *costs*, the counterparts to the equality of price with both average and marginal costs may be found in the following set of relationships:

Proposition 2.2″: If $n = n^0 = n^*$, then:

(i) $\Phi(\bar{q}) < \mathop{E}_{q}\{\Phi(q)\} < \Phi(q^*) = f(q^*) < \mathop{E}_{q}\{f(q)\}$

(ii) $\dfrac{1}{\bar{q}}\mathop{E}_{q}\{q\Phi(q)\} = \dfrac{1}{\bar{q}}\mathop{E}_{q}\{qf(q)\} > \Phi(q^*)$

(iii) $\mathop{E}_{q}\{\Phi(q)\} \text{ and } \dfrac{1}{\bar{q}}\mathop{E}_{q}\{q\Phi(q)\}$

are minimised over all n such that

$$\mathop{E}_{q}\{q\Phi(q)\} \geqslant \mathop{E}_{q}\{qf(q)\}$$

i.e. expected marginal cost – or expected price under competition – is less than minimum average cost and hence less than expected average cost; on the other hand, if price is weighted by quantity, then its expectation is equal to the corresponding weighted expectation of average cost and hence exceeds minimum average cost; furthermore, expected price – weighted or unweighted – cannot be reduced further without causing expected profit to become negative: minimising expected cost is equivalent to minimising expected price subject to that condition.

Let us comment briefly on these relationships. That expected marginal cost (price) exceeds marginal cost of expected output is not surprising: it is an immediate consequence of convexity of the marginal cost function. On the other hand, we were frankly surprised to discover that expected marginal cost would fall short of *minimum* average cost. In a competitive industry, this means that random fluctuations of demand will, under our assumptions, result in a fluctuating price that is, *on the average*, inferior to the price that would prevail with the same plants in the absence of uncertainty – i.e. $\Phi(q^*)$.[8] Consequently, a customer who purchases a fixed quantity, independently of the variations in market demand, will on the average pay a lower price, the greater the variance of Q. If he were contracting for sure delivery of that fixed quantity, a firm could offer it to him at a price $E\{\Phi(q)\} < \Phi(q^*)$: this customer would be subsidised by those whose demand is uncertain! How is this to be explained?

Our understanding of this apparent paradox is the following. Suppose that a known quantity K were added to the random quantity Q; expected demand is now equal to $\bar{Q} + K$, variance of demand is still equal to σ_Q^2. If expected output for each firm were maintained at the same level $\bar{q}$ as before, then n would increase by $K/\bar{q}$ and variance of output for each firm would fall from σ_Q^2/n^{*2} to

$$\frac{\sigma_Q^2}{\left(n^* + \dfrac{K}{\bar{q}}\right)^2};$$

consequently, expected total cost for the firm, and expected marginal cost, would decrease. This reduction would reflect a spreading of the same aggregate *variance* over a larger number of firms. It would thus be in the interest of the customers with uncertain demand (Q in total) to attract on the market additional customers with known stable demand (K in total);

[8] Of course the price under certainty might be reduced further by the choice of a different plant, with lower minimum average cost – for instance a less flexible plant. It is interesting to speculate that under appropriate assumptions about the class of average cost functions from which the firm chooses, $E\{\phi(q)\}$ might be precisely equal to minimum average cost for the less flexible plant that would be built under certainty – a topic on which we contemplate further investigations.

those new customers could, at the margin, be quoted a fixed price equal to expected marginal cost; such a price would be less than minimum average cost; the difference may be regarded as a subsidy used to attract them in the market.

The finding according to which expected marginal cost is less than minimum average cost (and hence than expected average cost) becomes less surprising when we remember – with the help of (ii) – that weighted expectations of marginal and average costs are equal, when the weights are given by quantity (output). In other words, our results show that the natural extensions of the static propositions must be stated in terms of *weighted* expectations. The quantity-weighted expectation of marginal cost exceeds $\Phi(q^*)$, which reflects appropriately the cost of uncertainty (to be felt most severely, in terms of marginal cost or price, for $q > \bar{q}$).

Furthermore, by proposition 2.2″(iii), the number of firms for which expected total cost is minimum is also the number of firms for which expected marginal cost (price) is minimum – no matter whether the expectations be weighted or not – under the constraint that expected profits for the firms be non-negative. This is the counterpart to the static proposition that competition leads to the smallest price at which a firm can break even.[9]

The results in 2.2′ and 2.2″ rest on the assumption that price will be set for each Q so as to equate supply and demand. An alternative arrangement would consist in fixing price once and for all and then allocating demand (output) among firms by the simple rule: $q = Q/n$. (This would have the advantage of relieving the consumers from price uncertainty.) If price is fixed at the quantity-weighted expectation of marginal cost,

$$\frac{1}{\bar{q}} \mathop{E}_{q} \{q\Phi(q)\},$$

and if n increases (decreases), whenever expected profit is positive (negative), then we know from 2.2′ and 2.2″ that the equilibrium value of n is n^* (and expected total cost is again minimised). Suppose now that price were fixed at expected marginal cost. Then:

Proposition 4.1: If

$$p = \mathop{E}_{Q} \left\{ \Phi\left(\frac{Q}{n}\right) \right\}$$

[9]We have not been able to ascertain whether at n^* unweighted expected *average* cost was minimum subject to non-negativity of expected profit. This is not very important, since the obvious counterpart to $\phi(q^*) = f(q^*)$ is (ii) in proposition 2.2″:

$$\frac{1}{\bar{q}} E\{q\phi(q)\} = \frac{1}{\bar{q}} E\{q f(q)\}.$$

and if n increases (decreases) whenever

$$\underset{Q}{\mathrm{E}}\left\{F\left(\frac{Q}{n}\right)\right\} < (>) p\frac{\bar{Q}}{n},$$

then in equilibrium $n < n^*$,

$$\Phi\left(\frac{\bar{Q}}{n}\right) < f\left(\frac{\bar{Q}}{n}\right)$$

and $p > \Phi(q^*)$.

This last proposition shows that sales at expected marginal cost, which led for $n = n^*$ to a price inferior to $\Phi(q^*)$ (applicable only to marginal customers – for otherwise expected profits would become negative), cannot be extended to the industry as a whole without so reducing the number of firms (in order to restore the non-negativity of profits) as to push price *above* $\Phi(q^*)$. Thus, the individual with a stable demand, who was implicitly subsidised by the market in the previous case, is now unduly penalised, since he is charged more than $\Phi(q^*)$ without having contributed to σ_Q^2.

5 Conclusion

Four major conclusions of empirical relevance may be drawn from our analysis.

(1)   Under demand fluctuations, free entry and competition may lead to excess capacity *on the average* ($\bar{q} < q^*$). Hence, any inference, drawn from average underutilisation of capacity, to the effect that imperfect or monopolistic competition prevails, is unwarranted if the data come from firms confronted with demand fluctuations.

(2)   Any inferences about competition in industries with fluctuating demand will typically need to be based on *weighted averages* (quantities weighted by price or prices weighted by quantity) – but such inferences will need to be carefully related to theoretical predictions, of the kind presented in 2.2″ above.

(3)   In an industry with uncertain future demand, one may expect the price on a forward market to fall below minimum average cost, if that price is to reflect expected marginal cost.

(4)   Under price rigidity, demand fluctuations should result in a (fixed) price exceeding minimum average cost.

Appendix

$$F(q) = \gamma + q - \frac{\alpha}{2}q^2 + \frac{\beta}{3}q^3 = \text{total cost for a firm} \qquad (A.1)$$

$$f(q) = \frac{\gamma}{q} + 1 - \frac{\alpha}{2}q + \frac{\beta}{3}q^2 = \text{average cost for a firm} \qquad (A.2)$$

$$f'(q) = -\frac{\gamma}{q^2} - \frac{\alpha}{2} + \frac{2\beta}{3}q \qquad (A.3)$$

$$\Phi(q) = 1 - \alpha q + \beta q^2 = F'(q) = \text{marginal cost for a firm} \qquad (A.4)$$

$$\Phi'(q) = 2\beta q - \alpha = F''(q) \geqslant 0 \quad \text{if } q \geqslant \frac{\alpha}{2\beta} \qquad (A.5)$$

$$\Phi''(q) = 2\beta = F'''(q) > 0 \qquad (A.6)$$

$$\Phi'''(q) \equiv 0 \equiv F''''(q) \qquad (A.7)$$

References

Hart, A.G. (1951). *Anticipations, Uncertainty and Dynamic Planning*, New York: Kelley

Krelle, W. (1961). *Preistheorie*. Tubingen: J.C.B, Mohr (Paul Siebe)

Nelson, R. (1961). Uncertainty, Prediction and Competitive Equilibrium. *Quarterly Journal of Economics*, 75: 41–62

Oi, W. (1961). The Desirability of Price Instability under Perfect Competition. *Econometrica*, 29: 58–64

Tisdell, C. (1963). Uncertainty, Instability, Expected Profit. *Econometrica*, 31: 243–47

Zucker, A. (1965). On the Desirability of Price Instability. *Econometrica*, 33: 437–41

12 Demand fluctuations, capacity utilisation and costs*

The impact of demand fluctuations on expected or average profits for a competitive firm was underlined by Walter Oi (1961), who showed the following: If a firm producing a single output under increasing marginal cost, equates (*ex post*) marginal cost to price, then expected (or average) profits increase with the variance of price.[1] An obvious implication of this result is that increased uncertainty of demand, because it increases expected profits, will attract new firms in the industry if there exist entrepreneurs motivated by profit expectations. This implication was pursued in 1967 by Drèze and Gabszewicz (henceforth D–G), who considered an industry consisting of identical firms supplying a single commodity under demand uncertainty, and defined a competitive equilibrium by the condition that expected profits for each firm be zero.

Under specific assumptions (a cubic cost function, a random demand with known symmetric density, and zero-price elasticity), they derived the following propositions:

1. In competitive equilibrium there is an optimum number of firms, each of which is operating with excess capacity on the average.
2. In competitive equilibrium the expected price is less than minimum average cost, and could not be reduced further without causing expected profits to become negative.

*American Economic Review, 66 (1976): 713–42, with Eytan Sheshinski.

[1]Two years later, it was remarked by Tisdell (1963) that when the same firm equates (*ex ante*) marginal cost to expected price, then expected profit is unaffected by price uncertainty. Various aspects of the firm's behaviour under uncertainty have been analysed in the recent works by Sandmo (1971) and Leland (1972). Their framework (a monopoly firm maximising expected utility) is quite different from ours.

3.   In competitive equilibrium expected marginal cost is equal to expected average cost when and only when the expectations are weighted by quantities.

4.   Under price rigidity a price equal to expected marginal cost (unweighted) exceeds minimum average cost when expected profits are zero.

They also remarked as an implication of these conclusions that various inferences drawn from static equilibrium theory do not apply to situations with demand uncertainty.

The present paper generalises the analysis of D–G in two ways. First, we show that all but one of their results hold under the more general assumptions of a cost function with differentiable, concave marginal cost and arbitrary demand density with zero-price elasticity. The proofs of these results are greatly simplified. This generalisation is presented in Section 2, following a reminder of some propositions from the static theory (Section 1). These two sections follow closely the presentation by D–G, to which the reader is referred for further comments.[2] Two interpretative comments made by D–G regarding the impact of the variance of demand on the number of firms and the impact of the coefficient of variation of demand on expected average cost are then formalised and substantiated in Section 3.

Second, we drop the assumption that all firms are identical. It is verified that the equality of expected marginal and average cost, weighted by quantity, remains valid with several types of plants. Such equality is a sufficient condition for most of the results in Section 2 which continue to hold for each type of plant (and in particular for the type that would be adopted in the absence of demand fluctuations). This important generalisation is presented in Section 4.

Finally, in a concluding section, we note that most positive results remain valid when demand is a function of price, when the commodity is storable, or even when the industry is monopolistic rather than competitive. The extension of the normative results is less straightforward, and raises more general issues of interpretation which are also discussed in the concluding section. The reader is referred to Section 5 for comments about the relevance of expected cost and expected profits.

1 Propositions from static theory

Consider an industry that produces a single commodity whose total quantity is denoted by Q. There are n identical firms in the industry, and there is no restriction on entry.[3] The output produced by each firm is denoted by q. Total cost for each firm, $F(q)$, is a function of the quantity it produces, and is

[2]We are grateful to Gabszewicz for permission to follow and to frequently quote that presentation.

[3]For convenience of the calculations we do not require n to be an integer. This simplification does not affect the results of Sections 1, 2, and 3 in an essential way, especially if n is large; see, however, note 11 below.

independent of the number of firms in the industry. The average cost curve, $f(q) = (1/q)F(q)$, is U-shaped and continuously differentiable:

$$f'(q) \lesseqgtr 0 \quad \text{as} \quad q \lesseqgtr q^*; \quad f''(q) > 0 \tag{1.1}$$

where $q^* > 0$ is the output for which average cost is minimum. We will also refer to q^* as *capacity output*. Marginal cost $g(q)$ is assumed to be increasing and convex:[4]

$$g'(q) > 0, \quad g''(q) \geqslant 0. \tag{1.2}$$

By definition

$$g(q) = \frac{\mathrm{d}F(q)}{\mathrm{d}q} = \frac{\mathrm{d}(qf(q))}{\mathrm{d}q} = f(q) + qf'(q). \tag{1.3}$$

From (1.1) and (1.3) it follows that:

$$g(q) \lesseqgtr f(q) \quad \text{as} \quad q \lesseqgtr q^*. \tag{1.4}$$

Total cost for the industry, $C(Q, n)$, depends on total output and on the number of firms in the industry. Under assumption 2, it is always efficient to divide equally any given output among all firms, so that $q = Q/n$ and

$$C = C(Q, n) = nF\left(\frac{Q}{n}\right) = nF(q). \tag{1.5}$$

There are two well-known propositions concerning industry equilibrium, which can be derived directly from assumptions 1–4.

> *Proposition 1.1:* For every Q, $C(Q, n)$ is minimum for n such that $f(q) = g(q)$; i.e. $q = q^*$. Total cost is minimised when each firm produces the output for which average cost is minimum and equal to marginal cost.

> *Proposition 1.2:* If q is such that $p = g(q)$, and if n increases (decreases) whenever $F(q) < (>)qg(q)$, then in equilibrium $f(q) = g(q) = p$ and $F(q) = pq$; i.e. competition and free entry lead to a price equal to minimum average cost, and hence to an optimal number of firms.

These propositions have been at the root of the following inferences about the structure of markets:

(1) $f(q) = g(q)$ is an indication of perfect competition and free entry;
(2) $f(q) > g(q)$ is an indication of imperfect competition;
(3) $f(q) < g(q)$ is an indication of limits to entry, or other restrictive practices.

---

[4] Actually, $g''(q) \geqslant 0$ is a *stronger* assumption than needed; the condition used below is $g'(q) - qg''(q) > 0$ or

$$\frac{qg''(q)}{g'(q)} > -1.$$

Our purpose now is to consider situations where demand for the industry is randomly fluctuating, and to investigate whether, in some sense, propositions 1.1 and 1.2 and the inferences derived from them hold in these situations.

2 Propositions for a simple model with uncertain demand

We assume at present that demand for the industry is a random variable with zero-price elasticity and a given expected value $\bar{Q}$; $E(Q) = \bar{Q} > 0$. Output is not storable and is accordingly equal to demand. More general cases will be discussed in Section 5. Firms are set up before the level of output is known. Output is then allocated equally among firms (for further discussion, see Drèze and Gabszewicz (1967, pp. 121–2)).

Let us first find the number of firms for which expected cost for the industry is minimised, and state the implications for the expected output produced by each firm and for expected cost. We shall then compare these results with a competitive equilibrium with free entry and maximisation of expected profits by firms.

The problem of finding the number of firms for which the expected total cost of producing a random output Q is minimum, can be stated as:[5]

$$\operatorname*{Min}_{n} \operatorname*{E}_{Q} [C(Q,n)] = \operatorname*{Min}_{n} \operatorname*{E}_{Q} \left[nF\left(\frac{Q}{n}\right) \right]. \tag{2.1}$$

Denote the solution to this problem by n^*, and by $\bar{q} = E(Q)/n^* = \bar{Q}/n^*$, the expected output for the firm at the optimum.[6]

The counterpart to proposition 1.1 is the following proposition, which states that cost minimisation implies that expected output for each firm is *less* than the output for which average cost is minimum:

Proposition 2.1: $\bar{q} < q^*$ or $f(\bar{q}) > g(\bar{q})$.

Proof: The first-order condition for a minimum of (2.1) using the identity $F(q) = qf(q)$ is

$$E(q^2 f'(q)) = 0 \tag{2.2}$$

---

[5] Henceforth, whenever no confusion can arise, we shall omit the subscript under the expectation sign.

[6] To ensure the existence of a positive n^* larger than one, some restrictions on the cost function $F(q)$ and the distribution of demand Q have to be placed. For example, suppose cost is quadratic: $F(q) = a + bq + cq^2$, with $a > 0$, $b > 0$, and $c > 0$ constants. Condition (2.3) then becomes $E[\phi(q)] = (c/n^{*2})E(Q^2) - a = 0$. To ensure that $n^* > 1$, it is necessary that $cE(Q^2) - a > 0$. On the questions of existence and uniqueness of the cost minimising number of firms in the more general model discussed in Section 4, see the authors' 1975 working paper (Drèze and Sheshinski, 1975).

or, using (1.3),

$$E[q(g(q) - f(q))] = E[\phi(q)] = 0 \tag{2.3}$$

where $\phi(q) = q(g(q) - f(q))$. Now, $\phi'(q) = qg'(q) > 0$ and $\phi''(q) = g'(q) + qg''(q) > 0$; i.e. $\phi(q)$ is an increasing, strictly convex function of q. By (1.4), $\phi(q^*) = q^*(g(q^*) - f(q^*)) = 0$. Hence

$$\phi(q) \geqslant \phi(q^*) + \phi'(q^*)(q - q^*) = \phi'(q^*)(q - q^*) \tag{2.4}$$

with strict inequality for $q \neq q^*$. Combining (2.3) and (2.4), it follows that

$$\phi'(q^*)E(q - q^*) < E[\phi(q)] = 0. \tag{2.5}$$

Hence, $E(q) = E(Q)/n^* = \bar{q} < q^*$. From (1.4) it then follows that $f(\bar{q}) > g(\bar{q})$.

Suppose now that the industry is competitive, with each firm producing the quantity for which marginal cost is equal to price: $p = g(q)$. Expected profits of the firm are given by:[7]

$$E[\Pi(q)] = E[qg(q) - F(q)] = E[q(g(q) - f(q))]. \tag{2.6}$$

It can be seen that (2.6) is a strictly decreasing function of n:

$$\frac{dE(\Pi)}{dn} = -\frac{1}{n}E[q^2 g'(q)] < 0. \tag{2.7}$$

Consequently, there is a unique number n^0 of firms for which expected profits are zero. Condition (2.3) is then satisfied, and we obtain the following counterpart to proposition 1.2.

Proposition 2.2: If n increases (decreases) whenever $E[\Pi(q)] > (<)0$, then equilibrium is stable and $n^0 = n^*$.

Proposition 2 implies that competition and free entry guided by maximisation of expected profits lead to the number of firms for which expected total cost is minimum. That is, competitive equilibrium is efficient.

We may conclude from propositions 2.1 and 2.2 that competition and free entry lead to *excess capacity* on the average (in the expectation sense, i.e. $\bar{q} < q^*$). This result may be illustrated with the aid of Figure 12.1. Suppose that the demand for each firm can assume the values $q^* - \delta$ and $q^* + \delta$ with equal probabilities, so that expected output is q^*. The marginal costs and prices corresponding to these outputs are p_0 and p_1, respectively. If the marginal cost curve $g(q)$ is convex, it is seen that $p_1 - p^* \geqslant p^* - p_0$. Now, at p_0, the firm's losses are evidently smaller than the area $abcd$, since $q^* - \delta$ and not q^* is the loss-minimising output at this price. On the other

---

[7]Note that when $p \equiv g(q)$, $\Pi(q) = \phi(q)$ and we are assuming that profits are a strictly convex function of output.

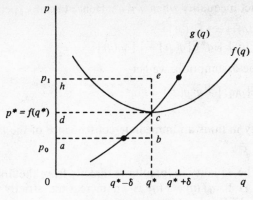

Figure 12.1

hand, at p_1, the firm's profits are larger than the area *dceh*, since $q^* + \delta$ and not q^* is the profit-maximising output at this price. Since the area *dceh* is not smaller than the area *abcd*, the firm's expected profits are necessarily positive. This demonstrates that expected output must be smaller than q^* in order for expected profits to be zero.

The next proposition shows that under competition, expected marginal cost is less than minimum average cost, and hence less than expected average cost. On the other hand, if marginal cost and average cost are weighted by quantity, then expected marginal cost is equal to expected average cost, and hence larger than minimum average cost. Furthermore, expected price, weighted or unweighted by quantity, cannot be reduced any further without causing expected profits to become negative.

Proposition 2.3: When expected profits are zero, then

(a) $g(\bar{q}) < E[g(q)] < g(q^*) = f(q^*) < E[f(q)]$

(b) $\dfrac{1}{\bar{q}} E[qg(q)] = \dfrac{1}{\bar{q}} E[qf(q)] > f(\bar{q}) > f(q^*)$

(c) $E[g(q)]$ and $\dfrac{1}{\bar{q}} E[qg(q)]$ are minimised over all n such that

$E[qg(q)] \geqslant E[qf(q)]$.

Proof (a): By equation (1.2), $g(q) \geqslant g(\bar{q}) + g'(\bar{q})(q - \bar{q})$, with strict inequality for $q \neq \bar{q}$. Hence

$$E[g(q)] > g(\bar{q}) + g'(\bar{q})E(q - \bar{q}) = g(\bar{q}). \tag{2.8}$$

We prove that $E[g(q)] < g(q^*)$ by contradiction. Assume that $E[g(q)] \geqslant g(q^*)$. Since $g'(q) > 0$, it follows that

$$F(q^*) \geqslant F(q) + (q^* - q)g(q) \tag{2.9}$$

for every q, with strict inequality when $q \neq q^*$. Hence taking expectations, we have from (2.9)

$$F(q^*) > E[F(q)] + q^*E[g(q)] - E[qg(q)]. \tag{2.10}$$

Using (2.3) and the assumption, we get

$$F(q^*) > q^*E[g(q)] \geqslant q^*g(q^*) = F(q^*) \tag{2.11}$$

a contradiction.

The last inequality in (a) is an immediate consequence of the fact that $f(q) > f(q^*)$ for all $q \neq q^*$. $\qquad\square$

Proof (b): The equality in (b) follows directly from the first-order condition (2.3). By (1.2), $qf(q) = F(q)$ is an increasing, strictly convex function of q. Hence $E[F(q)] > F(\bar{q})$ and

$$\frac{1}{\bar{q}}E[qf(q)] > f(\bar{q}) > f(q^*). \tag{2.12}$$
$$\square$$

Proof (c): In view of (2.7) and proposition 2.2, the condition $E[qg(q)] \geqslant E[qf(q)]$ is equivalent to $n \leqslant n^*$. The result then follows immediately from the fact that $E[g(q)]$ and $E[qg(q)]$ are strictly decreasing with n:

$$\frac{\mathrm{d}}{\mathrm{d}n}E[g(q)] = -\frac{1}{n}E[qg'(q)] < 0 \tag{2.13}$$

$$\frac{\mathrm{d}}{\mathrm{d}n}E[qg(q)] = -\frac{1}{n}E[qg(q) + q^2g'(q)] < 0. \tag{2.14}$$
$$\square$$

Proposition 2.3(a) may be illustrated with the aid of Figure 12.2. Suppose that the price may assume the values $p^* - \delta$ and $p^* + \delta$ with equal probability, so that expected price is equal to $p^* = f(q^*)$. The profit-maximising outputs corresponding to these prices are q_0 and q_1, respec-

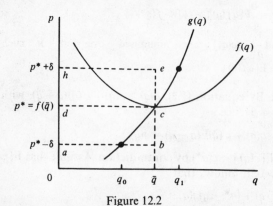

Figure 12.2

tively. Now, at $p^* - \delta$ the firm's losses are clearly smaller than the area $abcd$, since q_0 and not q^* is the loss-minimising output at this price. On the other hand, at $p^* + \delta$, the firm's profits are larger than the area $dceh$, since q_1 and not q^* is the profit-maximising output at this price. Since $abcd = dceh$, it is seen that expected profits are necessarily positive. Hence, when expected profits are zero, expected price must be smaller than p^*.[8]

Let us make some brief comments on these results. The fact that marginal cost of expected output is less than expected marginal cost is due to the convexity of the latter. It is more surprising that expected marginal cost, or expected price, is less than minimum average cost. Drèze and Gabszewicz explain this result in terms of the subsidy that could be offered to a stable buyer who purchases a fixed quantity. Such a buyer would increase expected demand but leave the variance of demand unchanged. Consequently, expected average cost and expected marginal cost would decrease. This is demonstrated in Section 3 below.

Finally, the equality of the quantity-weighted expectations of marginal cost and average cost provides the natural extension to the static propositions 1.1 and 1.2.

The results in propositions 2.2 and 2.3 rest on the assumption that for any level of demand, price is set so as to equate supply and demand. A possible alternative arrangement is to fix the price once and for all and to allocate the random demand among firms by the rule $q = Q/n$, for any Q. From the previous analysis it is clear that if the price is set at the level of the *quantity-weighted* expectation of marginal cost, $(1/\bar{q})\mathrm{E}[qg(q)]$, and if firms enter (leave) the industry whenever expected profits are positive (negative), then the stable equilibrium level of n is n^*.

Consider now the case of a fixed price equal to the unweighted expectation of marginal cost: $p = \mathrm{E}(g(q))$. Expected profits for the firm selling at this price are equal to

$$\mathrm{E}[\Pi(q)] = p\mathrm{E}(q) - \mathrm{E}[F(q)] = \mathrm{E}[g(q)]\mathrm{E}(q) - \mathrm{E}[qf(q)]. \qquad (2.15)$$

Suppose that firms enter (leave) the industry when expected profits are positive (negative). In order to show that there exists a stable equilibrium number of firms, one must verify that expected profits for each firm decrease as the number of firms increases. When price is set so as to equate supply and demand for any level of the latter, this condition is always satisfied. In the present case, however, an additional assumption is needed to that effect. The additional assumption (to be introduced in the next section) is equivalent to the condition that expected profits increase with the variability of demand (for given n).[9]

The following proposition shows that under the arrangement of a fixed price equal to expected marginal cost, the equilibrium number of firms,

[8]Note that convexity of marginal cost is not necessary for this result.
[9]That assumption is automatically satisfied by the cubic cost function used by D–G.

denoted by $\hat{n}$, is less and the expected output is larger than in the case when price is set so as to equate supply and demand for any level of the latter.

Proposition 2.4: If $p = E[g(q)]$ then in equilibrium (a) $\hat{n} < n^*$ and (b) $p > g(q^*)$.

Proof (a): The equilibrium, zero-profit condition becomes

$$E[\Pi(q)] = E[g(q)]E(q) - E[qf(q)] = 0. \tag{2.16}$$

Since $g(q)$ and q are by (1.2) positively correlated, $E[g(q)q] > E[g(q)]E(q)$. Hence, by (2.16),

$$E[q(g(q) - f(q))] > E[g(q)]E(q) - E[qf(q)] = 0. \tag{2.17}$$

It has already been shown in equation (2.7) that $E[q(g(q) - f(q))]$ is a strictly decreasing function of n. Comparing (2.3) with (2.17), conclusion (a) follows immediately. $\qquad\square$

Proof (b): It has also been shown that $qf(q)$ is an increasing, strictly convex function of q. Hence $qf(q) \geqslant \bar{q}f(\bar{q}) + g(\bar{q})(q - \bar{q})$ for all q, with strict inequality for $q \neq \bar{q}$. Consequently,

$$E[qf(q)] > \bar{q}f(\bar{q}). \tag{2.18}$$

From (2.16) and (2.18),

$$p = \frac{1}{\bar{q}}E[qf(q)] > f(\bar{q}) \geqslant f(q^*) = g(q^*). \tag{2.19}$$
$$\square$$

This last proposition shows that when all firms sell output at expected marginal cost, the number of firms is adjusted so as to push the price above $g(q^*)$, contrary to the case when, for any level of demand, price is set so as to equate supply and demand, where it was found that $E[g(q)] < g(q^*)$.

3 Changes in the distribution of demand

Changes in the distribution of demand can be usefully classified into changes in expected value and changes in variability. We shall now analyse the effect of such changes on the equilibrium number of firms and on the expected output and cost of each firm.

Consider the linear transformation of output

$$y = a\bar{Q} + b(Q - \bar{Q}) \tag{3.1}$$

where $a > 0$ and $b > 0$ are constants. When $a = b = 1$ then $y = Q$. The expected value of y and its variance are $a\bar{Q}$ and $b^2\sigma^2(Q)$ respectively, where $\sigma^2(Q)$ is the variance of Q. Accordingly, an increase in a implies an increase in the mean with unchanged variance, and an increase in b implies an increase in variance with unchanged mean.

The *coefficient of variation* is defined as the ratio of the standard error to the mean. Thus, the coefficient of variation of y is equal to $(b\sigma(Q))/a\bar{Q}$, and is seen to depend on the ratio b/a. One interpretation of changes in this coefficient is as follows. Suppose that there are m individual buyers, each of which has a random demand, y_i, with mean $\bar{Q}$ and variance $\sigma^2(Q)$. The mean of total demand,

$$\sum_{i=1}^{m} \bar{y}_i, \text{ is equal to } m \cdot \bar{Q}.$$

If individual demands are not correlated then the variance of total demand is $m\sigma^2(Q)$. Thus, the coefficient of variation is equal to $\sigma(Q)/\bar{Q}\sqrt{m}$, and is seen to decrease to zero as the number of buyers increases. We may note that this result holds even when demands are positively correlated, provided the correlation increases with the number of buyers at a rate smaller than $\sqrt{m}$.

Proposition 3.1: In equilibrium, (a) if the mean or the variance of output increases, the equilibrium number of firms increases; (b) if the coefficient of variation decreases (increases), expected output of each firm increases (decreases), and expected average cost decreases (increases).

Proof (a): Differentiating[10] equilibrium condition (2.3) with respect to a and n^*, using (1.3), yields

$$\mathrm{E}\left[qg'(q)\left(\frac{\partial q}{\partial a}da + \frac{\partial q}{\partial n}dn^* \right) \right] = 0. \tag{3.2}$$

From (3.1), $dq/da = \bar{q}$, and by definition, $dq/dn = -q/n^*$. Substituting into (3.2) and solving

$$\frac{dn^*}{da} = \frac{n^* \bar{q} \mathrm{E}[qg'(q)]}{\mathrm{E}[q^2 g'(q)]} > 0. \tag{3.3}$$

From (3.1), $dq/db = q - \bar{q}$. Hence, by implicit differentiation of (2.3), one finds

$$\frac{dn^*}{db} = \frac{n^* \mathrm{E}[qg'(q)(q - \bar{q})]}{\mathrm{E}[q^2 g'(q)]} > 0. \tag{3.4}$$

The inequality follows from the positive correlation between $qg'(q)$ and q:

$$\mathrm{E}[qg'(q)(q - \bar{q})] > \mathrm{E}[qg'(q)]\mathrm{E}(q - \bar{q}) = 0. \qquad \square$$

Proof (b): Differentiating $\bar{q}$ with respect to a/b, using (3.3) and (3.4),

---

[10]All derivatives will be evaluated at the point $a = 1$, $b = 1$ where $Y = Q$; this simplifies notation without affecting the reasoning.

one finds

$$\frac{d\bar{q}}{d(a/b)} = 2\bar{q}\left(1 - \frac{\bar{q}E[qg'(q)]}{E[q^2g'(q)]}\right) > 0. \tag{3.5}$$

The inequality follows from the previous argument.

The change in expected average cost is given by

$$\frac{dE[f(q)]}{d(a/b)} = E\left[f'(q)\frac{dq}{d(a/b)}\right]. \tag{3.6}$$

Using (3.1), (3.3), and (3.4), we can show that

$$\frac{dq}{d(a/b)} = 2\bar{q}\left(1 - \frac{qE[qg'(q)]}{E[q^2g'(q)]}\right) \tag{3.7}$$

which by (1.1) implies that $f'(q)$ and $dq/d(a/b)$ are negatively correlated. Thus,

$$E\left[f'(q)\frac{dq}{d(a/b)}\right] < E[f'(q)]\frac{d\bar{q}}{d(a/b)}. \tag{3.8}$$

Since $f'(q)$ and q^2 are, by (1.1), positively correlated, we have from (2.2) that

$$E(q^2)E[f'(q)] < E[q^2f'(q)] = 0 \tag{3.9}$$

which implies that $E[f'(q)] < 0$. The conclusion then follows from (3.5), (3.6), and (3.8).   □

We now return briefly to the discussion in Section 2 of a fixed price equal to unweighted expected marginal cost. Using (3.1), the assumption that expected profits of each firm, for a given number of firms, increase with the variance of demand is

$$\frac{dE[\Pi(q)]}{db} = E[(\bar{q}g'(q) - g(q))(q - \bar{q})] > 0. \tag{3.10}$$

Under this assumption it is seen that for a given distribution of output expected profits decrease as the number of firms increases:

$$\frac{dE[\Pi(q)]}{dn} = \frac{1}{n}E[(g(q) - \bar{q}g'(q))(q - \bar{q}) - \bar{q}^2g'(q)] < 0. \tag{3.11}$$

Proposition 2.4 can now be strengthened. Although under the fixed price arrangement expected marginal cost is larger than minimum average cost, still expected output is lower than capacity output, i.e. $\bar{q} < q^*$.

Differentiating (2.16):

$$E\left[\frac{\partial\Pi(q)}{\partial n}d\hat{n} + \frac{\partial\Pi(q)}{\partial b}db\right] = 0. \tag{3.12}$$

Using (3.10) and (3.11), we solve (3.12):

$$\frac{d\hat{n}}{db} = \frac{n^* E[(\dot{g}(q) - \bar{q}g'(q))(q - \bar{q})]}{E[g(q) - \bar{q}g'(q))(q - \bar{q}) - \bar{q}^2 g'(q)]} > 0 \tag{3.13}$$

from which it follows that

$$\frac{d\bar{q}}{db} = -\frac{\bar{q}}{\hat{n}}\frac{d\hat{n}}{db} < 0. \tag{3.14}$$

Since under certainty $\bar{q} = q^*$, with uncertainty, expected output is necessarily smaller than q^*.

4 Generalisation to different types of plants

In his early study of supply under uncertainty, Hart (1951) noted that demand fluctuations are best met by flexible plants, characterised by flatbottomed average cost curves. If a variety of plant designs is available, one may expect the design chosen under demand fluctuations to differ from the design chosen under known fixed demand. D–G (pp. 123, 133, and 138) recognise accordingly that the minimum average cost $f(q^*)$ corresponding to plants well suited to handle demand fluctuations is apt to exceed the price (minimum average cost) that would prevail under known fixed demand.

Actually, the problem of plant design is somewhat more complex. Under demand fluctuations and a variety of feasible plant designs, it will typically be efficient to build a variety of plants and to allocate output among them so as to minimise production costs. The assumption of identical firms and the uniform allocation of output among firms are both unrealistic, under demand fluctuations.[11]

When there exist plants of different design, it is important to recognise the possibility that some of them may be idle at low levels of demand. It is then natural to rely upon mathematical programming theory to characterise efficient investment and production decisions. This is most easily done in a discrete formulation. Consider m types of plant, characterised by the total cost functions $F_i(q_i), i = 1, \ldots, m$, with $F'_i(q_i) > 0$, $F''_i(q_i) \geqslant 0$. The industry demand Q is assumed to be a discrete variable, which may take any one of the r values $Q_j, j = 1, \ldots, r$, with respective probabilities P_j,

$$\sum_{j=1}^{r} P_j = 1.$$

Let there be n_i plants of type i, and let q_{ij} denote the output level of each

---

[11] A well-known example of chosen mixture of plant designs is provided by electricity production, where periodic and random fluctuations of demand are met by operating a variety of plants, with different ratios of average to marginal costs. See, for example, Massé and Gibrat (1964).

plant of type i when total demand is Q_j.[12] The problem of cost minimising is then stated as follows:

$$\operatorname*{Min}_{n_i, q_{ij}} \sum_i n_i \sum_j P_j F_i(q_{ij})$$

subject to

$$\sum_i n_i q_{ij} \geqslant Q_j \quad j = 1, \ldots, r \qquad (\lambda_j)$$

$$q_{ij} \geqslant 0 \quad i = 1, \ldots, m; j = 1, \ldots, r \quad (\mu_{ij})$$

$$n_i \geqslant 0 \quad i = 1, \ldots, m \qquad (\nu_i)$$

where the Greek letters in parentheses denote the dual variables associated with the constraints. By the Kuhn–Tucker theorem (Kuhn and Tucker, 1951), any solution to the above problem satisfies the following necessary conditions:[13]

$$n_i P_j F'_i(q_{ij}) - n_i \lambda_j - \mu_{ij} = 0, \quad \mu_{ij} q_{ij} = 0 \tag{4.1}$$

$$\sum_j P_j F_i(q_{ij}) - \sum_j q_{ij} \lambda_j - \nu_i = 0, \quad \nu_i n_i = 0. \tag{4.2}$$

These conditions imply

$$q_{ij} q_{hj} [F'_i(q_{ij}) - F'_h(q_{hj})] = 0, \quad i, h = 1, \ldots, m; j = 1, \ldots, r \tag{4.3}$$

$$n_i \mathrm{E}[F_i(q_i) - q_i F'_i(q_i)] = 0, \quad i = 1, \ldots, m. \tag{4.4}$$

Conditions (4.3) assert the equality of marginal costs for all the plants operating at any given time. Let $p_j = F'_i(q_{ij})$, $q_{ij} > 0$ denote the competitive price prevailing when $Q = Q_j$. Conditions (4.4) then assert the equality of expected total cost and expected revenue for each type of plant in use; this is the 'zero expected profits' condition. If plants of type i are to be operated at all levels of demand ($q_{ij} > 0 \forall j$), then (4.4) takes the familiar form

$$\mathrm{E}[q_i(f_i(q_i) - g_i(q_i))] = 0 \tag{4.5}$$

and proposition 2.2 applies.[14] Thus:

Proposition 4.1: (a) Competition and free entry guided by maximisation of expected profits sustain an efficient solution to problem (*P*); (b) for every type of plant i such that $q_{ij} > 0 \forall j$,

$$g_i(\bar{q}_i) < \mathrm{E}[g_i(q_i)] < g_i(q_i^*) = f_i(q_i^*) < \mathrm{E}[f_i(q_i)]$$

and $f_i(q_i^*) \bar{q}_i < \mathrm{E} F_i(q_i)$.

---

[12]We continue to ignore the condition that n_i be an integer – an approximation that is clearly less innocuous now than in Section 2. That identical plants should always produce the same output under increasing marginal cost is obvious.

[13]These necessary conditions are not sufficient, in particular because the maximand need not be convex in n_i and q_{ij}.

[14]Of course, when $q_i = 0$, average cost is not defined.

Proposition 4.1(b) has a very strong implication. In the absence of fluctuations (and of indivisibilities), a single type of plant would be built, namely that for which minimum average cost is minimum (in comparison with all other designs). With fluctuations, more flexible plants will be used. Still, some plants may correspond to the design that would be adopted in the absence of fluctuations. One may expect these 'efficient' plants to be operated (at some level) under all demand conditions. Then, it remains true that expected price is less than the price that would prevail in the absence of fluctuations, i.e. is less than the minimum minimorum of average cost. The reservation introduced at the beginning of the present section is thus unnecessary.

5 Conclusions and interpretation

The foregoing analysis hinges around the condition that expected profits for each firm are zero, a condition that reflects minimisation of expected cost, and that implies the strong inequalities of propositions 2.3–4.1. In this concluding section, we will reconsider that condition in three ways. First, we will remark that the condition remains meaningful outside of the narrow framework adopted thus far (a non-storable commodity with perfectly inelastic demand). Second, we will discuss the rationale for the expectation criterion (minimum expected cost, zero expected profits) underlying our analysis. Third, we will comment briefly on the implications of monopolistic behaviour.

In order for condition (2.3) ($\mathrm{E}[qg(q) - F(q)] = 0$) to entail zero expected profits, it is enough that price be equal to marginal cost at all levels of demand. This still allows price to be a function of quantity, and of other things as well (inventories for instance). Thus the assumptions that output is non-storable and that demand is independent of price are not required for proposition 2.3 so long as (2.3) holds. The (descriptive) conclusions from proposition 2.3 are thus valid under quite general supply and demand conditions, given competitive pricing and free entry guided by expected profits.

In this more general framework, efficiency considerations cannot be reduced to the elementary discussion of expected cost, since cost could always be reduced by curtailing demand. But the well-known results on efficiency of competitive allocations remain applicable.

Under uncertainty, competitive allocations are sustained by prices for contingent claims to commodities (on this notion, see for instance, Arrow (1953) or Guesnerie and de Montbrial (1974)). Using the discrete formulation of Section 4, we may replace the *r values* Q_j by a system of *r* demand *functions*, and interpret the index *j* as an index of 'states of the environment'. The notation P_j may be kept to denote the price of a claim to the numeraire (in terms of which costs and spot prices are measured), contingent on state *j*.

The expression

$$\sum_j P_j F(q_j)$$

now measures the present non-stochastic value of the total (stochastic) cost under the production strategy whereby q_j is produced in state j. Similarly, if $p_j = F'(q_j) = g(q_j)$ denotes the spot price of output in state j, then

$$\sum_j P_j q_j p_j = \sum_j P_j q_j g(q_j)$$

measures the present (non-stochastic) value of the (stochastic) revenue associated with the production strategy q_j at spot prices p_j. The condition

$$\sum_j P_j (q_j g(q_j) - F(q_j)) = 0$$

now asserts that the present value of revenue minus cost, i.e. the present value of profits, is zero. Under free entry,[15] this condition must be satisfied by competitive allocations, and these are Pareto optimal.

This line of reasoning provides a tight argument for the efficiency of investment guided by profit considerations. Note, however, that present values are computed with weights given by prices for contingent claims to the numeraire. These prices have all the properties of a probability measure, but reflect scarcity as well as probability considerations. Thus, all the expectations in the text need to be reinterpreted as present values.

In the absence of prices for contingent claims, the efficiency analysis of investment under uncertainty is much more complex and involves rather subtle issues of constrained optimality. The 'zero expected profits' condition must then be understood in terms of expected future (spot) prices and subjective probabilities. In order for expected profits to vanish *some* investors must be willing to bear the risks without compensation, i.e. must be risk neutral. Otherwise, free entry does not entail zero expected profits.

Similar remarks apply to the temporal interpretation of demand fluctuations. As already noted by D–G, 'everything that has been said about random fluctuations applies, mutatis mutandis, to fluctuations in time: one simply replaces the probability of a particular demand level by the relative frequency of its realization over time. Expectations become then arithmetical averages over time with discount rates providing a particular set of weights for relative frequencies' (p. 139). That is, P_j may now be interpreted as the discount factor applicable to time $j(j = 1, \ldots, r)$, with p_j still defining the spot price of output at time j. The expression

$$\sum_{j=1} P_j (p_j q_j - F(q_j))$$

now defines the present value of net revenue, and is again equal to zero

<hr />

[15] In general equilibrium theory, 'free entry' is introduced by assuming additivity of the production sets.

under competitive pricing and free entry. In order for the condition to be operational, however, firms must know the discount factors P_j and future spot prices p_j (or equivalently the futures prices $P_j p_j$). Otherwise, we are back to the uncertainty framework.

Under either interpretation of the model, monopolistic aspects may be brought into the analysis. Of course, if demand is totally inelastic to price, the monopolistic solution is not defined. When demand is a function of price, the monopolistic solution calls for the well-known equality of marginal cost and marginal revenue (*ex post*). Whatever pattern of output may result, the monopolist will still want to minimise cost. If one retains the criterion of maximisation of expected profits (or of present value of profits) the multiplant monopoly will still operate in such a way that

$$E[qg(q) - F(q)] = 0$$

or

$$n_i E[q_i(g_i(q_i) - f_i(q_i))] = 0 \cdot$$

Propositions 2.3 and 4.1(b) will continue to hold. Of course, the number or mixture of plants under the monopoly solution will differ from those obtaining under competition, with less investment in the former case than in the latter.

References

Arrow, K.J. (1953). Le rôle des valeurs boursières pour la répartition la meilleure des risques. *Econométrie*, pp. 41–7. Paris: CNRS. Translated (1964) as The Role of Securities in the Optimal Allocation of Risk-Bearing. *Review of Economic Studies*, 31: 91–6

Drèze, J.H. and J.J. Gabszewicz (1967). Demand Fluctuations, Capacity Utilisation and Prices. *Operations Res. Verfahren*, 3: 119–41 (Chapter 11 supra.)

Drèze, J.H. and E. Sheshinski (1975). *Industry Equilibrium under Uncertainty*, Working paper no. 59, IMSS, Stanford University (Chapter 13 infra.)

Guesnerie, R. and T. de Montbrial (1971). Allocation under Uncertainty: A Survey. In J.H. Drèze (ed.), *Allocation under Uncertainty: Equilibrium and Optimality*. London: Macmillan

Hart, A.G. (1951). *Anticipations, Uncertainty and Dynamic Planning*. New York: Kelley

Kuhn, K.W. and A.W. Tucker (1951). Non-Linear Programming. *Proc. Second Berkeley Symposium on Mathematical Statistics and Probability*, Berkeley: 481–92

Leland, H. (1972). Theory of the Firm Facing Random Demand. *American Economic Review*, 62: 278–91

Massé, P. and R. Gibrat (1964). Applications of Linear Programming to Investments in the Electric Power Industry. In J.R. Nelson (ed.), *Marginal Cost Pricing in Practice*, pp. 215–34. Englewood Cliffs: Prentice Hall

Oi, W. (1961). The desirability of Price Instability under Perfect Competition. *Econometrica*, 29: 58–64

Sandmo, A. (1971). On the Theory of the Competitive Firm under Price Uncertainty. *American Economic Review*, 62: 65–73

Tisdell, C. (1963). Uncertainty, Instability, Expected Profit. *Econometrica*, 31: 243–7

13 On industry equilibrium under uncertainty*

1 Introduction

Some time ago Stigler (1939) and Hart (1951) made the observation that demand fluctuations are best met by flexible plants, characterised by flat bottomed average cost curves. Actually, if a variety of plant designs are feasible, it may typically be efficient to build plants of different types and to allocate output among them so as to minimise expected total production costs. It is natural to inquire whether a competitive equilibrium will sustain such an efficient solution.

This question has been recently considered by Sheshinski and Drèze (S–D) (1976). In their model, an industry which consists of plants of different designs produces an output, the demand for which is randomly distributed. At each realisation of demand, the price of output is determined competitively so as to equate the output supplied by the firms present in the industry with the given level of demand. Entry and exit of firms is assumed to be governed by expected profits; that is, firms are risk neutral. The equilibrium number of firms is such that no firm in the industry has positive expected profits, and all potential entrants' expected profits, calculated at the equilibrium price distribution, are non-positive. S–D have analysed the characteristics of the equilibrium distributions of outputs and prices. They have also shown that any competitive equilibrium satisfies the *necessary*

Journal of Economic Theory, 33 (1984) (1): 88–97, with Eytan Sheshinski. This work was supported by National Science Foundation Grant SOC 75-21820-A01 at the Institute for Mathematical Studies in the Social Sciences, Stanford University. We would like to thank Kenneth Arrow, Claude Henry, Jean Jaskold Gabszewicz and Itzhak Katznelson for helpful discussions. This paper first appeared as Working paper no. 59, IMSS, Stanford University, Stanford, CA, 1975.

conditions for efficient production – defined as minimisation of the *expected cost* of meeting the random demand.

The purpose of this note is to prove that

(1)   the necessary conditions for efficiency are sufficient; accordingly, the set of competitive equilibria is non-empty and coincides with the set of efficient allocations (Section 2);

(2)   a dynamic process of free entry and exit of firms, guided by expected profits, is *quasi-stable* and every limit point is a competitive equilibrium (Section 3).

We also analyse the conditions for *uniqueness* of the competitive equilibrium, in which case it is stable. And we establish (Section 4) the stability result for the more general case of separable demand *functions* (instead of exogenous random demand).

2 Efficiency and equilibrium

We consider an industry consisting of numerous firms that produce a homogeneous output. Firms are identified by their cost structure, where each firm is assumed to belong to one of K possible *types*. Let $q_i \in \mathbb{R}_+$ be the *output* of a firm of type i and $F_i(q_i): \mathbb{R}_+ \to \mathbb{R}_+$ its total cost. It is assumed that the functions $F_i(\cdot)$ are monotone increasing, strictly convex and twice differentiable:[1]

$$F_i'(q_i) \geqslant 0 \quad \text{and} \quad F_i''(q_i) > 0, \quad \forall q_i \geqslant 0. \tag{2.1}$$

Each firm has a standard U-shaped (ditonic) average cost curve, i.e. there exists for each i a unique $q_i^* > 0$ such that

$$q_i F_i'(q_i) - F_i(q_i) \gtreqless 0 \quad \text{as } q_i \gtreqless q_i^*. \tag{2.2}$$

Assumptions (2.1) and (2.2) imply that $F_i(q_i) = K_i + G_i(q_i)$, where K_i is a positive constant and G_i is a strictly convex function.[2]

Let $n_i \in \mathbb{R}_+$ be the number of firms of type i, $i = 1, 2, \ldots, K$.[3] Clearly, cost minimisation requires that all firms of a given type produce the same output and hence incur the same costs. Thus, total costs for the industry, C, are given by

$$C = \sum_{i=1}^{K} n_i F_i(q_i). \tag{2.3}$$

Let $Q \in \mathbb{R}_+$ be the demand for the industry's output. Given any Q, it is

---

[1] At $q_i = 0$ these should be interpreted as the appropriate limits from the right. Actually, our analysis does not require F to be twice differentiable; it is enough that F has a Lipschitz continuous first derivative. The stronger assumption simplifies exposition.

[2] By convexity, $F_i(0) \geqslant F_i(q_i) - q_i F_i'(q_i)$. If $F_i(0) = 0$, then $q_i F_i'(q_i) - F_i(q_i) \geqslant 0$, contradicting (2.2); therefore $F_i(0) = K_i > 0$.

[3] Following S–D, we ignore the realistic condition that n_i should be an integer – a condition that would require an altogether different mathematical analysis.

assumed that production satisfies demand,

$$\sum_{i=1}^{K} n_i q_i \geqslant Q. \tag{2.4}$$

When $Q > 0$, (2.4) clearly requires that $n_j q_j > 0$ for some $j = 1, 2, \ldots, K$.

Given $\mathbf{n} = (n_1, n_2, \ldots, n_K)$ and Q, total costs, (2.3), are minimised subject to (2.4) if and only if the following conditions hold: $\exists p(\mathbf{n}, Q) \in \mathbb{R}_+$ such that

$$F_i'(q_i) - p(\mathbf{n}, Q) \geqslant 0 \quad \text{and} \quad q_i[F_i'(q_i) - p(\mathbf{n}, Q)] = 0, \quad \forall i, \tag{2.5}$$

and (2.4) is satisfied with equality.

Denote the solutions to (2.4)–(2.5) by $\hat{q}_i(p(\mathbf{n}, Q))$ or, in short, $\hat{\mathbf{q}}(\mathbf{n}, Q) = (\hat{q}_1(\mathbf{n}, Q), \hat{q}_2(\mathbf{n}, Q), \ldots, \hat{q}_K(\mathbf{n}, Q))$. Clearly, the $\hat{q}_i$ are continuous functions of $\mathbf{n}$ and Q.

Demand is assumed to be randomly distributed over a finite interval. Given the demand distribution and the functions $\hat{\mathbf{q}}(\mathbf{n}, Q)$, *expected total costs* are defined as a function of $\mathbf{n}$ by $L(\mathbf{n})$: $\mathbb{R}_+^K \to \mathbb{R}_+$:

$$L(\mathbf{n}) = \mathrm{E}[C(\mathbf{n}, Q)] = \sum_{i=1}^{K} n_i \mathrm{E}[F_i(\hat{q}_i(\mathbf{n}, Q))]. \tag{2.6}$$

Proposition 2.1: $L(\mathbf{n})$ is a convex function.[4]

Proof: Let

$$\psi_i(\mathbf{n}) = \mathrm{E}[\hat{q}_i F_i'(\hat{q}_i) - F_i(\hat{q}_i)]$$
$$= \mathrm{E}[\hat{q}_i(\mathbf{n}, Q) p(\mathbf{n}, Q) - F_i(\hat{q}_i(\mathbf{n}, Q))], \quad \forall i. \tag{2.7}$$

We shall show that for any $\mathbf{n}$ and $\mathbf{n}'$,

$$L(\mathbf{n}) \geqslant L(\mathbf{n}') + \sum_{i=1}^{K} (n_i' - n_i) \psi_i(\mathbf{n}'). \tag{2.8}$$

The right-hand side of (2.8) defines a supporting hyperplane to $L(\mathbf{n})$ at $\mathbf{n}'$, for any $\mathbf{n}'$.[5] Convexity of F_i implies that

$$F_i(\hat{q}_i(\mathbf{n}, Q)) \geqslant F_i(\hat{q}_i(\mathbf{n}', Q))$$
$$+ (\hat{q}_i(\mathbf{n}, Q) - \hat{q}_i(\mathbf{n}', Q)) F_i'(\hat{q}_i(\mathbf{n}', Q)), \quad \forall i. \tag{2.9}$$

---

[4]It was shown in the mimeographed version of this paper, released as CORE DP 7944, Louvain-la-Neuve, Belgium, that $L(\mathbf{n})$ is C^1.

[5]For $\mathbf{n} = \lambda \mathbf{n}' + (1 - \lambda)\mathbf{n}''$, $0 \leqslant \lambda \leqslant 1$, (2.8) implies directly

$$\lambda L(\mathbf{n}') + (1 - \lambda)L(\mathbf{n}'') \geqslant \lambda[L(\mathbf{n}) + \sum_i (n_i - n_i')\psi_i(\mathbf{n})]$$
$$+ (1 - \lambda)[L(\mathbf{n}) + \sum_i (n_i - n_i'')\psi_i(\mathbf{n})] = L(\mathbf{n}).$$

Thus,

$$L(\mathbf{n}) \geqslant \sum_{i=1}^{K} n_i E[F_i(\hat{q}_i(\mathbf{n}', Q) + (\hat{q}_i(\mathbf{n}, Q) - \hat{q}_i(\mathbf{n}', Q))F_i'(\hat{q}_i(\mathbf{n}', Q))]$$

$$= L(\mathbf{n}') + \sum_{i=1}^{K} (n_i - n_i')E[F_i(\hat{q}_i(\mathbf{n}', Q)) - \hat{q}_i(\mathbf{n}', Q)F_i'(\hat{q}_i(\mathbf{n}', Q))]$$

$$+ E\left[\sum_{i=1}^{K} (n_i \hat{q}_i(\mathbf{n}, Q) - n_i' \hat{q}_i(\mathbf{n}', Q))F_i'(\hat{q}_i(\mathbf{n}', Q)) \right]$$

$$= L(\mathbf{n}') + \sum_{i=1}^{K} (n_i' - n_i)\psi_i(\mathbf{n}')$$

$$+ E\left[p(\mathbf{n}', Q) \sum_{i=1}^{K} (n_i \hat{q}_i(\mathbf{n}, Q) - n_i' \hat{q}_i(\mathbf{n}', Q)) \right]$$

$$+ E\left[\sum_{i=1}^{K} (n_i \hat{q}_i(\mathbf{n}, Q) - n_i' \hat{q}_i(\mathbf{n}', Q))(F_i'(\hat{q}_i(\mathbf{n}', Q)) - p(\mathbf{n}', Q)) \right]$$

$$= L(\mathbf{n}') + \sum_{i=1}^{K} (n_i' - n_i)\psi_i(\mathbf{n}') + E\left[\sum_{i=1}^{K} n_i \hat{q}_i(\mathbf{n}, Q) \right.$$

$$\left. \times (F_i'(\hat{q}_i(\mathbf{n}', Q)) - p(\mathbf{n}', Q)) \right]$$

$$\geqslant L(\mathbf{n}') + \sum_{i=1}^{K} (n_i' - n_i)\psi_i(\mathbf{n}'). \tag{2.10}$$

$\square$

For each i, let $\bar{n}_i$ be the number of firms of type i which minimise total expected costs when $n_j = 0 \forall j \neq i$. By (2.2), $\forall i \exists \bar{n}_i > 0$, defined by

$$n_i E[F_i(Q/n_i)] \geqslant \bar{n}_i E[F_i(Q/\bar{n}_i)], \quad \forall n_i. \tag{2.11}$$

Clearly, $\psi_i = 0$ when $n_i = \bar{n}_i$ and $n_j = 0 \ \forall j \neq i$; and $\psi_i(\mathbf{n}) < 0$ for all $\mathbf{n}$ such that $n_i > \bar{n}$.

Definition 2.1: Let $N = \{\mathbf{n} | 0 \leqslant n_i \leqslant \bar{n}_i + \varepsilon, i = 1, 2, \dots, K\}$, where $\varepsilon > 0$ but otherwise arbitrary.[6]

Proposition 2.2: $\exists \mathbf{n}^* \in N$ such that $L(\mathbf{n}) \geqslant L(\mathbf{n}^*)$, $\forall \mathbf{n}$, i.e. $L(\mathbf{n})$ attains a minimum at $\mathbf{n}^*$.

Proof: The continuous function $L(\mathbf{n})$ attains a minimum on the compact set N – say at n^*. For all $n \notin N$, $L(n) > L(n^*)$. $\square$

Clearly, n^* satisfies the conditions

$$\psi_i(\mathbf{n}^*) \leqslant 0 \quad \text{and} \quad n_i^* \psi_i(\mathbf{n}^*) = 0, \quad \forall i. \tag{2.12}$$

---

[6]This particular definition is motivated by the remark in Section 3.

Definition 2.2: Let J^* be a subset of $\{1, 2, \ldots, K\}$ such that $j \in J^*$ if $\psi_j(\mathbf{n}^*) = 0$; let j^* be the cardinality of J^*.

Proposition 2.3: A sufficient condition that $\mathbf{n}^*$ be a *unique* minimum of $L(\mathbf{n})$ is that the j^* functions of $Q, \hat{q}_j(\mathbf{n}^*, Q)$, $j \in J^*$, be linearly independent, i.e. that the $j^* \times j^*$ matrix $E[\hat{q}_i \hat{q}_j]$, $i, j \in J^*$, has full rank.

Proof: If $L(\mathbf{n}) = L(\mathbf{n}^*)$ then, by (2.10) and (2.12), $n_i \psi_i(\mathbf{n}^*) \geqslant 0$, $\forall i$. Hence, $n_i = 0$, $\forall i$ such that $\psi_i(\mathbf{n}^*) < 0$. The argument in the proof of proposition 2.1 implies that if

$$L(\mathbf{n}) = L(\mathbf{n}^*) + \sum_{i=1}^{K} (n_i^* - n_i) \psi_i(\mathbf{n}^*),$$

then for any Q, $\hat{q}_i(\mathbf{n}, Q) = \hat{q}_i(\mathbf{n}^*, Q)$, $\forall i$. Hence, $\hat{q}_j(\mathbf{n}, Q) = \hat{q}_j(\mathbf{n}^*, Q)$, $\forall j \in J^*$. But,

$$\sum_{j \in J} n_j \hat{q}_j(\mathbf{n}, Q) = \sum_{j \in J} n_j^* \hat{q}_j(\mathbf{n}^*, Q),$$

i.e.

$$\sum_{j \in J} (n_j - n_j^*) \hat{q}_j(\mathbf{n}^*, Q) = 0$$

and the j^* functions $\hat{q}_j(\mathbf{n}^*, Q)$ are linearly dependent.   □

An example shows that this sufficient condition cannot in general be inferred from properties of the cost functions F_i alone, nor from properties of the demand distribution alone; both the cost functions *and* the demand distribution may be relevant.

Example: Let $F_i'(q_i) = a_i + b_i q_i$ for $i = 1, 2$, where a_i and b_i are constants. It is easily shown that if both plants operate in all states, then the determinant of the matrix $E(q_i q_j)$ is equal to

$$\left[\frac{(a_1 - a_2)^2}{(b_1 b_2)^2} \right] \text{Var}\,(p), \quad \text{where } \text{Var}(p) = E(p^2) - [E(p)]^2.$$

The condition for uniqueness is thus $a_1 \neq a_2$.

Yet, when Q is non-random, both types could be operated, even though $a_1 \neq a_2$, provided

$$\frac{F_1(q_1^*)}{q_1^*} = \frac{F_2(q_2^*)}{q_2^*}.$$

Thus, the condition $a_1 \neq a_2$ is not sufficient for uniqueness in that case.

Under *perfect competition*, each firm in the industry maximises profits when, for a given output price, p, (2.5) is satisfied, yielding output levels

$\hat{q}_i(\mathbf{n}, Q)$, $\forall i$. *Expected profits* of a firm of type i, given $\mathbf{n}$, are thus

$$E[p(\mathbf{n}, Q)\hat{q}_i(\mathbf{n}, Q) - F_i(\hat{q}_i(\mathbf{n}, Q))] = E[F_i'(\hat{q}_i)\hat{q}_i - F_i(\hat{q}_i)] = \psi_i(\mathbf{n}).$$

$$(2.13)$$

When firms are risk-neutral, the number of firms of each type is governed by expected profits. We therefore have:

Definition 2.3: In *competitive equilibrium* the number of firms, $\hat{\mathbf{n}}$ (and the corresponding $p(\hat{\mathbf{n}}, Q)$ and $\hat{q}_i(\hat{\mathbf{n}}, Q)$ for all i and for all Q), satisfies

$$\psi_i(\hat{\mathbf{n}}) \leqslant 0 \quad \text{and} \quad \hat{n}_i \psi_i(\hat{\mathbf{n}}) = 0, \quad \forall i. \tag{2.14}$$

Since $\hat{\mathbf{n}}$ satisfies (2.12), clearly, in a competitive equilibrium, expected total costs of the industry are minimised (see S–D, proposition 6).

3 Extension to separable demand functions and stability analysis

The foregoing analysis, and the earlier papers on which it rests, assume that demand is randomly distributed, independently of prices and costs. For many purposes, it would seem desirable to recognise that quantity demanded will be a function of price. A simple discrete formulation uses the concept of 'state of the environment'. Let $s = 1, \ldots, S$ denote a state, π_s its probability, p_s the price and Q_s the demand under state s. We have assumed so far that Q_s was given. Under the separable formulation,

$$Q_s = Q_s(p_s), \quad s = 1, \ldots, S. \tag{3.1}$$

More generally,

$$Q_s = Q_s(p_1, \ldots, p_s, \ldots, p_S), \quad s = 1, \ldots, S. \tag{3.2}$$

In this setting, minimisation of expected total cost is no longer meaningful, since costs can always be reduced by reducing quantities (and simultaneously raising prices to maintain equality of supply and demand). But it is still possible to define competitive equilibria.

Definition 3.1: A *competitive equilibrium* consists of a number of firms $\hat{\mathbf{n}}$, a vector of prices $\hat{\mathbf{p}} = (\hat{p}_1, \ldots, \hat{p}_s)$ and vectors of quantities $\hat{\mathbf{q}}_i = (\hat{q}_{i1}, \ldots, \hat{q}_{is})$, $i = 1, \ldots, K$, $\hat{\mathbf{Q}} = (\hat{Q}_1, \ldots, \hat{Q}_s)$, such that

$$\hat{Q}_s = \hat{Q}_s(\hat{\mathbf{p}}) = \sum_i \hat{n}_i \hat{q}_{is} \quad \forall s \tag{3.3}$$

$$\hat{\psi}_i = \sum_s \pi_s[\hat{q}_{is}\hat{p}_s - F_i(\hat{q}_{is})]$$

$$\geqslant \sum_s \pi_s[q_s\hat{p}_s - F_i(q_s)] \quad \forall q \in \mathbb{R}_+^S \, \forall i \tag{3.4}$$

$$\hat{\psi}_i \leqslant 0 \quad \text{and} \quad \hat{n}_i \hat{\psi}_i = 0 \quad \forall i. \tag{3.5}$$

Conditions (3.4) state that $\hat{q}_i$ is an optimal supply vector for a firm of type i, given the conditional prices $\hat{\mathbf{p}}$, where 'optimal supply' is still defined by maximisation of *expected profits*. Conditions (3.3) state that aggregate supply is equal, *in every state*, to the aggregate demand generated by prices $\hat{\mathbf{p}}$. Conditions (3.5) are the same as (2.4).

At a competitive equilibrium, the expected total cost of producing the vector of quantities $(\hat{Q}_1, \dots, \hat{Q}_S)$ is still minimum. We now prove that a competitive equilibrium exists, and can be reached through a natural process of entry and exit of firms.

Let $n_i(t)$ be the number of firms of type i at time t.

Definition 3.1: The dynamic process P for entry and exit of firms is given by

$$\dot{n}_i = \begin{cases} g_i(\psi_i), & n_i > 0 \\ \text{Max}\,\{0, g_i(\psi_i)\}, & n_i = 0 \end{cases} \quad \forall i \Bigg\} \tag{3.6}$$

and for all $t \geqslant 0$, $p_s(t)$ is such that

$$Q_s(p_s(t)) = \sum_i n_i q_{is}(p_s(t)), \quad s = 1, \dots, S,$$

where $\dot{n}_i = \mathrm{d}n_i(t)/\mathrm{d}t$, and where the functions $g_i : \mathbb{R}_+ \to \mathbb{R}_+$ are continuous, strictly increasing and absolutely bounded with $g_i(0) = 0$, $\forall i$.

In other words, we assume that new plants of type i are built whenever their expected profits are positive; but that plants of type i are scrapped, or at least not replaced, when their expected profits are negative. The rates of investment and of scrapping are assumed to be continuous monotone bounded functions of the levels of expected profits; whereas prices in each state adjust continuously to clear markets. This formulation is clearly an idealised representation of the investment process, requiring, in particular, unbiased profit expectations, and ignoring the discontinuous nature of physical investment. Of course, if such an idealised process were not quasi-stable, there would be little hope that actual investment processes converge to a competitive equilibrium.

Remark: If $\mathbf{n}(0) \in N$ then $\mathbf{n}(t) \in N$, $\forall t \geqslant 0$. Since $\psi_i < 0$ when $n_i = \bar{n}_i + \varepsilon$, by (3.6) $\dot{n}_i < 0$ at such points (on the boundary of N).

Theorem 3.1: Under assumptions (2.1) and (2.2), if the demand functions (3.1) are monotone non-increasing, continuous and piecewise C^1, then process P is quasi-stable.[7]

---

[7] The demand functions must have well-defined left and right derivatives. Process P is quasi-stable if and only if any limit point of any trajectory is an equilibrium.

Proof: We use theorem 6.1 of Champsaur *et al.* (C–D–H) (1977) which applies to differential equations with discontinuous right-hand sides. Our Lyapunov function is

$$\Lambda(\mathbf{n}(t)) = \Psi(\mathbf{n}(t), \mathbf{p}(t)) + \Gamma(\mathbf{p}(t))$$

$$= \sum_i n_i(t)\psi_i(\mathbf{p}(t)) + \sum_s \pi_s \int_{p_s(t)}^{\infty} Q_s(p_s(t))\mathrm{d}p_s. \tag{3.7}$$

This function is not everywhere differentiable, but it is continuous and it possesses right derivatives, constructed as follows:

(1)   The functions $q_{is}(p_s)$, defined implicitly by (2.5), are differentiable for all p_s such that $q_{is} > 0$; at $q_{is} = 0$, either $\partial q_{is}/\partial p_s = 0$, or $\partial q_{is}/\partial p_s^+ > 0$ and $\partial q_{is}/\partial p_s^- = 0$; in all cases, $\partial q_{is}/\partial p_s^+ (p_s - \partial F_i/\partial q_{is}) = \partial q_{is}/\partial p_s^- (p_s - \partial F_i/\partial q_{is}) = 0$;

(2)   The functions $p_s(\mathbf{n})$, defined implicitly by the equalities (2.4), i.e.

$$\sum_i n_i q_{is}(p_s) - Q_s(p_s) = 0,$$

have left and right derivatives given by

$$\frac{\partial p_s}{\partial n_i^+} = \frac{-q_{is}}{\sum_j n_j \dfrac{\partial q_{js}}{\partial p_s^-} - \dfrac{\partial Q_s}{\partial p_s^-}} \leqslant 0, \quad \frac{\partial p_s}{\partial n_i^-} = \frac{-q_{is}}{\sum_j n_j \dfrac{\partial q_{js}}{\partial p_s^+} - \dfrac{\partial Q_s}{\partial p_s^+}} \leqslant 0; \tag{3.8}$$

(3)   Writing $\partial q_{is}/\partial p_s^\circ, \partial p_s/\partial n_i^\circ$ for the directional derivatives ($+$ or $-$ as the case may be), we have

$$\frac{\mathrm{d}\Lambda}{\mathrm{d}t^+} = \sum_i \frac{\partial \Lambda}{\partial n_i^\circ}\dot{n}_i = \sum_i \psi_i \dot{n}_i + \sum_i n_i \sum_j \frac{\partial \psi_i}{\partial n_j^\circ}\dot{n}_j - \sum_s \pi_s Q_s(p_s)\sum_j \frac{\partial p_s}{\partial n_j^\circ}\dot{n}_j$$

$$= \sum_i \psi_i \dot{n}_i + \sum_{ij} n_i \dot{n}_j \sum_s \pi_s \frac{\partial p_s}{\partial n_j^\circ}\left[q_{is}(p_s) + \frac{\partial q_{is}}{\partial p_s^\circ}\left(p_s - \frac{\partial F_i}{\partial q_{is}}\right)\right]$$

$$- \sum_s \pi_s Q_s(p_s)\sum_j \frac{\partial p_s}{\partial n_j^\circ}\dot{n}_j$$

$$= \sum_i \psi_i \dot{n}_i + \sum_s \pi_s \sum_i n_i q_{is}(p_s)\sum_j \dot{n}_j \frac{\partial p_s}{\partial n_j^\circ} - \sum_s \pi_s Q_s(p_s)\sum_j \dot{n}_j \frac{\partial p_s}{\partial n_j^\circ}$$

$$= \sum_i \psi_i \dot{n}_i \geqslant 0. \tag{3.9}$$

It follows from (3.6) and (3.9) that

$$\frac{\mathrm{d}\Lambda}{\mathrm{d}t^+} = 0 \Leftrightarrow \dot{n}_i = 0 \quad \forall i. \tag{3.10}$$

In view of the above remark we may assume that $\mathbf{n}(t) \in N, \forall t \geqslant 0$. Since Λ is monotone continuous and N is a compact set, Λ converges as $t \to \infty$. Hence, Λ is a *Lyapunov function* as required by Champsaur *et al.* (1977, Theorem 6.1). The arguments in Section 5 of that paper may be reproduced to prove that the other assumptions of Theorem 6.1 are satisfied in our problem.[8]   □

It is of some interest that a suitable Lyapunov function is provided by the *sum* of the expected values of total profits $\Psi(\mathbf{n}, \mathbf{p})$ and consumers' surplus $\Gamma(\mathbf{p})$. The standard concept of consumers' surplus in unidimensional problems, i.e. the 'area under the demand curve', is of direct applicability under the separable formulation (3.1). Although the concept can be extended to multidimensional problems, it does not lead to a suitable Lyapunov function for the general formulation (3.2).

It should be noted that the expectation of consumers' surplus $\Gamma(\mathbf{p})$ is here introduced as a technical artefact leading to a suitable Lyapunov function. No particular welfare significance is attached to it. Indeed, a welfare analysis should be based on consumers' *expected utilities*, and should reflect the consumers' attitudes towards risk. The definition of $\Gamma(\mathbf{p})$ makes no reference to utilities and risk preferences. For the same reason, no claim is made that a competitive equilibrium is efficient from the viewpoint of consumers' preferences; counterexamples are easy to construct.

4 A concluding remark

The analysis in this paper, and its predecessors, rests on the explicit assumption that all firms maximise expected profits, using a common probability distribution on the states of the environment. Firms are assumed able to associate correctly output prices with states, given the levels of investment for the different types of plants. Hence, all firms are assumed to use a common probability distribution on prices. Yet, such price expectations need not be 'rational' to the extent that the common probability distribution on the states of the environment is arbitrary.

Although the model used in the paper is oversimplified, it might provide a useful vehicle for exploring the deeper issues arising when firms do not hold common expectations, or when firms base their decisions on criteria other than maximisation of expected profits (for instance, maximisation of an expected utility of profits, or of a market value).

References

Champsaur, P., J.H. Drèze and C. Henry (1977). Stability Theorems with Economic Applications, *Econometrica*, 45(2): 273–94

Hart, A.G. (1951). *Anticipations, Uncertainty and Dynamic Planning*, New York: Kelley

Sheshinski, E. and J.H. Drèze (1976). Demand Fluctuations, Capacity Utilisation and Costs, *American Economic Review*, 66: 731–42 (Chapter 12 supra.)

Stigler, G. (1939). Production and Distribution in the Short-Run, *Journal of Political Economy*, 47: 305–27

[8]Details were given in the mimeographed version of this paper, for the case where $Q_s(p_s) = Q_s \forall p_s$.

V Theory of the firm

14 Investment under private ownership: optimality, equilibrium and stability*

1 Introduction[1]

1.1 General equilibrium under uncertainty

The theory of equilibrium and efficiency of resource allocation, initially developed for a world of certainty, has been reinterpreted for a world of uncertainty, thanks to a suggestion made by Arrow (1953) and pursued further by Debreu (1959).[2]

An economy is defined by (i) a set of commodities, with the total resources (quantities of these commodities) initially available; (ii) a set of consumers, with their consumption sets and preferences; (iii) a set of producers, with their production sets. The resources, consumption sets and production sets define the physical environment. In a world of certainty, the environment is given. In a world of uncertainty, the environment depends upon uncertain events. Let these be determined by 'the choice that nature makes among a finite number of alternatives' (Debreu, 1959, p. 98).

The reinterpretation consists in defining a commodity not only by its physical properties (including the time and place at which it is available) but also by an event *conditional* upon which it is available. An allocation then

*From J.H. Drèze (ed.) (1974) *Allocation under Uncertainty: Equilibrium and Optimality*, pp. 129–66. London. Macmillan.

[1] I am grateful to Mordecai Avriel, Freddy Delbaen, Louis Gevers, Roger Guesnerie and Dieter Sondermann for helpful comments and discussions. Earlier work on this subject with Dominique de la Vallée Poussin led to the work by Drèze and de la Vallée Poussin (1971). Support of the Fonds de la Recherche Fondamentale Collective, Brussels, under contract No. 611 is gratefully acknowledged.
[2] See also Baudier (1954) and Borch (1960).

specifies the consumption of every consumer and the production of every producer, *conditional* on every event. Uncertainty means that these consumptions and productions may vary with the event that obtains.

Consumer preferences are defined over commodity vectors, that is, over plans specifying fully the consumption associated with every event. These preferences are introduced as a primitive concept. Underlying these preferences among consumption plans, there may exist subjective judgements about the likelihood of the various events and subjective attitudes towards risk, as well as conditional preferences among alternative consumptions given some event.

Production sets reflect the 'games against nature' to which the economy has access.

The interpretation of a price system is facilitated if one normalises prices by choosing as a unit the price of a numeraire commodity, available at time 0 (i.e. unconditionally). The price of a given commodity, defined conditionally on an event A, may then be interpreted as an insurance premium: the premium giving title to one unit of that commodity if, and only if, event A obtains. Thus a price system defines a full set of insurance premiums, one for each physical commodity conditionally on each event. In a market context, a price system is predicated upon the organisation of a full set of insurance markets.

With commodities and preferences so defined, the theory developed for a world of certainty is formally applicable to a world of uncertainty, without modification. In particular, the concepts of price equilibrium (or 'equilibrium relative to a price system') and Pareto-optimum, the existence and equivalence theorems, carry over.

1.2 Private ownership

A private ownership economy is completely described if, in addition to the consumption sets, preferences and production sets, one specifies, for each consumer, his resources and his shares of all firms (producers). Given a price system, the net value of a firm's production plan defines its profits; for each consumer the value of his initial resources plus his shares in the profits of all firms defines his budget constraint. Markets for shares can be substituted, to some extent, for insurance markets. Since the value of a firm is automatically equal to the market value of its production plan, one could replace the market for one of the firm's outputs by a market for shares of the firm. The price of that output would then be inferred from the price of the firm, instead of proceeding in the other direction. This operation could be repeated as many times as there are firms with linearly independent production plans. Similar remarks apply to the substitution of futures markets (and asset markets) for insurance markets.

When there exists a mixture of insurance markets, of futures markets, and of markets for shares and other assets, the question naturally arises whether together the prices on these markets provide the same information as the prices on a full set of insurance markets. This question is relevant for existing economies, which do indeed operate through such a mixture of markets.[3]

1.3 Unrealistic implications of competitive equilibria

A competitive equilibrium for a private ownership economy is defined by a price system and an allocation such that (a) the profits of each firm are maximised over its production set; (b) the consumption of each consumer is best, from the viewpoint of his preferences, over his budget set.

Such an equilibrium has two important properties. (i) The firms operate exactly in the same way as in a world of certainty. The price system provides all the information needed to guide their production and investment decisions. Profit maximisation amounts to choosing the conditional production plan with the highest insurance value, and collecting that insurance value at once. The firms need not make any probability judgements or adopt any attitude towards risk. Because the firms automatically maximise the wealth of their stockholders, no problem of control arises. (ii) Since the insurance markets on all events are cleared simultaneously at the outset, the occurrence of any event simply calls for realisation of the conditional plans, and no *new* adjustments are required.

These two properties may be contrasted with observed features of existing economies. (i′) Firms do engage continuously in activities designed to improve their assessments of the probabilities of future events. Sometimes, important debates take place, regarding the choice of investment policies, when these investments are surrounded by considerable uncertainty.[4] The control problems are obvious in small firms, especially family owned firms. In the case of large firms, such problems sometimes come out in the open, through proxy fights or takeover bids that point unmistakably to interactions between ownership and control. (ii′) The need to reconsider investment decisions in the light of new information is particularly obvious in times of change.[5] Revisions in international parities and monetary arrangements, new trade agreements, new public programs

---

[3]It is noteworthy that new financial assets are regularly created (e.g. shares in investment trusts, real estate certificates…).

[4]A particularly obvious example was provided in the late 1950s by the Belgian Steel Industry, which was then planning plant modernisation and capacity expansion. Whereas several major firms pooled their resources to build a large modern plant on the seashore, another firm planned instead to extend the capacity of its inland facilities. That plan was extensively debated between stockholders, management and financial institutions. A major argument in favour of the plan was the much shorter delay required for its realisation, as opposed to the new seashore complex. The plan was clearly perceived as a gamble on the rate of capacity utilisation in the 1960s, and opposing views were expressed about both the probabilities and the attitude towards risk that should guide the firm's policy. The plan was approved, and the firm faced severe financial difficulties in the late 1960s….

[5]The second half of 1971 provides a good example.

or forms of concern about the environment, temporary investment credits, are some key elements to which investment policies (and asset prices) must adjust. Clearly, the process does not reduce to realisation of predetermined conditional plans.

1.4 Outline of the chapter

Considering these shortcomings of the price information and insurance opportunities available in existing private ownership economies, it seems worthwhile to develop models which aim at capturing the essential operating features of these economies. Models of private ownership economies, with asset markets (in particular, with a stock market) but with restricted (in the limit, with no) insurance markets are natural candidates. The simplest models one can build involve a single commodity and two dates, with information about the true state of nature accruing at the later of these dates.

Among previous investigations of such models, the most relevant for my purposes here are those by Diamond (1967) and Stiglitz (1972). Diamond's paper concentrates on the special case where the firms choose only a scale of operation, and produce (conditional) outputs in exogenously given proportions. Some sections of Stiglitz's paper recognise output substitution, but describe them in terms of two parameters only (mean and variance of output). The results presented below are fully consistent with those of Diamond and Stiglitz but they are more general and explicitly linked to the underlying general equilibrium model.

The stability analysis presented in the second part of this paper and dealing with the issue raised under (ii') in Section 1.3 seems new. Because adjustment processes take place simultaneously at the level of markets for *assets* held by consumers, and at the level of investment decisions within firms, the standard literature on the dynamic stability of adjustment processes for commodity markets is not directly relevant, and a new theory is needed.

The plan of the paper is as follows. An economy with a stock market and no insurance markets is described in Section 2, where the notation and assumptions are also introduced. Section 3 is devoted to static analysis. An equilibrium concept, reflecting the special features of the economy, is introduced; equilibria are characterised and related to Pareto-optima. Section 4 gives three examples of equilibria that are not Pareto-optimal, and an example of a Pareto-optimum that is technologically inefficient. Section 5 is devoted to stability analysis, and contains a quite general convergence theorem. Applications of this theorem are discussed in Section 6. An application of the theory presented here to semi-public goods and some possible extensions are collected in a concluding section. Reference should also be made to a companion paper (Drèze, 1972), where some of these issues are approached with the tools of calculus, under differentiability assumptions. The results in the present paper are more general, but the two presentations are complementary.

2 The model

2.1 Consumers

The economy considered in this paper consists of I consumers, indexed $i = 1, \ldots, I$, and J firms, indexed $j = 1, \ldots, J$. There is a single physical commodity, but there are two periods of time, labelled 0 and 1 respectively. The true state of the world is unknown in period 0, but will be known in period 1. There are S mutually exclusive states, indexed $s = 1, \ldots, S$.

A *consumption plan* for consumer i is a non-negative vector in R^{S+1}: $x^i = (x^i_0, x^i_1, \ldots, x^i_S)$; x^i_0 denotes the consumption of i in period 0, x^i_s his consumption in period 1 if state s obtains. The consumption set of i is the non-negative orthant of the commodity space, R^{S+1}_+.

As a minimal survival requirement, it is assumed that future consumption is useless unless there is some current consumption (a stronger requirement could easily be introduced). Otherwise, R^{S+1}_+ is assumed to be completely ordered by a preordering $\succsim_i$, which is continuous, strictly convex and monotone. Monotonicity is a natural assumption, when there is a single physical commodity (but several periods and/or states). Convexity is needed for most results below, but strict convexity is used only once.[6]

Let $x^i_s = x^i_1$, $s = 1, \ldots, S$; strict convexity of preferences in the (x^i_0, x^i_1) plane is then equivalent to a 'diminishing marginal rate of time preference'. Let x^i_0 be fixed; strict convexity of preferences in the $(x^i_1, \ldots, x^i_S)$ space is then basically equivalent to risk aversion (for a detailed discussion of this point, see Guesnerie and de Montbrial (1974, Section 5.2)).

Assumption 2.1: $\succsim_i$ is representable by the continuous, non-decreasing function $U^i(x^i)$; $\bar{x}^i_0 = 0$ implies $U^i(x^i) \geqslant U^i(\bar{x}^i)$ for all $x^i \in R^{S+1}_+$; $\bar{x}^i_0 > 0$ implies that U^i is strictly quasi-concave at $\bar{x}^i$.

For some of the results in Section 3 and applications in Section 4, the stronger assumption of differentiability is needed.

Assumption 2.1': $\succsim_i$ is representable by the non-decreasing, twice continuously differentiable function $U^i(x^i)$; $\partial U^i/\partial x^i_0 > 0$; when $\bar{x}^i_0 = 0$, $\partial U^i/\partial x^i_s = 0 \forall s$ at $\bar{x}$; when $x^i_0 > 0$, U^i is strictly quasi-concave at $\bar{x}^i$.

---

[6] In step 2 of the proof of the convergence theorem 5.1. The role of strict convexity assumptions is not as clearly known in stability analysis as in the static theory, and it may well be that the strict assumption is not necessary.

Remarks 2.1

(i)   An example of a utility function satisfying assumptions 2.1 and 2.1′ is:

$$U(x) = x_0^{\alpha_0} \prod_{s=1}^{S} (x_s + c_s)^{\alpha_s},$$

$$\cdot \alpha_s > 0, \quad s = 0, 1, \ldots, S, \quad \alpha_0 < 1, \quad c_s > 0, \quad s = 1, \ldots, S.$$

(ii)   When U^i is strictly quasi-concave, it is also strictly increasing.

2.2 Producers

A production plan for firm j is a non-negative vector in R^{S+1}: $b^j = (a^j, b_1^j, \ldots, b_S^j)$, belonging to a production set Y^j; a^j denotes the input of firm j in period 0, b_s^j its output in period 1 if state s obtains; notice that inputs are treated as non-negative quantities. The following is assumed about Y^j:

Assumption 2.2: Y^j is closed and convex; $0 \in Y^j$; $\forall b^j \in Y^j, b_s^j > 0$ for some s implies $a^j > 0$. $\forall c \in R$, the set $\{b^j \,|\, b^j \in Y^j, a^j \leqslant c\}$ is compact.

For some applications in Section 6, a stronger assumption is needed, namely:

Assumption 2.2′: Y^j is defined by $f^j(b^j) \leqslant 0$, $b^j \geqslant 0$, where f^j is a twice continuously differentiable convex function, with $\partial f_j/\partial a_j < 0$, $\partial f_j/\partial b_s^j > 0$, and $f(0) = 0$.

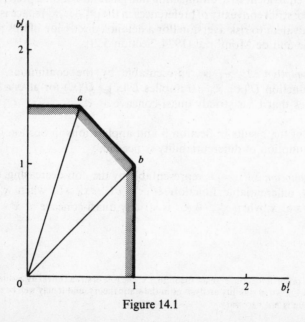

Figure 14.1

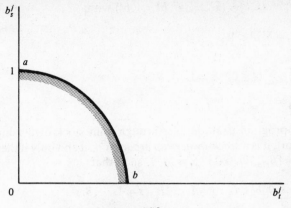

Figure 14.2

A few comments are in order about the interpretation of Y^j. Let there be two states, s and t, and consider a firm which has access to two basic activities, and to free disposal. With one unit of input, the first activity yields $1\frac{1}{2}$ units of output in state s and $\frac{1}{2}$ in state t, whereas the second yields 1 unit of output in both states. Let these two activities be subject to constant returns to scale. The production possibilities in the (b^j_s, b^j_t) plane, when $a^j = 1$, are then described by Figure 14.1, where point a corresponds to the first activity and point b corresponds to the second.[7]

As a further illustration, let the first activity yield 1 unit of b^j_s and 0 unit of b^j_t, the second activity yield 0 unit of b^j_s and 1 unit of b^j_t, when $a^j = 1$. Let, further, the input requirement be equal to the square of the output in the relevant state, for both activities. The production possibilities corresponding to $a^j = 1$ are then depicted in Figure 14.2. The production set of Figure 14.2 satisfies assumption 2.2′, and serves to illustrate how a continuous marginal rate of substitution among outputs may result from diminishing returns to a finite set of basic activities with fixed output proportions.

2.3 Stock-ownership programs

Let the *endowment* of the economy consist of an amount W_0 of initial resources.[8] A *feasible program* for the economy is then an $(I + J)$-tuple of

---

[7] The assumption of 'multiplicative uncertainty', on which the analysis of Diamond (1967) rests, would require the firm to have access to a single activity. In principle, 'multiplicative uncertainty' allows for the ratio b^j_s/b^j_t to vary with a^j; but these variations are constrained by the requirement that Y^j is convex. Under constant returns to scale, any variation is ruled out by convexity.

[8] Because no exchanges of future resources will be allowed, the endowment for period 1 may remain implicit in the consumer preferences and production sets of the firms.

vectors in R_+^{S+1}, $(x, b) = (x^1, \ldots, x^I, b^1, \ldots, b^J)$ with:

$$\sum_i x_0^i + \sum_j a^j \leqslant W_0 \tag{2.1}$$

$$\sum_i x_s^i - \sum_j b_s^j \leqslant 0, \quad s = 1, \ldots, S \tag{2.2}$$

$$b^j \in Y^j, \quad j = 1, \ldots, J. \tag{2.3}$$

A feasible program is attainable through joint stock-ownership of the firms – in short, it is a *stock-ownership program*[9] – if and only if there exists a matrix $\Theta = [\theta_{ij}]$, $\theta_{ij} \geqslant 0$,[10] $\sum_i \theta_{ij} \leqslant 1$, such that

$$x_s^i - \sum_j \theta_{ij} b_s^j \leqslant 0, \quad i = 1, \ldots, I, \quad s = 1, \ldots, S. \tag{2.4}$$

Condition (2.4) states that the consumption vector x^i can be attained through ownership of the shares $\theta_{ij}, j = 1, \ldots, J$, of all firms, where such ownership gives right to the same fraction θ_{ij} of firm j's output in every state, $j = 1, \ldots, J$.

A stock-ownership program will be denoted (x, b, Θ). As announced in the introduction, this paper deals exclusively with stock-ownership programs.

By definition, every stock-ownership program is feasible – but not all feasible programs can be attained through stock-ownership. Thus, when $J = 1$ (there is a single firm), conditions (2.4) impose that consumer i should receive the same fraction of society's output in every state – whereas (2.2) allows for these fractions to vary with the states, so long as their sum over all consumers does not exceed unity. In order for an arbitrary (feasible) program to be attainable through stock-ownership, it is necessary that the I vectors of future consumption $(x_1^i, \ldots, x_S^i)$, $i = 1, \ldots, I$, be contained in the (sub)space spanned by the J output vectors $(b_1^j, \ldots, b_S^j)$, $j = 1, \ldots, J$.[11]

An important implication of conditions (2.4) is the following:

Lemma 2.1: Under assumption 2.2, the set of feasible programs is convex. but the set of stock-ownership programs is not always convex.

Proof: The first proposition is well known and its proof is immediate. To prove the second proposition, let $\bar{b}_s^j > b_s^j > 0$ and $\bar{b}_s^k = b_s^k = 0$, $k \neq j$; let furthermore $\bar{\theta}_{ij} > \theta_{ij} > 0$ and $\bar{x}_s^i - \bar{\theta}_{ij} \bar{b}_s^j = 0$, $x_s^i - \theta_{ij} b_s^j = 0$. Then, $\forall \lambda \varepsilon (0, 1)$:

---

[9]Drèze (1972) has used instead the term 'private ownership program'; it was aptly pointed out to me that confusion with the standard concept of 'private ownership economy' should be avoided.

[10]$\theta_{ij} \geqslant 0$ rules out short-holdings of securities; that assumption seems more realistic, except in the very short run; dropping the assumption would not affect the results in this paper, so long as short-holdings are bounded.

[11]Taking the non-negativity constraints $\Theta \geqslant 0$ into account, the set of feasible stock-ownership programs is a convex polyhedron in the space spanned by the b^j.

$$\lambda \bar{x}^i_s + (1 - \lambda)x^i_s - (\lambda \bar{\theta}_{ij} + (1 - \lambda)\theta_{ij})(\lambda \bar{b}^j_s + (1 - \lambda)b^j_s)$$

$$= \lambda \bar{\theta}_{ij} \bar{b}^j_s + (1 - \lambda)\theta_{ij} b^j_s - (\lambda \bar{\theta}_{ij} + (1 - \lambda)\theta_{ij})(\lambda \bar{b}^j_s + (1 - \lambda)b^j_s)$$

$$= \lambda(1 - \lambda)(\bar{\theta}_{ij} \bar{b}^j_s + \theta_{ij} b^j_s - \bar{\theta}_{ij} b^j_s - \theta_{ij} \bar{b}^j_s)$$

$$= \lambda(1 - \lambda)(\bar{\theta}_{ij} - \theta_{ij})(\bar{b}^j_s - b^j_s) > 0. \qquad \square$$

The non-convexities introduced by conditions (2.4) may be illustrated graphically, with the help of Figures 14.3 and 14.4. For the case considered

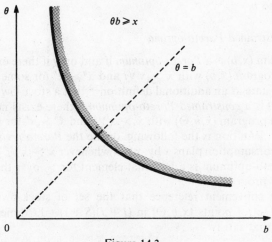

Figure 14.3

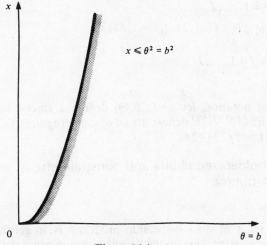

Figure 14.4

in the proof of the lemma, (2.4) reduces to $x_s^i - \theta_{ij}b_s^j \leqslant 0$, and we may drop all subscripts.

Let x be fixed; the feasible region in (b, θ) space is convex, being defined by a rectangular hyperbola (see Figure 14.3). Now, let x vary, and look at the intersection of the feasible region in (x, b, θ) space with the plane $\theta = b$ (the plane containing the x axis and the dotted line in Figure 14.3). That intersection is the complement of the convex set defined by $x \geqslant \theta^2 = b^2$ (see Figure 14.4). Putting Figures 14.3 and 14.4 together, one may visualise the feasible region in (x, b, θ) space as delineated by a sort of 'plough' with hyperbolic (convex) sections for fixed x and quadratic (concave) sections for fixed ratio of θ to b.

2.4 Constrained Pareto-optima

A feasible program (x, b) is a *Pareto-optimum* if and only if there exists no other feasible program $(\bar{x}, \bar{b})$ with $\bar{x}^i \succsim_i x^i \forall i$ and $\bar{x}^h \succ_h x^h$ for some h.

We shall now state as an additional definition[12] that a stock-ownership program (x, b, Θ) is a *constrained Pareto-optimum* if there exists no other stock-ownership program $(\bar{x}, \bar{b}, \bar{\Theta})$ with $\bar{x}^i \succ . x^i \forall i$ and $\bar{x}^h \succ_h x^h$ for some h.

An equivalent definition is the following: define the *Pareto preordering* over I-tuples of consumption plans x by: $x \succsim \bar{x}$ whenever $x^i \succsim_i \bar{x}^i \forall i$. Then, a constrained Pareto-optimum is a maximal element for $\succsim$ over the set of stock-ownership programs.

We recall for convenient reference that the set of stock-ownership programs is the set of points (x, b, Θ) in $(I + J)(S + 1) + IJ$ dimensional Euclidian space that satisfy:

$$\sum_i x_0^i + \sum_j a^j \leqslant W_0 \tag{2.1}$$

$$b^j \in Y^j, \quad j = 1, \ldots, J \tag{2.3}$$

$$x_s^i - \sum_j \theta_{ij}b_s^j \leqslant 0, \quad i = 1, \ldots, I, s = 1, \ldots, S \tag{2.4}$$

$$\sum_i \theta_{ij} \leqslant 1, \quad j = 1, \ldots, J \tag{2.5}$$

$$x, b, \Theta \geqslant 0. \tag{2.6}$$

For economy of notation, let $z = (x, b, \Theta)$ denote a stock-ownership program and $Z \subset R_+^{(I+J)(S+1)+IJ}$ denote the set of such programs, i.e. the set of z satisfying (2.1) and (2.3)–(2.6).

3 Stockholders' equilibria and constrained Pareto-optima

3.1 Outline of the section

The fact that the set Z of stock-ownership programs is, in general, not convex, places severe restrictions on the decentralisation properties of the

[12]A similar definition is used by Diamond (1967).

economy. Actually, it is not immediately clear how a suitable concept of equilibrium should be defined.

Drèze (1972) used the necessary optimality theorem for non-linear programming with differentiability (see, e.g., Mangasarian (1969, theorem 7.3.7)) to deduce from assumptions 2.1′ and 2.2′ necessary conditions for a constrained Pareto-optimum. As an alternative, one which does not use differentiability, I will consider here successively the set of reallocations that can be attained through the decisions of a single firm (3.2), then through exchanges of shares among individuals (3.3). In each case, a natural equilibrium concept will be borrowed from accepted theory. These concepts will then be combined to define a 'stockholders' equilibrium'. Properties of such equilibria, and their relationship to constrained Pareto-optima, will be studied (3.4).

The approach followed in this section also serves as a natural introduction to the stability analysis of Sections 5 and 6.

3.2 Pseudo equilibria for the firms

Given a stock-ownership program $\bar{z} = (\bar{x}, \bar{b}, \Theta)$, firm j can generate alternative programs by choosing in Y^j some alternative production plan $b^j \neq \bar{b}^j$. Whenever $a^j \neq \bar{a}^j$, the adjustment of the input level must somehow be accompanied by adjustments in the current consumptions of the consumers, if the production plans of the other firms remain fixed.

Denoting by $F^j(\bar{z})$ the set of stock-ownership programs attainable from a given starting point $\bar{z}$, through decisions of firm j and adjustments in current consumptions (the production plans of the other firms and the ownership matrix being given), we have:

$$F^j(\bar{z}) = \{z \mid z \in Z, b^k = \bar{b}^k \forall k \neq j, \Theta = \bar{\Theta}\}$$

$$= \{z \mid \sum_i x_0^i + a^j \leqslant W_0 - \sum_{k \neq j} \bar{a}^k; x_s^i - \bar{\theta}_{ij} b_s^j \leqslant \sum_{k \neq j} \bar{\theta}_{ik} \bar{b}_s^k,$$

$$i = 1, \ldots, I, s = 1, \ldots, S; b^j \in Y^j; x \geqslant 0\}. \tag{3.1}$$

The preferences of the consumers among such programs are representable by the continuous, quasi-concave,[13] monotonic functions

$$V^i(x_0^i, b_1^j, \ldots, b_S^j \mid \bar{z}) =_{\text{def}} U^i(x_0^i, \sum_{k \neq j} \bar{\theta}_{ik} \bar{b}_1^k + \bar{\theta}_{ij} b_1^j, \ldots,$$

$$\sum_{k \neq j} \bar{\theta}_{ik} \bar{b}_S^k + \bar{\theta}_{ij} b_S^j), \quad i = 1, \ldots, I. \tag{3.2}$$

$F^j(\bar{z})$ is also the set of feasible allocations for an economy, say $\mathscr{E}^j(\bar{z})$, with S public goods $(b_1^j, \ldots, b_S^j)$ and a single private good (x_0), where the preferences of the I consumers are defined by $(V^1, \ldots, V^I)$ and the

---

[13] When $\bar{\theta}_{ij} = 0$, V^i is still well defined and quasi-concave, but not strictly so.

constraints on production and distribution reduce to:

$$\sum_i x_0^i + a^j \leqslant W_0 - \sum_{k \neq j} \bar{a}^k \tag{3.3}$$

$$b^j \in Y^j \tag{3.4}$$

$$x_0^i \geqslant 0, \quad i = 1, \ldots, I. \tag{3.5}$$

All the results obtained for such an economy (see e.g. Drèze and de la Vallée Poussin (1971), Foley (1967), Malinvaud (1969a), Milleron (1972)) are thus valid in our context as well. In particular, a *pseudo equilibrium* for such an economy is defined by an allocation $\hat{z} \in F^j(\bar{z})$, and a set of I vectors $\phi^i \in R_+^{S+1}$, $\phi_0^i = 1$, such that:

(1) $V^i(x_0^i, b_1^j, \ldots, b_S^j) > V^i(\hat{x}_0^i, \hat{b}_S^j, \ldots, \hat{b}_S^j)$ implies

$$x_0^i + \sum_s \phi_s^i b_s^j > \hat{x}_0^i + \sum_s \phi_s^i \hat{b}_s^j, \quad i = 1, \ldots, I.$$

(2) $\hat{b}^j$ maximises $\sum_s b_s^j \left(\sum_i \phi_s^i \right) - a^j$ on Y^j.

The set of Pareto-optima for $\mathscr{E}^j(\bar{z})$, to be denoted $F_P^j(\bar{z})$, is defined as usual by:

$$F_P^j(\bar{z}) = \{ z \mid z \in F^j(\bar{z}), \not\exists \hat{z} \in F^j(\bar{z}), \hat{x}^i \succsim_i x^i \forall i, \hat{x}^h \succ_h x^h \text{ for some } h \}. \tag{3.6}$$

The following properties are well known.[14]

Proposition 3.1: Under assumptions 2.1 and 2.2, for all $\bar{z} \in Z$ with $\sum_i \bar{x}_0^i > 0$, $\mathscr{E}^j(\bar{z})$ is such that:

(i)   there exists a pseudo equilibrium;
(ii)   every pseudo equilibrium is a Pareto-optimum;
(iii)   with every Pareto-optimum $z \in F_P^j(\bar{z})$, one can associate a set of I vectors $\phi^i \in R_+^{S+1}$, $\phi_0^i = 1$, such that $\{z, \phi^i\}$ is a pseudo equilibrium.

The transposition of these results to our context is immediate. Using the monotonicity of $\succsim_i$, we may impose the equality conditions

$$x_s^i - \bar{\theta}_{ij} b_s^j = \sum_{k \neq j} \bar{\theta}_{ik} \bar{b}_s^k, \quad i = 1, \ldots, I, s = 1, \ldots, S. \tag{3.7}$$

Define then the vectors $\bar{\Pi}^i \in R_+^{S+1}$ by: $\bar{\Pi}_0^i = 1$, $\phi_s^i = \bar{\Pi}_s^i \bar{\theta}_{ij}$. It follows that

$$x_0^i + \sum_s \phi_s^i b_s^j > \hat{x}_0^i + \sum_s \phi_s^i \hat{b}_s^j \Leftrightarrow x_0^i + \sum_s \bar{\Pi}_s \bar{\theta}_{ij} b_s^j > \hat{x}_0^i + \sum_s \bar{\Pi}_s \bar{\theta}_{ij} \hat{b}_s^j$$

$$\Leftrightarrow \bar{\Pi}^i x^i > \bar{\Pi}^i \hat{x}^i. \tag{3.8}$$

We may then define a *pseudo equilibrium for firm j* (relative to $\bar{z}$) by an allocation $\hat{z} \in F^j(\bar{z})$, and a set of I vectors $\bar{\Pi}^i \in R_+^{S+1}$, $\bar{\Pi}_0^i = 1$, such that:

(1) $x^i \succ_i \hat{x}^i$ implies $\bar{\Pi}^i x^i > \bar{\Pi}^i \hat{x}^i, \quad i = 1, \ldots, I;$

[14]See the excellent survey paper by Milleron (1972). Milleron does not use the term 'pseudo equilibrium', introduced by Malinvaud, and refers instead to a 'Lindahl equilibrium'.

(2) $\quad \hat{b}^j$ maximises $\sum_s b_s^j \left(\sum_i \bar{\theta}_{ij} \bar{\Pi}_s^i \right) - a^j$ on Y^j.

As a corollary of proposition 3.1, we then have:

Theorem 3.1: Under assumption 2.1 and 2.2, and given any stock-ownership program $\bar{z}$ such that $\sum_i \bar{x}_0^i > 0$:

(i)   there exists a pseudo equilibrium for firm j, $j = 1, \dots, J$;

(ii)   every pseudo equilibrium for firm j belongs to $F_P^j(\bar{z})$;

(iii)   with every $z \in F_P^j(\bar{z})$, one can associate I vectors $\bar{\Pi}^i \in R_+^{s+1}$, $\bar{\Pi}_0^i = 1$, such that $\{z, \bar{\Pi}^i\}$ is a pseudo equilibrium for firm j.

The definition of a pseudo equilibrium for the firm states that the firm maximises the present value of its production plan, using shadow prices

$$\sum_i \bar{\theta}_{ij} \bar{\Pi}^i$$

obtained as weighted averages of individual shadow prices $\bar{\Pi}^i$ reflecting the consumption preferences of the shareholders, with the weights given by their respective ownership fractions.[15] Theorem 3.1 says that efficient production (investment) decisions by the firms imply the existence of such shadow prices.

The definition does not place any restrictions on the allocation among consumers of the adjustments in current consumption required to offset the adjustment in input level $a^j - \bar{a}^j$. Alternatively stated, the definition is consistent with arbitrary transfers of initial resources among consumers.[16]

3.3 Price equilibria for the stock market

Given a stock-ownership program $\bar{z} = (\bar{x}, \bar{b}, \bar{\Phi})$, exchanges of shares among individuals can generate alternative programs through the choice of an alternative ownership matrix $\Theta \neq \bar{\Theta}$ accompanied by adjustments in the current consumptions x_0^i, $i = 1, \dots, I$.

Let $E(\bar{z})$ denote the set of stock-ownership programs attainable, from a given starting point $\bar{z}$, through such exchanges (the production plans of all firms being given); we have:

$$E(\bar{z}) = \{z \mid z \in Z, b = \bar{b}\}$$
$$= \{z \mid \sum_i x_0^i \leqslant W_0 - \sum_j \bar{a}^j\}$$

[15]See the paper by Gevers (1974) on the (remote) possibility of obtaining these shadow prices, through majority voting, as weighted medians of the $\bar{\Pi}^i$.

[16]In the literature on public goods, some attention has been paid to the problem of existence of a pseudo equilibrium when the transfers of private goods are restricted; Foley (1967) has proved a theorem to that effect. A particular transfer mechanism, and its specific merits, are discussed by Drèze and de la Vallée Poussin (1971). Realism would call for individual contributions to $a^j - \bar{a}^j$ in proportion to the $\bar{\theta}_{ij}$.

$$x_s^i - \sum_j \theta_{ij} \bar{b}_s^j \leqslant 0, \quad i = 1, \ldots, I, s = 1, \ldots, S$$

$$\sum_i \theta_{ij} \leqslant 1, \quad j = 1, \ldots, J; \quad x, \Theta \geqslant 0 \}. \tag{3.9}$$

The preferences of the consumers among such programs are representable by the continuous, quasi-concave,[17] monotonic functions:

$$W^i(x_0^i, \theta_{i1}, \ldots, \theta_{iJ} | \bar{z}) =_{\text{def}} U^i \left(x_0^i, \sum_i \theta_{ij} \bar{b}_1^j, \ldots, \sum_i \theta_{ij} \bar{b}_S^j \right),$$
$$i = 1, \ldots, I. \tag{3.10}$$

$E(\bar{z})$ is also the set of feasible allocations for an exchange economy, say $\mathscr{E}(\bar{z})$, with $J + 1$ private goods, namely the shares of the J firms and current consumption, where the preferences of the I consumers are defined by $(W^1, \ldots, W^I)$ and the market clearing conditions reduce to:

$$\sum_i x_0^i \leqslant W_0 - \sum_j \bar{a}^j = \sum_i \bar{x}_0^i \tag{3.11}$$

$$\sum_i \theta_{ij} \leqslant 1 = \sum_i \bar{\theta}_{ij}, \quad j = 1, \ldots, J \tag{3.12}$$

$$x_0^i \geqslant 0, \quad i = 1, \ldots, I, \Theta \geqslant 0. \tag{3.13}$$

All the results obtained for such an economy are thus valid in our context as well. In particular, a *price equilibrium* for such an economy is defined by an allocation $\hat{z} \in E(\bar{z})$ and a (price) vector $\bar{p} \in R_+^{S+1}$, $\bar{p}_0 = 1$, such that

$$W^i(x_0^i, \theta_{i1}, \ldots, \theta_{iJ}) > W^i(\hat{x}_0^i, \hat{\theta}_{i1}, \ldots, \hat{\theta}_{iJ}) \text{ implies}$$

$$x_0^i + \sum_j \theta_{ij} \bar{p}_j > \hat{x}_0^i + \sum_j \hat{\theta}_{ij} \bar{p}_j.$$

The set of Pareto-optima for $\mathscr{E}(\bar{z})$, to be denoted $Ep(\bar{z})$, is defined as usual by:

$$E_p(\bar{z}) = \{ z \mid z \in E(\bar{z}), \not\exists \hat{z} \in E(\bar{z}), \hat{x}^i \succsim_i x^i \forall i, \hat{x}^h \succ_h x^h \text{ for some } h \}. \tag{3.14}$$

The following properties are well known:

Proposition 3.2: Under assumption 2.1, for all $\bar{z} \in Z$ with $\sum_i \bar{x}_0^i > 0$, $\mathscr{E}(\bar{z})$ is such that:

(i)   there exists a price equilibrium;
(ii)   every price equilibrium is a Pareto-optimum;
(iii) with every Pareto-optimum $z \in E_p(\bar{z})$ such that $x_0^i > 0 \forall i$, one can associate a price system $\bar{p}$, such that $(z, \bar{p})$ is a price equilibrium.

The transposition of these results to our context is obvious. Because the

---

[17]Strict quasi-concavity is not preserved by this transformation, when the vectors $\bar{b}^j$ are not linearly independent.

correspondence between the ownership fractions $(\theta_{i1}, \ldots, \theta_{iJ})$ and the consumption vector $(x_1^i, \ldots, x_S^i)$ is not one-to-one, the relation of the price vector for shares $\bar{p}$ to the shadow prices reflecting consumption preferences ($\bar{\Pi}^i$ of Section 3.2) is not entirely straightforward. For reasons that will become clear in 3.4, I will consider only the case where U^i is differentiable (assumption 2.1′). In that case, W^i is also differentiable, and

$$\frac{\partial W^i}{\partial \theta_{ij}} = \sum_s b_s^j \frac{\partial U^i}{\partial x_s^i}, \frac{\partial W^i}{\partial \theta_{ij}} \bigg/ \frac{\partial W^i}{\partial x_0^i} = \sum_s b_s^j \frac{\partial U^i}{\partial x_s^i} \bigg/ \frac{\partial U^i}{\partial x_0^i} = \sum_s b_s^j \Pi_s^i. \tag{3.15}$$

With differentiability of W^i, a price equilibrium $(z, \bar{p})$ has the property:

$$\frac{\partial W^i}{\partial \theta_{ij}} \bigg/ \frac{\partial W^i}{\partial x_0^i} \leqslant \bar{p}_j, \quad \theta_{ij}\left(\bar{p}_j - \frac{\partial W^i}{\partial \theta_{ij}} \bigg/ \frac{\partial W^i}{\partial x_0^i}\right) = 0.$$

Consequently:

Theorem 3.2: Under assumption 2.1′, with every $\hat{z} \in E_p(\bar{z})$ such that $\hat{x}_0^i > 0 \forall i$, one can associate I vectors $\bar{\Pi}^i \in R_+^{S+1}$, $\bar{\Pi}_0^i = 1$, and a vector $\bar{p} \in R_+^{S+1}$, $\bar{p}_0 = 1$, such that:

(i) $x^i \succ_i \hat{x}_i$ implies $\bar{\Pi}^i x^i > \bar{\Pi}^i \hat{x}^i$, $\quad i = 1, \ldots, I$;

(ii) $\sum_s b_s^j \Pi_s^i \leqslant \bar{p}_j, \theta_{ij}\left(\sum_s b_s^j \Pi_s^i - \bar{p}_j\right) = 0, \quad i = 1, \ldots, I, \; J = 1, \ldots, J.$

Conditions (i) and (ii) define portfolios of shares that are optimal from the viewpoint of the individual consumers, given the production plans of the firms and the (stock) market prices $\bar{p}$.

3.4 Stockholders equilibria

We can now combine the concepts and results of Sections 3.2 and 3.3. The definitions of pseudo equilibria for the individual firms and of price equilibria for the stock market can be combined in the following:

Definition 3.1: A stock-ownership program z is a *stockholders' equilibrium* if and only if:

(i)   for every firm j, there exist I vectors $\Pi^i(j)$ such that $\{z, \Pi^i(j)\}$ is a *pseudo equilibrium* for firm j (relative to z);

(ii)   there exists a (price) vector p such that (z, p) is a *price equilibrium* for $\mathscr{E}(z)$.

That is, a stockholders' equilibrium combines production plans in the individual firms which have the properties of pseudo equilibria for the corresponding public-goods economies $\mathscr{E}^j$, with an allocation of shares which has the properties of a price equilibrium for the corresponding exchange economy $\mathscr{E}$. In particular, the production plan of each firm is

Pareto-optimal, given the production plans of the other firms and the ownership matrix Θ; and the allocation of shares is Pareto-optimal, given the production plans of the firms. This definition provides, in my opinion, a natural concept of equilibrium for stock-ownership programs. Indeed, the firms have no incentive to change their production plans, and the consumers have no incentive to exchange shares, given the actions of the other agents. One could, of course, look for a stronger equilibrium concept, ruling out incentives for *simultaneous* adjustments in production plans and portfolios. But no natural definition of this stronger concept seems to present itself.

Two important properties of stockholders' equilibria may be stated at once.

Theorem 3.3: Under assumptions 2.1 and 2.2, and provided $W_0 > 0$, there exists a stockholders' equilibrium.

Proof: This follows as an immediate corollary of theorem 5.1 below. $\qquad\square$

Theorem 3.4: Under assumptions 2.1 and 2.2, every constrained Pareto-optimum z with $x_0^i > 0 \forall i$ is a stockholders' equilibrium.

Proof: Follows as an immediate corollary of theorem 3.1 (iii), and of proposition 3.2 (iii). $\qquad\square$

The converse of theorem 3.4 is not true: there exist stockholders' equilibria which are *not* constrained Pareto-optima. Examples are given in Section 4 below. This shortcoming of decentralised decision procedures reflects the non-convexity of the feasible set Z. Thus a price mechanism on the stock exchange and efficient decision procedures within individual firms will always *sustain* a Pareto-optimum, but could equally well sustain an allocation that is *not* Pareto-optimal.

Under differentiability, the price implications of a stockholders' equilibrium are sharper: the shadow price vectors $\Pi^i(j)$ in (i) of definition 3.1 do not depend upon j. That is, $\Pi^i(j) = \Pi^i(k), i = 1,\ldots,I, j,k = 1,\ldots,J$. This has an important implication for productive efficiency. Formally:

Theorem 3.5: Under assumptions 2.1' and 2.2, one can associate with every stockholders' equilibrium $\hat{z}$ such that $\hat{x}_0^i > 0 \forall i$ a set of I vectors $\hat{\Pi}^i \in R_0^{S+1}$, $\hat{\Pi}_0^i = 1$, and a vector $\hat{p} \in R_+^{S+1}$, $\hat{p}_0 = 1$ such that:

(i) $x^i \succ_i \hat{x}^i$ implies $\hat{\Pi}^i x^i > \hat{\Pi}^i \hat{x}^i, i = 1,\ldots,I$;

(ii) $\hat{b}^j$ maximises $\sum_s b_s^j \left(\sum_i \theta_{ij} \hat{\Pi}_s^i \right) - a^j$ on $Y^j, j = 1,\ldots,J$;

(iii) $\sum_s \hat{b}_s^j \hat{\Pi}_s^i \leqslant \hat{p}_j, \theta_{ij} \left(\sum_s \hat{b}_s^j \hat{\Pi}_s^i - \hat{p}_j \right) = 0, i = 1,\ldots,I, j = 1,\ldots,J$.

Proof: By definition 3.1, there exist J sets of I vectors $\Pi^i(j)$ satisfying (i) and (ii); by theorem 3.2, there exist I vectors Π^i and a vector p satisfying (i) and (iii). Let $\hat{p} = p$.

Under differentiability, with $\hat{x}^i_0 > 0$ and $\hat{\Pi}^i_0 = 1$, the inequality $\hat{x}^i_s > 0$ implies uniqueness of $\hat{\Pi}^i_s$ in (i). Accordingly for all i, s such that $\hat{x}^i_s > 0$,

$$\Pi^i_s(j) = \Pi^i_s = \hat{\Pi}^i_s, \quad j = 1,\ldots,J.$$

When $\hat{x}^i_s = 0$, we know that

$$\sum_j \hat{\theta}_{ij}\hat{b}^j_s = 0$$

(at a stockholders' equilibrium). Consequently, conditions (iii), which are satisfied by $(\hat{\Pi}^i, p)$, will be satisfied by $(\hat{\Pi}, p)$ provided $\hat{\Pi}^i_s \leqslant \Pi^i_s$. Similarly, conditions (ii), which are satisfied by $\Pi^i(j)$, will be satisfied by $\hat{\Pi}^i$ provided $\hat{\Pi}^i_s \leqslant \Pi^i_s(j)$: indeed, if $\hat{\theta}_{ij} = 0$, then $\hat{\Pi}^i_s$ is irrelevant to conditions (ii), for that j; if $\hat{b}^j_s = 0$, then

$$\sum_s b^j_s \sum_i \theta_{ij}\hat{\Pi}^i_s - a^j \leqslant \sum_s b^j_s \sum_i \theta_{ij}\Pi^i_s(j) - a^j$$
$$\leqslant \sum_s \hat{b}^j_s \sum_i \theta_{ij}\Pi^i_s(j) - \hat{a}^j$$
$$= \sum_s \hat{b}^j_s \sum_i \theta_{ij}\hat{\Pi}^i_s - \hat{a}^j.$$

We may thus define: $\hat{\Pi}^i_s = \mathrm{Min}\,\{\Pi^i_s,\ \Pi^i_s(j),\ j = 1,\ldots,J\}$. The vectors $\{\hat{p}, \hat{\Pi}^i\}$ so defined satisfy (i)–(iii). $\qquad\square$

Using theorem 3.5, it is easy to prove the following corollary, which states that a stockholders' equilibrium entails productive efficiency, not only for each firm considered in isolation, but for all firms considered simultaneously.

Corollary 3.1: Under assumptions 2.1′ and 2.2, every stockholders' equilibrium $\hat{z}$ such that $\hat{x}^i_0 > 0 \forall i$, is a Pareto-optimal element of the set $F(\hat{z}) = \{z \mid z \in Z, \Theta = \hat{\Theta}\}$.

In the absence of differentiability, $\Pi^i(j) \neq \Pi^i(k)$ in definition 3.1 may entail additional inefficiencies which are illustrated in example 4.4 below.

Conditions (i)–(iii) in theorem 3.5 are analogous to the necessary conditions derived from assumptions 2.1′ and 2.2′ given by Drèze (1972), where assumption 2.2′ is further used to state (ii) in the usual terms of marginal costs.

We may thus conclude that no additional necessary optimality conditions of a local nature can be deduced from assumptions 2.1 and 2.2.

4 Examples of inefficient equilibria

Four examples will now be presented, illustrating successively:

(i)   a stockholders' equilibrium that is not efficient, being a local optimum but not a constrained Pareto-optimum;
(ii)   a stockholders' equilibrium that is not efficient, being a saddle point;
(iii) a constrained Pareto-optimum with technologically inefficient production;
(iv)   a stockholders' equilibrium that is not technologically efficient, because the utility functions are not differentiable.

All four examples are constructed after the same pattern: there are 2 states, 2 consumers and 2 firms. These simplifications make it possible to present the examples graphically, by displaying the production possibilities of the firms when the input level is equal to one (this construction, underlying Figures 14.1 and 14.2, was explained in Section 2.2). The preferences of both consumers, for fixed current consumption x_0^i, are similarly represented by indifference curves in the space of future consumption under both states.

   Example 4.1: Equilibrium at a local optimum. In Figure 14.5 the production possibilities of firm j, when $a^j = 1$, are given by the triangle $0st$.[18]

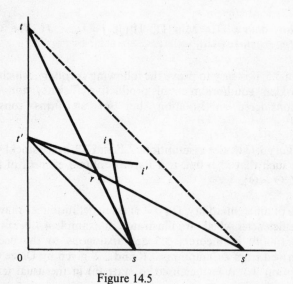

Figure 14.5

[18]In terms of the discussion in Section 2.2, the firm has access to two basic activities, defined respectively by points s and t.

With $\theta_{ij} = 1$, that firm is fully owned by individual i, whose preferences about future outputs are represented by the curve si. With the ratio $\bar{\Pi}^i_s/\bar{\Pi}^i_t$ corresponding to the slope of that indifference curve at point s, firm j maximises $\bar{\Pi}^i_s b^j_s + \bar{\Pi}^i_t b^j_t$ at point s, given $a^j = 1$. Thus, let $\bar{b}^j_s = \overline{0s}$, $\bar{b}^j_t = 0$.

Similarly, firm j' has the production set $0s't'$ when $a^{j'} = 1$, and is fully owned by individual i', whose preferences are represented by the curve $t'\,i'$. Again, firm j' maximises $\bar{\Pi}^{i'}_s b^{j'}_s + \bar{\Pi}^{i'}_t b^{j'}_t$ at point t', given $a^{j'} = 1$. Thus, let $\bar{b}^{j'}_s = 0$, $\bar{b}^{j'}_t = \overline{0t'}$.

Finally, let $\bar{\Pi}^i_s = \bar{\Pi}^{i'}_t$ and set $\bar{p}_j = \bar{\Pi}^i_s \bar{b}^j_s = \bar{p}_{j'} = \bar{\Pi}^{i'}_t \bar{b}^{j'}_t$. It follows that $\bar{p}_{j'} - \bar{\Pi}^i_s \bar{b}^{j'}_s - \bar{\Pi}^i_t \bar{b}^{j'}_t = \bar{p}_{j'} - \bar{\Pi}^i_s \bar{b}^{j'}_t > 0$, calling for $\bar{\theta}_{ij'} = 0$; similarly, $\bar{p}_j - \bar{\Pi}^{i'}_s \bar{b}^j_s - \bar{\Pi}^{i'}_t \bar{b}^j_t = \bar{p}_j - \bar{\Pi}^{i'}_s \bar{b}^j_s > 0$, calling for $\bar{\theta}_{i'j} = 0$. The allocation defined by $\bar{\theta}_{ij} = \bar{\theta}_{i'j'} = 1$, $\bar{\theta}_{ij'} = \bar{\theta}_{i'j} = 0$, with firm j producing at s and firm j' producing at t', is thus a stockholders' equilibrium.

The inefficiency of this allocation is obvious. Output in period 2 will be $\overline{0s} = \overline{0t}$ irrespective of which state obtains. With the same input level in each firm, but with firm j producing at point t and firm j' producing at s', output in period 2 would rise to $\overline{0s'} = \overline{0t}$ in either state – that is, it would double to no cost!

The economics of this situation are straightforward. Each firm produces optimally, *given the preferences of its owner*. With these production plans taken as given, and with the shares in both firms selling at the same price, the set of consumption plans available at a given cost is the line segment st'. Over this set, the optimal portfolio for i is at point s, for i' at point t'. Thus, each consumer carries an optimal portfolio, *given the production plans of the firms*. The inefficiency results from 'mismatching' between the production possibilities of the firms and the preferences of their owners.

There are two possible remedies to this situation. The first consists in changing the production plans of the firms, in the expectation that portfolio readjustments will follow. It may be argued that the 'opportunity-line' st' provides information about the direction of desirable changes in production plans. Examples 4.2 and 4.3 will show that such information may be missing (4.2) or misleading (4.3). It should also be noted that in order for this remedy to be effective, major changes in production plans are required: firm j must move above and to the left of point r, firm j' must move below and to the right of point r, in order for the adjustments to be beneficial.

The other remedy consists in changing the ownership fractions in the firms, in the expectation that modified ownership will lead to the desired adjustments in production plans. The initiative now lies with the consumers. But this requires additional information on their part: each consumer must know the production *set* of the other firm, not only its production *plan*. Furthermore, major changes in ownership fractions are again required: in order to exert enough influence on the decision within firm j' to move its production plan to the right of r, consumer i may have to acquire a majority interest.

The unprofitability of small moves confirms that the situation under consideration is a local optimum. Traditional market mechanisms, which are effective under convexity, are ineffective here. The first remedy might be implemented by managers disregarding the immediate interests of stockholders. The second remedy might be implemented (in a world with many small stockholders) through a proxy fight or a takeover bid.

Note, finally, that a merger would not help: with a single asset left, both consumers should consume a fixed proportion of output in both states, in spite of their diverging preferences.

Example 4.2: Equilibrium at a saddle point. This example is a variation of the previous one. The production possibilities of the two firms are unchanged, but the preferences of the two consumers are now represented by the indifference curves ri and ri' respectively (Figure 14.6). The analysis can be repeated, with $\bar{\theta}_{ij} = \bar{\theta}_{i'j'} = 1$ once more. Both firms are now in equilibrium at the same point r. But this equilibrium is unstable, in the sense that the slightest modification in ownership fractions will tilt the 'shadow prices' $(\Pi^i_s\theta_{ij} + \Pi^{i'}_s\theta_{i'j}, \ \Pi^i_t\theta_{ij} + \Pi^{i'}_t\theta_{i'j})$ and move firm j towards point t or firm j' towards point s'. This example depicts a 'saddle point' situation.

The global optimum calls for $\theta_{ij} = \theta_{i'j'} = \frac{1}{3}, \theta_{ij'} = \theta_{i'j} = \frac{2}{3}$ leading to the consumption plans u and u'. Thanks to the saddle point property, this optimum could easily be achieved through portfolio adjustments. Changes in production plans offer a less natural remedy, because at the point r the market opportunities for portfolio choices provide no information whatever about desirable production adjustments.

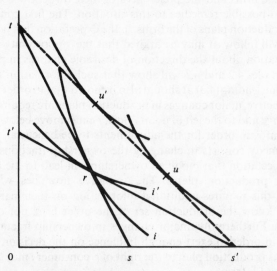

Figure 14.6

Example 4.3: Optimum with technological inefficiency. This example is another variation of example 4.1. The preferences of the two consumers are kept unchanged, but the production possibilities are modified. When $a^j = 1$, firm j can choose a production plan in the triangle $0st$; when $a^{j'} = 1$, firm j' can choose a production plan in the triangle $0s't'$ (Figure 14.7). Thus, firm j' is technologically less efficient than firm j. When $\theta_{ij} = \theta_{i'j'} = 1$, firm j produces at point s, firm j' at point t'. The import of this example is that *this situation may well define a genuine constrained Pareto-optimum*. Whereas firm j' would not produce at all in the presence of markets for contingent claims, the absence of such markets may justify its activity: the added opportunities for portfolio diversification compensate for its productive inefficiency. In order for consumer i' to be attracted by shares of firm j, the production plan of that firm should be moved above and to the left of point r – but this would be detrimental to consumer i, which explains why the initial situation may well define a constrained Pareto-optimum.[19]

This example shows that the opportunity line st' provides misleading, or at best irrelevant, information. If the management of firm j went by the shadow prices implicit in the opportunity line, it would move to point t, and there might result a local optimum with $\theta_{i'j} = \theta_{ij'} = 1$, firm j' producing at point s', and consumer i worse off than in the starting situation.

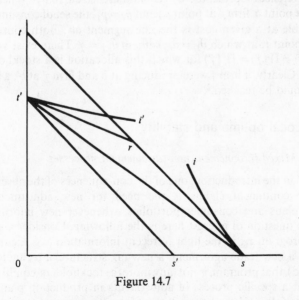

Figure 14.7

[19]Furthermore, with firm j producing to the left of r, consumer i might prefer to operate firm j' at point s'.

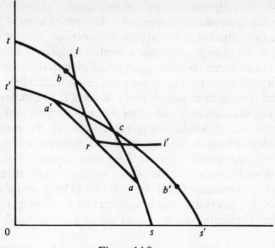

Figure 14.8

Example 4.4: Equilibrium with technological inefficiency. The last example illustrates the possible consequences of lack of differentiability. The production sets of the two firms are defined by $0st$ and $0s't'$ respectively, when $a^j = a^{j'} = 1$ (Figure 14.8). Both consumers have identical preferences represented by the indifference curve iri'. When firm j produces at point a, firm j' at point a', and $\bar{p}_j = \bar{p}_{j'}$, the set of consumption plans available at a given cost is the line segment aa'. Both consumers choose the point r, at which $\bar{\theta}_{ij} = \bar{\theta}_{i'j} = \bar{\theta}_{ij'} = \bar{\theta}_{i'j'} = \frac{1}{2}$. There exist vectors $\bar{\Pi}^i(j) = \bar{\Pi}^{i'}(j) \neq \bar{\Pi}^i(j') = \bar{\Pi}^{i'}(j')$ for which this allocation is a stockholders' equilibrium. Clearly, if firm j were producing at b and firm j' at b', a better allocation could be reached.[20]

5 Local optima and stability

5.1 Mixed tâtonnement/non-tâtonnement processes

As explained in the introduction, one of the consequences of the absence of markets for contingent claims is the need for new adjustments in production plans and consumer portfolios, whenever new information accrues. The question of interest here is the following. Consider a stock-ownership program z_0; in the light of recent information (e.g. a currency devaluation, a new trade agreement, a new tax structure, a technological discovery, etc.), that program, is not (any more) a stockholders' equilibrium. Suppose that a specific process of adjustments in production plans and consumer portfolios takes place; will the process converge to a new stock

[20]Note also the existence of a saddle point with both firms producing at point c.

ownership program and, if so, what will be the properties of the new program? (Will it be a stockholders' equilibrium? Will it be more efficient, in the Pareto sense, than the initial program?)

This topic is totally unexplored and the analysis here is very limited. It consists in establishing the convergence of a decentralised adjustment process, operating in discrete time through a sequence of realised exchanges of shares alternating with tentative revisions of the production plans of the firms. That is, the adjustments in consumer portfolios will proceed on a non-tâtonnement basis, whereas the adjustments in production plans will proceed on a tâtonnement basis.[21] The tâtonnement process seems natural for production (i.e. investment) decisions, which involve real resources and are irreversible. But stock-exchange adjustments are more realistically reflected in non-tâtonnement processes: portfolios are modified through trading, and existing institutions make no provisions for tâtonnements (except on special occasions, like takeover bids whereby a purchase price is announced conditionally on the supply of a given quantity).

The process defined below is thus a 'mixed tâtonnement/non-tâtonnement process'. It may be described informally as follows. Each 'morning' the stock exchange meets, and shares are exchanged until some equilibrium is reached, at which no further trading is forthcoming. Each 'afternoon' the firms revise their production plans, according to the preferences of their shareholders, taking into account the ownership fractions generated by the transactions that have actually taken place on the stock exchange in the morning; these plans are announced but not physically carried out until a final equilibrium is reached. The next 'morning', new stock exchange transactions take place, on the basis of information about the production plans chosen the previous afternoon. When, on some morning, no transactions take place on the stock exchange, the production plans of the firms are regarded as definitive and are carried out.

5.2 Individually rational and Pareto-optimal processes

In order to complete the description of the process, one should specify the properties of the stock exchange equilibrium reached in the morning and of the production decisions reached in the afternoon. I will assume that these decisions are always individually rational and Pareto-optimal (over the set of reallocations attainable through exchange of shares, or through the decisions of individual firms, respectively).

There are two reasons why individual rationality is a natural requirement to impose upon such a process. The first is that one cannot expect the process to converge towards a constrained Pareto-optimum, when the

---

[21] These features may be contrasted with those of the simultaneous tâtonnement process in continuous time defined and studied by Drèze (1972).

feasible set Z is not convex.[22] Considering that only a local optimum, or a saddle point, may be reached, one should guard against the possibility of ending up at an allocation which is worse than the starting point.[23] The only natural safeguard that I can think of is individual rationality of each move.

The second reason is that individually rational processes have a natural Lyapunov function, namely individual utilities. To see why this is important, consider exchanges of shares leading each morning to a competitive equilibrium on the stock exchange. Because preferences among portfolios are not strictly convex,[24] no reasonable assumptions will guarantee even local uniqueness of the competitive equilibrium. There is accordingly no natural way to base stability analysis on a Lyapunov function defined in the space of prices and/or quantities.

The other requirement – Pareto-optimality over the set of reallocations attainable at each step – could certainly be relaxed, but seems easier to justify (as will be done in the applications of Section 6) because the attainable set at each step is convex, so that procedures for reaching optima are available.

A major drawback of both requirements is the implicit assumption that the problem arising at each step will be solved as if that step were to be the last one; that is, no consideration of advantages to be realised at *later* steps is recognised. More specifically, acquisition of shares for the purpose of gaining control over a firm and changing its production plan, or choice of a disliked production plan susceptible of raising the price at which stock-holders will sell out, are implicitly ruled out by the requirements of individual rationality and Pareto-optimality. The process is thus better viewed as an illustration of the possibilities offered by decentralised, rational, but 'myopic', decisions, rather than as a description of the functioning of the stock exchange.[25]

Two definitions are needed to formalise the requirement of individual rationality. Given a stock-ownership program $\bar{z}$, I have defined in equation (3.1) the set $F^j(\bar{z})$ of reallocations attainable through decisions of firm j and adjustments in current consumption; and I have defined in equation (3.6) the subset $F_P^j(\bar{z})$ of $F^j(\bar{z})$ consisting of Pareto-optimal programs. Building upon these definitions, I will now define, and denote by $F_{IP}^j(\bar{z})$, the subset of $F^j(\bar{z})$ consisting of individually rational *and* Pareto-optimal programs:

$$F_{IP}^j(\bar{z}) = \{z \mid z \in F_P^j(\bar{z}), x^i \succsim_i \bar{x}^i \forall i\}. \tag{5.1}$$

Similarly, I have defined in equation (3.9) the set $E(\bar{z})$ of reallocations

[22]Indeed, no mathematical programming algorithm with such a strong property is currently available.

[23]Examples of seemingly sensible adjustment processes under which that perverse result may obtain can be constructed.

[24]See equation (3.10) and the remark surrounding that formula.

[25]The same remark applies to most dynamic models in mathematical economics.

attainable through exchanges of shares among consumers, and in (3.14) its Pareto-optimal subset, $E_P(\bar{z})$. I will now define, and denote by $E_{IP}(\bar{z})$, the subset of $E(\bar{z})$ consisting of individually rational *and* Pareto-optimal programs:

$$E_{IP}(\bar{z}) = \{z \mid z \in E_P(\bar{z}), x^i \succsim_i \bar{x}^i \forall i\}. \tag{5.2}$$

5.3 A convergence theorem

We are now ready to define a 'Mixed Tâtonnement/Non-Tâtonnement Process' for our economy. The process (P) is defined by a sequence of steps $q = 0, 1, 2, \ldots$.

At each step q, a stock ownership program z_q is generated. $z_0 \in Z$ is given, with positive current consumption $\forall i$, otherwise arbitrary. If q is odd, $z_q \in E_{IP}(z_{q-1})$. If q is even, z_q is the Jth element of a sequence $\{z_{q,j}\}$, $j = 1, \ldots, J$, where $z_{q,1} \in F^1_{IP}(z_{q-1})$,

$$z_{q,j} \in F^j_{IP}(z_{q,j-1}), \quad j = 2, \ldots, J;$$

that is z_q belongs to the composition of correspondences $F^J_{IP} \circ F^{J-1}_{IP} \circ \ldots F^1_{IP}(z_{q-1})$.
Thus:

Definition 5.1: The process (P) is defined by:

—an initial step: z_0 with $x^i_{00} > 0 \forall i$.
—a general step:
if q is odd, $z_q \in E_{IP}(z_{q-1})$
if q is even, $z_q \in F^J_{IP} \circ F^{J-1}_{IP} \circ \ldots F^1_{IP}(z_{q-1})$.[26]
—a termination rule:
if $z_q = z_{q-2}$, the process terminates.

Theorem 5.1: Under assumptions 2.1 and 2.2, the process (P) is well defined, its solution is bounded, and:

—either the process terminates at some q, and z_q is a stockholders' equilibrium,
—or the limit of any convergent subsequence of solutions, $\{z_{qv}\}$, $v \to \infty$, is a stockholders' equilibrium.

The proof of the theorem rests upon two lemmata.

Lemma 5.1: The correspondences $F^j(z)$ and $F^j_{IP}(z)$ are upper hemi-continuous, $j = 1, \ldots, J$.

---

[26] The results below would remain valid if one specified instead: 'if q is even, $z_q \in F^{\varphi_q J}_{IP} \circ F^{\varphi_q J-1}_{IP} \circ \ldots F^{\varphi_q 1}_{IP}(z_{q-1})$, where φ_q is an arbitrary permutation of the integers $1, \ldots, J$'. Although z_q may be affected by the order in which the production plans of the J firms are revised, convergence of the process is unaffected by that order (which may vary at each step, or be random, a.s.o.).

Proof: Let $\hat{z}^q \to \hat{z}^0$, $z^q \to z^0$, $q \to \infty$.

To prove that $z^q \in F^j(\hat{z}^q) \forall q$ implies $z^0 \in F^j(\hat{z}^0)$, it is enough to note that z^0 satisfies all the linear inequalities in the definition (3.1) and that Y^j is closed (assumption 2.2).

To prove that $z^q \in F^j_{IP}(\hat{z}^q) \forall q$ implies $z_0 \in F^j_{IP}(\hat{z}^0)$, one first notes that continuity of $\succsim_i$ implies $x^{i0} \succsim_i \hat{x}^{i0}$, so that z^0 is individually rational (relative to $\hat{z}^0$). There remains to prove that $F^j_{IP}(\hat{z}^0)$ does not own $\tilde{z}$ such that $\tilde{x}^i \succsim_i x^{i0} \forall i$, $\tilde{x}^h \succ_h x^{h0}$ for some h.

Suppose that such a $\tilde{z}$ exists. Then $\tilde{x}^h_0 > 0$ by assumption 2.1. Without loss of generality, we may assume that $\tilde{z}$ satisfies (2.1) and (2.4) in equality form, and that $\tilde{x}^i \sim_i x^{i0}$, $i \neq h$. Because $\tilde{z} \in F^j(\hat{z}^0)$, $\tilde{\Theta} = \hat{\Theta}^0$ and $\tilde{b}^k = \hat{b}^{k0} \forall k \neq j$, by (3.1). Define then a sequence $\{\tilde{z}^q\}$ as follows:

$$\tilde{\Theta}^q = \hat{\Theta}^q, \tilde{b}^{kq} = \hat{b}^{kq}, k \neq j; \quad \tilde{b}^{jq} = \tilde{b}^j;$$

$$\tilde{x}^{iq}_s = \sum_{k=1}^{J} \tilde{\theta}^q_{ik} \tilde{b}^{kq}_s \quad \forall i, s; \quad \tilde{x}^{iq}_0 \ni \tilde{x}^{iq} \sim_i x^{iq}, i \neq h;$$

$$\tilde{x}^{hq}_0 = \text{Max}\left\{0, W_0 - \sum_{k=1}^{J} \tilde{a}^q_k - \sum_{i \neq h} \tilde{x}^{iq}_0\right\}.$$

Whenever $\tilde{x}^{hq}_0 > 0$, then $\tilde{z}^q \in F^j(\hat{z}^q)$.

Let $B_\varepsilon(\cdot)$ denote the ball with radius ε centred at $(\cdot)$. There exist ε, $\delta = (I + J)\varepsilon$ and Q such that:

(i) $\tilde{x} \succ_h x$ for all $\tilde{x} \in B_\delta(\tilde{x}^h)$, $x \in B_\varepsilon(x^{h0})$;
(ii) $\tilde{x}^h_0 > \delta$;
(iii) $\forall q \geqslant Q$, $\tilde{x}^{iq} \in B_\varepsilon(\tilde{x}^i) \forall i \neq h$, $\tilde{b}^{kq} \in B_\varepsilon(\tilde{b}^k) \forall k \neq j$, so that $\tilde{x}^{hq} \in B_\delta(\tilde{x}^h)$;
(iv) $\forall q \geqslant Q$, $x^{hq} \in B_\varepsilon(x^{h0})$.

Properties (ii) and (iii) imply $\tilde{x}^{hq}_0 > 0$, $\tilde{z}^q \in F^j(\hat{z}^q)$, $\forall q \geqslant Q$. Properties (i), (iii) and (iv) imply $\tilde{x}^{hq} \succ_h x^{hq}$, $q \geqslant Q$. But $\tilde{x}^{iq} \sim_i x^{iq}$, $i \neq h$, by construction. This contradicts $z^q \in F^j_{IP}(\hat{z}^q)$ and the proof is complete.   □

Lemma 5.2: The correspondences $E(z)$ and $E_{IP}(z)$ are upper hemicontinuous.

Proof: Let $\hat{z}^q \to \hat{z}^0$, $z^q \to z^0$, $q \to \infty$.

To prove that $z^q \in E(\hat{z}^q) \forall q$ implies $z^0 \in E(\hat{z}^0)$, it is enough to note that z^0 satisfies all the linear inequalities in (3.9). That z^0 is individually rational (relative to $\hat{z}^0$) follows from continuity of $\succsim_i$, as noted in the proof of lemma 5.1. To complete the proof that $z^q \in E_{IP}(\hat{z}^q) \forall q$ implies $z^0 \in E_{IP}(\hat{z}_0)$, suppose, on the contrary, that $E_{IP}(\hat{z}^0)$ owns $\tilde{z}$ such that $\tilde{x}^i \succsim_i x^{i0} \forall i$, $\tilde{x}^h \succ_h x^{h0}$ for some h. Reasoning as in the proof of lemma 5.1, we define $\{\tilde{z}^q\}$ by:

$$\tilde{b}^q = \hat{b}^q; \quad \tilde{\Theta}^q = \tilde{\Theta}; \quad \tilde{x}^{iq}_s = \sum_j \tilde{\theta}_{ij} \tilde{b}^j_s \quad \forall i, s;$$

$$\tilde{x}^{iq}_0 \ni \tilde{x}^{iq} \sim_i x^{iq}, i \neq h; \quad \tilde{x}^{hq}_0 = \text{Max}\left\{0, W_0 - \sum_j \tilde{a}^q_j - \sum_{i \neq h} \tilde{x}^{iq}_0\right\}.$$

There exist ε, $\delta = (I + J)\varepsilon$ and Q with properties (i)–(iv) in the proof of lemma 5.1, leading to the same contradiction of $z^q \in E_{IP}(\hat{z}^q)$, $q \geq Q$. $\square$

Proof of theorem 5.1:

(1) $\forall z \in Z$, $E_{IP}(z)$ and $F_{IP}^j(z)$ are non-empty and contained in the compact set Z. Hence, $\forall q$, a solution z_q exists and is bounded. Because $x_{00}^i > 0$, it follows from assumption 2.1 and individual rationality that $x_{0q}^i > 0 \forall q, i = 1,\ldots,I$.

(2)   Let $\hat{z} \in Z$ with $\hat{x}_0^i > 0 \forall i$. $\forall z \in F_{IP}^j(\hat{z})$, either $z = \hat{z}$, or

$$\sum_i U^i(x^i) > \sum_i U^i(\hat{x}^i).$$

Indeed, $x^i \underset{\sim}{\succ}_i \hat{x}^i$ by individual rationality, so that

$$\sum_i U^i(x^i) \geqslant \sum_i U^i(\hat{x}^i),$$

with strict inequality if $x^i \succ_i \hat{x}^i$ for some i. Suppose that $x^i \sim \hat{x}^i \forall i$ but $x^h \neq \hat{x}^h$ for some h. Then $F^j(z)$, a convex set, owns $(z + \hat{z})/2 = \bar{z}$, and $\tilde{x}^i \underset{\sim}{\succ}_i x^i \forall i$, $\tilde{x}^h \succ_h x^h$, contradicting the Pareto-optimality of $z \in F_{IP}^j(\hat{z})$. Hence,

$$\sum_i U^i(x^i) = \sum_i U^i(\hat{x}^i)$$

implies $x^i = \hat{x}^i \forall i$. By (3.1) $x = \hat{x}$ implies $b^j = \hat{b}^j$ and $z = \hat{z}$.

(3)   Similarly, $\forall z \in E_{IP}(\hat{z})$, either $x = \hat{x}$, or

$$\sum_i U^i(x^i) > \sum_i U^i(\hat{x}^i).$$

This follows from the convexity of $E(\hat{z})$ and the reasoning under (2). Note further that $\forall z \in E_{IP}(\hat{z})$, $b = \hat{b}$ by (3.9).

(4) $\forall z \in F_{IP}^J \circ F_{IP}^{J-1} \circ \cdots F_{IP}^1 \circ E_{IP}(\hat{z}) =_{\text{def}} G(\hat{z})$ and $\forall z \in E_{IP} \circ F_{IP}^J \circ F_{IP}^{J-1} \circ \cdots$
$F_{IP}^1(\hat{z}) =_{\text{def}} H(\hat{z})$, either $x = \hat{x}$, $b = \hat{b}$ and $z \in E_{IP}(\hat{z})$, or

$$\sum_i U^i(x^i) > \sum_i U^i(\hat{x}^i).$$

This follows directly from (2) and (3).

(5)   Suppose that $z_q = z_{q-2}$. Because $z_q \in F_{IP}^j(z_q)$ with $x_{0q}^i > 0 \forall i$, there exist vectors Π_q^i such that $\{z_q, \Pi_q^i\}$ is a pseudo equilibrium for firm j (theorem 3.1), $j = 1,\ldots,J$. Because $z_q \in E_{IP}(z_q)$ with $x_{0q}^i > 0 \forall i$, there exists a vector p_q such that (z_q, p_q) is a price equilibrium (proposition 3.2); therefore, z_q is a stockholders' equilibrium.

(6)   Suppose next that an infinite sequence $\{z_q\}$ is generated. Because Z is compact, $\{z_q\}$ contains a convergent subsequence, say $\{z_{q_v}\}$; $\{z_{q_v}\}$ contains a subsequence $\{z_{q_\mu}\}$ such that $q_{\mu+1} - q_\mu$ is even $\forall \mu$; let $\rho = 1$ if q_μ is odd, $\rho = -1$ if q_μ is even; in either case, $\{z_{q_\mu+2\rho}\}$ contains a convergent subsequence, say $\{z_{q_\lambda+2\rho}\}$. Consider then the two converging subsequences:

$$\{z_{q_\lambda}\} \xrightarrow[\lambda \to \infty]{} \bar{z} = \lim_{v \to \infty} \{z_{q_v}\};$$

$$\{z_{q_\lambda+2\rho}\} \xrightarrow[\lambda \to \infty]{} \bar{\bar{z}}.$$

(7) $U^i(x^i_{q+1}) \geqslant U^i(x^i_q)$ by individual rationality. Because U^i is continuous and Z compact, U^i converges, so that $U^i(\bar{x}^i) = U^i(\bar{\bar{x}}^i) \forall i$.

(8)   When q_λ is odd, $z_{q_\lambda+2p} = z_{q_\lambda+2} \in H(z_{q_\lambda})$ (as defined under (4) above.) $H(z)$ is upper hemicontinuous, as a composition of upper hemicontinuous correspondences defined on compact sets (see, e.g. Zangwill (1969, lemma 4.2)). Consequently, $\bar{\bar{z}} \in H(\bar{z})$. By (7) and (4), $\bar{x} = \bar{\bar{x}}$, $\bar{b} = \bar{\bar{b}}$ and $\bar{\bar{z}} \in E_{IP}(\bar{z})$. It follows that $\bar{z} \in F^j_{IP}(\bar{z})$, $j = 1, \ldots, J$, $\bar{z} \in E_{IP}(\bar{z})$, with $\bar{x}^i_0 > 0 \forall i$. The reasoning under (5) shows that $\bar{z}$ is a stockholders' equilibrium.

(9)   When q_λ is even, $z_{q_\lambda+2p} = z_{q_\lambda-2}$ and $z_{q_\lambda} \in G(z_{q_\lambda-2})$ (as defined under (4) above). $G(z)$ is upper hemicontinuous, so that $\bar{\bar{z}} \in G(\bar{z})$. By (7) and (4), $\bar{x} = \bar{\bar{x}}$, $\bar{b} = \bar{\bar{b}}$ and $\bar{\bar{z}} \in E_{IP}(\bar{z})$. It follows that $\bar{z} \in E_{IP}(\bar{z})$, $\bar{z} \in F^j_{IP}(\bar{z})$, $j = 1, \ldots, J$, with $\bar{x}^i_0 > 0$, $\bar{z}$ is a stockholders' equilibrium, and the proof is complete.

5.4 Two remarks

Remark 5.1: In the proof of theorem 5.1, strict convexity of preferences is used only to rule out situations where $z \in F^j_{IP}(\hat{z})$ with

$$\sum_i U^i(x^i) = \sum_i U^i(\hat{x}^i)$$

but $z \neq \hat{z}$. Unless one specifies more narrowly how $z_{q,j} \in F^j_{IP}(z_{q,j-1})$ is selected, strict convexity is required to rule out cycling among indifferent programs.

The same difficulty has led me to define the process so that all firms in succession revise their production plans between two meetings of the stock exchange. I would have found it more general to allow for exchanges of shares between any pair of revisions of the production plans. But cycling among indifferent portfolios might then prevent convergence to a stockholders' equilibrium. Indeed, a subset of the consumers might hold a majority interest in firm j whenever that firm revises its production plan (calls a stockholders' meeting), and also hold a majority interest in firm j' whenever that firm revises its production plan, and switch indefinitely back and forth between these two portfolios through exchanges that are indifferent from the viewpoint of the remaining consumers. Such cycling cannot be excluded by strict convexity, as explained in connection with (3.10). But it would be ruled out by any kind of transaction costs.

Remark 5.2: Theorem 5.1 does not assert that process (P) converges. Non-convexity of the feasible set entails the possibility of multiple limit points among which all consumers would be indifferent. The convergence properties of the process are similar to those of mathematical programming algorithms for non-linear problems. Actually, the proof of theorem 5.1 was inspired by convergence theorems for mathematical programming algorithms (see, e.g., Zangwill (1969), or Avriel and Williams (1968)). Furthermore, the theorem implies the convergence of a simple algorithm for non-linear programming problems with bilinear constraints.

Consider indeed the following three problems ($\lambda^i \geqslant 0 \forall i$):

(P1) $\underset{(x,b,\Theta)}{\text{Max}} \sum_i \lambda^i U^i(x^i)$ subject to (2.1) and (2.3)–(2.6);

(P2) $\underset{(x,b)}{\text{Max}} \sum_i \lambda^i U^i(x^i)$ subject to (2.1), (2.3), (2.4) and (2.6),

given $\Theta = \bar{\Theta}$;

(P3) $\underset{(x,\Theta)}{\text{Max}} \sum_i \lambda^i U^i(x^i)$ subject to (2.1), (2.3), (2.5) and (2.6),

given $b = \bar{b}$.

Problems (P2) and (P3) are convex, problem (P1) is not. Consider the following algorithm for solving (P1):

initial step z_0
general step:
if q is odd, solve problem (P3), given $b = b_q$
if q is even, solve problem (P2), given $\Theta = \Theta_q$.
termination: if $z_q = z_{q-2}$, the algorithm terminates.

The convergence properties of this algorithm are covered by theorem 5.1. The algorithm consists in solving a sequence of *convex* programming problems, obtained upon linearising the bilinear constraints (2.3) – by keeping fixed b and Θ alternatively. This linearisation would be particularly helpful if Y^j were a polyhedron – in which case all the constraints in problems (P2) and (P3) would be linear.[27]

6 Applications

6.1 Competition on the stock exchange

Any application of theorem 5.1 must rest upon an institutional specification of the ways in which decisions within the firms are arrived at and

---

[27]This algorithm seems more appealing than the alternative contained in a previous, unpublished, version of this paper where it was suggested to solve at step $q + 1$ the following problem:

(P_q): $\underset{(x,b,\Theta)}{\text{Max}} \sum_i \lambda^i U^i(x^i)$

subject to (2.1), (2.4)–(2.6) and

$$x_s^i - \sum_j \theta_{ij} b_s^{jq} \left(1 + \log \frac{\theta_{ij} b_s^j}{\theta_{ij}^q b_s^{jq}} \right) \leqslant 0.$$

That algorithm would have similar properties. It is a special case of a more general theory developed by Avriel (1973).

Reference should also be made to recent work on bilinear programming, Konno (1971), which might open new possibilities for defining processes yielding constrained Pareto-optima rather than mere stockholders' equilibria exchanges of shares are carried out; that is, it must rest upon specific assumptions about the general step of process (P). I will discuss first the institutional specification of exchanges of shares (general step with q odd), then turn to decision-making within the firms (general step with q even), and finally compare my results with the simpler rule of market value maximisation by firms.

At step q, q odd, the set $E(z_{q-1})$ of reallocations attainable through exchanges of shares is the set of feasible allocations for an exchange economy $\mathscr{E}(z_{q-1})$ with $J+1$ private goods – the shares of the J firms and current consumption (see Section 3.3). Every *competitive equilibrium* for $\mathscr{E}(z_{q-1})$ is individually rational (relative to z_{q-1}) and Pareto-optimal (over $E(z_{q-1})$), and thus belongs to $E_{IP}(z_{q-1})$. Should a competitive equilibrium for $\mathscr{E}(z_{q-1})$ always exist, an institutional organisation of the stock exchange generating competitive equilibria would satisfy the requirements of the general step of (P) for odd q.

With monotonicity of preferences and $x_{0q}^i > 0$ for all i and all q, existence of a competitive equilibrium for $\mathscr{E}(z_{q-1})$ is readily ascertained (e.g. by means of the proposition of Debreu (1962, Section 4)).

Does the stock exchange generate competitive equilibria? That assumption would be somewhat too strong, in my opinion. During a meeting of the stock exchange, some trading typically takes place out of equilibrium, at prices which are successively adjusted until no further trading is forthcoming. The resulting allocation is a *price equilibrium*, not necessarily a competitive equilibrium. Of course, every price equilibrium for $\mathscr{E}(z_{q-1})$ is Pareto-optimal, over $E(z_{q-1})$, (see proposition 3.2); but not every price equilibrium is individually rational.

In a non-tâtonnement exchange process guided by price adjustments, individually irrational allocations can only result from (ill-advised) speculative behaviour.[28] As intimated in Section 5.2, theorem 5.1 may be viewed as a result on stability in the absence of speculation.

6.2 Decision-making within the firms

Let us now consider decision-making within the firms. At step q, q even, each firm in succession is called upon to choose a reallocation in $F_{IP}^j(\cdot)$. As explained in Section 3.2 above, that problem amounts to finding an individually rational and Pareto-optimal allocation for an economy $\mathscr{E}^j(\cdot)$ with S public goods and a single private good. Tâtonnement processes solving that problem, under assumptions 2.1' and 2.2', have been defined by Malinvaud (1969b) and Drèze and de la Vallée Poussin (1971).

---

[28]Looking at such a process as a game, with strategies defined by the net demands announced at each state as functions of past and current prices, one could also state that the α-core must be contained in the set $E_{IP}(\cdot)$ of individually rational and Pareto-optimal allocations (on the α-core concept, see Aumann (1967, Section 10)). Game theoretic analysis of economic adjustment processes is an intriguing but uncharted territory....

Using the differentiability assumptions, one may define

$$\Pi_s^i = \frac{\partial U^i}{\partial x_s^i} \Big/ \frac{\partial U^i}{\partial x_0^i},$$

i's marginal rate of substitution between x_s^i and x_0^i,

$$\gamma_s^j = -\frac{\partial f^j}{\partial b_s^j} \Big/ \frac{\partial f^j}{\partial a^j},$$

the marginal cost of b_s^j (in terms of a^j). The tâtonnement process – say (T^j)– studied by Drèze and de la Vallée Poussin (1971) is defined as follows (in continuous time, for all $t \geqslant 0$, with $\Theta \equiv \bar{\Theta}$):

$$\frac{db_s^j}{dt} = \begin{cases} \sum_i \bar{\theta}_{ij} \Pi_s^i(t) - \gamma_s^j(t), & b_s^j(t) > 0 \\[2mm] \mathrm{Max}\left[0, \sum_i \bar{\theta}_{ij} \Pi_s^i(t) - \gamma_s^j(t) \right], & b_s^j(t) = 0 \end{cases} \Biggr\} \; s = 1, \ldots, S; \tag{6.1}$$

$$\frac{da^j}{dt} = \sum_s \gamma_s^j(t) \frac{db_s^j}{dt}; \tag{6.2}$$

$$\frac{dx_0^i}{dt} = \bar{\theta}_{ij}\left[-\sum_s \Pi_s^i(t) \frac{db_s^j}{dt} + \sum_s \left(\frac{db_s^j}{dt} \right)^2 \right], \quad i = 1, \ldots, I. \tag{6.3}$$

This process (T^j) may be viewed as a procedure for collective choice during stockholders' meetings. Equation (6.1) indicates that production plans are adjusted according to the preferences Π_s^i of the stockholders, weighted by their respective ownership fractions $\bar{\theta}_{ij}$. (6.3) indicates that these adjustments are accompanied by transfers among stockholders, of which the first component is in the nature of an exact compensation for these adjustments, whereas the second component is in the nature of a dividend (per share). Under assumptions 2.1′ and 2.2′, the process (T^j) converges to an individually rational Pareto-optimum.[29]

The process requires that the stockholders reveal to the firm their consumption preferences. It is shown by Drèze and de la Vallée Poussin (1971) that the process entails incentives for correct revelation of these preferences. Looking at the process as a game, where individual strategies consist in the choice of revealed (as opposed to true) vectors $\Pi_s^i(t)$, one finds that correct revelation of preferences is the only minimax strategy, for every player or coalition; and that an equilibrium of the process is a Nash equilibrium of the game if, and only if, all consumers reveal their preferences correctly.[30]

[29] Drèze and de la Vallée Poussin (1971, theorem 1).
[30] See Drèze and de la Vallée Poussin (1971, theorems 3 and 4). The last statement must be qualified somewhat for goods s such that $b_s^j = 0$ – but the qualification is a minor one. It is also shown by Drèze and de la Vallée Poussin (1971) that the α-core of this game *coincides* with the set of individually rational and Pareto-optimal allocations.

The transfers (6.3) are indispensable to generate these incentives. Consider indeed the natural alternative

$$\frac{dx_0^i}{dt} = -\hat{\theta}_{ij}\frac{da_j}{dt}, \quad i = 1,\ldots,I. \tag{6.4}$$

It is readily verified that, at an equilibrium of the process ((6.1), (6.2), (6.4)), the game is *not* in Nash equilibrium. That is, market exchange of shares and production decisions based upon revealed preferences of stockholders imply incentives for *incorrect* revelation of preferences, in the absence of compensating transfers.

To sum up, theorem 5.1 proves the stability of a decentralised mixed tâtonnement/non-tâtonnement process based upon a stock exchange that generates individually rational price equilibria and decision procedures within the firms that generate efficient production plans, rendered individually rational through differentiated dividends (transfers). Reference to competitive equilibria and to the Malinvaud–Drèze–de la Vallée Poussin procedure for public goods, shows that the class of such processes is not empty. But the realism of these processes is severely limited, in particular because they ignore speculative transactions on the stock exchange and rely upon compensating transfers among stockholders of the firms.

6.3 Market value maximisation

The complexity of the tâtonnement process (T^j) may be contrasted with the simplicity of the recommendation typically found in the finance literature, namely that a firm should always adopt a revision of its production plan (an investment) that will increase its market value on the stock exchange.[31] The recommendation is based upon the explicit assumption that an increase in the market value of firm j may be viewed as an increase in the wealth of all stockholders of firm j, with prices of consumption goods unchanged. Such an increase should give the stockholders access to a preferred consumption plan. Consequently, any revision increasing market value is individually rational.

Within the present model, the assumption of unchanged prices for consumption goods is not acceptable. Indeed consumption goods reduce here to consumptions in the various states; in so far as they exist, the prices of those goods are implicit in the prices of shares on the stock exchange. It seems hardly meaningful to assume that consumption prices *implicit in stock prices* do not change when the market value of a given firm increases (even though the increase is due to a change in production plan).

The reasoning underlying the market value rule may still be pursued, within the present model, without assuming unchanged prices for con-

---

[31] See for example, Fama and Miller (1972, pp. 176ff., 299ff.).

sumption goods. Indeed the basic idea is that an adjustment in production plan is beneficial for all the stockholders of a firm, whenever it brings about a new situation where everyone has access to the consumption vector which he had *chosen* in the initial situation. This is the familiar 'revealed preference' criterion. A weaker criterion can be devised only through reference to the consumption preferences of the stockholders, the very reference which one would like to avoid. But the revealed preference criterion can, in principle, be applied even under price changes.

In order to make that criterion unambiguous, let us assume that the stock exchange generates competitive equilibria, and let us investigate under what conditions an adjustment in production plan is 'revealed individually rational'.

To that effect, consider a stock-ownership program $\bar{z}$, and a price vector for shares $\bar{p}$ such that $(\bar{z}, \bar{p})$ is a price equilibrium. Let firm 1 announce a change of its production plan from $\bar{b}^1$ to $\hat{b}^1$, and assume for simplicity that $\hat{a}^1 = \bar{a}^1$. Let this announcement be followed by a meeting of the stock exchange generating a new competitive price vector for shares, $\hat{p}$.

Let $\bar{\theta}_{i1} > 0$.[32] The consumption plan of consumer i in the old situation $\bar{z}$ was $\bar{x}^i$, with

$$\bar{x}^i_s = \sum_j \bar{\theta}_{ij} \bar{b}^j_s, \quad s = 1, \ldots, S.$$

In order for $\bar{x}^i$ to be available in the new situation, there must exist a vector of ownership fractions $(\hat{\theta}_{i1}, \ldots, \hat{\theta}_{iJ})$ such that:

(i) $\quad \theta_{i1} \hat{b}^1_s + \sum_{j=2}^{J} \hat{\theta}_{ij} \bar{b}^j_s \geqslant \sum_{j=1}^{J} \bar{\theta}_{ij} \bar{b}^j_s, \quad s = 1, \ldots, S.$

(ii) $\quad \sum_{j=1}^{J} (\hat{\theta}_{ij} - \bar{\theta}_{ij}) \hat{p}_j \leqslant 0.$

These conditions may also be expressed as follows. There must exist a vector $\beta \in R^J$,

$$\beta_j = \frac{\hat{\theta}_{ij} - \bar{\theta}_{ij}}{\bar{\theta}_{i1}},$$

such that:

(i') $\quad \hat{b}^1_s - \bar{b}^1_s \geqslant \beta_1 \bar{b}^1_s + \sum_{j=2}^{J} \beta_j \bar{b}^j_s, \quad s = 1, \ldots, S.$

(ii') $\quad \sum_{j=1}^{J} \beta_j \hat{p}_j \geqslant 0.$

Conditions (i') and (ii') state that the adjustment $(\hat{b}^1 - \bar{b}^1)$ must be greater than, or equal to, some linear combination of the new production plans, defining a portfolio (short sales permitted) with non-negative value at the new prices $\hat{p}$. In other words, *the adjustment in the production plan must have*

---

[32] If $\bar{\theta}_{i1} = 0$, consumer i cannot lose, since his portfolio entails unchanged consumption.

non-negative value at the consumption prices implied by the new stock prices.

This condition is quite different from the market value rule: $\hat{p}_1 > \bar{p}_1$ is neither sufficient nor necessary for (i')–(ii'). Conceivably, this new condition could be used as a starting point to define an individually rational adjustment process. But the condition does not possess the operational simplicity of the market value rule.[33]

7 Concluding remarks

Remark (1)

The analysis of the present paper could fruitfully be extended to a model involving several commodities, in period 0 and in period 1 under state *s*. Several commodities in period 0, with exchange opportunities for allocating these commodities, seems to call for an immediate and uninteresting extension. Several commodities in period 1, with limited (no) exchange opportunities for these commodities beyond those made possible by the markets for assets, raises more interesting issues. The analysis of temporary equilibrium under uncertainty (Grandmont, 1974; Sondermann, 1974) offers a natural and promising tool with which to approach these issues. Extensions of that analysis, in the direction of optimality and of equilibrium decisions for firms not endowed with preferences of their own, would be welcome.

Perhaps the most interesting and most accessible extension to several commodities will consist in distinguishing between labour and physical goods in an input vector a^j for firm *j*. A major interest of this distinction rests in the symmetrical treatment of human capital and physical capital that it permits. When physical capital is embodied in the inputs of a firm, the supplier of that capital surrenders control over its use to the firm. In the present model, such surrender is accompanied by a proportional right to the yield of the firm's capital, and should ideally be accompanied by a proportional weight in determining shadow prices guiding the use of the firm's capital.

When human labour is embodied in the inputs of a firm, there frequently results a creation of 'embodied human capital'. The productivity of a person who has worked for some time in a given firm is typically higher if he continues to work there, than if he shifts to some other occupation. But that extra productivity typically depends upon the state that obtains. The production (investment) decisions of a firm in a world of uncertainty are not only gambles with the physical capital of stockholders, they are also gambles with the embodied human capital of the firm's employees. Naive extensions of the model used in this paper point clearly towards the

---

[33]I have derived great benefit from discussion of this topic with my colleagues Jean Jaskold Gabszewicz and Jean-Philippe Vial, who had studied independently a related problem.

desirability of production decisions that aggregate not only the consumption preferences of the stockholders (in proportion to their shares), but also those of the employees (in proportion to the quantities of embodied human capital at stake). One may thus expect from this extension new insights into the intriguing problems of control for firms using both physical and human capital.

Remark (2)

The analysis of the present paper could fruitfully be extended to a model with more than two time periods. Serious consideration of such a model would raise a very difficult problem, which is ignored in Sections 5 and 6 above; namely the problem of *timing investment decisions*. Existing private ownership economies probably simulate, to some extent, the kind of adjustment process discussed in Section 5, where consumer portfolios are revised (through stock exchange transactions and other transfers of assets) in the light of new information about the environment and about the production plans of the firms, and investment decisions are revised in the light of new information about the environment and about asset prices. But these adjustments take place in real time and with limited information. At some stage, irreversible investment decisions are realised; that 'stage' must correspond to some step of an underlying adjustment process. Limit points are hardly ever observed, in real time, under sequential information about the environment. For this reason, and because carrying out an investment tomorrow is a typical alternative to carrying out the same investment today, the optimal timing of investment decisions raises a problem of enormous difficulty. What model could capture some essential aspects of that problem, in a framework amenable to analysis, is an open question.

Remark (3)

The set of private ownership programs defined by (2.1), (2.3)–(2.6) is analogous to the set of feasible programs for an economy with semi-public goods and 'consumer mobility'. As a particular case that admits of a straightforward interpretation in terms of (2.1) and (2.3)–(2.6), consider an economy with J regions (or 'clubs'). In each region, a vector of S 'semi-public' goods is produced; by 'semi-public' good is meant a good of which the total production in the region is at any time consumed in full by all the consumers present in that region, but *only* by these.[34] Let these semi-public goods be produced by means of a single input, that can be freely moved across regions. Denote by a^j the input used in region j, by b_s^j the amount of good s produced there, $s = 1, \ldots, S, j = 1, \ldots, J$, and let Y^j be the production set of region j. The I consumers of the economy consume (or supply) the

---

[34]Local police protection, public lighting, control of air pollution, street cleaning,... provide natural examples.

input (in quantities x_0^i) and consume the semi-public goods of the region where they reside. Let each consumer be free to move at no cost[35] across the regions, and denote by θ_{ij} the fraction of his time that consumer i spends in region j; thus,

$$\sum_j \theta_{ij} \leqslant 1, \quad i = 1, \dots, I.\text{[36]} \tag{7.1}$$

The total amount of semi-public good s consumed by i will then be

$$x_s^i = \sum_j \theta_{ij} b_s^j.$$

If the preferences of consumer i are completely represented by a preordering among vectors $x^i = (x_0^i, x_1^i, \dots, x_S^i)$ in R_+^{S+1}, then the problem of efficient production of the S semi-public goods in the J regions is formally equivalent to the problem of Pareto-optimality for stock ownership programs, with the *single* modification that (7.1) replaces (2.5). Most of the analysis in the present paper is directly applicable to the study of efficient production of semi-public goods.[37]

References

Arrow, K.J. (1953). Le rôle des valeurs boursières pour la répartition la meilleure des risques. In *Econométrie*, pp. 41–7. Paris: CNRS. Translated (1964) as The Role of Securities in the Optimal Allocation of Risk-Bearing. *Review of Economic Studies*, 31: 91–6

Aumann, R.J. (1967). *A Survey of Cooperative Games without Side Payments*, In M. Shubik (ed.), *Essays in Mathematical Economics*, pp. 3–27. Princeton: Princeton University Press

Avriel, M. (1973). Solution of Certain Non-Linear Programs Involving r-convex Functions. *Journal of Optimization Theory and Applications*, 11: 159–74

Avriel, M. and A.C. Williams (1968). Complementary Convex Programming. Mobil R. & D. Corporation, Progress Memorandum

Baudier, E. (1959). L'introduction du temps dans la théorie de l'équilibre général. *Cahiers Economiques*, December: 9–16

Borch, K. (1960). The Safety Loading of Reinsurance Premiums. *Skandinavisk Aktuarietidskrift*, 43: 163–84

Debreu, G. (1959). *Theory of Value*. New York: Wiley

—(1962). New Concepts and Techniques for Equilibrium Analysis. *International Economic Review*, 3: 257–73

[35]Transportation costs in this model would play a role analogous to transaction costs on the stock exchange in private ownership economies.

[36]The alternative constraints: $\theta_{ij} = \theta_{ij}^2$, $i = 1, \dots, I, j = 1, \dots, J$, imposing that each consumer resides in a single region, would of course create additional non-convexities.

[37]In particular, the examples of Section 4 admit of a natural interpretation in terms of relocating consumers i and i' between regions j and j' (town and suburbs?), and simultaneously modifying the supply of public goods in both regions.

Diamond, P.A. (1967). The Role of a Stock Market in a General Equilibrium Model with Technological Uncertainty. *American Economic Review*, 42: 759–76

Drèze, J.H. (1972). A Tâtonnement Process for Investment under Uncertainty in Private Ownership Economies. In *Mathematical Methods in Investment and Finance*, G.P. Szegö and K. Shell (eds.), pp. 3–23. Amsterdam: North Holland

Drèze, J.H. and D. de la Vallée Poussin (1971). A Tâtonnement Process for Public Goods. *Review of Economic Studies*, 38: 133–50

Fama, E. and M.H. Miller (1972). *The Theory of Finance*. New York: Holt, Rinehart and Winston

Foley, D.K. (1967). Resource Allocation and the Public Sector. *Yale Economic Essays*, 7: 45–98

Gevers, L. (1974). Competitive Equilibrium of the Stock Exchange and Pareto Efficiency. In J.H. Drèze (ed.), *Allocation under Uncertainty: Equilibrium and Optimality*, Ch. 10. London: Macmillan

Grandmont, J.M. (1974). On the Short-Run Equilibrium in a Monetary Economy. In J.H. Drèze (ed.) *Allocation under Uncertainty: Equilibrium and Optimality*, Ch. 12. London: Macmillan

Guesnerie, R. and T. de Montbrial (1974). Allocation under Uncertainty: A Survey. In J.H. Drèze (ed.), *Allocation under Uncertainty: Equilibrium and Optimality*, Ch. 4. London: Macmillan

Konno, H. (1971). Bilinear Programming: Part I: Algorithm for Solving Bilinear Programs; Part II: Application of Bilinear Programming. Stanford University, California, Technical Reports 9 and 10

Malinvaud, E. (1969a). *Leçons de théorie microéconomique*. Paris: Dunod

—(1969b). Procédures pour la détermination d'un programme de consommations collectives [mimeographed]. Paper presented at the European Meeting of the Econometric Society, Brussels

Mangasarian, O. (1969). *Non-Linear Programming*. New York: McGraw-Hill

Milleron, C. (1972). Theory of Value with Public Goods: A Survey Article. *Journal of Economic Theory*, 5: 419–77

Sondermann, D. (1974). Temporary Competitive Equilibrium under Uncertainty. In J.H. Drèze (ed.), *Allocation under Uncertainty: Equilibrium and Optimality*, Ch. 13. London: Macmillan

Stiglitz, J. (1972). On the Optimality of the Stock Market Allocation of Investment. *The Quarterly Journal of Economics*, 86: 25–60

Zangwill, W.I. (1969). *Non-Linear Programming, A Unified Approach*. Englewood Cliffs: Prentice Hall

15 Decision criteria for business firms*

1. Introduction and preview

1.1 Introduction

The economic theory of resource allocation was initially developed for a given environment, defined by (i) a set of commodities; (ii) a set of consumers, with their initial resources, consumption technology and preferences; (iii) a set of producers, with their initial resources and production technology. Actually, the environment is not given, but depends upon uncertain events. Research introduces new commodities and new technologies, resources are discovered or accidentally destroyed, consumer preferences are subject to unpredictable changes, the yield of production processes is affected by meteorological and random circumstances, and so on. An important conceptual clarification, introduced in the early fifties by Arrow (1953) and Savage (1954), consists in considering a set of alternative, mutually exclusive 'states of the environment', among which 'nature' will choose. This approach provides a more natural starting point for the economic theory of uncertainty than earlier formulations in terms of probability distributions for environmental characteristics or economic variables.[1] In particular, individual decisions and overall resource allocation remain

---

*A survey paper prepared for the 25th Anniversary of the Econometric Institute, Erasmus University, Rotterdam, 1982, and dedicated to the memory of the late P.J.M. van den Bogaard, as a tribute to his original thinking about group decisions (van den Bogaard and Theil, 1959; van den Bogaard and Versluis, 1962).
[1] Borch and Drèze stress this point in their introductions to collective volumes on uncertainty; see Borch and Mossin (1968, pp. xiv–xv) and Drèze (1974b, pp. xiv, 4).

298

amenable, under the new approach, to a unified treatment, into which the deterministic theory fits as a special case.[2]

Over the past 25 years, theoretical developments within the new framework have been conclusive on some issues, while other issues remain debated. Broadly speaking, the theories of consumer decisions, and of competitive equilibria with complete markets, have received lucid expositions, with successive contributions fitting neatly together. On the other hand, the theories of producer decisions and of equilibria with incomplete markets raise difficult, interrelated problems, which are less fully understood. Yet, the 'incomplete markets' case seems to be the more realistic alternative. The open problems are thus challenging. Further progress may be enhanced if we assess what we have learned so far, and what remains to be done.

1.2 A yardstick: complete insurance markets

The nature of the open problems is more easily understood if one reviews first the case of complete competitive markets. Let there be L physical commodities, indexed $l = 1, \ldots, L$, and S possible states of the environment, indexed $s = 1, \ldots, S$. A 'consumption plan' specifies the consumption of each commodity under each state. It may be viewed as a vector in R^{LS} (or equivalently as a set of S vectors in R^L). A 'production plan' specifies the production of each commodity under each state. A complete set of markets is a set of LS *insurance* markets, one for each commodity contingent on each state. A complete price system is a vector of insurance premia p in R^{LS}, where p_{ls} is a sure irrevocable payment giving right to one unit of commodity l if and only if state s obtains.[3]

If there existed a complete set of markets, each consumer could choose a consumption plan subject to a single budget constraint, connecting the insurance value of his receipts and expenditures. For such a consumer, uncertainty of receipts would be of little consequence. In particular, two assets of equal market value would be perfect substitutes (up to transaction costs), no matter how their returns are distributed over the states. The difficult choice for a consumer is the selection of a consumption plan (a state distribution of consumption bundles) among all those with a given value on the insurance markets. Subjective probabilities and risk tolerance influence that choice, and so would a possible dependence of tastes upon the state of the environment (see Section 2.2 below).

With a complete set of markets, every production plan has a well-defined insurance value. It seems then natural to assume that each producer

---

[2]See Debreu (1959, Ch. 7)

[3]Each commodity is dated. The temporal structure of this model, taking into account individual differences in information, has been detailed by Radner (1968, 1972, 1980); see also Guesnerie and Jaffray (1974).

maximises the insurance value of its production plan, which is also the profits and the market value of the firm. Any consumer owning a share of the firm will approve that choice.[4]

1.3 Statement of the problem

Unfortunately, the model of an economy with a complete set of insurance markets is an abstract idealisation. The very fact that business firms (producers) are concerned about uncertainty reveals that not all risks can be insured. I will accept that statement here as a valid empirical generalisation, and note for later reference that a standard explanation for this market failure is the presence of transaction costs (not only in organising markets but also in choosing transaction levels and monitoring moral hazards).[5]

The fact that insurance markets are incomplete has important consequences, the most widely discussed of which are the following

(i)   Being unable to sell revenue accruing under one state in order to consume more in another state, consumers are faced with a multiplicity of budget constraints. In the limiting case where no insurance at all is possible, revenues must cover expenditures in every state, and there are S independent budget constraints. If a consumer holds assets, the state distribution of their yields will matter to him, because the yield under each state affects a different budget constraint. Also, consumers may wish to exchange among each other shares of ownership in assets, in order to achieve a better allocation of risks through diversification.

(ii)   Being unable to sell their production plans on the insurance markets, business firms do not have uniquely defined profits; rather, a production plan induces a state distribution of profits.[6] The question then arises: *How does a firm choose among state distributions of profits?*

(iii)   In private ownership economies, business profits ultimately accrue to consumers, say as dividends. Also, consumers wish to trade shares of ownership in the firms, in order to reallocate risks among themselves. The prices of shares on the stock exchange act as a substitute for insurance markets in assigning a well-defined aggregate value to the production plan of each firm. A twofold corollary question then arises: *How do the preferences of shareholders, and the prices of shares on the stock exchange, influence the criterion by which a firm chooses among state distributions of profits?*

[4]See, however, Baumol (1962), Marris (1963), Penrose (1959) and Williamson (1964) for a different viewpoint.
[5]For a further discussion of the underlying issues, see e.g. Arrow (1970, Ch. 5).
[6]This statement assumes that commodity prices are uniquely determined conditionally on each state.

1.4 The answers of three alternative schools

The question, and its corollary, have concerned theorists of uncertainty, and of finance, over the past 15 years. The question comes up because producers, unlike consumers, are not human beings whose preferences may be taken as primitive data. Three types of answers have been given, which may be viewed as coming from 'nested' assumptions about the information available to producers.

One 'school' attempts at deriving each firm's decision criteria from the information contained in share prices. This approach has been developed, under the name of 'spanning', by Ekern and Wilson (1974), Leland (1974) and Radner (1974), among others, in a special issue of *The Bell Journal of Economics and Management Sciences*. It is reviewed and further clarified in a recent paper by Grossman and Stiglitz (1980). Special cases of this model include the case of 'multiplicative uncertainty', treated in the seminal paper by Diamond (1967); and the widely used 'Capital Asset Pricing Model' – see Mossin (1977) for a summary account and a few key references to a vast literature.

A second 'school' recognises that only under rather extreme assumptions will share prices contain all the information needed to guide business decisions. An attempt is then made at relating each firm's decision criteria to the preferences of its own shareholders. This approach has been developed by Drèze (1972, 1974a), Gevers (1974) and Grossman and Hart (1979).

A third 'school' recognises that consultation of shareholders is fraught with the same transaction costs as the organisation of insurance markets. Accordingly, it endows each business firm with preferences of its own, defined over state distributions of profits. These preferences depend neither on share prices nor on shareholder preferences. This approach is used in the general equilibrium models of Radner (1972, 1980) and Sondermann (1974), and in a number of partial equilibrium models, including among others Drèze (1980), Leland (1972) and Sandmo (1971).

1.5 Towards an integrated answer: preview and contents

My current view is that each 'school' contributes relevant considerations, which *should, and could*, be integrated to obtain a positive theory of firms' decisions under uncertainty suitable for the needs of economic analysis. I find it reasonable to assume that a firm will not adopt policies which could be identified as inefficient on the basis of information contained in stock market (or asset, or insurance) prices.[7] But this criterion alone will typically leave many questions unanswered. I next find it reasonable to assume that a firm will adopt policies beneficial to its shareholders, whenever their

---

[7]This idea is also central to the theory of investment of Tobin (1980, Ch. IV).

interests can be identified – as in the case of a proxy fight or take-over bid. But this form of consultation will typically be confined to major, infrequent policy decisions. There remain many less visible decisions involving uncertainties, for which it would be unrealistic to assume that firms will be risk-neutral. It is then tempting to endow the firm with a utility function of its own, on which these decisions will be based. This has the merit of preserving consistency, without which economic analysis is severely limited.

Of course, one would like to integrate these three levels of consideration into a single well-defined decision criterion. At first sight, the premises of the respective theories seem hard to reconcile. Yet, if one restricts attention to the characterisation of equilibria as distinct from behaviour out of equilibrium, it seems possible to view each proposed criterion as a special case of a general formulation: *In equilibrium, the decisions of each firm maximise the expected utility of profits, in terms of a utility function which is specific to the firm and is allowed to depend upon the state of the environment, the preferences of shareholders and the prices of shares on the stock market.* (The properties of the utility functions implied by theories of the first and second schools are spelled out in Section 2.)

This general formulation is an extension of the premise used by the third school. The utility function of a firm is no longer a primitive datum, but is shaped in part endogenously by the decisions of other firms and transactions on the stock exchange. This extension seems amenable to the methodology of general equilibrium theory, as developed in the 'abstract economy' formulation of Shafer and Sonnenschein (1975) – although technical difficulties of various kinds are bound to arise. *The message of this chapter is that any less general formulation would be unrealistic.*

Restricting attention to characterisations of equilibria has two implications. First, in the usual case where equilibrium is competitive, one ignores monopolistic aspects of behaviour. This simplification is also a clarification, as it has sometimes been unclear whether different conclusions were due to different criteria or to different assumptions about competitiveness. Second, one ignores behaviour out of equilibrium. This is a more severe limitation, since a decision criterion for the firm should prescribe its behaviour under all circumstances. However, the first 'school' has produced theories of equilibrium, with few results about stability or dynamics. It is doubtful that decisions based upon forecasts of price adjustments could generally admit of a utility representation. This question requires further investigation.

There is an element of tautology in saying that production decisions maximise expected utility, when the utility function itself depends upon the prevailing allocation. If production sets are convex, one can associate with every efficient decision a supporting hyperplane, thereby defining a direction of maximisation. The question under review is of course the extent to which theories of the stock market economy place restrictions on that direction. To that end, I will use the simplest possible model of an economy

Table 15.1

Theory	Utility function of the firm			Agrees with preferences of			Linear in profits given the state	Reflects market value	Pareto-optimality for shareholders	Reference to Section
	Firm-specific	State-dependent	Price-dependent	some shareholder	every shareholder	average				
Single owner firm	yes	yes	yes	yes	yes	yes	no	no	yes	2.2
Spanning complete	no	yes	yes	yes	yes	yes	yes	yes	yes	2.3.1
partial	yes	yes	yes	yes	yes	yes	yes	yes	yes	2.3.2
Multiplicative uncertainty	yes	yes	yes	yes	yes	yes	yes	yes	yes	2.3.3
CAPM	no	yes	yes	yes	yes	yes	yes	yes	yes	2.3.4
Efficiency for shareholders' preferences	yes	yes	yes	no*	no*	yes	yes	no	yes	2.4
Utility function of the firm	yes	yes	no	no	no	no	no	no	no	2.5
General formulation	yes	yes	yes	no*	no*	no*	no	no	no	2.6

*Still, in equilibrium, the utility function of the firm is influenced by the preferences of these shareholders.

with production and a stock market, namely the one-commodity, two-periods model introduced by Diamond (1967) and used in most of the models referred to above. After introducing the model (Section 2.1), I will discuss consumer choices (Section 2.2), and then review the three approaches mentioned above (Sections 2.3–2.5). My review will be limited to basic results, ignoring a number of more subtle issues treated in the literature, and making no attempt at bibliographical comprehensiveness. In all cases, I shall bring out an implicit utility function of the firm, and ask whether it is:

> firm-specific
> state-dependent
> price-dependent
> representative of the preferences of some, every or an average shareholder
> linear in profits given the state
> related to market value.

A summary presentation of the answers is given in Table 15.1. Only liminal conclusions are presented here, in Section 2.6. One important issue, not treated here, is the extent to which risk aversion is eliminated by large numbers of shareholders. Relevant contributions to that issue are found in the work of Arrow and Lind (1970), Hart (1979) and Malinvaud (1972).

1.6 Limitations of the model under review

Before proceeding further, I should insist on a major limitation of the model used in this survey. In a private ownership economy, business firms play three major roles. They produce the commodities which consumers buy; they create the jobs which workers fill; they invest in productive assets the resources which households save. At a competitive equilibrium, these three roles are coordinated through the price system. Under incomplete markets, other decision criteria and information channels are needed. The analysis of stock market economies privileges the third role. There may be good reasons for this, of a logical as well as historical nature.[8] But the other roles raise important issues as well, which have received less attention. For many households, uncertainty about the yield of savings is secondary relative to uncertainty about employment opportunities and labour income. In private ownership economies, labour contracts are the main instrument for the allocation of risks on human capital. Some implications of uncertainty for labour contracts have been investigated in the seminal work of Azariadis (1975), Baily (1977) and Gordon (1974) – see also the survey papers by Azariadis (1979) and Drèze (1979) and the general equilibrium analysis by Holmström (1981). Much remains to be done in this

---

[8]The question initially raised by Arrow (1953) was precisely the extent to which asset markets could replace insurance markets towards achieving an efficient allocation of risks.

important area.[9] Similarly, the way in which consumer preferences for specific commodities are communicated to producers in a world of uncertainty deserves further investigation, beyond the beginnings made in the analysis of rewards to innovation – as surveyed by Hirshleifer and Riley (1979) in their discussion of the economics of research and invention. Many issues remain to be understood, which cannot be captured in the simple model used here.

2 Nested models of decision criteria for business firms

2.1 A simple model

The simplest model of a stock market economy, namely the model with a single commodity and two periods, has received a lot of attention. In that model, it is assumed that the state of the world is unknown in period 0, when production, savings and portfolio decisions are made. The true state (indexed $s = 1, \ldots, S$) will be known in period 1. It will determine uniquely the output of each firm (given the decision made in period 0), and the consumption of each individual (given the portfolio choice made in period 0). There is a stock market, but no insurance markets.

Formally, a consumption plan for consumer i is a non-negative vector $x^i = (x_0^i, x_1^i, \ldots, x_s^i, \ldots, x_S^i)$, where x_0^i denotes consumption of the single commodity in period 0, and x_s^i consumption in period 1 under state s. Preferences among consumption vectors are representable by the quasi-concave utility function $U^i(x^i)$.

Similarly, a production plan for firm j is a non-negative vector $y^j = (y_0^j, y_1^j, \ldots, y_S^j)$ in Y^j, where y_0^j is the input level in period 0, and y_s^j the output level in period 1 under state s. The production set Y^j is convex and satisfies some technical assumptions (Y^j is closed and contains the origin; positive inputs are required for positive outputs; finite inputs lead to finite outputs).

The initial resources are owned by individuals in amounts $\bar{x}^i$, where $\bar{x}_0^i$ may include shares of past production. Ownership of the firms is shared among individuals in fractions θ_{ij},

$$\sum_i \theta_{ij} = 1.$$

Initial holdings, when relevant, are denoted $\bar{\theta}_{ij}$.

The physical and institutional constraints for this economy take the form:

$$\sum_i x_0^i + \sum_j y_0^j \leqslant \sum_i \bar{x}_0^i, \tag{2.1}$$

---

[9] A beginning has also been made at developing the alternative model of labour-managed firms in an uncertain environment; see in particular, Drèze (1976), Jensen and Meckling (1979) and Steinherr (1977).

$$x_s^i \leqslant \bar{x}_s^i + \sum_j \theta_{ij} y_s^j, \quad i = 1, \dots, m, s = 1, \dots, S, \tag{2.2}$$

$$y^j \in Y^j, \quad j = 1, \dots, n. \tag{2.3}$$

An important feature of this economy is that, in spite of the convexity of the production sets, the set of attainable consumption vectors defined by (2.1)–(2.3) is not always convex, due to the bilinear form of the constraints (2.2) – see Drèze (1974a, lemma 2.3). This feature reflects the need for simultaneous adjustments of the ownership shares θ_{ij} and production plans y^j to achieve certain consumption plans.

A price system on the stock market is a vector $p = (p_1, \dots, p_j, \dots, p_n)$ of R^n, in terms of which one can define budget constraints

$$x_0^i + \sum_j \theta_{ij}(p_j + y_0^j) \leqslant \bar{x}_0^i + \sum_j \bar{\theta}_{ij} p_j. \tag{2.4}$$

This formulation assumes that shareholders contribute the current inputs of the firms, thereby avoiding the need to introduce bond financing explicitly.

An equilibrium of production and exchange is a set of production plans and portfolios of shares with the 'Nash-property' that no firm and no consumer wishes to change its decision.

2.2 Portfolio choices by consumers

The problem faced by consumer i is to maximise $U^i(x^i)$ subject to (2.2) and (2.4). Quasi-concavity of utility is the standard assumption about consumer preferences under certainty. In the theory of individual decision-making under uncertainty, as developed by Ramsey (1931), von Neumann and Morgenstern (1944) and Savage (1954), it is assumed that preferences over consumption vectors are additive with respect to mutually exclusive events (sets of states). Formally, if A is any subset of $\{1, \dots, S\}$, let

$$x_A = {}_{\text{def}} (x_s)_{s \in A}, \quad x_B = {}_{\text{def}} (x_s)_{s \notin A}, \quad x = (x_0, x_A, x_B).$$

Then ('Sure thing principle'):

$$U^i(x_0, x_A, x_B) \geqslant U^i(x_0, x_A', x_B) \quad \text{if and only if}$$
$$U^i(x_0, x_A, x_B') \geqslant U^i(x_0, x_A', x_B') \quad \text{identically in } x_B'. \tag{2.5}$$

This condition implies

$$U^i(x^i) = \sum_s U_s^i(x_0^i, x_s^i), \tag{2.6}$$

with U^i defined up to a linear transformation.

That is, U^i is a separately additive, state-dependent utility function. It is state-dependent, because $U_s^i(x_0, x_s) = U_s^i(x_0', x_s')$ does not imply $U_t^i(x_0, x_s) = U_t^i(x_0', x_s')$; the reason being that consumption bundles do not describe consequences completely.[10] State-independent preferences, requiring additional assumptions, are representable by

$$U^i(x^i) = \sum_s \phi_s^i u^i(x_0^i, x_s^i) \tag{2.7}$$

where $\phi^i = (\phi_1^i, \ldots, \phi_S^i)$ is a (subjective) probability vector. Quasi-concavity of U^i now implies concavity of u^i, i.e. risk aversion. In the more general state-dependent formulation, ϕ_s^i is not identified, and U_s^i has the dimension of a probability times a conditional utility. Risk aversion given state s requires U_s^i to be concave.

Under differentiability of U^i, the following first-order conditions are necessary and sufficient for a solution of consumer i's portfolio choice problem:[11]

$$\theta_{ij}\left[\sum_s y_s^j \frac{\partial U_s^i}{\partial x_s^i} - (p_j + y_0^j)\sum_s \frac{\partial U_s^i}{\partial x_0^i}\right] = 0,$$

$$\sum_s y_s^j \frac{\partial U_s^i}{\partial x_s^i} - (p_j + y_0^j)\sum_s \frac{\partial U_s^i}{\partial x_0^i} \leqslant 0. \tag{2.8}$$

In this formulation, short sales are not allowed, which seems to be the more realistic assumption. Write Π_s^i for

$$\frac{\partial U_s^i}{\partial x_s^i} \Big/ \sum_t \frac{\partial U_t^i}{\partial x_0^i},$$

the marginal rate of substitution between future consumption contingent on state s and current consumption; (2.8) is then equivalent to

$$\sum_s y_s^j \Pi_s^i \leqslant p_j + y_0^j \tag{2.9}$$

with equality whenever $\theta_{ij} \neq 0$.

Conditions (2.8)–(2.9) embody an assumption of price-taking behaviour on the part of consumer i in his stock-market transactions.

If individual i were the single owner of firm j, then at an equilibrium of production and exchange he would wish the production plan y^j to solve

$$\underset{y^j \in Y^j}{\text{Max}} \sum_s U_s^i\left[\bar{x}_0^i + \sum_{k \neq j}\{\bar{\theta}_{ik}p_k - \theta_{ik}(p_k + y_0^k)\} - y_0^j,\right.$$

$$\left.\bar{x}_s^i + \sum_{k \neq j}\theta_{ik}y_s^k + y_s^j\right]. \tag{2.10}$$

In this case, the decision criterion of firm j would be to maximise the expected utility function U^i of the firm's owner, due account being taken of

[10]On this point, see Drèze (1961), Hirshleifer and Riley (1979, pp. 1387–9).
[11]More generally, conditions (2.8) could be stated in terms of subgradients. The constraint $\theta_{ij} \leqslant 1$ is ignored, but follows from $\theta_{kj} \geqslant 0$, $\sum_k \theta_{kj} = 1$.

the production plans of the other firms, of the share prices and of the portfolio equilibrium conditions (2.8). Obvious properties of this decision criterion appear in the first row of Table 15.1. Whether or not the production plan y^j also maximises the market value of firm j will in general depend upon the extensiveness of investment opportunities available to consumers, as illustrated in the sequel.

2.3 Decision criteria based upon share prices

This framework will now be used to review briefly the models where the share prices contain information susceptible of guiding the production decisions of all firms.

2.3.1 Complete spanning: Following Arrow (1953) and Radner (1974) for initial simplicity, assume that there exists a set of S firms (to be indexed $j = 1, \ldots, S$) with linearly independent output vectors. This is of course an extreme assumption; it will be relaxed slightly in Section 2.3.2 below.

In that case, an equilibrium price vector p for the stock exchange contains implicitly a price vector q in R^S for insurance contracts on the individual states. This can be seen as follows. Let B denote the $S \times S$ matrix with elements $B_{js} = y^j_s, j, s = 1, \ldots, S$. The matrix B has full rank. Write β^s for row s of B^{-1}, so that $\beta^s B = \delta^s$, the Kronecker vector with $\delta^s_s = 1$, $\delta^s_t = 0$ for $t \neq s$, $t = 1, \ldots, S$. We may interpret β^s as the portfolio (vector of shares in the S firms) giving right to one unit of output in state s and to nothing otherwise. The market value of this portfolio,

$$q_s = \sum_{j=1}^{S} \beta^s_j (p_j + y^j_0),$$

is the cost (on the stock exchange) of an insurance policy paying a unitary indemnity if and only if state s obtains.

In general, the portfolio β^s may fail to be non-negative, so that short sales must be permitted in order for this portfolio to be meaningful. Also, detailed exact information about the production plans $y^j_s, j, s = 1, \ldots, S$, is needed to compute β^s – two severe departures from realism.

Under these assumptions, an equilibrium of the stock exchange must satisfy two sets of conditions:

$$\text{for all } j, \quad p_j + y^j_0 = \sum_s q_s y^j_s; \tag{2.11}$$

$$\text{for all } i, \quad \text{for all } s = 1, \ldots, S, \quad \Pi^i_s = q_s. \tag{2.12}$$

If conditions (2.11) were not satisfied, there would be scope for riskless profitable arbitrages. If conditions (2.12) were not satisfied, the portfolio held by consumer i would not maximise his expected utility under the budget constraint (2.4). Furthermore, a shareholder taking the prices p_j and hence q_s as given will approve the production plan of firm j if and only if

$$\sum_s q_s y_s^j - y_0^j \geqslant \sum_s q_s y_s - y_0 \quad \text{for all } y \text{ in } Y^j. \tag{2.13}$$

If the firms adopt this price-taking behaviour, their production decisions and the portfolio decisions of the consumers result in a competitive equilibrium relative to the prices q_s for contingent claims to commodities.

It should be clear that conditions (2.11) and (2.13) are simply a characterisation of competitive equilibrium. It is not claimed that the implicit prices q_s would remain unchanged if firm j changed its production plan from y^j to y. If firm j is aware of the influence of its decisions on the prices, it may in fact choose to violate condition (2.13) – for the same reasons that monopolistic firms do not behave as price-takers in the certainty models. See Stiglitz (1972), Grossman and Stiglitz (1980) for further discussion of this issue.

Conditions (2.13) can be interpreted in terms of a utility function for firm j which is linear in profits given the states, with weights q_s common to all firms and representing also the preferences of all shareholders, in view of (2.12). The expected utility of the firm corresponds also to its market value, in view of (2.11). These properties are collected in line 2 of Table 15.1.

2.3.2 Partial spanning: A slightly less extreme set of assumptions is sufficient to obtain a well-defined decision criterion for the firms. Suppose that all the production sets Y^j belong to some linear subspace of R^{S+1} – say Z – with dimensionality $K + 1 < S + 1$. The essential steps of the foregoing argument can then be retraced in terms of a set of $K < S$ firms with linearly independent output vectors (spanning Z), and of K 'composite commodities' defined by K linearly independent vectors of R^S with implicit prices q_k. The foregoing analysis leads to a competitive equilibrium in these composite commodities.[12]

More precisely, let C be the $K \times S$ matrix defining these commodities (C_{ks} is the quantity of output in state s contained in composite commodity k). Every vector y^j in Y^j may be written as $\zeta^j C$, with implicit value $\sum_k q_k \zeta_k^j - y_0^j$. The production set of firm j is thus also $Z^j = \{(y_0^j, \zeta^j)|(y_0^j, \zeta^j C) \in Y^j\}$. The analogues of conditions (2.11)–(2.13) become

$$\text{for all } j, \quad p_j + y_0^j = \sum_k q_k \zeta_k^j; \tag{2.11'}$$

$$\sum_k q_k \zeta_k^j - y_0^j \geqslant \sum_k q_k \zeta_k - y_0 \quad \text{for all } (y_0, \zeta) \text{ in } Z^j. \tag{2.13'}$$

As for conditions (2.12), they become

$$\text{for all } i, \text{for all } k = 1, \ldots, K, \quad \sum_s C_{ks} \Pi_s^i = q_k. \tag{2.12'}$$

---

[12]However, Grossman and Stiglitz (1980) note that $K = S$ is required if the theory is to cover not only the production decisions but also the financial decisions.

This model is analogous to the 'characteristics' model of consumer demand theory.[13] The decision criterion for firm j can be stated in two ways (at a competitive equilibrium). One possibility is to define a utility function with arguments (y_0^j, ζ^j) in Z^j, linear in its arguments with weights q_k common to all firms. Another possibility is to note from (2.12')–(2.13') that the production plan of firm j maximises the expected utility of any and every one of its shareholders. These properties are listed in row 3 of Table 15.1.

2.3.3 Multiplicative uncertainty: In the seminal paper by Diamond (1967), it is assumed that the production set of firm j takes the simple form[14]

$$Y^j = \{y^j | y_s^j = b_s^j f^j(y_0^j), \quad s = 1, \ldots, S\}. \tag{2.14}$$

That is, firm j need only decide about its input level y_0^j; output in every state s is then fully determined. Also, the ratio of output in state s to output in state t is predetermined, being equal to b_s^j/b_t^j, independently of the firm's decision. Y^j is thus contained in a two-dimensional subspace of R^{S+1}.

In that case, if consumer i holds a non-null share θ_{ij} of firm j, his first-order condition for portfolio selection (2.9) reads

$$\sum_s \Pi_s^i y_s^j = \sum_s \Pi_s^i b_s^j f^j(y_0^j) = p_j + y_0^j. \tag{2.15}$$

Consumer i would also wish firm j to choose an input level y_0^j such that, if $f^j(y_0^j)$ is differentiable,[15]

$$\sum_s \Pi_s^i b_s^j \frac{\partial f^j}{\partial y_0^j} = 1. \tag{2.16}$$

Combining (2.15) and (2.16), we find that all shareholders will unanimously approve an input level y_0^j such that

$$\sum_s \Pi_s^i b_s^j = \left(\frac{\partial f^j}{\partial y_0^j}\right)^{-1} = \frac{p_j + y_0^j}{f^j(y_0^j)}. \tag{2.17}$$

In equilibrium, the market value of the firm provides all the information needed to verify the optimality of y_0^j, using (2.17). This result also follows from the 'spanning' theory. With a two-dimensional production set, a single share price contains all the requisite information ($K = 1$). The 'partial spanning' model holds for each firm separately, and its conclusions remain valid. In particular, the utility function of any one shareholder may again serve as a utility function for the firm, in so far as the production (i.e. input) decision is concerned – see row 4 of Table 15.1. The caveat about price-

---

[13]The analogy is developed by Drèze and Hagen (1978).
[14]The same assumption is made by Sandmo (1972), who points out the analogy with the concept of 'risk classes' as used by Modigliani and Miller (1958).
[15]More generally, condition (2.16) could be restated in terms of subgradients.

taking behaviour on the part of shareholders and firms introduced when discussing spanning remains appropriate here.

2.3.4 Mean-variance and the Capital Asset Pricing Model: Instead of introducing special assumptions regarding the production technology, one can introduce special assumptions regarding the preferences and endowments of consumers. This is the avenue followed successfully in the abundent literature on the Capital Asset Pricing Model (CAPM) – see, e.g. Modigliani and Pogue (1974) and Mossin (1977) for summary presentations. Assume that, for each consumer, the utility function (2.6) is quadratic and state-independent, with common probabilities ϕ:

$$U^i(x^i) = \sum_s \phi_s u^i(x_0^i, x_s^i) = \sum_s \phi_s [a_0^i x_0^i + a_1^i x_s^i - b_{00}^i (x_0^i)^2$$

$$- b_{01}^i x_0^i x_s^i - b_{11}^i (x_s^i)^2]. \tag{2.18}$$

Assume also that $\bar{x}_s^i = \bar{x}_1^i$, independently of s. Assume finally the existence of a safe asset, i.e. of a firm (indexed 0) with a state-independent output: $y_s^0 = y_1^0, s = 1, \ldots, S$. Write

$$\bar{y}^j \quad \text{for} \quad \sum_s \phi_s y_s^j, \quad \sigma_{jk} \quad \text{for} \quad \sum_s \phi_s (y_s^j - \bar{y}^j) y_s^k.$$

One then verifies that an equilibrium of the stock market satisfies

$$p_j = p_0 \bar{y}^j - R \sum_k \sigma_{jk} - y_0^j, \quad j = 1, \ldots, n, \tag{2.19}$$

where the scalar R, usually called 'market risk-aversion factor', is a function of the parameters of the individual utility functions and expected consumption levels. This is the familiar result (in the CAPM) that a firm's market value is equal to its expected profits, plus or minus a risk premium proportional to the covariance of its profits with aggregate resources.

Writing

$$z_s = \sum_j y_s^j + \sum_i \bar{x}^i$$

for aggregate resources, with expectation

$$\bar{z} = \sum_s \phi_s z_s,$$

we can rewrite (2.19) as

$$p_j = p_0 \sum_s \phi_s y_s^j - R \sum_s \phi_s y_s^j (z_s - \bar{z}) - y_0^j$$

$$= _{\text{def}} \sum_s q_s y_s^j - y_0^j, \tag{2.20}$$

$$q_s = \phi_s [p_0 - R(z_s - \bar{z})], \quad \sum_s q_s = p_0. \tag{2.21}$$

The weights q_s may be interpreted as prices for contingent claims to output. Under the assumptions of the CAPM, these prices are defined by a linear function of aggregate resources.

Another standard result in this model is that $\theta_{ij} = \theta_i$ for all $j > 0$: Each consumer holds the same fraction of all risky firms. It then follows that

$$x_s^i - \sum_t \phi_t x_t^i$$

is proportional to $z_s - \bar{z}$ and $\Pi_s^i = q_s$ for all i and s, so that

$$p_j = \sum_s \Pi_s^i y_s^j - y_0^j = \sum_s \left(\sum_i \theta_{ij} \Pi_s^i \right) y_s^j - y_0^j. \tag{2.22}$$

At a competitive production and exchange equilibrium, each firm maximises not only its market value but also the expected utility of each shareholder. It also maximises a common state-dependent utility function, which is linear in profits given the state – see row 5 of Table 15.1.

This conclusion must again be understood as a characterisation of equilibrium; if the firm were to change its production plan, the prices q_s would change, for the same reasons already mentioned in Section 2.3.1. In this case, however, the reactions of the prices q_s to changes in the production levels y_s^j can be predicted approximately within the model. If one assumed that p_0 and R would not be perceptibly affected by changes in y^j, one could rewrite (2.21) as

$$q_s = \phi_s \left[p_0 - R \sum_{k \neq j} \left(y_s^k - \sum_t y_t^k \phi_t \right) - R \left(y_s^j - \sum_t y_t^j \phi_t \right) \right]. \tag{2.23}$$

A firm taking into account the influence of its production plan on the prices q_s would choose a plan that does not maximise the expected utility of its price-taking stockholders – a point stressed by Stiglitz (1972).

2.4 Decision criteria based upon shareholders' preferences

Outside of the special cases where business firms inherit from the stock prices a well-defined decision criterion, it is natural to investigate the logical possibility of decentralised decisions compatible with shareholder preferences. For the simple model under review, this has been done by Drèze (1972, 1974a) and Grossman and Hart (1979); see also Gevers (1974), Milne and Starrett (1981).

Consider an economy with a stock exchange, where the smallest linear subspace of R^{S+1} containing the production set of firm j has dimensionality $K + 1$ exceeding the total number of firms. In other words, 'spanning' does not hold. No restrictions – beyond those of Section 2.2 – are placed on consumer preferences. Each stockholder i of firm j has a portfolio of shares θ_{ik} in the various firms, whose production plans y^k have been announced. Keeping θ_{ij}, θ_{ik} and y^k constant, all i and all k different from j, we can define the set of production plans for firm j which are Pareto-optimal from the viewpoint of its shareholders. Because these production plans determine simultaneously the 'dividends', hence the consumption, of all shareholders in the different states, the choice of a plan is comparable to the choice of a vector of public goods. Greater efficiency is achieved if the choice is accompanied by transfers among shareholders, which could be regarded as a form of trading in votes – see Grossman and Hart (1979, p. 301). A Pareto-optimal plan y^j is then characterised as follows:

$$\sum_s \left(\sum_i \theta_{ij} \Pi_s^i \right) y_s^j - y_0^j \geqslant \sum_s \left(\sum_i \theta_{ij} \Pi_s^i \right) y_s - y_0 \quad \text{for all } y \text{ in } Y^j.$$
(2.24)

The main result is that, under standard convexity assumptions, there exist production plans y^j and stock prices p_j for all firms, portfolios θ_{ij} and transfers of current resources among consumers, such that

(i)   each y^j is a Pareto-optimal production plan for firm j, given its set of shareholders, in the sense of (2.24);

(ii)   each portfolio vector θ_{ij} is optimal for consumer i, given the prices p_j and production plans y^j, in the sense of (2.9).

The resulting allocation is called 'stockholders equilibrium' by Drèze, 'competitive production-exchange equilibrium' by Grossman and Hart.[16] The new feature, in comparison with the special cases of Section 2.3, is that firms would need to collect information from their shareholders about their marginal rates of substitution Π_s^i, in order to verify the conditions (2.24). If there existed, explicitly or implicitly, prices q_s for contingent claims to commodities, these prices could be used, instead of

$$\sum_i \theta_{ij} \Pi_s^i,$$

to guide the production decisions. The absence of price information imposes on each firm the burden of collecting the relevant information from its shareholders. Because this 'consulting' of shareholders is needed in each firm, the transfer of information is less efficient. And it is indeed doubtful that this transfer actually takes place – for the same reasons of transaction costs which explain why insurance markets on all possible states do not exist.

At a 'stockholders equilibrium', if the production plans of the firms span a space Z of dimension $K + 1$, the marginal rates of substitution of all consumers are subject to K equality or inequality constraints (2.9) with identical coefficients. These constraints embody the information about production possibilities contained in the share prices. Accordingly, this information is automatically embodied in conditions (2.24). There is no need for each firm to consider it separately. Alternatively, the need to elicit

---

[16] The two models, which are not identical, are compared by Milne and Starrett (1981).

shareholders' preferences is reduced to $S-K$ dimensions (up to corner solutions). The ease with which the approach of this second 'school' incorporates the contributions of the first 'school' is clearly an important argument in its favour.

Conditions (2.24) may be interpreted locally in terms of utility functions which are firm-specific, state-dependent and linear in profits given the states, with weights

$$\sum_i \theta_{ij} \Pi^i_s;$$

see row 6 of Table 15.1. The weights

$$\sum_i \theta_{ij} \Pi^i_s$$

correspond to a weighted average of the marginal rates of substitution of shareholders. Gevers (1974, Section II) raises, but discards, the remote possibility that they could correspond to the preferences of a single manager, or of a median voter at a shareholders' meeting.

Under additional assumptions about internal operations in the firms, a global (out-of-equilibrium) interpretation is possible. Thus, if firm j adopted a decision rule of the form

$$\underset{y^j \in Y^j}{\text{Max}} \sum_i \lambda_{ij} \sum_s U^i_s \left[\bar{x}^i_0 + \sum_k (\bar{\theta}_{ik} - \theta_{ik}) p_k - \sum_{k \neq j} \theta_{ik} y^k_0 - \theta_{ij} y^j_0, \right.$$

$$\left. \bar{x}^i_s + \sum_{k \neq j} \theta_{ik} y^k_s + \theta_{ij} y^j_s \right] \tag{2.25}$$

then that firm would maximise globally a specific, state-dependent, *concave* utility function – uniquely defined by the choice of weights λ_{ij}. Note, however, that the resulting decisions need not be individually rational. An alternative internal rule, avoiding this difficulty but involving transfers of resources among shareholders, is analysed by Drèze (1974a, Section V), where a global stability result is proved. Here again, the informational requirements are formidable.

2.5 Utility functions for the firm

If one accepts the view that daily management of a business firm according to shareholders' preferences entails prohibitive transaction costs, the approach of the third 'school', whereby firms are endowed with a utility function of their own, becomes less unappealing.

Two basic criticisms may be advanced against this approach. First, it begs an important question, by failing to derive explicitly the decision criterion of the firm from explicit consideration of the preferences of individual agents, like shareholders, managers or employees. Second, although the axioms of consistent behaviour may be equally cogent for a firm as for an individual, the decisions of the firm are in the nature of group decisions; institutional rules of group decision easily result in violation of the axioms – as illustrated by the Condorcet paradox of majority voting, stressed by Gevers (1974).

I do not know of any compelling answer to these two criticisms, which have for many years prevented me from being a fellow-traveller of this 'school'. Yet, I have progressively become less sensitive to these criticisms, largely on 'operational' grounds.

First, it may be meaningful to regard a firm as an entity with a life of its own. One does observe that firms develop specific 'attitudes' to given problems – like product design, quality control, engineering techniques, personnel management, advertising style and the like. This requires, or reflects managerial efforts and internal training which tend to be self-reinforcing, and may at some stage be identified with 'preferences'. The same is true of risk attitudes, examples could be cited. From an 'operational' viewpoint, it may be unimportant to understand how such preferences are derived from the history of a firm and the initiatives of its individual members; if the preferences are meaningful, theory should recognise the fact.[17]

Second, it is true that a firm is a collection of individuals, whose actions may be mutually conflicting, and whose group decisions may be inconsistent. This problem exists also in the absence of uncertainty, if individual preferences (about work effort for instance) matter, or if transaction costs limit the flow of existing information. Yet most of our theories rest on assumptions of productive efficiency. Admittedly, these assumptions are less restrictive when we know that the basic information exists, even if poorly disseminated, than in the present context. From an 'operational' viewpoint, we would like to know how serious the departures from consistency may be. And we would certainly have less faith in results that are not robust in this respect.

Clearly, further research is needed on such topics as the theory of teams (see Marschak and Radner (1972)) or the principal–agent relationship (see Shavell (1979)). And empirical research on risk preferences of business firms would be very valuable.[18]

It was noted in the previous section that shareholders' preferences automatically reflect the information contained in share prices. There is unfortunately no straightforward argument to the effect that a firm's utility function will automatically reflect the information contained in share prices and expressed shareholders' preferences.[19] Such an argument would of

[17] A kindred justification has been given already by Sondermann (1974, p. 246).

[18] For a new suggestion towards empirical assessment of risk preferences, particularly of business firms, see Drèze (1981).

[19] A partial argument is that managers also own portfolios, and could be revoked by shareholders.

course be very valuable. More solid foundations for the firm's utility function are a prerequisite to such an argument.

2.6 Conclusions

A firm contemplating to start a new line of products may, or again may not, find in share prices on the stock market a clearcut evaluation of the new venture. If the products are genuinely new, or if information about the production plans of existing firms is fragmentary, the share prices will not provide the desired evaluation. These prices may still contain useful partial information, for instance about the advisability of buying up existing production facilities instead of building a new plant from scratch. If the decision to start the new line has major consequences for the firm's future, it may be appropriate to consult shareholders, for instance at an annual meeting; or to consult the 'stock market', for instance by incorporating the new venture separately, and undertaking the investment only if the issue of new shares is fully subscribed.[20] Once a decision to start the new line of products has been reached, many ancillary decisions remain to be taken, concerning production technology, product design, advertising, and so on. These ancillary decisions will be vested with management, and are not apt to be guided by share prices or shareholders' preferences. These decisions involve all sorts of uncertainties. Experience suggests that managers of many firms display a degree of risk aversion in reaching such decisions; otherwise, we could not account for the existence of insurance policies designed specifically to cover business risks, like machine break-downs, ship wreckages, bank hold-ups, and so on.[21]

On these grounds, I feel that theories based on utility functions for business firms do have an operational justification, at least as a first approximation, *if they make room for the information conveyed by share prices and an occasional consultation of shareholders.* The present survey stresses that possibility, by showing how alternative theories of the firm may be reinterpreted in utility terms.

To the extent that information conveyed by share prices or shareholders' preferences is of a local nature,[22] it implies linear, firm-specific weights for

---

[20]This form of consultation of potential shareholders is limited in scope, however, because the announcement that the venture will be discarded if the issue is undersubscribed distorts the information content of shareholders' responses.

[21]The possibility of risk neutrality through the spreading of given risks among a large number of shareholders was mentioned at the end of Section 1.5. It should, however, be noted that liquidity constraints may lead a risk neutral firm to behave as if it were risk averse, with a risk-aversion factor determined by technology; see Böhm (1980, Section 3.1.2) and Drèze and Marchand (1976, Section 5).

[22]To forestall a possible misunderstanding, I should specify that share prices or shareholders' preferences provide a local criterion in the sense that the criterion is associated with a given allocation; at a different allocation, prices and preferences would be different; on the other hand, the production plan of a firm with convex production set is globally optimal, relative to this criterion.

the alternative states. These weights combine a probability assessment and a marginal utility assessment. A clear example is provided by the Capital Asset Pricing Model, where marginal utility is a linear decreasing function of aggregate resources – see (2.21). This example provides a useful yardstick, against which specific conclusions can always be tested. More generally, probability assessments may vary across individuals and firms; this provides a further motivation to adopt firm-specific weights.

If the weights implied by share prices and/or shareholders' preferences were combined with a state-independent concave utility u^j reflecting the firm's risk aversion, an operational model would emerge, yielding the criterion

$$\underset{y^j \in Y^j}{\text{Max}} \left[\sum_s \phi_s^j u^j (y_s^j - y_0^j) \right]. \tag{2.26}$$

The operational merits of such a model would be further enhanced, if one assumed that the function u^j is quadratic, so that dynamic stochastic optimisation be amenable to the powerful theory of linear decision rules, as developed during the early years of the Econometric Institute.[23] With the weights assigned to alternative states behaving like a probability measure,[24] the results of Simon (1956) and Theil (1957, 1958) are directly applicable.

A prospective conclusion from the present survey is that the implications of a formulation like (2.26) seem worth investigating, both theoretically (in a general equilibrium framework) and empirically.

A positive conclusion from the present survey is that general equilibrium models, like those of Radner (1972) and Sondermann (1974), should allow a firm's utility function to depend upon share prices and shareholders' preferences; whereas partial equilibrium models should allow utility functions to be firm-specific and state-dependent.[25] Besides wondering whether such a formulation is general enough, we should know that nothing less general will do.

References

Arrow, K.J. (1953). Le rôle des valeurs boursières pour la répartition la meilleure des risques. In *Econométrie*, Paris: CNRS pp. 41–7. Translated (1964) as The Role of Securities in the Optimal Allocation of Risk-Bearing, *Review of Economic Studies*, 31: 91–6
—(1970). *Essays in the Theory of Risk-Bearing*, Amsterdam: North-Holland

[23] See Simon (1956) and Theil (1957, 1958).
[24] This property is established for prices of contingent commodities by Drèze (1971).
[25] These features may modify the conclusions reached in partial equilibrium models. For instance, the stability theorem for decentralised investment given by Drèze and Sheshinski (1984) does not generalise to the case where firms are risk averse or use different probabilities.

Arrow, K.J. and R.C. Lind (1970). Uncertainty and the Evaluation of Public Investment Decisions. *American Economic Review*, 60: 364–78

Azariadis, C. (1975). Implicit Contracts and Underemployment Equilibria, *Journal of Political Economy*, 83: 1183–202

—(1979). Implicit Contracts and Related Topics: A Survey, *CARESS Working Paper* 79–17, University of Pennsylvania

Baily, M. (1977). On the Theory of Layoffs and Unemployment, *Econometrica*, 45: 1043–63

Baumol, W.J. (1962). On the Theory of Expansion of the Firm, *American Economic Review*, 52: 1078–87

Bogaard, P.J.M. van den and H. Theil (1959). Macrodynamic Policy-Making: An Application of Strategy and Certainty Equivalence Concepts to the Economy of the United States 1933–1936, *Metroeconomica*, 11: 149–67

Bogaard, P.J.M. van den and J. Versluis (1962). The Design of Optimal Committee Decisions, *Statistica Neerlandica*, 16: 3

Böhm, V. (1980). *Preise, Löhne und Beschäftigung*, Tübingen: Mohr

Borch, K. and J. Mossin (eds.) (1968) *Risk and Uncertainty*, London: Macmillan

Debreu, G. (1959). *Theory of Value*, New York: Wiley

Diamond, P.A. (1967). The Role of a Stock Market in a General Equilibrium Model with Technological Uncertainty, *American Economic Review*, 57: 759–76

Drèze, J.H. (1961). Fondements logiques de la probabilité subjective et de l'utilité. In *La Décision*, Paris: CNRS, pp. 73–87 (Translated as Chapter 3 supra.)

—(1971). Market Allocation under Uncertainty, *European Economic Review*, 2: 133–65 (Chapter 6 supra.)

—(1972). A Tâtonnement Process for Investment under Uncertainty in Private Ownership Economies. In G.P. Szegö and K. Shell, (eds.), *Mathematical Methods in Investment and Finance*, Amsterdam; North-Holland, pp. 3–23

—(1974a). Investment under Private Ownership: Optimality, Equilibrium and Stability. In J.H. Drèze (ed.), *Allocation under Uncertainty: Equilibrium and Optimality*, London: Macmillan, pp. 129–66 (Chapter 14 supra.)

—(ed.) (1974b). *Allocation under Uncertainty: Equilibrium and Optimality*, London: Macmillan

—(1976). Some Theory of Labour Management and Participation, *Econometrica*, 44: 1125–39 (Chapter 18 infra.)

—(1979). Human Capital and Risk-Bearing, *The Geneva Papers on Risk and Insurance*, 12: 5–22 (Chapter 17 infra.)

—(1980). Demand Estimation, Risk Aversion and Sticky Prices, *Economics Letters*, 4: 1–6 (Chapter 7 supra.)

—(1981). Inferring Risk Tolerance from Deductibles in Insurance Contracts, *The Geneva Papers on Risk and Insurance*, 20: 48–52 (Chapter 5 supra.)

Drèze, J.H. and K. Hagen (1978). Choice of Product Quality: Equilibrium and Efficiency, *Econometrica*, 46: 493–513

Drèze, J.H. and M. Marchand (1976). Pricing, Spending and Gambling Rules for Non-profit Organisations. In R.E. Grieson (ed.), *Public and Urban Economics, Essays in Honor of William S. Vickrey*, Lexington, MA: Heath and Co., pp. 59–89 (Partim: Chapter 9 infra.)

Drèze, J.H. and E. Sheshinksi (1984). On Industry Equilibrium under Uncertainty, *The Journal of Economic Theory*, 33(1): 88–97 (Chapter 13 supra.)

Ekern, S. and R. Wilson (1974). On the Theory of the Firm in an Economy with Incomplete Markets, *Bell Journal of Economics and Management Science*, 5: 171–80

Gevers, L. (1974). Competitive Equilibrium of the Stock Exchange and Pareto Efficiency. In J.H. Drèze (ed.), *Allocation under Uncertainty: Equilibrium and Optimality*, London: Macmillan, pp. 167–91

Gordon, D.F. (1974). A Neo-Classical Theory of Keynesian Unemployment, *Economic Inquiry*, 12: 431–59

Grossman, S.J. and O.D. Hart (1979). A Theory of Competitive Equilibrium in Stock Market Economies, *Econometrica*, 47: 293–330

Grossman, S.J. and J.E. Stiglitz (1980). Stockholder Unanimity in Making Production and Financial Decisions, *The Quarterly Journal of Economics*, 94: 543–66

Guesnerie, R. and J.-Y. Jaffray (1974). Optimality of Equilibrium of Plans, Prices and Price Expectations. In J.H. Drèze (ed.), *Allocation under Uncertainty: Equilibrium and Optimality*, London: Macmillan, pp. 71–86

Hart, O.D. (1979). On Shareholder Unanimity in Large Stock Market Economies, *Econometrica*, 47: 1057–83

Hirshleifer, J. and J.G. Riley (1979). The Analytics of Uncertainty and Information: An Expository Survey, *Journal of Economic Literature*, 17: 1375–421

Holmström, B. (1981). Equilibrium Long-term Labor Contracts, DP 414, The Centre for Mathematical Studies in Economics and Management Science, Northwestern University

Jensen, M.C. and W.M. Meckling (1979). Rights and Production Functions: An Application to Labor-Managed Firms and Codetermination, *Journal of Business*, 52: 469–506

Leland, H. (1972). Theory of the Firm Facing Random Demand, *American Economic Review*, 62: 278–91

—(1974). Production Theory and the Stock Market, *The Bell Journal of Economics and Management Science*, 5: 125–44

Malinvaud, E. (1972). The Allocation of Individual Risks in Large Markets, *The Journal of Economic Theory*, 4: 312–28. Reprinted in J.H. Drèze (ed.), *Allocation under Uncertainty: Equilibrium and Optimality*, London: Macmillan, pp. 110–25

Marris, R. (1963). A Model of the Managerial Enterprise, *Quarterly Journal of Economics*, 72: 185–209

Marschak, J. and R. Radner (1972). *Economic Theory of Teams*, New Haven: Yale University Press

Milne, F. and D. Starrett (1981). Socially Optimal Investment Rules in the Presence of Incomplete Markets and Other Second Best Distortions, Technical Report no. 345, Institute for Mathematical Studies in the Social Sciences, Stanford, California

Modigliani, F. and M.H. Miller (1958). The Cost of Capital, Corporation Finance and the Theory of Investment, *American Economic Review*, 48: 261–97

Modigliani, F. and G.A. Pogue (1974). An Introduction to Risk and Return, *Financial Analysts Journal*, March: 68–80; April: 69–86

Mossin, J. (1977). *The Economic Efficiency of Financial Markets*, Lexington, MA: Heath and Co.

Neumann, J. von and O. Morgenstern (1944). *Theory of Games and Economic Behavior*, Princeton: Princeton University Press

Penrose, E.T. (1959). *The Theory of the Growth of the Firm*, New York: Wiley

Radner, R. (1968). Competitive Equilibrium under Uncertainty, *Econometrica*, 36: 31–58

—(1972). Existence of Equilibrium of Plans, Prices and Price Expectations in a

Sequence of Markets, *Econometrica*, 40: 289–303

—(1974). A note on Unanimity of Stockholders' Preferences among Alternative Production Plans, *The Bell Journal of Economics and Management Science*, 5: 181–6

—(1980). Equilibrium under Uncertainty. In K.J. Arrow and M.D. Intriligator (eds.), *Handbook of Mathematical Economics*, 2, Amsterdam: North-Holland, Ch. 20

Ramsey, F.P. (1931). Truth and Probability. In *The Foundations of Mathematics and Other Logical Essays*, London: Routledge and Kegan, pp. 156–98

Sandmo, A. (1971). On the Theory of the Competitive Firm under Price Uncertainty, *American Economic Review*, 61: 65–73

—(1972). Discount Rates for Public Investment under Uncertainty, *International Economic Review*, 13, 287–302. Reprinted in J.H. Drèze (ed.), *Allocation under Uncertainty: Equilibrium and Optimality*, London: Macmillan, pp. 192–210

Savage, L.J. (1954). *The Foundations of Statistics*, New York: Wiley

Shafer, W. and H. Sonnenschein (1975). Equilibrium in Abstract Economies without Ordered Preferences, *Journal of Mathematical Economics*, 2: 345–8.

Shavell, S. (1979). Risk Sharing and Incentives in the Principal and Agent Relationship, *The Bell Journal of Economics*, 10: 55–73

Simon, H.A. (1956). Dynamic Programming under Uncertainty with a Quadratic Criterion Function, *Econometrica*, 24: 74–81

Sondermann, D. (1974). Temporary Competitive Equilibrium under Uncertainty. In J.H. Drèze (ed.), *Allocation under Uncertainty: Equilibrium and Optimality*, London: Macmillan, pp. 229–53

Steinherr, A. (1977). On the Efficiency of Profit Sharing and Labor Participation in Management, *The Bell Journal of Economics*, 8: 543–55

Stiglitz, J. (1972). On the Optimality of the Stock Market Allocation of Investment, *The Quarterly Journal of Economics*, 86: 25–60

Theil, H. (1957). A Note on Certainty Equivalence in Dynamic Planning, *Econometrica*, 25: 346–9

—(1958). *Economic Forecasts and Policy*, Amsterdam: North-Holland

Tobin, J. (1980). *Asset Accumulation and Economic Activity*, Oxford: Blackwell

Williamson, O. (1964). *The Economics of Discretionary Behavior: Managerial Objectives in a Theory of the Firm*, Englewood Cliffs: Prentice Hall

16 (Uncertainty and) the firm in general equilibrium theory*

The firm fits into general equilibrium theory as a balloon fits into an envelope: flattened out! Try with a blown-up balloon: the envelope may tear, or fly away: at best, it will be hard to seal and impossible to mail.... Instead, burst the balloon flat, and everything becomes easy. Similarly with the firm and general equilibrium – though the analogy requires a word of explanation.

General equilibrium theory – GET for short – has two attributes. First, it defines *clearly* the boundary between economic analysis and the exogenous primitive data or assumptions from which it proceeds; that is, it defines a precise, self-contained 'model'. Second, it verifies the overall *consistency* of the economic analysis. A natural step in verifying overall consistency is to exhibit sufficient conditions for the *existence* of the proposed solutions, or 'equilibria'. This step is usually amenable to mathematical reasoning.

Still, I do not mean to *identify* general equilibrium theory with that potent cocktail of economics and mathematics known as mathematical economics. (To some, mathematical economics is merely a pleonasm; to others, it is a branch of mathematical pornography; the word cocktail, with its element of pornographic pleonasm, is purposely neutral.) Work in mathematical economics lacking the GET–attributes is abundant. Conversely, let me remind you of our friend Harry Johnson: he was a beautiful member of our GET-set, for he was skilful at integrating partial

*Text of the Harry Johnson Lecture, Royal Economic Society-Association of University Teachers of Economics Meeting, Bath, April 1984. I am grateful to H. Polemarchakis and H. Tulkens for helpful comments.

contributions into consistent general pictures; yet he needed little algebra, because he was a master at the declining art of expressing complex rigorous arguments in literate English.

The two attributes of General Equilibrium Theory stand out, for instance, in the classic work *Theory of Value* – hereafter referred to as TV (not inappropriately, given the recent successes of its author as a TV-star). In *Theory of Value*, an 'economy' is defined by a set of commodities; a set of consumers, individually described by their needs and abilities (consumption sets), their initial assets, and their tastes (preferences); and a set of producers of firms, individually described by their technological possibilities (production sets). These are the primitive data, which the economist treats as exogenous and does not seek to explain. Basically, they correspond to the *opportunities* and *motivations* of all agents – a structure which is even clearer in the 'abstract economies' approach; see Shafer and Sonnenschein (1975).

The point I wish to emphasise is that, in *Theory of Value* and related works, a firm is described *only* and *fully* by its production set, or technology; it has no idiosyncratic behavioural attributes whatever. The common motivation or decision criterion of all firms, namely *profit maximisation at given prices*, reduces management to profit calculations and comparisons. The arithmetic may be laborious – still, no behavioural identity, or managerial initiative is involved. The TV-firm is an anonymous computer, it has the behavioural depth of a flattened out balloon, it is the negation of managerial skill and management education. (I once read about 'the doubtless mythical review of *Lady Chatterley's Lover* in *Country Life* where the writer supposedly complained that much interesting material about being a gamekeeper was constantly interrupted by irrelevant personal experience' (Nixon, 1982). The TV-firm is like a platonic gamekeeper, endowed with a technology, but not susceptible of personal motivation and experience.)

This representation has been challenged, and various partial equilibrium contributions aim at extending it. Most notable among these is the Behavioural Theory of the Firm of Simon (1979), Cyert and March (1963). I shall not survey these contributions, but rather concentrate on the one area where formal extension is deliberately sought in a general equilibrium framework, namely uncertainty with incomplete markets. (It is also the one area with which I have some familiarity.)

Uncertainty is an intimate dimension of our daily lives. For some, it is the zest of life. Without uncertainty, the distinction between the present and the future is blurred; there are no surprises and no anticipations, hence no thrills; there is no scope for achievement, hence no rewards; and love, which always entails risks as well as the joy of discovery, loses its sharp edge. Yet, for others, uncertainty is the curse of life. It is so far those who feel threatened with loss of life or individual freedom, who have no assured shelter or subsistence, who lack job security and fear unemployment.

Uncertainty is thus an intimate dimension of economics as well. Decisions of households, firms or policy makers seldom entail fully deterministic consequences; uncertainty is 'generic'. (Still, many titles in economics include the precision 'under uncertainty', not even parenthetical; whereas it should be natural to include the warning 'under certainty', when appropriate.)

Uncertainty has been introduced formally into the model of *Theory of Value* by recognising that the primitive data or *environment* – in particular resources, tastes and technology – are not known and given, but are part of the unfolding history of the world. As of any future date, the world is apt to find itself in any one of several alternative, mutually exclusive *states* – each of which corresponds, among other things, to a history up to that date of resources, tastes and technology. Recognising that 'the environment is state-dependent' draws a credible boundary between the exogenous sources of uncertainty and economic analysis; we should be grateful to Savage (1953, 1954) and Arrow (1953) in particular for introducing that approach, which is more satisfactory than earlier formulations in terms of probability distributions of economic variables (like prices or incomes).

This is a model of 'Technological Uncertainty'. Recently economists have tackled the more subtle problem of 'Information', about which you will hear tomorrow from the horse's mouth, if I may refer colloquially to my thoroughbred friend of a younger generation (Stiglitz, 1984). (See also Hirshleifer and Riley (1979) who elaborate on the distinction, and relation, between uncertainty and information.)

A model where the environment is state-dependent is amenable to the same formal analysis as a model where the environment is given, if one is willing to assume the existence of a complete set of insurance markets, one for each physical commodity contingent on each state of the environment. In that case, business decisions reduce again to arithmetic, because each production plan has a well-defined present value on the insurance markets. In particular, a firm contemplating a new investment could simultaneously protect itself against demand uncertainties by selling its output at each date on futures market, and against supply uncertainties by purchasing insurance against output deficiencies, whether they be due to machine breakdowns, low labour productivity or mismanagement.

This is clearly an excessive idealisation. Existing insurance opportunities are limited by transaction costs, moral hazard, adverse selection and the like.[1] Incomplete markets are the rule, and firms come to life as they face the non-insurable uncertainties of history in the making. At once, they become concerned with forecasting and risk taking, which involve more than arithmetic (fortunately, say the econometricians and decision theorists). But as firms come to life, they fit less easily into the envelope of general

---

[1] Note also that the set of potential buyers on a long-term futures market may include as yet unborn consumers... .

equilibrium theory: there is today no formal description of 'live' firms which is both generally accepted and suitable for the purposes of general equilibrium theory.

This is unfortunate, because it hampers the development of general equilibrium theory, in all the directions where business uncertainties are essential; and these include investing, pricing, hiring, colluding, etc.,....At the same time, progress seems at hand, to the extent that most of the descriptions which have been used can be suitably reconciled and integrated, as I hope to show now.

1 Stock market economies and equilibria

A simple model has proved very useful to clarify these issues, namely the temporary general equilibrium model of a stock-market economy, introduced by Diamond (1967) in the spirit of Arrow's (1953) initial suggestion. (This is a streamlined model, as could be expected. Indeed, models basically play the same role in economics as in fashion: they provide an articulated frame on which to show off your material to advantage...; a useful role, but fraught with the dangers that the designer may get carried away by his personal inclination for the model, while the customers may forget that the model is more streamlined than reality.)

There are two periods, the present (0) and the future. There are finitely many (S) possible states, indexed $s = 1, \ldots, S$. The true state is unknown in the present, but will be known in the future. There is a given set J of firms, indexed $j = 1, \ldots, J$. A production plan for a firm j is an $(S + 1)$-dimensional vector $\mathbf{y}^j = (y_0^j, y_1^j, \ldots, y_S^j)$, consisting of an input level y_0^j in the present and a vector of state-dependent outputs $y_1^j, \ldots, y_S^j$ in the future. The set of technologically feasible production plans is a given convex set Y^j in $R_- \times R_+^S$. The problem of the firm is to choose a production plan $\mathbf{y}^j$ in Y^j.

There are no markets for contingent claims. But there is a stock market, where shares of stock in the various firms are traded at prices $\mathbf{p} = (p_1, \ldots, p_J)$. The price p_j is the market value of firm j, i.e. the price of a 100 per cent share of that firm.

There is a given set I of consumers, indexed $i = 1, \ldots, I$. A consumption plan for consumer i is an $(S + 1)$-dimensional vector $\mathbf{x}^i = (x_0^i, x_1^i, \ldots, x_S^i)$ in R_+^{S+1}, specifying a current consumption level x_0^i and a future consumption level x_s^i in state s, $s = 1, \ldots, S$. Consumer i has well-defined, continuous, convex, monotone preferences over consumption plans. These preferences reflect simultaneously time preferences, probability beliefs, attitudes to risk and interactions between states and consumption. They are represented by the utility function $u^i(x_0^i, x_1^i, \ldots, x_S^i)$, here assumed differentiable for convenience. (See, e.g. Hirshleifer (1966) or Drèze (1982) for details.)

Also, each consumer i has an initial endowment of consumption goods $\boldsymbol{\omega}^i = (\omega_0^i, \omega_1^i, \ldots, \omega_S^i)$ in R_+^{S+1}, and of shares of stock in the firms $\boldsymbol{\theta}^i = (\bar{\theta}^{i1}, \ldots, \bar{\theta}^{iJ})$, where $\bar{\theta}^{ij} \geq 0$ for all i, j and $\sum_i \bar{\theta}^{ij} = 1$ for all j.

With no markets for contingent claims, the only possibility for consumers to transfer resources between the present and the future, or between different states in the future, is to modify their initial portfolios of shares by trading on the stock market. These transactions, leading to the new portfolio $\theta^i = (\theta^{i1}, \ldots, \theta^{iJ})$ in R_+^J, determine the final consumption levels[2]

$$x_0^i = \omega_0^i + \sum_j p_j(\bar{\theta}^{ij} - \theta^{ij}) + \sum_j \theta^{ij} y_0^j \geq 0; \tag{1.1}$$

$$x_s^i = \omega_s^i + \sum_j \theta^{ij} y_s^j, \quad s = 1, \ldots, S. \tag{1.2}$$

Condition (1.1) is a budget constraint, stating that current consumption is equal to the value of initial resources,

$$\omega_0^i + \sum_j p_j \bar{\theta}^{ij},$$

minus the cost of the final portfolio,

$$\sum_j p_j \theta^{ij},$$

and i's share of the initial dividends (or fund raising) in the firms where he is a shareholder. Condition (1.2) states that future consumption is the sum of initial resources ω_s^i and the dividends accruing to the portfolio,

$$\sum_j \theta^{ij} y_s^j.$$

The problem of consumer i is to choose the portfolio θ^i that maximises $u^i(x_0^i, x_1^i, \ldots, x_S^i)$ subject to the current budget constraint $(x_0^i \geq 0)$, with $\mathbf{x}^i$ defined by (1.1)–(1.2).[3]

An *equilibrium of the stock-market economy* consists of a price vector $\mathbf{p}$, a set of feasible portfolios $(\theta^i)_{i \in I}$ and a set of feasible production plans $(\mathbf{y}^j)_{j \in J}$, such that:

(i)   the stock market clears: for all j, $\sum_i \theta^{ij} = 1$;
(ii)   each consumer is in equilibrium, given the prices $\mathbf{p}$ and the production plans $(\mathbf{y}^j)$: θ^i maximises $u^i(\mathbf{x}^i)$ subject to (1.1) and (1.2);
(iii)   each firm is in equilibrium: $\mathbf{y}^j$ is the best production plan in Y^j – *in a sense that remains to be defined*.

When a business firm is unable to sell its production plan on insurance markets, it does not have well-defined profits; rather, a production plan induces a state-distribution of gross profits, $(y_1^j, \ldots, y_S^j)$ in the simple model under review. The question then arises: *How does a firm choose among alternative state-distributions of profit?* (For instance, how did McGraw Hill decide that it was worth their while to acquire DRI for a hundred

---

[2] In addition, $1 \geq \theta^{ij} \geq 0$ must hold for each j; no inequality constraint is stated on x_s^i, $s = 1, \ldots, S$, because ω_s^i and y_s^j (all j) are non-negative by assumption.

[3] In view of the equalities (1.1)–(1.2), consumption is uniquely determined by the portfolio choice, for given production plans of the firms.

million dollars – presumably without the benefit of DRI model simulations to guide the decision? How did General Motors recently decide how much to bid for Jaguar? How will A.T. and T. decide how much to bid for the British Post Office, when it is put up for sale? How did that French firm specialising in industrial conditioning and packaging decide to diversify into services by opening a chain of funeral parlours?)

The question arises because firms, unlike consumers, are not human beings whose preferences could be introduced as primitive data. Economists have come to accept that a person's attitude towards risks is part of that person's identity, together with her attitude towards tea bags, rock music or central heating. But not so with business firms, which have no personal tastes for what they produce, and no visceral reactions to uncertainty.[4]

Thus, risk preferences belong with human agents. In Diamond's model, business profits ultimately accrue to consumers as dividends (or capital gains). The risk preferences of consumers manifest themselves through portfolio choices, and are reflected in stock prices. In turn, the prices of shares on the stock market act as a partial substitute for insurance markets, in assigning a well-defined aggregate value to the production plan of each firm. This raises the more specific question: *Do the preferences of shareholders, and the prices of shares on the stock market, influence the choices of firms among alternative state distributions of profits?*

These questions have occupied theorists of uncertainty, and of finance, over the past 15 years. In a survey two years ago, published in a book with the unlikely title *Current Developments in the Interface* (Drèze, 1982) and reprinted in a volume of essays on *Economic Decisions under Uncertainty* (Drèze, 1986a), I found it helpful to classify their contributions in three 'nested' groups, as follows. (See also Grossman and Stiglitz (1980) and Milne and Starrett (1981).)

2 Decision criteria for business firms

It was noted above that the stock market assigns a well-defined aggregate value to the production plan of a firm. This value is often referred to as 'the market value of the firm'. By analogy with financial decisions, production decisions are sometimes presented (in textbooks or the oral tradition) as *maximising the market value of the firm*. This is the first group or approach.

In order for this criterion to be operational, a firm should know whether a given modification to its production plan will increase or decrease market value. If that information is to be found in stock-market prices, there must exist some portfolio of shares, whose net value is indicative of the incremental value of the proposed modification. Special assumptions are

[4]This issue does not arise under complete markets because each production plan has a well-defined insurance value, so that profit maximisation is a well-defined universal criterion.

needed to prove the existence of market portfolios conveying the necessary information, for all possible modifications of a firm's plan. The assumptions underlying the *Capital Asset Pricing Model* are sufficient – but highly restrictive; the more general assumptions underlying the *Arbitrage Pricing Model* are not sufficient. Diamond's assumption of multiplicative uncertainty, which corresponds to the *Risk Classes* of Modigliani and Miller (1958), is also sufficient but equally restrictive. Both approaches are special cases of the so-called *Spanning Theory*, which applies when the production set of each firm is contained in a space spanned by the production plans of existing firms.[5]

That special, restrictive assumptions are needed, to render the market value criterion operational, should not surprise us. Indeed, to say that the market value is an operational criterion is to say that business management is again a matter of arithmetic, in contradiction to the observation that firms are directly concerned with forecasting and risk taking.

Recognising that stock prices (market values) do not always convey the information needed to guide production and investment decisions, a second group of theorists (namely, Grossman and Hart (1979) and Drèze (1947b)) have investigated the possibility that stockholders' preferences may guide these decisions directly. (When that approach is presented to a Business School audience, it is typically greeted with sneers or laughter; fortunately, 'le ridicule ne tue pas'.)

When spanning prevails, all consumers holding portfolios which are optimal from the viewpoint of their consumption preferences (given the production plans of the firms and the stock-market prices) will unanimously approve production decisions maximising market value. *In the absence of spanning*, there is room for disagreement – for example between shareholders favouring more venturesome decisions, and those favouring more conservative decisions. It seems natural to require that business firms should at least respect *unanimous* wishes of their shareholders.

In Diamond's model, shareholder i prefers production plan $\hat{\mathbf{y}}^j$ over $\mathbf{y}^j$ if and only if his resulting consumption has higher utility, that is if and only if[6]

$$u^i[\mathbf{x}^i + \theta^{ij}(\hat{\mathbf{y}}^j - \mathbf{y}^j)] > u^i(\mathbf{x}^i). \tag{1.3}$$

This leads to a criterion of *Nash–Pareto-optimality*: the production plan $\mathbf{y}^j$ is best for firm j, given its ownership $\boldsymbol{\theta}^j = (\theta^{1j}, \dots, \theta^{Ij})$, if there does not exist an alternative plan $\hat{\mathbf{y}}^j$ in Y^j preferred to $\mathbf{y}^j$ by all shareholders, that is, by all consumers i with $\theta^{ij} > 0$ (more generally, preferred by some shareholders and deemed indifferent by the remaining ones).

[5]Technically, the Capital Asset Pricing Model has the 'spanning property' in the space of the two 'characteristics' (namely, mean and variance) in terms of which preferences can be represented. See Drèze and Hagen (1978) for details.

[6]The inequality (1.3) follows from substituting $\hat{\mathbf{y}}^j$ for $\mathbf{y}^j$ in (1.1)–(1.2), keeping all other right-hand variables unchanged.

The Pareto aspect (for the owners of a given firm) is clear; the Nash aspect comes from the feature that the portfolios of consumers, and the production plans of other firms, are treated as given and fixed in the definition. As a consequence, Nash–Pareto-optimality does not entail full Pareto-optimality: it could be that simultaneous changes in the production decisions of several firms, or simultaneous changes in portfolios and in production decisions, would lead to Pareto-superior allocations; examples are given by Drèze (1974b), where it is shown that the set of feasible allocations in this economy is in general *not* convex.

The Nash–Pareto criterion just defined has two attractive features. First, it preserves the consistency of decentralised decisions. As we shall see below, under standard (TV) assumptions, *there exist stock prices, portfolios and production plans defining an equilibrium of the stock-market economy, where the production plan of each firm is a Nash–Pareto-optimum for its own* shareholders.

Second, the Nash–Pareto criterion is consistent with market value maximisation, under either complete or partial spanning. That is, whenever information contained in stock prices reveals that a potential modification of firm *j*'s production plan would increase market value, there will be unanimous approval of the modification by the shareholders. This also implies that formal elicitation of shareholders' preferences will be superfluous, in that case.

On the other hand, the Nash–Pareto criterion has two drawbacks. First, it only establishes a very partial ordering among production decisions, leaving many issues undecided. Because most decision situations call for definite choices, the criterion must be supplemented by a specification of how undecided issues are resolved. Second, consultation of shareholders is unwieldy, time consuming and costly. The relevance of this criterion thus seems limited to major, infrequent decisions (for instance, fixed investment financed by equity issues).

These two drawbacks explain why many authors assume outright the existence of a *Utility Function of the Firm*, defined *exogenously* over state-distributions of profits. That assumption appears in numerous partial equilibrium analyses, and in the general equilibrium work of Radner (1972, 1980) and Sondermann (1974) among others. It is justified by the fact that firms have to decide on many issues, for which stock prices are uninformative and consultation of shareholders impossible, but where consistent decisions remain a goal.

The approach of this third group has been criticised on the already mentioned grounds that firms have no physical identity in which risk preferences could be rooted. Also, provision should be made for the utility function of a firm to reflect its ownership structure, the resulting share-holders' preferences and/or the information contained in stock prices, when appropriate; that is, provision should be made for integrating the three approaches.

Let me quote the conclusions of my 1982 survey:

> A firm contemplating to start a new line of products may, or
> again may not, find in share prices on the stock market a
> clearcut evaluation of the new venture. If the products are
> genuinely new, or if information about the production plans of
> existing firms is fragmentary, the share prices will not provide
> the desired evaluation. These prices may still contain useful
> partial information, for instance about the advisability of
> buying up existing production facilities instead of building a
> new plant from scratch. If the decision to start the new line has
> major consequences for the firm's future, it may be appropriate
> to consult shareholders, for instance at an annual meeting; or
> to consult 'the stock market', for instance by incorporating the
> new venture separately, and undertaking the investment only if
> the issue of new shares is fully subscribed.[7] Once a decision to
> start the new line of products has been reached, many ancillary
> decisions remain to be taken, concerning production
> technology, product design, advertising, and so on. These
> ancillary decisions will be vested with management, and are
> not apt to be guided by share prices or shareholders'
> preferences. These decisions involve all sorts of uncertainties.
> Experience suggests that managers of many firms display a
> degree of risk aversion in reaching such decisions; otherwise,
> we could not account for the existence of insurance policies
> designed specifically to cover business risks, like machine
> breakdowns, ship wreckages, bank hold-ups, and so on.[8]
> On these grounds, I feel that theories based on utility functions
> for business firms do have an operational justification, at least
> as a first approximation, *if they make room for the information
> conveyed by share prices and an occasional consultation of
> shareholders.* (Drèze, 1982, p. 44)

Leland (1978) has suggested that the manager of a firm could be himself a
shareholder. If the utility of the firm is simply the utility of the manager,
then maximisation of that utility implies Pareto-optimality for the
shareholders, since the manager is one of them. And we have seen that
Pareto-optimality for the shareholders entails consistency with market

---

[7]This form of consultation of potential shareholders is limited in scope, however, because the
announcement that the venture will be discarded if the issue is undersubscribed distorts the
information content of shareholders' responses.

[8]The possibility of risk neutrality through the spreading of given risks among a large number
of shareholders was mentioned at the end of Section 1.5 (Drèze, 1982). It should however be
noted that liquidity constraints may lead a risk neutral firm to behave as if it were risk averse,
with a risk-aversion factor determined by technology; see Böhm (1980, Section 3.1.2) or Drèze
and Marchand (1976, Section 5).

value maximisation, to the extent that it is defined.[9] In this way the three approaches become 'nested', and the preferences of a single individual – the manager – define a utility function for the firm, which meets the requirements of the three approaches just reviewed.

There remain problems, however. First, the identity of the manager is exogenously given, independently of the ownership structure of the firm. Thus a majority of shareholders could not appoint its own manager. Second, it is assumed that the manager is a shareholder of the firm, without explicit reference to his portfolio choices. In particular, diversification between the risks on labour income and on property income might discourage the manager from owning stock in his own firm. Third, although it is true that a manager shareholder maximising his own utility brings about Nash–Pareto-optimality, it may still be the case that his preferences are quite at variance with those of a majority of shareholders. For instance, he could be a very competent manager, while shunning risks in so far as his own finances are concerned. It would then be natural for him to consult shareholders on decisions involving major uncertainties, while holding no stock and working for a fixed salary. Should he fail to do so, it would be natural for the shareholders to impose a policy line, or to replace him.

These shortcomings point to the desirability of seeking to integrate the three approaches in a way which brings more explicitly to the foreground the interaction between the portfolio choices of consumers, the decision criteria of the firms and the practice of management.

3 Control and delegation

Recently, I have followed another avenue towards integrating the three approaches to decision criteria for the firms. It is in a sense more institutional, starting as it does from a naïve observation of some legal and administrative aspects of business management. This alternative avenue was developed in the 1983 Jahnsson Lectures, to be published under the title *Labour Management and Labour Contracts* (Drèze, 1986b). It may be summarised as follows.

Modern corporations are typically organised under legal systems which vest the ultimate authority with shareholders, reaching majority decisions at general meetings (with the possibility of qualified majorities for special decisions, like modifications to the company's statute). Because general meetings of shareholders are unwieldy, provision is made for partial delegation of authority to a Board of Directors, comprising a small number of members, elected by the shareholders. The Board typically decides about its own *modus operandi*. Each year, the Board requests from the general meeting of shareholders endorsement of its decisions. Because Directors

[9]This consistency will also obtain if the firm owns a portfolio of shares, as in the model of Sondermann (1974).

could not conveniently meet every day, the Board in turn delegates some authority to managers, under the responsibility of one or more members of the Board (the President, or Deputy Directors,...).

It is somewhat surprising, but definitely intriguing, that this mode of organisation can easily be fitted into the abstract formalism of general equilibrium theory (under an assumption which does not seem unduly restrictive), and covers earlier approaches as special cases.

To start with a simple example, suppose that a corporation has been formed, with the provision that the Board of Directors will consist of the four largest shareholders, and that decisions (of some significance) must be approved by all the directors and by a majority of shareholders. An abstract version of this example runs as follows.

Given the ownership of firm j, as defined by the I-tuple of ownership fractions $\theta^j = (\theta^{1j}, \ldots, \theta^{ij}, \ldots, \theta^{Ij})$ resulting from the portfolio choices of the consumers, there exists for firm j a *Control Group* (the Board of Directors), say $I^j(\theta^j)$, a subset of the shareholders (a subset of $\{1, \ldots, i, \ldots, I\}$, with $\theta^{ij} > 0$ for each i in the subset). For two feasible production plans of firm j, say $\mathbf{y}^j$ and $\hat{\mathbf{y}}^j$ in Y^j, we shall say that $\mathbf{y}^j$ is *preferred to $\hat{\mathbf{y}}^j$ by firm j if $\mathbf{y}^j$ is preferred to $\hat{\mathbf{y}}^j$ by all the members of the control group and by some set $\hat{I}^j(\theta^j)$ of shareholders' representing more than fifty percent of the ownership;*[10] more concisely, $\mathbf{y}^j$ is preferred to $\hat{\mathbf{y}}^j$ by firm j (given θ^j) if it is preferred by *some majority group* (of shareholders) *including $I^j(\theta^j)$*. (An important aspect of the definition is that the majority deciding to choose $\mathbf{y}^j$ over $\hat{\mathbf{y}}^j$ may be different from the majority choosing $\mathbf{y}^j$ over some third alternative $\tilde{\mathbf{y}}^j$ – but all members of the same control group must in either case belong to the decisive majority.)

This stipulation is sufficient to give content to condition (iii) in the definition of an equilibrium of the stock-market economy, namely:

(iii′) $\mathbf{y}^j$ is a best production plan in Y^j, i.e. there does not exist an alternative plan $\hat{\mathbf{y}}^j$ and a majority group of shareholders $\hat{I}^j(\theta^j)$ including the control group $I^j(\theta^j)$, such that $\hat{\mathbf{y}}^j$ is preferred to $\mathbf{y}^j$ by all members of $\hat{I}^j(\theta^j)$.[11]

I now submit that the precise rules determining who belongs to the control group (who becomes a Director), *as a function of the ownership of the firm*, may properly be treated as an exogenous primitive datum by the general equilibrium theorist. His problem is only to verify whether or not the rules are consistent, meaning here conducive to existence of an equilibrium, under reasonable assumptions about the other primitive data of the economy.

---

[10]The simple majority rule

$$\sum_{i \in \hat{I}^j(\theta^j)} \theta^{ij} > 0.5$$

could be replaced by any other majority rule.

[11]In applying this definition, it is understood as before that shareholder i prefers $\hat{\mathbf{y}}^j$ to $\mathbf{y}^j$ if and only if he prefers the resulting consumption plan, i.e. if and only if $u^i(\mathbf{x}^i + \theta^{ij}\hat{\mathbf{y}}^j - \theta^{ij}\mathbf{y}^j) > u^i(\mathbf{x}^i)$.

To elucidate the existence issue, let me begin with a simple intermediate proposition. Ignoring momentarily the dependence of the control group on the ownership of the firm, I shall consider first the case where for each firm the control group is given a priori (as was the case for the manager, in the work of Leland reviewed in Section 2 above), and members of the control group always own a positive share of the firm.

Proposition 3.1: Assume that for each *j*, the control group is given a priori; then, under standard (TV) assumptions, there exists an equilibrium for the stock-market economy.

This proposition, proved in the manuscript of the 1983 Jahnsson Lectures, is a new existence result, not covered by those of Drèze (1974b) or Grossman and Hart (1979) which ignore majority approval but require transfers among shareholders of a kind not frequently encountered (or imaginable, for that matter) in the financial world.

It is perhaps not a surprising result, given that decisions within each firm are reached by majority voting with a fixed set of veto players. It is well known that existence of veto players eliminates the Condorcet paradox of voting, a paradox stressed in our context by Gevers (1974). Majority voting with veto leads to a decision criterion for each firm which is a partial ordering, free of intransitivities (though not necessarily transitive), and consistent (where defined) with the preferences of veto players. These properties, combined with standard TV assumptions, are sufficient to prove existence. The technical argument follows the approach of Shafer and Sonnenschein (1975) to 'Equilibrium in Abstract Economies Without Ordered Preferences'.

Of course, it is not congruent with general equilibrium methodology to assume that the control group is given a priori, independently of the ownership of the firm. As repeatedly stressed before, we would like the control group to reflect ownership (as in my example of a Board of Directors comprising the four leading shareholders). To handle this more general case, two assumptions are needed – a minor technical one, and a major institutional one.

The technical assumption (hereafter, Assumption B) is meant to preclude indeterminacies arising if a firm becomes inactive, and nobody cares to hold its stock. We still need to verify that inactivity is a 'best' plan for that firm. The easiest way of covering that loophole consists in assuming that *some* initial shareholders of the firm never divest themselves completely of their stock. A more satisfactory (weaker) assumption, which is also more demanding technically, only requires that somebody always be prepared to hold the stock *at a zero price*.

The important assumption is the institutional one, which imposes a degree of continuity in the exogenous rule determining how changes in ownership affect the composition of the control group. Here are three equivalent statements of the proposed assumption, couched in increasingly abstract terms.[12]

Assumption A.1: Let $I^j(\theta^j)$ be the control group associated with the ownership vector θ^j; for all $\hat{\theta}^j$ sufficiently close to θ^j, $I^j(\hat{\theta}^j)$ is included in $I^j(\theta^j)$.

Assumption A.2: For all i, the set of ownership vectors θ^j such that consumer i belongs to $I^j(\theta^j)$ is closed.

Assumption A.3: The correspondence I^j which associates with every ownership vector θ^j a control group $I^j(\theta^j)$ is upper semi-continuous in the discrete topology.

These three statements are formally equivalent and will be referred to as Assumption A. A general existence result is:

Theorem 3.1: Under standard (TV) assumptions and assumptions A, B, there exists an equilibrium for the stock-market economy.

In this proposition, control groups reflect ownership, and the decisions of the firms reflect ownership and control. This is a genuine 'general equilibrium' result. It rests on reasonable assumptions, and covers most previous results as special cases (as the reader can easily verify).[13]

Before stating further generalisations, a word of comment about assumption A is in order. Perhaps the more transparent statement is A.2, which says: if you belong to the Board of Directors for every ownership vector in a sequence converging to θ^j, then you also belong for θ^j itself. For example, if you belong to the Board provided you own *more than* 5 per cent of the shares, you should also belong if you own *exactly* 5 per cent. This requirement is not vacuous – but it does not seem unduly restrictive either; and it is interesting to discover that it is consistent with decentralised portfolio choices, and decentralised decisions by firms, to the extent of implying existence of equilibria.

Examples of statutes verifying Assumption A include Boards of Directors consisting of every shareholder holding at least α per cent of the stock; or consisting of the k leading shareholders; or consisting of the set of leading shareholders holding together β per cent of the stock, and so on (with appropriate tie-breaking rules). These examples are illustrated in

---

[12]I am grateful to Bernard Cornet for suggesting the more abstract formulations.

[13]In particular, if $I^j(\theta^j)$ consists of all consumers owning at least 'one share' of stock, we are back to the Nash–Pareto criterion of the second group: if $I^j(\theta^j)$ consists of a single manager shareholder (possibly identified a priori), we are back to Leland's version of a utility function of the firm.

Figures 16.1, 16.2 and 16.3 respectively, for the case of three shareholders – see the Appendix.

The main drawback of the proposed decision criterion (majority vote among shareholders with veto right for Directors) is the requirement of *unanimity among the Directors*. This is of course a much weaker requirement than unanimity *among the shareholders*. Also, over the small group of Directors, side payments could (and sometimes do) take place to facilitate agreement. More importantly, perhaps, the proposed criterion is easily generalised to a two-tier majority rule. For instance, the Board of Directors could reach decisions through majority voting, with a veto right for the Chairman of the Board, or for some particular subset of the Board. This extension is immediate, when the subset with veto power is again determined in a manner verifying Assumption A. (Note that a veto right is conveniently exercised by controlling the agenda of meetings and putting to a vote preferred changes only.)

An interesting extension, which available time does not permit discussing in detail, consists in recognising formally the existence of *partial delegation of authority*. Thus, the shareholders might endow the Board of Directors with *final authority over a set of issues*, whereas issues outside that set would still require approval by a majority of shareholders. In turn, the Board could delegate to management final authority over a subset of issues from its own sphere of authority.

Work in progress shows that such delegations are consistent with existence of decentralised equilibria, provided two conditions are met:

(i)   every person or group receiving delegation belongs to the group granting delegation (i.e. the manager is a Director and Directors are shareholders);

(ii)   the set of issues over which delegation is granted, relative to a given production plan, is a convex subset of the production set (actually, of the set for which the body granting delegation has final authority), and depends *continuously* upon the reference plan.

Under all the forms of *control* and *delegation* referred to here, the decision criterion of a firm defines a partial ordering over production plans. In general, the ordering is not complete nor representable by a concave utility function. But it satisfies the two conditions used in the existence theorem for abstract economies; namely, a continuity condition ('the preference correspondence has open graph') and a convexity condition ('a production plan never belongs to the convex hull of the set of plans preferred to it'). These properties are sufficient for many purposes, a claim illustrated by the following application.

4 Labour contracts

As noted above, the model of Diamond is highly streamlined. Although it captures an important aspect of private ownership economies, namely the interaction of production decisions and portfolio choices, still it ignores essential aspects of business organisations. In particular, it leaves out labour altogether, to concentrate exclusively on capital. It is striking that, in the sixties and early seventies, so much attention was devoted to portfolio problems, and so little attention to labour contracts, in spite of the fact that uncertainties about labour income are much more significant than capital gains or losses, for most people.[14]

This is perhaps revealing of the geographical concentration of our GET-set. In my experience, when European economists from different countries meet socially, there comes a time when they discuss salaries. When American economists meet socially, they eventually discuss the stock market; whereas Israeli or Indian economists discuss credit conditions. (Incidentally, this observation relates to Milton Friedman's (1964) celebrated 'Tenured Income Hypothesis', claiming that the standard of living of University Teachers of Economics is the same all over the world, but the number of jobs they hold is inversely proportional to the country's wealth. Friedman may well be right after all, in spite of the fact that living conditions are more attractive in Bath than in Buffalo and that Jerusalem is a safer city than Chicago.)

It was left for income-conscious European economists, like Costas Azariadis (1975) and Martin Baily (1975), working in the efficient environments of North-American Universities, to restore priorities by drawing attention to labour contracts as instruments of risk sharing.

I need not remind you of the contents of implicit contracts theories of 'wages and employment under uncertain demand'. Oliver Hart (1983) devoted his Review of Economic Studies Lecture at your 1983 meeting to this topic. Let me, however, remind you of one significant assumption in the presentation by Oliver Hart and in all the antecedent literature: each firm has well-defined preferences over state distributions of profits, representable by a concave utility function....

It is an obvious task for general equilibrium theorists to bring the partial equilibrium analysis of labour contracts in harmony with production decisions of the firms and portfolio choices of their owners; in other words, to introduce labour inputs in the Diamond model, and study the existence and properties of equilibria defined simultaneously for the stock market, the markets for labour contracts, and the decentralised decisions of firms and households; with the firms now choosing labour contracts as well as production plans, and with the households now supplying labour as well as holding portfolios. This is clearly a more ambitious, yet realistic programme. It belongs to the core of my 1983 Jahnsson Lectures. It is germane to the 'institutional' approach developed above for decision criteria of the firms, since negotiated labour contracts are the most commonplace

---

[14]On this point, see Drèze (1979).

institutional device for private risk-sharing arrangements between labour and capital in Western economies.

There are by now a number of alternative models of labour contracts in the literature.[15] Some are more easily fitted than others into the general equilibrium framework considered here. A simple model goes as follows.

There is a single type of labour.[16] Each firm offers a labour contract, which specifies the quantity of work to be performed in the initial period, as well as in the future period under every state (that is, it specifies a vector of state-dependent labour times or retention probabilities); the contract also specifies the hourly wage, both now and tomorrow in every state. The decision of the firm becomes a pair consisting of a production plan and a labour contract. Such a decision implies an initial investment or dividend, as the case may be; and a vector of state-dependent future dividends, defined for each state by the value of output minus the wage bill. A decision d^j is best for firm j if there exists no alternative decision $\bar{d}^j$ deemed preferable by a majority of shareholders including the control group, *and by a majority of workers as well.* This approach looks at labour contracts as negotiated with labour, and subject to approval by majority voting at a meeting of all workers. (If one wishes, a control group with veto rights can be introduced among the workers as well, for instance a group consisting of the union representatives. Other approaches to labour's endorsement of the contract are conceivable. For instance, a new contract could be chosen in the convex hull of all existing contracts, thereby generalising the standard condition of a satisfactory utility level for identical workers; or the contract could have to be such as to generate an adequate labour supply. See Drèze (1986b) for precisions.)

At the same time, households make joint decisions about their portfolios of assets and their labour supply, choosing among the labour contracts offered by the different firms. Pending wage rigidities, easily handled along the now familiar lines of equilibrium theory with price rigidities and quantity rationing,[17] *an equilibrium for the stock-market economy with labour contracts* consists of a vector of share prices **p**, and a set of decisions for each consumer and each firm, such that:

(i)   the stock market clears;
(ii)   the market for labour contracts *in each firm* clears;
(iii)   each consumer is in equilibrium (in terms of portfolio choice and labour supply), given the share prices **p**, the dividend prospects of each firm, and the terms of the available labour contracts;
(iv)   each firm is in equilibrium, in the sense that: no alternative feasible decision (production plan and labour contract) would be preferred by a

[15]See Azariadis (1979) and Ito (1982) for recent surveys.
[16]Explicit treatment of several types of labour raises no difficulty. Also, workers are *not* assumed identical in what follows.
[17]Cf. Drazen (1980) or Grandmont (1977).

majority of shareholders and a majority of workers, including the (endogenously defined) control group(s).

Under assumptions similar to those of the previous theorem, such an equilibrium exists!

On several previous occasions (Drèze, 1976, 1979), I have characterised firms as fulfilling three roles: they realise physical investments, that match consumer savings; they create jobs, which consumers fill; they produce commodities, which consumers buy. The work reviewed here integrates the first two aspects in a general equilibrium theory. Formal analysis of the third aspect, in a general equilibrium model with uncertainty and incomplete markets, remains an open challenge.

5 Conclusions

What is to be concluded from this presentation? I will offer six brief remarks, on the following theme:

If we are willing to assimilate general equilibrium theory to a cardboard box rather than to an envelope, firms can fit into such a box without being flattened out – and general equilibrium theory is not an empty box! Let me elaborate in steps.

(1)   The existence results quoted above indicate that firms can be fitted into general equilibrium theory, in a way which draws a reasonable boundary between economic analysis and the exogenous environment, and which leads to verify the overall consistency of an economic analysis based on relatively weak assumptions.

        The boundary has been shifted by treating as exogenous the rules whereby control of a firm is related to its endogenously determined ownership, instead of treating control as altogether exogenous.

(2)   Of course, the results presented here should not be viewed as the final word on the subject. My only claim is that these results cover previous approaches as special cases. This justifies taking stock of these results, in the hope that they may stimulate further research in an area which should, in my opinion, retain due attention.

(3)   The resulting decision criteria of the firm are somewhat hybrid, reflecting as they do nested majority decisions with veto rights, possibly combined with partial delegation of authority (and tie-breaking rules). In general, the resulting preferences will not be representable by a concave utility, and will depend upon the overall allocation (portfolio choices and production plans of the other firms). But the preference correspondences have open graph, and a decision never belongs to the convex hull of the set of preferred decisions.

        The implications of this kind of preferences for other problems (in particular, properties of supply correspondences or of efficient labour contracts) *remain to be investigated.*

        As an immediate implication, the set of equilibria for the stock-market economy will be larger and more diversified than, say, under spanning –

the set may be more like a box with a non-empty interior than like an envelope with measure zero.

(4)   The equilibria under consideration are Nash–Pareto-optima, but not full Pareto-optima, as was to be expected given the non-convexity of the problem, already stressed ten years ago.

(5)   The equilibria under consideration have a competitive flavour, in that portfolio choices are based on stock prices and announced production plans. Although the rules determining membership in the control groups (Boards of Directors) are typically public knowledge, no allowance is made for portfolio choices *aimed at participation in control* – a question worth pursuing. Similarly, delegation of authority should be linked to the growing literature on 'principal–agent' problems.[18]

(6)   The approach followed here, and in particular the technical treatment of the existence problem in terms of abstract economies without ordered preferences, is quite robust. This has been illustrated by the ease with which labour contracts could be fitted into the Diamond model – a step of some substantive interest in itself. *There remain many open issues* in temporary general equilibrium theory calling for analysis with uncertainty and business decisions. Hopefully, a robust approach to these decisions may permit new developments.

[18]Cf. Shavell (1979).

Appendix

The figures below illustrate rules, for defining control groups, which satisfy Assumption A. The figures are drawn for three shareholders, whose ownership fractions $(\theta^1, \theta^2, \theta^3)$ in some firm add up to 1 and thus belong to the triangle with vertices at $(1, 0, 0)$, $(0, 1, 0)$ and $(0, 0, 1)$; i.e. to the unit simplex of R^3.

In Figure 16.1, the rule defining the control group is: 'shareholder i belongs to the control group $I(\theta)$ if and only if $\theta^i \geqslant 0.25$'.

In the inner triangle with heavy boundary, this condition is satisfied for each $i = 1, 2, 3$. That triangle (boundary included) is thus the set of ownership structures θ for which $I(\theta) = \{1, 2, 3\}$. Immediately to the right of the inner triangle, one finds a trapezium defining the set of ownership structures for which $I(\theta) = \{1, 2\}$. That set is closed (contains its boundary) on three sides, but it does not contain the face which belongs to the boundary of the inner triangle. (On that face, $\theta^3 = 0.25$ so that 3 belongs to $I(\theta)$.) Similar remarks apply to the trapezia for $\{1, 3\}$ and $\{2, 3\}$. Finally, the lozenges containing the vertices of the simplex correspond to one-person control groups. They are closed on the two sides which also belong to the boundary of the simplex, but open on the interior sides.

In Figure 16.2, the rule defining the control group is: '$I(\theta)$ consists of the single largest shareholder; if two or more shareholders have equal holdings, unsurpassed by others, they all belong'. Formally, $I(\theta) = \{i|\theta^i \geqslant \theta^j \forall j\}$.

The construction is analogous to that of Figure 16.1. $I(\theta) = \{1, 2, 3\}$ at the single point $(1/3, 1/3, 1/3)$, marked with a heavy dot. $I(\theta) = \{1, 2\}$ along the solid line from $(1/3, 1/3, 1/3)$ to $(1/2, 1/2, 0)$. Outside of the set of measure zero corresponding to ties, there is a single person in the control group. Thus, 1 belongs to that group for all values of θ in the closed tetrahedron

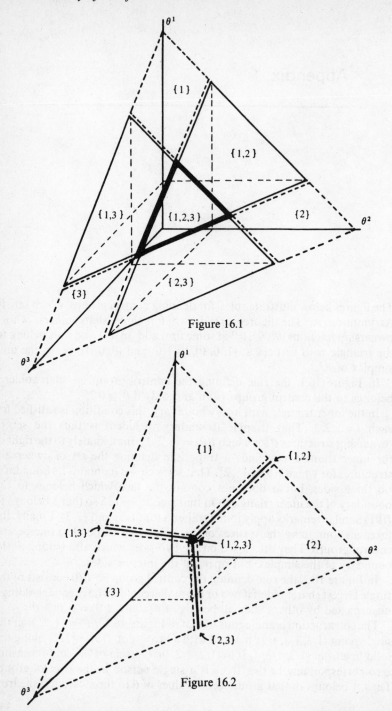

Figure 16.1

Figure 16.2

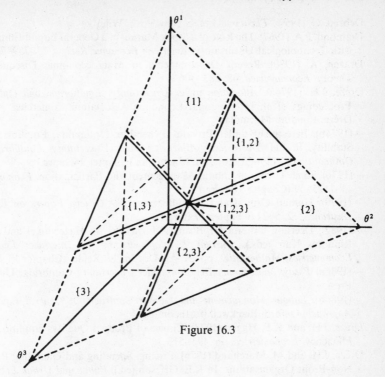

Figure 16.3

corresponding to the upper part of the figure; he is the only member of the control group for all values of θ in the interior of that tetrahedron or on the sides contained in the boundary of the simplex.

In Figure 16.3, the rule is: '$I(\theta)$ is the smallest group of shareholders owning together at least 1/3 of the shares; if two or more distinct groups meet this condition, $I(\theta)$ is the union of their members'. The interpretation of the figure is left to the reader.

References

Arrow, K.J. (1953). Le rôle des valeurs boursières pour la répartition la meilleure des risques. In *Econométrie*, pp. 41–8. Paris: CNRS. Translated (1964) as The Role of Securities in the Optimal Allocation of Risk-Bearing. *Review of Economic Studies*, 31: 91–6

Azariadis, C. (1975). Implicit Contracts and Underemployment Equilibria. *Journal of Political Economy*, 83: 1183–202

—(1979). Implicit Contracts and Related Topics: A Survey. CARESS Working Paper 79–17. University of Pennsylvania

Baily, M. (1975). Wages and Employment under Uncertain Demand. *Review of Economic Studies*, 41: 37–50

Böhm, V. (1980). *Preise, Löhne und Beschäftigung*. Tübingen: Mohr

Cyert, R.M. and J.G. March (1963). *A Behavioral Theory of the Firm*. Englewood Cliffs: Prentice Hall

Debreu, G. (1959). *Theory of Value.* New York: Wiley

Diamond, P.A. (1967). The Role of a Stock Market in a General Equilibrium Model with Technological Uncertainty. *American Economic Review,* 57: 759–76

Drazen, A. (1980). Recent Developments in Macroeconomic Disequilibrium Theory. *Econometrica,* 48: 283–306

Drèze, J.H. (1974a). *Allocation under Uncertainty: Equilibrium and Optimality.* Proceedings of an International Economic Association Conference, ed. J.H. Drèze, London: Macmillan

—(1974b). Investment under Private Ownership: Optimality, Equilibrium and Stability. In J.H. Drèze (ed.), *Allocation under Uncertainty: Equilibrium and Optimality,* pp. 129–66. London: Macmillan (Chapter 14 supra.)

—(1976). Some Theory of Labour Management and Participation. *Econometrica,* 44: 1125–39 (Chapter 18 infra.)

—(1979). Human Capital and Risk Bearing. *The Geneva Papers on Risk and Insurance,* 12: 5–22 (Chapter 17 infra.)

—(1982). Decision Criteria for Business Firms. In M. Hazewinkel and A.H.G. Rinnooy Kan (eds.), *Current Developments in the Interface: Economics, Econometrics, Mathematics,* pp. 27–51. Dordrecht: Reidel (Chapter 15 supra.)

—(1986a). *Essays on Economic Decisions under Uncertainty.* Cambridge University Press

—(1986b). *Labour Management and Labour Contracts: A General Equilibrium Approach.* Oxford: Blackwell (forthcoming)

Drèze, J.H. and K.P. Hagen (1978). Choice of Product Quality: Equilibrium and Efficiency. *Econometrica,* 46: 493–513

Drèze, J.H. and M. Marchand (1976). Pricing, Spending and Gambling Rules for Non-Profit Organisations. In R.E. Grieson (ed.), *Public and Urban Economics,* Essays in Honour of William S. Vickrey, pp. 58–89, Lexington, Mass: Lexington Books (Partim: Chapter 19 infra.)

Friedman, M. (1964). Private communication

Gevers, L. (1974). Competitive Equilibrium of the Stock Exchange and Pareto Efficiency. In J.H. Drèze (ed.), *Allocation under Uncertainty: Equilibrium and Optimality,* pp. 167–91. London: Macmillan

Grandmont, J.M. (1977). Temporary General Equilibrium Theory. *Econometrica,* 45: 535–73

Grossman, S.J. and O.D. Hart (1979). A Theory of Competitive Equilibrium in Stock Market Economies. *Econometrica,* 47: 293–330

Grossman, S.J. and J.E. Stiglitz (1980). Stockholder Unanimity in Making Production and Financial Decisions. *Quarterly Journal of Economics,* 94: 543–66

Hart, O. (1983). Optimal Labour Contracts under Asymmetric Information: An Introduction. *Review of Economic Studies,* 50: 3–35

Hirshleifer, J. (1966). Investment Decision under Uncertainty: Applications of the State Preference Approach. *Quarterly Journal of Economics,* 80: 252–77

Hirshleifer, J. and J.G. Riley (1979). The Analytics of Uncertainty and Information: An Expository Survey. *Journal of Economic Literature,* 17: 1375–421

Ito, T. (1982). Implicit Contract Theory: A Critical Survey. Discussion Paper 82–164. Minneapolis: University of Minnesota

Leland, H. (1978). Information, Managerial Choice and Stockholder Unanimity. *Review of Economic Studies,* 45: 527–34

Milne, F. and D. Starrett (1981). Socially Optimal Investment Rules in the Presence of Incomplete Markets and Other Second-best Distortions. Technical Report 345, Institute for Mathematical Studies in the Social Sciences. Stanford, California

Modigliani, F. and M.H. Miller (1958). The Cost of Capital, Corporation Finance and the Theory of Investment. *American Economic Review*, 48: 261–97

Nixon, W.M. (1982). Two Faces of Bardsay. *Yachting World*, June: 52–3

Radner, R. (1972). Existence of Equilibrium of Plans, Prices and Price Expectations in a Sequence of Markets. *Econometrica*, 40: 289–303

—(1980). Equilibrium under Uncertainty. In K.J. Arrow and M.D. Intriligator (eds.), *Handbook of Mathematical Economics*, vol. 2, pp. 923–1006. Amsterdam: North-Holland

Savage, J.L. (1953). Une axiomatisation du comportement raisonnable face à l'incertitude. In *Econométrie*, pp. 29–34. Paris: CNRS

—(1954). *The Foundations of Statistics*. New York: Wiley

Shafer, W. and H. Sonnenschein (1975). Equilibrium in Abstract Economies Without Ordered Preferences. *Journal of Mathematical Economics*, 2: 345–8

Shavell, S. (1979). Risk Sharing and Incentives in the Principal and Agent Relationship. *The Bell Journal of Economics*, 10: 55–73

Simon, H.A. (1979). Rational Decision-Making in Business Organisations. *American Economic Review*, 69: 493–513

Sondermann, D. (1974). Temporary Competitive Equilibrium under Uncertainty. In J.H. Drèze (ed.), *Allocation under Uncertainty: Equilibrium and Optimality*, pp. 229–53. London: Macmillan

Stiglitz, J.E. (1984). Information and Economic Analysis. F.W. Paish Lecture, RES-AUTE Meeting, Bath

VI Human capital and labour contracts

17 Human capital and risk-bearing*

1 Forms of risk-sharing

The economic theory of decision-making under uncertainty and risk-bearing rests on the assumption that individual agents behave consistently. If preferences do not depend upon the state of nature and if there exist opportunities for gambling at fair odds (say, on the stock market, or through private bets), then consistent behaviour implies aversion, or at least neutrality, towards economic risks (cf. Drèze (1971)). Casual empiricism confirms that risk aversion is indeed the rule: most individuals seem eager to shed their risks, even at unfair odds.

These risks take many forms, and affect an individual's health, his wealth, his liability, etc. Risk-shedding is achieved mainly through diversification, exchange or insurance. Each one of these three devices is limited in scope.

Diversification consists in splitting a risk into components with limited stochastic dependence, thereby reducing the total variance. Asset portfolios provide an example. But diversification entails costs of information and transactions. And an element of stochastic dependence is always present on the level of general economic activity: collective risks (as opposed to individual risks) cannot be eliminated through diversification.[1]

Exchange sometimes enables strongly risk-averse individuals to sell their risks to other agents who are more tolerant or endowed with complementary risks. Futures markets enable buyers and sellers to shed price

*This essay was presented originally as the Second Annual Lecture of the Geneva Association, at the Institut d'Etudes Politiques in Paris, on 16 March 1979.
[1]On this notion, see Allais (1953). I have given an implicit definition: Risks are 'individual' or 'collective' according as they can, or cannot, be eliminated through diversification.

uncertainties (but not quantity uncertainties). Equity financing is a way of selling business risks. But exchange must take place before the relevant information becomes available (once a lottery is drawn, there is no market any more for its tickets). Consequently, information could be harmful! When I drew attention to this apparent paradox in *Economie Appliquée* some twenty years ago, I was not fully aware of its significance, which has been brought out by Hirshleifer and recently discussed by Arrow in the First Annual Lecture of the Geneva Association (Drèze, 1960; Hirshleifer, 1971; Arrow, 1978). As noted by Arrow, there may arise conflicts between efficiency in production and efficiency in risk sharing. These conflicts are sometimes resolved by exchanging risks before pooling the relevant information, but producing afterwards.

Mutual *insurance* is a form of diversification. Commercial insurance involves an exchange followed by diversification. (The policy holder sells his risks to a company which resorts to diversification in a systematic and scientific way, through reinsurance if necessary.) But here again there are limitations. Transaction costs may absorb up to 50 per cent of the premium for small risks. Diversification typically relies on actuarial experience.[2] And insurance is subject to the paramount limitations of moral hazard and adverse selection. When the probabilities of a casualty are to some extent influenced by the policy holder, or are better known to him than to the company, the scope for insurance is reduced. This explains why insurance against celibacy or divorce is so uncommon.

In the words of Arrow (1965): 'The insurance policy might itself change incentives and therefore the probabilities upon which the insurance company has relied. Thus, a fire insurance policy for more than the value of the premises might be an inducement to arson or at least to carelessness.' Borch (1979) uses game theory to measure the cost of moral hazard for policy holders through higher premiums.

2 Risks affecting human capital and opportunities for sharing these risks

This short overview is useful for appraising the distinction between risk-sharing opportunities for physical capital on the one hand and for human capital on the other. The concept of 'human capital' entered economics some fifteen years ago, to denote the present value of a stream of labour income (Becker, 1964). Because future labour incomes are uncertain, human capital bears risks, which fall under three headings. Some risks are *physical* – death, accidents, illness. Insurance coverage of these risks is well developed, at the individual, group and social level. Other risks are

---

[2]Still, Borch (1977) gives a racy account of the contract whereby Lloyds of London insured the Cutty Sark whisky company against capture of the monster in Loch Ness, for a premium of 2.5 per thousand.

economic; they result from the *endogenous* and *exogenous* uncertainties affecting labour income. The endogenous uncertainties concern an individual's proficiency at work: qualifications, creativity, drive, sociability,... The exogenous uncertainties concern the *demand* for the labour services offered by an individual: high demand at times of full employment, but low demand at times of underemployment; a demand which assigns to a particular type of labour a higher or lower value, depending upon business conditions and industrial structures.

Risks surrounding individual abilities are particularly hard to shed. Diversification is ruled out, short of a dual personality. Exchange has disappeared, together with slavery. As for insurance, it is particularly curtailed, in this area, by the problems of subjective assessment, moral hazard and adverse selection. A singer can easily take out insurance against throat cancer, but not against hostile audiences or new 'musical' styles. Insurance companies do not protect students against insufficient grades, employees against lack of promotion or authors against stubborn editors.

In the case of the self-employed, the distinction between endogenous and exogenous economic uncertainties is not always clearcut. When a supermarket drives the local grocery store out of business, is that evidence of carelessness or bad luck? Perhaps the presumption of carelessness would be enhanced if the grocer carried insurance against business failure? And one would like to know what provisions, if any, the insurance contract contained regarding price policy, advertising, service quality, etc.

A self-employed person has no effective way of shedding his professional risks other than through salaried employment – possibly in trades where income variability is largely unrelated to individual productivity (like in the case of unskilled workers or tenured professors). The relationships between risk aversion and income distribution have not yet been fully charted. Shortly before the revival of the theory of decision-making under uncertainty, Friedman and Kuznets (1945) expressed some surprise at their discovery of a positive rank correlation between mean and variance of income from independent professional practice. They sought an explanation for this phenomenon on the demand side, but could find none. A few years later, Friedman (1953) presented in Paris his explanation of the dispersion in personal incomes through attitudes towards risks.

My main interest here centres on risks arising from the demand for labour. These may consist in uncertainty about wage levels, especially in the long run; or in uncertainty about labour demand at given wages, especially in the short run. This last phenomenon, namely unemployment risk, will be my main – and timely – concern. A wage- or salary-earner may be uncertain about short-run labour demand at three levels, namely: the firm, the trade or sector, and the economy as a whole. Risks arising at firm level are largely diversifiable, whereas those arising at an economy-wide level are definitely 'collective'. In between, the two types of risks are mixed in varied proportions. When the labour demand of a particular firm changes, there may be some doubt, at least temporarily, as to whether the change is specific to the firm, or is of a broader nature. This obvious remark illustrates a recurrent theme in the recent literature on anticipations, namely the difficulty in distinguishing the individual and the collective components of observed disturbances (for instance, of distinguishing changes in relative prices from changes in the general price level); as we shall see below, this difficulty is relevant for the policing of labour contracts (Fischer, 1977).

Here again, the scope for *diversification* is almost nil. A given person seldom works for several firms, or in several trades, simultaneously. And the risks arising from general business conditions cannot be diversified, by definition.[3] As for *exchange*, it takes the form of labour contracts, with more or less elaborate guarantees for the workers (concerning wage rates, hours, employment stability, dismissal notice, severance pay,...). I will discuss this topic at some length below. I would like to state, however, that successful execution of the contract is predicated upon solvency of the firm. Bankruptcy insurance is hampered again by the problems of moral hazard and adverse selection already mentioned in the case of the self-employed. From the workers' viewpoint, *insurance* typically takes the form of unemployment compensation, in a social security framework. The provisions (amount, duration,...) are thus fixed by collective rules instead of privately agreed contracts.

3 Risk tolerance of firms and workers

There exists a marked difference between the risk-sharing opportunities applicable to human capital, which are narrowly limited; and those applicable to physical capital, which are quite extensive. Financial intermediation has made an important contribution, through the creation of negotiable securities. Unlike human capital, financial assets are divisible and free of transportation costs. This opens up opportunities for diversification which are substantial (although still imperfect). In particular, financial diversification operates across firms, sectors and even nations.

As noted by Meade (1972): 'While property owners can spread their risks by putting small bits of their property into a large number of concerns, a worker cannot put small bits of his effort into a large number of different jobs. This presumably is a main reason why we find risk-bearing capital hiring labour rather than risk-bearing labour hiring capital.' To be sure, labour management does not rule out equity financing (Drèze, 1976a). But Meade's point is well taken, and applies also to such forms of compensation as gratuities or sharecropping (Stiglitz, 1974).

For these reasons, I believe that risk tolerance is greater:

---

[3] Let us note, for further reference, that uncertainty about rates of monetary inflation, without any real counterpart, could be covered by escalator clauses (indexing).

– for owners of non-human capital than for owners of human capital;
– for corporations than for the self-employed;
– for firms than for workers.

It would be worthwhile to test the first of these propositions by measuring risk aversion, as defined by Arrow (1965) and Pratt (1964), first on the basis of stock market valuations; and secondly on the basis of insurance contracts subscribed by broad groups of individuals (like all automobile owners, or home owners). The latter measurement could be carried out, from the files of insurance companies, relying upon the theory of optimal insurance discussed below.

The second proposition is illustrated by the behaviour of the self-employed who pay a high price to reduce their professional risks; I am referring in particular to farmers, who resort to technically inefficient diversification of production activities as a substitute for assets diversification.

The third proposition plays an important role in what follows, and deserves a word of explanation. According to what criteria do business firms make decisions under uncertainty? This is a debated issue, about which opinions differ. Some work rests on the assumption that firms are risk-neutral.[4] The implicit rationale for this assumption is that portfolio diversification by shareholders eliminates the individual risks specific to a firm. But collective risks are still there; they are measured, say, by the covariance between the profits of a given firm and national income. Furthermore, many business firms insure individual risks (fire, machine breakdown, theft,...), thereby revealing their risk aversion. This may be explained, at least in part, by the *linkage of risks*. Thus a liquidity crisis may call for costly emergency measures (selling inventories at discount prices, curtailing turnover, using expensive credit margins,...). In the more acute cases of bankruptcy, fixed assets are apt to be sold on disastrous terms. Accordingly, business firms are not entirely risk-neutral. But many risks which are serious for individuals are innocuous for firms – because stock ownership permits portfolio diversification by owners of non-human capital, who have an opportunity to invest their wealth in low-risk assets.

4 Sharing income risks: an example

In order to assess the implications of the difference in risk aversion between workers and firms, let us consider the example of the steel industry in Luxembourg. Everywhere in Europe – and Luxembourg is no exception – the steel industry faces sizeable demand fluctuations, which result in commensurate fluctuations in the degree of capacity utilisation. There are

---

[4]See for instance Drèze (1976b) and the references there to Drèze and Gabszewicz (1967), Sheshinski and Drèze (1976) or Tisdell (1968). Malinvaud (1972) shows that efficiency requires firms to be neutral towards individual risks.

in Luxembourg a number of steel workers who have few alternative employment opportunities in the short run. If their wages were set each year (month) at a level equating labour supply to industry demand, these wages would fluctuate with demand. At this time (March 1979), they would have to be low enough for steel workers to be indifferent to working or staying home; at which point excess supply disappears by definition! On the other hand, at times of strong demand and high prices for steel products, wages would also be very high. When will such a situation prevail again? This question is surrounded by considerable uncertainty.

The arrangement which I have just described would of course entail serious drawbacks for steel workers, especially if they are young and have no savings. How could this arrangement be improved? A first approach – which provided the motivation for my work on equilibrium with price rigidities (Drèze, 1975) – would consist in seeking improvement through mutual insurance. Workers from steel works, hotels and vineyards could pool and share their income, fully or partly; this form of diversification would reduce individual risks. This approach must however fulfil certain conditions, in order to be successful. Suppose that wages of steel workers become low enough to make them indifferent to working or staying home. In the framework of mutual insurance, this means 'working and contributing one's earnings to the mutual fund' or 'staying home and nevertheless receiving benefits from the mutual fund' – a perfect example of moral hazard! In order to set things straight, the group must agree about a wage rate below which its members may refuse to work while remaining eligible for their share of the pool. This brings in a form of downward wage rigidities, and in particular a minimum wage.

Actually, the mutual insurance approach retains the drawback of restricting diversification to owners of human capital. Why not extend the mutual arrangement to owners of physical capital? Since they are more risk-tolerant, they could buy a share of the risks borne by workers, for a suitable premium. This looks good – but perhaps a bit difficult to organise. Indeed, one must somehow control whether each member of the group contributes the agreed-upon share of his earnings. (A fixed contribution would contradict the very idea of mutual insurance.) This calls for checking the amount of earnings with the employer. In the steel industry, employers are joint stock companies. Why not invite the steel company to join the mutual insurance group, both as a seller of insurance and as a controller (of earnings)? So far so good – but then, it may no longer be necessary for the steel company to pay its workers, collect a share of their earnings as insurance premium, and finally pay out an insurance benefit. It would seem easier, and more attractive from the tax angle (in Luxemboug) to immediately register the final amount as a wage. This brings in rigid wages, independent of business conditions, paid out directly by the employer.

There remains a problem, however. Suppose again that the marginal value product of labour is such that workers would rather go hunting and eating quail than working and earning this marginal product. Under flexible wages, they would be voluntarily unemployed. Under rigid wages, they prefer to work. So the employer will use authority and lay them off. Rigid wages and involuntary unemployment have thus replaced flexible wages and voluntary unemployment – without any change in the real situation (employment level), but with a transfer of risks from the workers to the firms.

5 Implicit labour contracts and contractual equilibria

We have just rediscovered the concept of 'implicit labour contract', introduced five years ago by Azariadis (1975), Baily (1974) and Gordon (1974), and soon followed by Barro (1977), Grossman (1977) and others (Azariadis, 1977; Feldstein, 1976; Gordon, 1976, 1977; Polemarchakis and Weiss, 1978). The idea is simple. Suppose that a firm faces a demand (price) subject to random fluctuations. At a given level of labour input, the marginal value product of labour will also be random. Should a worker receive a wage equal to the marginal value product of his labour, the *variance* of earnings would entail for him a loss of utility. The firm may then offer him a fixed wage, inferior to his expected marginal value product, but more attractive than the random wage, both for the risk-averse worker and for the risk-tolerant firm. Both parties have incentives to sign a contract specifying a fixed wage, unaffected by demand fluctuations. It is an employment contract, coupled with an implicit insurance contract.[5] The worker earns a wage equal to the marginal value product of his labour, plus an insurance benefit in case of adverse business conditions, but minus an insurance premium in case of favourable business conditions. The insurance contract is underwritten by the firm itself, and not by an insurance company, because the firm has immediate access to the information required in order to monitor the contract (the marginal value product of labour); the insurance company would be confronted with a moral hazard problem.

In the simplest model, initially considered by Azariadis and Baily, the firms are risk-neutral[6] and the length of the working week is fixed. When demand (price) is very low, the value of the output of the last (marginal) worker is inferior to his disutility of working. The implicit contract calls then for laying off temporarily a number of workers just sufficient to raise the value of the output of the marginal worker back to parity with the disutility of work; this adjustment is mutually advantageous.[7] This 'implicit

[5]For some authors, like Grossman (1978a), the term 'implicit' is due to the illegality of involuntary servitude – a common law principle dear to married men.
[6]When firms are somewhat risk-averse, wages should undergo slight variations – which can be ignored in the presence of transaction costs.
[7]Indeed, the savings accruing to the firm through temporary lay-offs permit an increase in the fixed wage rate.

contracts' model leads to stability of the real income of employed workers, but to instability of employment. Stability of real, as opposed to nominal income, calls for tying wages to the consumer price index.

Extensive reliance upon this type of contract could, according to some of the aforementioned authors, explain why wages do not reflect the cyclical fluctuations of the *marginal* value product of labour, i.e. why wages are rigid in the short run. In this way, a phenomenon which plays an important role in Keynesian macroeconomics would receive rational microeconomic foundations. (Unlike Keynes however, our authors do not assume that employment is at all times such as to equate the rigid wage, to the marginal value product of labour.)

The most sophisticated version of this model is due to Holmström (1979), in a general equilibrium framework with two periods and uncertainty about the state of nature in the second period. A 'contractual equilibrium' includes labour contracts specifying a first period wage and, for each state of nature in the second period, a wage and a rate (probability) of unemployment. Holmström assumes that competition on a homogeneous labour market in the first period brings about a unique wage (for all workers and all firms). In the second period, once the state of nature becomes known, two situations may arise. If labour demand is high, wages go up and full employment is obtained at a unique wage rate. If labour demand is low, wages are downward rigid and some of the workers are laid off. In equilibrium, expectations are rational, and there exist no alternative wage contracts simultaneously more appealing to workers and firms. The fact that wages are rigid downwards but not upwards follows from the assumption that workers could break their first period contract if another firm offered them a higher wage (illegality of involuntary servitude).

Holmström proves existence of a *'contractual equilibrium'* for an economy with a single commodity, an arbitrary number of risk-neutral firms with convex production sets, and a continuum of identical workers with concave preferences.

He then considers a sequence of competitive (Walrasian) spot equilibria – without futures markets or insurance markets. He shows that wages and employment in the second period are never higher at competitive spot equilibria than at contractual equilibria, whereas the expected utility of workers is higher or at least equally high at contractual equilibria. The first result follows from the fact that efficient labour contracts keep workers employed so long as their marginal product is at least high enough to compensate them for the disutility of working. The second result is due to the fact that downwards wage rigidity reduces the variance of labour incomes, in comparison with the sequence of competitive spot equilibria. In order to do better still, one should introduce insurance markets, or a working week of variable length. With reference to this last point, one could imagine that lay-offs would affect all the workers of a given firm symmetrically as they would take them in turns. This is equivalent to variable hours.

6 Unemployment compensation and seniority rights

These results demonstrate the relevance of the concept of 'implicit labour contract' and of risk-bearing for a better understanding of some aspects of labour markets. I will now introduce some variations on this theme, then turn to a normative discussion of risk-sharing through labour contracts.

An element duly stressed in the literature has not thus far been mentioned, namely unemployment compensation under social security provisions. Let us first investigate their rationale, in the general framework introduced so far.[8] I think that this rationale rests at least in part with the residual risk aversion of business firms and with their bankruptcy risks. The first point explains why firms, especially small firms, find it more advantageous to participate in a national scheme than to guarantee themselves a replacement income to their temporarily laid off workers. The second point explains why workers find it more advantageous to receive such replacement income from a national agency than from possibly insolvent firms. (Note furthermore that an outside agency must take over when a worker is permanently dismissed. The least able workers are the main beneficiaries of unemployment compensation.)

Now, social unemployment insurance has two implications which are important for our discussion. First, unemployment compensation must be added to the disutility of labour in defining the opportunity cost of employment. It is well known that unemployment benefits do influence the supply of labour, because some persons find it more appealing to draw these benefits than to earn more through work. The law does not always succeed in denying them unemployment benefits. But these benefits also influence the demand for labour by firms. We saw earlier that efficient implicit contracts keep employment at a level where the product of a marginal worker is at least equal to the disutility of working. Actually, this product must be at least equal to the *sum* of the disutility of labour and the unemployment benefits.

An implicit contract which is efficient from the viewpoint of a firm and its workers treats unemployment compensation as an external benefit, which is advantageously internalised by temporary lay-offs at times of slack demand. This result holds so long as the marginal cost of unemployment benefits is not borne by the firm and its workers. Such is generally the case in Europe; I understand that it is also the case for most American firms, in spite of partial adjustment of social security contributions to a firm's past record regarding employment stability.[9] Accordingly, Baily (1977), Feldstein (1974) and Grossman (1978a, 1978b) feel that unemployment compensation schemes have a negative impact on employment stability, an impact which is conducive to inefficiency. Unemployment insurance is thus

---

[8]Curiously, this point is not treated in the papers dealing with implications of social unemployment insurance – cf. Baily (1977), Feldstein (1976) and Grossman (1978b).
[9]Cf. Feldstein (1976, fn. 25); Baily (1977, p. 1058).

plagued by moral hazard both because it reduces effective labour supply and because it adds to instability of labour demand.

A second implication of unemployment compensation schemes is their negative impact on incentives to reduce temporarily the length of the working week at times of excess labour supply. Suppose that a firm wishes to reduce by 10 per cent the total number of man hours worked by its employees. If it reduces by 10 per cent the length of the working week (say from 40 to 36 hours), no unemployment compensation is involved. If instead 10 per cent of the workers are laid off, they will collect unemployment compensation; the firm and its employees should find it advantageous to internalise these external benefits. This remark may help to explain the relative rigidity of working hours through spells of unemployment.[10]

Another phenomenon, emphasised by Grossman (1977, 1978a) and Holmström (1979), is the common practice of seniority rights. They may take the form of higher wages, or higher employment stability[11] for the workers with higher seniority within the firm.

Seniority rights may be justified on productivity grounds, since more senior workers have acquired more experience on the job. The theory of implicit contracts provides an additional explanation. If a worker is employed, sometimes for a wage inflated by an insurance benefit and sometimes for a wage deflated by an insurance premium, it is important that a proper balance should exist between both types of periods. But in periods of high labour demand, workers employed under a previous contract have an incentive to change firm, thereby dodging the implicitly agreed upon premium (moral hazard!) to start afresh in another firm at a higher wage. Seniority rights combat this incentive and promote workers' stability, without violating the illegality of involuntary servitude.

As for firms, their incentives to honour implicit contracts are typically sought in the desire to acquire a reputation of reliability, which induces stable workers to contract with them. Note, however, that this motivation disappears when a firm closes down, since any goodwill acquired in this way disappears with the firm. It should not surprise us that workers dismissed by such firms react as victims defrauded of an implicit right to employment stability – i.e. as the party wronged through violation of the implicit contract.

7 Empirical relevance of the implicit contracts theory

The main points made so far are listed in the left side of Table 17.1 in Appendix, which aims at bringing out their interrelations. The right side concerns the normative analysis, to which I shall soon turn. Prior to that,

[10]Feldstein (1976, p. 938) refers to union contracts requiring that firms lay-off workers instead of reducing average hours per week.
[11]Feldstein (1976, p. 938) refers also to union contracts with inverted seniority provisions, whereby the more senior workers have the option of being laid off *first* instead of last.

however, I would like to comment briefly upon the realism and empirical relevance of the implicit contracts theory.

I have been concerned with implications of the absence, in our economies, of adequate opportunities for spreading or insuring the economic risks of human capital. Needless to say, the explanations contributed by the theory of risk-bearing have a partial character and do not exhaust the topics under discussion. The theory of implicit labour contracts should not lead anyone to believe that the massive unemployment observed today in several countries is 'implicitly voluntary'. Neither should one neglect the role of adjustment costs, stressed for instance by Oi (1962), or of the increasing returns to working time, stressed by Feldstein (1976) in explaining the cyclical rigidity of hours worked.

The first question to be raised about the empirical relevance of the theory concerns the extent to which labour contracts actually include an (implicit) insurance policy. This question is not easy to answer, because the provisions of the insurance policy are clearly defined only under the extreme (and unrealistic) assumption that firms are risk-neutral, in which case labour incomes should be non-stochastic – also for temporarily laid-off workers, which is seldom the case. In general, some variability in labour incomes remains appropriate, and a quantitative yard-stick should be developed against which observed variability could be gauged. Separate measurements of risk aversion by firms and workers, as already advocated in Section 3, would here be called for.

Casual empiricism reveals substantial variations as between countries, sectors, firms and types of labour. Thus, escalator clauses protecting real income are more extensive in some countries than others – see Azariadis (1978). Income stability is much greater in some industrial sectors (automobile) than others (textiles). Large firms seem to offer more guarantees than small firms. Most conspicuous perhaps is the difference in status between blue collar wage-earners, and white collar salary-earners who are seldom laid off temporarily. To the best of my knowledge, a systematic analysis of these differences is still lacking; it should include other elements beside risk-bearing – as in the theories of labour market segmentation; see Cain (1976). Such an analysis is a prerequisite to proper assessment of the empirical relevance of the implicit contracts theory.

A second empirical question to be raised about this theory concerns the extent to which implicit labour contracts lead to privately efficient employment policies – i.e. to policies whereby the marginal value product of labour is always equal to its private opportunity cost. Some authors, in particular Barro (1977) and Grossman (1978b), defend that assumption. I would tend to side with Fischer (1977), who questions it. Fischer's reservations derive from moral hazard. On the one hand, the disutility of working is hardly observable and firms would be reluctant to insure workers against fluctuations in labour supply; on the other hand, firms may be tempted to misrepresent their labour demand. My own reservations are of a different nature. I regard implicit contracts as bearing on commodities with multiple characteristics, where the characteristics (state distributions of wages and rates of unemployment) are not given but must be chosen by the firms. And we know that competitive mechanisms can correctly guide the decisions about quantities for a given set of commodities, but not the choice of characteristics for these commodities. The set of feasible combinations of quantities and qualities is not convex, and the presumption of efficiency is therefore unwarranted.[12]

8 Normative analysis: productive efficiency and optimal insurance

Turning to the normative analysis, I must point out that the existing literature consists of *partial* equilibrium models with many periods – as in the work of Baily (1974) or Azariadis (1975) – and general equilibrium models with *two periods* – as in the work of Holmström (1979). Yet the time dimension is just as important, for our problem, as general interdependence. Clearly, the wage of a shop attendant does not vary with the sales volume from hour to hour or day to day. What we are concerned with is the cyclical pattern of wages and employment. Equally clearly, the attendant will be dismissed if the shop closes down. A difficult issue is to know when closing down the shop is justified, due account being taken of the labour contract. Normative analysis of this issue should rest on general equilibrium models with several periods, uncertainty and incomplete insurance markets. Such models have not yet been treated in the literature, to the best of my knowledge. I will accordingly base my normative discussion on two theoretical contributions of more limited scope: the theory of productive efficiency under certainty; and the theory of optimal insurance for given risks.

The theory of Pareto-efficiency requires that labour inputs be so allocated that (i) the marginal value product of labour be the same in all its uses, i.e. in all firms, and (ii) the marginal value product of labour be just sufficient to compensate for the marginal disutility of working.

The first equality requires mobility of workers between firms, so as to continuously reorient labour towards the most productive activities. Seniority rights hamper mobility and may discourage workers from changing firms. Indeed a worker may be reluctant to give up his seniority rights, without full immediate compensation, even though his future productivity may be superior elsewhere.

The second equality is violated when the implicit contract is ineffective, so that firms equate the marginal value product of labour to a rigid wage;

---

[12]The non-convexities result from simultaneous modifications in the contract and the personnel of a given firm – see Drèze and Hagen (1978); or in the contract and the equipment of that firm – see de Kerchove (1976).

and again when the implicit contract is privately efficient, with firms equating the marginal value product of labour to its opportunity cost, consisting of disutility of work plus unemployment compensation. The second equality may also require cyclical fluctuations in hours worked, reflecting cyclical fluctuations in demand. This point is quite obvious for small countries, who cannot control the cyclical fluctuations in world demand. When the world demand for Belgian labour diminishes, whereas the Belgian labour supply is unchanged, labour inputs in Belgium should go down. If the rationing of supply is not achieved through price adjustments (lower wages), because fluctuations in real income are costly for risk-averse workers, then labour supply must be subjected to quantity rationing. But quantity rationing through shorter hours is socially more efficient than quantity rationing through unemployment.

I will come back in my concluding section to some means whereby one could hopefully reduce the gap between our practice and these norms of Paretian efficiency. Prior to that, I still want to quote the two main results from optimal insurance theory, proved respectively by Borch (1960) and Arrow (1970b).

Borch has demonstrated the following proposition:[13] 'If the insured and the insurer are both risk-averters and there are no transaction costs, then any non-trivial Pareto-optimal policy stipulates benefits which increase with the loss, but in such a way that an increase in the loss never be fully insured.'

This proposition, applied to the collective risks of general business conditions, would require universal sharing of these risks, with no one fully insulated. Yet downward rigid real wages insulate employed workers from the collective risks of insufficient world demand, deterioration in terms of trade, etc. A similar conclusion is reached by Azariadis (1978) in his paper on escalator clauses. In the case of collective risks ('real' shocks), only partial indexing of money wages is justified.

A different conclusion holds for individual risks, which disappear at the collective level through compensation or diversification. Azariadis recommends full indexing of money wages against purely monetary disturbances. This is consistent with the theorem of Arrow (1970b) on optimal insurance of individual risks: 'If an insurance company is willing to offer any insurance policy against loss desired by the buyer at a premium which depends only on the policy's actuarial value, then the policy chosen by a risk-averting buyer will take the form of 100 per cent coverage above a deductible minimum.'

The reasoning in the proof of this proposition applies to the case of income risks as well. In the case of individual risks, insurance at a premium depending only upon actuarial value makes sense. Full coverage above a deductible minimum becomes full downwards rigidity of real incomes not

[13] I am quoting here the formulation by Arrow (1970b, p. 216).

exceeding a given level (like in the case of full indexation up to a given ceiling). The level of income up to which full downwards rigidity applies plays the same role here as the level of wealth net of deductible losses in Arrow's formulation.

9 Suggestions for possible improvements

In the light of these remarks, I wish to suggest some avenues along which improvements to our institutions could be sought. All my suggestions aim at alleviating the rigidities of these institutions.

(a) *Income flexibility.* The theory of optimal insurance suggests that individual incomes should be independent of individual risks, but not of collective risks. This calls for indexing wages and salaries on national income at current prices, rather than on consumer prices. Thus, any monetary disturbance without real effects would automatically be offset by proportional adjustments in wages and salaries. On the other hand, in a recession, the fall in real national income would be shared by all, as required by Borch's theorem.

This suggestion is conceptually simple, yet difficult to implement. Indeed, arithmetic indexation of all earnings on national income would leave no room for adjustments in income shares. In order to retain some flexibility, one could for instance subtract from the rate of change of national income at current prices, the rate of change in productivity, whose contribution could be redistributed freely. Alternatively, one could index earnings up to a ceiling amount, in order to leave room for some redistribution of personal incomes. Arrow's theorem allows for such a ceiling, which plays the same role as a deductible minimum. Failure to index tax brackets has roughly similar effects and might find here a rationale which deserves further study.

Another difficulty is that official data on national income are published with considerable delay – one year or more. In contrast, the consumer price index admits rapid measurement. My colleague Steinherr (1978) has suggested tying wages and salaries to a price index of value added – an index which aims at tracking the ratio of nominal to real national income. This is an interesting suggestion, which meets the objective as well as the objections just mentioned. Another possibility would be to use the rate of unemployment in order to curb escalator clauses during recessions. This rate has the merit of being measured without lags and of being generally familiar. But the best way of using it for our purposes remains to be defined.

(b) *Flexibility of hours worked.* I have indicated above why some flexibility in hours per week might be desirable, to absorb cyclical fluctuations in demand. I have also indicated how standard unemployment compensation schemes impose a penalty on this way of rationing labour supply. The penalty would disappear if unemployment benefits were proportional to the number of hours of involuntary unemployment (the standard working week minus hours effectively worked). But this suggestion may have its drawback, because workers would feel motivated to oppose reductions in the standard working week, even when such reductions are required for full employment.[14]

(c) *Employment stability*. I have also indicated how unemployment compensation, because it enters into the private opportunity cost of labour, tends to destabilise employment (lay-offs internalise an external benefit). On the other hand, when the marginal cost of unemployment compensation is borne by the firm, the destabilising effect disappears. This is the reason why some authors, like Feldstein (1976), have suggested that contributions to unemployment compensation schemes should be geared to the past record of firms. A record of employment stability would lead to low contributions, and conversely. This principle has found little application in Europe, where it should be studied carefully.

(d) *Labour mobility*. Among the sources of conflict between productive efficiency and risk-sharing, I have mentioned seniority rights. They help in monitoring implicit labour contracts, but they discourage the mobility of workers between firms. Perhaps these rights could become transferable, whenever those concerned find it agreeable? Consider a declining firm, where a senior worker is entitled to collect two years of severance pay. Suppose that another firm were prepared to hire that worker. His seniority rights could be transferred to the new firm, subject to payment by the old firm of an appropriate premium.[15] This is a particular aspect of a broader issue, namely the accountancy of seniority rights. Whereas most fringe benefits are covered by contributions which are paid out on a flow basis, other benefits, like severance pay, never appear in the books of a firm, and are not covered by specific reserves.[16] Is this practice logical? The problem seems worth studying.

10 Conclusion

The central problem discussed in this paper is that of reconciling efficient risk-sharing with decentralised incentives for efficient use of labour inputs in private ownership market economies with incomplete insurance markets.

In Western Europe, the current recession illustrates dramatically the significance of this problem, and the limitations of the institutions which have emerged to cope with it.

[14]See Drèze and Modigliani (1981).
[15]This provision appears in the definition of contractual equilibria by Drèze and Greenberg (1980).
[16]I understand that severance pay is covered by specific contributions in Italy.

Table 17.1 *The scope for spreading or insuring economic risks borne by human capital is very limited, in our economies*

Assumptions	Institutions	Operating characteristics (rigidities)	Evaluation		Improvements (flexibility)
Workers are more risk averse than firms	Implicit labour contracts	Escalator clauses	OPTIMAL INSURANCE	Universal sharing of collective risks	Wages indexed on nominal national income
		Downwards wage rigidity and excessive temporary lay-offs		Justification of downwards wage rigidity for individual risks	Incomes indexed up to ceiling amount, possibly through income tax
Firms cannot spread collective risks and sometimes go bankrupt	National schemes of unemployment compensation		PRODUCTIVE EFFICIENCY	Equality of marginal value product and marginal disutility of labour	Contributions geared to past record of firms
		Substantial rigidity in hours per week		Cyclical flexibility in hours per week	Benefits proportional to hours of involuntary unemployment
Illegality of involuntary servitude		Seniority rights		Labour mobility	Seniority rights transferable and covered by specific reserves

Our theoretical understanding of the problem has been enhanced by important recent contributions, like those surveyed here, but it is still far from complete. The theory of risk-bearing has been applied more systematically to business decisions about physical or financial investment than to decisions about human resources; yet the potential usefulness of the theory seems to be even greater in the latter area.

It was suggested above that multiperiod general equilibrium would be an important step towards better understanding of the problems raised by risk-bearing and human resources. I may perhaps add, by way of conclusion, that the range of issues discussed here is still very narrow and leaves out important dimensions, like investment in human capital, incentives for effort and other qualitative aspects of work, the interactions of decisions on physical capital and human resources, etc.

These broader issues provide additional motivation to develop more comprehensive theoretical models.

References

Allais, M. (1953). L'extension des théories de l'équilibre économique général et du rendement social au cas du risque, *Econometrica*, 21: 269–90.

Arrow, K.J. (1965). *Aspects of the Theory of Risk-Bearing*, Helsinki: Yrjö Jahnsson Foundation

—(1970a). *Essays in the Theory of Risk-Bearing*, Amsterdam: North-Holland

—(1970b). On optimal insurance policies. *Essays in the Theory of Risk-Bearing*, Amsterdam: North-Holland, pp. 212–19

—(1978). Risk allocation and information: Some recent theoretical developments, *Geneva Papers on Risk and Insurance*, 8: 5–19

Azariadis, C. (1975). Implicit contracts and underemployment equilibria, *Journal of Political Economy*, 83: 1183–202

—(1977). Gordon on unemployment theory, *Journal of Monetary Economics*, 3: 253–5

—(1978). Escalator clauses and the allocation of cyclical risks, *Journal of Economic Theory*, 18: 119–55

Baily, M.N. (1974). Wages and employment under uncertain demand, *Review of Economic Studies*, 41: 37–50

—(1977). On the theory of layoffs and unemployment, *Econometrica*, 45: 1043–63

Barro, R.J. (1977). Long-term contracting, sticky prices and monetary policy, *Journal of Monetary Economics*, 3: 305–16

Becker, G. (1964). *Human Capital: A Theoretical and Empirical Analysis with Special Reference to Education*, New York: Columbia University Press

Borch, K. (1960). The safety loading of reinsurance premiums, *Skandinavisk Aktuarietidskrift*, pp. 163–84

—(1977). The monster in Loch Ness. In A. Aykaç and C. Brumat (eds.), *New Developments in the Applications of Bayesian Methods*, Amsterdam: North-Holland, Ch. 16

—(1979). The price of moral hazard, Mimeo, Norwegian School of Economics, Bergen

Cain, G.G. (1976). The challenge of segmented labor market theories to orthodox theory: A survey, *Journal of Economic Theory*, 14: 1215–57.

Drèze, J.H. (1960). Le paradoxe de l'information, *Economie Appliquée*, 13: 71–80 (Translated as Chapter 4 supra.)

—(1971). Market allocation under uncertainty, *European Economic Review*, 2: 135–65 (Chapter 6 supra.)

—(1975). Existence of an exchange equilibrium under price rigidities, *International Economic Review*, 16: 301–20

—(1976a). Some theory of labor management and participation, *Econometrica*, 44: 1125–39 (Chapter 18 infra.)

—(1976b). Decision-making under uncertainty: The lessons from economic analysis, with reference to financial markets, mimeo, Institut International d'Etudes Bancaires et Monétaires, Genève

Drèze, J.H. and J. Jaskold Gabszewicz (1967). Demand fluctuations, capacity utilization and prices, *Operations Research Verfahren*, 3: 119–41 (Chapter 11 supra.)

Drèze, J.H. and J. Greenberg (1980). Hedonic coalitions: Optimality and stability, *Econometrica*, 48(4): 987–1003

Drèze, J.H. and K.P. Hagen (1978). Choice of product quality: Equilibrium and efficiency, *Econometrica*, 46(3): 493–513

Drèze, J.H. and F. Modigliani (1981). The trade-off between real wages and employment in an open economy, *European Economic Review*, 15: 1–40

Feldstein, M. (1974). Unemployment compensation, adverse incentives and distributional anomalies, *National Tax Journal*, 37: 231–44

—(1976). Temporary layoffs in the theory of unemployment, *Journal of Political Economy*, 84: 937–52

Fischer, S. (1977). Long-term contracting, sticky prices and monetary policy, a comment, *Journal of Monetary Economics*, 3: 317–23

Friedman, M. (1953). La théorie de l'incertitude et la distribution des revenus selon leur grandeur, *Econométrie*, Paris: CNRS, pp. 65–79

Friedman, M. and S. Kuznets (1945). *Income from Independent Professional Practice*, New York: National Bureau of Economic Research

Gordon, D.F. (1974). A neo-classical theory of Keynesian unemployment, *Economic Inquiry*, 12: 431–59

Gordon, R.J. (1976). Aspects of the theory of involuntary unemployment. In K. Brunner and A.M. Meltzer (eds.), *The Phillips Curve and Labor Markets*, Amsterdam: North-Holland

—(1977). Aspects of unemployment theory: Reply to Azariadis, *Journal of Monetary Economics*, 3: 257–60

Grossman, H.I. (1977). Risk shifting and reliability in labor markets, *Scandinavian Journal of Economics*, 79: 187–209

—(1978a). Risk shifting, layoffs, and seniority, *Journal of Monetary Economics*, 4: 661–86

—(1978b). Risk shifting, the dole and layoffs, Working Paper 78–21, Brown University, Providence, RI

Hirshleifer, J. (1971). The private and social value of information and the reward to inventive activity, *American Economic Review*, 61: 561–74

Holmström, B. (1979). Equilibrium long-term labour contracts, mimeo, Svenska Handelshögskolan, Helsinki

Kerchove, A.M. de (1976). Fluctuations de la demande, capacité de production et rémunération du facteur travail, mimeo, Institut des Sciences Economiques, Louvain

Malinvaud, E. (1972). The allocation of individual risks in large markets, *Journal of Economic Theory*, 4: 312–28

Meade, J. (1972). The theory of labor-managed firms and of profit sharing, *Economic Journal*, 82: 402–28

Oi, W. (1962). Labour as a quasi-fixed factor, *Journal of Political Economy*, 70: 538–55

Polemarchakis, H.M. and L. Weiss (1978). Fixed wages, layoffs, unemployment compensation, and welfare, *American Economic Review*, 68: 909–17

Pratt, J.W. (1964). Risk aversion in the small and in the large, *Econometrica*, 32: 127–36

Sheshinski, E. and J.H. Drèze (1976). Demand fluctuations, capacity utilization, and costs, *American Economic Review*, 66: 731–42 (Chapter 12 supra.)

Steinherr, A. (1978). A new proposal for wage indexation, *Bulletin de l'IRES*, 49: 1–16

Stiglitz, J. (1974). Incentives and risks in sharecropping, *Review of Economic Studies*, 41: 219–55

Tisdell, C.A. (1968). *The Theory of Price Uncertainty, Production and Profit*, Princeton, NJ: Princeton University Press

18 Some theory of labour management and participation*

1 Labour management

One hundred years ago, the first edition of the *Eléments d'Economie Politique Pure* by Léon Walras was half-way through printing. This anniversary provides special justification for the presentation of a Walras lecture at our congress. It also places a special burden on the author of the lecture to rationalise the choice of his pet-subject through appropriate references to the life and works of Walras. I will in due course provide such rationalisation for my topic, which is the pure theory of labour management and participatory economies.

This topic currently arouses a great deal of interest – at various levels. For some, labour management, or self-management, is a global project of political, social and economic organisation. For others, it is a form of organisation that meets a basic human aspiration and should be fostered wherever possible, through modest as well as ambitious projects. For our purpose here, a labour-managed economy is an economy where production is carried out in firms organised by workers who get together and form collectives or partnerships. These firms hire non-labour inputs, including capital, and sell outputs, under the assumed objective of maximising the welfare of the members, for which a simple proxy is sometimes found in the return (value added) per worker. The capital can be either publicly or privately owned. To permit easier comparison, I will base this presentation on private ownership.

*Walras lecture delivered at the Third World Congress of the Econometric Society, Toronto, August 1975. The comments and suggestions of Volker Böhm, Maurice Marchand, John Roberts and Henry Tulkens are gratefully acknowledged.

Such economies have been studied by Vanek (1970) whose *General Theory of Labour-Managed Market Economies* extends comprehensively the seminal contributions of Ward (1958) and Domar (1966); and by Meade (1972) who presents a lucid, concise review of that work, as well as his own views on 'The Theory of Labour-Managed Firms and Profit-Sharing'.

I would like to report here on my attempts at studying labour-managed economies with the general equilibrium methodology. The outcome of these attempts may serve as a yardstick to assess the usefulness of the approach introduced by Walras one hundred years ago.

Although my presentation will be largely informal, it rests upon technical analysis that will be made available separately. The presentation will consist of three parts. In the first part, I define a Walrasian equilibrium for a labour-managed market economy and contrast its properties with those of a competitive equilibrium. Next, I discuss the choice of working conditions under labour management and profit maximisation. Finally, I take up some of the more intriguing problems raised by risk-bearing

2 A market economy

In defining a labour-management equilibrium, my basic model will be largely, but not entirely, borrowed from Walras' final edition – not the fourth, 'definitive' edition of 1926, but the truly 'definitive' posthumous edition of 1959, known as *Theory of Value* (Debreu (1959)).

I will thus take as given a list of perfectly divisible commodities – goods and labour services – described by their physical characteristics, their date, and their location. Also given is a set of individuals, who will be consumers, workers, and property owners. They are identified by an initial endowment, a consumption set, and a preference relation on that set. It is convenient to assume that all preferences are complete, transitive, and strongly monotonic (meaning that individuals prefer more consumption to less, but prefer less labour to more).

On the production side, I will depart from the standard Walrasian model in *Theory of Value*, which uses as a starting point a given set of 'producers' or firms. Instead, I want to allow for the free association of workers into production cooperatives. To that end, I describe the pure technological knowledge of the economy by means of a production set Y in the commodity space. This pure knowledge is freely accessible to all, even if its use requires inputs of qualified labour (by engineers, skilled technicians, econometricians, etc.). This free access, or free entry, condition is reflected in the technical assumption that Y contains the origin and that Y satisfies additivity.[1]

In order to describe production possibilities via pure technological

[1]To quote: 'Insofar as Y represents technological knowledge, it is clear that two production plans separately possible are jointly possible' (Debreu, 1959, p. 41).

knowledge, one must assume that all scarce inputs are listed as commodities. In a real economy at a given time, some of these inputs take the form of initial assets that are neither divisible nor reproducible. In the standard model these assets belong to firms and remain hidden behind the individual production sets. Here they are treated as physical goods, but I do not assume convexity of the production sets, so as to allow for indivisibilities. The two formulations are equivalent, except that the number of firms is given – and irrelevant – in the standard model, whereas it is indeterminate here. Instead, there is an unlimited number of 'potential firms'.

A feasible allocation for the economy is a set of consumption plans, one for each consumer in his consumption set, and of production plans, one for each potential firm in its production set, such that demand equals supply for each good and each type of labour.

In order to define a competitive equilibrium for that economy, one introduces a vector of prices, one for each good, and a vector of wages, one for each type of labour. A feasible allocation, a price vector and a wage vector together define a competitive equilibrium provided two conditions are met: first, the production plan of every potential firm must yield maximum profit over its production set, given prices and wages. Under our assumptions, these profits are zero for all firms. Second, the consumption plan of every consumer must be best for his preferences over the budget set defined by prices, wages and his initial resources.

3 Labour-management equilibrium

Under labour management, firms are organised by workers, who buy and sell physical goods at market prices and share among themselves the 'value added' in production. Maximisation of value added per worker replaces maximisation of profit as an objective for the firm, thereby yielding a new set of equilibrium conditions for production. The shares in value added replace salaries as determinants of individual incomes, thereby yielding a new definition of individual budget sets and new equilibrium conditions for labour supply and consumption. Each firm, that is each production cooperative, must now decide how its value added is to be shared among its members. Following Marx and Vanek (for once they agree), I assume that shares in value added may vary with the type of labour performed. Thus, labour that is physically more exacting or requires more training may receive a higher share than common 'abstract' labour, the relative weights being 'somehow' determined firm by firm. For a given type of labour, individual shares are proportional to quantity supplied. An individual's total share is thus a weighted sum of the quantities of the different types of labour he performs. Value added per worker is value added per equivalent number of full time common workers (where 'full time' means some given number of hours).

An equilibrium for a labour-managed market economy consists of a feasible allocation, a price vector for physical goods and, within each firm, a set of weights defining value shares for the different types of labour, such that two conditions hold. First, the production plan of every potential firm must yield maximum value added per worker (as just defined), given the prices and labour weights. Second, the consumption plan of every consumer (a plan which also specifies his labour supply) must be best for his preferences over the budget set defined by prices, unit shares in value added, and his initial resources.

On the assumption that production possibilities are the same under profit maximisation and under labour management, the following propositions are readily established (Drèze, 1974).

(1) With every labour-management equilibrium, one can associate a vector of salaries such that the given allocation, the given prices, and these salaries, together, define a competitive equilibrium.

(2) The set of allocations that can be sustained, under suitable redistribution of initial resources, as competitive equilibria and as labour management equilibria, are identical, and coincide with the set of Pareto-optima.

In other words, maximising average value added gross of wages, or maximising total value added net of competitive wages, leads to the same general equilibrium solutions. These propositions are intuitively plausible when it is realised that the definition of budget sets implies perfect mobility of labour across firms. In equilibrium, either labour mobility or competitive labour markets lead to labour incomes geared to marginal productivity.

The propositions are useful in establishing the compatibility of labour management with efficiency. Conditionally on equilibrium, they establish compatibility of labour management with profit maximisation, within a given economy or even within a single firm. The propositions also permit reliance upon the more developed theory of competitive economies to study such questions as existence, uniqueness, stability and continuity of labour-management equilibria.

These conclusions are reminiscent of those reached by Barone (1908) and his followers about *The Economic Theory of Socialism* (Lange (1938)). In both cases, the conclusions illustrate the merits and limitations of static equilibrium analysis, which provides very clear answers to oversimplified questions. In our case, the correct answer had been reached through partial analysis by Vanek and Meade. But the general equilibrium reasoning is simpler, more rigorous, and, of course, more general. Yet the questions are too narrow. Meaningful comparisons between economic systems should recognise the differences in productivity associated with the respective incentive schemes. Also, these comparisons should not deal only with equilibrium allocations; they should also deal with such issues as the ability of alternative systems to generate equilibria, or to generate satisfactory adjustments to disequilibrium situations, or to generate alternative solutions (like underemployment or monopolistic equilibria).

The analyses of Vanek (1970) and Meade (1972, 1974) deal with such issues. I have not attempted to approach them from a general equilibrium viewpoint. The incentives problem is not easily reducible to formal analysis, and the comparative advantages of general equilibrium theorists are still confined to statics, not to dynamics.

Instead, I have pursued through static analysis two issues which are stressed both in the literature and in the debates among social leaders. One issue concerns investment decisions under uncertainty, especially uncertainty about future employment conditions. I will return to that issue shortly. The other one, to which I now turn, concerns decisions about working conditions.

4 Choice of working conditions

Vanek insists that such aspects of working conditions as speed, intensity and duration of work, the design of tools or working posts, and so on, would be chosen differently under labour management than under profit maximisation. He even sees in this property a major claim to superiority for labour-managed economies. The urgency with which some social leaders advocate labour control over working conditions and the repeated occurrence of industrial relations conflicts on this very matter confirm the plausibility of his claim. Yet there is an alternative view – more popular perhaps in Chicago than in Ithaca – namely that working conditions more advantageous, on balance in terms of both costs and benefits, to workers would be consistent with profit maximisation, in the absence of wage rigidities.

The standard model, used so far, ignores this problem because it proceeds from a given list of commodities and hence from given types of labour and given working conditions.[2]

Choice of working conditions is a special case of the general problem of choice of product quality, which is logically the same for an input (labour) as for an output (consumer good). The 'hedonic characteristics' approach to consumer demand provides a useful framework to discuss that problem. That framework has indeed permitted ingenious empirical work by Thalers and Rosen (1973), who measure implicit prices for some characteristics of working conditions, such as on-the-job safety. The special, but tractable, case of linear technology is sufficient to treat our problem.

Three remarks are in order. First, when there are many different commodities and few characteristics (the case considered in the index-number literature), competitive pricing of commodities entails competitive implicit pricing of characteristics, and quality choices guided by profits at these implicit prices inherit the general efficiency of competitive solutions.

[2] Or else one should assume that working conditions can differ from one worker to the next in the same shop, which would be totally unrealistic.

Second, when there are fewer commodities than characteristics, choosing product quality is like choosing a vector of semi-public goods. To illustrate, the menu served at a congress banquet is a public good from the viewpoint of congress participants, and should satisfy the well-known 'Samuelson (1954) conditions' in order to be efficient. There is a difference, however. Consumers choose the quantities consumed – possibly zero. It could be that (1) quality choice is efficient, given the quantities consumed; and (2) optimal quantities are consumed, given the quality; but (3) simultaneous changes in quality and quantities would permit a global improvement. An example of such simultaneous change was witnessed recently when the French railroads replaced some dining cars by self-service facilities, where simpler courses are bought by a larger set of customers. The non-convexities associated with these simultaneous changes mean that locally efficient quality choices need not be globally efficient.

The same remark applies to working conditions. Such characteristics as duration or intensity of work in a given shop are public goods from the viewpoint of the workers, and they should satisfy the relevant 'Samuelson conditions'. But these conditions guarantee only local efficiency, since a change in working conditions accompanied by a simultaneous change in labour force might result in global improvement.[3] This problem arises in labour-managed, capitalist or socialist economies alike. Like all the problems arising from non-convexities, it does not admit of simple solutions, given the present stage of our knowledge.

Third, we still want to know whether profit-maximising working conditions are at least locally efficient from the viewpoint of the workers, in the absence of implicit prices for work characteristics. The technical answer (and I am quoting here from Drèze and Hagen (1978)) is that they need not be, even under wage flexibility.

Thus, consider an assembly line, where workers would collectively prefer a lower speed of operation, even if their income absorbed the full reduction in value added. This does not imply that the same output could then be produced for a smaller wage bill. Indeed, it might happen that labour supply, at the lower speed of operation and lower hourly wages, is insufficient to produce the same output. In the technical analysis, based upon a Slutsky equation for quality changes, the source of the possible discrepancy is broken down in two components, namely: (1) the labour supply of an individual worker may well be affected by a compensated change in working conditions, and (2) the aggregation over workers of labour supply and of preferences for working conditions obey different rules, possibly leading to an aggregation bias.

The theory thus vindicates the claim that competitive profit maximisation does not imply an efficient choice of working conditions. Labour

---

[3]Such a simultaneous change occurs, for instance, when unskilled workers are replaced by more skilled workers or when men are replaced by women.

management, at least labour control over working conditions, seems to offer a natural remedy. But the theoretical answer has a sobering tone. First, the differences may be slight, a conclusion that is suggested by technical analysis of the two components just mentioned. The difference may even vanish, if a sufficient variety of types of labour entails implicit prices for all the hedonic characteristics of working conditions. Second, labour control over working conditions may be hard to design, since a 'public goods' problem must be solved in order for efficiency, even local efficiency, to obtain. I should also mention, for future reference, that working conditions may have hedonic relevance for consumers as well as for workers. Opening hours of shops, banks, post offices, etc., provide an obvious example. This adds a new dimension to the analysis.

As far as the usefulness of theory is concerned, it may be claimed that theory is indispensable to clarify a disputed issue. Note that the clarification comes from a recent development in demand analysis that has not been fully integrated into general equilibrium theory.

5 Firms as coalitions of agents

This discussion of working conditions, like that of Walrasian equilibrium, assumes perfect divisibility of labour and absence of externalities. This enables workers to distribute their work over several firms, or to choose individually the length of their working day. It assumes that labour is anonymous: who you work with matters neither in terms of productivity nor in terms of preference. I regard as potentially more appealing the alternative 'coalition production economies' approach of Hildenbrand (1970), Böhm (1974), Oddou (1976) and Sondermann (1974). Under that approach, one simply assumes that the production possibilities of a given coalition S of agents are described by a production set $Y(S)$ in the commodity space. The correspondence assigning a production set to every coalition describes fully the production possibilities of the economy.

The potential usefulness of that approach for the study of production under labour management goes approximately as follows. We recognise that labour-managed firms are typically associations of individuals pooling their labour on a full time basis. A partition of the set of agents, or coalition structure, defines a set of labour-managed firms. Each firm (coalition) may then choose a production plan in its production set. Given market prices for physical goods, that production plan should maximise value added. In each firm, value added is distributed among members of the coalition, thereby defining individual incomes, budget sets and demand for consumption goods. Equilibrium prices for physical goods have the property that supply equals demand for these goods, i.e. the production and consumption plans are feasible.

For additional generality, the production set of each coalition can be defined, not in the commodity space, but in an enlarged space with coordinates indexed by physical goods, the labour contributions of all members of the coalition, and the characteristics of working conditions. The chosen production plan should then maximise value added given the labour inputs and working conditions, while the latter should be chosen through some appropriate group decision rule. Also, individual consumption sets and preferences can be defined, not in the commodity space, but on the set of coalitions and for each coalition in the enlarged space. Who you work with and how work is organised are then objects of preference.

A model with precisely these features appears in the work of Greenberg (1975) on local public goods. Replace firms by 'communities' and working conditions by 'living conditions', and the model just described admits of an almost complete reinterpretation in terms of city formation and local public goods production. Greenberg's work contains a number of interesting game-theoretic results for this model.

Starting with the textbook case of a single physical good, Greenberg and I (1980) have also studied an equilibrium concept inspired by some remarks of Meade (1972) about the 'rules which are appropriate for the running of all forms of labour cooperatives'. Two of these rules bear on the process of coalition formation. Meade suggests that 'a new partner should enter the concern only if two conditions are fulfilled, namely: (a) that the new partner wishes to come in and (b) that the old partners wish to accept him'. He adds, 'what is not perhaps quite obvious, that there must be two analogous conditions for the withdrawal of an existing partner from a cooperative, namely: (a) that the partner concerned wishes to leave and (b) that he should obtain from the remaining partners permission to withdraw' (p. 421). Meade's justification for this last rule goes as follows. A labour cooperative using fixed equipment must raise financial capital. 'As partners withdraw, the remaining partners are left to hold the debt.' 'It is not a true participatory cooperative if any individual partner can without any obligation just walk out and leave his other partners with the full debt burden' (p. 422).

Consider then a solution defined by a coalition structure and, for each coalition, a feasible choice of labour inputs, working conditions, and imputation among members of the output, here assumed composed of a single consumption good. Let that solution fulfill two conditions: (1) the solution is Pareto-optimal within coalitions; and (2) no individual could change coalition in a way consistent with Meade's rules.[4] Call such a solution an 'individually stable contractual equilibrium'. If preferences are continuous, given any coalition, and if the production correspondence is compact-valued, there exist individually stable contractual equilibria.

[4]More technically: (1) for no coalition does there exist an alternative choice (of labour inputs, working conditions and imputation of output) that would be preferred by all members. (2) For no pair of coalitions does there exist a transfer of one individual from the first coalition to the second, a transfer of resources in either direction, and feasible choices in the two new coalitions, that would be preferred by all members of these two coalitions.

Under the additional assumptions that preferences are convex, given any coalition, and that the production correspondence is convex-valued, a stronger result holds. Consider an arbitrary sequence of solutions, each of which is Pareto-optimal within coalitions and derived from its predecessor by the move of a single individual from one coalition to another one, in a way consistent with Meade's rule. Such a sequence always converges to an individually stable contractual equilibrium.

This is not a very deep result. It uses a weak solution concept, which does not imply efficiency, contrary perhaps to an earlier conjecture of Tiebout (1956). But it is an encouraging result, to the extent that the model is very general, the assumptions are minimal, and cooperative game theory seems to provide a natural framework to study the process of coalition formation and the imputation of value added – or, more generally, to deal with indivisibilities and externalities.

6   Uncertainty

Let us now turn to some of the intriguing problems raised by uncertainty. An important distinction is that between risks embodied in physical capital and risks embodied in human capital. The nature of the risks is the same in both cases, namely uncertainty about the future value of an existing asset. In both cases there exist relatively risky assets – like a supertanker, an aircraft engineer, or a Bayesian econometrician – and relatively safe assets – like a house, a mechanic, or a computer programmer. But a crucial difference is that physical assets are transferred by outright sales, whereas human assets are not. Furthermore, institutions designed to share the risks embodied in physical assets are more developed, in most Western economies, than institutions designed to share risks embodied in human assets. Similarly, the theory of efficient allocation of risk bearing is more developed for physical capital than for human capital. I will, accordingly, discuss at some length risk bearing for physical capital in a labour-managed economy, then conclude with a brief remark about risks embodied in human capital, a remark inspired by explicit consideration of future labour inputs.

My basic model is again largely, but not entirely, borrowed from Debreu's *Theory of Value*, where uncertainty is treated along the 'states of nature' approach introduced by Arrow (1953). Following several authors in the field of finance, I consider only two time periods: period 1 (now), when the true state of nature is unknown, and period 2 (then), when the true state will be known. And I consider a single commodity in period 2. The description of production and consumption is the same as in *Theory of Value*, but financial institutions are different. Thus, a production plan is defined by a vector of inputs in period 1 and a vector of conditional output levels in period 2, one for each possible state. Production sets, in the space of inputs and conditional outputs, describe the uncertain returns to investment and the technological substitution possibilities among alternative state-distributions of outputs. For instance, drilling for oil in the North Sea is a production activity. The level of investment is closely related to the number of drillings. The returns, measured by the richness of the fields discovered, depend upon the unknown state of nature. By choosing the location and depth of the drillings, alternative state distributions of returns are generated from a given investment level. Similarly, a consumption plan specifies a vector of consumption (and work) in period 1 and a vector of consumption levels in period 2 conditionally on the state of nature. Individual preferences are defined over consumption plans.

Instead of assuming, as in *Theory of Value*, the existence of a complete set of markets for trading in contingent claims, I will adopt the more realistic financial institutions of a stock market economy. There exist spot markets for all commodities in period 1; there exist no insurance markets for trading now in contingent outputs then; there is a given, finite set of business firms, each one identified with a production set; these firms undertake the investments and finance them by issuing shares and defaultless bonds; and there is a stock market, where shares of all firms are traded. Individual savings are invested in these shares or in bonds.

In this model, as remarked by Leland (1975) and Hagen (1973), a share in a firm may be regarded as a commodity with as many hedonic characteristics as there are states of nature. Individuals choose portfolios of shares that are best for their consumption preferences over the relevant budget sets. The remarks made earlier about choice of product quality in the hedonic characteristics model apply here to the choice of investments. With fewer firms (commodities) than states (characteristics), the set of feasible allocations is not convex, and competitive market value maximisation is not always efficient. The 'Samuelson conditions' which are necessary for local efficiency imply, for each firm, the existence of shadow prices for conditional future outputs, defined as averages of the corresponding marginal rates of substitution in consumption, weighted by individual share holdings. Although these conditions are difficult to implement in practice, as noted by Gevers (1974), they define unambiguously rules of management necessary for Pareto efficiency in a stock market economy. Also, the relationship of shadow prices to consumer preferences provides a useful criterion for comparing alternative systems.

7 Financing the labour-managed firms

The counterpart of this model for labour-managed economies is obtained by imposing different financial institutions on the same physical model. I continue to rule out insurance markets for future conditional outputs. For simplicity I reason at once for a given set of firms, ignoring the process through which they are formed. Spot markets are now restricted to physical goods. Labour inputs give right to shares in value added. But value added is uncertain, being defined by output in period 2, which depends upon the state of nature. Shares in value added are shares in uncertain future output, just like the shares of stock in the previous model.

If investment were financed entirely by retained earnings or defaultless bonds, shares in value added would, in fact, be levered shares of stock. An economy where these shares are held by the workers and cannot be traded is a more constrained version of the stock market economy, where the stock market has been eliminated, and where the workers engaged in a production activity must bear all the risks associated with that production. This additional constraint is clearly undesirable. As remarked by Meade (1972, p. 426): 'While property owners can spread their risks by putting small bits of their property into a large number of concerns, a worker cannot put small bits of his effort into a large number of different jobs. This presumably is a main reason why we find risk-bearing capital hiring labour rather than risk-bearing labour hiring capital.'

Vanek (1974) also recognises this problem, and he develops an alternative specification, whereby labour-managed firms are financed by a combination of three financial instruments, namely bonds, negotiable shares of stock issued on the market and non-negotiable shares of stock issued to the workers. It is implicit in Vanek's specification that control of the firms remains vested with the workers only.[5]

Two possibilities should be distinguished, according as to whether the shares issued on the capital market are similar to those held by the workers or they are allowed to be different.

Efficiency analysis of the first case is straightforward. It is always desirable for a labour-managed firm to issue on the market shares representing 100 per cent of future output and to divide the proceeds of the sale among the workers, who may then allocate freely their income between current consumption and a diversified portfolio acquired on the stock market. The workers cannot gain from tying up part of their income in a risky asset that cannot be traded.

Furthermore, efficient production plans are sustained by shadow prices for conditional future outputs, defined as averages of the corresponding marginal rates of substitution in consumption, as weighted by individual shareholdings.

These are precisely the conditions already encountered in the stock market economy. The analysis developed for the certainty case may be repeated. But the equivalence among solution sets now holds for efficient allocations, rather than for equilibrium allocations, which are less naturally defined.

In this simple model, where asset diversification by firms and future

---

[5]Vanek also considers a situation in which the stock market is replaced by a central investment agency holding all the shares in the labour-managed firms. As indicated at the beginning, I do not pursue that suggestion here, in order to maintain simple terms of comparison.

labour inputs are ignored, an efficient allocation of risk bearing in private ownership labour-managed economies requires the organisation of a stock market, so as to permit portfolio diversification. Given the existence of a stock market, efficiency of production decisions requires that control rights be vested with the shareholders.

To illustrate, suppose that a group of sailors and derrickmen sets about drilling for oil in the North Sea. Their output could be very valuable or worthless. By issuing shares of stock, the workers' collective can transfer its financial risk to others and receive a sure payment, which is in the nature of a wage. Once the uncertain output has been sold, it matters little to the workers that drilling be carried out at one place or another, and the risk preferences of shareholders (who are directly concerned) might as well be decisive (subject to earlier remarks about working conditions).

There is no reason why the members of labour-managed firms should bother to carry risks that can easily be shed. Furthermore it would be inefficient here to let the risk preferences of the workers interfere with production decisions, for the same reason that it is inefficient under certainty to let their consumption preferences interfere with production decisions.

These conclusions are not surprising, since all the risks considered thus far are in the nature of capital risks, borne by shareholders, and management according to the preferences of those concerned, is in the true spirit of self-management. Theory leads here to conclusions that differ from those anticipated by the proponents of the model – a useful role, provided one recognises the limitations of the model and of an efficiency analysis that still lacks a convincing counterpart in equilibrium analysis.

8 Asset diversification

Consider now the second possibility, where shares issued on the capital market differ from those held by the workers. This would be the case, say, if workers issued common stock and held preferred stock. Three remarks are in order.

First, it would again be more efficient, from the viewpoint of the workers, to issue all the stock, both preferred and common, on the market and to let individual workers reinvest their incomes as they please.

Second, we must now specify how future output should be divided between common stock and preferred stock. Asset diversification entails the new possibility of specifying a division that varies with the state of nature. Efficiency would require a state-dependent division of returns such that, for every state, the average marginal rate of substitution in consumption, weighted by individual shareholdings, be the same for holders of preferred stock as for holders of common stock.

This condition, which holds whether preferred stock is negotiable or not, is easy to understand in theory but hard to apply in practice. The theoretical rationale is the following. We are concerned with the division of a given output, conditional on some state, between two groups of shareholders. If one group valued that conditional output more than the other group, it should receive a larger fraction of the said output and compensate the other group in terms of current income. Both groups would then stand to gain.

If this condition were satisfied, both groups would agree about production decisions. Indeed, the consumption preferences of both groups would imply the same shadow prices for conditional future output.

But it is not easy to see how this condition could be satisfied in practice, except in the simplest cases. For sharper exposition, let the workers hold the preferred shares and capital owners hold the common shares. If both groups displayed similar risk preferences, the labour incomes implied by an efficient division should be characterised by the same degree of uncertainty as diversified portfolios – neither more, nor less. For risks that are absorbed by capital markets at no premium, labour incomes should be certain, as under a salary system with 100 per cent unemployment insurance. For risks that sell at a premium on capital markets, i.e. socially significant risks, labour incomes should not be certain, but should bear their share of global uncertainties. Perhaps a form of indexation of labour incomes on national income (rather than consumer prices) would be a first step towards fulfilling the condition under review.

Third, if the division of returns between preferred stock and common stock does not satisfy the efficiency condition just discussed then the two groups no longer agree about production decisions. Efficient production decisions are sustained by shadow prices, defined as weighted averages of the marginal rates of substitution of both workers and capital owners. Each group is weighted by the fraction of output accruing to it. Inside each group individuals are weighted by their shareholdings. That is, efficiency calls for participation of both capital and labour in defining criteria for managerial decisions affecting the future incomes of both groups. Under an efficient division of returns, the interests of both groups are concordant. More generally, these interests are combined in a very simple way – an arithmetic average, with weights measuring the respective interests at stake. But the weights vary from state to state, so that simplicity is more apparent than real.

9 Participation

More generally, when firms use labour inputs and capital inputs both now and in the future, we have automatically two assets, labour and capital, irrespective of how investment is financed. The problem of specifying the division of output between labour and capital, for every state of nature, always arises, whether capital hires labour or labour hires capital.

The solution suggested by efficiency analysis is still the same. For every firm and every state, the average marginal rates of substitution in consumption of the workers and of the capital owners should be the same, implying that they agree about production decisions. State-dependent wages or dividends, as the case may be, should see to that.

But these conditions should be considered together with those defining the quantity of labour to be performed in every firm under every state. Pareto efficiency requires that the marginal product of labour in any state be equal to a marginal rate of substitution between work and income, obtained as a weighted average over workers. These natural conditions are not compatible with decentralised incentives when efficient rules for the division of output are adopted.

When labour hires capital it would not be in the interest of workers to equate their marginal rate of substitution between work and income to the marginal product of their labour unless that marginal product accrued entirely to them. But efficient risk-bearing typically requires another division.[6]

When capital hires labour, the wage rates required for efficient risk bearing are not equal, *ex post*, to the marginal product of labour. Wages that serve a function of income insurance cannot simultaneously measure labour productivity. Hence, these wages do not sustain, *ex post*, the efficient allocations as decentralised competitive equilibria. This conclusion should not surprise us, since we know from experience that wage rigidities, recognised here as desirable to alleviate income uncertainties, may result in efficient underemployment equilibria.

We now have two reasons why the division of future output between labour and capital may fail to bring both groups in agreement about production and investment decisions. First, the required division would be hard to define in practice. Second, it would be incompatible with decentralised incentives. We may thus expect the need to reconcile the interests of both groups through some form of participatory decision-making, of the kind outlined in my discussion of asset diversification.

Tentative as this conclusion may still be, I regard it as providing theoretical justification for the participation of both labour and capital – whether it be publicly or privately owned – in decisions affecting the future of the firm and hence of its workers and capital owners.

More speculatively, I regard productive organisations or firms as serving a triple role. They produce commodities desired by consumers, they provide employment opportunities filled by workers, and they provide physical investment opportunities for the capital held by people or society.

It is remarkable that conditions exist under which the three roles can be filled efficiently through decentralised decisions sustained by prices. Under more general conditions, when the price system is not fully operative, it is only natural that more elaborate forms of participatory decision-making are required to bring the three roles into harmony.

[6]This problem has been recognised in the related context of sharecropping (see, for example, Stiglitz (1974)).

10 Walras on labour management

Would Léon Walras have accepted that conclusion in 1875, after due briefing on the concept of Pareto efficiency? Before going to Lausanne, he had taken a keen interest in the development of producers' cooperatives in France. In 1865, a set of Walras (1865) lectures on the subject was given in Paris. This led to his appointment as Director of the Caisse d'Escompte des Associations Populaires. In his autobiographical notice, reprinted by Jaffé (1965), Walras explains his endeavours to convince (I translate) 'cooperative members that they should keep to the economic principles applicable to all firms and regard themselves as fulfilling a dual role, as workers and as entrepreneurs; that consequently they should accept the prices of commodities and the wages of labour as determined by market forces; as for the residual difference between revenue and costs, they should allocate it among capital owners, who alone have a claim on profits because they alone absorb losses.' As a Director of the Caisse d'Escompte, Léon Walras extended credit to cooperatives producing straw hats, walking sticks, umbrella handles, and other valuable commodities. (I translate) 'Unfortunately, these cooperatives insisted on low selling prices and high wages, and showed little concern for their capital, less still for the capital they borrowed. None of them succeeded or paid back its loans.' This experience was not forgotten by Walras, who kept referring to it in his later correspondence and defending the viewpoint just quoted.

The first part of this paper confirms the view that the prices of commodities and the remuneration of labour play the same role, and lead to the same equilibrium solutions, under labour management as under profit maximisation. The second part indicates that decentralised profit maximisation will in general fail to be compatible with efficient decisions about working conditions. The third part suggests that efficient risk bearing and efficient production under uncertainty will typically require more elaborate forms of participatory decision-making. Walras cannot be blamed for having omitted to qualify his statements. Instead, he should be praised for having innovated a methodology susceptible of leading to these qualifications and hopefully of throwing, in the future, additional light on issues that could only be treated superficially today.

References

Arrow, K.J. (1953). Le rôle des valeurs boursières pour la répartition la meilleure des risques. In *Econométrie*, pp. 41–7. Paris: CNRS. Translated (1964) as The Role of Securities in the Optimal Allocation of Risk-Bearing. *Review of Economic Studies*, 31: 91–6

Barone, E. (1908). Ministerio della produzione nello stato collectivisto. *Giornale*

Degli Economisti, 37: 269–93, 391–414. Translated (1935) as The Ministry of Production in the Collectivist State. In F.A. von Hayek (ed.), *Collectivist Economic Planning*, pp. 245–90. London: Routledge

Böhm, V. (1974). The Core of an Economy with Production. *Review of Economic Studies*, 61: 429–36

Debreu, G. (1959). *Theory of Value*. New York: Wiley

Domar, E. (1966). The Soviet Collective Farm as a Producer Co-operative. *American Economic Review*, 56: 734–57

Drèze, J.H. (1974). The Pure Theory of Labour-Managed and Participatory Economies, Part I: Certainty. CORE Discussion Paper 7422, Université Catholique de Louvain

Drèze, J.H. and K. Hagen (1978). Choice of Product Quality: Equilibrium and Efficiency. *Econometrica*, 46(3): 493–513

Drèze, J.H. and J. Greenberg (1980). Hedonic Coalitions: Optimality and Stability. *Econometrica* 48(4) 987–1003

Gevers, L. (1974). Competitive Equilibrium of the Stock Exchange and Pareto Efficiency. In J.H. Drèze (ed.), *Allocation under Uncertainty: Equilibrium and Optimality*, pp. 167–91. New York: Macmillan

Greenberg, J. (1975). Pure and Local Public Goods: A Game Theoretic Approach [mimeo]. The Hebrew University of Jerusalem

Hagen, K. (1973). On the Optimality of the Competitive Market System in an Economy with Product Differentiation, Discussion Paper, Norwegian School of Economics and Business Administration, Bergen

Hildenbrand, W. (1970). Existence of Equilibria for Economies with Production and a Measure Space of Consumers, *Econometrica*, 18: 608–23

Jaffé, W. (1965). *Correspondence of Léon Walras and Related Papers, I–III*, Amsterdam: North-Holland

Lange, O. (1938). On the Economic Theory of Socialism. In: *On the Economic Theory of Socialism*, B.E. Lippincott (ed.), Minneapolis: University of Minnesota Press (second printing 1948) 57–143

Leland, H. (1975). Quality Choice and Competition, Working Paper 29, Berkeley: University of California

Meade, J.E. (1972). The Theory of Labour-Managed Firms and of Profit-Sharing, *Economic Journal*, 82: 402–28

—(1974). Labour-Managed Firms in Conditions of Imperfect Competition, *Economic Journal*, 84: 817–24

Oddou, C. (1976). Théorèmes d'existence et d'équivalence pour des économies avec production, *Econometrica*, 44: 265–81

Samuelson, P.A. (1954). The Pure Theory of Public Expenditures, *Review of Economics and Statistics*, 36: 387–9

Sondermann, D. (1974). Economies of Scale and Equilibria in Coalition Production Economies, *Journal of Economic Theory*, 8: 259–91

Stiglitz, J. (1974). Incentives and Risk in Sharecropping, *Review of Economic Studies*, 41: 219–55

Thalers, R. and R. Rosen (1973). The Value of Saving a Life: Evidence from the Labour Market, Discussion Paper 74–2, Rochester, NY: University of Rochester

Tiebout, C. (1956). A Pure Theory of Local Expenditures, *Journal of Political Economy*, 64: 416–24

Vanek, J. (1970). *The General Theory of Labour-Managed Market Economies*,

Ithaca, NY: Cornell University Press

—(1974). Uncertainty and the Investment Decision under Labour Management and their Social Efficiency Implications, Discussion Paper 83, Ithaca, NY: Cornell University

Walras, L. (1865). *Les associations populaires de consommation, de la production et de crédit*, Leçons publiques faites à Paris en janvier et février 1865, Paris: E. Dentu

—(1926). *Eléments d'Economie Politique Pure*, édition définitive, Paris: Pichon, Lausanne: Rouge.

Ward, B. (1958). The Firm in Illyria: Market Syndicalism, *American Economic Review*, 48: 566–89

VII Public decisions

19 Pricing, spending and gambling rules for non-profit organisations*

1 Introduction and conclusions

1.1 Questions

During our association with universities in Europe and in the United States, we have encountered many questions apt to challenge economists, for instance:

1. Should prices charged in university hospitals reflect (marginal) costs alone, or include a monopolistic markup?
2. Should faculty salaries be determined by a standard scale, or vary with the alternative opportunities of faculty members? (For instance, should the respective salaries of a medical doctor and of a biologist, doing similar work in a research laboratory, reflect the higher opportunity cost of the medical doctor?)
3. How should a university allocate its resources among alternative uses, like education and research?
4. Should universities enjoying an endowment fund aim at spending income and maintaining capital, or at accumulating part of the income, or at depleting the fund at some optimal rate?
5. What rate of discount should be used by a university for decisions about plant and equipment?
6. What should be the attitude of a university toward portfolio risk? Should universities adopt less conservative investment policies than, say, managers of private trust funds? (This was once intimated by officers of a Foundation Oriented toward Research and Development; that foundation has recently reduced its spending, due to a sharp decline in market value of endowment.)

*From a joint paper with Maurice Marchand, published in 1976 in a volume of essays in honour of William Vickrey. Sections 3 and 4 of the original paper are omitted here because they are unrelated to uncertainty.

All these questions arise because universities operate under a budget constraint, the level of which is not always set optimally; produce public goods (research); and are sometimes required to sell services below cost (education in state universities).

Similar questions are faced by all non-profit organisations aiming at public service rendered under a budget constraint.

Pricing rules for such organisations have been derived from the first-order conditions for (constrained) Pareto-optimality by Boiteux (1956), in a model related to that investigated thirty years earlier by Ramsey (1927). A straightforward extension of that model to the case of public goods provides the natural framework to answer the questions listed above. Various simplifications must be introduced in order to translate the theoretical answers into operational rules. The purpose of the present chapter is to develop these extensions and simplifications, and to draw conclusions for problems of pricing, resource allocation, and risk bearing in non-profit organisations.

1.2 Answers

Within the limitations of the model studied below,[1] we obtain the following answers to the questions listed above:

1.   A university operating under a binding budget constraint should operate, on the markets for private goods and services, like a profit-maximising monopolist, except that the university should blow up all price elasticities by a constant factor $1/\bar{y}(>1)$; that factor should be such that the budget constraint be satisfied; in particular, the university should engage in price discrimination whenever possible.

2.   A university should adopt the personnel policies of a discriminating monopsonist, except that the university should blow up by the same factor $1/\bar{y}$ the price elasticity of labour supply; outside opportunities are relevant only to the extent that they result in higher price elasticities of supply; for a given type of labour, a lower price elasticity of supply will imply a lower level of employment and a higher excess of marginal productivity over salary.[2]

3.   If the university produces public goods, it should aim at equating (across public goods) the ratios of marginal cost to marginal value, where marginal value is defined by the sum over all consumers of their marginal demand price (willingness to pay) for the public good; this ratio should furthermore be equal to $(1 - \bar{y})$, under the budget constraint; the rules defined under (1) for private goods and under (3) for public goods characterise efficient resource allocation unambiguously.

4.   The same principles apply to intertemporal allocation; intertemporal efficiency will not (except by accident) result in maintaining capital; in particular, expenditures might exceed receipts in periods where income

[1]One major limitation is the assumption that the rest of the economy behaves competitively.
[2]The authors have discovered that the price elasticity of labour supply was very low in their own case. Accordingly, few details about question 2 are given below.

from sources other than endowment are abnormally low, and conversely; intertemporal efficiency does not require that endowment income be defined.

5.   By further application of the same principles, the internal rate of discount to be used in a university should be equal to the relevant market rate plus $\bar{y}$ times its elasticity; the relevant market rate may be either a borrowing rate or a lending rate, as the case may be.

6.   Portfolio choices by a university producing a public good should be guided by a risk-aversion function defined as the sum of (i) the elasticity (with respect to quantity) of the marginal value of the public good, and (ii) minus the output elasticity of the marginal cost of the public good; that sum should furthermore be multiplied by the ratio of average to marginal cost in order to obtain the relative risk-aversion function, or by output times the reciprocal of marginal cost to obtain the absolute risk-aversion function.

We believe that these answers provide theoretically sound approximations to optimal decision rules for non-profit organisations (NPOs). Practical application of these rules still requires a knowledge of cost and demand parameters that is typically not available. We hope that our theoretical analysis may stimulate further work on the measurement problems.

1.3 Organisation of the chapter

The chapter is organised as follows. The Ramsey–Boiteux models are extended to the case of public goods in Section 2. The role of income transfers in that model is discussed and illustrated in Section 3, which is in the nature of a digression. The results are applied to problems of pricing and resource allocation in Section 4. In Section 5, the model is simplified and extended, so as to permit a discussion of risk preferences. Section 5 is largely independent of Sections 3 and 4 and may be read after Section 2.

Bibliographical remark. The idea of extending the models of Ramsey and Boiteux to public goods is not new. Our results in Section 2 parallel those of Diamond and Mirrlees (1971), Stiglitz and Dasgupta (1971) and Atkinson and Stern (1974). Systematic discussions of budget constraints for producers appear in the work of Bronsard (1971) and Kolm (1970). A recent survey of this and related work – e.g. by Baumol and Bradford (1970) and Bergson (1972) – is given by Guesnerie (1975).

2 Pricing and public goods production under a budget constraint

2.1 The model

Following Boiteux (1956), we consider an economy consisting of m individuals, indexed $k = 1, \ldots, m$; v private firms, indexed $h = 1, \ldots, v$; and a public sector. There are n private goods, indexed $i = 1, \ldots, n$, with market prices $p_1, \ldots, p_i, \ldots, p_n$, consumed or supplied by the individuals, the private firms and the public sector, in respective quantities q_i^k, x_i^h, y_i, $i = 1, \ldots, n, k = 1, \ldots, m, h = 1, \ldots, v$; these quantities are also denoted $q^k, x^h,$ y in vector notation. The nth good is used as numeraire ($p_n = 1$). In addition, we introduce l public goods indexed $j = 1, \ldots, l$. These goods are produced by the public sector, and consumed by the individuals, in (identical) quantities $z_j, j = 1, \ldots, l$. For simplicity, we assume that the production possibilities of the private firms are independent of the production of public goods. The more general case presents no special difficulty (see, e.g. Sandmo (1972)).

Individual preferences are assumed representable by quasi-concave, twice continuously differentiable utility functions $U^k(q^k, z)$. Each individual is assumed to maximise utility under the budget constraint

$$p \cdot q^k - r^k = 0 \tag{2.1}$$

where r^k denotes the 'income' of individual k. Incomes are measured in terms of the numeraire. In the model of this section, we follow Boiteux in assuming that individual incomes are policy variables, which can be redistributed freely under the single constraint that their sum be equal to the net profits of the private and public sectors, as per equation (2.6) below.

First-order conditions for consumer equilibrium imply, together with (2.1):

$$\frac{U_i^k}{U_n^k} = \frac{p_i}{p_n}, \quad i = 1, \ldots, n,$$

$$\sum_i p_i \frac{\partial q_i^k}{\partial r^k} = 1,$$

$$\sum_i p_i \frac{\partial q_i^k}{\partial p_a} + q_a^k = 0, \quad a = 1, \ldots, n-1;$$

$$\sum_i p_i \frac{\partial q_i^k}{\partial z_j} = 0, \quad j = 1, \ldots, l, k = 1, \ldots, m, \tag{2.2}$$

where U_i^k denotes the partial derivative of U^k with respect to q_i^k.

The production sets of private firms are assumed representable by concave, continuously differentiable production functions $f^h(x^h)$. Each firm is assumed to maximise its profits $p \cdot x^h$ under the constraint $f^h(x^h) = 0$, taking p as given. The first-order conditions imply

$$\frac{f_i^h}{f_n^h} = \frac{p_i}{p_n}, \quad i = 1, \ldots, n,$$

$$\sum_i p_i \frac{\partial x_i^h}{\partial p_a} = 0, \quad a = 1, \ldots, n-1, \tag{2.3}$$

where f_i^h denotes the partial derivative of f^h with respect to x_i^h.

The public sector has a production set in the space of private and public goods, here assumed representable by the twice continuously differentiable production function $g(y, z)$. The budget constraint of the public sector takes the form

$$b - p \cdot y = 0 \tag{2.4}$$

where b is some given number. Partial derivatives of the production function g with respect to y_i or z_j will be denoted g_i or g_j, a concise notation that should not cause confusion.

The physical constraints, or market clearing conditions, are

$$\sum_k q^k - y - \sum_h x^h = 0. \tag{2.5}$$

Together, they imply a constraint on the sum of individual incomes

$$p \cdot \sum_k q^k = \sum_k r^k = p \cdot y + p \cdot \sum_h x^h = b + \sum_h (p \cdot x^h). \tag{2.6}$$

2.2 First-order conditions

The problem of defining a constrained Pareto-optimum may be written as

$$\operatorname*{Max}_{p,r,y,z} \sum_k \lambda^k U^k [q^k(p, r^k, z), z]$$

subject to

(α) $\sum_k q^k(p, r^k, z) - y - \sum_h x^h(p) = 0$

(β) $g(y, z) = 0$

(γ) $b - p \cdot y = 0$

where the greek letters denote Lagrange multipliers and where the first order conditions and constraints on the behaviour of individuals and private firms are implied by the symbols $q^k(p, r^k, z), x^h(p)$, which denote demand or supply functions.

Remarks

1. The demand and supply functions of individuals and private firms embody the implicit assumption of competitive behaviour in the private sector.

2. In this formulation, non-negativity conditions are ignored. A more courageous formulation, using the Kuhn–Tucker conditions, would not change the nature of our results.

3. Using both prices (p) and quantities (z) as decision variables – constrained by (α) – is convenient for exposition. If non-negativity conditions were recognised, a number of private goods (not supplied by the public sector) would cease to enter as policy instruments.

The first-order conditions are

$$(p_a)\sum_k\sum_i \lambda^k U_i^k \frac{\partial q_i^k}{\partial p_a} - \sum_i \alpha_i\left(\sum_k \frac{\partial q_i^k}{\partial p_a} - \sum_h \frac{\partial x_i^h}{\partial p_a}\right) + \gamma y_a = 0,$$

$$a = 1,\ldots,n-1.$$

$$(r^k)\,\lambda^k \sum_i U_i^k \frac{\partial q_i^k}{\partial r^k} - \sum_i \alpha_i \frac{\partial q_i^k}{\partial r^k} = 0, \quad k = 1,\ldots,m.$$

$$(y_i)\,\alpha_i - \beta g_i + \gamma p_i = 0, \quad i = 1,\ldots,n$$

$$(z_j)\sum_k \lambda^k\left(U_j^k + \sum_i U_i^k \frac{\partial q_i^k}{\partial z_j}\right) - \sum_i \alpha_i \sum_k \frac{\partial q_i^k}{\partial z_j} - \beta g_j = 0, \qquad j = 1,\ldots,l.$$

Using (2.2), one may rewrite the conditions (r^k) and then (p_a) as follows:

$$\frac{\lambda^k U_n^k}{p_n} = \sum_i \alpha_i \frac{\partial q_i^k}{\partial r^k} \tag{2.7}$$

$$\sum_i \alpha_i\left[\sum_k\left(\frac{\partial q_i^k}{\partial p_a} + q_a^k \frac{\partial q_i^k}{\partial r^k}\right) - \sum_h \frac{\partial x_i^h}{\partial p_a}\right] = \gamma y_a. \tag{2.8}$$

Because the first-order conditions are homogeneous of degree zero in the Lagrange multipliers, $(\alpha, \beta, \gamma, \lambda)$, one may multiply these by an arbitrary non-null scalar. It is convenient to define $\bar{\alpha} = \alpha p_n/\beta g_n$, $\bar{\gamma} = \gamma p_n/\beta g_n$, $\bar{\lambda} = \lambda p_n/\beta g_n$. After this transformation, conditions (y_i) become

$$\bar{\alpha}_n + \bar{\gamma} p_n = p_n, \quad \bar{\alpha}_i = \frac{g_i}{g_n} p_n - \bar{\gamma} p_i, \quad i = 1,\ldots,n. \tag{2.9}$$

Let n be the index of an input (to the public sector), in terms of which costs and productivities will be measured. When i is the index of an output, $(g_i/g_n)p_n$ defines the marginal cost of good i. When i is the index of an input, $(g_i/g_n)p_n$ defines the marginal value productivity of factor i. We find it convenient to write $Cm_i =_{\text{def}}(g_i/g_n)p_n$, and to phrase our interpretation for the case where Cm_i is the marginal cost of output i. We leave to the reader the appropriate rephrasing needed when Cm_i is the marginal productivity of input i.

The terms in brackets in (2.8) are the partial derivatives, with respect to p_a, of the compensated market demand functions for y_i, $i = 1,\ldots,n$. Denote these terms by $\partial \hat{y}_i/\partial p_a$, where the symbol $\hat{\ }$ indicates that the demand function is compensated. By conditions (2.2) and (2.3),

$$\sum_i p_i \frac{\partial \hat{y}_i}{\partial p_a} = 0.$$

Multiplying (2.8) by

$$\frac{p_n}{\beta g_n},$$

adding

$$(\bar{\gamma} - 1)\sum_i p_i \frac{\partial \hat{y}_i}{\partial p_a}$$

to the left-hand side and using (2.9), we obtain

$$\sum_i (Cm_i - p_i)\frac{\partial \hat{y}_i}{\partial p_a} = \bar{\gamma} y_a. \tag{2.10}$$

These are precisely the 'Ramsey–Boiteux conditions' for optimal pricing under a budget constraint. In the absence of public goods, $\bar{\gamma}$ should be such that $p \cdot y = b$. With public goods, we go back to conditions (z_j) and rewrite them successively as follows, using (2.2), (2.7), and (2.9):

$$\sum_k \frac{U_j^k}{U_n^k}(\lambda^k U_n^k) = \beta g_j + \sum_i \alpha_i \sum \frac{\partial q_i^k}{\partial z_j}$$

$$p_n \sum_k \frac{U_j^k}{U_n^k}\left[\sum_i \bar{\alpha}_i \frac{\partial q_i^k}{\partial r^k}\right] = \frac{g_j}{g_n}p_n + \sum_i \bar{\alpha}_i \sum_k \frac{\partial q_i^k}{\partial z_j} \tag{2.11}$$

$$p_n \sum_k \frac{U_j^k}{U_n^k}\left[1 - \bar{\gamma} + \sum_i (Cm_i - p_i)\frac{\partial q_i^k}{\partial r^k}\right] = Cm_j - \sum_i (p_i - Cm_i)\sum_k \frac{\partial q_i^k}{\partial z_j}.$$

Following standard notation in the literature on public goods, we will denote the amount of numeraire that individual k would be just willing to pay for one additional unit of public good j by

$$\pi_j^k = p_n \frac{U_j^k}{U_n^k}.$$

We will also denote by $\partial \hat{y}_i / \partial z_j$ the partial derivative, with respect to z_j, of the compensated market demand function for y_i:

$$\frac{\partial \hat{y}_i}{\partial z_j} = \sum_k \left(\frac{\partial q_i^k}{\partial z_j} - \pi_j^k \frac{\partial q_i^k}{\partial r^k}\right). \tag{2.12}$$

Indeed, $-\pi_j^k$ is the income adjustment that would exactly compensate individual k for a unit increase in z_j.

With this notation, (2.11) may be written as

$$\sum_k \pi_j^k = \frac{1}{1 - \bar{\gamma}}\left[Cm_j - \sum_i (p_i - Cm_i)\frac{\partial \hat{y}_i}{\partial z_j}\right]. \tag{2.13}$$

Together, conditions (2.4), (2.10), and (2.13) define the rules for pricing and public goods production that should be followed in the public sector.

2.3 Interpretation

In the absence of a budget constraint, optimal production of public goods would be defined by the 'Samuelson conditions':

$$\sum_k \pi_j^k = Cm_j.$$

This result would coincide with (2.13) if $\bar{\gamma}$ (hence γ, the Lagrange Multiplier associated with the budget constraint) were equal to zero, in which case (2.10) would also hold with $p_i = Cm_i$, $i = 1,\ldots,n$. In general, however, this solution will not be consistent with (2.4), calling for $\bar{\gamma} \neq 0$, prices different from marginal costs, and

$$\sum_k \pi_j^k \neq Cm_j.$$

Furthermore, $0 < \bar{\gamma} < 1$ under the plausible assumption that b exceeds the (probably negative) profits that the public sector would make if no budget constraint were imposed (first-best optimum).[3] In terms of (2.13), the impact of the budget constraint on production rules for public goods is twofold:

1.   The marginal cost of public good j is corrected by a term reflecting the difference in net profits from private goods production that would accrue to the public sector if output of z_j were increased by one unit; these profits are evaluated by means of the compensated demand functions, for reasons valid in connection with (2.10) and (2.13) alike, and discussed in the original text; the signs of these adjustments to marginal costs are a priori indeterminate.

2.   Denote by Cm_j the marginal cost of public good j adjusted for the difference in profits; then

$$\sum_k \pi_j^k = \frac{Cm_j}{1-\bar{\gamma}} > Cm_j$$

(since $\bar{\gamma} > 0$). The cost at market prices is inflated by a factor $(1-\bar{\gamma})^{-1}$ to reflect the fact that production of public good j: (a) uses real resources, in an amount measured by Cm_j, and (b) uses resources from the public sector, whose social opportunity cost is higher than if they were used in the private sector (because of the budget constraint).

If all cross-elasticities are negligible, the analogy between conditions (2.10) and (2.13) can be made more apparent by rewriting them as:

---

[3] Under this assumption, $dL/db = -\gamma < 0$, where L stands for the Lagrangian of our maximisation problem. From the signs of the derivatives of L with respect to initial endowments of the nth good given respectively to the private and public sectors, one also infers that $\alpha_n > 0$ and $\beta g_n > 0$. Since

$$\bar{\gamma} = \frac{\gamma}{\beta g_n} = 1 - \frac{\alpha_n}{\beta g_n}$$

it then follows that $0 < \bar{\gamma} < 1$.

$$\bar{\gamma} = \frac{p_i - Cm_i}{p_i} |\hat{\eta}_{y_i p_i}| \tag{2.14}$$

$$\bar{\gamma} = \frac{\sum_k \pi_j^k - Cm_j}{\sum_k \pi_j^k} |\hat{\eta}_{z_j z_j}| \tag{2.15}$$

where $\hat{\eta}$ stands for the compensated demand elasticity

$(\hat{\eta}_{z_j z_j} = 1)$.

3 Risk preferences and portfolio selection in NPOs[4]

3.1 Approach

Until now, we have used a deterministic approach. This was a natural starting point and a satisfactory framework to study pricing rules and some resource allocation problems. However, intertemporal decisions usually involve uncertainty in an essential way. This is particularly true for decisions relating to capital assets, like portfolio choices.

The theory of general equilibrium has been extended to uncertainty by the introduction of 'states of the world' in the definition of commodities (see Arrow, 1964). If there existed markets and prices for all commodities contingent on all states, the analysis in the foregoing section would be complete and would not call for a specific extension to uncertainty. Our rules (2.10) and (2.13) could govern pricing and spending on all commodities (including assets) contingent on all states.

When there are no markets for contingent commodities but markets for (some) assets, an analysis of constrained Pareto-optimality is still possible (see, e.g., Drèze, 1974). One could insert NPOs in a 'state model with incomplete markets' and deal explicitly with issues of risky physical investments, portfolio choices, participation of NPOs in control by stockholders, a.s.o. We feel that an analysis of that kind would be very much worth conducting, but it lies beyond the scope of the present chapter.

There is a more pedestrian, but more operational, approach to some problems of choice under uncertainty, which has been found particularly useful to study portfolio decisions: namely, the analysis of risk preferences in terms of a utility function U and the absolute risk-aversion function U''/U' (or the corresponding relative risk-aversion function (see Pratt, 1964)). This approach is quite satisfactory for analysis of individual decisions, especially in two-asset models. It is not directly applicable to firms, whose preferences

[4]The authors wish to thank Kåre Hagen for a helpful discussion of the material in this section. Work on this problem was started at the University of Chicago in 1968 by one of the authors, who benefited greatly from discussions with Merton Miller.

should be inferred from those of the individuals ultimately concerned (as workers or stockholders). We will now show how it can be applied to NPOs, in a reasonably operational and rigorous way, but at the cost of severe simplifications.

The derivation of risk-aversion functions for NPOs serves two purposes. First, it provides an adequate tool to study those questions which can be answered in terms of a risk-aversion function (like portfolio decisions in a world with two assets, or equivalently in a world where the separation theorem holds (see Merton, 1971)). Second, the analysis of a relatively simple case might serve as a guide for more difficult cases.

In order to place the specific elements of risk bearing by NPOs in proper perspective, we shall first recall the interpretation of the absolute risk-aversion function. We return next to the model of Section 2, simplify it, extend it to uncertainty, and derive risk-aversion functions for NPOs.

3.2 Risk aversion and protfolio selection

The interpretation of the risk-aversion functions is most easily perceived in terms of a simple portfolio (or asset management) problem. Consider an individual, whose preferences among risky prospects are defined by a cardinal utility function for wealth $U(w)$, and who has the option of purchasing, at price p, an asset with random return ξ, satisfying $E(\xi) = \mu$ and $V(\xi) = \sigma^2$. Denote by r his initial wealth and by θ the number of units of the risky asset bought. Then:

$$U(w) = U[r + \theta(\xi - p)]. \text{ Let}$$
$$\bar{U} =_{\text{def}} U[r + \theta(\mu - p)].$$
(3.1)

Using a Taylor-series expansion, we may write:

$$\underset{\xi}{E} U[r + \theta(\xi - p)] = \bar{U} + E(\xi - \mu)\bar{U}'\theta + \frac{E(\xi - \mu)^2}{2}\bar{U}''\theta^2 + \text{Rem}$$

$$\cong \bar{U} + \frac{\sigma^2}{2}\bar{U}''\theta^2.$$
(3.2)

The first-order condition for a maximum of EU with respect to θ, as obtained from (3.2), is:

$$\bar{U}'(\mu - p) + \sigma^2\bar{U}''\theta = 0, \quad \frac{\mu - p}{\sigma^2\theta} = -\frac{\bar{U}''}{\bar{U}'},$$
(3.3)

up to third-order terms. Thus, the absolute investment θp in the risky asset is inversely proportional to the absolute risk aversion $-\bar{U}''/\bar{U}'$ and the relative investment $\theta p/r$ is inversely proportional to the relative risk-aversion function $-r\bar{U}''/\bar{U}'$. In both cases, the proportionality factor is the reciprocal of the coefficient of variation per unit of investment, i.e. $(\sigma^2/(\mu - p))/p$.

Furthermore, if the price paid for the risky asset varies with the number of units bought, so that $p = p(\theta)$, then (3.3) becomes

$$\bar{U}'\left(\mu - p - \theta \frac{dp}{d\theta}\right) + \sigma^2 \bar{U}''\theta = 0, \quad \frac{\mu - p(1 + \eta_{p\theta})}{\sigma^2 \theta} = \frac{-\bar{U}''}{\bar{U}'}. \tag{3.4}$$

This generalisation admits of the usual economic interpretation.

Finally, if utility is not a function of wealth, but rather of some commodity z produced by means of the production function g using wealth as input, $z = g(w)$, then $V(w) = U[g(w)]$. Define: $\bar{V}(r, \theta) = U[g(r + \theta(\mu - p))]$. It is then readily verified that:

$$\bar{V}_r = \bar{U}_z g', \quad \bar{V}_{rr} = \bar{U}_{zz}(g')^2 + \bar{U}_z g''$$

$$\frac{\bar{V}_{rr}}{\bar{V}_r} = \frac{\bar{U}_{zz}}{\bar{U}_z} g' + \frac{g''}{g'}, \tag{3.5}$$

where all derivatives of g are taken at $w = r + \theta(\mu - p)$ and those of U at $z = g(r + \theta(\mu - p))$.

Thus, the absolute risk-aversion function for the input (wealth) is the sum of two terms: (i) the absolute risk-aversion function (utility-wise) for the produced commodity (divided by marginal cost, for scaling); (ii) the logarithmic derivative of the marginal productivity of the input, which has the same interpretation as an absolute risk-aversion function (production-wise) for the input. This additive decomposition will be used in the sequel.

We also note for further reference that

$$\bar{V}_{rrr} = \bar{U}_{zzz}(g')^3 + 3\bar{U}_{zz}g'g'' + \bar{U}_z g''', \tag{3.6}$$

thereby establishing the 'third-order' nature of the term $U_{zz}g'g''$.

3.3 A model of portfolio selection by NPOs

We now introduce a simplified version of the model of Section 2, and generalise to public goods the analysis in the preceding subsection.

Consider the model of Section 2 with *a single private good*, hence no private firms, *a single public good* and *no transfers*. We may identify the private good with the individual incomes ($q^k = r^k$) and with the budget constraint of the NPO ($y = b$); and we may express the amount of public good z as an explicit function of the input level $b, z = g(b)$. Then $U^k(q^k, z) = U^k[r^k, g(b)]$.

We now introduce the possibility, for each individual *and* for the NPO, to acquire a risky asset with random return ξ, satisfying $E(\xi) = \mu$ and $V(\xi) = \sigma^2$.[5] Let the number of units of this asset acquired by individual k be θ^k, the number acquired by the NPO be θ; the total 'investment' in the risky

[5] Following standard practice in portfolio analysis, we assume unanimous agreement about $E(\xi)$ and $V(\xi)$.

asset is then

$$\theta + \sum_k \theta^k.$$

As a convenient shortcut to the more explicit analysis that was recommended in section 3.1, we assume that the risky asset is acquired at a price

$$p = p\left(\theta + \sum_k \theta^k\right)$$

expressed in the same units as r^k and b. For an open economy, p may be interpreted as a price prevailing on an international capital market. In a closed economy, p may be interpreted as the cost (in terms of r^k or b) of producing the risky asset.[6]

Taking the risky investment into account, we obtain '*ex post* incomes' $q^k = r^k + \theta^k(\xi - p)$ and *ex post* output of the public good $z = g(b + \theta(\xi - p))$, yielding the utility levels $U^k[r^k + \theta^k(\xi - p), g(b + \theta(\xi - p))]$, where

$$p = p\left(\theta + \sum_k \theta^k\right).$$

We denote again $U^k[r^k + \theta^k(\mu - p), g(b + \theta(\mu - p))]$ by $\bar{U}^k$ and obtain from a Taylor-series expansion

$$\mathop{E}_{\xi} U^k = \bar{U}^k + \frac{\sigma^2}{2}[\bar{U}^k_{rr}(\theta^k)^2 + 2\bar{U}^k_{rz}\theta^k\theta g' + \bar{U}^k_{zz}(g')^2\theta^2$$
$$+ \bar{U}^k_z g''\theta^2] + \text{Rem.} \tag{3.7}$$

Our analysis will be greatly simplified, both conceptually and expositionally, by the assumption that $\bar{U}^k_{rz} = 0 \forall k$, *meaning that* $-\bar{U}^k_{rr}/\bar{U}^k_r$ *is independent of* z. This assumption is far from innocuous, considering that U^k is defined up to a *linear* transformation (our assumption is more restrictive than additive *ordinal* preferences). But it may be argued that in the real world:

1. $\theta^k = 0$ for most beneficiaries of the public goods produced by a specific NPO; $\bar{U}^k_{rz}$ then drops out of (3.7);
2. portfolio diversification would anyhow enable an NPO to hold assets with returns only mildly correlated with those of assets held by the said beneficiaries, a feature not recognised in our simplified model; the term $\bar{U}^k_{rz}$ would then be multiplied by covariances, not by variances; and
3. the cross derivatives U^k_{rz} could not be measured empirically, so that a more general analysis would have academic interest only.

---

[6]An average cost interpretation is natural if the risky asset is incorporated as a new business venture (with the individuals and the NPO supplying the equity capital); a marginal cost interpretation could easily be formalised, with the added complication of an explicit assignment (among individuals and the NPO) of the initial ownership and profits; that complication is of no immediate interest for our purpose in this section.

3.4 A risk-aversion function of NPOs

A gambling rule for the NPO will now be defined by solving the problem

$$\underset{\theta}{\text{Max}} \sum_k \lambda^k \underset{\xi}{\text{E}} U^k \text{ subject to } p = p\left(\theta + \sum_k \theta^k\right), \quad \frac{\partial \text{E}U^k}{\partial \theta^k} = 0. \qquad (P)$$

The first-order condition for a maximum is

$$0 = \frac{\text{d}\sum_k \lambda^k \text{E}U^k}{\text{d}\theta} = \frac{\partial\sum_k \lambda^k \text{E}U^k}{\partial\theta} + \frac{\partial\sum_k \lambda^k \text{E}U^k}{\partial p}\frac{\text{d}p}{\text{d}\theta} \qquad (3.8)$$

where

$$\frac{\partial \text{E}U^k}{\partial\theta} = \bar{U}_z^k g'(\mu - p) + \sigma^2\left[\{\bar{U}_{zz}^k(g')^2 + \bar{U}_z^k g''\}\theta + \frac{3}{2}\bar{U}_{zz}^k g'g''(\mu - p)\theta^2 \right.$$
$$\left. + \bar{U}_{rz}^k\theta^k\{g' + g''\theta(\mu - p)\}\right] \qquad (3.9)$$

$$\frac{\partial \text{E}U^k}{\partial p} = -\bar{U}_r^k\theta^k - \bar{U}_z^k g'\theta - \sigma^2\left[\frac{3}{2}\bar{U}_{zz}^k g'g''\theta^3 + \bar{U}_{rz}^k\theta^k\theta^2 g''\right]$$
$$+ \frac{\partial \text{E}U^k}{\partial\theta^k}\frac{\text{d}\theta^k}{\text{d}p}. \qquad (3.10)$$

Upon using our assumption $\bar{U}_{rz}^k = 0$ and the conditions $\partial \text{E}U^k/\partial\theta^k = 0$, neglecting the third-order terms $\bar{U}_{zz}^k g'g''$, writing once more π^k for $\bar{U}_z^k/\bar{U}_r^k$ and inserting (3.9)–(3.10) into (3.8), we obtain:

$$0 = \sum_k \lambda^k\bar{U}_r^k\left\{\pi^k g'\left(\mu - p - \theta\frac{\text{d}p}{\text{d}\theta}\right) - \theta^k\frac{\text{d}p}{\text{d}\theta} + \sigma^2\theta g'\left[\frac{\bar{U}_{zz}^k}{\bar{U}_r^k}g'\right.\right.$$
$$\left.\left. + \frac{g''}{g'}\pi^k\right]\right\}. \qquad (3.11)$$

If the NPO views with indifference transfers of income among individuals; more generally, if the NPO assigns weights

$$\frac{\lambda^k\bar{U}_r^k}{\lambda^m\bar{U}_r^m}$$

to marginal income transfers that are uncorrelated (over individuals) with the terms inside the curly brackets, then a final form of the first-order condition (3.8), or (3.11), is:

$$\frac{\mu - p - \theta\dfrac{\text{d}p}{\text{d}\theta} - \dfrac{\sum_k \theta^k}{g'\sum_k \pi^k}\dfrac{\text{d}p}{\text{d}\theta}}{\sigma^2\theta} = \frac{-g'}{\sum_k \pi^k}\sum_k \frac{\bar{U}_{zz}^k}{\bar{U}_r^k} - \frac{g''}{g'}$$

$$\frac{\mu - p(1 + \eta_{p\theta}^\tau)}{\sigma^2\theta} = \frac{-1}{Cm}\left(\frac{1}{\sum_k \pi^k}\frac{\partial\sum_k \pi^k}{\partial z} - \frac{1}{Cm}\frac{\text{d}Cm}{\text{d}z}\right) \qquad (3.12)$$

where: $Cm = 1/g'$ is the marginal cost of the public good

$$\frac{dCm}{dz} = \frac{d(1/g')}{dz} = \frac{-1}{(g')^2}\frac{dg'}{dz} = \frac{-1}{(g')^2}\frac{dg'}{dr}\frac{dr}{dz} = \frac{-g''}{(g')^3}$$

$$\eta_{p\theta}^\tau = \frac{\theta^\tau}{p}\frac{dp}{d\theta}, \quad \theta^\tau = \theta + \frac{\sum_k \theta^k}{g'\sum_k \pi^k} = \theta + \frac{Cm}{\sum_k \pi^k}\sum_k \theta^k$$

and where use has been made of $\bar{U}_{rz}^k = 0$ to write

$$\frac{\bar{U}_{zz}^k}{\bar{U}_r^k} = \frac{\partial \pi^k}{\partial z}.$$

According to formula (3.12) the absolute risk-aversion function for the NPO is obtained as a sum of two terms, that are directly comparable to the two terms in formula (3.5). The output elasticity of marginal cost is directly measurable within the NPO; the elasticity of willingness to pay for the public good is less directly measurable but the information required for that measurement is not so different from that required to evaluate

$$\sum_k \pi^k.$$

The corresponding relative risk-aversion function is obtained upon multiplying by the input level b. By definition, b is also equal to output z times average cost Ca. The relative risk-aversion function is then

$$-\frac{zCa}{Cm}\left(\frac{1}{\sum_k \pi^k}\frac{\partial \sum_k \pi^k}{\partial z} - \frac{1}{Cm}\frac{\partial Cm}{\partial z}\right) = \frac{-Ca}{Cm}(\eta_{\Sigma \pi^k \cdot z} - \eta_{Cm \cdot z})$$

where the η are elasticities.

When $dp/d\theta = 0$, then the absolute risk aversion of the NPO is simply equated to $\mu - p/\sigma^2\theta$ as in (3.3). When $dp/d\theta \neq 0$, the elasticity of supply of the risky investment comes in – as in (3.4). The elasticity formula $\eta_{p\theta}^\tau$ takes into account the difference in relative valuation between resources used in the public and private sectors, namely

$$\frac{\sum_k \pi^k}{Cm}.$$

As before, individual price elasticities are deflated by the ratio of marginal cost to marginal valuation of the public good. This refinement is not likely to make an essential difference in possible applications of formula (3.12).

In spite of the numerous simplifications made in this section, we regard the right-hand side of formula (3.12) as the most useful approximation to a risk-aversion function for NPOs that we could suggest. We note that, under increasing returns to scale in production, an NPO could conceivably display a positive risk preference.

As a further hint toward interpretation, we mention the case of a single individual (or identical individuals) who regards the private and public goods as perfect substitutes. His risk-aversion function for gambles with the resources of the public sector would differ from his risk aversion for gambles with his private resources by the term $\eta_{Cm \cdot z}$ (output elasticity of marginal cost). The public sector would thus be more, or less, risk averse than the individual, according as diminishing, or increasing, returns prevailed in production.

We conclude with the remark that further work on this subject is much needed. Indeed, we find in (3.12) that the absolute risk-aversion function of an NPO is given by the logarithmic derivative of

$$\frac{\sum_k \pi^k}{Cm}$$

with respect to b. Going back to formulae (2.9) and (2.13), we find that (in the absence of adjustments to marginal costs for a difference in net profits)

$$\frac{\sum_k \pi_j^k}{Cm_j}$$

is equal to

$$\frac{1}{1 - \bar{\gamma}} = \frac{\alpha_n + \gamma p_n}{\alpha_n},$$

where α_n and γ are the Lagrange multipliers associated respectively with the market clearing constraint on good n and with the budget constraint. Indeed,

$$\frac{\sum_k \pi_j^k}{Cm_j}$$

is a measure of the relative value of inputs inside and outside the public sector. And a transfer of risks between the NPO and the private sector is a gamble about a transfer of inputs between the NPO and the private sector. The assumptions made in this section enable us to write

$$\frac{d}{db} \log\left(\frac{\sum_k \pi_j^k}{Cm}\right)$$

as

$$\frac{1}{Cm} \frac{d}{dz} \log\left(\frac{\sum_k \pi_j^k}{Cm}\right).$$

In the more general model of Section 2, a change in b would result in a vector of changes in p, r, y and z, so that

$$\frac{d}{db} = \frac{\partial}{\partial p}\cdot\frac{dp}{db} + \frac{\partial}{\partial r}\cdot\frac{dr}{db} + \frac{\partial}{\partial y}\cdot\frac{dy}{db} + \frac{\partial}{\partial z}\cdot\frac{dz}{db}.$$

In order to take into account all these effects, one should analyse the differential of the system formed (say, in Section 2) by conditions (α), (β), (γ), (p_a), (r^k), (y_i) and (z_j), and try to obtain a formula for the logarithmic derivative of

$$\frac{\alpha_n + \gamma p_n}{\alpha_n}$$

with respect to b. Research on such technical problems could, in our opinion, be pursued under foundation support.

References

Arrow, K.J. (1964). The Role of Securities in the Optimal Allocation of Risk-Bearing, *Review of Economic Studies*, 31: 91–6

Atkinson, A. and N. Stern (1974). Pigou, Taxation and Public Goods, *Review of Economic Studies*, 41: 119–28

Baumol, W. and D. Bradford (1970). Optimal Departures from Marginal Cost Pricing, *American Economic Review*, 60: 265–83

Bergson, A. (1972). Optimal Pricing for a Public Enterprise, *Quarterly Journal of Economics*, 36: 518–41

Boiteux, M. (1956). Sur la gestion des monopoles publics astreints à l'équilibre budgétaire, *Econometrica*, 24: 22–40

Bronsard, C. (1971). *Dualité microeconomique et théorie du second-best*, Louvain: Vander

Diamond, P. and J. Mirrless (1971). Optimal Taxation and Public Production. *American Econometric Review*, 61: 8–27, 261–78

Drèze, J.H. (1974). Investment under Private Ownership: Optimality, Equilibrium and Stability. In J.H. Drèze (ed.), *Allocation under Uncertainty: Equilibrium and Optimality*, pp. 129–66. London: Macmillan (Chapter 14 supra.)

Guesnerie, R. (1975). On Second-Best Pareto-Optimality in a Class of Models. CEPREMAP [unpublished]

Kolm, S.C. (1970). *Théorie des contraintes de valeur*. Paris: Dunod

Merton, R.C. (1971). Optimum Consumption and Portfolio Rules in a Continuous Time Model. *Journal of Economic Theory*, 3: 373–413

Pratt, J.W. (1964). Risk Aversion in the Small and in the Large. *Econometrica*, 32: 122–36

Ramsey, F.P. (1927). A Contribution to the Theory of Taxation, *Economic Journal*, 37: 47–61

Sandmo, A. (1972). Optimality Rules for the Provision of Collective Factors of Production. *Journal of Public Economics*, 1: 149–57

Stiglitz, J. and P. Dasgupta (1971). Differential Taxation, Public Goods and Economic Efficiency, *Review of Economic Studies*, 38: 151–74

20   Econometrics and decision theory[*]

This is a written version of the Presidential Address delivered at the Second World Congress of the Econometric Society, Cambridge, September 10, 1970.

The oral presentation was introduced by the following remark: There is a substantial difference between the science of writing a cookbook and the art of cooking a good dinner. A similar difference exists between the task of writing a presidential address and that of presenting it at a Congress. I did consult many econometric cookbooks over the summer in preparing this address, but today I will present it in the spirit in which a dinner is served. So I begin by announcing the

MENU
Appetizers

Consommé Savage
(U.S.D.A. Monopole Brut 1970)

Arrow–Debreu Salad
(Château L'Efficience)

The Reverend's Sole
(Château Schlaifer 1959)

Sliced Filet of Simultaneous Equations
...à la façon du Chef[1]
(Château Tintner 1930)

---

[*]Reprinted from *Econometrica*, 40 (1972): 1–17, with permission of the Econometric Society.
[1]Served under limited information.

Sequential Stochastic Fruitcup
(U.S.D.A. Monopole Brut 1980)

———

Mignardises

The address was dedicated to William Vickrey, who introduced me to econometrics. The notes were not included in the oral presentation.

1 Appetizers

This address will review a development which lies in the future as much as in the past, and still calls for a tone of sober and subdued confidence. It is a development which I foresaw as my friends and colleagues at Carnegie Tech were 'Planning production, inventories and work force' (Holt *et al.*, 1960), while French engineers were putting 'Marginal cost pricing in practice' (Nelson, 1964); the picture became sharper after I became acquainted with Savage's view of 'The foundations of statistics' (Savage, 1954), and then discovered how Arrow (1953) could deduce from it 'The role of securities in the optimal allocation of risk bearing' and how Schlaifer (1959) could extend it to 'Probability and statistics for business decisions'.

My theme will be that we should now regard as a realistic challenge the formal analysis of decision problems in economics, resting on a specification of ends and means firmly rooted in economic theory, incorporating a probabilistic treatment of econometric information, and making use of the possibilities offered by mathematical programming techniques to compute optimal policies.

2 Consommé Savage (U.S.D.A. Monopole Brut 1970)

'Knowledge is useful if it helps to make the best decision', noted Marschak (1953, p.1) in the opening sentence of 'Studies in econometric method'. The decisions of concern to us are the economic decisions of households, firms and public authorities. These decisions are typically made under uncertainty. Formal analysis of decisions under uncertainty rests on logical foundations that were clearly set forth in Savage's book in terms of three basic concepts: the states, which describe the environment; the consequences, which describe what happens to the decision-maker; and the acts, which are functions assigning a consequence to each state (or to sets of states called events). A decision problem calls for choosing a most preferred element from a given set of acts.

Consistency of preferences is usually identified with the existence of a preordering, among the objects of choice, which is simple – that is, complete and transitive. A natural extension of this requirement to the realm of uncertainty leads Savage to postulate: (i) a simple preordering among acts, conditionally on any non-null event; (ii) a simple preordering among consequences; and (iii) a simple preordering among events.

Under appropriate technical precautions, these postulates imply the powerful 'moral expectation theorem': the preordering among consequences is representable by a real-valued function, defined up to a linear transformation – call it 'utility' or 'loss'; the preordering among events is uniquely representable by a probability measure; and the preordering among acts is then representable by their expected utility, so that an optimal act maximises expected utility over the feasible set.[2]

In the light of this theorem, a decision problem under uncertainty can be logically decomposed into the following four steps: (i) define the set of acts; (ii) define a utility on the consequences; (iii) define a probability measure on the events; and (iv) find an act which is maximal with respect to expected utility.

This decomposition, permitting each of the four steps to be attacked independently, is useful for applications and research strategy alike. At the cost of oversimplification, let me suggest that positive economics should assist in defining the set of acts (that is, the range of alternatives and their consequences conditionally upon the states); that normative economics should assist in defining the utility; that statistics and econometrics should bring empirical observations to bear upon the assessment of probabilities; and that techniques of mathematical programming should assist in finding an optimal act.

I may now restate my theme more specifically. Recent advances in statistical and econometric methodology enable us to derive from empirical observations a probability measure on the relevant events for many decision problems; this new possibility challenges us to state our decision problems formally; the directions in which normative economics should be

[2]This theory is usually presented with reference to 'games against nature' as opposed to 'games of strategy' or 'games of strength and skill'. One reason for this distinction is the following: (i) the events must be defined with interpersonal objectivity, if the theory is to remain operational; (ii) the choice of strategy by a player, in a game of strategy or in a game of strength and skill, is not always observable (especially when mixed strategies are used); (iii) consequently, the probability measure associated with the events used in describing these games may depend upon the strategy chosen by the decision-maker. I personally hold the view that the theory outlined in the text can be generalised in a natural way so as to cover the three (collectively exhaustive) types of games. The generalisation consists in (i) providing an operational test whereby one can identify sets of acts having at least one *common* optimal strategy; (ii) restricting the postulates that imply a qualitative probability to such sets of acts. One then defines probability measures on the events *conditionally* upon the choice of a strategy by the decision-maker, and one verifies that the moral expectation principle governs the choices among strategies as well as the choices among acts. The weaker postulates underlying this reformulation also allow the ordering among consequences to become conditional upon the state that obtains, a useful generalisation in itself. This viewpoint is developed in my unpublished Ph.D. dissertation (1958); a summary presentation of the generalised theory is given by Drèze (1961); a non-technical presentation is given by Drèze (1960). An application of this approach to choices affecting the decision-maker's probability of survival is given by Drèze (1963).

extended in order to meet that challenge and the specific mathematical programming problems with which we are confronted can be sharply defined. This is a limited but well-defined area of research that deserves to be systematically explored.

By way of illustration, let me rise to my natural level of incompetence, and invade that most serious-minded of our substantive fields, agricultural economics.

In response to short-term random fluctuations in yields and long-term trends in productivity, and of course under due political pressure, many countries have engaged in programs of price support for basic agricultural commodities, accompanied by government-held buffer stocks. Typical policies consist in choosing a level for the price paid to farmers and a level for the wholesale price (or for the buffer inventory). The consequences of policy choices include the direct costs of the support and buffer program, its incidence on the welfare of consumers and agricultural producers, and all kinds of indirect effects, through the prices and outputs of substitutes, migration between farms and cities, and so on. The inventory levels resulting from one year's decisions are part of the initial conditions affecting the following year's decisions. Imperfect predictability characterises not only agricultural yields but also the responses of farmers and consumers to price changes, the future states of the economy, and so on.

Such programs may be continued, or redesigned, or discontinued upon disposal of the existing inventories; in any case, rational decisions would call for an analysis in four steps: (i) specification of the range of feasible policies and of a model linking the policy instruments to their consequences; (ii) definition of a criterion function (utility) encompassing the various dimensions of the consequences; (iii) specification of the joint probability density function of the unknown parameters in the model; and (iv) sequential stochastic maximisation of the expected value of the criterion function over the set of feasible policies.

Of course, this is not the way in which we proceed nowadays. In some cases, there will be no formal analysis whatever; in those cases where formal analysis is attempted, it will typically consist in computer simulation of some simple policy, using a random generator of annual yields reflecting historical experience, but proceeding conditionally as regards other parameters (such as trends, demand elasticities, and the like). The criterion function will typically be some discounted net sum of consumers' surplus plus producers' surplus minus direct costs of the program. Such simulations are clearly valuable (see, e.g., Reutlinger (1970)), and they are a significant step in the right direction. But we should prepare ourselves to do better: first, by relating more tightly the specification of the criterion function to general economic theory (recognising, for instance, the role of private speculators, the efficiency aspects of the program, and so on); second, by treating in probabilistic terms all the unknown parameters of the model, instead of proceeding conditionally on point estimates for some of these;

and third, by searching for optimal decision rules by mathematical programming techniques.

My remarks will successively point to the directions for research in normative economics connected with the first task; to the new possibilities offered by Bayesian statistics as regards the second task; and to some of the specific problems in stochastic sequential optimisation associated with the third task.

3 Arrow-Debreu Salad (Château l'Efficience)

By way of introduction to my first topic, I will recall some relevant propositions from welfare economics under certainty. We start from consumers' sovereignty, and take consumers' tastes as given. In the absence of externalities and of consumer saturation, a competitive equilibrium is a Pareto-optimum; under additional convexity assumptions on preferences and production possibilities, one can associate with every Pareto-optimum a price system and a distribution of initial resources for which the allocation is also competitive. Accordingly, profit maximisation at given prices by firms (producers) is compatible with productive and allocative efficiency; equilibrium prices reflect the marginal values of consumers and can, for instance, guide evaluations of costs and benefits, at least locally. These two propositions hold in any institutional framework. But when there are externalities, or when the prevailing allocation is not a competitive equilibrium, they lose their generality. In some cases, one may resort to the methodology of second-best, or constrained Pareto-optimality, to define efficiency conditions. This has been done successfully for a few specific situations, in which it has typically been found that the possibility of carrying out lump-sum transfers among consumers would preserve the separation of the efficiency problems from the distributive problems. In other cases, it seems more meaningful to approach group decisions by means of solution concepts that are not reducible to decentralisation through prices, but have distinct claims to realism. An example of such a concept is the core, which has been studied extensively; for some specific models, the analysis has interesting implications for allocative efficiency.

This is still a narrow basis from which to proceed towards policy decisions in industrial states and developing countries alike. But narrow as it may be, that basis has the merit to exist; it is a rigorous and well-articulated theoretical model. The underlying assumptions are clearly defined; as Koopmans (1957, p. 28) remarked, 'their importance is emphasised by the strength of the conclusions that can be derived from them'. The frontiers of our knowledge are sharply defined, inviting 'the construction of economic knowledge through a sequence of models'.

The possibility of extending these results to a world of uncertainty was first suggested in Arrow's pioneering paper 'The role of securities in the optimal allocation of risk bearing' (Arrow, 1953). Arrow's results for an exchange economy were extended by Debreu (1959) to a private ownership economy with production, and then by Radner (1968) to the case in which different agents have different information. Letting again the uncertainties be described by a set of states, a consumption plan for a consumer now specifies the quantity of each commodity to be consumed under each state of the world: it is a vector in an enlarged commodity space, obtained as the Cartesian product of the traditional commodity space and the state space. A production plan for a producer is similarly defined. Taking again as given the preferences of consumers among consumption plans, the propositions of welfare economics under certainty carry over directly to this model. In particular, the correspondence between Pareto-optima and competitive equilibria is preserved, with price systems now defined as vectors in the enlarged commodity space. The interpretation of such price systems is straightforward: the price of commodity c under state s, in terms of today's numeraire, is the price to be paid today for one unit of commodity c, to be claimed if and only if state s obtains; it is the price of a claim to one unit of commodity c contingent on the occurrence of state s, and may be interpreted as an insurance premium. Given such a price system, that is, given a full set of insurance markets for all commodities and all states, profit maximisation at given prices by firms is again efficient, and prices provide appropriate marginal valuations of costs and benefits.[3]

Of course, in an economy extending over time and with continuous random variables entering the definition of the states, a full system of prices for contingent claims can only be an idealisation that ignores the costs of computations, communication, and market organisation. In real economies, the possibilities of exchanging contingent claims are limited, and the corresponding prices are neither unique nor directly observable: they exist only in the latent form of marginal rates of substitution for consumers or of transformation for producers. The welfare economics of uncertainty are accordingly the welfare economics of second-best, or

---

[3]Thus, in the Arrow–Debreu model, the information provided by the price system reduces the decision problems of firms and public authorities to mere optimisation under certainty. There is, however, an alternative formulation of this conclusion, which runs as follows. It is readily verified that, under appropriate normalisation, the prices for contingent claims to any given commodity have all the formal properties of a probability measure on the events (including the rules of conditional probability). Let us for simplicity abstract from time considerations. Choose a numeraire, normalise the prices for contingent claims to the numeraire so that they add up to unity, and call these prices 'market probabilities'. The price of a claim to commodity c contingent on state s may then be viewed as the 'market probability' of state s times the price at which commodity c would exchange against the numeraire, should state s obtain; call this last price the 'utility of commodity c under state s'. The value of a plan, at the market prices for contingent claims, has become the 'expected utility' of that plan, in terms of the 'market probabilities' and 'utilities' just defined. Under this alternative formulation, the information provided by the price system amounts to the definition of a 'utility function' for firms and public authorities. The utility function so defined is the same for all firms; it is linear in profit for any given state, but with a different proportionality constant for each state. For further details, see Drèze (1971).

constrained Pareto-optimality, under restricted exchange opportunities. The time has come when this type of normative economics could, and should, be developed. Some beginnings have already been made, as in some work of Diamond (1967), Foley (1970), Hahn (1971) and Radner (1968).

In the specific context of uncertainty, recent work on consumption decisions (Drèze and Modigliani, 1972; Hakansson, 1970) and portfolio selection (Markowitz, 1959) provides some of the required building blocks.[4] But the analysis of production decisions raises altogether new problems. By contrast to the certainty theory, efficiency of production decisions under uncertainty with limited insurance opportunities seems hard to analyse without reference to the prevailing institutional framework. For instance, in private ownership economies with a stock market, many risks accepted by firms are ultimately borne by stockholders, and one would like to relate explicitly the decisions of the firms to the preferences of stockholders, a feature that is specific to private ownership economies, and may well call for appropriate criteria of group decisions within the firms.

These remarks may seem quite remote from my illustrative decision problem about price support and buffer stocks. But in fact they are not remote at all. The only reason that such programs are considered, and are not trivial to manage efficiently, is the absence of markets where agricultural output could be traded 'contingently' on yields and other determinants of supply or demand (notice that futures markets do *not* fulfil the same functions). A rigorous normative analysis of the problem would require an assessment of the available opportunities for allocating risk-bearing, of the additional opportunities offered by the program, and of the efficiency conditions for a constrained Pareto-optimum under the limited exchange opportunities. Pending such an analysis, any discussion of the merits of the program remains somewhat vague, and only suboptimal policies can be defined.

Before leaving this topic, I would like to draw attention to the dual nature of the tasks just assigned to normative analysis: the inductive aspect, concerned with discovering the functioning and shortcomings of existing institutions, is just as important as the deductive aspect, concerned with discovering the corresponding second-best efficiency conditions. Theoretical analysis is needed to clarify the testable implications of restricted exchange opportunities, but empirical analysis is indispensable to bring the theory to bear upon realistic decision problems.

4 The Reverend's Sole (Château Schlaifer 1959)

In the formal analysis of realistic decision problems, we will typically work with a model specifying the relationship among decision variables,

---

[4]Of particular interest to me, in this connection, has been the search for conditions under which the decisions about consumption can be separated from the portfolio choices, with current consumption chosen first, on the basis of a 'certainty-equivalent' rate of return, and the portfolio choices coming thereafter. See Drèze and Modigliani (1966, 1972).

exogenous variables and dependent variables; typically again, these relationships will not be exact, but will contain random terms. We may be uncertain about the structure of the model, the numerical values of its parameters and the future values of exogenous or random variables. In terms of the moral expectation theorem, all these sources of uncertainty combine to define the states. We would like to summarise our imperfect information in a probability measure on the states. We would also like to bring empirical observations to bear upon the numerical assessment of that probability measure. The tool which has been developed over the past fifteen years to accomplish precisely this purpose goes under the name of Bayesian statistics. Its logical basis is very simple.

Consider a set of states, a partition of that set into events B_i, and a probability measure which assigns to B_i the probability $P(B_i)$. Consider next an observation x, and a statistical model specifying, for all x and B_i, the conditional probability $P(x|B_i)$. It then follows from Bayes' theorem that:

$$P(B_i|x) = \frac{P(B_i) \cdot P(x|B_i)}{\Sigma_j P(B_j) \cdot P(x|B_j)}.$$

Bayes' theorem is the formula through which an empirical observation x is brought to bear upon the assessment of a probability measure on the states. There are two inputs to this formula. The first input is $P(B_i)$, the probability measure defined on the states *prior* to the observation; if $P(B_i)$ is the same for all i, then $P(B_i|x)$ is proportional to $P(x|B_i)$, and we say that our prior measure is non-informative. The second input is $P(x|B_i)$, the likelihood of the observation; if $P(x|B_i)$ is the same for all i, then $P(B_i|x)$ is equal to $P(B_i)$, and the observation is non-informative; when this property holds for all x, the B_i are called 'observationally equivalent'. These are the two inputs. The output of the formula is a posterior probability measure which combines our prior information with that supplied by the observation; it is the probability measure that will be used for decision purposes.

This procedure is very general; it enables us to combine various types of information, like cross-section and time-series observations or judgemental probabilities and sample evidence; and it enables us to define probability measures on the states on the basis of observations alone, starting from prior ignorance.

It is of course a long distance from these simple principles to operational statistical procedures, but substantial contributions have already been made towards bridging the gap. The work of Schlaifer (1959), Raiffa and Schlaifer (1961), Pratt *et al.* (1965) and several of their associates has been particularly significant in this respect. For a number of standard data generating processes (like binomial, Poisson and normal sampling), they have defined families of prior densities on the process parameters having the useful property that posterior densities belong to the same families and are characterised by parameters that can be readily computed as functions of the corresponding parameters of the prior densities on the one hand and of sufficient statistics summarising the sample information on the other hand. With these families of 'natural conjugate densities', 'the kernel of the prior density combines with the sample kernel in exactly the same way that two sample kernels combine' (Raiffa and Schlaifer, 1961, p. 49). Typically, a limiting member of the natural conjugate family may be regarded as non-informative about the process parameters. When one wishes to incorporate in the analysis prior information which is not equivalent to what might have been learned from a hypothetical previous sample generated by the same process, it is sometimes possible to extend the natural conjugate family by introducing additional parameters. Otherwise, one must resort to specific algebraic or numerical analysis; in such cases, one loses the reproductive properties which make natural conjugate analysis so attractive; and one faces the practical limitations of numerical analysis, especially when many variables are involved.

A further step consists of preposterior analysis, which is concerned with the design of experiments. By studying the attributes of the posterior density prior to the observation, and relating these attributes to optimal decisions, it is sometimes possible to compute the expected value of sample information and thereby to encompass data collection in the formal analysis.

5 Sliced filet of Simultaneous Equations... à la façon du Chef* (Château Tintner, 1930)

I would like to review some features of this approach in the specific econometric context of simultaneous equations models. I will do this mostly on the basis of my own work (Drèze, 1962, 1968; Drèze and Morales, 1970), but I wish to acknowledge the decisive stimulation provided by others who have worked in the same area, in particular V.K. Chetty (1968), R. Harkema (1969), G. Kaufman (1970), T. Kloek (Kloek and Harkema, 1970), J. Kmenta (Zellner *et al.*, 1966), T.J. Rothenberg (1963) and A. Zellner (1970); and I wish to thank my closer associates, Juan-Antonio Morales, Michel Mouchart, and Jean-François Richard, who frequently provided specific assistance as well as intellectual encouragement.

My interest in Bayesian analysis of simultaneous equations arose naturally in 1961, as I taught econometrics to a group of students trained in Bayesian statistics. My starting point consisted of the paper by Fisher (1962) on 'Estimation in the linear decision model' and the paper by Theil and Goldberger (1961) on 'Pure and mixed statistical estimation in economics'. In addition, a paper by Frank Fisher (1961), 'On the cost of approximate specification in simultaneous equation estimation' pointed to a natural application of Bayesian methods: in case of doubt about the prior specification, why not introduce stochastic constraints on the structural parameters, instead of deterministic constraints?

*Served under limited information

Consider the structural system $By + \Gamma z = u$, with reduced form $y = \Pi z + v$, and let Σ and Ω denote the parameters of the structural and reduced form disturbances respectively. The structural parameters are thus (B, Γ, Σ) and the reduced form parameters (Π, Ω). The identification problem arises because the likelihood can be written as a function of reduced form parameters only, whereas the correspondence between structural and reduced form parameters is many-to-one. That problem is traditionally solved by restricting a priori the range of the parameters in such a way that a one-to-one correspondence emerges. More generally, one can define a prior density function $f(B, \Gamma, \Sigma)$ on the space of structural parameters, and combine it with the sample likelihood by means of Bayes' theorem to obtain the posterior density $f(B, \Gamma, \Sigma \mid Y, Z) \propto f(B, \Gamma, \Sigma) L(Y, Z \mid B, \Gamma, \Sigma)$. *This operation is well defined, whether the model is identified or not. But conditionally on a set of values for the reduced form parameters, the prior and posterior densities of B are identical:*

$$f(B \mid \Pi, \Omega, Y, Z) \underset{Y,Z}{\equiv} f(B \mid \Pi, \Omega).$$

This identity reveals that all non-singular matrices B are observationally equivalent: the observations are informative about the reduced form parameters alone. The identity provides a simple and general statement of the identification problem. Indeed, exact identifying restrictions correspond to the special case where $f(B \mid \Pi, \Omega)$ has all its mass concentrated at a single point.

From the Bayesian viewpoint, classical identification theory is really concerned with local uniqueness of posterior modes. For a system of m equations identified by means of exclusion restrictions, a necessary condition for identification of a given equation is that at least $m - 1$ variables be excluded from it, and a sufficient condition is that a certain submatrix from Π should have full rank. The Bayesian counterpart of these conditions states that the coefficients of a given equation will have locally unique posterior modes if and only if the prior density has locally unique modes for at least $m - 1$ of these coefficients and the *very same* rank condition is fulfilled. Thus, a prior density with finitely many modes carries essentially the same identification power as it would with all its mass concentrated at a single point.[5]

This remark should bring comfort to those who regard underidentification as the natural state of an econometric model: indeed, stochastic prior information, even if imprecise, should enable them to proceed with structural estimation. Turn now to overidentification. In principle, deterministic restrictions are maintained, even if they conflict with the observ-

---

[5]Unlike the other statements in the text, this result is not quoted from my papers (Drèze, 1962, 1968; Drèze and Morales, 1970). I have only recently become aware of this close analogy between the classical conditions for identification through exclusion restrictions and their Bayesian counterpart. This analogy was clarified through discussion with Morales, Mouchart, and Richard. More complete results on this point will be presented in a forthcoming paper.

ations: the prior information dominates the sample information. In contrast, stochastic prior information gets combined with sample information through Bayes' theorem; neither type of information dominates the other, but both count in proportion to their respective precisions.

As a final remark about identification, let me note that locally unique posterior modes need not be relevant for decision purposes. Consider a decision problem in which the criterion function involves the square of a structural coefficient; examples are easy to find. We are then interested in the second moments of the posterior density. But we know, for instance, that even moments of two-stage least-squares estimators exist only up to an order not exceeding the degree of overidentification of the equation being estimated; and even less can be claimed about limited information maximum likelihood estimators (Mariano, 1969). We shall keep this problem in mind as we review some more specific results about Bayesian inference.

Space limitations impose selectivity, so I shall only discuss a limited information approach. When we study a single equation from a system under limited information, we ignore all the a priori information about the remaining equations, except for the classification of variables into endogenous ones and exogenous ones. In a Bayesian approach, this means using a non-informative prior density about the parameters of these remaining equations. Non-informative prior densities on variances and covariances are a persistent headache, the classical work of Jeffreys (1961) notwithstanding. Fortunately, the nature of our problem suggests unambiguously how we should proceed. Indeed, let there be m endogenous and n exogenous variables, and let the structural disturbances be jointly normally distributed with zero expectation and covariance matrix Σ, identically and independently for all observations. If we want our prior density to be constant-valued over the space of structural regression coefficients (B, Γ), and to remain constant-valued if we perform the non-singular integrand transformation from Γ to Π, then the joint prior density $f(B, \Gamma, \Sigma)$ is *uniquely* defined by its kernel

$$|\Sigma|^{-(m+n+1)/2}$$

and

$$f(B, \Gamma, \Sigma^{-1}) \propto |\Sigma|^{(m+1-n)/2}.$$

Combining this prior density with the likelihood leads to a posterior density which can be factored into: a normal density for Γ, conditionally on B and Σ^{-1}; a Wishart density for Σ^{-1}, conditionally on B; and a constant-valued marginal density for B (as was to be expected in the absence of identifying prior information). This factorisation permits analytical integration with respect to all the parameters except those of a single equation. In order to identify that equation, we may combine at will deterministic and stochastic types of prior information. In particular, the extended natural conjugate prior family is conditionally normal for the regression coefficients given the residual variance, and marginally gamma for that variance; this is also the form in which information would arise from, say, a regression analysis of cross-section data immune from simultaneity bias.

For illustrative purposes, I shall consider the case of identification through exclusion restrictions; the more general case of a natural conjugate prior is both logically and computationally analogous. And I shall discuss only the marginal posterior density for the regression coefficients of the endogenous variables appearing in one equation, say β_Δ. That marginal density, $f(\beta_\Delta \mid Y, Z)$, is obtained upon further analytical integration, first with respect to the non-zero regression coefficients of exogenous variables – let there be $n - n_*$ of these – and next with respect to the residual variance; it is defined by

$$f(\beta_\Delta \mid Y, Z) \propto \frac{(\beta_\Delta W_{\Delta\Delta} \beta'_\Delta)^{(T-m+1)/2}}{(\beta_\Delta W^*_{\Delta\Delta} \beta'_\Delta)^{(T-m+1+n+n^*)/2}} \, d\beta_\Delta,$$

where $W_{\Delta\Delta}$ and $W^*_{\Delta\Delta}$ are the familiar matrices of cross-products of least-squares residuals appearing in the variance ratio from which limited information maximum likelihood (LIML) estimators are computed. Actually, our posterior kernel differs from the variance ratio to be maximised for LIML estimation in one respect only, namely the different exponents in the numerator and denominator.

The difference in exponents results from the fact that our density is a marginal one: had we instead looked for the conditional density of β_Δ, given that the other parameters in our equation take their modal or mean values, then the two exponents would have been equal, as in the LIML case. The difference in exponents has an important implication: the posterior moments of β_Δ exist up to the degree of overidentification, whereas the small sample moments of LIML estimators of β_Δ do not exist. When the likelihood function has a complicated algebraic expression and involves many nuisance parameters, or when there are strong interdependences among parameters, marginal densities may be quite different from conditional densities; the marginal densities are usually the relevant ones, and will be more reliable – but they are sometimes difficult to obtain analytically. The posterior mode of β_Δ can be computed in almost the same way as LIML estimators, but so far moments can only be evaluated by numerical integration techniques. The numerical integration involves quadratic forms which are easy to evaluate. In general, a posterior density based directly upon the likelihood function is much more tractable than the sampling distribution of a modal value of that function, which involves the maximisation operator.

These points are vividly illustrated by the overidentified version of the demand equation in Tintner's (1952) two-equation model of the US meat market. After normalisation, β_Δ consists of a single element, β_{12}, the price coefficient in the demand function. The model uses three exogenous variables, so that $m + 1 - n = 0$, and our prior density embodies no other information than the exclusion restrictions. The sample consists of 23 observations. Figure 20.1 depicts, as a function of β_{12}, the variance ratio in a form to be maximised for limited information maximum likelihood estimation; notice first that the integral of this function does not converge: *conditionally* on the model (or mean) values of Γ and Σ^{-1}, β_Δ does not have a proper density; notice also that the function is constant, up to computer accuracy, over the whole range from 4 to 7. (Tintner has computed a LIML estimator of 5.8, Goldberger has recomputed that estimator as 4.8, with an asymptotic standard error of 5.7; the two-stage least-squares estimator is 1.6, with an asymptotic standard error of 0.6; the ordinary least-squares estimator is 1.0.) Figure 20.2 gives the posterior marginal density of β_{12}, obtained under the *very same* prior information. It has a mode of 2.46, a mean of 2.96 and a standard deviation of 2.9 (over the range of integration). The contrast between the two figures is the contrast between a conditional

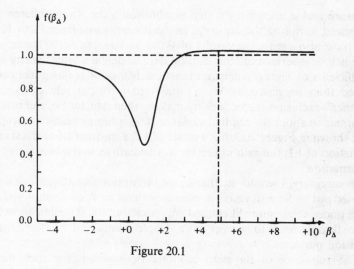

Figure 20.1

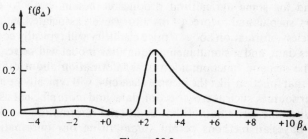

Figure 20.2

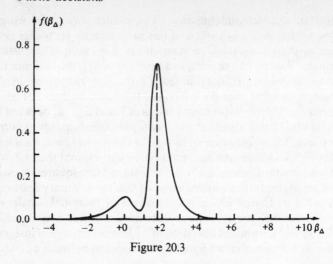

Figure 20.3

measure and a marginal density; algebraically, the whole difference has consisted in raising the exponent in the denominator from 11 to 12....

I have also used some results of Wold and Jureen's (1953) analysis of Swedish time-series and cross-section data to define a prior density on the coefficients of Tintner's demand function. My prior is much less concentrated than suggested by Wold's standard errors; it relaxes somewhat Tintner's exclusion restrictions by making them stochastic; and it is non-informative about the residual variance. The resulting posterior density of β_{12}, shown in Figure 20.3, has a mode of 1.7, a mean of 1.6 and a standard deviation of 1.1; the gain in precision is, of course, due to the use of prior information.

In summary, I would say that limited information analysis can now be carried out under a Bayesian approach with no more computational effort than under a maximum likelihood approach; but the Bayesian approach is more flexible, leads to sharper finite sample results, and is better suited for decision purposes.

The relevance of Bayesian econometric methods for such decision problems as my illustrative example is obvious enough. The price elasticity of demand for some agricultural product comes in, both to evaluate consumers' surplus and to forecast inventory levels associated with specific price policies; information about a price elasticity will typically come from time-series data, and a simultaneous equations model will be required to identify the demand function; additional information about other parameters of that function, like the income elasticity, will typically be available from other sources, such as cross-section data, and more efficient use will be made of the time-series data if that additional information is taken into account. Bayesian methods permit summarising our information in a posterior marginal density on the price elasticity; that density may be used for calculating expected values associated with specific policies; this procedure is much more satisfactory than the alternative of proceeding conditionally on some point estimate of the price elasticity of demand.

6 Sequential stochastic fruitcup (U.S.D.A. Monopole Brut 1980)

There remains now to comment briefly about the prospects for computing optimal policies. My example may serve as a starting point. To be specific, let us assume that demand functions and storage costs are linear, let us take agricultural inputs as given, and let us further ignore indirect effects. In the suboptimisation problem outlined above, the criterion function combining consumers' and producers' surpluses with direct costs of the program will be a quadratic function of the policy variables, with stochastic coefficients. The range of feasible policies will be defined by inequality constraints, like the non-negativity and storage constraints on inventories.

The resulting optimisation problem may seem relatively simple, but real difficulties are associated with its sequential nature. Indeed, assume for a moment that we were only concerned with a one-period problem, some value being attached to terminal inventory; the total value of end-of-period inventory could for instance be given as a quadratic function of inventory level, with stochastic coefficients. We would then need only to solve a quadratic programming problem, a rather simple one at that. But how could the value of terminal inventory be given to us, when terminal inventory of the first period is simply the starting inventory for the second period? It is only by solving the second period's problem that we could specify the terminal value for the first period's problem; and in order to solve the second period's problem, we need a value for the second period's terminal inventory, which can only be obtained by solving the third period's problem, and so on. This is the horizon problem. We start with an indefinite future; in looking for an optimal solution, we must either solve the problem over the infinite future, or we must show that if the problem is truncated in a certain way at a certain point, and an optimal solution to the finite problem is found, then there will always exist a continuation to the finite solution which leads to a global optimum.

Solving the problem over the infinite future would be easy in the absence of constraints on the policy variables: the Simon–Theil certainty equivalence theorem for unconstrained quadratic optimisation (Simon, 1956; Theil, 1964) could be invoked and would justify replacing all stochastic parameters by their expected values; stationarity assumptions might then permit computing optimal decision rules. But there are constraints: buffer stocks cannot become negative, and one certainly hopes that they will vanish at some point!

Truncating the problem would be easy if the price elasticity of demand were zero and holding costs were linear: the problem would then reduce to a stochastic warehousing problem, for which horizon rules and forward-working algorithms have been defined.[6] But certainly the price elasticity is different from zero.

To the best of my knowledge, standard algorithms for sequential stochastic problems exist neither in the quadratic case with constraints nor in the linear case with more than two periods; the model of two-period stochastic linear programming, or linear programming with recourse (Wets, 1969), is an interesting one, of genuine mathematical interest, and some of the results obtained for that problem may eventually help in attacking N-stage problems (Jagannathan, 1968); but as of now, N-stage algorithms are not available.

Unless we had the rare good fortune to discover that our specific problem is discussed in the inventory literature (Hadley and Whitin, 1963) there would seem to be few avenues worth exploring. The main ones are Markov programming (Blackwell, 1962) and stochastic control theory (Kushner, 1967) (sometimes also referred to under other names). The first avenue clearly holds some promise; of course, it would require a discrete formulation of our problem; but the approximations involved, if any, might be tolerable. Of greater concern would be the realism of the stationarity assumptions on which that theory rests. Stochastic control theory seems less promising in terms of operational algorithms, but it might help with analytical characterisations of optimal policies.

Before generating too much enthusiasm about these possibilities, however, we should realise fully the implications of imperfect knowledge about the model parameters in sequential stochastic problems. The density function of such parameters will frequently be the posterior marginal density of some statistical or econometric investigation. At each stage, additional observations will be available to revise these densities, and the revisions will seldom be given by simple formulae. The marginal densities, as of the first period, of parameters for more distant periods can only be specified through preposterior analysis. More importantly, the conditional densities of the stochastic coefficients pertaining to each period will depend upon all the intervening observations, even if the random terms themselves have a Markovian property. To top it all, these intervening observations will themselves depend upon the decisions made in earlier periods. Consequently, full optimisation would call for taking into consideration the expected value of the information generated by the decisions, in addition to the expected value of the direct consequences of the decisions. To be concrete, a

[6]Thanks to its simplicity, the warehousing model provides a neat illustration of sequential stochastic problems. Rules for optimal truncation (horizon rules) can be defined in terms of the densities of the unknown parameters (prices and costs, in this case). The rules consist in placing bounds on the expected value of terminal inventory for the relevant period. Bounds can also be placed on the expected value of the first period's terminal inventory by considering only the first n periods, $n \geqslant 2$. As n becomes larger, the bounds are brought towards each other in a monotonic way. This is the basis for defining forward-working algorithms. For further details, see Charnes *et al.* (1966).

monopolist may wish to depart from the price which maximises expected profit, simply to learn more about his demand function. Our experience with the mathematical programming problems associated with such situations is too meagre to permit further considerations now, but it is obvious that the difficulties will be great and the challenge lasting. In the meantime, we will live with suboptimisation and continue to solve proximate problems, following the suggestion already voiced by Arrow (1957) in his presidential address fourteen years ago.

7 Mignardises

To have identified certain problems is only a first step towards solving them, and I realise that my remarks have covered more problems than results. But my main purpose was to review the broad picture as I see it today. To repeat once more, we are still a long way from operational routines for a formal analysis of economic decision problems under uncertainty, but the goal is in sight, and the task is challenging. The challenges come on several fronts: normative economics, statistical methods of econometrics, and mathematical programming. I have no doubt that these challenges will be answered; this is just a matter of time. When problems of practical relevance and scientific importance are clearly defined, they attract talent. The problems of decision-making under uncertainty have all these attributes.

I thus feel tempted to conclude this address with a note of optimism. But optimism about an exciting subject is too easily wishful. So, to those who will extend the work in this area, I had better refrain from promising success. I will simply offer the modest advice that they are sure to learn a great deal from looking at real-life problems; and I will make the modest promise that it will be a lot of fun.

References

Arrow, K. (1953). Le rôle des valeurs boursières pour la répartition la meilleure des risques. In *Econométrie*, pp. 41–8. Paris: CNRS. Translated (1964) as The Role of Securities in the Optimal Allocation of Risk-Bearing. *Review of Economic Studies*, 31: 91–6

Arrow, K. (1957). Statistics and Economic Policy. *Econometrica*, 25: 523–31

Blackwell, D. (1962). Discrete Dynamic Programming. *The Annals of Mathematical Statistics*, 33: 719–26

Charnes, A., J.H. Drèze and M.H. Miller (1966). Decision and Horizon Rules for Stochastic Planning Problems: A Linear Example. *Econometrica*, 34: 307–30

Chetty, V.K. (1968). Bayesian analysis of Haavelmo's models. *Econometrica*, 36: 582–602

Debreu, G. (1959). *Theory of Value*. New York: Wiley

Diamond, P. (1967). The Role of a Stock Market in a General Equilibrium Model with Technological Uncertainty. *American Economic Review*, 57: 759–76

Drèze, J.H. (1958). Individual Decision Making under Partially Controllable Uncertainty. Unpublished Ph.D. Dissertation, Columbia University

—(1960). Les probabilités subjectives ont-elles une signification objective? *Economie Appliquée*, 13: 55–70

—(1961). Les fondements logiques de l'utilité cardinale et de la probabilité subjective. In *La Décision*, pp. 73–87. Paris: CNRS (Translated as Chapter 3 supra.)

—(1962). The Bayesian Approach to Simultaneous Equations Estimation. ONR Research Memorandum 67, The Technological Institute, Northwestern University

—(1963). L'utilité sociale d'une vie humaine. *Revue Française de Recherche Opérationnelle*, 23: 93–118

—(1968). Limited Information Estimation from a Bayesian Viewpoint. CORE Discussion Paper 6816, Université Catholique de Louvain

—(1971). Market Allocation under Uncertainty. *European Economic Review*, 2: 133–65 (Chapter 6 supra.)

Drèze, J.H. and F. Modigliani (1966). Epargne et consommation en avenir aléatoire *Cahiers du Séminaire d'Econométrie*, 9: 7–33 (Partim: Chapter 10 supra.)

—(1972). Consumption Decisions under Uncertainty. *Journal of Economic Theory*, 5: 308–35 (Chapter 9 supra.)

Drèze, J.H. and J.A. Morales (1970). Bayesian Full Information Analysis of the Simultaneous Equations Model. CORE Discussion Paper 7031, Université Catholique de Louvain

Fisher, F. (1961). On the Cost of Approximate Specification in Simultaneous Equation Estimation. *Econometrica*, 31: 139–70

Fisher, W. (1962). Estimation in the Linear Decision Model. *International Economic Review*, 3: 1–29

Foley, D.K. (1970). Economic Equilibrium with Costly Marketing. Working Paper 52, Department of Economics, Massachusetts Institute of Technology

Hadley, G. and T.H. Whitin (1963). *Analysis of Inventory Systems*, Englewood Cliffs: Prentice-Hall

Hahn, F. (1971). Equilibrium with Transaction Costs. *Econometrica*, 39: 417–39

Hakansson, N. (1970). Optimal Investment and Consumption Strategies under Risk for a Class of Utility Functions. *Econometrica*, 38(5): 587–607

Harkema, R. (1969). A Class of Tractable Prior Distributions on Structural Parameters of Simultaneous Equation Systems. Report 6919, Econometric Institute, Rotterdam

Holt, C.C., F. Modigliani, J.F. Muth and H.A. Simon (1960). *Planning Production, Inventories and Workforce*. Englewood Cliffs: Prentice-Hall

Hood, W.C. and T.C. Koopmans (1953). *Studies in Econometric Method*. New York: Wiley

Jagannathan, R. (1968). A Solution Procedure for a Class of Multi-Stage Linear Programming Problems under Uncertainty. Management Science Research Report 146, Carnegie-Mellon University

Jeffreys, H. (1961). *Theory of Probability*, 3rd edn. Oxford: Clarendon Press

Kaufman, G. (1970). Posterior Inference for Structural Parameters Using Cross-Section and Time-Series Data. Paper presented at the Second World Congress of the Econometric Society, Cambridge, September 1970

Kloek, T. and R. Harkema (1970). A Limiting Bayesian Approach to Simultaneous Equation Systems. Report 7004, Econometric Institute Rotterdam

Koopmans, T.C. (1957). *Three Essays on the State of Economic Science.* New York: McGraw-Hill

Kushner, H.J. (1967). *Stochastic Stability and Control.* New York: Academic Press

Mariano, R.S. (1969). On Distributions and Moments of Single-Equation Estimators in a Set of Simultaneous Linear Stochastic Equations. Econometric Series Report 2, Institute for Mathematical Studies in the Social Sciences, Stanford University

Markowitz, H.M. (1959). *Portfolio Selection.* New York: Wiley

Marschak, J. (1953). Economic Measurements for Policy and Prediction. In W.C. Hood and T.C. Koopmans (eds.), *Studies in Econometric Method,* pp. 1–26. New York: Wiley

Nelson, J.R. (ed.) (1964). *Marginal Cost Pricing in Practice.* Englewood Cliffs: Prentice-Hall

Pratt, J., H. Raiffa and R. Schlaifer (1965). *Introduction to Statistical Decision Theory.* New York: McGraw-Hill

Radner, R. (1968). Competitive Equilibrium under Uncertainty. *Econometrica,* 36: 31–58

—(1970). Problems in the Theory of Markets under Uncertainty. *American Economic Review,* 60: 454–60

Raiffa, H. and R. Schlaifer (1961). *Applied Statistical Decision Theory,* Cambridge, Mass: MIT Press

Reutlinger, S. (1970). A Simulation Model for Evaluating National Buffer Stock Programs. Paper presented at the Second World Congress of the Econometric Society, Cambridge, September 1970

Rothenberg, J.T. (1963). A Bayesian Analysis of Simultaneous Equation Systems. Report 6315, Econometric Institute, Rotterdam

Savage, L.J. (1954). *The Foundations of Statistics.* New York: Wiley

Schlaifer, R. (1959). *Probability and Statistics for Business Decisions; An Introduction to Managerial Economics under Uncertainty.* New York: McGraw-Hill

Simon, H.A. (1956). Dynamic Programming under Uncertainty with a Quadratic Criterion Function. *Econometrica,* 24: 74–81

Theil, H. (1964). *Optimal Decision Rules for Government and Industry.* Amsterdam: North-Holland

Theil, H. and A. Goldberger (1961). Pure and Mixed Statistical Estimation in Economics. *International Economic Review,* 2: 65–78

Tintner, G. (1952). *Econometrics.* New York: Wiley

Wets, R.J.-B. (1969). Stochastic Programs with Recourse: A Survey. Mathematical Note 614, Boeing Scientific Research Laboratories

Wold, H. and L. Jureen (1953). *Demand Analysis.* New York: Wiley

Zellner, A. (1970). Bayesian and Non-Bayesian Analysis of Simultaneous Equation Models. Paper presented at the Second World Congress of the Econometric Society, Cambridge, September 1970

Zellner, A., J. Kmenta and J.H. Drèze (1966). Specification and Estimation of Cobb-Douglas Production Function Models. *Econometrica,* 34: 784–95

Index